PRINCIPLES OF CORPORATE TAXATION

Second Edition

Douglas A. Kahn
Paul G. Kauper Emeritus Professor of Law
University of Michigan Law School

Jeffrey H. Kahn
Harry W. Walborsky Professor of Law
Florida State University College of Law

CONCISE HORNBOOK SERIES™

WEST
ACADEMIC
PUBLISHING

The publisher is not engaged in rendering legal or other professional advice, and this publication is not a substitute for the advice of an attorney. If you require legal or other expert advice, you should seek the services of a competent attorney or other professional.

© 2010 Thomson Reuters
© 2019 LEG, Inc. d/b/a West Academic
     444 Cedar Street, Suite 700
     St. Paul, MN 55101
     1-877-888-1330

Printed in the United States of America

ISBN: 978-1-63460-336-2

To the memory of Gladys Lavitan
–DK

To John Lopatka,
"Nil Ego Contulerim Jocundo Sanus Amico."
–JK

Preface

Principles of Corporate Income Taxation is a contracted and updated version of the one volume Hornbook, *Corporate Income Taxation* (6th ed.) that we authored together with Terrence G. Perris. This Concise Hornbook is designed as an aide to a student who is taking a course in corporate taxation or business planning.

A significant source of tax law is the Internal Revenue Code. Regulations, administrative decisions, and judicial decisions also are primary sources of tax law. The book discusses all of those sources and how they contribute to creating a body of corporate income tax principles. In addition, the book contains numerous examples to illustrate how the tax law is applied and how the various provisions interact. Those examples will help the student's understanding of the subject.

Following the general structure for the Concise Hornbook series, this book is meant as a study aide to supplement the student's casebook and notes. We have minimized our use of citations. We have not included citations to acquiescences and nonacquiescences; and when we have cited a revenue ruling, we have cited only the number of the ruling and have omitted references to the cumulative bulletins. Those citations are readily available, of course, from a variety of easily accessible on line and hard-copy sources.

Corporate taxation is a complex subject, and not every detail or exception can be covered in a corporate tax course. We have endeavored to provide as much depth and coverage as are consistent with the "concise" nature of the book series. Since the book is designed for students, we have restricted its scope to topics that are covered in most corporate tax courses. For example, we have omitted coverage of consolidated returns and the limitations on certain tax benefits for multiple corporations. If a student needs information about an area omitted from this text or needs more detailed discussion of an area, we recommend that the student consult our Hornbook. Indeed, readers will note that the Concise Hornbook itself occasionally cross-references to our Hornbook in certain instances where we think the reader might be interested in more extensive treatment of a particular topic.

The book does include discussion of a few areas that are omitted from, or covered only briefly in, some corporate tax courses. Corporate divisions and reorganizations are covered. In addition, there is some coverage of a corporation's acquisition of the tax attributes of another corporation and of the limitations on a corporation's utilization of acquired or retained tax attributes.

The organization of the book does not follow the chronological life of a corporation. Instead, the book begins by examining the tax consequences of a corporation's making distributions to its shareholders either on account of or in redemption of their stock. Each instructor will choose the organization of his or her course that suits that instructor best. Whether or not the instructor adopts the organization used in this book, the book will be a useful aide to the student. The book need not be read cover to cover. A student can select the chapter that deals with the material to be covered in class at that time. Each chapter (and parts of chapters) can stand on its own and be read independently of the rest of the book.

Unless otherwise stated, all "§" signs used in this text refer to section numbers of the Internal Revenue Code of 1986, as amended. Any reference in this text to the Code refers to the Internal Revenue Code of 1986.

DOUGLAS A. KAHN
JEFFREY H. KAHN

May 2019

Summary of Contents

PREFACE V

Chapter One. Introduction 1

Chapter Two. Distributions to Shareholders: § 301
    Distributions 9

Chapter Three. Distributions in Redemption of Stock 41

Chapter Four. Complete Liquidation of a Corporation 89

Chapter Five. Taxable Purchase and Sale of a
    Corporate Business 111

Chapter Six. Distribution of Stock and Section 306
    Stock 131

Chapter Seven. Organization of a Corporation 155

Chapter Eight. Corporate Divisions 199

Chapter Nine. Reorganizations 251

Chapter Ten. Acquisition or Retention of Tax
    Attributes 319

Chapter Eleven. S Corporations 359

TABLE OF CASES 399

TABLE OF INTERNAL REVENUE CODE SECTIONS 401

TABLE OF TREASURY REGULATIONS 409

TABLE OF REVENUE RULINGS 415

TABLE OF MISCELLANEOUS DECISIONS 417

INDEX 419

Table of Contents

PREFACE V

Chapter One. Introduction...1
¶ 1.01   Overview...1
¶ 1.02   General Tax Treatment of C Corporations 2
¶ 1.03   Nonrecognition...4
¶ 1.04   Rescission Doctrine...5
¶ 1.05   What Organizations Constitute a Corporation? 6
¶ 1.06   Diagraming Transactions...8

Chapter Two. Distributions to Shareholders: § 301
Distributions 9
¶ 2.01   Introduction...9
¶ 2.02   Amount Distributed...11
¶ 2.03   Definition of "Dividend"...12
¶ 2.04   Dividend—Received Deduction for Corporate
          Shareholders 17
¶ 2.05   Treatment of Dividend to a Noncorporate
          Shareholder..18
¶ 2.06   Earnings and Profits—in General 18
¶ 2.07   Effect of Discharge of Indebtedness on E and P 22
¶ 2.08   Effect of § 301 Distributions on E and P 22
¶ 2.09   Distribution of Corporation's Stock or Bonds 28
¶ 2.10   Amendments to § 312 and Depreciation Deductions......28
¶ 2.11   § 301 Distributions to 20 Percent Corporate
          Shareholder..31
¶ 2.12   Distributions to Shareholders in Excess of Earnings
          and Profits...33
¶ 2.13   Extraordinary Dividends to a Corporate
          Shareholder..34
¶ 2.14   Basis of Property Distributed to Shareholders..............36
¶ 2.15   Distributing Corporation's Recognition of Gain or
          Loss: General Utilities Doctrine 37
¶ 2.16   Current Status of General Utilities................................37
¶ 2.17   Disguised and Constructive Dividends 38

Chapter Three. Distributions in Redemption of Stock 41
¶ 3.01   Introduction...41
¶ 3.02   Attribution of One Individual's or Entity's Stock
          Ownership to a Different Individual or Entity..............43
¶ 3.03   Tax Consequences of Stock Redemption 48

¶ 3.04   Purchase or Dividend Treatment?—Standards Set at
          the Shareholder Level 53
    ¶ 3.04.1 § 302(b)(1)—Not Essentially Equivalent to a
          Dividend 53
        ¶ 3.04.1.1   Redemption of Voting Stock.........................54
        ¶ 3.04.1.2   Redemption of Nonvoting Stock 56
        ¶ 3.04.1.3   Hostility Among Shareholders.....................58
    ¶ 3.04.2 Substantially Disproportionate Redemptions.........59
    ¶ 3.04.3 Termination of Shareholder's Interest 62
        ¶ 3.04.3.1   Preclusion of Family Attribution.................62
        ¶ 3.04.3.2   Waiver of Attribution by an Entity 66
¶ 3.05   Partial Liquidations—Standards Set at the Corporate
          Level 67
    ¶ 3.05.1 Tax Consequences to Shareholder-Distributee.......67
    ¶ 3.05.2 Definition of Partial Liquidation.............................69
¶ 3.06   Gain or Loss Recognized by Distributing
          Corporation 72
¶ 3.07   Distribution in Redemption of Stock That Was
          Included Within the Gross Estate of a Decedent for Federal
          Estate Tax Purposes...73
¶ 3.08   Effect of Redemption of Stock on Corporation's
          Earnings and Profits 75
¶ 3.09   Extraordinary Dividend to a Corporate Distributee
          Resulting from a Stock Redemption or Partial
          Liquidation..78
¶ 3.10   Redemption of Stock of One Shareholder as a
          Dividend to Other Shareholders..79
¶ 3.11   Constructive Redemption—the Sale of Corporate
          Stock Either to a Subsidiary Corporation or to a Sister
          Corporation 80
    ¶ 3.11.1 Brother-Sister Corporations....................................81
    ¶ 3.11.2 Parent-Subsidiary Corporations 85
    ¶ 3.11.3 Overlap with § 351...87

Chapter Four. Complete Liquidation of a Corporation 89
¶ 4.01   Introduction..89
¶ 4.02   A Liquidating Corporation's Recognition of Gain or
          Loss 91
    ¶ 4.02.1 The Operation of Subsection (d)(1) 93
        ¶ 4.02.1.1   Non-Pro Rata Distributions........................94
        ¶ 4.02.1.2   Disqualified Property 95
    ¶ 4.02.2 The Operation of Subsection (d)(2)—the Anti-
          Stuffing Provision 96
¶ 4.03   Shareholder's Treatment in an Ordinary Liquidation ...98
¶ 4.04   Reincorporations 98

¶ 4.05   Liquidation of a Controlled Subsidiary Corporation 100
    ¶ 4.05.1 Requisites for Nonrecognition for Parent
           Corporation 101
           ¶ 4.05.1.1 Insolvency Exception..................................102
           ¶ 4.05.1.2 Distribution on All Classes of Stock..........103
           ¶ 4.05.1.3 Taxpayer's Deliberate Violation of a
                    § 332 Requirement.....................................103
           ¶ 4.05.1.4 Parent's Basis in Property Received in
                    the Liquidation...104
           ¶ 4.05.1.5 Parent's Acquisition of Subsidiary's Tax
                    Attributes 104
           ¶ 4.05.1.6 Example 104
    ¶ 4.05.2 Minority Shareholders...105
    ¶ 4.05.3 Taxation of the Liquidating Subsidiary 105
    ¶ 4.05.4 Partial or Full Satisfaction of Subsidiary's
           Indebtedness to Its Parent Corporation.......................108

**Chapter Five. Taxable Purchase and Sale of a
Corporate Business** **111**
¶ 5.01   Introduction..111
¶ 5.02   Sale of Assets 111
¶ 5.03   Sale of Stock 113
    ¶ 5.03.1 Sale of Stock Followed by Liquidation of
           Target 114
    ¶ 5.03.2 Section 338 Election..115
¶ 5.04   Section 338(h)(10) Election 120
¶ 5.05   New T's Basis in Its Assets 122
¶ 5.06   Section 336(e) Election 125

**Chapter Six. Distribution of Stock and Section 306
Stock**.. **131**

A.   STOCK DIVIDENDS

¶ 6.01   Introduction..131
¶ 6.02   The Nature of Stock Dividends 132
¶ 6.03   Historical Background—Eisner v. Macomber..............132
¶ 6.04   Section 305—in General...133
¶ 6.05   Stock Dividend Equivalents 139
¶ 6.06   Treatment of a Taxable Stock Dividend.......................141
¶ 6.07   Basis of Stock Received as a Tax-Free Dividend
    Under § 305(a) 142

B. PREFERRED STOCK BAILOUTS
AND SECTION 306 STOCK

¶ 6.08   Introduction..144
    ¶ 6.08.1 Definition of "Section 306 Stock" 146
    ¶ 6.08.2 Disposition of Section 306 Stock 150
    ¶ 6.08.3 Exemption from § 306 Treatment.........................153

Chapter Seven. Organization of a Corporation **155**
¶ 7.01   Introduction..155
¶ 7.02   Basic Rules Apart from § 351......................................156
¶ 7.03   Basic Overview of § 351(a) 157
¶ 7.04   Basis Limitation Rules 160
¶ 7.05   § 351 Requirements—Business Purpose and
    Continuity of Interest..163
¶ 7.06   § 351 Requirements—"Persons in Control
    Immediately After the Exchange" 164
    ¶ 7.06.1 Accommodation Transfers 165
    ¶ 7.06.2 "Immediately After" 166
¶ 7.07   § 351 Requirements—the Transferor Must Transfer
    "Property"...168
¶ 7.08   § 351 Requirements—the "Exchange" Requirement 169
¶ 7.09   § 351 Requirements—Transfers "Solely in Exchange
    for Stock" 170
¶ 7.10   Contribution to Capital 171
¶ 7.11   The Receipt of "Boot," Part I (in General) 172
    ¶ 7.11.1 Nonqualified Preferred Stock................................175
    ¶ 7.11.2 Controlled Corporation's Recognition of Gain or
        Loss..179
¶ 7.12   The Receipt of Boot, Part II (Corporate Assumption
    of Transferor Liability and Netting of Obligations) 179
    ¶ 7.12.1 Tax Avoidance Purpose...181
    ¶ 7.12.2 Liabilities in Excess of Basis................................182
    ¶ 7.12.3 Liabilities That Would Give Rise to a
        Deduction 186
    ¶ 7.12.4 Avoiding § 357(c) 187
    ¶ 7.12.5 Liabilities in Excess of Fair Market Value............190
¶ 7.13   The Receipt of Boot, Part III (Corporate Obligations
    to Shareholder) 191
¶ 7.14   Overriding § 351 192
    ¶ 7.14.1 Statutory Overrides—Depreciation Recapture
        (§ 1245) 192
    ¶ 7.14.2 Statutory Overrides—Related Party
        Transactions (§ 1239)..193
    ¶ 7.14.3 Statutory Overrides—Reallocations by the
        Commissioner (§ 482) 193

¶ 7.14.4 Statutory Overrides—Anti-Bailout Rule I
(§ 304) 194
¶ 7.14.5 Statutory Overrides—Anti-Bailout Rule II
(§ 306) 195
¶ 7.15   Non-Statutory Overrides...196
¶ 7.15.1 Non-Statutory Overrides—Assignment of
Income 196
¶ 7.15.2 Non-Statutory Overrides—the Tax Benefit
Rule..197
¶ 7.15.3 Non-Statutory Overrides—Business Purpose
Test and Court Holding Doctrine................................197

Chapter Eight. Corporate Divisions................................... **199**
¶ 8.01   Introduction...199
¶ 8.02   Types of Corporate Divisions 200
¶ 8.03   Nonrecognition Treatment and the Potential for Tax
Avoidance 201
¶ 8.04   An Overview of §§ 355 and 356....................................203
¶ 8.05   "Stock or Securities" 205
¶ 8.06   Distribution of a Controlling Interest 206
¶ 8.07   The "Device" Test...207
¶ 8.08   The Five-Year Active Trade or Business
Requirement..211
¶ 8.08.1 Active Conduct of a Trade or Business................212
¶ 8.08.2 Active Conduct of a Trade or Business Through
a Subsidiary 215
¶ 8.08.3 The Five-Year Requirement.................................216
¶ 8.08.4 Division of an Integrated Business and the
Problem of "Expansions" 217
¶ 8.08.5 Corporate Divisions Followed by Corporate
Acquisitions..219
¶ 8.09   Nonstatutory Requirements—Business Purpose and
Continuity of Interest...220
¶ 8.09.1 Business Purpose 221
¶ 8.09.2 Continuity of Interest 224
¶ 8.10   Boot..227
¶ 8.10.1 Excess Securities Boot 228
¶ 8.10.2 Stock Boot...229
¶ 8.10.3 Nonqualified Preferred Stock Boot 231
¶ 8.11   Tax Consequences for Shareholders When Boot Is
Distributed 231
¶ 8.11.1 § 356—General Rules 231
¶ 8.11.2 § 356—Amount and Characterization of Gain......232
¶ 8.11.3 § 356—Special Problems in Split-Offs with
Boot..232

¶ 8.11.4 § 356—Testing for Dividend Equivalency 233
¶ 8.12   Basis Calculation 236
¶ 8.13   Taxation of the Distributing Corporation 237
    ¶ 8.13.1 Not Pursuant to a Reorganization 238
    ¶ 8.13.2 Pursuant to a Reorganization 240
    ¶ 8.13.3 Gain Recognition Required by § 355(d) and (e).....241
        ¶ 8.13.3.1 § 355(d) 241
        ¶ 8.13.3.2 § 355(e) 246
¶ 8.14   Earnings and Profits...249

Chapter Nine. Reorganizations...................................... **251**
¶ 9.01   Introduction...251
¶ 9.02   General Tax Consequences of Mergers and
Acquisitions That Qualify as Reorganizations 252
¶ 9.03   Reorganizations—Extra-Statutory Requirements 254
    ¶ 9.03.1 Continuity of Proprietary Interest......................254
    ¶ 9.03.2 Continuity of Business Enterprise......................258
    ¶ 9.03.3 Other Extra-Statutory Doctrines.........................261
¶ 9.04   Overview of the Statutory Requirements of
Reorganizations 261
    ¶ 9.04.1 A Reorganizations 262
    ¶ 9.04.2 B Reorganizations 264
    ¶ 9.04.3 C Reorganizations 271
    ¶ 9.04.4 Triangular Reorganizations 276
    ¶ 9.04.5 Triangular Mergers..279
        ¶ 9.04.5.1 Forward Triangular (Subsidiary) Merger
((a)(2)(D)) 279
        ¶ 9.04.5.2 Reverse Triangular (Subsidiary) Merger
((a)(2)(E)) 281
    ¶ 9.04.6 D Reorganizations..284
        ¶ 9.04.6.1 Divisive D Reorganizations.......................285
        ¶ 9.04.6.2 Acquisitive D Reorganizations...................285
    ¶ 9.04.7 E Reorganizations 288
        ¶ 9.04.7.1 Exchange of Stock for Stock......................289
        ¶ 9.04.7.2 Exchange of Bonds for Stock.....................291
        ¶ 9.04.7.3 Exchange of Bonds for Bonds 291
        ¶ 9.04.7.4 Exchange of Stock for Bonds.....................291
    ¶ 9.04.8 F Reorganizations 292
    ¶ 9.04.9 G Reorganizations..293
¶ 9.05   A Closer Look at Statutory Reorganizations Including
Determination of Basis..293
    ¶ 9.05.1 Tax Treatment of Simple A Reorganizations 295
    ¶ 9.05.2 Tax Treatment of Simple B Reorganizations 296
    ¶ 9.05.3 Tax Treatment of Triangular B
Reorganizations 297

¶ 9.05.4 Tax Treatment of Simple C Reorganizations 299
¶ 9.05.5 Tax Treatment of Triangular C
          Reorganizations 300
¶ 9.05.6 Tax Treatment of Triangular A Reorganizations:
          Forward and Reverse Triangular Mergers 303
¶ 9.05.7 Acquisitive D Reorganizations 307
¶ 9.06   Tax Treatment of Shareholders Who Receive Boot in
          Qualifying Reorganization 309
¶ 9.07   Tax Treatment of Target Corporation (Distribution
          of Appreciated Assets) 312
¶ 9.08   The Rise of § 351 Exchanges as an Alternative to a
          Reorganization 314

Chapter Ten. Acquisition or Retention of Tax
   Attributes **319**
¶ 10.01   Introduction..320

A. ACQUISITION OF TAX ATTRIBUTES

¶ 10.02   Introduction..322
¶ 10.03   Liquidation of Subsidiary Corporations 323
¶ 10.04   Acquisitive Reorganizations.......................................323
¶ 10.05   Triangular Reorganizations 323
¶ 10.06   Taxable Years and Carrybacks 325
¶ 10.07   Net Operating Losses 326
¶ 10.08   Earnings and Profits...327

B. STATUTORY LIMITATIONS

¶ 10.09   Introduction..329
¶ 10.10   The § 382 Limitation—Overview 330
¶ 10.11   Objective of § 382 Limitation 331
¶ 10.12   Events That Cause the Application of the
          Limitation..332
¶ 10.13   The Amount of the § 382 Limitation 342
¶ 10.14   Continuity of Business Requirement...........................346
¶ 10.15   Insolvent Corporations 346
¶ 10.16   Recognized Built-In Gains and Losses 347
¶ 10.17   The § 383 Limitation on Carryovers of Net Capital
          Losses and of Certain Tax Credits 351
¶ 10.18   Limitation on Offsetting Preacquisition Losses and
          Credits of One Corporation Against Another's Built-In
          Gains...351
¶ 10.19   Acquisitions Made to Evade or Avoid Income Tax—
          § 269..355

C.   NON-STATUTORY LIMITATION ON SURVIVAL OF TAX ATTRIBUTES

¶ 10.20   The De Facto Dissolution Doctrine 356

Chapter Eleven. S Corporations **359**
¶ 11.01   Small Businesses—Introduction 360
¶ 11.02   Subchapter S—Introduction 361
¶ 11.03   Application of Subchapter C to S Corporations 362
¶ 11.04   Eligibility, in General 363
¶ 11.05   Qualified Subchapter S Subsidiary ("QSSS" or "QSub") 365
¶ 11.06   Trusts as Shareholders 365
¶ 11.07   One Class of Stock Requirement, in General 367
¶ 11.08   Debt as a Second Class of Stock 368
¶ 11.09   Call Options and Warrants as a Second Class of Stock 369
¶ 11.10   Buy-Sell Arrangements 370
¶ 11.11   Difference in Amounts or Timing of Actual Distributions 370
¶ 11.12   Election 371
¶ 11.13   Taxable Year 372
¶ 11.14   Taxation of the S Corporation 372
¶ 11.15   Earnings and Profits 373
¶ 11.16   Pass-Through of Tax Items, in General 373
¶ 11.17   Shareholder's Basis—Adjustments 375
¶ 11.18   Order of Adjustments to Shareholder's Basis 377
¶ 11.19   Limitations on Deductions, in General 377
¶ 11.20   At Risk and Passive Activity Loss Limitations 378
¶ 11.21   Distributions to Shareholders—No Earnings and Profits 379
¶ 11.22   Distributions to Shareholders—Accumulated Adjustments Account (AAA) 380
¶ 11.23   Distributions to Shareholders of Property 382
¶ 11.24   Distributions to Shareholders During Post-Termination Transition Period 383
¶ 11.25   Termination of S Election—Revocation 384
¶ 11.26   Termination of S Election—Cessation of Qualification 384
¶ 11.27   Termination of S Election—Passive Investment Income 385
¶ 11.28   New S Election After Termination 385
¶ 11.29   S Termination Year 386
¶ 11.30   Taxation of Passive Investment Income 386
¶ 11.31   Purpose and Operation of § 1374 388
¶ 11.32   LIFO Recapture Amount 393

¶ 11.33 Qualified Business Income Deduction.............................394
    ¶ 11.33.1 Amount of the Deduction 394
    ¶ 11.33.2 Qualified Business Income 394
    ¶ 11.33.3 Combined Qualified Business Income.................395
    ¶ 11.33.4 Qualified Trade or Business 396
    ¶ 11.33.5 Threshold Amount..397
    ¶ 11.33.6 Anti-Abuse Rules...397

TABLE OF CASES 399

TABLE OF INTERNAL REVENUE CODE SECTIONS 401

TABLE OF TREASURY REGULATIONS 409

TABLE OF REVENUE RULINGS...415

TABLE OF MISCELLANEOUS DECISIONS...417

INDEX 419

PRINCIPLES OF CORPORATE TAXATION

Second Edition

Chapter One

INTRODUCTION

Analysis

Para.

1.01   Overview

1.02   General Tax Treatment of C Corporations

1.03   Nonrecognition

1.04   Rescission Doctrine

1.05   What Organizations Constitute a Corporation?

1.06   Diagraming Transactions

¶ 1.01 OVERVIEW

A corporation is a fictional entity. For many jural purposes, including for tax purposes, it has a separate legal existence apart from its owners. The owners of a corporation (i.e., those who have an indirect interest in its assets) are those who hold shares of its stock and are referred to as "shareholders." Creditors of the corporation also have an interest in the corporation's assets, but it is of a different nature than that held by the shareholders.

Since a corporation is a common form of conducting business, it became necessary to determine how the tax law should treat corporations. One possibility was to treat a corporation as a separate entity from its shareholders and to tax the corporation on its income. A different approach (referred to as the "conduit" or the "aggregate" approach) would be to treat the corporation as merely a representative of the aggregate of the interests of the shareholders in the assets held in the corporation's name; under that conduit approach, the corporation's income would pass through to the shareholders and be taxed directly to them. The choice was made to treat a corporation as a distinct entity, separate from its shareholders, and to tax the corporation on its income. This is referred to as an entity approach and results in a double taxation of the corporation's income; it is taxed once to the corporation when it is earned and is taxed again to the shareholders when the earnings (less taxes) are distributed to them. The conduit approach has been applied to partnerships, which do not pay any federal income taxes

1

and all of whose income is passed through to its partners who pay a single income tax thereon.

For tax purposes, corporations can be divided into subcategories. There are foreign corporations and domestic corporations. A domestic corporation is one "created or organized in the United States or under the law of the United States or of any State."[1] A foreign corporation is one that is not domestic.[2] This book deals only with domestic corporations. Most of the rules applicable to domestic corporations also apply to those foreign corporations that are subject to United States taxation, but additional rules apply to the foreign entities.

Certain corporations are permitted to make an election to pass their income through to their shareholders, and those corporations generally are not taxed on their income. Those electing corporations are referred to as "S corporations."[3]

All corporations that are not classified as S corporations are referred to as "C corporations."[4] C corporations are so named because many of the tax provisions that apply specifically to them are set forth in Subchapter C of Chapter 1 of Subtitle A of the Internal Revenue Code (§§ 301 to 385). Except for Chapter Eleven, which addresses S corporations, this book will deal exclusively with domestic C corporations.[5] Note that most of the provisions of Subchapter C also apply to S corporations and their shareholders.[6]

¶ 1.02 GENERAL TAX TREATMENT OF C CORPORATIONS

A C corporation is taxed on all of its income reduced by deductions that are allowed by the Code. While individuals have a standard deduction allowance, corporations do not and also do not have an exemption allowance. So, every dollar of income that is not reduced by a specific deduction is taxable.

Prior to 2018, in lieu of the regular corporate tax, a C corporations might be subject to a larger Alternative Minimum Tax; but the 2017 Tax Cuts and Jobs Act repealed the Alternative

---

[1] § 7701(a)(4).

[2] § 7701(a)(5).

[3] § 1361(a)(1).

[4] § 1361(a)(2).

[5] Certain entities that are taxed as corporations are given special tax treatment by the Code. For example, life insurance companies and real estate investment trusts (REITs) have specific provisions addressed to them. This text will not discuss those entities and will focus on ordinary domestic C corporations.

[6] § 1371(a).

Minimum Tax for corporations. So for taxable years beginning after 2017, there is no Alternative Minimum Tax for corporations.

Prior to 2018, graduated multiple tax rates applied to C corporations. The 2017 Tax Cuts and Jobs Act eliminated multiple tax rates for corporations. For taxable years beginning after 2017, there is a single rate of 21% on all of a corporation's taxable income.[7] The corporation's taxable income is determined in the same manner as that of an individual taxpayer; but some provisions apply differently to corporations than they do to individuals; and some provisions apply exclusively either to individuals or to corporations.

The concept of distinguishing itemized and nonitemized deductions does not apply to corporations, and the concept of adjusted gross income also is inapplicable.

A corporation is not allowed a deduction for distributions it makes to a shareholder on account of the shareholder's stock.[8] The taxation of the corporation on its income together with the denial of a deduction for the distributions it makes to shareholders who are taxed on that distribution results in the double taxation of corporate income. Currently, the tax law provides some relief from that double taxation by applying capital gain tax rates to the income that noncorporate shareholders recognize from certain dividend income.[9]

Noncorporate taxpayers are taxed at lower tax rates on long-term capital gain income than on other income. Currently, the preferential lower rates on net capital gains do not apply to corporations. So, corporations pay ordinary income tax rates on capital gains. Corporations are permitted to deduct capital losses only from capital gains; they are not permitted to deduct any amount of capital losses from ordinary income. Consequently, the only benefit that capital gain characterization has for a corporation is to permit it to deduct capital losses from those gains.

Subject to several exceptions, a C corporation is not permitted to use the cash receipts and disbursement method of accounting for reporting its taxable income.[10] The 2017 Tax Cuts and Jobs Act expanded the principal exception that allows a C corporation to use the cash receipts and disbursements method. If a corporation's

---

[7]   § 11(b).

[8]   Of course, a corporation can make deductible payments to a person who is a shareholder in a capacity other than as a shareholder. For example, a corporation could employ a shareholder, and the wages paid for that person's services may qualify as a deductible business expense under § 162.

[9]   § 1(h)(11).

[10]   § 448. A farming business and a qualified personal service corporation are permitted to use the cash receipts and disbursements method. § 448(b)(1), (2). A qualified personal service corporation is defined in § 448(d)(2).

average annual gross receipts for the three-year period immediately preceding the taxable year does not exceed $25,000,000, the corporation can use the cash receipts and disbursement method of accounting.[11] A C corporation, other than a personal service corporation, can elect to adopt a calendar or fiscal year of its choice to report its income.[12] A personal service corporation and an S corporation are required to use a calendar year unless certain conditions are satisfied.[13] A personal service corporation is a corporation whose principal activity is the performance of personal services that are substantially performed by "employee-owners."[14]

The 2017 Tax Cuts and Jobs Act Adopted § 167(j) imposing a limit on the amount of deduction permitted for business interest. The deduction for the taxpayer's business interest is limited to the sum of: (1) the business interest income of the taxpayer for that year, 10% of the taxpayer's "adjusted taxable income" for that year, plus (3) taxpayer's floor plan financing interest (i.e., interest on financing for the acquisition of motor vehicles held for sale or lease). Business interest is interest paid or accrued on a debt allocable to a trade or business (but does not include investment interest). Business interest income is interest income properly allocable to a trade or business (but does not include investment income). Certain businesses are not treated as a trade or business for this purpose. The trade or business of performing services as an employee is excluded, and an election is permitted to exclude a real property trade or business and a farming business from this provision. § 163(j)(7). Adjusted taxable income is the taxable income of the taxpayer with the adjustments listed in § 163(j)(8). This limitation on interest deduction does not apply to a business whose average annual gross receipts for the three preceding taxable years does not exceed $25,000,000. § 163(j)(3). If the limitation of § 163(j) disallows a deduction of business interest, the disallowed amount is carried forward and treated as business interest paid or accrued in the next year. § 163(j)(2).

¶ 1.03 NONRECOGNITION

The Code includes a number of provisions that exclude or defer the recognition of realized gain. The provisions deferring the recognition of gain are referred to as "nonrecognition provisions." Many of the nonrecognition provisions apply to transactions involving corporations or corporate stock. Much of corporate tax

---

[11]   § 448(b)(3), (c)(1). If the corporation is a tax shelter, it cannot use the cash receipts and disbursement method of accounting. § 448(a)(3).

[12]   § 441.

[13]   §§ 441, 1378.

[14]   An "owner-employee" is defined in § 269A(b)(2) as modified by § 441(i)(2).

practice consists of structuring transactions so as to comply with the requirements of one or more of those nonrecognition provisions without sacrificing the business objectives of the parties. The nonrecognition provisions are central elements of the corporate tax system. Consequently, a sizeable portion of a corporate tax course and this book is focused on those provisions.

The justification for the Code's permitting nonrecognition of gain for certain transactions is that Congress did not wish the imposition of income tax liability to deter the restructuring of the form in which a business or businesses are conducted, or of changes in the types of ownership interests of the shareholders, where the restructuring is intended to increase efficiency and thereby might benefit the economy and the public.[15] However, we will see that the provisions allowing nonrecognition for a change of ownership interests are quite generous in many respects. Another consideration that may have impacted the decision to adopt some of the nonrecognition provisions lies in the alternative approaches that might have been taken to the taxation of a corporation—i.e., treating a corporation either as a separate and distinct entity from its shareholders or as a mere alter ego of its shareholders. As previously noted, for many significant purposes, Congress chose to treat the corporation as a separate entity and taxed it on its income. But Congress was aware that a corporation is not entirely independent of its shareholders. By allowing some transfer of assets between a corporation and its shareholders to take place without incurring an immediate tax, Congress impliedly accommodated the alter ego aspect of a corporation. In effect, the tax system is a compromise system in which a corporation and its shareholders are treated as separate entities for most, but not for all, purposes.

¶ 1.04 RESCISSION DOCTRINE

If a transaction is rescinded in the same taxable year of the taxpayer in which it took place, the tax law treats the situation as if the transaction had never occurred provided that the parties are essentially in the same economic position that they would have occupied if the transaction had never occurred. A rescission refers to the abrogation, cancellation, or voiding of a contract that has the effect of releasing the contracting parties from further obligations to each other and restores the parties to the relative positions they would have occupied had no contract been made. A rescission may be made by mutual agreement of the parties, by one of the parties with

---

[15]   One commentator proposed that the true purpose of providing the nonrecognition provisions was to remove tax as a deterrent to the "redeployment of corporate assets." David E. Shores, "Continuity of Business Enterprise: A Concept Whose Time Has Passed," 63 The Tax Lawyer 471 (2010).

the other's consent if sufficient grounds exist, or by applying to a court for a decree of rescission.[16]

However, if the rescission takes place in a taxable year subsequent to the one in which the transaction occurred, it will not change the consequences of the prior year. To prevent the consequences of the transaction, the rescission must be made in the same year that the transaction took place. This treatment accords with the annual accounting concept pursuant to which the tax consequences of a taxable year are determined by the facts that exist at the end of the year.

The rescission doctrine is established by administrative rulings and case law. See Rev. Rul. 80–58, Rev. Rul. 74–501, PLR 200752035, PLR 200533002, *Penn v. Robertson*, 115 F.2d 167 (4th Cir. 1940). Note that the IRS will not rule on the question of whether the rescission doctrine applies to a transaction.[17]

¶ 1.05 WHAT ORGANIZATIONS CONSTITUTE A CORPORATION?

Since corporations are taxed differently from other organizations, and since numerous types of organizations exist, it is important to determine which organizations are to be taxed as a corporation. The question arises especially in connection with unincorporated businesses. For example, will a business venture that is operated in partnership form or by a trust be taxed as a corporation or as a partnership or trust?

The Code does not provide a definition of the term "corporation."[18] However, § 7701(a)(3) states that "the term 'corporation' includes associations, joint stock companies, and insurance companies." The most controversial term in that list was "associations"; much litigation ensued as to whether an unincorporated business organization was an "association" taxed as a corporation.[19] Originally, the determination of whether an unincorporated organization was taxable as a corporation was based on a resemblance test—that is, the characteristics of the specific

---

[16] Rev. Rul. 80–58. See also, *Penn v. Robertson*, 115 F.2d 167 (4th Cir. 1940).

[17] Rev. Proc. 2018–3 (Sec. 3.02(8)).

[18] While not defined in the Code, it is defined in Treas. Reg. § 301.7701–2(b).

[19] The history of that litigation is instructive. There were periods during which the government sought to impose association characterization (and thus corporate taxation) on organizations in order to impose double taxation on the organization's earnings. There also were periods during which corporate characterization provided tax benefits to an organization (for example, allowed more liberal deferred compensation arrangements for employees who also were shareholders); and that led to a reversal of litigating roles in which the taxpayers sought association characterization and the government resisted.

organization were examined to determine whether they resembled those of a corporation more than those of an unincorporated entity. This resemblance test was adopted by the Supreme Court in its 1935 decision of *Morrissey v. Commissioner*,[20] and Treasury promulgated regulations applying that test.

Over the years, unincorporated organizations became more sophisticated and complex, and the established lines of purported difference between a corporation and such entities became unreliable markers for distinguishing them. The states' adoption of laws permitting the establishment of Limited Liability Companies (LLCs) and Limited Liability Partnerships (LLPs) especially impacted on this issue and made the old lines of distinction obsolete.

Beginning in 1997, the regulations were changed to provide an eligible organization (referred to as an "eligible entity") the power to elect whether to be taxed as a corporation.[21] The current regulations are referred to as the "check the box" regulations. Under these regulations, an eligible entity with two or more members can elect to be taxed either as a corporation (i.e., as an association taxable as a corporation) or as a partnership. An eligible entity with a single owner can elect either to be taxed as a corporation or to be disregarded as an entity that is separate from its owner (i.e., the entity is treated as a nullity for federal income tax purposes even though it has jural existence for state business and property law purposes).[22] A single-member eligible entity that is not taxed as a corporation is sometimes referred to as a "tax nothing."

To be an eligible entity, it must first be an organization that is treated as a business entity for federal income tax purposes.[23] A business entity qualifies as an "eligible entity" if it is not classified as a corporation by Treas. Reg. § 301.7701–2(b)(1) or (3) through (8).[24] Examples of business entities that are classified as corporations, and therefore for which an election is not available, are incorporated organizations, insurance companies, certain (but not all) foreign entities, real estate investment trusts (REITS), and publicly traded partnerships that are treated as a corporation by § 7704. So, an incorporated organization will be treated as a corporation, and no election out of that characterization is permitted.

---

[20]   296 U.S. 344 (1935).

[21]   Treas. Reg. §§ 301.7701–2 through 301.7701–3. The validity of these regulations was sustained by the Sixth Circuit. *Littriello v. United States*, 484 F.3d 372 (6th Cir. 2007).

[22]   Treas. Reg. § 301.7701–3(a).

[23]   Treas. Regs. §§ 301.7701–2(a) and 301.7701–3(a).

[24]   Treas. Reg. § 301.7701–3(a).

If a domestic eligible entity fails to make an election, the default rule is to treat the organization as a partnership if it has more than one member or as a tax nothing if it has only one member.[25] There are a different set of default rules for foreign eligible entities.

¶ 1.06 DIAGRAMING TRANSACTIONS

It is often difficult to visualize the transactions that are the subject of a tax inquiry. This is as true for tax practitioners as it is for students who are taking a tax course. It is helpful to diagram the original position of the corporations and shareholders and then to make new diagrams for each transaction that takes place to show how the positions of the parties have changed. Tax practitioners make diagrams as a matter of course. It is essential to applying the tax principles to a problem that the nature of the transactions is clearly in focus, and diagraming helps in that regard.

---

[25] Treas. Reg. § 301.7701–3(b)(1).

Chapter Two

DISTRIBUTIONS TO SHAREHOLDERS: § 301 DISTRIBUTIONS

Analysis

Para.

2.01   Introduction

2.02   Amount Distributed

2.03   Definition of "Dividend"

2.04   Dividend—Received Deduction for Corporate Shareholders

2.05   Treatment of Dividend to a Noncorporate Shareholder

2.06   Earnings and Profits—in General

2.07   Effect of Discharge of Indebtedness on E and P

2.08   Effect of § 301 Distributions on E and P

2.09   Distribution of Corporation's Stock or Bonds

2.10   Amendments to § 312 and Depreciation Deductions

2.11   § 301 Distributions to 20 Percent Corporate Shareholder

2.12   Distributions to Shareholders in Excess of Earnings and Profits

2.13   Extraordinary Dividends to a Corporate Shareholder

2.14   Basis of Property Distributed to Shareholders

2.15   Distributing Corporation's Recognition of Gain or Loss: General Utilities Doctrine

2.16   Current Status of General Utilities

2.17   Disguised and Constructive Dividends

¶ 2.01 INTRODUCTION

Alice, an individual, is a shareholder of Acme Corporation. Even if Alice is the only shareholder of Acme Corporation, corporate law and the federal tax code treat the two as separate tax entities. How does Alice get money out of her investment in Acme Corporation? Alice could sell her stock to a third party and thus terminate some or all of her investment in Acme Corporation. Instead, Alice could sell her stock to the corporation in what is called a "stock redemption." Alternatively, Alice could have Acme Corporation pay her a salary for services provided to Acme Corporation, or pay rent for a building that Alice owns, or pay a royalty for a patent that Alice controls.

Where we will begin, however, is with the common corporate distribution to Alice as a shareholder of Acme Corporation. In this context, we use the term "distribution" to refer to a transfer of corporate assets to a shareholder where the corporation does not receive any of its stock in exchange. Since such distributions are subject to § 301 of the Code, we often refer to them as § 301 distributions. If the corporation receives shares of its stock from the shareholder in exchange for the property transferred to the shareholder, that is referred to as a "stock redemption." As we will see, in certain circumstances a corporation's purchase of its stock in a stock redemption will be ignored and the transaction will be treated as a § 301 distribution.[1] In some contexts, a corporation's distribution of property to a shareholder, whether a § 301 distribution or a stock redemption, is referred to as a "nonliquidating distribution" or, if it is made in complete liquidation of the corporation, as a "liquidating distribution."

In common parlance and for general corporate law purposes, most distributions from a corporation are referred to as a "dividend." However, for federal tax purposes, the word "dividend" is a term of art that is specifically defined in the Code. The tax definition of a dividend is separate and independent of the characterization of a corporate distribution to shareholders for state corporate law purposes. Unless indicated otherwise, as used hereafter, the term "dividend" will refer to a dividend for federal tax purposes. A distribution made on a share of stock, which may or may not be a dividend, is referred to in this book as a "§ 301 distribution." It is important not to assume that every distribution made by a corporation on its stock is a dividend, and so it is useful to refer to such distributions by some name other than "dividend" in order to keep in focus that additional determinations must be made to see if it qualifies as a dividend.

Assume Alice comes into your office and states that Acme Corporation has distributed assets to her. She would like to know her tax consequences on account of receiving that distribution. The correct answer will depend on several factors:

(1) the amount distributed to her;

(2) whether the distribution was made to her in her capacity as a shareholder;

(3) whether and to what extent the distribution to her constitutes a dividend for federal tax purposes.

---

[1]   See ¶ 3.01, infra.

Dividends received by a shareholder constitute ordinary income regardless of whether the shareholder is an individual, a corporation, or some other entity.[2] As we shall see, in the event that a corporation's distribution to a shareholder in his or her capacity as a shareholder does not qualify as a dividend, it typically will be treated as a return of capital (reducing basis in the stock held by the shareholder) or as a capital gain to the extent that the amount distributed exceeds the shareholder's basis.

¶ 2.02 AMOUNT DISTRIBUTED

Section 301 deals with distributions made by a corporation to its shareholders on account of their stock holdings. As discussed above, such a distribution may or may not constitute a "dividend" for federal tax purposes, and so it is not desirable to refer indiscriminately to all such distributions as dividends. Accordingly, we will refer to a distribution that is made to a shareholder on account of the shareholder's stock holdings as a "§ 301 distribution."

The amount distributed as a § 301 distribution to a shareholder is equal to the amount of money plus the fair market value of "property" in kind received by the shareholder.[3] This amount is reduced (but never below zero) by the sum of the liabilities assumed or accepted by the shareholder[4] pursuant to the distribution.[5] For purposes of § 301, the term "property" is defined in § 317(a) as "money, securities and any other property" other than stock in the distributing corporation or rights to acquire that stock.[6] Thus,

---

[2]　§ 301(c)(1).

[3]　§ 301(b)(1).

[4]　Treas. Reg. § 1.301–1(g) states that a liability will not reduce the amount distributed unless assumed by the shareholder within the meaning of § 357(d). The liabilities to which this provision can apply are divided into two categories. One is a "recourse" liability—i.e., a liability that the owner of the property has a personal obligation to repay. For this purpose, a recourse liability is not deemed to have been assumed by the transferee unless the latter has agreed to and is expected to satisfy the obligation. It does not matter if the transferor also continues to be liable for payment of the obligation. § 357(d)(1)(A). A second type of liability is a "nonrecourse" liability. A nonrecourse liability is one that encumbers property and that the owner has no obligation to repay. Accordingly, the creditor's only recourse if the debt is not repaid is to foreclose on the encumbered property. For this purpose, a transferee who takes property subject to a nonrecourse liability is deemed to have assumed that liability. § 357(d)(1)(B). However, if the nonrecourse liability is also secured by property not transferred to the shareholder, the amount of the nonrecourse liability that is treated as assumed may be reduced by the amount of the debt that the owner of the other assets securing the debt agrees with the transferee to satisfy and is expected to do so. No more than the fair market value of such other property securing the debt can reduce the liability deemed to have been assumed by the transferee. § 357(d)(2).

[5]　§ 301(b)(2).

[6]　Although the statutory definition of property for this purpose specifically excludes stock of the distributing corporation, as we shall see in Chapter Six when we

property can include, among other examples, land (improved or unimproved), tangible and intangible personalty including bonds and obligation notes of the distributing corporation, inventory, and stock of a corporation other than the distributing corporation.

Ex. (1) Corporation X has two equal shareholders, A, an individual, and P Corporation. Corporation X holds unimproved Blackacre with a fair market value of $10,000 and a basis to X of $2,000. X distributes $10,000 cash to A and Blackacre to P Corporation. The amount distributed to each shareholder is $10,000. Note that it is irrelevant for purposes of determining the amount distributed whether the shareholder is an individual or a corporation. Also, note that the basis that the distributing corporation holds in the property is irrelevant when determining the amount distributed to the shareholder.

Ex. (2) The same facts as in Example (1) except that Blackacre is encumbered by a $4,000 mortgage and P Corporation takes the distribution of Blackacre subject to that mortgage debt.[7] The mortgage debt is not secured by any other property. The amount distributed to P Corporation is $6,000—that is, the $10,000 fair market value of Blackacre less the $4,000 liability which P Corporation accepted. Since P did not assume personal liability for the debt, it is a nonrecourse debt in P's hands. For the purpose of determining the amount distributed by X to P, it does not matter whether P assumes the debt or merely takes the property subject to the encumbrance on it.

¶ 2.03 DEFINITION OF "DIVIDEND"

The characterization of a distribution as a dividend is significant. A dividend is treated as ordinary income to the distributee, but the Jobs and Growth Tax Relief Act Reconciliation Act of 2003 (hereinafter referred to as the "JGTRRA") amended the Code to tax most dividends to noncorporate taxpayers at capital gain rates, which currently will usually be a 20% rate. While there are

---

study stock dividends, there are instances when the tax treatment of such stock distributions will be covered by § 301.

[7] As used in this book, if property is received "subject to" a liability, the debt was not assumed by the recipient, and so is a nonrecourse liability in the recipient's hands. If the transferee "assumes" the debt, the transferee has accepted personal liability for its payment. That is the typical manner in which those terms are employed, but the term "assumes" is given a special meaning in § 357(d), which meaning has been extended to § 301 by the regulation discussed in n. 4 of this chapter.

some exceptions to that treatment, even when taxed at capital gain rates, a characterization of a transaction as a dividend is important.[8]

A dividend for tax purposes is defined in § 316(a) as a: "distribution of property made by a corporation to its shareholders" out of either earnings and profits (oftentimes referred to as "e and p") accumulated after February 28, 1913,[9] or current earnings and profits for the taxable year. Distributions are deemed to be made out of the most recently accumulated earnings and profits (that is, the corporation's e and p are allocated in the reverse chronological order from which they were obtained by the corporation).

The phrase "earnings and profits" is a term of art for federal tax purposes. The method for determining e and p is described in ¶¶ 2.06 to 2.11. The extent to which a distribution to a shareholder constitutes a dividend turns upon the amount of earnings and profits allocated to that distribution under a bifurcated standard, viz., (i) the current e and p of the distributing corporation for the taxable year (determined at the end of the taxable year without making any reduction for distributions made during that taxable year) are first allocated pro rata to the distributions made during the current taxable year, and (ii) if the total distributions during the taxable year exceed the current e and p, then the e and p accumulated after February 28, 1913, are allocated to such distributions according to their chronological order of distribution.

Note that the earnings and profits for a current year are isolated from the earnings and profits that were accumulated in prior years, and so there are two classes or groupings of earnings and profits, which are often referred to respectively as "current e and p" and "accumulated e and p." Note also that the allocation systems for the two classes of earnings and profits are different. Current e and p are allocated pro rata to distributions made during the year—the timing of the distributions has no effect on the allocation of current e and p. Timing is everything, however, for the allocation of accumulated e and p.

Ex. (1)   At the beginning of its Year Two calendar year, X Corporation, which reports on a calendar year basis, had no accumulated e and p. On January 1, Year Two, X distributed $20,000 cash to shareholder A. On December 30, Year Two, X distributed $20,000 cash to shareholder B. In Year Two, X earned a $10,000 profit (after-taxes), and the current e and p of the X Corporation for Year Two

---

[8]   See ¶ 2.05.

[9]   This peculiar date was chosen because the Sixteenth Amendment to the Constitution became effective on February 25, 1913; therefore, the end of the month was chosen as a dividing line.

(computed at the end of the year) amounted to $10,000. Since there were earnings and profits in the current year, and since the total amount distributed that year ($40,000) is greater than X's current *e and p*, the current *e and p* of $10,000 must be allocated pro rata to the distributions made during Year One.

The method for allocation of current *e and p* is set out in Treasury Regulation § 1.316–2(b): "that proportion of each distribution which the total earnings and profits of the year bears to the total distributions made during the year shall be regarded as out of the earnings and profits of that year." In this example, the calculation is:

$$\frac{\$10{,}000 \text{ (current } e \text{ and } p)}{\$40{,}000 \text{ (total distributions)}} = 25\%$$

Thus, 25 percent of each distribution comes out of current *e and p* so that $5,000 ($20,000 × 25 percent) is allocated to each distribution.

An alternative (and sometimes easier) method for determining the amount of current *e and p* allocated to each distribution is that since the distributions were equal, half the current *e and p* ($5,000) is allocated to A's distribution and half the current *e and p* ($5,000) is allocated to B's distribution. A and B each have $5,000 of dividend income.

Ex. (2) Same facts as Example (1) except that the distribution to B was $80,000 cash. Under the regulation's formula, the calculation is:

$$\frac{\$10{,}000 \text{ (current } e \text{ and } p)}{\$100{,}000 \text{ (total distributions)}} = 10\%$$

Thus, 10% of each distribution comes out of X's current *e and p* or $2,000 ($20,000 × 10 percent) for A and $8,000 ($80,000 × 10%) for B. A has dividend income of $2,000; and B has dividend income of $8,000.

Under our alternative calculation system, which is merely another means of reaching the same result, X's current *e and p* are allocated pro rata so 80% ($80,000/$100,000) of X's current *e and p*, $8,000, will be allocated to B and 20% ($20,000/$100,000) of X's current *e and p*, $2,000, will be allocated to A. Note again that the timing of the two distributions has no effect on the calculation.

Ex. (3)   At the beginning of calendar Year Three, Y Corporation had accumulated *e and p* of $1,200. Y reports its income on a calendar year basis. For Year Three, Y had current *e and p* of $10,000. On June 6, Year Three, Y distributed $3,000 cash to shareholder C; and on November 8, Year Three, Y distributed $9,000 cash to shareholder D. The regulation's formula for allocating current *e and p* is:

$$\frac{\$10,000 \text{ (current } e \text{ and } p)}{\$12,000 \text{ (total distributions)}} = 83.33\%$$

Thus, 83.33% of each distribution comes out of Y's current *e and p* or $2,500 ($3,000 × 83.33 percent) for C and $7,500 ($9,000 × 83.33%) for D. Similarly, under our alternative method of calculation, the $10,000 current *e and p* are allocated 25 percent ($2,500) to the June 6 distribution to C and 75 percent ($7,500) to the November 8 distribution to D.

Y's $1,200 accumulated *e and p* are then allocated to the distributions in the order made, i.e., $500 is allocated to the balance of the June 6 distribution that was made to C ($3,000 minus the $2,500 current *e and p* that were allocated to that distribution), and the remaining $700 of accumulated *e and p* are allocated to the November 8 distribution that was made to D.[10] Thus, C had a dividend of $3,000 and D had a dividend of $8,200. In tabular form, the allocation is as follows:

Date	Amount Distributed	Allocat'n of Curr. e and p	Allocat'n of Accum. e and p	Total Alloc. of e and p	Amount of Dividend
June 6	$3,000	$2,500	$500	$3,000	$3,000
Nov. 8	$9,000	$7,500	$700	$8,200	$8,200

So far, we have studied corporations with operations that have been successful; but obviously not all businesses are consistently successful. The next few examples illustrate the allocation of *e and p* when the corporation either has been historically unprofitable but has current earnings, or is unprofitable in the year of the distribution but has positive accumulated *e and p*.

Ex. (4)   At the beginning of its calendar Year Four, X Corporation, which reports on a calendar year basis, had accumulated *e*

---

[10]   Treas. Reg. § 1.316–2(c), Ex.

and p of *negative* ($50,000), i.e., a deficit e *and* p. On January 1, Year Four, X distributed $20,000 cash to shareholder A. On December 30, Year Four, X distributed $20,000 cash to shareholder B. In Year Four, X Corporation earned a $10,000 profit (after-taxes), and the current e *and* p of the X Corporation for Year Four (computed at the end of the year) amounted to $10,000. Even though X has negative accumulated e *and* p, the e *and* p of the current year must be allocated pro rata to the distributions made during Year Four. Since the distributions were equal, half the current e *and* p ($5,000) is allocated to A's distribution and half the current e *and* p ($5,000) is allocated to B's distribution. A and B each have $5,000 of dividend income. Note that the answer would be the same if X's accumulated e *and* p at the beginning of the year had been zero.

Ex. (5)   At the beginning of the calendar Year Six, Y Corporation, which reports on a calendar year basis, had accumulated earnings and profits of $40,000. On July 1, Year Six, Y distributed $40,000 cash to its shareholder, individual A. In Year Six, Y operated at a deficit and had a deficit e *and* p for that taxable year of ($10,000). Since Y has no current e *and* p for Year Six, only Y's accumulated e *and* p were available for allocation in order to create a dividend. However, the losses during the year must be taken into account when determining the amount of accumulated e *and* p that are available at the time that the distribution was made. Generally, a corporation's aggregate loss for the entire year is allocated pro rata throughout the year, but the current year's loss will be allocated differently if the losses that occurred in the portion of the year prior to the distribution can be shown.[11] In this example, assume the shareholder chooses to use the pro rata method, and thus half the losses are deemed to have taken place by July 1 (the halfway point of the year). Thus, Y is deemed to have lost $5,000 by July 1. Those losses reduce accumulated e *and* p, and so Y is deemed to have $35,000 accumulated e *and* p on July 1 when the distribution to A takes place. Accordingly, only $35,000 of the amount distributed to A is a dividend.

When a corporation has more than one class of stock outstanding and when one or more of those classes are given preferential rights to receive dividends prior to the corporation's paying a dividend on

---

[11]   Treas. Reg. § 1.316–2(b). In effect, the taxpayer has the option to use a pro rata method or to determine the actual amount of loss in the period preceding the § 301 distribution.

the other classes, should the allocation of current *e and p* take those preferential rights into account? The problem arises only if the total amount distributed in a taxable year exceeds the aggregate of the distributing corporation's accumulated and current *e and p*. In Revenue Ruling 69–440, the Commissioner determined that current *e and p* should be allocated first to distributions made in satisfaction of preferential rights; and only the remaining current *e and p* are allocated to the distributions that are not made in satisfaction of such preferential rights.

¶ 2.04 DIVIDEND—RECEIVED DEDUCTION FOR CORPORATE SHAREHOLDERS

A dividend paid to a corporate shareholder is ordinary income to the corporate shareholder and does not qualify for the capital gains rates that apply to noncorporate shareholders. In any event, corporations, unlike individuals, are not given any special tax rates for their capital gains. However, corporate shareholders are given tax relief for their dividend income if certain qualifications are satisfied.

When a dividend is paid by a taxable *domestic* corporation to a corporate shareholder, the corporate shareholder is granted a deduction, sometimes referred to as a "dividend-received deduction," in an amount equal to some specified percentage of the dividend. Ordinarily, the deduction will be equal to 50 percent of the amount of the dividend.[12] The net result of this deduction is that only 50 percent of the dividend paid to the corporate shareholder is taxed. Since the tax rate payable by a corporation currently is 21 percent (note that the capital gains rate on qualified dividends does not apply to corporations), the maximum marginal nominal rate that can be applied to a corporate shareholder's receipt of a dividend that qualifies for the 50 percent dividend-received deduction is 10.5 percent (i.e., a tax of 21 percent on 50 percent of the dividend received).

If a corporate shareholder owns 20 percent or more of the voting rights and of the value of the outstanding stock of a domestic distributing corporation[13] (hereinafter sometimes referred to as a "20-percent owned corporation"), the amount of the dividend-received deduction is increased from 50 percent to 65 percent for a dividend paid to that shareholder.[14] The maximum effective rate on a dividend

---

[12]   § 243(a)(1). The 2017 Tax Cuts and Jobs Act changed the rates of the dividend received deduction, and the current rates are set forth in this book.

[13]   Certain nonvoting preferred stock is not taken into account when determining whether the 20% ownership rule is satisfied. §§ 243(c)(2), 1504(a)(4).

[14]   § 243(c). However, there are circumstances in which the amount of either the 50 percent or 65 percent dividend-received deduction is reduced. See, e.g., §§ 246 and 246A.

for which an 65 percent dividend-received deduction is allowed is 7.35 percent (i.e., a tax of 21 percent on 35 percent of the dividend).

In certain prescribed circumstances (mainly dividends paid among members of an "affiliated group"), a corporate shareholder is permitted to deduct an amount equal to the entire dividend received—thus, permitting a receipt of the dividend without imposing any tax at all.[15]

¶ 2.05 TREATMENT OF DIVIDEND TO A NONCORPORATE SHAREHOLDER

Prior to the adoption of the JGTRRA in 2003, a dividend to a shareholder, whether the shareholder was a corporation or an individual, was taxed at ordinary income rates. As noted above, corporate shareholders were treated differently in that typically only a fraction of a dividend was taxed to them. The 2003 Act did not change the treatment of corporate shareholders, but it made a significant change in the treatment of dividends paid to noncorporate shareholders.

While a dividend paid to a noncorporate shareholder is still treated as ordinary income, in most circumstances it will be taxed at capital gain rates. Currently, the tax rate that most frequently will be applied to an individual's dividend income is a 20 percent rate. The significance of treating it as ordinary income even though it may be taxed at capital gain rates arises primarily when the individual shareholder has capital losses that year. An individual's capital losses cannot be deducted from the dividend except to the extent that they could be deducted from any ordinary income.[16]

Not all dividends qualify for the capital gain rate treatment. Dividends that do qualify are classified as "qualified dividend income." To qualify, the dividend must be paid from a domestic corporation (other than one that is tax exempt or a mutual savings bank) or from a limited class of foreign corporations.[17]

¶ 2.06 EARNINGS AND PROFITS—IN GENERAL

Although an extremely important concept, one of the mysteries of federal income taxation is that the Internal Revenue Code does not include a definition of the term "earnings and profits." While § 312

---

[15] § 243(a)(2), (3).

[16] A noncorporate taxpayer can deduct up to $3,000 of his net capital losses against ordinary income. § 1211(b).

[17] The provision does not apply to shareholders who are nonresident aliens. Among other exceptions, the provision does not apply if the shareholder has not held the stock on which the dividend was paid for a specified period of days. § 1(h)(11)(B)(iii).

does provide illustrations of adjustments to be made in determining earnings and profits, that section is by no means exclusive. In Revenue Procedure 2015–3 (Sec. 3.45), the Service stated that it will not rule on the determination of a corporation's *e and p*. The guidelines for determining *e and p* are set forth in Revenue Procedure 75–17.

The basic purpose of *e and p* is to serve as a measuring rod of the amounts available to a corporation for distribution to its shareholders without impairing its capital. Thus, *e and p* are analogous to the corporate law concept of retained earnings. The adjustments made to *e and p*, however, are frequently different from those used in corporate law; and it should never be assumed that a corporation's retained earnings are identical to its *e and p*.

Why does it matter for tax purposes whether a corporation is impairing its capital? Congress adopted a system under which all distributions are deemed to be made from corporate earnings to the extent thereof, and any excess distributions are treated as having been made from the capital that the shareholders had contributed to the corporation. In other words, the notion is that all amounts shareholders receive from their corporation are to be taxed as dividend income until the corporation has nothing left except the capital that the shareholders contributed to it, after which any further distributions constitute a return of the shareholders' capital investment.

Any item included in the corporation's gross income and recognized for tax purposes typically will increase the corporation's *e and p*; yet increases to *e and p* are not linked exclusively to taxable income since property received tax-free by the corporation is nevertheless available for distribution to shareholders without impairing capital. For example, a corporation's receipt of tax-free interest from a state obligation will increase its *e and p*. The interest is permanently excluded from taxable income, and is not merely deferred to a later date. However, realized gain of a corporation on which taxation is *deferred* by operation of a nonrecognition statute, such as § 1031, will not increase *e and p*.[18] Similarly, a corporation's realization of a loss, the recognition of which is deferred, will not reduce *e and p*. The increase or decrease in *e and p* will take place when (and if) the corporation recognizes the deferred gain or loss. Note that it is important to distinguish between provisions that merely defer gain or loss recognition and provisions that permanently exclude income or loss from any tax consequence. The latter typically will be taken into account in determining *e and p*

---

[18]   § 312(f)(1).

when the gain or loss is realized; while a deferred gain or loss will not affect *e and p*.

A corporate expenditure or loss will reduce the corporation's capacity to make distributions to its shareholders, and as a result such expenditures or losses typically reduce *e and p* even when they are not deductible from gross income for income tax purposes. For example, capital losses that exceed capital gains, losses disallowed under § 267, and payment or accrual of federal income tax liability will reduce a corporation's *e and p* even though those items are not deductible by the corporation. This provision does not apply to capital expenditures since they do not cause a reduction of the amount available for distribution to shareholders.

Since the excess of a corporation's losses over its income reduces its *e and p*, it would duplicate that reduction if a carryover of any part of the excess loss for taxable income purposes were to reduce *e and p* again when deducted in a subsequent year. To prevent that duplication, a deduction of a net operating loss or capital loss carryforward or carryback will not reduce *e and p*.

The Commissioner maintains that, except where a statutory exception is applicable, a corporation's *e and p* should be determined by the same accounting method as is properly employed in determining the corporation's taxable income.[19] Thus, the Commissioner argues that a cash method corporation may reduce *e and p* for its tax liabilities only when they have been paid by the corporation.[20]

Ex. (1)   X Corporation owned Blackacre, unimproved land, with a basis of $200,000. Blackacre was condemned by the state, and X received $350,000 cash for it. To replace Blackacre, X promptly purchased Whiteacre, unimproved land, for $300,000. While X realized a gain of $150,000 on the condemnation sale of Blackacre, X elected under § 1033 not to recognize $100,000 of that gain; and so X recognized only $50,000 of the realized gain. Although X paid $300,000 for Whiteacre, its basis in Whiteacre is only $200,000. In effect, the $100,000 of realized but unrecognized gain from the condemnation sale of Blackacre is deferred by building that potential gain into the basis of Whiteacre. As a consequence of the sale of Blackacre, X will increase its *e and p* by $50,000—i.e., by the amount of gain that was not deferred. If X were to sell Whiteacre in a subsequent year, any gain

---

[19]   Treas. Reg. § 1.312–6(a).

[20]   While earlier judicial decisions divided over this question, the most recent decisions adopt the Commissioner's view. See, e.g., Mazzocchi Bus Co. *v.* Commissioner, 14 F.3d 923 (3d Cir. 1994).

recognized by X on that sale would increase its *e and p* at that time; so the deferred gain from the sale of Blackacre potentially will increase X's *e and p* at some future date when Whiteacre is sold.

Ex. (2)   Y Corporation owned Greenacre with a basis of $70,000 and a value of $50,000. Y transferred Greenacre to one of its shareholder in exchange for all of that shareholder's Y stock, having a value of $50,000. The exchange was not treated as a § 301 distribution because the shareholder's interest in Y was terminated by the transaction. While Y realized a loss of $20,000 on the distribution, it was denied recognition of that loss by § 311(a). The loss is not merely deferred; it is disallowed permanently. Consequently, Y will reduce its *e and p* by the $20,000 loss it realized even though that loss was not recognized.

Note that the decline in value of Greenacre in Y's hands represents a decline in the amount that could be distributed to shareholders without using up any of the contributed capital that Y has. Because of the doctrine of realization, that decline in value had not previously been reflected in Y's *e and p*. When Y disposed of Greenacre, the decline in the property's value must be reflected in *e and p* at that time or it will never be taken into account. Consequently, the loss that Y realized on the disposition of Greenacre reduces Y's *e and p* in order to properly reflect what amount is available for distribution to shareholders without impairing Y's capital.

Ex. (3)   In Year One, Z Corporation had a net operating loss of $100,000, which Z carried forward to future years. Z will reduce its Year One *e and p* by that $100,000 loss even if it means that Z will have a deficit *e and p* then. In Year Two, before taking the net operating loss carryover into account, Z had taxable income of $25,000 and current *e and p* of the same amount. While Z can use $25,000 of its $100,000 net operating loss carryover to reduce its taxable income to zero, Z's *e and p* will be increased by $25,000 without any reduction for the net operating loss carryover deduction. Since the entire $100,000 loss reduced Z's *e and p* in Year One, it would be double counting if it were to reduce it again when any of the carryover loss is applied in a subsequent year; and the tax law does not allow that to occur.

¶ 2.07 EFFECT OF DISCHARGE OF INDEBTEDNESS ON E AND P

Unless an exception applies, a discharge of a solvent corporation's indebtedness will cause the corporation to recognize income; so no basis adjustment to the corporation's assets will be made; and the corporation's *e and p* will be increased by the amount of the discharged debt. On the other hand, an insolvent corporation will not recognize income from having its debt discharged except to the extent that the discharged debt causes the solvency of the debtor corporation.[21] To the extent that an insolvent corporation's discharged debt does not cause it to recognize income, some tax attributes of the debtor corporation (including its basis in its properties) may be reduced by § 108(b).[22] To the extent that an amount of a forgiven debt of an insolvent corporation is excluded from income but does not cause a reduction of that corporation's basis in its properties, that amount will increase the debtor corporation's *e and p*.

¶ 2.08 EFFECT OF § 301 DISTRIBUTIONS ON E AND P

The purpose of *e and p* is to measure the amount that a corporation has available to distribute to its shareholders without impairing its capital. When a corporation with positive earnings and profits makes a § 301 distribution of an asset to a shareholder, the *e and p* of the distributing corporation must be reduced to reflect the fact that the distributed asset is no longer available for distribution to shareholders. The reduction of *e and p* for a distribution to shareholders cannot reduce the corporation's *e and p* below zero.[23] In other words, a distribution to a shareholder can reduce a positive *e and p* of the distributing corporation, but it can neither cause a negative *e and p* nor increase the amount of a negative *e and p*.

If a corporation suffers an operating loss, the amount of the loss reduces its *e and p* even if that causes a deficit *e and p* or increases the amount of the corporation's deficit in *e and p*. The loss does not alter the amount of capital that shareholders invested in the corporation, but reflects the fact that the corporation no longer possesses that amount of capital. Subsequent earnings of the

---

[21]   § 108(a).

[22]   Section 312(*l*)(1) provides that a corporation's *e and p* are not affected by a discharge of an indebtedness of the corporation to the extent that under § 1017 the amount forgiven causes a reduction in the corporation's basis in some of its assets. When an insolvent corporation's basis in its properties is to be reduced because of § 108(b), the amount and timing of such reduction is determined by § 1017.

[23]   § 312(a).

corporation will restore the corporation's capital and so will reduce the accumulated deficit until it reaches zero. Once the accumulated *e and p* reach zero, any additional earnings will cause a positive *e and p*. The situation is quite different when a corporation with a zero or deficit *e and p* makes a distribution to its shareholders.

To the extent that a § 301 distribution exceeds the corporation's positive *e and p*, it is treated as a return of the distributee's capital (as discussed later in this chapter, this will reduce the basis in his or her stock or cause a recognition of gain on the stock). Unlike the operating loss situation, the distribution does not represent a decline in the corporation's capital that shareholders are entitled to have recouped by subsequent corporate earnings. That is the reason that distributions cannot reduce a corporation's *e and p* below zero, but operating losses can do so.

The manner for determining the effect of a § 301 distribution on a corporation's *e and p* is described below.

A corporation's distribution of cash to a shareholder that is made on account of the shareholder's stock reduces a positive *e and p* by the amount of money that was distributed.[24] The consequence of a corporation's distributing property in kind to a shareholder depends upon whether the property is appreciated (appreciated property is property whose fair market value exceeds the basis that the property owner has therein). If unappreciated property is distributed in kind to a shareholder, the distributing corporation's *e and p* are reduced by the basis that the distributing corporation had in such property immediately prior to the distribution.[25] If the property that is distributed in kind is an appreciated asset, then the distributing corporation's *e and p* are first *increased* by the amount of such appreciation in the hands of the distributing corporation and are then *reduced* by the fair market value of the distributed property.[26] Note that the end result of those two calculations is to reduce the *e and p* by the basis of the property. Why then does § 312(b) require a taxpayer to first increase the *e and p* by the appreciation? The answer is that the amount of appreciation will increase the corporation's *current e and p*, and the reduction for the fair market value of the distribution will reduce the corporation's *accumulated e and p*.

If a shareholder-distributee takes distributed property subject to a liability or assumes a liability of the distributing corporation, the determination of the amount of reduction of the distributing corporation's accumulated *e and p* must take those liabilities into

---

[24]   § 312(a)(1).

[25]   § 312(a)(3).

[26]   § 312(b).

account.[27] In general, the amount of reduction of accumulated *e and p* that was described in the paragraph above must be reduced by the amount of liabilities that were assumed or accepted by shareholder-distributees.

Ex. (1) As of January 1, Year One, X Corporation had accumulated *e and p* of $5,000. X had two equal shareholder individuals, A and B. In Year One, X earned net income (after taxes) of $8,000, and X's current *e and p* for Year One also was $8,000. On July 1, Year One, X distributed $3,000 cash to A and $3,000 cash to B. X made no other distributions to its shareholders in that year. Note that you determine current *e and p* without any reduction for the distributions during the year. Since current *e and p* exceed the total amount distributed, all of the distributions are dividends. The cash distributions reduce X's accumulated *e and p*. Accordingly, X's $5,000 accumulated *e and p* are increased by the $8,000 of *e and p* that X earned in Year One and are reduced by the $6,000 that X distributed to its shareholders.

$5,000.00

8,000.00

(6,000.00)

$7,000.00

As of January 1, Year Two, X has accumulated *e and p* of $7,000.

Ex. (2) As of January 1, Year One, X had an accumulated *e and p* deficit of ($12,000). X had two equal shareholders, individuals A and B. In Year One, X earned net income (after taxes) of $8,000, and X's current *e and p* for Year One also were $8,000. On July 1, Year One, X distributed $5,000 cash to A and $5,000 cash to B. X made no other distributions to its shareholders in that year. Since X had current *e and p* of $8,000 in Year One, that amount (determined at the end of the year) is allocated pro rata to the distributions that X made in Year One. Therefore A and B each have dividend income of $4,000 in Year One. Alternatively, applying the method for determining dividends that is adopted in the regulations, 80% of each distribution is a dividend; and that also nets a dividend of $4,000 to each shareholder. What effect do the cash distributions have on X's accumulated *e and p*—that is,

---

[27] § 312(c).

what are X's accumulated *e and p* as of January 1, Year Two?

Under § 312(a), X can reduce its *e and p* only "to the extent" that X has a positive *e and p*. The corporation's *e and p* that is to be reduced under § 312(a) is its accumulated *e and p* since current *e and p* is a concept that is used only for the purpose of applying the bifurcated standard that § 316(a) employs for determining dividends. The question is whether the limitation in § 312(a) of a reduction of *e and p* "to the extent thereof" limits the amount of reduction of X's *e and p* to the amount of positive accumulated *e and p* that X had on July 1, Year One, when the distributions to the shareholders were made. If that were so, the distributions would not reduce X's *e and p* at all, since X had a deficit accumulated *e and p* at all times during Year One (the entire amount of *e and p* that X earned in Year One ($8,000) was less than the negative amount of *e and p* ($12,000) that X had at the beginning of the year). If that construction were adopted, X's accumulated *e and p* as of January 1, Year Two would be a deficit of ($4,000) i.e., X's deficit *e and p* of ($12,000) would be reduced by the $8,000 that X netted in Year One, and there would be no reduction of *e and p* for the July 1 distributions. Clearly, that construction of § 312(a) is inconsistent with the purposes of the *e and p* concept, and it has *not* been adopted.

Since $8,000 of the amounts distributed by X is treated as having been paid out of X's *e and p* because of the bifurcated standard employed by § 316(a), the distributions should reduce X's *e and p* by $8,000. In other words, that amount of X's earnings is treated by § 316 as having been paid out to X's shareholders, and so that amount of earnings is no longer available for a future distribution to shareholders. Therefore, only the amount of current *e and p* that was not deemed to have been distributed to the shareholders should be added to X's accumulated *e and p*. Since all of X's $8,000 of current *e and p* was allocated to the distributions that were made to X's shareholders, none of those earnings is added to X's accumulated *e and p*.[28] X's accumulated *e and p* as of January 1, Year Two, therefore, are a deficit of ($12,000).

---

[28]   This interpretation has been adopted by the Commissioner in Rev. Rul. 74–338 and by the Tax Court and the Seventh Circuit in Anderson v. Commissioner, 67 T.C. 522 (1976), acq. 1979–2 C.B. 1, aff'd per curiam, 583 F.2d 953 (7th Cir. 1978).

Ex. (3)   As of January 1, Year One, Y Corporation had accumulated
e and p of $20,000. D is the sole shareholder of Y. On July
1, Year One, Y distributed to D unimproved land
(Blackacre) in which Y had a basis of $10,000. The fair
market value of Blackacre was $3,000, and Blackacre was
not encumbered. Y made no other distributions to its
shareholder in that year. In Year One, Y had current *e and
p* of $13,000. Since Blackacre is a depreciated asset, Y will
reduce its accumulated *e and p* by the *basis* of Blackacre
($10,000).[29] Accordingly, Y's accumulated *e and p* as of
January 1, Year Two, is $23,000 as the following
computation shows:

> $20,000.00—accumulated *e and p*
>
> $13,000.00—*e and p* earned in Year One
>
> ($10,000.00)—basis of Blackacre
>
> $23,000.00—*e and p* as of 1/1/Year Two

Ex. (4)   The same facts as those stated in Example (3) except that,
at the time of distribution, Blackacre was subject to a
mortgage in the amount of $1,200, and D took Blackacre
from Y subject to that mortgage. The liability to which
Blackacre was subject reduces the reduction of Y's *e and p*
that is allowed because of the distribution of Blackacre to
D.[30] Therefore, Y's accumulated *e and p* are reduced by
$8,800:

> $10,000.00—basis
>
> ($1,200.00)—liability
>
> $8,800.00—reduction of *e and p*

As of January 1, Year Two, *Y* has accumulated *e
and p* of $24,200 as shown below:

> $20,000.00—accumulated *e and p*
>
> $13,000.00—*e and p* earned in Year One
>
> ($8,800.00)—reduction of *e and p*
>
> $24,200.00—*e and p* as of 1/1/Year Two

---

[29]   § 312(a)(3).

[30]   § 312(c). Treas. Reg. § 1.312–3.

Ex. (5) The same facts as those stated in Example (4) except that the fair market value of Blackacre at the time of distribution to D was $22,000. Since Blackacre was an appreciated asset, Y must add to its $13,000 of current *e and p* the amount by which Blackacre is appreciated ($12,000). Y's current *e and p* therefore is $25,000 ($13,000 + $12,000). Note that this calculation ignores the mortgage liability.

> $22,000.00—fmv
>
> ($10,000.00)—basis
>
> $12,000.00—appreciation

Therefore, ignoring the effect on current *e and p* that any tax liability that Y will incur from distributing Blackacre will have, Y had $25,000 of current *e and p* for Year One ($13,000 + $12,000 = $25,000).

Y will reduce its accumulated *e and p* by the fair market value ($22,000) of Blackacre since Blackacre is an appreciated asset.[31] The amount of this reduction of *e and p* is reduced by the $1,200 of mortgage liability to which Blackacre was subject.[32] So, Y will reduce its accumulated *e and p* by $20,800:

> $22,000.00—fmv
>
> ($1,200.00)—liability
>
> $20,800.00—reduction of *e and p*

As of January 1, Year Two, Y has accumulated *e and p* of $24,200 as shown below:

> $20,000.00—accumulated *e and p*
>
> $25,000.00—*e and p* earned in Year One
>
> ($20,800.00)—*reduction of e and p*
>
> $24,200.00—*e and p* as of 1/1/Year Two

---

[31]   § 312(b)(2).

[32]   § 312(c).

¶ 2.09 DISTRIBUTION OF CORPORATION'S STOCK OR BONDS

If a corporation distributes its own stock to a shareholder in a transaction to which § 301 applies because of § 305(b) (discussed in Chapter Six), *e and p* are reduced by the fair market value of the portion of the stock to which § 301 applies.[33] If § 301 does not apply to a corporation's distribution of stock (or rights to its stock), the corporation's *e and p* are not affected.[34]

If a corporation distributes its own bond or other debt obligation to a shareholder and if the issue price of the debt instrument is at least as great as its principal amount, the distributing corporation's *e and p* are reduced by the principal amount of the debt instrument.[35] However, if the issue price of a distributed debt instrument is less than its principal amount, or more specifically if the issue price is less than the "stated redemption price at maturity," the distributing corporation's *e and p* will be reduced by the issue price, and the difference between the issue price and the stated redemption price at maturity will be treated as original issue discount.[36]

¶ 2.10 AMENDMENTS TO § 312 AND DEPRECIATION DEDUCTIONS

In 1984 and again in 1986, Congress modified § 312 to make a corporation's earnings and profits more accurately reflect its economic status. If applicable, most (but not all) of those modifications will increase the size of a corporation's *e and p*. For example, for purposes of calculating *e and p*, § 312(n)(5) prohibits the use of the installment method in reporting income from an installment sale; consequently, the entire gain from an installment sale is added to *e and p* in the year in which the sale occurs.

Generally, tangible property acquired after 1986 is required to be depreciated under the Modified Accelerated Cost Recovery System (MACRS) set forth in § 168. Under MACRS, most tangible personal property can be depreciated on the double declining balance method

---

[33]   Treas. Reg. § 1.312–1(d).

[34]   § 312(d).

[35]   § 312(a)(2). While § 312(d) prevents a reduction of *e and p* for certain distributions of a corporation's security if it does not cause gain recognition to the distributee, that occurs only when the security is distributed in exchange for a security of at least equal principal amount. See §§ 354(a)(2), 355(a)(3), 356(d).

[36]   §§ 312(a)(2), (o), 1273 and 1275(a)(4). For the meaning of "issue price," "stated redemption price at maturity," and "original issue discount," see § 1273. The amount of original issue discount will be allocated among the remaining years of the debt and will be includible in the taxable income of the distributee and will be deductible by the distributing corporation in accordance with the usual rules that are applicable to debt instruments that are issued at a discount.

switching to straight line depreciation in the first year in which straight line will yield a greater allowance.[37] The recovery period for depreciating an asset is set forth in tables provided by the statute.[38] Certain types of property are required to be depreciated under an "alternative depreciation system" provided by § 168(g). Under the alternative system, only straight line depreciation can be used, and special recovery periods are applied. These recovery periods typically are longer than the period allowed under MACRS and are never shorter.

Section 312(k)(3) requires that the *e and p* of a corporation that is depreciating tangible property be determined by computing the corporation's depreciation under the alternative depreciation system established in § 168(g)(2) and (3). Thus, for purposes of determining *e and p*, depreciation will be computed on a straight line basis and, the recovery periods employed typically will be longer than those employed by regular MACRS depreciation.

The adjustment to *e and p* for a corporation's gain or loss on the sale of recovery property may differ from the corporation's gain or loss as determined for taxable income purposes. This difference arises because the corporation's basis for *e and p* purposes is determined by adjusting basis for the depreciation allowed or allowable for *e and p* purposes, which can differ from the amount of depreciation allowable for other tax purposes. In determining a corporation's gain or loss on the disposition of depreciable property, the corporation therefore can have a basis in its properties for *e and p* purposes that is different from its basis for the purposes of determining its taxable income.[39]

Ex. The X Corporation was formed on February 6, Year One; and X reports its income on the calendar year basis. X has two equal shareholders—A and B, both of whom are individuals.

On March 10, Year One, X purchased a computer for use exclusively in its business. The computer is classified as 5-year property for purposes of MACRS. X paid $30,000 for the computer, and X made no other purchases in Year One. X did not elect to take bonus depreciation under § 179. Pursuant to MACRS, X took a depreciation deduction in Year One of $6,000 (i.e., 40% × $30,000 × $1/2$ = $6,000). This deduction is determined by using a 5-year recovery period and the half-year convention and by employing the double declining balance method.

---

[37]   § 168(b)(1).

[38]   § 168(c).

[39]   § 312(f)(1) (penultimate sentence).

For purposes of determining the impact that the deductions taken for the computer have on X's *e and p*, X must depreciate the computer over a 9-year recovery period and must use the straight line method.[40] Thus, for *e and p* purposes, the depreciation rate for Year One is $1/9$ for half of a year (on account of the half-year convention) which equals $1/18$ or 5.56 percent. Thus, the total depreciation for Year One for *e and p* purposes is $1,666.67, significantly lower than the $6,000 of deduction allowable in determining X's taxable income for that year.

On January 2, Year Two, X sold the computer for $25,000. For taxable income purposes, X's allowable depreciation for the computer for Year Two is $4,800 ($24,000 × 40% × $1/2$), and X took a deduction in that amount. X's adjusted basis in the computer at the time of the sale is $19,200 ($30,000—$6,000—$4,800). X had a gain of $5,800 on the sale of the computer ($25,000—$19,200), and all of that gain is ordinary income under § 1245.

For *e and p* purposes, X's depreciation for Year Two is only $1,666.67. Using a 9-year recovery period on a straight-line method for $1/2$ of the year, X's *e and p* depreciation in Year Two is the same as it was in Year One. For *e and p* purposes, X's adjusted basis in the computer at the time of sale is $26,666.66 ($30,000—$1,666.67—$1,666.67). For *e and p* purposes, X recognized a loss of ($1,666.66). X's current *e and p* are reduced by that $1,666.66 loss.

Since the amount of deductions allowable for taxable income purpose is different than the amount of deductions allowed for *e and p* purposes, X has two separate bases to be used in measuring gain or loss on the disposition of the computer—one basis for *e and p* purposes and one for taxable income purposes.

The determination of *e and p* is a highly complex matter, and the above material does not encompass all of the problems involved. Additional references to *e and p* are made subsequently in this book in connection with specific transactions.

As a consequence of the modifications to *e and p* calculation that Congress made in 1984 and 1986, typically a larger amount of a corporation's § 301 distributions will constitute dividend income to its distributees. This may result in an increase in a distributee's tax liability since, as discussed in ¶ 2.12, a nondividend § 301 distribution is treated either as a nontaxable return of capital or as a capital gain. However, if the distributee is a corporate shareholder, the availability of a dividend-received deduction under § 243(a)

---

[40]   §§ 312(k)(3) and 168(g).

might make it more advantageous to the distributee to have the § 301 distribution characterized as a dividend. This is especially so if the corporate distributee has a low basis in its stock and if it has a 20 percent or more ownership interest in the distributing corporation so that the dividend-received deduction allowed to it by § 243(c) will be 65 percent of the amount of dividend received instead of the more usual 50 percent deduction.

¶ 2.11 § 301 DISTRIBUTIONS TO 20 PERCENT CORPORATE SHAREHOLDER

Congress did not wish its expansion of the definition of *e and p* to provide a 20 percent corporate shareholder with a greater amount of dividends that qualify for the dividend-received deduction. Accordingly, Congress added the current version of § 301(e) to make dividend treatment inapplicable for § 301 distributions to a 20 percent corporate shareholder to the extent that the distribution was a dividend because of certain provisions of § 312 that were designed to expand a corporation's *e and p*.

Except to the extent exempted by regulation, § 301(e) makes the provisions of § 312(k) and (n), other than § 312(n)(7), inapplicable when determining whether a section 301 distribution to a 20 percent corporate shareholder constitutes a dividend or a return of capital. A 20 percent corporate shareholder is a corporation that owns (after applying certain stock attribution rules)[41] stock in the distributing corporation representing either: (1) at least 20 percent of the voting power of the distributing corporation's outstanding stock, *or* (2) at least 20 percent of the total value of the distributing corporation's outstanding stock (exclusive of nonvoting stock that is limited and preferred as to dividends).[42] When § 301(e) applies, the distributing corporation's *e and p* are determined as if § 312(k) and (n), other than (n)(7), do not exist; but this operates *only* for purposes of determining how much of the amount received by a 20 percent corporate shareholder is a dividend and how much is a return of capital. This provision has no effect on the *e and p* of the distributing corporation for purposes of determining the characterization of § 301 distributions to shareholders who are not a 20 percent corporate shareholder. Thus, the distributing corporation must maintain two separate *e and p* accounts—one for 20 percent corporate shareholders and one for all other purposes.

---

[41]   Under the applicable stock attribution rules, stock owned by persons falling within specified relationships to the corporate shareholder is treated as owned by the corporate shareholder. §§ 301(e)(2), 318. See ¶ 3.02.

[42]   § 301(e)(2).

Two of the transactions covered by § 301(e) are installment sales and depreciation. Section 312(n)(5) prevents a corporation from using the installment method in computing its *e and p*. However, § 301(e) states that solely for purposes of determining the taxable income (and the basis adjustment of the distributing corporation's stock) of 20 percent corporate shareholders, the *e and p* of the distributing corporation are determined as if § 312(n) did not apply. Thus, for 20 percent corporate shareholders, the adjustment to the *e and p* of the distributing corporation for making an installment sale will be computed under the installment method.

Ex. The X Corporation reports its income on a calendar basis. X has two equal shareholders—individual A and the O corporation. As of January 1, Year One, X had no accumulated *e and p*.

On July 1, Year One, X sold Blackacre to an unrelated person for an installment note in the principal amount of $100,000; the note provided for payments of $10,000 of principal plus an adequate amount of interest each year for ten years, beginning with a payment in December of Year One. X had a basis of $20,000 in Blackacre, and so X realized a gain of $80,000 on the installment sale. X did not hold Blackacre for sale to customers in the ordinary course of its business, and so the sale of Blackacre qualified for installment reporting. X did not elect out of installment reporting. For taxable income purposes, X reports the $80,000 gain it realized on the sale of Blackacre on the installment method; so 80 percent of each installment payment of principal that X receives on the installment note constitutes income to X. X had no other gains or losses that year.

On December 31, Year One, X received a payment of $10,000 principal on the installment note. In addition, X received a payment of $5,000 for interest on the installment debt. X had no other income or deductions in that year. So, X reported taxable income of $13,000 for Year One; $8,000 of X's income was the gain it recognized upon receiving the $10,000 principal payment on the installment note, and $5,000 of X's income was the interest payment it received from the debtor. However, X's *e and p* for Year One is $85,000 since § 312(n)(5) prevents X from using the installment method in computing its *e and p*. For *e and p* purposes, X must include in Year One the entire $80,000 gain it realized on the sale of Blackacre.

In Year One, X distributed $10,000 cash to A and $10,000 cash to O. Since X had $85,000 of current *e and p* in Year One (ignoring the effect of any tax liability), the $10,000 distributed to A is dividend income. However, the characterization of the distribution to O is quite different.

Since O is a 20 percent corporate shareholder, the taxable income that O recognized from the receipt of the § 301 distribution is determined by computing X's *e and p* without applying § 312(k) and (n), other than (n)(7).[43] After excluding the operation of § 312(n)(5), X had current *e and p* of only $13,000 in Year One; X's *e and p* are computed by applying the installment method. So, only $6,500 of the $10,000 distributed to O is dividend income (i.e., $1/2$ of the $13,000 of X's current *e and p* (as computed without § 312(n)(5)) are allocated to the distribution to O).

As discussed in ¶ 2.10, § 312(k)(3) requires that depreciation of tangible property be determined by applying the alternative depreciation system of § 168(g)(2). However, § 301(e), which applies when determining the effect that a § 301 distribution has on the taxable income of a 20 percent corporate shareholder, requires that the *e and p* of the distributing corporation be determined without applying § 312(k) and (n), other than (n)(7). Thus, the same system that the distributing corporation uses to determine the effect of depreciation deductions on its taxable income will be used to determine the effect on its *e and p* for the purpose of characterizing the § 301 distribution to a 20 percent corporation shareholder.

¶ 2.12 DISTRIBUTIONS TO SHAREHOLDERS IN EXCESS OF EARNINGS AND PROFITS

The amount distributed to a shareholder in excess of the current and accumulated earnings and profits of the corporation that are allocated to that distribution (hereinafter referred to as "the excess distribution") is treated as follows:

The excess distribution reduces the basis of the shareholder's stock in the corporation, and to the extent that such basis is available, the excess distribution is not included in the shareholder's gross income.[44] There is a question as to which stock's basis is to be used for this purpose. Should only the basis of the stock on which the distribution was made be used, or can basis of other stock held by the shareholder be used? That issue is unsettled. However, a proposed regulation that was promulgated in January, 2009, states that the excess distribution is to be applied pro rata, on a share by share basis, to each share of the shareholder's stock that is within the class of stock on which the distribution was made.[45] For this purpose, it appears that a class of stock is determined by reference to the stock's economic rights to distributions rather than to rights with respect to

---

[43]   § 301(e).

[44]   § 301(c)(2).

[45]   Prop. Reg. § 1.301–2(a).

corporate governance.[46] The 2009 proposed regulations are not effective unless and until finalized.

If the excess distribution is greater than the shareholder's basis in his stock, it will be treated as gain from the sale or exchange of property.[47] As noted in the paragraph above, there is a question as to the basis of which stock is to be used; and, if finalized, the 2009 proposed regulations will provide that the basis of each share of stock will be treated as separate and distinct from that of each other share of stock, such that a distribution can produce capital gain on some shares even as there remains unrecovered basis on other shares.[48]

Ex. On January 1, Year One, X Corporation had no accumulated earnings and profits. For that year, X had current earnings and profits of $5,000. On July 5, Year One, X distributed $15,000 to shareholder A, and X made no other distributions that year. A had a basis of $3,000 in his stock of X, all of which was common stock. A recognized ordinary dividend income of $5,000 (on account of the current *e and p*). The excess distribution of $10,000 reduced A's basis in his stock of X from $3,000 to zero, and A recognized $7,000 as capital gain income.

¶ 2.13 EXTRAORDINARY DIVIDENDS TO A CORPORATE SHAREHOLDER

In certain circumstances, a *corporate* shareholder's receipt of an "extraordinary dividend" on a share of stock that the corporate shareholder had held for two years or less at the time that the dividend was declared can cause a reduction of the shareholder's basis in that share of stock or can cause the shareholder to recognize additional income.[49] The reduction of the shareholder's basis in that share of stock is made at the beginning of the "ex-dividend date" for the extraordinary dividend.[50] The "ex-dividend date" is the first day after the extraordinary dividend was declared that a purchaser of the share of stock on which the extraordinary dividend was declared would purchase that stock ex-dividend (i.e., the dividend would be

---

[46]   Cf. Prop. Reg. § 1.302–5(b)(2).

[47]   § 301(c)(3).

[48]   This is consistent with what the Treasury described as "the cornerstone" of the proposed regulations—i.e., "that a share of stock is the basic unit of property that can be disposed of and, accordingly, the result of a transaction should generally derive from the consideration received in respect of that share." Preamble to the 2009 Proposed Regulations, 74 Fed. Reg. 3509 (2009).

[49]   § 1059(a). While § 1059 does not directly affect dividends to noncorporate shareholders, JGTRRA does cause it to have an indirect effect. Any loss on a sale of stock recognized by a noncorporate shareholder will be treated as long-term capital loss to the extent of the aggregate extraordinary dividends that the shareholder had received on that stock. § 1(h)(11)(D)(ii).

[50]   § 1059(d)(1).

paid to the seller and not to the purchaser).[51] The amount of the reduction of the corporate shareholder's basis in the share of stock equals the amount of the extraordinary dividend on that share that effectively is taken out of the corporate shareholder's taxable income by virtue of the dividend-received deduction allowed to the shareholder because of that dividend by §§ 243, 244, or 245. This amount is referred to as the "nontaxed portion of [the] dividend."[52]

A corporate shareholder's basis in a share of stock cannot be reduced below zero under this provision. Instead, if the nontaxed portion of an extraordinary dividend exceeds the basis that, at the time of the ex-dividend date, the corporate shareholder had in the share of stock on which the dividend was paid, the excess amount is treated as gain from the sale of that share of stock.[53] Typically, that will be a capital gain. The gain is recognized in the taxable year in which the extraordinary dividend was received.[54]

For purposes of this provision, an "extraordinary dividend" is defined in § 1059(c). The term includes a dividend on a share of stock the amount of which equals or exceeds a percentage, referred to as the "threshold percentage," of the corporate shareholder's basis in that share of stock. Instead of using its basis in the share of stock, the corporate shareholder can use the fair market value that the stock had on the day before the ex-dividend date if the shareholder can establish that value.[55] The size of the "threshold percentage" depends upon the type of stock on which the dividend was paid. If the dividend was paid on a share of preferred stock, the threshold percentage is five percent (5%). If the dividend was paid on any other type of stock, the "threshold percentage" is ten percent (10%).[56]

Ex. X Corporation, which has been in existence for more than five years, has two equal shareholders, Individual A and Z Corporation. A and Z each own 100 shares of common stock of X, in which they have a basis of $1,000 per share. X has no other stock outstanding. In Year One, X paid a cash dividend of $100 on each share of its outstanding stock. Z had held its X stock for 1 year and six months at the time that the dividend was declared. X had ample earnings and profits, so the entire amount distributed to its shareholders constituted a dividend. X and Z are both domestic corporations. As a consequence of receiving the dividend, A and Z will each have $10,000 of ordinary income.

---

51   § 1059(d)(4).
52   § 1059(a)(1), (b).
53   § 1059(a).
54   § 1059(a)(2).
55   § 1059(c)(4).
56   § 1059(c)(2).

However, Z will have a dividend-received deduction of $6,500 under § 243 (i.e., $65 dividend-received deduction for each $100 of dividend paid on each share of Z's stock in X). The fair market value of the X shares of stock was less than the basis that Z had in those shares. Since the amount of the dividend received by Z on each share of its X stock ($100) equals 10% of its basis in that share ($1,000), the dividend on each share of Z's stock is an extraordinary dividend; and since Z had held the X stock for less than 2 years when the dividend was announced by X, § 1059(a) is applicable. The nontaxed portion of the $100 dividend that Z received on each share of its X stock is $65 since that is the amount of dividend-received deduction that Z obtained for the $100 it received on each share. Consequently, Z's basis in each share of its X stock is reduced by $65. As of the ex-dividend date (the date on which Z's shares of X stock first became ex-dividend), Z's basis in each share of its X stock is $935. Section 1059 has no effect on A's basis in his X stock since A is not a corporation.

In certain statutorily defined circumstances, dividends paid on the same share of stock within a specified time period are aggregated and treated as a single dividend for purposes of determining whether they were "extraordinary." For example, dividends that are received by a taxpayer on the same share of stock and have ex-dividend dates within the same 85 consecutive day period are aggregated and treated as a single dividend for this purpose.[57]

In addition to extraordinary dividends arising from a § 301 distribution, § 1059 can also apply to a corporate shareholder's receipt of a corporate distribution pursuant to a partial liquidation or a non-pro rata stock redemption, or of certain boot in a corporate reorganization, but only to the extent that such distributions are treated as a dividend to the corporate shareholder.[58] In such cases, the amount that constitutes a dividend is treated as an extraordinary dividend to which § 1059 applies regardless of how long the shareholder had held the redeemed stock.

¶ 2.14 BASIS OF PROPERTY DISTRIBUTED TO SHAREHOLDERS

A shareholder's basis in property received from the corporation as a § 301 distribution is equal to the fair market value of the property at the time of distribution.[59] Note that the basis of the

---

[57]   § 1059(c)(3)(A).

[58]   § 1059(e)(1). The circumstances in which a stock redemption or partial liquidation will be treated as a dividend will be discussed in Chapter Three.

[59]   § 301(d).

property distributed to a shareholder as a § 301 distribution is identical to the amount deemed to be distributed to the shareholder under § 301(b) except that no adjustment is made because of liabilities assumed or accepted by the shareholder.

¶ 2.15 DISTRIBUTING CORPORATION'S RECOGNITION OF GAIN OR LOSS: GENERAL UTILITIES DOCTRINE

The *General Utilities* doctrine is the name given to the now largely defunct tax rule that a corporation does not recognize a gain or a loss on making a liquidating or nonliquidating distribution of an appreciated or depreciated asset to its shareholders. The roots of the doctrine can be traced to a regulation promulgated in 1919 that denied realization of gain or loss to a corporation when making a liquidating distribution of an asset in kind. In *General Utilities & Operating Co. v. Helvering*,[60] the Supreme Court adopted a nonrecognition rule for dividend distributions that are made in kind. In deference to that decision, the rule for nonrecognition of gain or loss on a corporate distribution of property in kind to a shareholder, whether made in liquidation or not, commonly has been referred to as the *General Utilities* doctrine. Congress codified the doctrine in the Internal Revenue Code of 1954. With few exceptions, the original provisions of the Code provided that a distributing corporation did not recognize a gain or loss on making a distribution in kind to its shareholders.

Over the years, Congress adopted numerous exceptions to the general rule of nonrecognition of *gain* so that even before the Tax Reform Act of 1986 was adopted, the general rule had become that a corporation recognized a gain on making a distribution of an appreciated asset (for example, as a dividend, a stock redemption, or a partial liquidation), and only in narrowly defined circumstances was gain not recognized. The *General Utilities* doctrine had been sufficiently eroded by 1986 that one could reasonably have concluded that the "General" had by that time already been reduced in rank to no more than a "Major."

¶ 2.16 CURRENT STATUS OF GENERAL UTILITIES

Under current law, beginning with the amendments made by the Tax Reform Act of 1986, a corporation that makes a distribution (whether a § 301 distribution or one made to redeem stock) to its shareholders of appreciated property (other than its own stock or

---

[60]   296 U.S. 200 (1935).

obligations) will recognize gain as if it had sold that property for its fair market value.[61] However, if a corporation makes a nonliquidating distribution of depreciated property (i.e., property that has a basis greater than its fair market value), the corporation is not permitted to recognize a loss on that distribution.[62] In this context, the term "nonliquidating distribution" refers to a distribution by a corporation to a shareholder, whether a § 301 distribution or a distribution in exchange for the corporation's stock, that is not made in complete liquidation of the corporation. So, as to nonliquidating distributions, the current version of the Code retains the *General Utilities* doctrine insofar as that doctrine precludes the distributing corporation's recognition of a loss, but the Code repudiates the doctrine insofar as the recognition of gain is concerned.

If an encumbered asset is distributed by a corporation to a shareholder who receives the asset subject to that liability or if a shareholder assumes a liability of the corporation in connection with the receipt of a distributed asset, then for purposes of determining the distributing corporation's gain on making that distribution, the fair market value of the distributed asset is deemed to be no less than the amount of such liability.[63]

No gain is recognized by a corporation on distributing its own stock or its own debt instrument. Under § 1032, a corporation does not recognize a gain or loss on the disposition of its own stock. Neither does a corporation recognize a gain or loss on the sale or exchange of its own debt instrument for no more than its face amount because that transaction is essentially one in which the corporation is borrowing funds and the distributee is merely a lender.

¶ 2.17 DISGUISED AND CONSTRUCTIVE DIVIDENDS

A shareholder may have dividend income without a direct "distribution of property" to him. A "disguised" or "constructive" dividend may arise when a closely held corporation confers an economic benefit on a shareholder. A bargain sale by a corporation to its shareholder, for example, might constitute a corporate distribution to the shareholder in the amount of the difference between the purchase price and the fair market value of the property

---

[61] § 311(b)(1).
[62] § 311(a).
[63] §§ 311(b)(2), 336(b).

sold.[64] If so, it will constitute a dividend to the extent that earnings and profits are available.

"Loans" purportedly made to a shareholder may also be disguised dividends if there is no intention that the so-called "loans" be repaid.[65] The actual intention of the parties as to whether the "loan" is to be repaid is a question of fact.[66] There may also be a deemed distribution for below-market interest loans.[67]

A corporation may deduct under § 162(a) the amount paid as salary or bonus to a shareholder-employee (or to a member of his family) for services rendered if the amount is reasonable compensation for the work performed.[68] If the amount paid as salary or bonus is unreasonably large, the excess over a reasonable sum will be treated as a disguised § 301 distribution to the shareholder-employee, and no deduction will be allowed to the corporation therefor.[69] The classification of such payments as § 301 distributions has generally had minimal effect on the shareholder-distributee, who usually will include the amount received in his gross income regardless of whether it is treated as a dividend or as compensation for services.[70] On the other hand, the classification is often important to the distributing corporation as it will determine whether the "payment" is a deductible expense or a nondeductible distribution.

A corporation (especially an S corporation) might pay a low wage to an employee who is also a shareholder in order to reduce

---

[64]   Treas. Reg. § 1.301–1(j). For example, in Honigman v. Commissioner, 466 F.2d 69 (6th Cir. 1972), a corporation's sale of property to a second corporation controlled by a minority shareholder of the selling corporation was held to be a dividend distribution to the minority shareholder where the selling price was found to be less than the property's value.

[65]   See Estate of Taschler v. United States, 440 F.2d 72 (3d Cir. 1971); Chared Corp. v. United States, 446 F.2d 745 (5th Cir. 1971); Commissioner v. Makransky, 321 F.2d 598 (3d Cir. 1963); Williams v. Commissioner, 627 F.2d 1032 (10th Cir. 1980); Crowley v. Commissioner, 962 F.2d 1077 (1st Cir. 1992).

[66]   For a list of some significant factors that are taken into account in determining whether there was an intention that a purported loan to a shareholder be repaid, see Jaques v. Commissioner, 935 F.2d 104 (6th Cir. 1991), aff'g T.C. Memo 1989–673.

[67]   § 7872.

[68]   E.g., Transport Mfg. & Equip. Co. v. Commissioner, 434 F.2d 373 (8th Cir. 1970).

[69]   Treas. Reg. § 1.162–8.

[70]   The characterization issue is now more complex on account of President Bush's tax cuts in JGTRRA, described in ¶ 2.03. Prior to those cuts, the income would have been taxed at ordinary rates whether classified as a dividend or compensation for services (although the characterization would affect the amount of social security tax and other employment taxes that are payable). Since some dividends are now taxed at a lower maximum rate than salaries, this makes the issue more complex. The salary is deductible by the corporation and the dividend is not, but the salary will be taxed at higher rates by the shareholder-employee than the dividend. The optimal classification will depend on the tax brackets of both the shareholder and the corporation.

employment taxes (such as FICA and FUTA). In such cases, the IRS may rely on the substance versus form doctrine to recharacterize dividends to that employee/shareholder as wages.[71]

Recognizing the issue, however, is much easier than coming up with a clear and simple solution on what constitutes excessive compensation. Courts have attempted to use multi-factor tests, looking at, among other things, the employee's qualifications and the nature and scope of the employee's work.[72] Lately, these tests have been criticized as unhelpful.[73] In the end, what is reasonable compensation under § 162 is a factual question.[74]

---

[71]   See Rev. Rul. 74–44.

[72]   See, e.g., Edwin's Inc. v. United States, 501 F.2d 675 (7th Cir. 1974).

[73]   See Exacto Spring Corporation v. Commissioner, 196 F.3d 833 (7th Cir. 1999). In Exacto Spring, Judge Posner advocated a single "independent investor" test. See also Menard, Inc. v. Commissioner, 560 F.3d 620 (7th Cir. 2009).

[74]   One rule that, in general, has been rejected by most courts and even the Service is the so-called "automatic dividend" rule. The fact that a successful corporation does not pay dividends will not be sufficient on its own to treat some payments to shareholder-employees as deemed distributions. See Rev. Rul. 79–8. But see Charles McCandless Tile Service v. United States, 422 F.2d 1336 (Ct. Cl. 1970).

Chapter Three

DISTRIBUTIONS IN REDEMPTION OF STOCK

Analysis

Para.

3.01   Introduction

3.02   Attribution of One Individual's or Entity's Stock Ownership to a Different Individual or Entity

3.03   Tax Consequences of Stock Redemption

3.04   Purchase or Dividend Treatment?—Standards Set at the Shareholder Level

3.05   Partial Liquidations—Standards Set at the Corporate Level

3.06   Gain or Loss Recognized by Distributing Corporation

3.07   Distribution in Redemption of Stock That Was Included Within the Gross Estate of a Decedent for Federal Estate Tax Purposes

3.08   Effect of Redemption of Stock on Corporation's Earnings and Profits

3.09   Extraordinary Dividend to a Corporate Distributee Resulting from a Stock Redemption or Partial Liquidation

3.10   Redemption of Stock of One Shareholder as a Dividend to Other Shareholders

3.11   Constructive Redemption—the Sale of Corporate Stock Either to a Subsidiary Corporation or to a Sister Corporation

¶ 3.01 INTRODUCTION

If Alice sells her corporate stock to another person, the transaction typically will be treated as a purchase and sale in which Alice recognizes a capital gain or loss. There are exceptions, but that is the most common treatment of such sales. How then should a corporation's redemption of its stock be treated—as a purchase or as a § 301 distribution to the distributees in which the distributee's transfer of shares of stock to the corporation is ignored? The stock redemptions discussed in this chapter are not connected to a complete liquidation. Complete liquidations are discussed in Chapter Four.

The tax law treats some stock redemptions the same as if the redeemed shares were purchased by a third party, and treats other stock redemptions as § 301 distributions. For the most part, it is an all or nothing proposition in that the redemption will be treated either entirely as a purchase or entirely as a § 301 distribution.[1]

For purposes of the Code, a stock redemption occurs when a corporation acquires its own stock from a shareholder in exchange for property whether or not the corporation then retires the acquired stock or holds it as treasury stock.[2] A stock redemption is equivalent to a sale of stock by a shareholder to the corporation that issued the stock. Under the normal treatment of sales of property, a shareholder would report a gain or loss for the difference between the net redemption price and the shareholder's basis; and since the stock typically will qualify as a capital asset, the shareholder's profit (or loss) would be characterized as a capital gain (or loss). However, in certain circumstances, the net result of a corporation's redeeming a portion of the stock holdings of a shareholder may more closely resemble a dividend than a sale and will be treated accordingly.

Ex. A owned the entire 200 shares of outstanding stock of the X Corporation. X had accumulated earnings and profits of $200,000. A sold 100 shares of his X stock to X for $150,000. Thus, A owned 100 percent of the outstanding stock of the X Corporation before and after the sale, and the net effect of the "sale" was that A withdrew $150,000 from the corporation. The $150,000 is treated as a § 301 distribution to A. To the extent that earnings and profits of X are allocable to the distribution, it will constitute a dividend to A.

Prior to 1954, purchases of its own stock by a corporation were treated as sales unless "essentially equivalent to the distribution of a taxable dividend." Decisions as to whether a redemption was or was not essentially equivalent to a dividend analyzed the redemption from two different viewpoints:

- from the point of view of the shareholder to determine whether the redemptions were substantially disproportionate since proportional redemptions resemble a dividend; and

- from the point of view of the corporation to determine whether there was a legitimate business purpose for making the redemption.

While the essentially equivalent test has been retained in § 302(b)(1), the present Code provides additional tests, the

---

[1]   One exception to the all or nothing treatment arises under § 303, which applies to the redemption of certain stock that was included in a decedent's gross estate. Section 303 is discussed in ¶ 3.07.

[2]   § 317(b).

satisfaction of any of which precludes dividend treatment. Some of these additional tests look at the position of the shareholder whose stock is being redeemed and some of them look at the position of the distributing corporation. As to § 302(b)(1), it differs from its pre-1954 antecedent in that it rests solely on the proportionality of the redemption.

Section 302(d) provides that, unless a specific statutory exception is applicable, a corporation's redemption of a shareholder's stock will be treated as a § 301 distribution to the shareholder rather than as a purchase of the stock. In other words, § 301 treatment is the default rule if no specific statutory rule providing purchase treatment is applicable. If § 301 treatment applies, the entire amount paid in redemption of the stock (and not merely the excess of the amount paid over the shareholder's basis) will constitute a § 301 distribution. The several specific statutory exceptions to § 302(d) are discussed in succeeding paragraphs; but since the application of many of those exceptions depends upon the amount of stock actually or constructively owned by the shareholder involved, the rules of attribution of stock ownership are discussed first. Stock attribution rules are rules that treat one person as the owner of corporate stock that is actually owned by someone else.

¶ 3.02 ATTRIBUTION OF ONE INDIVIDUAL'S OR ENTITY'S STOCK OWNERSHIP TO A DIFFERENT INDIVIDUAL OR ENTITY

When stock ownership is a factor in determining corporate tax consequences, not only will the stock owned by the specific shareholder be significant but frequently the stock owned by an individual or entity having a close relationship to the specific shareholder may also be taken into account. Whether a person has constructive ownership of stock not directly owned by him is determined by technical statutory rules of attribution, and the tests employed are objective rather than subjective. For purposes of determining whether a stock redemption is a sale or a § 301 distribution, the rules of attribution set forth in § 318 control.[3]

Unless rules of attribution are specifically made applicable to a provision of the Internal Revenue Code, no constructive ownership (other than sham arrangements that involve actual rather than constructive ownership) will pertain to that provision. Section 318(a) specifically applies only to those provisions "to which the rules contained in this section are expressly made applicable." The Code contains a number of attribution rules, which have different scopes

---

3   § 302(c)(1).

but operate in similar fashion. In some instances, a provision of the Code will adopt rules of attribution contained in another section but will establish specific modifications.

The congressional purpose for providing explicit statutory rules of stock attribution is to foster predictability and to avoid the uncertainty created by having ad hoc judgments made as to the extent of the autonomy of members of a family or other related group. For that reason, the statutory rules are applied strictly without reference to the actual independence of the parties involved. For example, the fact that family members are at odds with each other does not prevent the stock of one from being attributed to the other; there is no "bad blood" exception to the operation of the attribution rules of § 318.

Section 318 provides for attribution in four separate settings:

(1)   Family attribution: an individual is deemed to own the stock owned, directly or indirectly, by or for his spouse, children, grandchildren, and parents;

(2)   Attribution from an entity to its beneficiaries or owners:

    (a)   Stock owned (directly or indirectly) by or for a partnership, trust, or estate is considered to be owned proportionately by its partners or beneficiaries.

    (b)   A portion of stock owned (directly or indirectly) by or for a corporation will be deemed owned by a shareholder having a 50 percent or greater interest in the corporation in proportion to the shareholder's percentage interest in the corporation. The percentage interest in the corporation is determined by the value of the stock involved rather than by voting power. In determining a shareholder's percentage interest in a corporation (let us call it the X Corporation) the X stock owned by others that is attributed to the shareholder by § 318 is taken into account.[4]

(3)   Attribution to an entity from its beneficiaries or owners:

    (a)   Stock owned (directly or indirectly) by or for a partner or a beneficiary of a trust or an estate is

---

[4]   § 318(a)(5)(A); and Treas. Reg. § 1.318–1(b)(3).

deemed to be owned by the partnership, trust, or estate.

(b) Stock owned (directly or indirectly) by or for a shareholder having 50 percent or more in value of the stock of another corporation is considered to be owned by the latter corporation. In determining whether a shareholder satisfies that 50 percent or more interest requirement, stock owned by others that is attributed to the shareholder by § 318 is taken into account. § 318(a)(5)(A).

(4) Options:

The holder of an option to acquire stock (or an option to acquire another option to acquire stock) is deemed the owner of the stock that is subject to the option. Stock warrants and convertible debentures are treated as options.

Ex. (1) X Corporation has 100 shares of stock outstanding of which A and B each own 30 shares, and C and D each own 20 shares. A is the grandmother of B. C and D are not related to each other or to A or B. X owns 200 shares of stock of the Z Corporation. A owns 50 shares of Z stock, and B owns 10 shares of Z stock. The 30 shares of X stock that B owns are attributed to his grandmother, A, under the family attribution rule of § 318(a)(1). Consequently, A is treated as owning 60 shares of X stock (60 percent of X's outstanding stock)—30 shares outright and 30 shares by attribution from B. Since A satisfies the 50 percent of value requirement, 60 percent of the 200 shares of Z stock that X owns (i.e., 120 shares) are attributed to A. In addition, the 10 shares of Z stock that B owns are attributed to A. A therefore is deemed to own 180 shares of Z stock—50 shares outright, 120 shares by attribution from X, and 10 shares by attribution from B.

Note that A's 30 shares of X stock are not attributed to her grandson, B; and so none of X's shares of Z stock are attributed to B because B does not have a 50 percent or greater interest in X.

The 50 shares of Z stock that A owns outright are attributed to X by § 318(a)(3)(C). The 10 shares of Z stock that B owns are not attributed to X by § 318(a)(3)(C) because B does not have the requisite 50 percent or greater interest in X. However, the 10 shares of Z stock that B owns are attributed to A by family attribution; and, since A is treated as actually owning those shares, those 10 shares of Z stock are reattributed from A to X by § 318(a)(3)(C). X therefore is deemed to own 260 shares of Z stock—200 shares outright and 60 shares by attribution from A.

There are exceptions to these general rules. For example, for attribution to and from estates, a person who has only a future interest in an estate does not qualify as a beneficiary of the estate. The holders of the present interests in the estate are attributed the estate's stock that otherwise would have been attributed to the holders of the future interests.[5] This treatment of future interests applies only to estates and does not apply to trusts.

For trusts, if all or part of the trust income is taxed to the grantor of the trust, then that portion of the stock held by the trust is deemed owned by the grantor. Also, for attribution *to* trusts, stock owned by a contingent beneficiary whose interest in the trust (computed actuarially) is five percent or less of the value of the trust assets is ignored.[6] The interest of such a beneficiary is referred to as a "remote contingent interest." While stock held by a beneficiary who has only a remote contingent interest in a trust is not attributed to the trust, the converse is not true. A portion of any stock held by the trust is attributed to the remote contingent beneficiary according to the value of his proportionate interest in the trust.

Ex. (2)   F's estate owns 200 shares of stock of the Z Corporation. Pursuant to F's will, A is entitled to 40 percent of F's estate. Of the remaining 60 percent of F's estate, B has a life interest and C has the remainder interest (a future interest). By attribution, A is deemed to own 80 shares of the Z stock that F's estate owns (40% × 200 shares). The remaining 120 shares of Z stock that F's estate owns are attributed to B, who has a present interest in 60 percent of the estate. None of the Z shares that F's estate owns are attributed to C since C's interest in the estate is a future interest.

The rules of § 318 are applied strictly, and if parties do not come within those rules, there is no attribution among them. For example, under § 318 there is no attribution among brothers and sisters; and the stock owned by a grandparent is not attributed to a grandchild; although the stock held by a grandchild is attributed to his grandparent.

---

5   Treas. Reg. § 1.318–3(a), Ex.(1)(a).
6   § 318(a)(3)(B)(i).

With certain exceptions, a party is deemed to have actual ownership of stock that has been attributed to him; the attributed stock may then be reattributed to a third party.[7]

Ex. (3)   A is a beneficiary of a trust owning 100 shares of stock in X Corporation. A's actuarially determined interest in the trust is 75 percent; A is deemed to own 75 shares of the stock of X held by the trust. Since A is regarded as the actual owner of those 75 shares, the ownership of the 75 shares will be reattributed from A to his wife, W. Therefore, the trust owns 100 shares of X, and A and W are each deemed to own 75 shares of X. Note that A is deemed to own the stock only for specific purposes (such as § 302); for example, A is not deemed to own that stock for purposes of applying certain nonrecognition provisions such as the § 351 provision for transfers to a controlled corporation.

There are two circumstances in which constructively owned stock will not be reattributed to a third party:

(1)   Stock that is constructively owned by an individual because of family attribution rules (§ 318(a)(1)) is not reattributed from that individual to another member of his family. § 318(a)(5)(B). However, the stock may be reattributed from that individual to an entity (such as a trust of which the individual is a beneficiary).

(2)   Stock that is attributed *to* an entity from a beneficiary or owner is not reattributed *from* the entity to another beneficiary or owner.[8] This amendment eliminated the previously troublesome problem of so-called "sideways attribution," e.g., if stock were attributed from a beneficiary to a trust or estate and then a portion of such stock were reattributed to another beneficiary of the trust or estate, there would be "sideways attribution" from one beneficiary to the other of part of the first beneficiary's stock holdings.

Ex. (4)   A and B are equal beneficiaries of an estate that has 100 shares of stock of the Y Corporation. A and B are not related. B individually owns 40 shares of stock of Y. Fifty of the 100 shares of Y stock held by the estate are constructively owned by A and are reattributed from A to his wife, W. The 50 shares constructively owned by W are not reattributed to S, W's son by a prior marriage, since W's constructive ownership was the product of family

7   § 318(a)(5)(A).
8   § 318(a)(5)(C).

attribution. The 40 shares of Y stock held by B are attributed to the estate, which is deemed to own 140 shares of Y stock. However, none of the 40 shares attributed to the estate are reattributed to A.

¶ 3.03 TAX CONSEQUENCES OF STOCK REDEMPTION

In determining whether a stock redemption qualifies as a purchase of the stock or whether it is to be treated as a § 301 distribution, the Code establishes two sets of standards—one set of which views the transaction from the shareholder's perspective and one set of which views the transaction from the distributing corporation's perspective. The word "purchase" is used to distinguish a distribution in redemption that is not covered by § 301 from one that is so covered. If treated as a purchase, the difference between the amount distributed to the shareholder and his basis in the redeemed shares will constitute a recognized gain or loss (typically, but not always, a capital gain or loss).

Note that the importance of § 302 was diminished (although not eliminated) by the 2003 amendment to the Code that applied capital gains rates to most dividend income received by an individual. While dividends are ordinary income, they may be taxed at capital gain rates.

Prior to the 2003 amendment, individuals generally preferred to avoid § 301 treatment in order to obtain the favorable capital gains tax rate. Now, even though most dividends to individuals are taxed at the same rate as capital gains, there are still important differences in the tax treatments of the two that can matter in certain circumstances. If a redemption is treated as a purchase, the taxpayer will be able to use his basis in the redeemed stock to measure the amount of gain recognized on the transaction.[9] Also, capital gains, unlike ordinary income, can be reduced by capital losses. If a redemption is not treated as a purchase of the stock, then the entire amount distributed by the corporation to the shareholder (not merely the excess of the amount distributed over the shareholder's basis in the redeemed stock) is treated as a § 301 distribution and is classified as ordinary income to the extent that the distribution does not exceed the corporation's current and accumulated earnings and profits. Also, foreign taxpayers will prefer purchase treatment because they are not taxed by the United States on most capital gains earned in the United States, whereas dividends earned in the United States are

---

[9] Only the basis of the redeemed shares is used to measure the amount of recognized gain. Prop. Reg. § 1.304–2(c), Ex. (1).

ordinarily subject to a United States withholding tax (unless exempted by tax treaty).

The capital gains rate treatment that the 2013 amendment added to the Code does not alter the landscape for corporate shareholders. Since corporations are taxed at the same rate on capital gains and ordinary income, corporations generally prefer dividend treatment in order to qualify for the dividend-received deduction.

If a portion of a shareholder's stock is redeemed by the corporation, and the amounts received from the corporation are characterized by § 302(d) as a § 301 distribution, for some time there was concern that, since the shareholder no longer owns the redeemed stock, the shareholder's unused basis in the redeemed shares would be lost. The regulations relieved much of that fear by providing that the shareholder's unused basis will be allocated to other stock in that corporation held by the same shareholder.[10] However, that regulatory treatment will be changed dramatically if proposed regulations that were promulgated in January, 2009, are finalized in their current form. The 2009 proposed regulations are discussed later in this chapter.

The following two examples illustrate the workings of the current regulations. The altered treatment adopted by the 2009 proposed regulations is discussed immediately after these two examples.

Ex. (1)   X redeemed 100 shares of its stock from Individual A, its sole shareholder, for $50,000. All of X's outstanding stock was of the same class. X had e and p in excess of $80,000. A had a basis of $20,000 in the redeemed stock, and he had a basis of $14,000 in the remaining stock of X that he retained. The $50,000 paid to A was determined to be a dividend to A. A's $20,000 basis in the redeemed shares is allocated to his remaining shares of X for which he therefore has a $34,000 basis after the redemption is completed. The current regulations do not make clear how the basis is allocated among the individual shares of stock.

Ex. (2)   Y Corporation had 100 shares of stock outstanding of which H owned 45 shares and W owned the remaining 55 shares. Y had e and p in excess of $200,000. H and W are a married couple, and each had a basis of $1,000 per share in the Y stock. Y redeemed H's 45 shares of Y stock and paid H $90,000 for those shares. No § 302(c)(2) election was made to prevent the attribution of W's stock to H. Since W's 55

---

[10]   Treas. Reg. § 1.302–2(c).

shares of Y stock are attributed to H, the $90,000 that H received is treated as a § 301 distribution and qualifies as a dividend. Under current regulations, the $45,000 basis that H had in the redeemed shares is added to W's basis in her 55 shares; and so, after the redemption, W has a basis of $100,000 in her 55 shares of Y stock.

The 2009 proposed regulations treat this transaction very differently. The proposed regulations do not permit the transfer of H's unused basis to W. We describe below how the proposed regulations deal with the unused basis.

The 2009 proposed regulations adopt a complex scheme for the treatment of stock redemptions that constitute § 301 distributions because of § 302(d). While the proposed regulations better accord with tax policy than do the current regulations, which do not address many of these issues, they will be more difficult to administer. A Treasury official stated that Treasury plans to reexamine the issues addressed in the 2009 regulations,[11] and so it is far from certain that the final regulations will be unchanged. Let us now focus briefly on the treatment of § 302(d) redemptions by the 2009 proposed regulations.[12]

If the deemed § 301 distribution creates any excess distribution (i.e., the amount of the distribution in excess of the corporation's *e and p*), it is allocated pro rata on a share-by-share basis to each share of stock held by the shareholder that is of the same class as the stock that was redeemed.[13] The excess distribution is allocated among both the redeemed shares and the retained shares of the same class. The amount allocated to each share will reduce the basis of that share. If the amount allocated to a share exceeds the basis of that share, the difference will be a gain recognized on that share (typically a capital gain).

Immediately after the bases of the shares have been reduced (and any gain recognized), a constructive recapitalization under § 368(a)(1)(E) is deemed to take place in which the shareholder exchanged both the redeemed shares and the retained shares of the same class for new shares of the corporation.[14] No gain or loss is recognized from the exchanges made pursuant to that constructive recapitalization. The constructive recapitalization is merely a

---

[11] 225 Daily Tax Report G-2 (Nov. 21, 2013).

[12] The 2009 proposed regulations deal with more than § 302(d) redemptions, but that is the focus of this part of the book.

[13] Prop. Reg. § 1.302–5(a)(1). For this purpose, class is determined by reference to economic rights to distribution rather than by rights with respect to governance. Prop. Reg. § 1.302–5(b)(2).

[14] Prop. Reg. § 1.302–5(a)(2).

fictional device to change the basis of the retained shares so that part of those shares reflects the unused basis of the redeemed shares and part of those shares reflects the unused basis of the retained shares. For convenience, let us refer to the retained shares that were deemed to have been exchanged in the constructive recapitalization as the "old retained shares" and let us call the retained shares held after the constructive recapitalization as the "new retained shares." The new retained shares will then be divided into at least two separate blocks in determining the basis of those shares. One block of the new retained shares will have the holding period and unused basis that the redeemed shares had remaining after any reduction of that basis because of the excess distribution allocated to those shares. The other block of the new retained shares will have the holding period and unused basis that the old retained shares had after any reduction of that basis because of the excess distribution allocated to those shares. The division of the shares into several blocks is made proportionately according to the fair market values of each block.

It will not be necessary to divide the new retained shares into several blocks if all of the shares that shareholder held at the time of the redemption had the same value and the same holding period. There can be more than two blocks of the new retained shares if either the redeemed shares or the old retained shares consisted of more than one block of stock because of a difference in holding period or basis.

The following example, which is taken from the proposed regulations,[15] illustrates how that system operates.

Ex. (3)   H and W, husband and wife, each own 100 shares (50%) of the outstanding stock of the X Corporation. The 100 shares that H held were divided into two blocks because H had a different basis in each block. H had a basis of $100 in 50 of the shares that he held (Block 1). H had a basis of $200 in the remaining 50 shares he held (Block 2). On December 31, Year One, X redeemed all 50 shares of Block 2 stock for $300 cash. X had no current or accumulated *e and p* in Year One. Under § 302(d), the entire $300 is treated as a § 301 distribution. Since X had no *e and p*, the amount allocated to each share will reduce the basis of that share and any excess will cause gain recognition.

Since Block 1 and Block 2 are of equal value, 50% of the $300 (i.e., $150) is allocated to Block 1 (the old retained shares). H had a basis of $100 in the shares in that Block 1. The $150 distribution allocated to that Block 1 will reduce

---

[15]   Prop. Reg. § 1.302–5(e), Ex. (1).

H's basis in those shares to zero and cause H to recognize a gain of $50. The remaining $150 of the distribution is allocated to Block 2. That will reduce H's basis in Block 2 to $50, and will not cause H to recognize any additional income. H is then deemed to transfer the stock of both Block 1 and Block 2 to X in exchange for the new retained shares of stock. The new retained shares will be divided into two blocks. Block 3 will be deemed to have been received in exchange for Block 1 (the old retained shares) and Block 4 will be deemed to have been received in exchange for Block 2 (the redeemed shares). Since Blocks 1 and 2 were of equal value, one-half of the new retained shares will be deemed to have been received for Block 1 shares and one-half for Block 2 stock. Thus, there will be an equal number of shares in Blocks 3 and 4. So, the shares in Block 3 will have a basis of zero (the unused basis of the old retained shares) and the shares in Block 4 will have a basis of $50 (the same as the unused basis of the redeemed shares).

What happens if all of the shares of the same class that a shareholder holds are redeemed? In that case, there will be no retained shares, and so none of the unused basis can be shifted to new retained shares. The proposed regulations provide that, in such a case, the shareholder realizes a loss on the redeemed shares in the amount of the unused basis.[16] This realized loss is deferred and is recognized at a date referred to in the proposed regulations as the "inclusion date."

The inclusion date (i.e., the date on which the deferred loss is recognized and can be deducted) is the earliest date on which one of several listed events occurs.[17] One such date is the first date on which the redeemed shareholder would satisfy § 302(b)(1), (2), or (3) if the facts and circumstances that exist at the end of that later date had existed immediately after the redemption took place. Subsections 302(b)(1), (2), and (3) are the principal provisions that operate to treat a stock redemption as a purchase rather than as a § 301 distribution when certain conditions are satisfied; and those subsections are discussed in ¶¶ 3.04.1 to 3.04.3. Thus, once facts exist that would have characterized the redemption as a purchase if they had existed immediately after the redemption, the deferred loss will be recognized. Another date that can be used if it occurs first is the date

---

[16]　Prop. Reg. § 1.302–5(a)(3).
[17]　Prop. Reg. § 1.302–5(b)(4).

on which all of the stock of the redeeming corporation becomes worthless.[18]

¶ 3.04   PURCHASE OR DIVIDEND TREATMENT?—STANDARDS SET AT THE SHAREHOLDER LEVEL

The Code defines three circumstances where a shareholder's position vis-à-vis his fellow shareholders is so changed by a redemption that it is treated as a purchase of that shareholder's stock. Two of these provisions rest on objective ascertainable standards, and they are sometimes referred to as "safe-harbor" provisions. The third provision rests on a vaguer standard that is less susceptible to predictability.

There also are two provisions that provide purchase treatment without regard to whether there was a change in the shareholder's position. One of those is the treatment of partial liquidations described in ¶ 3.05. Another provision concerns a redemption of stock of a regulated investment company. In 2010, Congress added § 302(b)(5) to the Code. That provision provides purchase treatment for the redemption of publicly offered stock of a regulated investment company if two conditions are satisfied. The two conditions are: (1) the company issues only stock that is redeemable upon the demand of the shareholder, and (2) the redemption is made upon the shareholder's demand.

¶ 3.04.1   § 302(b)(1)—Not Essentially Equivalent to a Dividend

The first of these three circumstances is a version of the pre-1954 test, viz., redemptions "not essentially equivalent to a dividend" are treated as purchases.[19] Prior to the Supreme Court's 1970 decision in *United States v. Davis*,[20] the courts split in their interpretation of that phrase. One line of cases adopted a "flexible net effect" test that incorporated a "business purpose" test—i.e., whether the redemption was designed to serve a legitimate business purpose of either the corporation itself or of the shareholders. In *Davis*, the Supreme Court held that the existence or absence of a business purpose for making a redemption was not relevant to the determination of whether § 302(b)(1) was applicable. Instead,

---

[18]   Prop. Reg. § 1.302–5(b)(4)(i)(B). The 2009 proposed regulations contain provisions dealing with other aspects of the deferred loss treatment provision including the treatment of a successor corporation to the redeeming corporation. There also are special provisions for a corporate shareholder whose stock is redeemed. We do not discuss those additional provisions of the proposed regulations.

[19]   § 302(b)(1).

[20]   397 U.S. 301, reh. denied, 397 U.S. 1071 (1970).

following a second line of cases, the Supreme Court adopted a "strict net effect" test, i.e., whether the circumstances resulting from the redemption are significantly different from the circumstances that would have resulted if a dividend had been distributed. Under this test, a pro rata or nearly pro rata redemption of a shareholder's stock will not qualify.[21] The Court also held that in determining whether a redemption is sufficiently disproportionate, the stock attribution rules of § 318 are applicable.

In *Davis*, the Court held that to qualify as not essentially equivalent to a dividend under § 302(b)(1), a redemption of a shareholder's stock must result in a "meaningful reduction of the shareholder's proportionate interest in the corporation." A reduction of a shareholder's proportionate interest in the corporation has been deemed to refer to any of the following: a reduction of a shareholder's voting interest, that is, a loss of some important element of control; a reduction of the shareholder's dividend rights; a reduction in the shareholder's percentage interest in the proceeds of a complete liquidation of the corporation; or a reduction of some combination of the above.

The courts and the Commissioner have been fairly liberal in applying the § 302(b)(1) standard.[22] Although far from exhaustive, two typical situations where § 302(b)(1) could apply should be noted.[23] In discussing that provision in this book, we examine separately the redemption of voting and nonvoting stock.

¶ 3.04.1.1   *Redemption of Voting Stock*

When voting stock of a majority shareholder is redeemed, the courts and the Commissioner have looked primarily to the control of the shareholder after the redemption to determine whether a meaningful reduction has occurred. The Commissioner's view is that a reduction of a majority voting interest to a voting interest of no more than 50 percent will be sufficient for § 302(b)(1) but that a reduction of voting interest to a percentage that is greater than 50 percent will not qualify.[24] The percentage interest of a shareholder is determined after applying § 318 stock attribution rules.

---

[21]   Treas. Reg. § 1.302–2(b).

[22]   See, e.g., Rev. Rul. 77–426 (redemption of five percent of the nonvoting preferred stock of a shareholder who had no actual or constructive ownership of voting common stock qualified for purchase treatment under § 302(b)(1)).

[23]   For a thorough examination of the operation of the § 302(b)(1) provision see Douglas A. Kahn, *Stock Redemptions: The Standards For Qualifying As A Purchase Under Section 302(b)*, 50 Fordham L. Rev. 1, 17–27 (1981).

[24]   See Rev. Rul. 78–401; Rev. Rul. 77–218; Rev. Rul. 75–502; TAM 199934001.

The Eighth Circuit held in a two-to-one 1973 decision in *Wright v. United States*,[25] that a reduction of a shareholder's voting interest from 85 percent to 61.7 percent was a meaningful reduction because under state law a two-thirds vote was required to authorize a merger, consolidation or liquidation, or to amend the articles of incorporation, and the shareholder therefore lost the power to make those decisions unilaterally.[26] In Rev. Rul. 78–401, the Commissioner rejected the holding in *Wright* and stated that such a reduction was not meaningful when there is no indication that any of the types of corporate action that require a two-thirds vote are contemplated for the near future.

Ex. (1)   X Corporation had 100 shares of voting common stock outstanding of which A owned 60 shares, B owned 10 shares, and C owned the remaining 30 shares. A, B, and C are not related. X redeemed 5 shares of A's stock after which A owned 55/95 or 57.9 percent of X's outstanding stock. Since A owns more than 50 percent of X's stock after the redemption, § 302(b)(1) will not apply; and the amount paid by X in redemption of those 5 shares will be treated as a § 301 distribution to A.

Ex. (2)   The same facts as those stated in Example (1) except that X redeemed 20 shares of A's stock instead of redeeming only 5 shares. After the redemption, A owns 40/80 or 50 percent of X's outstanding stock. While the issue is not free of doubt, it is likely that the redemption will be treated as a purchase of A's 20 shares of stock rather than as a § 301 distribution. In a 1975 ruling, the Commissioner held that a redemption that reduced a shareholder's majority interest to a 50 percent interest, where he thereby had only veto power, is not essentially equivalent to a dividend and so is treated as a purchase.[27]

A minority shareholder whose percentage interest of common stock is reduced by a redemption may not have lost a significant voting interest, since he already lacked control, unless his prospects of sharing control by joining with a small number of shareholders is diminished by the redemption.[28] Because a shift in voting rights is of

---

[25]   482 F.2d 600 (8th Cir. 1973).

[26]   Similarly, in Henry T. Patterson Trust v. United States, 729 F.2d 1089 (6th Cir. 1984), the Sixth Circuit held that a reduction of a shareholder's percentage interest from an 80 percent interest to a 62.8 percent interest was a meaningful reduction to which § 302(b)(1) applies.

[27]   Rev. Rul. 75–502.

[28]   See Rev. Rul. 76–364; Rev. Rul. 84–114. For example, if before the redemption, the shareholder needed only one other shareholder to join with him to exercise control, and after the redemption the shareholder needed to have four other shareholders join

less importance to a minority shareholder than to one who has lost voting control, a reduction of dividend rights and liquidation interests is a more significant factor for a minority shareholder.

Ex. (3)   The same facts as those stated in Example (1) except that X redeemed 5 shares of C's stock and did not redeem any of A's stock. The redemption of C's 5 shares of X stock reduced her interest from 30 percent to 25/95 or 26.3 percent. Since, both before and after the redemption, C had only a minority interest, the crucial consideration is that C's dividend and liquidation rights were reduced. It is likely that the redemption will be treated as a purchase, but that result is not certain.

If a minority shareholder owns only a minuscule percentage of a corporation's stock, a non-pro-rata redemption of any number of his shares of common stock that reduces his percentage interest to any extent should qualify under § 302(b)(1). For example, in Rev. Rul. 76–385, a reduction of a shareholder's percentage interest from .0001118 percent to .0001081 percent, a reduction of only 3.3 percent, was determined to qualify for § 302(b)(1) treatment. A non-pro-rata redemption of even one share from such a shareholder bears no similarity to a dividend.

¶ 3.04.1.2   *Redemption of Nonvoting Stock*

The redemption of nonvoting stock where the shareholder has no control over the decision to redeem and where the redemption is disproportionate to the shareholder's voting stock holdings is the very circumstance that the Senate gave as an illustration of the need to have a flexible exception to dividend treatment in the Code.[29] The determination of whether a shareholder lacks control should rest on the same polices as were discussed above in connection with the redemption of voting stock.

If, after applying attribution, a shareholder owns only nonvoting stock, a redemption of all or any part of the shareholder's stock ordinarily should be covered by § 302(b)(1).[30] Since the shareholder has no voting rights, the reduction of his right to participate in dividend distributions and in liquidating distributions cannot be compensated by his exercise of control over the corporation.

If, after applying attribution rules, a shareholder owns both voting and nonvoting stock, the question how the tax law should treat

---

with him to exercise control, that redemption can be seen as causing a significant loss of voting power.

[29]   S.Rep. No. 1622, 83d Cong., 2d Sess. 44–45 (1954).

[30]   Treas. Reg. § 1.302–2(a).

a redemption of the nonvoting stock is unsettled. But the proper treatment in some circumstances seems reasonably clear. For example, if, after the redemption, the shareholder has (or is deemed to have after applying attribution rules) more than 50 percent of the voting power of the corporation's stock, there seems no reason to allow purchase treatment for the redemption.[31] Also, if the shareholder has (or is deemed to have) the same proportion of the corporation's outstanding voting and nonvoting stock after a redemption as before, a redemption of all of the corporation's outstanding nonvoting stock would not alter the shareholder's proportionate rights to dividends or liquidation proceeds and so should be treated as a § 301 distribution.[32] If the shareholder owns (or is deemed to own) voting and nonvoting stock in different proportions, and if the shareholder does not have voting control, the issue becomes more difficult to resolve.

Although it is difficult to predict with certainty the outcome of the application of § 302(b)(1) to many types of situations, in the following examples, the authors have indicated how they believe the provision should be applied.

Ex. (4)   X Corporation had outstanding 1,000 shares of voting common stock and 100 shares of nonvoting preferred stock, none of which was section 306 stock. A owned 60 shares of X's nonvoting preferred stock, and B owned the remaining 40 shares. All of the 1,000 shares of X's voting common stock were owned by C. A, B and C are not related. X redeemed 30 shares of A's nonvoting preferred stock and 20 shares of B's nonvoting preferred stock. The amounts paid by X to A and B should qualify for purchase treatment under § 302(b)(1) because each of them had a meaningful reduction of their rights to dividend and liquidating distributions, and they lack control of the corporation that would have enabled them to cause the corporation to compensate them for that reduction.

Ex. (5)   The same facts as those stated in Example (4) except that A is the spouse of C. Since C's voting stock is attributed to A by family attribution, A is deemed to have control of X after the redemption. The amount paid to A in redemption of his 30 shares of preferred stock should be treated as a § 301 distribution, but the amount paid to B should be treated as a purchase of his redeemed shares.

---

[31]   An Example in the 2009 proposed regulations provides some support for this view. Prop. Reg. § 1.302–5(e), Ex. (3).

[32]   Id.

Ex. (6)   The same facts as those stated in Example (4) except that (1) B owns 400 shares (40 percent) of X's voting common stock and C owns the remaining 600 shares, and (2) X redeems all of its outstanding nonvoting preferred stock. The redemption of A's 60 shares of preferred stock should qualify for purchase treatment. But the redemption of B's 40 shares of preferred stock should be treated as a § 301 distribution. After the redemption, B continues to be entitled to 40 percent of any distribution X makes to its shareholders, whether a liquidating distribution or a dividend distribution.

¶ 3.04.1.3   *Hostility Among Shareholders*

There is a question whether hostility or "bad blood" among persons listed in § 318 precludes the attribution of stock or otherwise influences a determination of dividend equivalence.[33] As to the attribution rules themselves, stock will be attributed under § 318 regardless of the hostility among the parties involved.[34] This construction conforms with the legislative purpose for adopting § 318. The question remains, however, as to what effect family hostility has on the operation of § 302(b)(1).

The "bad blood" or hostility in a family group could be regarded as a factual circumstance to be considered in determining whether a redemption is meaningful. Under this approach, if the redemption of stock of a shareholder would qualify as a meaningful redemption if it were not for the attribution of stock to him from his relatives, the fact that there is animosity between the family members is a factor to be weighed in favor of qualifying the redemption under § 302(b)(1). This position was adopted by the First Circuit in *Haft Trust v. Commissioner*,[35] but was repudiated by the Fifth Circuit in *Metzger Trust v. Commissioner*.[36]

It is noteworthy that Treas. Reg. § 1.302–2(b) lends mild support to the *Haft Trust* decision. The regulation states that the question of dividend equivalence for a redemption "depends upon the facts and circumstances of each case" and that merely "[o]ne of the facts to be considered in making this determination is the constructive stock ownership of such shareholder under section 318(a)." This statement

---

[33]   There is also the question of whether attribution can be judicially expanded to cover friendly relations not listed in § 318. For a discussion of that issue, see Kahn, Kahn, Perris, Lehman, Corporate Income Taxation (7th ed.) at Section 3.04.1 (hereinafter cited as Corporate Income Taxation Hornbook).

[34]   Metzger Trust v. Commissioner, 693 F.2d 459, 467 (5th Cir. 1982); Cerone v. Commissioner, 87 T.C. 1 (1986).

[35]   510 F.2d 43, 48 (1st Cir. 1975), vacating 61 T.C. 398 (1973).

[36]   693 F.2d at 466–67.

of the regulation was quoted with approval by the Sixth Circuit in *Henry T. Patterson Trust v. United States.*[37]

The Tax Court's position, as reflected by the majority decision in *Metzger Trust v. Commissioner*,[38] on this issue is that if, after applying the attribution rule, a shareholder's percentage interest in the corporation is not reduced at all, then family hostility is not to be taken into account; but if the taxpayer's interest is reduced to any extent, then family hostility might be taken into account. The Fifth Circuit, while affirming the Tax Court's decision, repudiated the Tax Court's suggestion that family hostility can be taken into account in determining whether a reduction of a shareholder's proportionate interest, no matter how small, constitutes a meaningful reduction; but the court noted that the hostility issue was not presented by the facts before them.[39] The Fifth Circuit believed that to give any weight to family hostility would be inconsistent with the Supreme Court's decision in *Davis*.

¶ 3.04.2 Substantially Disproportionate Redemptions

Under § 302(b)(2), if the redemption of any one shareholder's stock complies with certain prescribed objective tests demonstrating that the redemption is substantially disproportionate, the distribution in redemption of that shareholder's stock will constitute a purchase. In applying these tests, the attribution rules of § 318 are employed to determine the amount of stock owned or deemed to be owned by the shareholder.[40] The standards that the shareholder must satisfy to qualify are:

- Immediately after the redemption, the shareholder must own less than 50 percent of the voting power of all classes of stock entitled to vote.

- The percentage of outstanding voting stock of the corporation owned by the shareholder immediately after the redemption must be less than 80 percent of the percentage of outstanding voting stock of the corporation owned by the shareholder immediately prior to the redemption. Another way to phrase this requirement is that the redemption must reduce the shareholder's percentage of voting stock by more than 20 percent.

---

37   729 F.2d 1089, 1095 (6th Cir. 1984).

38   76 T.C. 42 (1981), aff'd 693 F.2d 459 (5th Cir. 1982).

39   Metzger Trust, 693 F.2d at 466–67 nn. 13 and 16.

40   § 302(c)(1).

- The shareholder's percentage of outstanding common stock of the corporation (whether voting or nonvoting) before and after the redemption must also meet the 80 percent requirement set forth in the preceding paragraph. If there is more than one class of common stock, the 80 percent requirement is measured according to the fair market value of the common stock.[41]

Section 302(b)(2) applies only to redemptions of voting stock or to redemptions of both voting and nonvoting stock; it does not apply to redemptions solely of nonvoting stock (whether common or preferred).[42]

A literal construction of § 302(b)(2) would make it inapplicable to a redemption of only voting preferred stock since the third requirement that the shareholder's percentage of outstanding common stock be reduced by more than 20 percent could not be satisfied. However, where a shareholder has no actual or constructive ownership of common stock but does own voting preferred stock, the Commissioner ruled in Rev. Rul. 81–41[43] that a redemption of a sufficient amount of the shareholder's voting preferred stock can qualify for the § 302(b)(2) safe harbor.

Ex. (1) The X Corporation had 400 shares of common voting stock outstanding; A owned 200 shares, and B owned 200 shares. A and B are not related parties. X had earnings and profits of over $50,000. X redeems 100 shares of A's stock for $20,000 cash. A owns less than 50 percent of the voting stock of X immediately after the redemption; consequently, the first test of § 302(b)(2) is satisfied. A owned 50 percent of the voting stock of the corporation immediately before the redemption, and he owns 33⅓ percent (100/300) after the redemption. Since his percentage of interest in both voting and common stock after the redemption (33⅓ percent) is less than 80 percent of his interest before the redemption (80% × 50% = 40%), the redemption of A's stock is deemed a purchase rather than a dividend.

Ex. (2) The Y Corporation had 600 shares of common voting stock outstanding. C and D each owned 300 shares. C and D are not related. Y had *e and p* of $40,000. Y redeems 100 shares of C's stock for $20,000 cash. While C owns less than 50

---

[41] § 302(b)(2)(C).

[42] Treas. Reg. § 1.302–3(a). If only nonvoting stock is redeemed, the requirement that the shareholder's percentage of voting stock be reduced by more than 20 percent cannot be satisfied.

[43] 1981–1 C.B. 121.

percent of Y's stock after the redemption, the second test of § 302(b)(2) is not satisfied. C owned 50 percent of Y's common voting stock before the redemption, and C owns 40 percent (200/500) of that stock after the redemption took place. Thus, C's percentage ownership of Y's voting (and common) stock after the redemption was exactly 80 percent of the percentage ownership that he had prior to the redemption, and § 302(b)(2) will not apply unless C's percentage interest after the redemption was *less than* 80 percent of his percentage interest before the redemption.[44]

Even if a stock redemption is substantially disproportionate at the time that the redemption occurs, it will not qualify for § 302(b)(2) treatment if it is made pursuant to a plan the purpose or effect of which is a series of redemptions ultimately resulting in a stock ownership that is not substantially disproportionate to the holdings that existed at the time that the plan was initiated.[45]

If a shareholder owns both voting common stock and nonvoting stock and if a redemption of shares of the shareholder's common stock qualifies as substantially disproportionate so that § 302(b)(2) applies, § 302(b)(2) will also apply to a simultaneous redemption of that shareholder's nonvoting stock.[46]

Ex. (3)   X corporation had outstanding 400 shares of voting common stock and 100 shares of nonvoting preferred stock, none of which is section 306 stock.[47] A owned 200 shares of X's voting common stock and all 100 shares of X's nonvoting preferred stock. On the same date, X redeemed from A 100 shares of A's common stock and 60 shares of his preferred stock. The redemption of the voting common stock from A qualifies as a purchase under § 302(b)(2) since A owned 50 percent of X's voting common stock before the redemption and only 33 1/3 percent afterwards. Since the redemption of A's common stock qualified for purchase treatment under § 302(b)(2), the simultaneous redemption of 60 shares of A's preferred stock also is treated by § 302(b)(2) as a purchase.

---

[44]   However, since the redemption deprived C of a veto position, there is a question whether the redemption might qualify as a purchase by virtue of § 302(b)(1); the regulations expressly leave that question open. Treas. Reg. § 1.304–2(c), Ex. (1).

[45]   § 302(b)(2)(D).

[46]   Treas. Reg. § 1.302–3(a). This provision does not apply to the redemption of so-called section 306 stock. Id. Section 306 stock is discussed in Chapter Six.

[47]   Section 306 stock is described in § 306(c) and is subject to undesirable tax treatment on its sale or redemption.

¶ 3.04.3 Termination of Shareholder's Interest

Section 302(b)(3) provides that a redemption of a shareholder's stock will constitute a purchase if the redemption terminates the shareholder's stock interest in the corporation. Except as provided in § 302(c)(2), described below, the attribution rules of § 318 are employed to determine whether a shareholder's stock interest has been terminated by a redemption.[48]

Ex. (1)   X Corporation had outstanding 400 shares of common voting stock and 200 shares of preferred nonvoting stock. The 400 shares of common stock were owned by A, and the 200 shares of preferred stock were owned by B. A and B are not related parties. X redeems B's 200 shares of preferred stock for $10,000 cash. Section 302(b)(2) is inapposite because only nonvoting stock was redeemed. Section 302(b)(3) is applicable, and the redemption will be treated as a purchase.

A complete termination of a shareholder's stock need not be effected in a single transaction in order to qualify under § 302(b)(3). The termination can be accomplished through a series of redemptions provided that they are made pursuant to a firm and fixed single plan.

¶ 3.04.3.1   *Preclusion of Family Attribution*

Section 302(c)(2)(A) mitigates the stringent operation of the attribution rules by providing that the family attribution rules of § 318(a)(1) do not apply to redemptions terminating a shareholder's interest in a corporation if certain requisites are satisfied. These requisites are:

- Immediately after the redemption the distributee has no interest in the corporation (including an interest as an officer, director, or employee) other than an interest as a creditor. In some cases, an interest in a subsidiary or parent of a corporation is treated as an interest in the corporation itself. Similarly, an interest in a successor corporation to the corporation will be treated as an interest in the corporation itself.[49]

- The distributee does not acquire any such interest (other than stock acquired by bequest or inheritance) within ten years after the redemption.

---

[48]   § 302(c)(1).

[49]   Treas. Reg. § 1.302–4(c). For the meaning and application of the "successor corporation" provision, see Rev. Rul. 76–496; PLR 9018028.

- The distributee files an agreement attached to his tax return for the year in which the redemption occurred, in which agreement the distributee promises to notify the district director of any interest he may acquire in the corporation (or successor corporation) within the ten-year period, and such notification shall be made within 30 days after the interest is acquired.[50]

The agreement of a distributee to prevent family attribution rules from operating is sometimes referred to as a "waiver" of family attribution. The term "waiver" is a peculiar choice since that term suggests the voluntary release of a valuable right whereas the family attribution rules that are "waived" are detrimental to the distributee.

If a distributee who executes an agreement under § 302(c)(2)(A) retains or acquires a forbidden interest in the distributing corporation (other than stock acquired by bequest or inheritance) within the ten-year period in contravention of the statutory requirement, then the provisions of § 302(c)(2)(A) will not apply, and a tax deficiency may be assessed for the year in which the redemption occurred. There is a question as to the type of interest that is prohibited to the distributee by the statute. The Tax Court has held that the type of interest at which the statutory prohibition is aimed is one that provides the distributee with either a substantial financial stake in the corporation (i.e., a proprietary interest as contrasted to a creditor's interest) or with control over the operations of the corporation.[51] It seems likely that that is the object of the statutory prohibition. However, the IRS and the Ninth Circuit have adopted a more expansive construction.

It is unsettled whether the determination of whether an interest acquired or retained by a distributee is within the prohibited category turns solely on the relationship of the distributee to the distributing corporation (for example, the status of being an employee of the corporation) or whether it turns upon a factual determination as to whether the distributee's interest provides him with either a substantial financial stake in the corporation or control over the operations of the corporation. For example, if a distributee performs services for the corporation within the proscribed period, is that sufficient to bar § 302(c)(2) or does the prohibition rest on a determination that the distributee's salary or fees are sufficiently large to give the distributee a substantial financial interest in the corporation?

---

[50]   Treas. Reg. § 1.302–4(a).

[51]   E.g., Cerone v. Commissioner, 87 T.C. 1, 31 (1986); Estate of Lennard v. Commissioner, 61 T.C. 554, 561 (1974).

The Tax Court maintains that not all employment relationships between the distributing corporation and the distributee will bar § 302(c)(2).[52] The Tax Court will impose the prohibition only if the distributee's employment relationship is one that provides the distributee with a substantial financial stake in the corporation or with managerial control.

In *Lynch v. Commissioner*,[53] after the redemption, the distributee was retained by the corporation under a consulting agreement. The Tax Court determined that by serving under the consulting agreement, the distributee was acting as an independent contractor and not as an employee. The court then stated: "In particular, where the interest retained is not that of an officer, director, or employee, we must examine the facts and circumstances to determine whether a prohibited interest has been retained under § 302(c)(2)(A)(i)."[54] The Tax Court held that the facts of that case did not support the Commissioner's contention that the distributee's compensation gave him a substantial financial interest in the corporation or that he retained managerial control. Accordingly, the Tax Court allowed the distributee in *Lynch* to use § 302(c)(2).

The Ninth Circuit reversed the Tax Court's decision in *Lynch*.[55] The Ninth Circuit rejected the Tax Court's view that the extent of the distributee's financial interest or control was relevant, and the court rejected the view that there is a different standard for independent contractors than for employees. In an opinion by Judge Hall, the Ninth Circuit said:

> We reject the Tax Court's interpretation of section 302(c)(2)(A)(i). An individualized determination of whether a taxpayer has retained a financial stake or continued to control the corporation after the redemption is inconsistent with Congress' desire to bring a measure of certainty to the tax consequences of a corporate redemption. We hold that a taxpayer who provides post-redemption services, either as an employee or an independent contractor, holds a prohibited interest in the corporation because he is not a creditor.

Judge Hall used selected quotations from the Committee Reports to the 1954 Code to support her conclusion that a proper

---

[52]   Seda v. Commissioner, 82 T.C. 484, 488 (1984) (reviewed by the court); Lynch v. Commissioner, 83 T.C. 597, 605 (1984), reversed, 801 F.2d 1176 (9th Cir. 1986); *Cerone*, 87 T.C. at 31.

[53]   83 T.C. at 597.

[54]   83 T.C. at 605.

[55]   801 F.2d 1176 (9th Cir. 1986). See also PLR 8944076 in which the Commissioner adopted the Ninth Circuit's position on this issue.

construction of § 302(c)(2)(A) is one that rests on an inflexible objective standard rather than on a facts and circumstances test. The statements quoted by the court relate to the safe harbor provisions of § 302(b); they were not aimed at subsection (c)(2). Judge Hall's view that Congress intended to preclude factual inquiries in determining whether family attribution rules can successfully be waived cannot be reconciled with the last sentence of § 302(c)(2)(B) (discussed below) which expressly establishes a subjective test. Section 302(c)(2)(B) precludes the operation of one of the bars to the waiver provision if a certain transaction "did not have as one of its principal purposes the avoidance of Federal income tax."

A distributee does not acquire a forbidden interest under § 302(c)(2)(A) merely by being entitled to a fair rent from the corporation for the use of property owned by the distributee.[56] In such event, the position of the distributee as a landlord is similar to that of a creditor. However, if the distributee's right to rent either is subordinated to the claims of general creditors or is dependent upon future earnings of the corporation, the Commissioner might contend that the distributee has a prohibited interest and thus cannot qualify under § 302(c)(2).[57]

If a stock interest in the distributing corporation is acquired within the proscribed 10-year period by a person whose stock interest is attributed to the distributee by § 318(a), will the distributee be treated as having acquired that stock interest and thereby lose the § 302(c)(2) bar to family attribution? If the attribution to the distributee of the acquired interest in the corporation is attributable to family attribution, then the terms of § 302(c)(2) prevent that attribution from taking place, and so the waiver of family attribution is not lost.[58] However, if the attribution of the acquired interest is attributable to a provision of § 318(a) other than family attribution, it is likely that the distributee will be deemed to have acquired that interest and thereby have lost the bar to family attribution.[59]

Section 302(c)(2)(B) makes the waiver inapplicable (1) if a portion of the redeemed stock was acquired by the distributee during the previous ten years from a person whose stock ownership would (at the time of the distribution) be attributed to the distributee under § 318(a); or (2) if a third person owns stock of the corporation (at the

---

[56]   Rev. Rul. 77–467.

[57]   See Treas. Reg. § 1.302–4(d). Compare Dunn v. Commissioner, 615 F.2d 578 (2d Cir. 1980).

[58]   Rev. Rul. 71–562. See also PLR 9144017.

[59]   See Rev. Rul. 71–562 implying that such an acquisition will cause the loss of a § 302(c)(2) waiver if the acquired interest is attributed to the distributee by some provision of § 318(a) other than family attribution.

time of redemption) the ownership of which is attributable to the distributee under § 318(a) and such stock was acquired from the distributee within the previous ten-year period unless the third person's acquired stock is redeemed in the same transaction. Neither of the above two provisions applies if the acquisition referred to in (1) or the disposition referred to in (2) did not have federal income tax avoidance as one of its principal purposes.[60] The Service announced in Rev. Proc. 2018–3, Sec. 3.01(47) that it will not rule on the question of whether an acquisition or disposition of stock was motivated by tax avoidance within the meaning of § 302(c)(2)(B) unless the facts and circumstances are materially identical to one of six rulings listed in the footnote below.[61]

¶ 3.04.3.2   *Waiver of Attribution by an Entity*

Under § 302(c)(2)(C), for purposes of applying § 302(b)(3), the complete termination safe-harbor, an entity can waive family attribution rules if all of the individuals through whom stock ownership (deemed to be held through family attribution) that would otherwise be reattributed to the entity join in making the waiver.[62] The types of entities that can utilize the waiver of family attribution rules are an estate, trust, partnership, or corporation.

To qualify for the waiver, the conditions of § 302(c)(2)(A) must be satisfied by the entity itself and by all of the persons to whom (in the absence of a valid waiver) stock of the corporation, at the time of the redemption, would otherwise be attributed under the family attribution rules of § 318(a)(1) and which stock would then have been reattributed to the entity under § 318(a)(3). Those beneficiaries or owners of equity interests who are required to comply with the conditions of § 302(c)(2)(A) are referred to as "related persons." All related persons must comply with those conditions for the entity's waiver to be effective. In addition, each related person must agree to be jointly and severally liable for a deficiency resulting from an acquisition by the entity or a related person of a prohibited interest in the redeeming corporation within ten years after the redemption.

Ex. (2)   X Corporation had 100 shares of stock outstanding. H owned 50 shares; W–1 (H's first wife) owned 10 shares; and W–2 (H's second wife) owned 40 shares. H was divorced from both W–1 and W–2. Upon H's death, his will provided a pecuniary bequest to his brother, B, and he left his

---

[60]   § 302(c)(2)(B) (last sentence).

[61]   Rev. Ruls. 85–19, 1985–1 C.B. 94; 79–67, 1979–1 C.B. 128; 77–293, 1977–2 C.B. 91; 57–387, 1957–2 C.B. 225; 56–556, 1956–2 C.B. 177; 56–584, 1956–2 C.B. 179.

[62]   For a discussion of the law prior to the adoption of § 302(c)(2)(C), see Corporate Income Taxation Hornbook at Section 3.04.3.2.

residuary estate to S (a son of H and W–1) and D (a daughter of H and W–2). X redeemed from H's executor all 50 shares of X's stock held by H's estate, and that redemption did not qualify for § 303 treatment.[63] The executor wishes to invoke § 302(c)(2)(C) and prevent the attribution of the stock held by W–1 and W–2 to their respective children since those shares will be reattributed to the estate. If both S and D join with the estate in making the election to waive the family attribution rules and agree to joint and several liability for deficiencies, the redemption of the estate's stock can qualify as a purchase by virtue of § 302(b)(3) provided that neither the estate, nor S, nor D acquires a prohibited interest in X within the proscribed ten-year period. It is not necessary that B join in the election since no stock of X will be attributed to B by family attribution rules. However, if only D consented to join with the estate and S refused, the waiver would not be effective.

¶ 3.05 PARTIAL LIQUIDATIONS—STANDARDS SET AT THE CORPORATE LEVEL

As noted earlier in this chapter, prior to 1954 the determination of whether a stock redemption qualified as a purchase was made by viewing the transaction either from the perspective of the shareholder or from the perspective of the distributing corporation. The 1954 Code established two separate sections to deal with those two perspectives. The shareholder's perspective was dealt with in § 302(b). The perspective of the distributing corporation (i.e., whether the distributing corporation had a legitimate business reason for redeeming the stock) initially was dealt with in § 346. A redemption that qualified for purchase treatment under § 346 was referred to as a "partial liquidation."

¶ 3.05.1 Tax Consequences to Shareholder-Distributee

Today, a distributee's treatment upon receiving a distribution in partial liquidation is described in § 302(b)(4).[64] This provision applies only to a distribution made to a noncorporate shareholder. For this purpose, any stock held by a partnership, estate, or trust is treated as if it were held proportionately by its partners or beneficiaries.[65]

---

[63]   Section 303 is discussed at ¶ 3.07.

[64]   For a detailed description of the partial liquidation law prior to the enactment of § 302(b)(4), see Corporate Income Taxation Hornbook at Section 3.05.

[65]   § 302(e)(5).

Those entities are described as "pass-thru entities."[66] A so-called "S" corporation[67] is another type of pass-thru entity, but it is not included in the list of entities whose stock holdings are deemed to be held by their partners or beneficiaries. Consequently, it appears that a distribution to an S corporation pursuant to a partial liquidation will not qualify for purchase treatment under § 302(b)(4). The shareholders of an S corporation will therefore have § 301 treatment for such partial liquidations unless one of the other provisions for purchase treatment is applicable.

The exclusion of S corporations from the special provision that applies to other pass-thru entities likely occurred because the previously existing § 1371(a)(2) provided that in an S corporation's capacity as a shareholder, it was treated as an individual. So, there was no need to provide a special treatment in § 302. However, § 1371(a)(2) was repealed in 1996. The failure to amend the pass-thru provision in § 302 to include S corporations may be due to an oversight.

If the distribution in redemption of the stock of a noncorporate shareholder qualifies as one made pursuant to a partial liquidation as defined in § 302(e), the distribution will be treated as an amount realized on the sale or exchange of the distributee's stock under § 302(a). As such, the distributee's gain typically will be a capital gain.

While a distribution in redemption of stock held by a corporate shareholder can qualify as part of a partial liquidation, it will not thereby qualify for purchase treatment under § 302(b)(4). Consequently, a redemption of a corporate shareholder's stock will be treated as a § 301 distribution unless § 302(b)(1), (2) or (3) is applicable or unless the redemption is made pursuant to a complete liquidation of the distributing corporation.[68] As noted above, in determining whether stock is held by a noncorporate shareholder, the stock held by a partnership, estate, or trust is treated as held proportionately by its partners or beneficiaries.[69] This means that the tax treatment of a distribution made pursuant to a partial liquidation in redemption of stock held by a partnership, trust, or estate can be divided so that a portion of the distribution will be treated as a purchase of stock under § 302(b)(4) and the balance of

---

[66]   Id.

[67]   See Chapter Eleven.

[68]   To the extent that the distribution in partial liquidation to a corporate shareholder is treated as a dividend that is "nontaxed" because of a dividend-received deduction or similar deduction, it can cause a reduction of the distributee corporation's basis or gain recognition under § 1059. See ¶ 3.09.

[69]   § 302(e)(5).

the distribution that is attributable to corporate partners or beneficiaries will be treated as a § 301 distribution unless § 302(b)(1), (2), or (3) is applicable.

¶ 3.05.2 Definition of Partial Liquidation

A partial liquidation is defined in § 302(e). Section 302(e) contains both a general "not equivalent to a dividend" standard and a safe harbor provision that grants partial liquidation characterization if specified requirements are met.

Section 302(e)(1) adopts the general definition of "not essentially equivalent to a dividend" that covers corporate contractions. Section 302(e)(1)(A) explicitly states that dividend equivalence is to be determined at the corporate rather than at the shareholder level. Section 302(e)(1)(B) contains the requirement that a distribution in partial liquidation of a corporation must be made pursuant to a plan that was adopted either in the taxable year of distribution or in the immediately preceding taxable year.

The objective safe harbor resides in § 302(e)(2), (3), and (4). The objective test established by § 302(e)(2)–(4) is only a safe harbor; a genuine corporate contraction can qualify as a partial liquidation even though it does not comply with the requirements set forth in § 302(e)(2)–(4). The standards established by the § 302(e)(2)–(4) safe harbor are that:

- immediately prior to the distribution, the corporation conducted at least two trades or businesses, both of which had been actively conducted during the five-year period prior to the distribution[70] and neither of which had been acquired by the corporation during that five-year period in a taxable transaction;

- the distribution is attributable to the corporation's ceasing to conduct one or more of such trades or businesses; and

- the corporation continued the active conduct of at least one of such trades or businesses after the distribution.

---

[70] The requirement of § 302(e)(2) and (3) that two or more businesses or trades have been actively conducted for five years prior to the distribution and that at least one of them be actively conducted after the liquidation is similar to the "active business" test employed in § 355 for corporate divisions. § 355(b). The regulations promulgated under the old section covering partial liquidations, § 346, adopted by reference the regulations promulgated under § 355 for the interpretation of the phrase "active conduct of a trade or business." Presumably, the regulations that will be promulgated under § 302(e) also will refer to the § 355 regulations on this issue. The active business test of § 355 is examined in Chapter Eight.

A distribution attributable to the corporation's ceasing to conduct a trade or business includes:

(1) a distribution of the proceeds from the sale of such trade or business; or

(2) a distribution in kind of the assets of such trade or business; or

(3) a distribution in kind of some of the assets of such trade or business plus a distribution of the proceeds from the sale of the remaining assets of such trade or business.[71]

In order to qualify under § 302(e)(2), the assets (or the proceeds from the sale of the assets) of the terminated trade or business must be distributed to the shareholders but they need not be distributed pro rata.[72] Unless the distribution is made pro rata among the corporation's shareholders, it must be made in redemption of stock of the corporation. If the distribution is made pro rata among the shareholders, no redemption is required in order to qualify for exchange treatment as a distribution in partial liquidation of the corporation.[73] In such cases, each shareholder will be deemed to have surrendered that number of shares of the distributing corporation the fair market value of which equals the amount distributed to that shareholder.[74] Of course, only the distributions that are made to noncorporate shareholders can qualify for the purchase treatment provided by § 302(b)(4).

In Section 4.01(25) of Rev. Proc. 2018–3, the Commissioner announced that ordinarily he will not rule on whether a distribution will qualify as a distribution in partial liquidation unless it results in a 20 percent or greater reduction in (1) gross revenue, (2) net fair market value of assets, and (3) employees. This provision does not apply to a partial liquidation that qualifies for the safe harbor provision of § 302(e)(2).

One question that can arise is what amount of working capital can be attributed to a liquidated business and so distributed to shareholders under the protection of § 302(e). In Section 3.01(48) of Rev. Proc. 2018–3, the Commissioner announced that he will not rule on the question of the amount of working capital of a terminated business that may be distributed in partial liquidation.

---

[71]   Treas. Reg. § 1.346–1(b)(2).

[72]   § 302(e)(4).

[73]   Rev. Rul. 90–13.

[74]   Rev. Rul. 77–245.

Ex. (1)   X Corporation has operated a retail clothing business since Year One. In Year Twenty, X purchased the assets of a hardware business for $100,000 cash, and thereafter conducted both the retail clothing business and the hardware business. In Year Twenty-Three, X sold the hardware business to a third party and distributed the net proceeds to its shareholders in proportionate redemption of part of their X stock. Since the hardware business was acquired by X in a taxable exchange within the five-year period prior to distribution, § 302(e)(2) is inapplicable. It is possible that the redemption will qualify as a corporate contraction pursuant to § 302(e)(1), but that is unlikely.

Ex. (2)   At the beginning of Year Fourteen, P Corporation owned all of the outstanding stock of S Corporation, and P had owned all of the stock of S since Year One. P and S had each actively engaged in a business since Year One. In Year Fourteen, P decided to liquidate the business that S conducted. Accordingly, in that year, P sold its S stock to an unrelated party and distributed the proceeds to its shareholders in redemption of some of the shares of their P stock. The Commissioner ruled that since P did not itself directly conduct the business that S conducted, P's distribution of the proceeds of its sale of the S stock did not qualify as a partial liquidation.[75] If instead of selling the S stock and distributing the proceeds, P had distributed the S stock directly to its shareholders in a pro rata redemption of some shares of their P stock, the Commissioner maintains that the redemption would not qualify as a partial liquidation for the same reason that a distribution of the proceeds of the sale of the S stock cannot qualify.[76] However, the distribution of all of S's stock to P's shareholders might qualify as a nonrecognition transaction under § 355.[77]

Ex. (3)   The same facts as in Example (2) except that instead of selling or distributing the S stock, P proceeded as follows. P caused the liquidation of S and the liquidating distribution of S's assets to P. As noted in Chapter Four, the liquidation of S will not cause either P or S to recognize a gain or loss because of the provisions of §§ 332 and 337. P then sold the assets it acquired from S to an unrelated party and distributed the proceeds among its shareholders in a pro

---

[75]   Rev. Rul. 79–184.

[76]   Id.; Rev. Rul. 75–223.

[77]   See Chapter Eight for a discussion of § 355.

rata redemption of some shares of P's stock. The Commissioner ruled that the distributions by P in redemption of some shares of its stock qualified as a partial liquidation.[78] The Commissioner reasoned that as a consequence of § 381 (see the discussion in Chapter Ten), the P Corporation inherited all of the tax attributes of S upon the liquidation of the latter, and so P should be viewed after the liquidation as if P itself had always operated the business that had in fact been conducted by S. Since P is deemed to have conducted S's business for the requisite time period, the active business requirement was satisfied.

The Commissioner's treatment of the three situations described in Examples (2) and (3) above is instructive. The substance of each of those three transactions is very much the same, and yet the form in which the transaction is conducted can alter the tax consequences dramatically. While the tax law's predilection to elevate substance over form is widely recited, there are numerous examples where significant tax consequences hinge on the choice of the form of a transaction, and the above examples are merely one illustration of the importance of form. The reader should understand how difficult it is in many circumstances to determine whether the form of a transaction will be disregarded for tax purposes.

¶ 3.06 GAIN OR LOSS RECOGNIZED BY DISTRIBUTING CORPORATION

Section 311(b) requires that a corporation recognize a gain on making a distribution of appreciated property in a distribution to which § 302 (and certain other sections) is applicable. Consequently, a corporation will recognize as gain the amount of appreciation of an asset distributed pursuant to a partial liquidation or a stock redemption. A corporation will not recognize a loss on distributing depreciated property to a shareholder pursuant to a partial liquidation or a stock redemption.[79] As previously noted, the same rules apply to a corporation's § 301 distribution of an appreciated or a depreciated asset.

---

[78]   See Rev. Rul. 75–223.

[79]   § 311(a).

¶ 3.07 DISTRIBUTION IN REDEMPTION OF STOCK THAT WAS INCLUDED WITHIN THE GROSS ESTATE OF A DECEDENT FOR FEDERAL ESTATE TAX PURPOSES

In order to assist the representatives of a decedent's estate to satisfy obligations incurred on account of the decedent's death, Congress has granted the redemption of corporate stock that was included in a decedent's gross estate for federal estate tax purposes a special exemption from dividend treatment, provided that certain statutory requisites are satisfied. This treatment is provided by § 303.

The provisions of § 303 are primarily of importance to owners of stock of a closely held corporation and, when applicable, permit the withdrawal of funds from such corporation upon the death of a stockholder without causing taxable dividends to the recipient. While the current dividend tax rate lessens the importance of § 303, it still plays a significant role in estate planning.

Section 303 provides that a corporation's redemption of stock that was included in a decedent's gross estate for federal estate tax purposes[80] will be deemed a distribution in full payment of the stock, (thus excluded from § 301) if the following conditions are satisfied.

(1)   The estate tax value of the stock of the redeeming corporation that is included in the decedent's gross estate for estate tax purposes is greater than 35 percent of the difference between the value of the decedent's gross estate and the aggregate amount of deductions allowable under §§ 2053 and 2054 (i.e., deductions from the gross estate that are allowable for funeral and administrative expenses, claims against the estate, debts, and casualty and theft losses).[81] For convenience, the difference between the decedent's gross estate and the deductions allowable under §§ 2053 and 2054 is sometimes referred to as the decedent's "adjusted gross estate" even though that term is not used in § 303.[82]

Under § 303(b)(2)(B), where stocks of two or more corporations were included in the decedent's gross

---

[80]   Comparable relief is provided for the redemption of stock that was the subject of a generation-skipping transfer under § 2611 occurring at the same time and as a result of the death of an individual. § 303(d).

[81]   § 303(b)(2)(A).

[82]   Section 6166(b)(6) uses essentially the same concept, and terms it "adjusted gross estate."

estate, the values of the stocks of those several corporations are combined in determining whether the more than 35 percent of adjusted gross estate test is satisfied, provided that only the stock of a corporation that had at least 20 percent of the value of its outstanding stock included in the decedent's gross estate can be included in the aggregate group.[83]

(2)   Section 303 treatment applies only to redemptions of stock of a shareholder whose interest in property acquired from the decedent is directly reduced (or indirectly through a binding obligation to contribute) by any payment of death taxes or of funeral and administration expenses that qualify as allowable deductions under § 2053 (or § 2106 for a nonresident alien); and § 303 applies only to the extent that the shareholder whose stock is being redeemed is liable for the payment of those death taxes and funeral and administration expenses.[84]

(3)   Section 303 applies only to distributions made in redemption of stock of the type described above within a certain time period.[85]

(4)   The maximum amount of corporate distributions that can be excluded from dividend treatment under § 303 is the sum of the death taxes (both federal and state) imposed on account of the decedent's death (including interest thereon), and the funeral and administrative expenses that are allowable as estate tax deductions under § 2053 (or § 2106 if the decedent was neither a resident nor a citizen of the United States).[86]

---

[83]   In determining whether stock included in a decedent's gross estate satisfies the 20 percent test so that it will be aggregated with other such stocks in applying the more than 35 percent test, stocks held by the decedent and his spouse as joint tenants, tenants by the entirety, tenants in common or as community property are treated as if they were included in the decedent's gross estate. § 303(b)(2)(B). In other words, for purposes of applying the 20 percent test for combining stock values, and only for such purpose, the value of the decedent's spouse's share of stocks held by the decedent and his spouse in any type of co-ownership is treated as if it were included in the decedent's gross estate. No other attribution rules are applicable. Estate of Byrd v. Commissioner, 388 F.2d 223 (5th Cir. 1967).

[84]   § 303(b)(3).

[85]   The time period is usually four years after the death of the taxpayer, but, in some cases, can be extended beyond that period. § 303(b)(1). For a detailed discussion of the time period allowed, see Corporate Income Taxation Hornbook at Section 3.09.

[86]   § 303(a). Since interest owed on death taxes is included in the ceiling of the amount of stock to which § 303 can apply, the ceiling can continue to increase after the decedent's death as interest on the death taxes accrues.

When a shareholder receives "new stock" in a corporation, the basis of which is determined by reference to the basis of "old stock" that was included in the decedent's gross estate and that qualified for redemption under § 303, then the "new stock" may also be redeemed under § 303(c).

It is worth emphasizing that while the rationale for enacting § 303 (and its predecessors) was to provide liquidity for an estate, the operation of § 303 is not limited to circumstances in which liquidity is a problem. Section 303 may be employed to advantage even though the estate has sufficient liquid assets.

A shareholder incurs little or no income tax liability as a consequence of having stock redeemed under § 303 because, under § 1014, the shareholder's basis in the redeemed stock equals the estate tax value of that stock. The price at redemption normally will not be greatly in excess of that value, so that the shareholder will recognize gain, if any, only on the appreciation that occurs after the estate tax valuation date. Typically, any such gain would be long-term capital gain.[87]

¶ 3.08 EFFECT OF REDEMPTION OF STOCK ON CORPORATION'S EARNINGS AND PROFITS

A redemption of stock that constitutes a § 301 distribution has the same effect on the corporation's *e and p* as does a § 301 distribution to a shareholder that is not made in redemption of stock.[88] A different rule applies to a redemption that qualifies for purchase treatment. Under § 312(n)(7), a redemption that constitutes a purchase of a shareholder's stock under § 302(a) or under § 303 reduces *e and p* by an amount that is not in excess of the ratable share of the corporation's accumulated *e and p* at the time of the redemption that is attributable to the redeemed shares of stock. The legislative history indicates that Congress intended that the total reduction in *e and p* under this pro rata approach should not in any event exceed the amount distributed in redemption of the stock.[89]

Ex. (1) A and B formed X Corporation and each contributed $10,000 cash for 100 shares of the stock of X. After two years of operation, X had accumulated *e and p* of $18,000, and the net worth of X was $50,000. X then redeemed A's 100 shares of stock for $25,000 cash. The 100 redeemed shares constituted 50 percent of X's outstanding stock. Under

---

[87] See § 1223(9).

[88] See ¶ 2.08.

[89] H.R. Rep. No. 861, 98th Cong., 2d Sess. 838 (1984). For a discussion of the rationale of this approach, see Corporate Income Taxation Hornbook at Section 3.07.

§ 312(n)(7), the reduction in *e and p* of X is the redeemed stocks' ratable share of *e and p*. The amount of reduction is $9,000 (50% × $18,000).

One issue concerning a stock redemption's effect on *e and p* is whether a redemption that is treated as a purchase reduces the amount of current *e and p* that is applicable to a § 301 distribution that is made in the same taxable year. The Tax Court and the Seventh Circuit held in *Anderson v. Commissioner*[90] that a corporation's current *e and p* are first allocated to its § 301 distributions made during that taxable year without diminution because of any redemption or liquidating distributions made during that taxable year. The courts further held that any excess current *e and p* remaining after allocation to the current § 301 distributions is added to the accumulated *e and p* of the corporation.[91] Only a portion of the excess current *e and p*, determined according to the portion of the year that had expired at the time of the redemption, is added to the corporation's accumulated *e and p* at the time of the redemption.[92]

Ex. (2) As of January 1, Year One, X Corporation had 100 shares of stock outstanding and had no positive or deficit accumulated *e and p*. Individuals A and B each owned 30 shares of X's stock and individual C owned the remaining 40 shares. A, B and C are unrelated. In Year One, X had current *e and p* of $100,000. On July 1, Year One, X redeemed C's 40 shares of stock. X distributed $84,000 to C in redemption of his stock. Since that redemption terminated C's interest, it is treated as a purchase. § 302(b)(3). On December 6, Year One, X distributed $35,000 cash to A and a like amount to B. So, X's § 301 distributions to its shareholders in Year One totaled $70,000.

X's current *e and p* of $100,000 are first allocated to the $70,000 of § 301 distributions that it made to A and B, and so A and B each have dividend income of $35,000. That leaves $30,000 of X's current *e and p* to be included in X's accumulated *e and p* for the next year. However, under § 312(n)(7), the redemption of C's stock will cause a reduction of 40 percent of the amount of accumulated *e and p* that X had at the time that the redemption took place on July 1. (The stock that was redeemed constituted 40 percent of X's outstanding stock.) The question then is how much of

---

[90]   67 T.C. 522, 569–570 (1976), aff'd per curiam, 583 F.2d 953 (7th Cir. 1978).

[91]   Id.; Rev. Rul. 74–33. See also GCM 39570; PLR 8342012.

[92]   Rev. Rul. 74–338.

the *e and p* that X earned in Year One was accumulated as of July 1. According to the Commissioner, the portion of the $30,000 of X's current *e and p* that was not allocated to the § 301 distributions is deemed to have been accumulated on a pro rata daily basis in that year. Since the redemption of C's stock took place at the mid-point of the year, one-half of X's $30,000 of available current *e and p* (the current *e and p* in excess of § 301 distributions) is deemed to have been accumulated as of July 1. So, one-half of $30,000 or $15,000 of *e and p* was accumulated at the time of the redemption of C's stock. The accumulated *e and p* are then reduced by 40 percent of $15,000 which equals $6,000.[93] Therefore, as of January 1, Year Two, X has accumulated *e and p* of $24,000 ($30,000 minus $6,000).[94]

How should a redeemed stock's ratable share of *e and p* be determined when the corporation has more than one class of stock outstanding, especially if one of the outstanding classes of stock has priority for the allocation of dividends or liquidation proceeds? Should *e and p* be apportioned among the several classes of stock in such manner as to reflect those priorities?

The Conference Committee's Report[95] to the Tax Reform Act of 1984,[96] which is the Act in which § 312(n)(7) was adopted, states that, in allocating *e and p* to a redemption of one class of stock that is treated as a purchase, effect should be given to the priorities that the several classes of stock possess. In the example given in the Conference Report, the preference utilized to make the allocation was for both dividends and liquidating proceeds.[97] Thus, the Conference Committee's determination does not rest on the value of the different classes of stock, but rather on a weighing of their rights to share in dividends and liquidating distributions.

An example set forth in the Conference Report and later repeated in the Blue Book involves the redemption of a class of nonvoting common stock that had a 2–1 preference for dividends and liquidating distributions over a class of voting common stock; and the corporation had no other stock outstanding. The Conference Report and the Blue Book state that a redemption of all of the nonvoting

---

[93] § 312(n)(7).

[94] Rev. Rul. 74–338.

[95] H.R.Rept. No. 161, 98th Cong., 2d Sess. at 840 (1984).

[96] The Tax Reform Act of 1984 was one division of the Deficit Reduction Act of 1984.

[97] The Blue Book to the Tax Reform Act of 1984 contains essentially the same statement and example as does the Conference Report. See General Explanation of the Revenue Provisions of the Deficit Reduction Act of 1984 at 181 (Joint Committee Print, 1984).

stock in that example will reduce the corporation's *e and p* by two-thirds ($^2/_3$), subject to the limitation that the reduction cannot exceed the value of the property distributed.

¶ 3.09 EXTRAORDINARY DIVIDEND TO A CORPORATE DISTRIBUTEE RESULTING FROM A STOCK REDEMPTION OR PARTIAL LIQUIDATION

As previously noted, all or part of the amounts distributed to a shareholder pursuant to a stock redemption or a partial liquidation may constitute a § 301 distribution. Some or all of the amount treated as a § 301 distribution can constitute dividend income to the distributee. If the distributee is itself a corporation, the dividend can qualify the distributee for a dividend-received deduction under § 243 (or §§ 244 or 245). If, under § 1059, such a dividend is treated as an "extraordinary dividend" to the corporate distributee, the amount of the "nontaxed portion" of the dividend will reduce the corporate distributee's basis in its stock of the distributing corporation or will cause the corporate distributee to recognize a gain[98] (typically, any such gain will be a capital gain). There are four circumstances in which a dividend recognized by a corporate distributee as a consequence of a stock redemption will automatically constitute an extraordinary dividend, and so will trigger § 1059. Those four circumstances are:

(1) If the dividend to the corporate distributee resulted from a partial liquidation as defined in § 302(e), the dividend will be treated as extraordinary.[99]

(2) If the dividend to the corporate distributee resulted from a stock redemption that was not pro rata to all shareholders, the dividend will be treated as extraordinary.[100]

(3) If the distribution to the corporate distributee was a dividend because of the attribution by § 318(a)(4) of stock that was subject to an option to acquire, the dividend will be treated as extraordinary.[101]

---

[98]   § 1059(a). See ¶ 2.13.

[99]   § 1059(e)(1)(A)(i).

[100]   § 1059(e)(1)(A)(ii).

[101]   § 1059(e)(1)(A)(iii)(I).

(4) If the dividend treatment to the corporate distributee was caused by the application of § 304(a), the dividend will be treated as extraordinary.[102]

¶ 3.10 REDEMPTION OF STOCK OF ONE SHAREHOLDER AS A DIVIDEND TO OTHER SHAREHOLDERS

A corporation's redemption of one shareholder's stock will not usually constitute a constructive distribution to the corporation's other shareholders.[103] This is true even if the redemption of the retiring shareholder's stock is part of a plan under which either an outside party or the other shareholders acquire control of the corporation. Indeed, there need be no constructive dividend to the surviving shareholders even though the redemption of the retiring shareholder's stock is pursuant to a plan under which part of the retiring shareholder's stock is redeemed and the remaining shares are purchased by the surviving shareholders.[104]

In Rev. Rul. 69–608, the Commissioner described seven different situations in which stock of a retiring shareholder was redeemed, and the Commissioner noted which of those situations would result in a constructive dividend to the surviving shareholders and which would not. The examples given in Rev. Rul. 69–608 demonstrate the Service's view that a redemption of a retiring shareholder's stock will constitute a constructive distribution to the surviving shareholders only if the surviving shareholders had a "primary and unconditional" obligation to purchase the redeemed shares. The following example is taken from that ruling.

Ex. (1) A and B own all of the outstanding stock of the X Corporation. A and B execute an agreement that, in the event that B leaves the employ of X, B will sell his stock to A; and A will purchase the X stock owned by B at a price determined in the agreement. B subsequently terminated his employment and, pursuant to the agreement, tendered his X stock to A. Instead of purchasing the stock himself, A caused X to assume the contract and to redeem the stock held by B. Since A had a primary and unconditional obligation to purchase B's stock at the time that the

---

[102]   § 1059(e)(1)(A)(iii)(II). Section 304 is discussed at ¶ 3.11.

[103]   See Rev. Rul. 69–608; Rev. Rul. 58–614; Enoch v. Commissioner, 57 T.C. 781 (1972); Bennett v. Commissioner, 58 T.C. 381 (1972); Smith v. Commissioner, 70 T.C. 651 (1978); Edenfield v. Commissioner, 19 T.C. 13 (1952); Holsey v. Commissioner, 258 F.2d 865 (3d Cir. 1958). See also Everett L. Jassy, *The Tax Treatment of Bootstrap Stock Acquisitions: The Redemption Route vs. The Dividend Route*, 87 Harv. L. Rev. 1459 (1974).

[104]   Id.

contract was assigned to X, the amount distributed by X to B in redemption of B's stock will constitute a constructive distribution to A.

¶ 3.11 CONSTRUCTIVE REDEMPTION— THE SALE OF CORPORATE STOCK EITHER TO A SUBSIDIARY CORPORATION OR TO A SISTER CORPORATION

The net result of a shareholder's selling stock of a controlled corporation to a subsidiary of that corporation or to another corporation that is also controlled by the selling shareholder may be similar to a dividend distribution. For example, A owns the 200 outstanding shares of stock of P Corporation. P owns all of the outstanding stock of S Corporation. A sells 100 shares of P's stock to S for $50,000 cash. The net result of this "sale" is that A retains 100 percent control of P and has withdrawn $50,000 cash from a subsidiary of P. The only person other than A who holds P stock is S, and P owns all of S's outstanding stock.

Currently, a corporation's purchase of stock of a parent or of a sister corporation is subject to the provisions of § 304. Before examining the tax treatment of such sales, it is useful to specify the terms used to identify each of the two corporations that are involved in the transaction. The corporation that purchases the stock of a parent or sister corporation is referred to as the "acquiring corporation." The corporation whose stock is sold to the acquiring corporation is called the "issuing corporation."

The statutory pattern for sales that fall within § 304 is to treat them as constructive redemptions. If the stock is sold to a sister corporation, the redemption is deemed to have been made by the acquiring corporation of its own stock.[105] If the stock is sold to a subsidiary corporation, the redemption is deemed to have been made by the issuing corporation (i.e., the parent corporation).[106]

The application of § 304 depends upon whether the persons selling the stock are in "control" of both the issuing and the acquiring corporations or whether the issuing corporation is in "control" of the acquiring corporation.[107]

"Control" refers to actual or constructive ownership of stock possessing at least 50 percent voting power *or* 50 percent of the total value of all outstanding shares. Section 318 stock attribution rules

---

[105]   § 304(a)(1).

[106]   § 304(a)(2).

[107]   § 304(a)(1), (2).

are applied in determining control, but the 50 percent limitation contained in § 318(a)(2)(C) and (a)(3)(C) is modified by substituting a five percent limitation in those two provisions.[108] If a shareholder owns at least five percent of a corporation but less than 50 percent, only a portion of the stock held by that shareholder, equal to his percentage of the value of the corporation's outstanding stock, is attributed to the corporation under § 318(a)(3)(C).[109]

If the requisite control is held so that § 304 applies and causes the transaction to be treated as a redemption, then it becomes necessary to determine whether the constructive redemption is to be treated as a § 301 distribution or as a purchase. That determination is made by applying to the stock of the issuing corporation the §§ 302 and 303 rules that apply to ordinary redemptions.[110] In applying § 302 rules to the stock of the issuing corporation, a modified version of § 318 attribution rules is applied, but the modification to § 318 that is employed for this purpose is different from the modification that is employed in determining control.[111]

If the transaction constitutes a § 301 distribution, then it becomes necessary to determine the earnings and profits that are allocated to that distribution. The current statutory scheme is first to apply the *e and p* of the acquiring corporation; and, if that *e and p* is less than the amount of the distribution, then apply the *e and p* of the issuing corporation. Those rules for applying *e and p* are the same whether the sale of the stock was made to a sister corporation or to a subsidiary corporation.

The above discussion provides the reader with a general map of the statutory scheme. The following discussion provides a more detailed picture of the provision.

¶ 3.11.1 Brother-Sister Corporations

If one or more persons are in control of each of two corporations and neither of the two corporations controls the other, and if in return for property one of the controlled corporations (the acquiring corporation) acquires stock of the other controlled corporation (the issuing corporation) from the person or persons in control, § 304 treats the exchange as a redemption by the acquiring corporation of its own stock. Sections 302 and 303 are then applied to determine whether the amount received by a seller will be treated as a purchase of the stock that the seller transferred or instead as a § 301

---

[108]   § 304(c).

[109]   See § 304(c)(3)(B)(ii).

[110]   § 304(a), (b)(1).

[111]   § 304(b)(1).

distribution. The determination of whether § 302(b) applies to treat the transaction as a purchase is made by referring to the stock of the issuing corporation even though it is the acquiring corporation that is deemed to have redeemed its own stock.[112]

Section 304(a)(1) provides that the characterization of the exchange as either a purchase or as a § 301 distribution will be determined by applying §§ 302 and 303. To qualify as a purchase under § 302, one of the five provisions of § 302(b) must be satisfied. For purposes of applying § 302(b) to determine whether the exchange will be treated as a purchase or as a § 301 distribution, reference is made to the stock of the issuing corporation (i.e., the corporation whose stock was "sold" to the acquiring corporation).[113] In determining whether the exchange comes within § 302(b), the attribution rules of § 318 are applicable, except that the 50 percent limitation contained in § 318(a)(2)(C) and (a)(3)(C) is disregarded. Note that, unlike the substitution of a five percent limitation when determining control under § 304(c), the determination of whether § 301 applies to a distribution is made by disregarding the 50 percent limitation entirely.[114]

The thrust of the brother-sister rules is to treat a shareholder's sale of a corporation's stock to its sister corporation as an exchange of stock of the issuing corporation for fictitious shares of stock of the acquiring corporation followed immediately by a redemption of the fictitious stock of the acquiring corporation. No gain or loss is recognized on the constructive exchange of stocks because § 351 is deemed to apply to that constructive exchange. Under §§ 358 and 1223(1), the shareholder obtains a basis and holding period in his fictional stock of the acquiring corporation that is equal to the basis and holding period he had in the shares of stock of the issuing corporation that he transferred to the acquiring corporation. The Code states only that stock of the acquiring corporation is deemed to have been received by the shareholder in the exchange; it does not state what character the fictitious shares are deemed to have. However, the proposed regulations that were promulgated in 2009 state that the fictitious stock of the acquiring corporation that the shareholder is deemed to have received in the exchange is *common* stock. Prop. Reg. § 1.304–2(a)(3). The characterization as common stock is significant if the redemption is treated as a § 301 distribution in which case the amount distributed to the shareholder is allocated among the distributee's shares of stock to determine the basis of retained shares and the additional gain recognized (if any). According

---

[112]   Id.

[113]   § 304(b)(1).

[114]   Id.

to the 2009 proposed regulations, the amount distributed is to be allocated among all of the shareholder's stock of the same class as the stock that was deemed to have been redeemed

If the constructive redemption of the fictional shares is treated as a § 301 distribution, then all of that § 301 distribution will be a dividend to the shareholder if it does not exceed the combined *e and p* of the issuing and acquiring corporations.[115] If the amount of the § 301 distribution exceeds the combined *e and p* of the two corporations, then the excess distribution will reduce the shareholder's basis of the acquiring corporation's stock, and any amount in excess of the stock's basis will be a gain to the shareholder.[116]

If the constructive redemption is treated as a purchase under § 302(b) or § 303, the transferor's gain or loss is measured by his basis in the fictional shares of the acquiring corporation that are deemed to have been redeemed.[117] The acquiring corporation's basis in the issuing corporation's stock that it acquired from the transferors will equal the amount it paid for those shares.

Ex. (1)   At the beginning of Year One, A, an individual, owned all 100 shares of the outstanding stock of Corporation X and all 100 shares of the outstanding stock of Corporation Y. Since, for purposes of § 304, A is in control of both X and Y, a sale by A of stock of either corporation to the other corporation would be subject to § 304(a)(1). A had a basis of $1,000 in each share of X and Y stock. The value of the X shares was $2,000 per share. X had accumulated *e and p* of $15,000, and apart from the transaction in question X earned current *e and p* of $8,000 in Year One. X made no distributions in that year. Y had no accumulated *e and p*, and, apart from the transaction in question, Y had a deficit of $20,000 for its current *e and p* in Year One.

---

[115]   § 304(b)(2). If the shareholder (the transferor) who transferred stock to the acquiring corporation is itself a corporation, and if the amount received by the corporate shareholder is treated as a § 301 distribution, the amount that is treated as a dividend to the shareholder will qualify the shareholder for a dividend-received deduction under § 243. Any such dividend will constitute an extraordinary dividend under § 1059(e)(1)(A)(iii)(II). See Prop. Reg. § 1.304–2(c), Ex. (3).

[116]   § 301(c)(2), (3). As noted in ¶ 3.03 in connection with a stock redemption that is treated as a § 301 distribution, there is an issue of which shares of the shareholder's stock should be used when determining basis. Since the transaction in question is recast as a stock redemption by the acquiring corporation of its own stock, the rules concerning stock redemptions that are discussed in ¶ 3.03 are applicable. You will recall that the 2009 proposed regulations, which as of this writing have not been finalized, treat the fictitious shares as common stock of the acquiring corporation.

[117]   Treas. Reg. § 1.304–2(a). See Prop. Reg. § 1.304–2(c), Ex. (1).

In March of Year One, A sold ten shares of X stock to Y for $20,000 cash. This sale is covered by § 304(a)(1). It is treated as a transfer of ten shares of X stock to Y in exchange for fictitious shares of Y stock having the same value as the ten shares of X stock, followed immediately by Y's redemption of those fictitious shares for $20,000. The constructive exchange of X stock for fictitious shares of Y stock does not cause recognition of gain or loss because of § 351. The constructive redemption of the fictitious shares of Y stock will be treated as a § 301 distribution of $20,000 from Y to A. Under § 304(b)(1), the characterization of the constructive redemption is made by applying § 302 principles to A's change of ownership of X stock. Since, after applying § 318 attribution rules, A owns 100% of X stock before and after the transaction, it will be treated as a § 301 distribution from Y.

The allocation of *e and p* is made by first applying the *e and p* of Y (the acquiring corporation). Since Y had no *e and p*, the *e and p* of X is then applied. The $8,000 of X's current *e and p* and $12,000 of its accumulated *e and p* will be allocated to the $20,000 distribution that Y made to A. Consequently the $20,000 distributed to A will constitute a dividend to him. At the beginning of Year Two, X will have accumulated *e and p* of $3,000, and Y will have an accumulated *e and p* deficit of $20,000.

A's basis in the fictitious shares of Y stock that he is deemed to have received in exchange for the ten shares of X stock that he transferred to Y is equal to the $10,000 basis that A had in the X shares that he transferred to Y.[118] Since the constructive redemption of those fictitious shares is treated as a § 301 distribution to A, A's $10,000 basis in those fictitious shares is added to A's $100,000 basis in his 100 shares of Y's stock.[119] So, after the transaction is completed, A has a basis of $110,000 in his 100 shares of Y's stock. Note that it is the transferor's basis in the acquiring corporation's stock that is increased. Under § 362, Y's basis in the ten shares of X stock that it acquired from A is $10,000—the same basis that A had therein. A's basis in the 90 shares of X stock that he continues to own is unchanged—i.e., A has a $90,000 basis in those shares. Note that A's basis in his Y stock would be determined differently if the 2009 proposed regulations are finalized.

---

[118] § 362(a).

[119] Treas. Reg. §§ 1.302–2(c); 1.304–2(a).

¶ 3.11.2 Parent-Subsidiary Corporations

If, in exchange for property, an acquiring corporation acquires the stock of the issuing corporation from a shareholder of the issuing corporation, and the issuing corporation controls[120] the acquiring corporation, the transaction is treated by § 304(a)(2) as a distribution in redemption of the stock of the issuing corporation. For purposes of determining whether the "redemption" qualifies as a purchase under § 302(b), the stock position of the issuing corporation is determinative.[121] If the distribution to the shareholder is deemed a § 301 distribution, the amount of that distribution that is a dividend is determined as if the amount distributed to the shareholder were distributed by the acquiring corporation to the extent of its *e and p* and then by the issuing corporation to the extent of its *e and p*.[122] Thus, the rules for determining whether a constructive redemption results in a § 301 distribution and, if so, the amount of *e and p* that is applied to it are the same for both parent-subsidiary and brother-sister transactions.

However, there are differences in other aspects of the manner in which § 304(a)(2) (the parent-subsidiary provision) applies and the manner in which § 304(a)(1) (the brother-sister provision) applies. For example, if the transaction is treated as a § 301 distribution to the transferor, the transferor's basis in the transferred stock is added to his basis in his remaining shares of the issuing corporation's stock in the case of a § 304(a)(2) (parent-subsidiary) transaction;[123] whereas, the transferor's basis in the transferred shares is added to the transferor's basis in his stock of the acquiring corporation in the case of a § 304(a)(1) (brother-sister) transaction. So, it is important to determine whether the transaction is to be treated as a brother-sister or a parent-subsidiary transaction. In the event of an overlap, which occurs if the transaction fits within both § 304(a)(1) and § 304(a)(2), the Code provides that the parent-subsidiary rules of § 304(a)(2) take priority.[124]

Ex. (2)   As of January 1, Year One, P Corporation had 100 shares of voting common stock outstanding all of which were owned

---

[120] The term "control" is defined at § 304(c). See ¶ 3.11.

[121] § 304(b)(1). The question of whether purchase treatment applies is determined by reference to the issuing corporation's stock regardless of whether the transaction is a sale to a sister corporation (a § 304(a)(1) transaction) or a sale to a subsidiary corporation (a § 304(a)(2) transaction).

[122] § 304(b)(2). This rule applies to sales to a sister corporation as well as to a subsidiary corporation.

[123] The allocation to the shares of the issuing corporation's stock is described in ¶ 3.03. Note that the method of allocation will be changed if the 2009 proposed regulations are finalized.

[124] § 304(a)(1).

by individual K. K had a basis of $100 in each share of P's stock. As of January 1, Year One, P had accumulated *e and p* of $10,000, and P had no current *e and p* in Year One. P made no distributions in Year One. S Corporation had 100 shares of common voting stock outstanding of which P owned 60 shares and M (an unrelated individual) owned 40 shares. As of January 1, Year One, S had accumulated *e and p* of $14,000, and S earned current *e and p* of $30,000 in Year One. On July 1, Year One, K sold 30 shares of his P stock to S for $40,000 cash. K had a basis of $3,000 in those 30 shares of stock. S made no other purchases or distributions in Year One.

Under § 304(a)(2), the "sale" of the stock to S is treated as a redemption by P of 30 shares of its stock. Since the constructive redemption is not protected by § 302(a), it is treated as a § 301 distribution of $40,000 to K. Under § 304(b)(2), the amount of that distribution that is a dividend is determined first by applying the *e and p* of S (the acquiring corporation) and then, if the acquiring corporation's applicable *e and p* are less than the amount of the distribution, the *e and p* of P (the issuing corporation) are applied.[125] In this case, S has sufficient *e and p* to cause the entire $40,000 that was paid to K to be treated as dividend income.

K has $40,000 dividend income in Year One. Since this transaction is treated as a redemption by P (even though it was the *e and p* of S that caused the payment to K to be a dividend), K's basis ($3,000) in the 30 shares of P stock that were constructively redeemed is added to K's basis in the 70 shares of P's stock that he continues to hold. So, K will have a basis of $10,000 in the 70 shares of P's stock that he holds.

The $40,000 that S paid to K will reduce S's accumulated *e and p*. So, as of January 1, Year Two, S will have accumulated *e and p* of $4,000, computed as follows:

$14,000.00—*e and p* at beginning of year

$30,000.00—*e and p* earned during year

($40,000.00)—§ 301 distribution to K

$4,000.00—accumulated *e and p*

---

[125] § 304(b)(2).

P's *e and p* will not be affected by this transaction. According to a ruling by the Service, S acquires a basis of $40,000 in the 30 shares of P's stock that S acquired from K—i.e., it acquired a basis in those shares equal to the amount it paid for them.[126] That ruling seems to the authors to be overly generous to taxpayers, but there is not yet any contrary authority.

¶ 3.11.3   Overlap with § 351

Section 351 is the principal Code provision that deals with the tax treatment to a transferor of transferring property to a controlled corporation in exchange for the corporation's stock plus other property. In Chapter Seven, dealing with transfers to a controlled corporation, we discuss the overlap of §§ 304 and 351 in certain areas. This overlap created problems in statutory construction because gain recognized under § 351(b) usually will be characterized as a capital gain while § 304 often results in the recognition of ordinary income. The question of which provision has priority was resolved by the addition to the Code in 1982 of subsection (b)(3) of § 304. Subject to two exceptions, § 304 will take priority over § 351(b).

---

[126] Rev. Rul. 80–189.

Chapter Four

COMPLETE LIQUIDATION
OF A CORPORATION

Analysis

Para.

4.01   Introduction
4.02   A Liquidating Corporation's Recognition of Gain or Loss
4.03   Shareholder's Treatment in an Ordinary Liquidation
4.04   Reincorporations
4.05   Liquidation of a Controlled Subsidiary Corporation

¶ 4.01 INTRODUCTION

In the prior two chapters, we discussed the tax consequences of a corporation's making nonliquidating distributions to shareholders, which include distributions made pursuant to a partial liquidation. In this context, nonliquidating distributions refer both to distributions made to shareholders on account of their stock and also to transfers of corporate property in exchange for the corporation's own stock. In this Chapter, we will examine the tax treatment of distributions made pursuant to the complete liquidation of a corporation. References in this book to a "liquidating distribution" refer to a distribution made pursuant to a complete liquidation of the corporation.

In general, a corporate distribution to a shareholder pursuant to its complete liquidation is treated as an exchange of the shareholder's stock for the distribution.[1] This exchange typically will result in a capital gain or loss for the shareholder since the stock will usually be a capital asset in his hands. There are situations, however, where the shareholder will not recognize a gain or loss, or where a gain or loss will be ordinary income. Generally, the liquidating distribution will be a taxable event to the liquidating corporation.[2]

These general rules are subject to several exceptions at both the shareholder and the corporate levels. In particular, at the shareholder level:

---

[1]   § 331(a).
[2]   § 336(a).

(1)   A parent corporation generally does not recognize gain or loss on the complete liquidation of a subsidiary of which it owns 80% or more of the stock.

(2)   The complete liquidation of a corporation may be ignored for tax purposes if the business of the liquidating corporation is reincorporated into another corporation that is controlled by essentially the same persons who controlled the liquidating corporation.[3]

At the corporate level, the liquidating corporation will recognize a gain on making a liquidating distribution of appreciated property[4] unless the liquidation qualifies as a tax-free exchange.[5] Examples of liquidations that qualify as a tax-free exchange are complete liquidations of certain controlled subsidiary corporations and liquidations that qualify as part of a reorganization.[6] As used in tax law, a "reorganization" is a term of art that refers to specifically defined transactions that are described and discussed in Chapter Nine.

Subject to several exceptions, a liquidating corporation will recognize a loss on making a liquidating distribution of depreciated property.[7] In that respect, a liquidating distribution differs from a nonliquidating distribution in which a distributing corporation can never recognize a loss because of § 311(a). If the liquidation qualifies as a tax-free exchange, neither a gain nor a loss can be recognized; but, even if the liquidation is not part of a tax-free exchange, a loss will not be recognized in certain circumstances.[8]

Before discussing these various provisions, we should consider what constitutes a complete liquidation for tax purposes. The Code does not define a "complete liquidation." The regulations, however, provide that for tax purposes,

> [a] status of liquidation exists when the corporation ceases to be a going concern and its activities are merely for the purpose of winding up its affairs, paying its debts, and distributing any remaining balance to its shareholders. A liquidation may be completed prior to the actual dissolution of the liquidating corporation. However, legal dissolution of

---

[3]   See ¶ 4.04.

[4]   Appreciated property is property whose fair market value is greater than its basis.

[5]   § 336(a).

[6]   §§ 332, 337, 336(a), (c).

[7]   § 336(a), (d). The extent to which a corporation's recognition of loss is subjected to limitations is discussed in ¶ 4.02. Depreciated property is property whose basis is greater than its fair market value.

[8]   Id.

the corporation is not required. Nor will the mere retention of a nominal amount of assets for the sole purpose of preserving the corporation's legal existence disqualify the transaction.[9]

Presumably, the definition set forth in that regulation is applicable for tax purposes to all liquidations, even though the regulation is promulgated under the statute dealing with the liquidation of certain subsidiary corporations.

¶ 4.02 A LIQUIDATING CORPORATION'S RECOGNITION OF GAIN OR LOSS

Prior to 1986, the tax law adhered to the now largely defunct *General Utilities* doctrine by usually precluding a liquidating corporation from recognizing a gain or loss on making liquidating distributions. As a consequence of amendments made to the Code by the Tax Reform Act of 1986, § 336(a) provides that a liquidating corporation will recognize gain or loss on making liquidating distributions as if the property were sold to the distributee at its fair market value. The characterization of the gain or loss turns upon the normal rules that would apply if the distributed property had been sold to the shareholder.

Ex. (1)   X Corporation has three equal shareholders—A, B, and Y. A and B are individuals, and Y is a corporation. Pursuant to its complete liquidation, X distributes all of its assets to its three shareholders. X distributes Blackacre (unimproved land) to A. Blackacre has a value of $120,000 and is subject to a mortgage liability of $20,000. X has a basis of $45,000 in Blackacre. X recognizes a gain of $75,000 on that distribution ($120,000 minus the $45,000 basis). The gain will likely be either a capital gain or a § 1231 gain. The mortgage liability does not affect the amount of X's gain.

X distributes depreciable equipment to Y. X had used the equipment in its business for several years. The equipment has a value of $100,000, and is not subject to any liability. X has a basis of $32,000 in the equipment. X recognizes a gain of $68,000, which will be ordinary income to the extent that the § 1245 recapture of depreciation rule applies and likely will be § 1231 gain to the extent of the balance of its

---

[9]   Treas. Reg. § 1.332–2(c). A corporation that has been dissolved for state corporate law purposes may nevertheless continue to exist for tax purposes if it (or trustees on its behalf) continue to engage in some business activity or if it retains valuable assets. E.g., Messer v. Commissioner, 438 F.2d 774 (3d Cir. 1971); Hersloff v. United States, 310 F.2d 947 (Ct. Cl. 1962).

gain, if any. The recognition of the gain is not affected by the fact that the distributee is a corporation since no nonrecognition rule is applicable.

X distributes to B Whiteacre (unimproved land) having a value of $100,000 and a basis of $112,000. X's basis in Whiteacre reflected the fact that X had purchased that property for $112,000 several years earlier.[10] Whiteacre was held by X for use in its business. X recognizes a § 1231 loss of $12,000 on that distribution because, as we will see, none of the limitations on the deduction of losses is applicable here. Note that losses and gains must be treated separately rather than netted against each other because the recognition of losses is subject to limitations that do not apply to gains.

There are a number of exceptions to the recognition requirement of § 336(a). Three of those exceptions apply to both gains and losses, and the remaining ones apply only to losses.

The first exception is that a liquidating subsidiary corporation *usually* does not recognize gain or loss on making a distribution to its parent if § 332 applies to the liquidation.[11] Section 332 and the operation of this exception are discussed in ¶ 4.05.

A second exception is that a corporation will not recognize a gain or loss on making a liquidating distribution of "qualified property" pursuant to a tax-free "reorganization."[12] "Reorganization" is a term of art in tax law. The definition and treatment of reorganizations are discussed in Chapter Nine.

A third exception is that a corporation does not recognize gain or loss on making a liquidating distribution (or any other type of distribution) of "qualified property" pursuant to a corporate division to which § 355(a)(1) provides nonrecognition.[13] Corporate divisions are discussed in Chapter Eight.

The remaining exceptions apply only to the liquidating corporation's recognition of losses on distributing depreciated property. Depreciated property is property whose basis is greater than its fair market value. These exceptions are set forth in § 336(d). It is doubtful that there ever was a defensible rationale for the § 336(d) limitations, especially given the manner in which they

---

[10]   Since X purchased the property, it can have a basis in it that exceeds its value. See § 362(e). Presumably, the value of Whiteacre declined after X purchased it.

[11]   §§ 337(a), 336(d)(3). The limited circumstances in which a subsidiary can recognize a gain are described in ¶ 4.05.3.

[12]   See Chapter Nine; §§ 336(c), 361(c).

[13]   § 355(c).

operate.[14] Moreover, in light of the adoption of § 362(e) in 2004, the limitations of § 336(d) not only no longer serve any useful purpose, but they now can also cause results that conflict with congressional policy.[15] Since they have not yet been repealed, let us consider how those limitations operate.

There are three limitations on losses imposed by § 336(d). Two of the limitations are set forth in § 336(d)(1), and the third limitation is set forth in § 336(d)(2). The apparent purpose for adopting those limitations, or at least for adopting two of them, was to prevent the doubling of loss deductions by transferring depreciated property to a controlled corporation. The potential for doubling a loss in that manner was effectively eliminated by the 2004 adoption of § 362(e); but the § 336(d) limitations have not been repealed.

¶ 4.02.1 The Operation of Subsection (d)(1)

Subsection (d)(1) applies only to liquidating distributions that are made to a shareholder who is a related person within the meaning of § 267. Note that while § 267(a)(1) denies a deduction for losses realized on sales between related parties, that provision, by its own terms, does not apply to corporate liquidations. If the shareholder is an individual, he is a related person if, after applying certain stock attribution rules,[16] he owns more than 50% in value of the liquidating corporation's outstanding stock.[17] If the shareholder is itself a corporation, the shareholder will be a related person if, after applying stock attribution rules, the two corporations are members of the same "controlled group" as defined in §§ 267(f) and 1563(a). Two corporations are members of a controlled group if they are members of parent-subsidiary controlled group, a brother-sister controlled group, or a combined group.[18]

A parent-subsidiary controlled group is one or more chains of corporations connected by a common parent where either more than 50% in value of each corporation's (other than the parent corporation) outstanding stock or more than 50% of the total voting power of each corporation's (other than the parent corporation) outstanding voting stock is owned by one or more of the other corporations in the chain. In addition, the common parent corporation must own stock having

---

[14]   See Douglas A. Kahn and Jeffrey H. Kahn, *Prevention of Double Deductions of a Single Loss: Solutions in Search of a Problem*, 26 Va. Tax Rev. 1 (2006).

[15]   Id.

[16]   The stock attribution rules are set forth in § 267(c).

[17]   § 267(b)(2).

[18]   § 1563(a).

more than 50% of the voting power or more than 50% of the value of the outstanding stock of at least one corporation in the chain.[19]

A brother-sister controlled group is two or more corporations if five or fewer persons (who are individuals, estates, or trusts) own stock having either more than 50% of the voting power or more than 50% of the value of the outstanding stock of each corporation.[20]

A combined group is three or more corporations each of which is a member or a parent-subsidiary group or a brother-sister group, and one of which is the common parent of the parent-subsidiary group and also is one of the corporations in the brother-sister group.[21]

A liquidating corporation is not barred by subsection (d)(1) from recognizing a loss on all distributions to related persons. There are only two situations in which that provision prevents a corporation from recognizing a loss. The first is where the distribution is not made pro rata to the shareholders. The second is where the depreciated distributed property is "disqualified property." We discuss each of those two provisions below.

¶ 4.02.1.1   *Non-Pro Rata Distributions*

The pro rata requirement refers to depreciated property on which a loss is realized. In most liquidations, the entirety of the corporation's properties will be distributed pro rata among its shareholders, but that will not prevent subsection (d)(1) from denying recognition of a loss. To satisfy the pro rata rule, the distribution of the depreciated property itself must be made pro rata.

Ex. (2)   X Corporation had 100 shares of voting common stock outstanding of which A owned 60 shares, B owned 15 shares, and Y owned the remaining 25 shares. Y is a corporation, and the other two shareholders are individuals. In liquidation, X distributed Whiteacre (unimproved land) to A. X had a basis of $120,000 in Whiteacre, which had a value of $90,000. Also in liquidation, X distributed $22,500 cash to B and $37,500 cash to Y. Although X realized a loss of $30,000 on the distribution of Whiteacre, it did not recognize any of that loss because of § 336(d)(1). While the total liquidating distributions were made pro rata, the distribution of Whiteacre (the depreciated asset) was not made pro rata; and it was made to a related person.

---

[19]   §§ 336(d)(1)(A), 267(b)(3), (f), 1563(a).
[20]   § 1563(a)(2).
[21]   § 1563(a)(3).

What is the purpose of the pro rata rule? One possible purpose is to prevent the recognition of loss when the depreciated asset remains in the hands of a related person so that the pro rata rule could be viewed as merely reinstating § 267(a)(1)'s application to corporate liquidations.[22] However, if that were the purpose of the provision, there would be no reason to allow the recognition of a loss from a distribution to a related person when the distribution was pro rata. The difficulty with ascribing a congressional purpose to the adoption of the pro rata rule is that it operates so poorly to implement any possible purpose that its structure conflicts with any purpose one might suggest.[23]

¶ 4.02.1.2   *Disqualified Property*

Subsection (d)(1) also bars a liquidating corporation from recognizing a loss on a distribution of "disqualified property" to a related person regardless of whether the distribution was made pro rata. Disqualified property is property that was acquired by the liquidating corporation within five years of the distribution either in an exchange to which § 351 applies or as a contribution to the corporation's capital. Section 351 generally provides nonrecognition of gain or loss for transfers of property to a controlled corporation in exchange for stock of the controlled corporation.[24] Note that there is no requirement that property have been depreciated at the time that the controlled corporation acquired it for it to be treated as disqualified property; it is necessary only that it have been acquired during the requisite five-year period either in a § 351 exchange or as a contribution to capital.

Ex. (3) In Year One, in an exchange that qualified for nonrecognition under § 351, A transferred Blackacre to the X Corporation in exchange for shares of X's stock. The value of Blackacre was $900,000 at the time of the exchange, and A had a basis of $850,000 in Blackacre. So, Blackacre was an appreciated asset at the time of the § 351 exchange. In Year Three, X liquidated and distributed its assets to its shareholders. At that time, X had 100 shares of stock outstanding, of which A owned 40 shares and B owned the remaining 60 shares. At that time, Blackacre's value had fallen to $750,000; and X still had a basis of $850,000 in the property. So, Blackacre was a depreciated asset at the time of the liquidation. X distributed a 40% interest in Blackacre to A and a 60% interest in Blackacre to B. The liquidating

---

[22]   See Bittker & Eustice at ¶ 10.05[3][a].

[23]   See Douglas A. Kahn and Jeffrey H. Kahn, *Prevention of Double Deductions of a Single Loss: Solutions in Search of a Problem*, 26 Va. Tax Rev. 1, 18, 35–37 (2006).

[24]   The operation of § 351 is explained in Chapter Seven.

distributions of Blackacre were thus made pro rata between the corporation's shareholders, and the pro rata requirement was satisfied.

X realized a loss of $100,000 on the liquidating distributions of Blackacre. Forty percent of that loss ($40,000) is recognized by X since it was realized from a distribution to A who is not a related person. X is denied recognition for the $60,000 of loss (60% of its loss) that is attributable to the liquidating distribution that was made to B since B is a related person and Blackacre is disqualified property. It does not matter that Blackacre was not a depreciated asset at the time that X acquired it. It is disqualified property because it was acquired by X in a § 351 exchange that took place within five years of the date on which the liquidating distribution was made.

¶ 4.02.2 The Operation of Subsection (d)(2)—the Anti-Stuffing Provision

Subsection (d)(2) also applies to property that was acquired by a liquidating corporation in either a § 351 exchange or a contribution to capital; but the provision applies only to the extent that the acquired property was depreciated at the time that the liquidating corporation acquired it.[25] Subsection (d)(2) is sometimes referred to as the "anti-stuffing provision." Unlike subsection (d)(1), whose application rests exclusively on objective factors, subsection (d)(2) applies only if a principal purpose of the liquidating corporation's acquisition of the depreciated asset was to recognize a loss on the disposition of that property in connection with a liquidation.[26]

While subsection (d)(2) does not explicitly set a time limit for the period during which it can apply, it does state that if the depreciated asset was acquired within two years of the date on which the corporation adopted a plan of liquidation, the asset will be treated as having been acquired for the tainted purpose except as provided otherwise in regulations.[27] Despite the ominous language of that provision, its legislative history indicates that the two-year period merely creates a rebuttable presumption that will be disregarded if there is a clear and substantial relationship between the contributed property and the conduct of the corporation's current or future business enterprises.[28] In other words, if there is a good business reason for the depreciated property's having been transferred to the

---

[25] § 336(d)(2)(A).
[26] § 336(d)(2)(B)(i)(II).
[27] § 336(d)(2)(B)(ii).
[28] H.R. Rep. No. 99–841, pt.2 at II–200 to 201 (1986) (Conf. Rep.).

corporation, the presumption will be negated. The legislative history also states that subsection (d)(2) generally will not apply to property acquired within the first two years of the corporation's existence.[29]

The presence of a presumption for property acquired within the proscribed two-year period would not, by itself, show that acquisitions obtained more than two years before the plan of liquidation was adopted are necessarily excluded from the subsection (d)(2) limitation; but the legislative history indicates that the provision should be applied to such acquisitions "only in the most rare and unusual cases."[30]

If applicable, subsection (d)(2) causes a reduction of the liquidating corporation's basis in the acquired asset, but only for the purpose of determining a loss. The effect of the provision is to reduce the amount of loss that the corporation otherwise would have realized. The significance of doing this by reducing the corporation's basis is that it will reduce the corporation's loss from a sale of the asset as well as from distributing it in liquidation. Recall, however, that the provision is restricted to sales or distributions by liquidating corporations since its application depends upon satisfying the subjective requirement that the property had been placed in the corporation in anticipation of its recognizing the built-in loss in connection with a liquidation. So, for the provision to apply to a sale of property, the sale must be connected with a liquidation.

If subsection (d)(2) applies, the amount of reduction of the corporation's basis in the asset is equal to the amount by which the asset was depreciated at the time of acquisition (i.e., it is equal to the built-in loss of the asset).[31] Recall however, that the basis is reduced only for the purpose of determining the amount of the corporation's loss on the disposition of the asset.

If both subsection (d)(1) and (d)(2) apply to the same liquidating distribution, subsection (d)(1) has precedence.[32] The order of priority is significant because subsection (d)(1) disallows the entire amount of loss realized on a liquidating distribution to a related person whereas subsection (d)(2) disallows only the amount that does not

---

[29]   Id.

[30]   H.R. Rep. 99–841, pt. 2 at II–200 (1986) (Conf. Rep.). See also Staff of Joint Comm. on Taxation, 100th Cong., General Explanation of the Tax Reform Act of 1986 (Joint Comm. Print 1987) (subsequently referred to as the "Blue Book for the Tax Reform Act of 1986").

[31]   § 336(d)(2)(A). The corporation's basis in the property is reduced by the excess of the basis that the corporation otherwise would have had in the property immediately after acquiring it over the fair market value of the property at that time. Id.

[32]   See Blue Book for the Tax Reform Act of 1986 n. 86.

exceed the built-in loss at the time of the corporation's acquisition of the property.

As we shall see, the addition to the Code of § 362(e) in 2004 deprives subsection (d)(2) of much of its significance.[33] However, while § 362(e) prevents subsection (d)(2) from operating in many circumstances, the sad fact is that subsection (d)(2) can still apply in certain circumstances; and when it does, it actually contravenes congressional polices that were behind the adoption of § 362(e).[34]

¶ 4.03 SHAREHOLDER'S TREATMENT IN AN ORDINARY LIQUIDATION

In the absence of a statutory exception, a distribution of assets to a shareholder pursuant to a complete liquidation of the corporation is treated as a payment for the shareholder's stock.[35] The net amount received by the shareholder in excess of his basis in his stock will usually be taxed as capital gain, and the excess of the shareholder's basis in his stock over the net amount received by him will usually constitute a capital loss.[36] A shareholder's gain or loss on liquidating distributions is computed on each share of stock separately.[37] Thus, whether the gain or loss on a share of stock is a long-term or short-term capital gain or loss depends upon the length of time that share of stock had been held by the shareholder. The basis in the hands of the shareholder of property distributed in kind in a liquidation in which gain or loss is recognizable is equal to the fair market value of the property at the time of distribution.[38]

¶ 4.04 REINCORPORATIONS

The liquidation provisions apply only when the assets of a corporation are distributed in "complete liquidation." The substance of that requirement is not satisfied if a significant portion of the liquidating corporation's assets is transferred (before or after the liquidation) to another corporation (new or previously existing) that is controlled by the same persons who controlled the liquidating

---

[33]   See ¶ 7.04.

[34]   Id.

[35]   § 331(a).

[36]   The net amount received by a shareholder in liquidation is the amount of cash plus the fair market value of property distributed to him less any liabilities that he assumes or to which the property transferred to him is subject. Losses recognized by a shareholder on the liquidation of the corporation usually will be deductible as capital losses under § 165(c)(2), subject to the limitations imposed on the deduction of capital losses by § 1211 and subject to the carryover permitted for capital losses by § 1212.

[37]   Treas. Reg. § 1.331–1(e).

[38]   § 334(a). This provision does not apply to the liquidation of a controlled subsidiary to which § 332 applies. § 334(b). See ¶ 4.05.

corporation.[39] In such a case, the purported liquidation may be recharacterized as something else and the amounts distributed to the shareholders that was not reincorporated may be treated as § 301 distributions. Transactions of this type are referred to as "reincorporations"—i.e., the apparently liquidated corporation was effectively reborn as a different corporation with essentially the same ownership and attributes, and so the different corporation is treated as a continuation of the liquidated one. The reincorporation device is primarily of use to shareholders who are not corporations or that are a corporation that does not control the liquidating corporation.

Two of the simplest forms of "reincorporation" are illustrated in the following examples:

Ex. (1)   A, an individual, is the sole shareholder of Corporation X, which operates a jewelry business and has also acquired some investment assets over the years. A liquidates X, forms new corporation Y, and transfers the operating assets to Y while retaining the investment assets.

Ex. (2)   A, an individual, is the sole shareholder of Corporation X, which operates a jewelry business and has also acquired some investment assets over the years. X forms a new subsidiary Y, transfers the operating assets of the jewelry business to Y in exchange for Y stock, and retains the investment assets. No gain or loss is recognized on that exchange because of § 351. A then liquidates X, acquiring the Y stock together with the investment assets.

Historically, shareholders in the situations exemplified above have hoped to obtain three principal benefits from liquidation and reincorporation. First, to the extent the transaction left the shareholders holding some assets that had been owned by X, but were not reincorporated in Y, they hoped to avoid having their receipt of those assets taxed as a dividend distribution from X. Rather, they hoped to reduce the amount of gain recognized by their basis in the X stock and then to have that gain taxed at significantly more favorable capital gains rates.[40] Second, to the extent that X had accumulated earnings and profits, they hoped to be able to obtain a "fresh start" by transferring the business to a corporation with no accumulated *e and p*. Finally, if the shareholder's basis in the corporation's stock was greater than its value, the liquidation would provide the shareholder with a loss deduction. Prior to the 1986 congressional repudiation of the *General Utilities* doctrine, this type

---

[39]   Treas. Reg. § 1.331–1(c).

[40]   This latter benefit currently has less significance since capital gains rates apply to most dividends to noncorporate shareholders.

of plan was made more attractive by the then *General Utilities* rule that a corporation did not recognize gain on distributing an appreciated asset pursuant to a complete liquidation. So long as most dividends received by individuals continue to be taxed at capital gains rates, there is much less purpose to converting dividend income into capital gains; but in many factual circumstances there will still be much to be gained from a reincorporation if it is not successfully challenged.

Naturally, the Commissioner has not been willing to permit taxpayers to reduce their taxation in this manner. At times, he has contended that the transaction should be taxed as being, "in substance," a dividend distribution subject to the rules of §§ 301 and 302.[41] At other times, he has contended that the transaction should be taxed as being, "in substance," a "reorganization" that involves a distribution of "boot"[42] to the shareholders, subject to the special rules of § 368 and § 356. We examine the often complex rules associated with reorganizations in Chapter Nine.

¶ 4.05 LIQUIDATION OF A CONTROLLED SUBSIDIARY CORPORATION

Since 1935, the tax laws have reflected a congressional policy to permit the liquidation of a controlled subsidiary corporation without causing any adverse tax consequences to the parent corporation. This exemption removes a tax impediment to the exercise of business judgment in rearranging and simplifying the corporate structure of an enterprise, and it conforms with the tax-free treatment provided for certain exchanges made pursuant to a "reorganization."[43]

Under § 332, no gain or loss will be recognized to a parent corporation for receiving distributions of property in liquidation of its subsidiary, provided that certain requisites are satisfied.[44] In that event, the parent corporation will succeed to the tax attributes of the subsidiary; e.g., the parent will absorb the subsidiary's earnings and profits and net operating losses and will assume the subsidiary's basis in its assets.[45]

---

[41] E.g., Telephone Answering Serv. Co. v. Commissioner, 63 T.C. 423 (reviewed by the entire court), aff'd per curiam, 546 F.2d 423 (4th Cir. 1976); Rev. Rul. 76–429. Cf. Rev. Rul. 61–156; Breech, Jr. v. United States, 439 F.2d 409 (9th Cir. 1971); Gallagher v. Commissioner, 39 T.C. 144 (1962).

[42] "Boot" refers to property received in a nonrecognition type of transaction that does not qualify for nonrecognition treatment.

[43] See Chapter Nine.

[44] Rev. Proc. 90–52 sets forth a checklist of information to be included in a request for a ruling on the applicability of § 332 to a transaction.

[45] §§ 381 and 334(b)(1).

Note that cash qualifies as "property" that can be distributed tax-free to a parent corporation pursuant to § 332.[46]

¶ 4.05.1 Requisites for Nonrecognition for Parent Corporation

The requisites for tax-free treatment under § 332 for the parent corporation are:

(1) The parent corporation must have owned stock having at least 80 percent of the total combined voting power of the voting stock of the liquidating subsidiary and having a value equal to at least 80 percent of the value of the total outstanding stock of the subsidiary, except that nonvoting, nonparticipating, nonconvertible preferred stock with limited redemption and liquidation rights is not taken into account.[47] The parent corporation must have possessed the requisite percentage of the subsidiary's stock for a continuous period commencing on the date on which the plan of liquidation was adopted and terminating on the date on which the subsidiary's assets were distributed to the parent corporation.[48] If the parent corporation is a member of a consolidated group that files a consolidated return, the parent corporation is deemed to own all of the stock of the liquidating corporation that is owned by all other members of the group.[49]

(2) The liquidating subsidiary corporation must either:

    (a) within one taxable year,[50] have distributed its assets in complete cancellation or redemption of *all* its outstanding stock;[51] or

---

[46] See Cherry-Burrell Corp. v. United States, 367 F.2d 669 (8th Cir. 1966).

[47] §§ 332(b)(1), 1504(a)(2), (4). However, such preferred stock will not be excluded from consideration if its redemption or liquidation rights exceed its issue price plus a reasonable redemption or liquidation premium. § 1504(a)(4)(C).

[48] § 332(b)(1).

[49] Treas. Reg. § 1.1502–34

[50] The Commissioner has ruled that the "taxable year" referred to in § 332(b)(2) and (3), dealing with the time limits for the distribution of a subsidiary corporation's assets, refers to the taxable year of the distributing corporation. Rev. Rul. 76–317.

[51] § 332(b)(2). The Commissioner has ruled that, while this alternative requires that all the subsidiary's property be distributed within one taxable year, the year of distribution can be a different year from the year in which the plan was adopted. Rev. Rul. 71–326. In Rev. Rul. 71–326, § 332(b)(2) was held to apply to a liquidation where the distribution of the subsidiary's assets took place in a taxable year three years after the year in which the plan of liquidation was adopted and there were legitimate business reasons for the delay.

(b) have distributed its assets in complete cancellation or redemption of *all* of its outstanding stock in accordance with a plan of liquidation under which all the transfers are to be completed within three years after the close of the taxable year in which the first distribution is made under the plan.[52]

When liquidation is not completed within one taxable year and the parent corporation seeks the refuge of § 332, the Commissioner requires that the parent corporation waive the statute of limitations on assessment and collection for each taxable year within the period of liquidation; and the Commissioner may also require the parent corporation to file a bond containing such terms as the Commissioner specifies.[53]

¶ 4.05.1.1   *Insolvency Exception*

The requirement that the liquidating subsidiary distribute its assets in cancellation or redemption of all its outstanding stock has caused some surprising consequences under which the § 332 treatment is lost. One of those consequences is that § 332 will not apply to the liquidation of a subsidiary that is insolvent. Since creditors must be paid before any distribution can be made on the liquidating corporation's outstanding stock, an insolvent corporation will be unable to make any distribution on its stock. Treas. Reg. § 1.332–2(b) requires that the liquidating subsidiary make at least partial payment on its stock that the parent corporation owns for § 332 to apply to the liquidation. If none of the subsidiary's distributions is applicable to its stock, the liquidation is not covered by § 332;[54] and the parent corporation can recognize a gain or loss on the liquidation.[55] As we shall see, in that case, the subsidiary corporation also can recognize a gain or loss on distributing appreciated or depreciated assets.[56]

---

[52]   § 332(b)(3). PLR 9723044 provides an example of this alternative. In that ruling, P owned all of the stock of S. Pursuant to a plan of liquidation, S distributed all of its assets to P, except that S retained bare legal title to some items of intellectual property, but P received the beneficial interest in that intellectual property. All of the business thereafter was conducted by P. P retained one share of S's stock, and the remaining shares were cancelled. The final liquidation was to be completed within 3 years. The Commissioner ruled that § 332 applied to the distribution of S's assets to P.

[53]   § 332(b), Treas. Reg. § 1.332–4(a).

[54]   Rev. Rul. 68–602.

[55]   Section 267(a)(1) does not apply to a complete liquidation.

[56]   Id. Also, since § 332 does not apply, neither does the limitation on loss recognition in § 336(d)(3).

¶ 4.05.1.2   *Distribution on All Classes of Stock*

In addition, courts have construed the requirement that distributions be made by the subsidiary on *all* its stock to mean that if distributions are not made on any one class of the subsidiary's stock, § 332 does not apply.

In H.K. Porter Co. v. Commissioner,[57] the liquidating corporation had outstanding voting common stock and nonparticipating preferred stock that provided voting rights only in a few special circumstances. All of the liquidating corporation's stock (both common and preferred) was held by a parent corporation. The subsidiary corporation was liquidated and its assets were distributed to the parent corporation. The amount of liquidating distributions made to the parent was less than the liquidation preference that was provided for the parent's preferred stock. So, all of the liquidating distributions were made on the subsidiary's outstanding preferred stock, and no distribution was made on the subsidiary's outstanding common stock. The court held that § 332 did not apply. Since the liquidating distribution to the parent was less than its basis in its preferred stock, the parent was allowed to recognize a loss on its preferred stock.

In 2005, Treasury adopted the *Porter* position when it promulgated Prop. Reg. § 1.332–2(b) which states, "Section 332 applies only when the recipient corporation receives at least partial payment for each class of stock that it owns in the liquidating corporation."

¶ 4.05.1.3   *Taxpayer's Deliberate Violation of a § 332 Requirement*

In some instances a taxpayer might desire to remove a subsidiary's liquidation from the reach of § 332. For example, the parent's basis in its stock of the subsidiary may be greater than the net value of the subsidiary's assets, and the parent might therefore wish to make the liquidation a taxable transaction so that it could recognize a loss on the exchange. In a pre-1954 Code case, *Commissioner v. Day & Zimmermann, Inc.,*[58] the parent corporation's sale or disposition of some of the subsidiary's stock immediately prior to liquidation, in order to reduce its stock ownership below 80 percent, disqualified the liquidation from coverage under the antecedent to § 332. Of course, the sale of such stock would fail to disqualify the liquidation from § 332 if the sale

---

[57]   87 T.C. 689 (1986).

[58]   151 F.2d 517 (3d Cir. 1945).

were not bona fide.[59] The Tax Court also has stated that § 332 can be deliberately avoided by a corporation.[60]

¶ 4.05.1.4   *Parent's Basis in Property Received in the Liquidation*

The general rule is that the parent corporation's basis in the properties it receives from the § 332 liquidation of the subsidiary will be the same as the basis that the subsidiary had in those properties.[61] There are two exceptions to that rule. If the subsidiary recognized a gain or loss on making the distribution,[62] the parent's basis in the property on which gain or loss was recognized will equal the fair market value of that property.[63] The second exception applies in certain circumstances where the subsidiary is a foreign corporation.[64]

¶ 4.05.1.5   *Parent's Acquisition of Subsidiary's Tax Attributes*

If § 332 applies to a liquidation, the parent will inherit all or some of the subsidiary's positive or negative accumulated *e and p* and of its other tax attributes.[65] The manner in which the subsidiary's *e and p* and other tax attributes are inherited by the parent corporation is discussed in Chapter Ten.[66]

¶ 4.05.1.6   *Example*

Ex. (1)   P Corporation owned all of the outstanding stock of the S Corporation, and both are domestic corporations. S had no debts owing to P. In Year One, S liquidated and distributed all of its assets to P, which also assumed S's liabilities. At the time of liquidation, S had accumulated *e and p* (including the *e and p* that it earned in the year of liquidation) of $240,000, and P had positive accumulated *e and p*. P had a basis of $50,000 in the S stock. The total value of the assets that were transferred as liquidating distributions was $800,000 of which $200,000 was cash. S had liabilities of $70,000, all of which were assumed by P.

---

[59]   Cf. Hodge v. Commissioner, T.C. Memo 1970–280; Associated Wholesale Grocers, Inc. v. United States, 927 F.2d 1517 (10th Cir. 1991).

[60]   George L. Riggs, Inc. v. Commissioner, 64 T.C. 474, 489 (1975).

[61]   § 334(b).

[62]   The limited circumstances in which a subsidiary can recognize a gain on making a liquidating distribution to its parent are described in ¶ 4.05.3.

[63]   § 334(b)(1)(A).

[64]   § 334(b)(1)(B).

[65]   § 381(a), (c)(2).

[66]   See § 381(c)(2)(B).

The liquidation satisfied the requirements for § 332 treatment.

While P realized a gain of $680,000 from the liquidation, P did not recognize any of that gain because of § 332. As we shall see below, S did not recognize a gain or loss on making the liquidating distribution even if some of the distributed properties were appreciated or depreciated.[67] P's basis in the properties in kind that it received is the same basis that S had in those properties.[68] The basis that P had in its S stock disappears and is of no consequence. P inherits the $240,000 accumulated *e and p* that S had at the time of its liquidation.

¶ 4.05.2 Minority Shareholders

If the conditions described above are satisfied, § 332 provides a tax exclusion only for a controlling parent corporation. When § 332 is applicable to a parent corporation, but there also are minority shareholders of the liquidating corporation, § 332 does not afford any relief to the minority shareholders.[69] The minority shareholders typically will recognize gain or loss on their receipt of liquidating distributions. One exception is that a minority shareholder may not recognize gain or loss on receiving stock of the parent corporation in the transaction when the liquidation is accomplished by merging the subsidiary into the parent.[70] As discussed in the next section, in no event can the liquidating corporation recognize a loss on making a distribution of depreciated property to a minority shareholder in a § 332 liquidation.[71]

¶ 4.05.3 Taxation of the Liquidating Subsidiary

The general rule is that a corporation recognizes gain or loss on making a liquidating distribution of appreciated or depreciated property.[72] As noted earlier in this chapter, there are several exceptions to that recognition requirement, and one of the exceptions

---

[67] § 337(a).

[68] § 334(b).

[69] Treas. Reg. § 1.332–5. The term "minority shareholders" refers to shareholders who do not own the requisite 80% control and are not deemed to own such control through the consolidated return regulations.

[70] §§ 368(a)(1)(A), 354(a). While Treas. Reg. § 1.332–2(d), (e) Ex. treats "an upstream merger" of a subsidiary into its parent as a liquidation, it can also be treated as a reorganization. Performance Systems, Inc. v. United States, 382 Fed. Supp. 525 (M.D. Tenn. 1973), aff'd 501 F.2d 1338 (6th Cir. 1974).

[71] § 336(d)(3).

[72] § 336(a). See ¶ 4.02.

applies to liquidating distributions made by a controlled subsidiary to its parent corporation if § 332 applies to the liquidation.

Section 337(a) provides that a corporation does not recognize gain or loss on making a distribution of property to an "80-percent distributee" pursuant to a complete liquidation to which § 332 applies.[73] An "80-percent distributee" is a corporation that meets the 80-percent stock ownership requirements of § 332(b).[74] In determining whether the 80-percent stock ownership requirement is satisfied, a parent corporation that is a member of a consolidated group is not treated as owning stock of the liquidating corporation that is owned by other members of that consolidated group—i.e., only stock actually owned by the parent corporation is taken into account.[75]

The nonrecognition rules of § 337 for the liquidating corporation are supplemented by a special rule set forth in § 336(d)(3). Section 336(d)(3) provides that, in the case of any liquidation to which § 332 applies, the liquidating subsidiary shall not recognize any *losses* realized in connection with distributions to *any* of its shareholders— even minority shareholders. The purpose of the provision is to prevent a subsidiary from obtaining loss recognition by distributing all of its depreciated assets to its minority shareholders and thereby evading the nonrecognition requirement of § 337. This provision does not apply to a distribution to an 80-percent distributee if § 337 nonrecognition does not apply to that distribution.[76]

It is likely that the nonrecognition provision of § 337(a) overrides common law doctrines such as the anticipatory assignment of income doctrine and the tax benefit rule. For example, in Rev. Rul. 74–396, the Commissioner determined that the tax benefit rule did not apply to a § 332 liquidation where the distributee's basis in the distributed property is determined under § 334(b)(1). While this ruling preceded the Supreme Court's decision in *Hillsboro Nat'l Bank v. Commissioner*,[77] it is unlikely that the *Hillsboro*[78] case will alter that

---

[73]   Subject to exceptions, this nonrecognition provision does not apply if the 80-percent distributee is either a tax exempt entity or a foreign corporation. § 337(b)(2), 367(e)(2).

[74]   § 337(c).

[75]   § 337(c).

[76]   § 336(d)(3). For example, § 337 nonrecognition sometimes does not apply to a distribution to an 80-percent distribute that is a tax-exempt organization. § 337(b)(2).

[77]   460 U.S. 370 (1983).

[78]   The Supreme Court's decision in the Hillsboro Nat'l Bank case is sometimes referred to as the "Bliss" case.

result. Note that the recapture of depreciation provisions do not apply to § 332 liquidations.[79]

Subject to certain exceptions, the disposition of an installment obligation on which income was being reported on the installment method generally will cause the transferor to recognize income in the amount of the deferred gain.[80] One of the exceptions is that income will not be recognized when an installment obligation is distributed by a liquidating subsidiary corporation in a distribution to which § 337(a) applies.[81]

When a corporate distributee's receipt of a liquidating distribution qualifies for nonrecognition under § 332 and the subsidiary recognized no gain or loss on the distribution, the distributee's basis in the distributed property equals the basis that the subsidiary had therein.[82] However, the basis of any other shareholder (including minority shareholders) in property received from a corporation being liquidated under § 332 is equal to the fair market value of that property at the time of distribution.[83]

Ex. (2)   On January 1, X Corporation had 1,000 shares of common voting stock outstanding. P Corporation owned 900 shares of X stock having a basis of $90,000 (which it had acquired ten years earlier), and B, an individual shareholder, owned 100 shares of X stock having a basis of $10,000. P and X report their income on a calendar year basis. As of January 1, P had accumulated *e and p* of $300,000, and X had accumulated *e and p* of $50,000. In the year in question, X had no earnings or losses. On March 1, the shareholders of X resolved that X should distribute all of its assets in redemption of its outstanding stock, and the redemption was completed by August 5.[84] The liquidating distributions to P consisted of property having a fair market value of $135,000; and B received property having a fair market value of $15,000. Section 332 excludes the entire $45,000

---

[79]   §§ 1245(b)(3), 1250(d)(3), and 291(a)(1).

[80]   § 453B.

[81]   § 453B(d).

[82]   § 334(b). This provision does not apply in certain circumstances where the liquidating subsidiary is a foreign corporation. § 334(b)(1)(B).

[83]   § 334(a). Similarly, if the subsidiary recognized a gain or loss on a § 332 distribution to an 80-percent distributee (which can occur, for example, when the 80-percent distributee is a tax-exempt entity), the basis of a distributed asset in the hands of the distributee equals its fair market value. § 334(b)(1).

[84]   Where all of the assets of the liquidating corporation are transferred within one taxable year, the shareholders' resolution authorizing the distributions of those assets in redemption of the outstanding stock constitutes an adoption of a plan of liquidation for purposes of satisfying the Code's requirement that one be adopted. § 332(b)(2).

gain realized by P from the latter's gross income. However, B will recognize the $5,000 gain realized by her on the liquidating distribution. B's basis in the assets she received will equal the fair market value of those assets. P's basis in the assets that it received from X will be the same as the basis that X had in those assets. The basis that P had in its 900 shares of X stock disappears and has no tax relevance. X's accumulated *e and p* is reduced by an amount equal to ten percent of its *e and p* ($5,000).[85] The remaining $45,000 of X's accumulated *e and p* is added to P's accumulated *e and p*, which then becomes $345,000.[86]

¶ 4.05.4 Partial or Full Satisfaction of Subsidiary's Indebtedness to Its Parent Corporation

When a liquidating subsidiary is indebted to its parent corporation, a portion of the distributions made to the parent pursuant to the liquidation constitutes payment in satisfaction of the debt rather than distributions in redemption of stock. Creditors of a liquidating corporation have priority over shareholders. When a shareholder is also a creditor, the priority requires that distributions first be allocated to the satisfaction of the subsidiary's debt and that only the remaining balance, if any, be available for redemption of stock.

Under § 337(b)(1), if § 332 applies to a liquidation, the liquidating subsidiary will not recognize a gain or loss on the distribution of appreciated or depreciated assets in satisfaction of its debt to a corporate shareholder that qualifies as an 80-percent distributee within the meaning of § 337(c). You will recall, however, that if the subsidiary is insolvent so that no distribution is made on its stock, then neither § 332 nor § 337 will apply.

If a liquidating subsidiary makes a payment in kind on a debt owing to a person that is not an 80-percent distributee, the subsidiary can recognize gain or loss.

Section 332 has no application to a parent's receipt of payment on the subsidiary's debt whether or not the subsidiary is solvent.[87] When the payment made to the parent on the debt exceeds the latter's basis in the debt (e.g., when prior to the parent's acquisition of control of the subsidiary, the parent purchased bonds of the subsidiary at a discount and that purchase was not made in anticipation of subsequently acquiring control of the subsidiary), the

---

[85]   § 312(n)(7).

[86]   Treas. Reg. § 1.381(c)(2)–1(c)(2).

[87]   Treas. Reg. § 1.332–7.

parent will recognize a gain.[88] If the payments are less than the parent's basis, the parent is allowed a bad debt deduction or, if no payment is received, a deduction for worthless securities.[89]

Where § 332 is inapplicable because the subsidiary is insolvent, the parent is entitled to a loss deduction for the worthless stock of the subsidiary.[90] Section 165(g)(3) usually will grant an ordinary loss deduction to the parent rather than a capital loss.

If, because of § 337(b)(1), no gain or loss is recognized by a subsidiary corporation on making a transfer of property in satisfaction of its debt to its parent, the parent corporation's basis in such property is equal to the basis that the subsidiary had therein.[91] This transferred basis rule will apply even when the parent corporation recognized a gain on receiving the distribution.

---

[88] Under current tax law, there are limited circumstances in which a parent can have a basis in its subsidiary's debt that is less than the principal amount of that debt. See § 108(e)(4).

[89] Rev. Rul. 59–296; Rev. Rul. 68–602; Rev. Rul. 70–489.

[90] § 165(g). See Treas. Reg. § 1.332–2(b).

[91] § 334(b).

Chapter Five

TAXABLE PURCHASE AND SALE OF A CORPORATE BUSINESS

Analysis

Para.

5.01   Introduction

5.02   Sale of Assets

5.03   Sale of Stock

5.04   Section 338(h)(10) Election

5.05   New T's Basis in Its Assets

5.06   Section 336(e) Election

¶ 5.01 INTRODUCTION

Corporate businesses are typically bought and sold in one of two ways: Either the corporation sells its assets (after which it may or may not be liquidated); or the shareholders sell their shares (after which the purchaser may or may not liquidate the acquired corporation). This chapter discusses the general patterns of taxation applied to these two methods of buying and selling corporate businesses when the transaction does not qualify as a reorganization.[1] Reorganizations are discussed in Chapter Nine.

¶ 5.02 SALE OF ASSETS

Assume purchasing corporation (P) desires to purchase the business of target corporation (T), which is owned by a single individual stockholder (A). The following two examples briefly discuss the basic tax results when P purchases the business via an asset sale.

Ex. (1)   T has one business asset which has a fair market value of $600,000. T's adjusted basis in the asset is $350,000. A's basis in his T stock is $200,000. P purchases T's asset using $600,000 cash. T will recognize $250,000 gain on that

---

[1]   For a more detailed discussion of these topics, see Corporate Income Taxation Hornbook at Chapter Four, Part B.

transaction. T liquidates and transfers the $600,000 cash[2] to A. A will recognize a gain on $400,000 on the complete liquidation of T. Note that there are two instances of taxation—one at the corporate level when the assets are sold and one at the shareholder level when T liquidates. P will take T's former business asset with a fair market value basis of $600,000.

Ex. (2)   Same facts as Example (1). A decides to liquidate T prior to the asset sale and then A will sell the business asset to P for $600,000. The tax results are the same.[3] T will recognize $250,000 gain and A will recognize $400,000 gain on the liquidation. As in Example (1), there are two levels of taxation. There will be no additional gain recognized by A on the sale of the assets to P because A's basis in those assets will equal their fair market value. Again, P will take T's former business asset with a fair market value basis of $600,000.

When a corporation sells many or all of its assets directly to a purchaser, the total purchase price must be allocated among the purchased assets in order to determine the gain or loss recognized by the seller on each asset and in order to determine the purchaser's basis in each asset. If the transferor and transferee agree in writing as to the allocation of the purchase price of an asset or its fair market value, that will be binding on both parties unless the allocation or fair market value is not appropriate.[4] If the sale constitutes an "applicable asset acquisition"[5] in which the assets that constitute a trade or business[6] of the seller are acquired, then § 1060(a) requires that the purchase price be allocated among the assets according to the "residual method" of allocation as that method is set forth in the regulations under § 338(b)(5).[7]

The residual method, as discussed in Treas. Reg. § 1.338–6(b), divides T's assets into seven categories or "Classes" and allocates the

---

[2]   T will incur a tax liability on the sale which will reduce the amount distributable to A in liquidation. For convenience of computation, in this example we will ignore the reduction that taxes will cause to the amount distributed to A.

[3]   For convenience in this example, we will ignore the tax liability on making its liquidation distribution.

[4]   § 1060(a). This provision applies if the sale constitutes an "applicable asset acquisition," which term is defined in n. 5, infra.

[5]   An applicable asset acquisition is one in which the purchaser's basis in the acquired assets is determined wholly by the consideration paid by the purchaser for those assets except that a transaction does not lose its taxable status merely because § 1031 (like-kind exchanges) applies to part of the transaction. § 1060(c).

[6]   The standards for determining whether a corporation's sale of assets constitutes the sale of a trade or business are explained in Treas. Reg. § 1.1060–1(b)(2).

[7]   Treas. Reg. § 1.338–6(b).

purchase price first to the value of Class I assets, and then any unallocated price to the value of Class II assets, and so on through Class VI assets. Any residue of the price remaining after the allocation to the first six Classes is then allocated to the assets in Class VII regardless of the value of those assets. This creates a priority of allocation and provides that any premium paid in excess of the value of the corporation's assets is allocated to Class VII assets, which consist of goodwill and going concern value. The classifications are:

Class I assets:	cash and general deposit accounts in banks, savings and loan associations (and similar depository institutions).
Class II assets:	actively traded personal properties, certificates of deposit, and foreign currency.
Class III assets:	assets that are required to be marked to market at least annually and certain debt instruments.
Class IV assets:	stock in trade, inventory, and property held primarily for sale to customers in the ordinary course of a trade or business.
Class V assets:	all assets that are not included in any of the other Classes.
Class VI assets:	all "§ 197 intangibles" (as defined in § 197(d)) other than those in the nature of goodwill and going concern value.
Class VII assets:	goodwill and going concern value.

¶ 5.03 SALE OF STOCK

Let us review the basic tax consequences when a purchasing corporation (P) purchases the business of a target corporation (T) via a stock acquisition.

Ex. (1)   T has one business asset, which has a fair market value of $600,000. T's adjusted basis in the asset is $350,000. The single individual owner of T, A, has a basis in his T stock of $200,000. A sells his T stock to P for $600,000 cash. A recognizes a gain of $400,000 on the sale. No gain is recognized by T and thus, unlike the asset sale, there is only one level of taxation (the shareholder level). P has a fair market value basis of $600,000 in the T stock. However, T still has a $350,000 basis in the business asset.

The repudiation by Congress of the *General Utilities* doctrine has created a tax bias in favor of purchasing stock of a target corporation (and making no § 338 election) rather than purchasing the target's assets. If the target's assets are purchased, there will be a tax imposed on the recognition of the unrealized appreciation of the target's assets; and, in order for the shareholders of old target promptly to obtain the proceeds of that sale, they will have to recognize a second tax on the appreciation of their stock when they distribute the proceeds in liquidation of the target.[8] On the other hand, if the purchaser acquires the stock of the target, there will only be a single tax, which is imposed on the recognition of the previously unrealized appreciation of that stock. In the latter case, the target's basis in its assets will be unchanged, and so the unrealized appreciation in those assets will effectively be recognized either when the target sells its assets or because of a lower amount of annual depreciation for them. However, the tax cost for having a reduced basis in the target's assets in a stock purchase will be incurred in years subsequent to the year of acquisition; while the tax cost for recognizing a gain when the target is liquidated after an asset sale will be incurred immediately. Because of the time value of money, there is a significant benefit in deferring the imposition of a tax cost to a future date. So, in many circumstances, there can be a cost saving to purchasing and selling stock of a target rather than its assets. The benefit of this saving can be allocated between the purchaser and the seller by altering the price to be paid for the stock.[9]

¶ 5.03.1 Sale of Stock Followed by Liquidation of Target

Prior to the 1954 Code, judicial doctrine established that, when (in a taxable transaction or series of transactions) a party acquired all (or virtually all) of the stock of a corporation (sometimes referred to as the "target") for the purpose of liquidating the target corporation and thereby obtaining its assets, and when the target corporation was in fact promptly liquidated, the substance of the transaction was considered to be a purchase of the target corporation's assets through the medium of acquiring its stock. Upon liquidation of the target corporation, no gain or loss was recognized by the purchaser, and the purchaser's basis in the distributed property was equal to the

---

[8]   Recognition of gain by a parent corporation will not occur if the target can be liquidated under § 332 or pursuant to a reorganization provision, but even then minority shareholders often would recognize their gain.

[9]   Notwithstanding the tax benefits derived from a stock sale, many purchasers insist on an asset sale in order to avoid the risk that the target will have undisclosed liabilities (including tax liabilities) that the purchaser will have to bear. An indemnification agreement from the sellers will not always be sufficient security to undertake that risk.

purchase price paid for the stock. This judicial principle is commonly referred to as the "Kimbell-Diamond" rule in deference to a landmark decision on this issue.[10]

As applied to the purchase of stock by a *corporation*, the "Kimbell-Diamond" rule was codified in the "old version" (i.e., the pre-1982 version) of § 334(b)(2) of the 1954 Code[11] with some modifications. In 1982, Congress repealed the old version of § 334(b)(2) and replaced it with a new § 338.[12] As we shall see, § 338 provides many of the benefits of the "Kimbell-Diamond" rule without the requirement that the target corporation be liquidated.

¶ 5.03.2   Section 338 Election

Section 338 is a complex elective provision whose desirability, and therefore its significance, was reduced when Congress later repudiated the *General Utilities* rule. Because of its reduced significance, we have provided in this book only a brief sketch of how the provision operates.

Section 338 applies only if a purchasing corporation (P) makes a "qualified stock purchase" of the stock of a target corporation (T). Section 338 does not apply to a stock purchase by an individual or any enterprise that is not taxed as a corporation for federal income tax purposes.[13]

Generally, a "qualified stock purchase" refers to a corporation's "purchase"[14] of a controlling interest (an 80% voting and value test) in a target corporation within a twelve-month acquisition period.[15] In

---

[10]   Kimbell-Diamond Milling Co. v. Commissioner, 14 T.C. 74 (1950), aff'd, 187 F.2d 718 (5th Cir. 1951).

[11]   Internal Revenue Code of 1954, Ch. 736, Sec. 334(b)(2), 68A Stat. 1, 105.

[12]   Tax Equity and Fiscal Responsibility Act of 1982, Pub. L. No. 97–248, Sec. 224, 96 Stat. 324, 485–90.

[13]   While individuals can form a corporation for the purpose of having it make a § 338 qualified stock purchase, the purchase will be treated as having been made by the individuals (rather than by the corporation) if the facts indicate that the corporate purchaser was a transitory entity whose existence was short-lived or if P promptly liquidates T or disposes of the T stock. Treas. Reg. § 1.338–3(b)(1).

[14]   The term "purchase" is defined in § 338(h)(3) and is given a restricted meaning. In general, a purchase is an acquisition of stock in which (i) the basis of the stock in the hands of the purchaser is not determined in whole or in part by reference to the transferor's basis, (ii) the acquisition was not one of the nonrecognition exchanges listed in the statute and regulations, and (iii) the stock was not acquired from a person from whom stock would be attributed to the purchaser under the § 318 attribution rules, other than § 318(a)(4).

[15]   § 338(d)(3). The requisite stock purchase can take place in a single transaction or as a series of stock purchases that occur within the twelve-month acquisition period. Except as provided otherwise by regulation, when stock of a target corporation is purchased by corporations that are members of the same affiliated group (as defined in § 1504), such stock is treated as having been purchased by one corporation. § 338(h)(8). Accordingly, the aggregate purchases of the target corporation stock by

such cases, P is given an election under § 338(g) to have the tax consequences of the transaction be determined under a special set of rules.[16] An election to have § 338 apply is sometimes referred to as a "§ 338 election" or as a "§ 338(g) election."

If P makes a valid election under § 338(g),[17] T will be deemed to have sold to an unrelated person all of its assets at fair market value in a single transaction at the close of the date on which P acquired the requisite control of T through a "qualified stock purchase."[18] The date on which P acquired the requisite control of T is referred to as the "acquisition date."[19] T will realize gain or loss on any appreciated or depreciated assets that it holds on the acquisition date. T will recognize all of its realized gain or loss from the constructive sale.[20]

Unless a special election is made under § 338(h)(10),[21] a § 338(g) election will not affect the amount of gain or loss recognized by the shareholders of T on the sale of their stock to P.

The acquisition date is deemed to be the last day of T's existence. At the beginning of the next day, a new T Corporation is treated as having come into existence, and new T is deemed to have purchased from an unrelated person the assets that were deemed to have been sold by old T.[22] As we will see, the basis that new T acquires in those assets is not necessarily the same as the purchase price that old T is deemed to have received for them. The T Corporation that existed

---

several members of an affiliated group will be counted in determining whether there has been a qualified stock purchase.

[16]   The statute establishes so-called consistency rules under which, in certain defined circumstances in which a qualified stock purchase takes place, even though P does not make a § 338 election, the provisions of § 338 will be applied as if P had made the election regardless of whether P desires to have that section apply. § 338(e), (f). The statute authorizes Treasury to establish exceptions so that a deemed election will not be imposed in certain circumstances. Pursuant to that authority, the current regulations narrow the scope of the consistency rules and provide a different consequence when they apply—i.e., § 338 treatment will apply only if an *actual* election is made. Treas. Reg. § 1.338–8. Under the regulations, the consequences of causing the consistency rules to apply relates to the basis of property. Given the complexity of the consistency rules and the reduction of their significance by the regulations, the authors have chosen not to cover those rules in this book. For a detailed discussion of the consistency rules, see Douglas Kahn, *Section 338 and its Foolish Consistency Rules—the Hobgoblin of Little Minds*, 14 Quinnipiac L. Rev. 31 (1994).

[17]   For § 338 to apply, P must make an election not later than the 15th day of the 9th month beginning after the month in which the acquisition date occurs. § 338(g)(1). Once made, the election is irrevocable. § 338(g)(3).

[18]   § 338(a)(1); Treas. Reg. § 1.338–1(a)(1).

[19]   § 338(h)(2).

[20]   Prior to 1986, much (or all) of the gain or loss realized by T on this constructive sale of its assets was not recognized because of the operation of the old version of § 337.

[21]   Section 338(h)(10) is discussed in ¶ 5.04.

[22]   § 338(a)(2); Treas. Reg. § 1.338–1(a)(1).

prior to the day after the acquisition date is referred to as "old T," and the T Corporation that exists on the day after the acquisition date is referred to "new T." Old T and new T are treated as two distinct corporations.

The amount realized by old T on the constructive sale of all of its assets is referred to as the "aggregate deemed sales price" or by the acronym, "ADSP."[23] The ADSP for a deemed sale of a target's assets is designed to equal approximately the aggregate fair market value of those assets. However, rather than permitting appraisals to be made of the values of the target's assets, the regulations provide a formula that constructs the value of the target's assets by a computation that utilizes the amount paid by P for T's stock and by taking into account T's liabilities, including the tax liabilities incurred by T as a consequence of the constructive sale.[24] This formula is sometimes referred to as the "ADSP formula." In general, the formula provides that the ADSP is the sum of: (1) the "grossed-up amount realized" on the sale to P of P's "recently purchased target stock" plus (2) the liabilities of the target, which may include any tax liability resulting from the deemed sale of target's assets.[25]

"Recently purchased target stock" is stock of the target that is held by the purchasing corporation (P) on the acquisition date and was purchased by P during the 12-month acquisition period.[26] The 12-month acquisition period is the 12-month period beginning with the date of the first purchase of stock included in the qualified stock purchase.[27]

The grossed-up amount realized is the amount realized on the sale to P of the recently purchased target stock (i.e., the amount P paid for that stock) divided by the percentage of recently purchased stock (determined by value on the acquisition date). The resulting

---

[23] Treas. Reg. § 1.338–1(a)(3).

[24] § 338(h)(11); Treas. Reg. § 1.338–4.

[25] Treas. Reg. § 1.338–4(b)(1)(i), (d). The liabilities of T that are taken into account in computing the ADSP are those liabilities that, under general tax principles, would be included in old T's amount realized if old T had sold its assets to an unrelated person for consideration that included an acceptance or assumption of those liabilities. Treas. Reg. § 1.338–4(d). This treatment of T's liabilities is an application of the well known *Crane* (or *Tufts*) doctrine.

The ADSP is subject to redetermination when needed to reflect events that occur after the acquisition date and that affect the amount of the purchase price for the recently purchased stock (such as the discovery or maturity of a liability not previously taken into account). Treas. Reg. § 1.338–4(b)(2)(ii), 7(a).

[26] § 338(b)(6)(A).

[27] A qualified stock purchase is described in the text to n. 14, supra.

figure is reduced by the selling costs incurred by the shareholders in connection with the sale of the recently purchased target stock to P.[28]

Since the size of ADSP is dependent upon the amount of liabilities that old T had on the acquisition date, which includes the tax liability that old T incurred from the deemed sale of its assets, and since the amount of old T's tax liability from the deemed sale is dependent upon the size of the ADSP, those two figures are dependent on each other. One means of calculating the ADSP and old T's tax liability is to use a trial and error method.[29] However, the regulations provide an algebraic solution to the computational difficulty of determining those two figures, and so the cumbersome trial and error method can be avoided.[30]

The ADSP is allocated among old T's assets to determine the gain or loss recognized on each asset from the deemed sale.[31] The regulations explain how the ADSP is allocated among old T's assets.[32]

The ADSP formula is designed to approximate the value of old T's assets. By grossing up the amount realized from the sale to P of the recently purchased target stock[33] (i.e., the amount P paid for the T stock it acquired in the 12-month or so period ending on the acquisition date), the formula obtains a figure approximately equal to the *net value* of T's assets on the acquisition date. When T's liabilities are added to that figure, the sum represents the *fair market value* of those assets.

Absent an election under § 338(h)(10), or a contractual agreement for the selling shareholders to bear the tax from the constructive sale of old T's assets, the federal income tax on any gain recognized by old T on the constructive sale of its assets on the acquisition date will not be borne by the shareholders of old T even if old T was a member of a consolidated group.[34] If old T was a member of a consolidated group, it must file a separate short-year tax return in which it reports the income or loss from the constructive sale of its assets on the acquisition date.[35] Since T is controlled by P (the purchasing corporation) by the time of the acquisition date, the

---

[28]   Treas. Reg. § 1.338–4(c)(1).

[29]   Treas. Reg. § 1.338–4(e).

[30]   Treas. Reg. § 1.338–4(g), Exs. (1)–(3).

[31]   Treas. Reg. § 1.338–4(e).

[32]   Id. and Treas. Regs. § 1.338–6 and –7.

[33]   The purchasing corporation's "recently purchased target stock" is stock of the target that is held by the purchasing corporation (P) on the "acquisition date" and that was purchased by P during the "12-month acquisition period." § 338(b)(6)(A).

[34]   Of course, the selling price of the stock can be negotiated so that all or a part of the tax burden will effectively be borne by the shareholders of old T.

[35]   See Treas. Reg. § 1.338–10(a)(2).

incidence of a tax on old T's constructive sale of its assets will fall on P rather than on the shareholders of old T who sold their stock to P; and this will be true even when old T was a member of a consolidated group.[36]

The ADSP formula is used only for purposes of determining the amount of gain or loss that old T recognized on the constructive sale of its assets; it is not used in determining the aggregate basis that new T has in its assets after the constructive sale is deemed to have taken place. New T's basis is determined by a different formula discussed below.

As previously mentioned, on the day after the acquisition date, new T is deemed to have purchased from an unrelated person all of the assets that old T was deemed to have sold on the prior day.[37] The "T" that makes this constructive purchase is treated as a new corporation.[38] For most income tax purposes (but not for all), the election causes T to be treated as two separate corporations.[39] There is old T, which sells all of its assets at the end of the acquisition date and which ceases to exist at that time. Then, there is new T, which is treated as a new corporation that purchases the assets of old T on the day after the acquisition date.[40] The taxable year of old T closes on the acquisition date, and the taxable year of new T begins on the next day.[41] Thus, all of the earnings and profits, net operating loss and capital loss carryovers, and most other income tax attributes of old T cease to exist after the acquisition date. However, old T's carryover losses that are otherwise available as deductions can be deducted from any gain recognized by old T in its final taxable year (ending on the acquisition date), and so such carryover losses can be deducted from the net gain that old T may have recognized on the constructive sale of all of its assets.[42]

Nevertheless, for purposes other than the income tax and for some income tax purposes, especially for rules relating to the relationship of the corporation to its employees, old T and new T will

---

[36]   See id. and § 338(h)(9).

[37]   § 338(a)(2).

[38]   Id.

[39]   Treas. Reg. § 1.338–1(b). Since new T is a new corporation, it can adopt a new taxable year and a new method of accounting without regard to the taxable year and method of accounting employed by old T. Treas. Reg. § 1.338–1(b)(1). New T can elect to depreciate its depreciable assets under § 168 as a new purchaser under whatever method and convention it chooses without regard to the elections that had been made by old T. Id.

[40]   Treas. Reg. § 1.338–2(c)(17).

[41]   See Treas. Reg. § 1.338–10(a).

[42]   Treas. Reg. § 1.338–10(a)(2)(iii).

be treated as one taxpayer.[43] Also, new T is liable for old T's federal income tax liabilities, including old T's liability for income taxes incurred because of the constructive sale of all of its assets on the acquisition date.[44]

New T's aggregate basis in the assets that it is deemed to have purchased from old T is determined according to the formula established by § 338(b) and set forth in greater detail in Treas. Reg. § 1.338–5. The manner in which new T's aggregate basis in its assets is determined is discussed at ¶ 5.05. The aggregate basis of new T's assets is sometimes referred as the "adjusted grossed-up basis" or by the acronym, "AGUB."[45] The manner in which AGUB is allocated among new T's assets to determine the basis of each asset is set forth in Treas. Regs. § 1.338–6 and –7.

Since 1986, the year in which the *General Utilities* doctrine was eliminated, an election to have § 338 apply has required the immediate recognition of the target's unrealized gain on its assets. Accordingly, there are fewer circumstances in which it will be desirable to make that election, and § 338 has more limited significance than it had prior to 1986. A circumstance in which a § 338 election may be desirable arises when the target has a large amount of net operating loss carryovers or other tax-saving attributes from prior years. Those carryover losses or other attributes can be deducted from income recognized by old T, or credited against the tax payable by old T, from the constructive sale of its assets on the acquisition date.[46] However, when an election under § 338(h)(10) is available, there are circumstances in which that election is desirable. Section 338(h)(10) is described in ¶ 5.04.

¶ 5.04 SECTION 338(h)(10) ELECTION

Under § 338, a corporation (or corporations) that sells the target's stock (the "seller") is granted an election under § 338(h)(10) effectively to treat the stock sale as a sale of the target's assets in certain circumstances. This election is permitted only if there was a deemed sale of the target's assets under § 338.[47] Also, a § 338(h)(10) election can be made for a target only if the target is (1) a member of

---

[43]   Treas. Reg. § 1.338–1(b). For example, for purposes of determining the FICA and FUTA taxes on wages of employees, old T and new T are treated as one taxpayer, and new T must use the same employer identification number that old T had. Treas. Reg. § 1.338–1(b)(3).

[44]   Treas. Reg. § 1.338–1(b)(3)(i).

[45]   Treas. Reg. § 1.338–1(a).

[46]   Treas. Reg. § 1.338–10(a)(2)(iii).

[47]   If a valid § 338(h)(10) election is made for T, that election is treated as simultaneously also making a § 338 election for T. Treas. Reg. § 1.338(h)(10)–1(c)(4).

a selling consolidated group,[48] (2) a member of a selling affiliated group filing separate returns,[49] or (3) an S corporation.[50]

A § 338(h)(10) election must be made jointly by the purchasing corporation (P) and either the selling consolidated group, the selling affiliate, or the shareholders of the S corporation, as the case may be.[51] The election must be made no later than the 15th day of the 9th month beginning after the month in which the acquisition date occurs.[52]

When a valid § 338(h)(10) election has been made for a target (T), old T is treated as having sold all of its assets in one transaction at the close of the acquisition date. On the constructive sale of its assets, old T is treated as having received an amount determined under a formula. The amount deemed to have been received by old T for its assets is referred to as the "aggregate deemed sales price" or by its acronym, "ADSP." The operation of that formula is described earlier in ¶ 5.03.2. As noted in ¶ 5.03.2, the ADSP formula takes old T's liabilities, including the tax liability from the deemed sale, into account.[53] However, since the tax liability arising from the deemed sale of old T's assets in a § 338(h)(10) transaction typically will be borne by the selling shareholders of old T, those liabilities are excluded from ADSP when § 338(h)(10) is elected.[54]

Immediately after the deemed sale of its assets, T is deemed to have distributed all of the proceeds pursuant to a complete liquidation to the members of the selling consolidated group, the selling affiliate, or S corporation shareholders . The liquidation and distribution are deemed to have taken place while old T is still owned

[48]　A "selling consolidated group" is a group that includes T as a member and that files a consolidated return for the period that includes T's acquisition date. Treas. Reg. § 1.338(h)(10)–1(b)(2).

[49]　In the case of a sale by a selling affiliated group, the § 338(h)(10) election applies only to a sale of stock by a "selling affiliate." A "selling affiliate" is a domestic corporation that does not file a consolidated return with the target and that owns on the acquisition date an amount of stock of a domestic target that satisfies the stock-holding requirements of § 1504(a)(2). Treas. Reg. § 1.338(h)(10)–1(b)(3). The requirements of § 1504(a)(2) are that the selling affiliate own stock possessing at least 80% of the voting power of T's outstanding stock and having a value equal to at least 80% of the aggregate value of T's outstanding stock.

[50]　Treas. Reg. § 1.338(h)(10)–1(c)(1). S Corporations are discussed in Chapter Eleven.

[51]　In the case of an S corporation, all of the shareholders (including those who did not sell any shares of the target's stock) must consent to the § 338(h)(10) election for it to be valid because even the non-selling shareholders will include in their income their share of the target's gain from the constructive sale of its assets. Treas. Reg. § 1.338(h)(10)–1(c)(3).

[52]　Treas. Reg. § 1.338(h)(10)–1(c)(3).

[53]　Treas. Reg. § 1.338–4(d).

[54]　Treas. Reg. § 1.338(h)(10)–1(e), Exs (4), (5).

by the selling consolidated group or by the selling affiliate (or by its shareholders if T is an S corporation).[55] The constructive liquidation of old T is treated as an actual liquidation, and the appropriate tax rules are applied accordingly.[56] Old T ceases to exist, and new T comes into existence the next day.

If the § 338(h)(10) election is valid, no gain or loss is recognized by the selling consolidated group, the selling affiliate, or by the shareholders of a target that is an S corporation, for the sale of the target's stock that is part of a qualified stock purchase.[57] Instead, those sellers will be liable for the gain from old T's deemed sale of its assets. Thus, if T's stock was sold by a selling consolidated group, the group must file a consolidated return for the period that includes the acquisition date.[58] If, instead, T was an S corporation, its gain or loss from the deemed sale of its assets will pass through to its shareholders.[59] If T's deemed liquidating distribution is made to a selling affiliate, the tax incurred by T on the deemed sale of its assets will be borne by the selling affiliate as a transferee of T's assets. Old T is liable for its tax liability for gain recognized on the deemed sale, and so its shareholders take on that liability as transferees of old T's assets in the constructive liquidation.

¶ 5.05 NEW T'S BASIS IN ITS ASSETS

Section 338(a)(2) and (b)(1) provide that T's assets are deemed to be purchased on the day after the acquisition date by a new corporation (new T). New T's basis in its assets is determined by a formula that arrives at a figure called "the adjusted grossed-up basis" or by its acronym "AGUB" which is determined as of the beginning of the day after the acquisition date.[60] AGUB is used for both regular § 338 elections and § 338(h)(10) elections. The AGUB for new T is equal to the sum of:

(1)   the grossed-up basis of P's recently purchased stock,

(2)   the basis of P's nonrecently purchased stock, and

(3)   the liabilities of new T.[61]

---

[55]   Treas. Reg. § 1.338(h)(10)–1(d)(4).

[56]   Treas. Reg. § 1.338(h)(10)–1(d)(4).

[57]   Treas. Reg. § 1.338(h)(10)–1(d)(5)(i).

[58]   Treas. Reg. § 1.338(h)(10)–1(d)(7)(i).

[59]   § 1366; Treas. Reg. § 1.338(h)(10)–1(d)(5)(i).

[60]   Treas. Reg. § 1.338–5(b)(2)(ii).

[61]   Treas. Reg. § 1.338–5(b)(1). If subsequent events occur that affect the determination of the price paid for the constructive sale of old T's assets, such as the discovery of liabilities not previously taken into account, the AGUB will be redetermined accordingly. Treas. Reg. § 1.338–5(b)(2)(ii).

The following definitions are necessary to determine how new T's basis in its assets is determined.

(a) *Recently Purchased Stock.* The term "recently purchased stock" means any T stock that is held by P (or by an affiliate of P) on the acquisition date and that was purchased by P during the twelve-month acquisition period.[62] Unless otherwise indicated, any reference in this discussion to an acquisition by P will include acquisitions by affiliates of P since, under § 338(h)(8), acquisitions made by an affiliated group are treated as having been made by one corporation unless the regulations provide otherwise.

(b) *Nonrecently Purchased Stock.* The term "nonrecently purchased stock" means any T stock that is held by P (or by an affiliate of P) on the acquisition date and that is not recently purchased stock.[63] P can elect to recognize gain on its nonrecently purchased stock and thereby obtain a basis equal to its fair market value.

(c) *Grossed-Up Basis of Recently Purchased Stock.* For purposes of determining AGUB, the "grossed-up basis" of recently purchased stock is defined in § 338(b)(4) as follows: an amount equal to the basis of P's recently purchased stock in T at the beginning of the day after the acquisition date, multiplied by a fraction, the numerator of which is 100 percent minus the percentage of stock (by value) attributable to P's nonrecently purchased stock in T, and the denominator of which is the percentage of stock (by value) attributable to P's recently purchased stock in T.[64] The resulting figure is increased by any of P's acquisition costs, such as brokerage fees, that would be added to P's basis in the stock under normal tax principles.[65]

Note that, when a § 338(h)(10) election is made, new T's basis in all of its assets will be approximately equal to their fair market value. That is because, when a § 338(h)(10) election is made, P *must* recognize gain on the appreciation of its nonrecently purchased stock.[66]

---

[62] § 338(b)(6)(A). For this purpose, "purchase" is defined in § 338(h)(3).

[63] § 338(b)(6)(B).

[64] Treas. Reg. § 1.338–5(c).

[65] Id.

[66] Treas. Reg. § 1.338(h)(10)–1(d)(1).

In the examples below, no election was made to apply
§ 338(h)(10), and assume that there were no selling or acquisition
costs.

Ex. (1)   P purchased 100 percent of T's stock for 200 under a
               qualified stock purchase and made a timely § 338 election.
               At the time of the sale of the stock, T had no liabilities, and
               T had a basis of 120 in its assets. The deemed sale of T's
               assets did not cause any tax liability to T because of a net
               operating loss carryover that T had. The amount at which
               T's assets are deemed to have been purchased is the
               grossed-up basis of the recently purchased T stock, which
               equals 200. After the acquisition date, new T has a basis of
               200 in its assets. If P had purchased 85 percent of T's stock
               for 170, and had not previously acquired any of T's stock,
               the grossed-up basis of the recently purchased T stock
               would still be 200—i.e., 170 × 100/85 = 200.

Ex. (2)   Assume the same facts as in Example (1) except that P
               purchased 10 percent of T's stock five years earlier for 5 and
               purchased the other 90 percent for 180 under a qualified
               stock purchase. The grossed-up basis of the recently
               purchased T stock is 180—i.e., 180 × (100−10)/90. After the
               acquisition date, new T has a basis of 185 in its assets (the
               sum of 180 for the recently purchased T stock plus 5 for the
               nonrecently purchased T stock), although the fair market
               value of T's assets is 200. The built-in gain in new T's assets
               is attributable to P's nonrecently purchased stock of T.

Ex. (3)   Assume the same facts as in Example (1) except that P
               purchased 10 percent of T stock five years earlier for 5 and
               purchased recently only 80 percent of the T stock for 160
               under a qualified stock purchase. The grossed-up basis of
               the recently purchased T stock is 180—i.e., 160 ×
               (100−10)/80. Note that the grossed-up basis for the recently
               purchased T stock includes the fair market value of the 10
               percent of T stock not owned by P on the acquisition date.
               Note also that the stock that is not owned by P is not
               included in nonrecently purchased stock. The reference to
               nonrecently purchased stock is to stock held by P on the
               acquisition date that was not purchased during the twelve-
               month acquisition period; it does not refer to stock held by
               other shareholders. After the acquisition date, new T has a
               basis of 185 in its assets (the sum of 180 for the recently
               purchased T stock plus 5 for the nonrecently purchased T
               stock).

An election is provided under § 338(b)(3) pursuant to which the basis of new T's assets may be determined by stepping-up the basis of the T stock held by P at the acquisition date that was not purchased during the twelve-month acquisition period (i.e., the nonrecently purchased stock). The stepped-up basis is to be determined under regulations[67] and is applicable if P elects to recognize gain as if such nonrecently purchased stock were sold on the acquisition date.[68]

The "AGUB" must be allocated among new T's assets to determine the basis in each asset. Section 338(b)(5) delegates to Treasury the determination of the manner in which that allocation will be made. In Treas. Reg. § 1.338–6(b), Treasury adopted the so-called "residual method" of allocating the deemed purchase price among the assets for the purposes of allocating both AGUB and ADSP. The residual method is discussed in ¶ 5.02.

¶ 5.06 SECTION 336(e) ELECTION

The Tax Reform Act of 1986 added § 336(e) to the Code authorizing Treasury to promulgate regulations granting a parent corporation an election that is similar to § 338(h)(10) for certain sales, exchanges, or distributions of stock of a subsidiary. Final regulations were promulgated by Treasury in 2013 and amended in 2017.[69] The general thrust of § 336(e) and the regulations is to provide such an election when the purchaser of the target corporation is not itself a corporation that acquired 80 percent of the target corporation's stock (by vote and value) in a qualified stock purchase and thus qualifies for the election provided under § 338. In other words, the objective is to provide treatment similar to that of § 338(h)(10) even when the purchaser is not a single corporation or a group of affiliated corporations filing a consolidated return. With one exception, if a transaction qualifies for both a § 338 election and a § 336(e) election, only the § 338 election is available.[70] If a corporate seller is a member of a consolidated group of corporations, the entire group is treated as a single seller regardless of which members sold their target stock.[71]

---

[67]   See Treas. Reg. § 1.338–5(d).

[68]   A deemed sale of nonrecently purchased stock under a § 338(b)(3) election requires P to recognize gain, but it does not permit P to recognize a loss.

[69]   Treas. Reg. §§ 1.336–1 to –5.

[70]   Treas. Reg. § 1.336–1(b)(6)(ii)(A). The one exception occurs when a deemed sale of target's assets because of a § 336(e) election results in a disposition of a subsidiary's stock that qualifies for § 338. Treas. Reg. § 1.336–1(b)(6)(ii).

[71]   Treas. Reg. § 1.336–2(g)(2).

The operation of the § 336(e) regulations is complex. We will describe only the basic structure set forth in the regulations. If an election is made to apply § 336(e), it is irrevocable.[72]

When a corporation, or shareholders of an S corporation, sells, exchanges, or distributes sufficient stock (basically 80 percent of vote and value) in a subsidiary in a transaction that constitutes a "qualified stock disposition," § 336(e) provides an election to treat that transaction as a disposition of all of the assets of the subsidiary, and no gain or loss will be recognized on the sale, exchange, or disposition of the target's stock. A qualified stock disposition is a transaction or series of transactions in which the stock of a domestic corporation is sold, exchanged, distributed, or any combination thereof within the 12-month disposition period, which is the 12-month period beginning with the first date of sale, exchange or distribution of stock included in the qualified stock disposition.[73] To qualify for this provision, the stock that is sold, exchanged, or distributed during the 12-month disposition period must possess at least 80% of the voting power of the target corporation's stock and have a value equal to at least 80% of the total value of the target's outstanding stock.[74]

For purposes of this provision, a "target" is a domestic corporation the stock of which is sold, exchanged or distributed in a qualified stock disposition. "Old target" refers to target for the period ending with the disposition date, and "new target" refers to target for subsequent periods.[75] The disposition date for a target is the first date on which there is a qualified stock disposition of the target's stock.[76]

If a qualified stock disposition takes place, the seller or S corporation shareholders are given an election to treat the transaction as a sale by the target corporation of all of its assets. The requirements for making the election are set forth in Treas. Reg. § 1.336–2(h). The effect of the election is to prevent any gain or loss from being recognized on the stock that was sold, exchanged or disposed of as part of the qualified stock disposition.[77] Instead, old target is deemed to have sold all of its assets in a single transaction to an unrelated person on the close of the disposition date.[78] Old

---

[72]   Treas. Reg. § 1.336–2(a).
[73]   Treas. Reg. § 1.336–1(b)(6), (7).
[74]   Treas. Reg. § 1.336–1(b)(6).
[75]   Treas. Reg. § 1.336–1(b)(3).
[76]   Treas. Reg. § 1.336–1(b)(8).
[77]   Treas. Reg. § 1.336–2(b)(1)(i)(A).
[78]   Treas. Reg. § 1.336–2(b)(1)(i)(A).

target recognizes all of the gain and, with several exceptions, the losses from that deemed sale of its assets.[79]

The amount realized by old target on the deemed sale of its assets is the aggregate deemed asset disposition price, hereinafter referred to as the ADADP.[80] In general, the ADADP is the sum of the grossed-up amount realized on the sale, exchange or distribution of recently disposed stock of target plus the liabilities of old target, determined at the beginning of the day after the disposition date.[81] Recently disposed stock is stock in the target that is disposed of by the seller, a member of the seller's consolidated group, or an S corporation shareholder during the 12-month disposition period and is not held by any such person immediately after the close of the disposition date.[82] The manner for determining the grossed-up amount realized on the sale, exchange or distribution of recently purchased stock is set forth in Treas. Reg. § 1.336–3(c). The ADADP is allocated among the assets of old target to determine gain or loss on each asset in accordance with Treas. Reg. §§ 1.338–6 and –7—i.e., in the same manner that constructive amounts received are allocated for purposes of a § 338 election.[83]

Section 336(e) does not apply to the sale of stock by a minority shareholder, and so a minority shareholder will recognize gain or loss on such sales.[84] A minority shareholder will not recognize gain or loss on stock of the target that is retained by that shareholder.[85] For this purpose, a minority shareholder is a shareholder of old target who is neither a seller, a member of seller's consolidated group, or an S corporation shareholder.[86]

Although target is a single corporation, if a valid § 336(e) election is made, old target and new target are generally treated as two separate corporations.[87] Unlike the situation with a § 338(h)(10) election, subject to one exception, old target is not deemed to liquidate as a result of a § 336(e) election.[88]

After the deemed sale by old target of its assets, the basis that new target acquired in those assets needs to be determined. New target's basis in the assets is referred to as the adjusted grossed-up

---

[79]   Treas. Reg. § 1.336–2(b)(1)(i)(B).

[80]   Treas. Regs. §§ 1.336–2(b)(1)(i)(A), –3(a).

[81]   Treas. Reg. § 1.336–3(b).

[82]   Treas. Reg. § 1.336–1(b)(17).

[83]   Treas. Reg. § 1.336–3(a).

[84]   Treas. Reg. § 1.336–2(d)(2).

[85]   Treas. Reg. § 1.336–2(d)(3).

[86]   Treas. Reg. § 1.336–2(d)(1).

[87]   Treas. Reg. § 1.336–2(g)(1).

[88]   Treas. Reg. § 1.336–2(b)(2)(i)(A).

basis and is hereafter referred to as AGUB. The AGUB for old target is determined in the same manner that AGUB is determined for purposes of § 338,[89] and the determination of that figure is described in ¶ 5.05, supra. See Treas. Reg. § 1.338–5. The AGUB is allocated among new target's assets in the same manner that it is allocated for purposes of § 338 by Treas. Reg. § 1.338–6.[90] In that regulation, Treasury adopted the so-called residual method for allocation, and that method is described in ¶ 5.02, supra.

The aggregate amount of the subsidiary's stock can be disposed of in a variety of ways. Some of the stock could be sold or exchanged and some could be distributed to the parent corporation's shareholders as § 301 distributions. All forms of dispositions within the 12-month disposition period are counted; however, there are certain dispositions that are excluded and cannot be taken into account.[91]

A § 336(e) election is made unilaterally by the parent corporation. If a valid election is made, the consequences are similar to those that apply to a § 338(h)(10) election. The subsidiary (the old subsidiary) is deemed to have sold all of its assets to a third corporation. The old subsidiary will recognize any gain that was realized on that constructive sale of its assets. If the qualified stock disposition did not include any distributions to the parent's shareholders, then the subsidiary also will recognize any loss it realized on the constructive sale of its assets. However, to the extent that a distribution to the parent's shareholders is part of the qualified stock disposition, then a percentage of the subsidiary's realized loss is not recognized.[92]

The selling and purchase price of the old subsidiary's constructive sale of its assets are determined by formulas that are similar to the ones used in determining the deemed selling and purchase price in a § 338 election. The manner of determining the deemed selling price and the basis of the assets that are deemed to have been sold is set forth in Prop. Reg. §§ 1.336–3 and 1.336–4.

Generally, the old subsidiary is treated as having distributed all of its assets to the parent in liquidation before the close of the day in which the qualified stock disposition took place.[93] In most cases, this constructive liquidation will qualify as a § 332 liquidation in which no gain or loss is recognized by the parent or the old subsidiary. The

89   Treas. Reg. § 1.336–4(a).
90   Id.
91   Treas. Reg. § 1.336–1(b)(6)(i).
92   Prop. Reg. § 1.336–2(b)(1)(i)(B)(2), (2)(i)(B)(2).
93   Prop. Reg. § 1.336–2(b)(1)(iii).

parent will inherit all of the tax attributes of the old subsidiary (e.g., its earnings and profits and net operating losses) under § 381. Consequently, the tax consequences of any gain or loss recognized by the old subsidiary on the constructive sale of its assets will be borne by the parent corporation.

Chapter Six

DISTRIBUTION OF STOCK AND SECTION 306 STOCK

Analysis

A. *STOCK DIVIDENDS*

Para.

6.01   Introduction

6.02   The Nature of Stock Dividends

6.03   Historical Background—Eisner v. Macomber

6.04   Section 305—in General

6.05   Stock Dividend Equivalents

6.06   Treatment of a Taxable Stock Dividend

6.07   Basis of Stock Received as a Tax-Free Dividend Under § 305(a)

B.   *PREFERRED STOCK BAILOUTS AND SECTION 306 STOCK*

6.08   Introduction

A. STOCK DIVIDENDS

¶ 6.01 INTRODUCTION

A "stock dividend" refers to a corporation's distribution to its shareholders of shares of the corporation's own stock or rights to acquire its own stock. There is a difference between a stock dividend and a "stock split;" although they are similar in many ways. A stock dividend constitutes a capitalization of the corporation's earnings so that the retained earnings shown on the corporation's balance sheet are reduced by the amount of the stock dividend, and that same amount is added to the balance sheet's statement of the corporation's capital stock. In effect, a stock dividend shifts some of the corporation's retained earnings to its paid in capital, but the corporation's assets continue to be held by it with no diminution.

A stock split also does not cause any change in the assets owned by the corporation. However, in contrast to a stock dividend, a stock split (whether positive or negative) merely changes the number of outstanding shares of the class of stock that was split in such manner that the shareholders continue to own the same percentage of that class of stock; and no change is made to the corporation's balance sheet statement of retained earnings or the aggregate dollar amount of its capital stock. It is the latter aspect of not changing the balance sheet's statement of the corporation's retained earnings that distinguishes a stock split from a stock dividend, but the economic effect of the two types of transactions often is the same.

A stock dividend is subject to special considerations that do not apply to distributions of property in kind. There are compelling reasons not to tax stock dividends unless the transaction is of such nature that a failure to tax it could be abused as a device to avoid dividend income. In Part A of this chapter, we will examine the circumstances in which stock dividends are taxed and those in which they are not. In Part B of this chapter, we will examine circumstances where certain stock received pursuant to a stock dividend (or received in connection with a reorganization or corporate division) is subject to special (generally unfavorable) treatment when disposed of by the shareholder. The stock that is subject to that special treatment on disposition is referred to as "section 306 stock" because it is § 306 of the Code that prescribes its treatment.

¶ 6.02 THE NATURE OF STOCK DIVIDENDS

Unlike ordinary § 301 distributions, a stock dividend does not sever a corporate asset from the holdings of the corporation and pass it to a shareholder as a return on his stock. A stock dividend *may* cause a reallocation of the stockholders' aggregate rights in the corporation, but not all stock dividends have that effect. The fact that the corporation's ownership of assets remains intact after the distribution of the stock dividend and the fact that its net worth is not affected raise a question as to whether, as a matter of tax policy, such distributions should constitute gross income to the shareholder-distributees. A brief history of the tax law's treatment of stock dividends is worth relating.

¶ 6.03 HISTORICAL BACKGROUND— EISNER V. MACOMBER

Congress first sought to treat a stock dividend as gross income to the shareholder in section 2(a) of the Revenue Act of 1916. In *Eisner v. Macomber*,[1] a case involving a proportional dividend of common stock by a corporation that had only common stock outstanding, the Supreme Court held that the congressional attempt to tax stock dividends was void because such a tax would contravene the constitutional mandate that direct taxes be apportioned according to population. In so holding, the Court determined that the

---

[1]   252 U.S. 189 (1920).

receipt of a stock dividend in that case did not constitute "income" as that term is used in the Sixteenth Amendment; and so the tax was not protected by that amendment. In effect, the Court treated the tax as a direct tax on the shareholder's stock; and since not protected by the Sixteenth Amendment and not apportioned among the states by population, it was prohibited by the constitution.

The Court reasoned that the stock dividend in that case did not provide the taxpayer with anything more than she already possessed; her percentage interest in the corporation was the same after the proportional stock dividend as it was before. The effect of the stock dividend was merely to crystallize the corporation's accumulated earnings by converting retained earnings into capital stock. As a consequence of the decision in *Macomber*, Congress excluded stock dividends from taxation in the Revenue Act of 1921.

The Court held that the 16th Amendment applies only when income is severed (i.e., derived) from capital. This severance requirement is referred to as the doctrine of "realization." The vitality of the *Macomber* decision that realization is a constitutional requirement has been widely thought to have dissipated over the years, and most commentators believe that the decision no longer reflects the Court's position and should be disregarded.[2] In general, realization still constitutes a prerequisite to tax incidence, but today the doctrine may be based more on tax policy considerations than on constitutional demands.

¶ 6.04　SECTION 305—IN GENERAL

Prior to the adoption of the 1954 Code, the decisions concerning the taxability of stock dividends had engendered confusion and uncertainty. In the 1954 Code, Congress brought greater clarity and certainty to this area by enacting § 305. Under § 305(a), a corporation's distribution to its shareholders of its own stock or rights to acquire its stock is excluded from the shareholder's gross income unless one of the exceptions set forth in § 305(b) is applicable. This exclusion from gross income applies only to stock distributed to a shareholder *qua* shareholder—i.e., on account of his stock holdings.

The 1969 Tax Reform Act retained the general rule of § 305(a) that gross income does not include distributions of stock or stock rights to shareholders in respect of their stock; but under the amended version of that section, the number and scope of the exceptions to the general rule of tax exclusion were substantially expanded. These exceptions are designed to impose income tax in

---

[2]   See Edwin S. Cohen, et al., *A Technical Revision of the Federal Income Tax Treatment of Corporate Distributions to Shareholders*, 52 Colum. L. Rev. 1, 10 (1952).

most (but not all) situations in which the proportionate interest of the shareholders in the assets or earnings of the corporation is altered. In applying these exceptions, note that a reference in § 305 to "stock" includes rights or warrants to acquire stock and that the term "shareholder" includes a holder of rights, warrants, or convertible securities.[3] If a stock dividend is taxable under one of these exceptions, the amount included in gross income is the fair market value of the distributed stock or stock rights at the time of distribution.[4]

The first of these exceptions, § 305(b)(1), provides that, whenever a shareholder has an election to receive either stock or property, the distribution of stock pursuant to the shareholder's election is treated as a § 301 distribution. This exception applies to a stock dividend distribution if *any one* shareholder had an election to receive either stock or property regardless of whether the distributee himself had such an election; the exception applies irrespective of whether the election was exercisable before or after the declaration of distribution.[5]

Ex. (1)   Y Corporation had 1000 shares of voting common stock outstanding, of which D owned 900 shares and E owned 100 shares. Y had no other shares outstanding. At all relevant times, Y had *e and p* in excess of $200,000. Y distributed an additional 90 shares of its stock to D and offered E the option of receiving either 10 additional shares of Y stock or $10,000 cash. The fair market value of Y's stock was $1,000 per share. E elected to take the 10 shares of stock rather than the cash. Since one of the shareholders, E, had an election to receive property in lieu of the stock dividend for 100% of the stock she received, all of the stock distributed to both shareholders is a § 301 distribution that is taxable as dividend income since Y has ample *e and p*. So, D has $90,000 of dividend income, and E has $10,000 of dividend income.

Ex. (2)   X Corporation had 100 shares of voting common stock outstanding of which A owned 40 shares, B owned 40 shares, and C owned 20 shares. X had no other shares of stock outstanding. A, B, and C are unrelated individuals. X has accumulated *e and p* of more than $50,000. X distributed a stock dividend of ten shares of its voting common stock, and those ten shares were allocated four shares each to A and B and two shares to C. The distributed

---

[3]   § 305(d); Treas. Reg. § 1.305–1(d).

[4]   Treas. Reg. § 1.305–1(b)(1).

[5]   Treas. Reg. § 1.305–2(a).

shares had a value of $1,000 per share. At the time of distribution, A was given the right to have three shares of the stock she received as a dividend redeemed by X for cash for their fair market value; neither B nor C was given any such right. A did not elect to have any of her shares redeemed. X made no other distributions in the year in which the stock dividend was paid. The right of A to have three shares of her stock dividend promptly redeemed is treated as an option to receive cash in lieu of those three shares. Thus, A had an option to receive 75 percent of her stock dividend as cash. So, under § 305(b)(1), 75 percent of the value of the shares of stock distributed to each shareholder is treated as a § 301 distribution to that shareholder.[6] Since X has sufficient *e and p*, all of the § 301 distributions constitute dividend income. A and B each recognized $3,000 of dividend income, and C recognized $1,500 of dividend income.

The second exception to exclusion from income is set forth in § 305(b)(2). Section 305(b)(2) provides that a distribution (or a series of distributions) that has the effect of some shareholders receiving property while others receive an increase in their proportionate interest in the assets or the *e and p* of the corporation will be treated as a § 301 distribution. Thus, where a corporation has two classes of common stock outstanding, each share of which participates equally in the assets and earnings of the corporation, a stock dividend paid on one class will constitute gross income to the recipients if a cash (or property in kind) dividend is paid on the other class of stock.[7]

The applicability of this exception does not depend upon there being a prearranged plan to distribute cash or property to some stockholders and to increase the proportionate interest of other stockholders; it is sufficient that that is the net effect of the distributions.[8] If stock is distributed to some shareholders and cash or property is distributed to other shareholders, and if this results in a change in the shareholders' relative interests in the assets or earnings of the corporation, the exception will apply even though the distributions were not made pursuant to an integrated plan and were

---

[6]   Rev. Rul. 90–68 modifying Rev. Rul. 83–68. In Rev. Rul. 83–68, the corporation was not required to redeem tendered stock but had always done so, and the Service ruled that that was sufficient to trigger the exception. Rev. Rul. 90–68 repudiated that aspect of Rev. Rul. 83–68, but otherwise approved of that ruling's method of applying the exception. Rev. Rul. 90–68 did hold that in appropriate circumstances a consistent pattern of redeeming tendered stock would be sufficient to trigger the exception, but held that the facts of Rev. Rul. 83–68 did not justify an application of the exception.

[7]   Treas. Reg. § 1.305–3(e), Ex.(1).

[8]   Treas. Reg. § 1.305–3(b)(2).

not made simultaneously. If there is a time lag of more than 36 months between the distribution of the cash or property and the distribution of the stock, the exception will *not* apply *unless* both sets of distributions were made pursuant to a prearranged plan.[9]

Ex. (3)   Z Corporation has two classes of stock outstanding—Class A voting common stock and Class B nonvoting common stock. Class A and Class B stock have the same par value, and the classes share in dividend income and liquidation proceeds in ratio to their par values. At all relevant times in this question, Z had ample *e and p.*

In Year One, Z distributed to the shareholders of Class A stock a stock dividend of 100 shares of Class A stock, having a fair market value of $10,000. Z made no distributions to the Class B shareholders in Year One or in a prior year. Z made no distributions to any of its shareholders in Year Two. In Year Three, Z distributed $10,000 cash to the Class B shareholders. When the distribution of Class A stock was made in Year One, there was no plan to make a distribution to the Class B shareholders at a future date. Z made no distribution to the Class A shareholders in Year Three.

The distribution of 100 shares of Class A stock to the Class A shareholders in Year One will constitute a § 301 distribution to those shareholders under § 305(b)(2) and will be treated as a taxable dividend. The Class A shareholders proportionate interest in the earnings and assets of Z were increased by the stock dividend, and cash was distributed to the Class B shareholders within three years of that stock dividend. It does not matter that there was no plan to make the two distributions since they occurred within 36 months of each other.

Note that the Class A shareholders will not know that they recognized $10,000 of income in Year One until the Class B shareholders receive a cash dividend in Year Three.

Section 305(d)(2) treats holders of stock rights or of convertible securities as shareholders for purposes of applying that section. Therefore, payment of a stock dividend to common shareholders will be treated as a § 301 distribution if there is outstanding a debt issue, upon which interest has been paid, which is convertible into shares of common stock unless the convertible debt has an anti-dilution provision so that the number of shares of common stock into which it may be converted are increased to reflect the dilution of common

---

[9]   Treas. Reg. § 1.305–3(b)(4).

shares caused by the stock dividend.[10] If instead of a convertible debt instrument, the corporation had outstanding convertible preferred stock on which cash dividends had been paid, the result would be the same.[11]

Not all distributions of cash to one group of stockholders and stock to another group cause the stock dividends to be taxed under § 305(b)(2). For example, § 305(b)(2) generally is not triggered by distributions of cash in lieu of a fractional share of a stock dividend to which the distributee would otherwise be entitled.[12] The cash paid in lieu of a fractional share usually is treated as a payment in redemption of stock, the consequences of which are determined under § 302. For another example of cash and stock distributions that do not trigger § 305(b)(2) because the stock distribution did not increase the shareholders' proportionate interests in the assets or *e and p* of the corporation, see Treas. Reg. § 1.305–3(e), Ex.(2) and Ex.(3).

Ex. (4)　Y Corporation has two classes of stock outstanding—Class A common stock and Class B preferred stock. The preferred stock, which is not convertible, provides a priority for both dividend and liquidation proceeds, but does not provide for any participation in the corporation's earnings and assets in excess of the preferred stock's preferential rights. In Year One, Y distributed a stock dividend on its Class A stock of one share of Class A stock for each two shares of Class A stock that were outstanding. At the same time, Y paid a cash dividend on its preferred stock. The stock dividend that was paid to the Class A stockholders does *not* constitute a § 301 distribution to them because the stock dividend did not increase their proportionate interest in the assets or earnings and profits of the Y Corporation, and so § 302(b)(2) is inapplicable.[13]

Section 305(b)(2) applies whenever there is property distributed to some shareholders and other shareholders receive an increase in their proportionate interest in the earnings or assets of the corporation. The statute does not state that the value of the property and the increase in proportionate interests in the corporation have to be equivalent. It is an open question whether some rule of proportionality will be applied.

Section 305(b)(3) provides that any distribution in which some common shareholders receive preferred stock while other common

---

[10]　Treas. Reg. § 1.305–3(d), (e), Ex.(4).

[11]　Id.

[12]　Treas. Reg. § 1.305–3(c). See Rev. Proc. 77–41.

[13]　See Treas. Reg. § 1.305–3(e), Ex.(2).

shareholders receive common stock will be treated as a § 301 distribution to all the distributees. The legislative history is rather sparse on this provision, which was evidently designed to require income inclusion in situations where a distribution results in a change of the proportionate interests of the shareholders in the growth of the corporation.

What is meant by common stock and preferred stock in this context? Preferred stock is defined in Treas. Reg. § 1.305–5(a) as stock that, compared to other classes of stock, is limited in its rights and privileges (generally associated with dividend and liquidation priorities) and that does not participate to a significant extent in corporate growth.[14] Even if the stock has a right to participate in earnings and assets above the stock's preference rights, it will be deemed to be preferred stock if the facts and circumstances at the time the stock dividend occurred make it reasonable to conclude that no additional participation will take place.[15] The parties designation of stock as either preferred or common is a factor to be considered but is not decisive of the characterization of the stock.[16] Preferred and common stocks are mutually exclusive categories; so stock that is not preferred is common stock, and vice versa.

For purposes of applying § 306, a related Code section,[17] the Service has ruled that stock (regardless of whether voting or nonvoting) that is subject to a ceiling *either* as to the amount of dividends payable thereon *or* as to the amount it can receive from a liquidation does not qualify as "common stock."[18] It appears likely that that definition will also apply for purposes of § 305. Stock that is not "common" stock will be treated as preferred stock.

The fourth exception is set forth in § 305(b)(4). Section 305(b)(4) treats as a § 301 distribution any distribution made with respect to preferred stock except an increase in conversion ratios to take account of dividends or splits made on the stock into which the preferred may be converted. As noted above, "preferred stock" is defined in Treas. Reg. § 1.305–5(a) as stock that in relation to other classes of stock enjoys certain limited rights and privileges but does not participate in corporate growth to any significant extent. The limitation on participation in growth is the principal feature of preferred stock.[19]

---

[14] For a similar definition of preferred stock, see § 351(g)(3)(A). See also § 305(e)(5)(B).

[15] Treas. Reg. § 1.305–5(a).

[16] See CCA (Chief Counsel Advice) 201236025.

[17] Section 306 is discussed at ¶ 6.08.

[18] Rev. Rul. 79–163; Rev. Rul. 82–191.

[19] See also Treas. Reg. § 1.305–5(d), Ex.(9); Rev. Rul. 79–163; Rev. Rul. 82–191.

Ex. (5)   X Corporation has voting common stock and nonvoting nonconvertible preferred stock outstanding. X distributes 100 shares of preferred stock, having a value of $20,000, to the preferred stock shareholders. The stock dividend to the preferred stock shareholders is a § 301 distribution to them of $20,000.

Section 305(b)(5) makes the disproportionate distribution test of § 305(b)(2) applicable to distributions of convertible preferred stock. In order to avoid treatment as a § 301 distribution, the Secretary of the Treasury or his delegate must be satisfied that the net effect of the transaction will not be a shift in the proportionate interests of the shareholders in the assets or *e and p* of the corporation. The Senate Report and the regulations state that the essential factors in making this determination are the length of time during which the conversion privilege may be exercised and whether the terms of the stock (such as the dividend rate and redemption provisions are consistent with the market since that will affect the likelihood that the conversion right will be exercised.[20] If the period for conversion is relatively short, e.g., four months, the indicated presumption is that some shareholders will exercise their conversion privilege, thereby increasing their interest in the corporation, while other shareholders will not. On the other hand, a conversion period of 20 years raises a presumption that substantially all shareholders will exercise the conversion privilege, and there will be no change in proportionate interests. The regulations merely restate the two extreme examples noted in the legislative history (e.g., four months and 20-year periods in which to convert). Where the line is to be drawn between these two extremes is not indicated either by the regulations or by the legislative history.

¶ 6.05 STOCK DIVIDEND EQUIVALENTS

Congress was aware that § 305(b) does not cover all of the possible corporate transactions in which the proportionate interests of shareholders may be altered. Instead of declaring a stock dividend that would be taxable under § 305(b), a corporation could employ a different technique (such as a recapitalization or a redemption) having the same effect as the type of stock dividend to which § 305(b) applies. In 1969, in anticipation of renewed attacks on the regulations that would be issued to deal with such other transactions, Congress adopted § 305(c), which instructs the Treasury to issue regulations under which a change in conversion ratio, a change in redemption price, a difference between redemption price and issue

---

[20]   Another factor to be taken into account is whether the terms of the stock (such as dividend rate and redemption provisions) are consistent with the market since that will affect the likelihood that the conversion right will be exercised.

price, a redemption that is treated as a distribution to which § 301 applies, or any transaction (including a recapitalization) having a similar effect on the interests of any shareholder shall be treated as a distribution with respect to any shareholder whose proportionate interest in the earnings and profits or assets of the corporation is increased by such change, difference, redemption, or similar transaction.

Note that § 305(c) merely instructs the Treasury to issue regulations that characterize certain types of transactions as a distribution to one or more of the shareholders. Section 305(c) does not treat the constructive distributions as income to the distributee; they will be so treated only if one of the exceptions set forth in § 305(b) applies to the constructive distribution.

While, as to redemptions, § 305(c) was aimed at *periodic* redemptions, potentially it could make all disproportionate redemptions, including isolated transactions, that are treated as § 301 distributions subject to constructive dividend treatment since the percentage interest of a shareholder whose stock is not redeemed is increased by the redemption of the others' stock. The legislative history of the 1969 Act indicates that subsection (c) does not apply to isolated redemptions,[21] and the regulations have excluded isolated redemptions from § 305(c).[22] There are good reasons for imposing constructive dividend treatment on those redemptions that are designed to avoid the election exception of § 305(b)(1),[23] but there is little justification for imposing such treatment on isolated transactions motivated by legitimate goals of business or estate planning; and the regulations do not do so.

Ex. The total outstanding stock of X Corporation is 100 shares of common stock and ten shares of preferred stock. At all relevant times, the fair market value of X's common stock was $10 per

---

[21]   The Senate Committee Report indicated that a corporation's redemption of 15 percent of its shares from a 70 percent shareholder will not cause a 30 percent shareholder to recognize a constructive dividend. S. Rep. No. 552, 91st Cong., 1st Sess. 154 (1969).

[22]   Treas. Reg. § 1.305–3(e), Exs. (10) and (11).

[23]   For example, suppose that a corporation having four common stock shareholders has an optional stock redemption program under which, instead of distributing its *e and p* as dividends, it offers to redeem an amount of its shareholders' common stock, as determined by the corporation's earnings. In that event, a redemption of some shares of the stock of two shareholders who accept the offer and who thereby are deemed to have received a § 301 distribution will cause the other two shareholders whose stock was not redeemed to recognize income from a constructive stock distribution that is treated as a § 301 distribution by § 305(b)(2). Treas. Reg. § 1.305–3(e), Ex. (11). If the redemption of the two shareholders' stock did not constitute § 301 distributions to them, the constructive distributions to the other two shareholders would not fall under § 305(b)(2) and so would not constitute a § 301 distribution to them unless some other event triggered one of the § 305(b) exceptions.

share and the fair market value of X's preferred stock was $50 per share. X had accumulated *e and p* in excess of $10,000. A is the owner of the ten shares of X's preferred. Each share of preferred stock is convertible into five shares of common. At the expiration of each calendar year, the conversion ratio is automatically increased by one share of common for each share of preferred. Thus, at the expiration of each year, A's preferred stock is convertible into ten additional shares of X common stock. The increase in the conversion ratio each year is treated as a stock dividend paid on the preferred stock and so is taxable under § 305(b)(4). A receives a § 301 distribution equal to the fair market value of ten shares of X's common stock at the expiration of each calendar year (i.e., $100 per year). The accumulated *e and p* of X is reduced each year by the constructive $100 § 301 distribution to A. A's basis in his ten shares of preferred stock is increased by $100 (i.e., $10 per share) at the end of each calendar year.

¶ 6.06 TREATMENT OF A TAXABLE STOCK DIVIDEND

When a stock dividend is excluded from § 305(a) because it falls within one of the exceptions set forth in § 305(b), the stock dividend is treated as a § 301 distribution to the distributee. The amount distributed will equal the fair market value of the distributed stock at the date of distribution.[24]

The basis of stock received by a corporate or individual shareholder as a dividend subject to § 301 will equal the fair market value of the stock at the date of distribution.[25]

The accumulated *e and p* of a distributing corporation are reduced by the fair market value of the distributed stock that is taxed to the distributee under § 305(b).[26] A distributee's holding period for stock acquired as a dividend subject to § 305(b) will commence on the day following the date that the dividend was received by the distributee.[27]

Ex. The total outstanding stock of X Corporation was 100 shares of common stock. X had accumulated *e and p* of more than $100,000. A owned 50 shares and B owned 50 shares. The X Corporation declared a stock dividend of one share of $50 par preferred stock for each outstanding share of common. The fair

[24] § 301(b)(1). See also Treas. Reg. §§ 1.305–1(b)(1); 1.305–2(b), Ex.(1).
[25] § 301(d).
[26] Treas. Reg. § 1.312–1(d).
[27] Rev. Rul. 66–7; Rev. Rul. 99–5.

market value of the preferred stock was $50 per share. A was given an option by the X Corporation to receive either the 50 shares of $50 par preferred stock or $2,500 cash, and A elected to take the preferred stock. Under § 305(b)(1), A and B each received a § 301 distribution in an amount equal to the fair market value of the 50 shares of the preferred stock ($2,500) that they received, and the accumulated *e and p* of the X Corporation is reduced by an amount equal to the fair market value of the 100 shares of preferred stock ($5,000). A and B have a basis in the distributed preferred stock equal to the stocks' fair market value at the date of their acquisition, and their holding period for the distributed stock will commence the day after their date of acquisition.

¶ 6.07 BASIS OF STOCK RECEIVED AS A TAX-FREE DIVIDEND UNDER § 305(a)

If a distribution of stock or stock rights ("new stock") is excluded from income by § 305(a), then § 307(a) allocates a portion of the basis of the "old stock" in respect of which the distribution was made to the distributed new stock or stock rights.[28] The basis allocation between the old stock and the new stock (or stock rights) is made according to their respective fair market values determined immediately after the distribution.[29] Where shares of the old stock were acquired at different dates for different costs, the basis of each separately acquired lot of such old stock must be allocated separately to the new stock or rights received thereon.[30]

For purposes of determining whether capital gains or losses recognized on the subsequent disposition of new stock or stock rights acquired in a tax-free distribution under § 305 are long-term or short-term gains or losses, the holding period of such new stock or stock rights includes the period for which the shareholders held the old stock with respect to which the distribution was made (i.e., the holding period of the "old" stock is tacked on to the holding period of the "new" stock or stock rights).[31] However, if stock rights are distributed tax-free under § 305, and the distributee exercises those rights and purchases new stock, the holding period of the purchased

---

[28]   See Rev. Rul. 72–71.

[29]   Treas. Reg. § 1.307–1(a), (b), Ex.

[30]   Rev. Rul. 71–350.

[31]   § 1223(4). Note that there is a possibility that stock rights or stock acquired through the exercise of such rights may constitute section 306 stock. § 306(d); Treas. Reg. § 1.306–3(b).

new stock commences with the date on which the stock rights were exercised.[32]

The method of basis allocation established by § 307 is illustrated by the following example.

Ex. A owned 100 shares of common stock of X Corporation since Year One, and A had a basis of $50 per share (or a total basis of $5,000) in his stock. In Year Eleven, X declared a stock dividend of $5 par preferred stock for each outstanding share of common stock, and A received 100 shares of $5 par preferred stock, which was excluded from A's gross income by § 305. The fair market value of A's common stock immediately after the distribution was $95 per share (a total fair market value of $9,500 for the 100 shares). The fair market value of the $5 par preferred stock at the date of distribution was $5 per share (or a total of $500 for the 100 shares). The $5,000 basis of the common stock is allocated as follows:

Basis of preferred:

$$\frac{500 \ (\text{fmv pref})}{500 \ (\text{fmv pref}) + 9{,}500 \ (\text{fmv com})} \times \ \$5{,}000 = \$250$$

Total basis allocated to preferred or $2.50 basis in each share of preferred stock.

Basis of common:

$$\frac{9{,}500 \ (\text{fmv com})}{500 \ (\text{fmv pref}) + 9{,}500 \ (\text{fmv com})} \times \ \$5{,}000 = \$4{,}750$$

Total basis allocated to common or $47.50 basis in each share of common stock.

With one exception, the allocation of basis between the old and new stock or stock rights is mandatory. The sole exception is when a corporation distributes stock rights, the fair market value of which at the time of distribution is less than 15 percent of the fair market value of the old stock at such time.[33] In this latter event, no basis will be allocated to the stock rights (which will therefore have a zero basis) unless the shareholder elects to allocate basis in the normal manner, and the election can be made only by attaching a statement

---

[32]   § 1223(5).
[33]   § 307(b).

to that effect to the shareholder's tax return for the year in which the rights are received.[34]

B. PREFERRED STOCK BAILOUTS AND SECTION 306 STOCK

¶ 6.08 INTRODUCTION

Section 306, which was first adopted as part of the Internal Revenue Code of 1954, causes part or all of the amount realized from the disposition of certain stock that had been acquired in tax-free transactions, including stock received as a tax-free stock dividend, to be taxable as either ordinary income or as a § 301 distribution, rather than as capital gain. The reason for its adoption was to deal with the then existing potential for using preferred stock as a device to "bail-out" earnings of a corporation in a manner that caused much lower tax consequences to the shareholders than would have been incurred if the earnings were simply distributed to them as dividends. Dividends, of course, usually constitute ordinary income to a shareholder who receives them. Prior to 2003, dividend income was taxed at the same rates as other ordinary income, but that is not the case for qualified dividends from a corporation under current law.

Noncorporate shareholders received tax relief for most dividend income by an amendment made to the 1986 Code by the Jobs and Growth Tax Relief Reconciliation Act of 2003, which added § 1(h)(11) to the Code. Section 1(h)(11) applies capital gain rates to most (but not to all) dividends received by noncorporate shareholders.[35] Moreover, § 306(a)(1)(D) extends that capital gain rate treatment to income recognized on the disposition of section 306 stock. Those amendments have reduced the significance of § 306, but the provision is still important for a number of reasons.

First, not all dividends to noncorporate shareholders qualify for the capital gain rates; and so, for dividends that do not qualify, the pre-2003 circumstances are unchanged.[36] Second, even post-2002 dividends are treated as ordinary income, and there are circumstances where actual capital gain treatment, beyond just the lower tax rate, would be preferable—e.g., where the shareholder has capital losses he would like to deduct.[37] Third, if the shareholder is a corporation, the capital gain rate provision does not apply; and for a disposition other than a redemption, the shareholder's income will not qualify for the dividend-received deduction provided by § 243.

---

[34]   Treas. Reg. § 1.307–2.

[35]   This provision is discussed in ¶ 2.05.

[36]   See ¶ 2.05.

[37]   Id.

Finally, the preferred stock bail-out scheme permits a shareholder to utilize part of his basis in his stock to prevent the recognition of income for some of the money he receives from the corporation; whereas, all of the money he received will be income to him if § 306 applies. In sum, § 306 retains significant continuing vitality.

The nature of the "preferred stock bail-out" scheme and the operation of § 306 are described below. In those descriptions, we will ignore the impact that the 2003 amendment applying capital gain rates to dividends has on the significance of § 306.

Section 306 applies to certain stock referred to as "section 306 stock." Section 306 stock can be acquired as a result of a stock dividend or as the result of a reorganization or division of a corporation.[38] In this section of the book, we will focus on section 306 stock that was obtained through a stock dividend. The consequence of having section 306 stock is the same regardless of whether the stock was acquired in a stock dividend or in a reorganization or division.

If left unchecked, a crafty shareholder of a closely held corporation could abuse the general rule of § 305(a), which excludes from gross income a corporation's distribution of its own stock to its shareholders. For example, in a year prior to 1954 when § 306 was adopted, where A was the sole shareholder of X Corporation, which had accumulated *e and p* of over $150,000, A could have caused X to distribute on A's common stock a dividend of nonvoting preferred stock having a fair market value of $100,000, and A could then sell the preferred stock to B, an unrelated party, for $99,000.[39] X would then redeem the preferred stock seriatim over a five-year period. In effect, A would have withdrawn $99,000 from the corporation, and the excess of that amount over his basis in the preferred stock would be taxed to him at long-term capital gain rates. The cost to A of transmuting the withdrawal of a dividend, then taxed at ordinary income rates, to a capital gain of a smaller amount is the extra $1,000 paid to B by the corporation when the preferred stock is redeemed plus the dividends paid to B on the preferred stock during the five-year period prior to final redemption; and that cost is borne by the corporation without tax consequence to A. Section 306 was adopted to close that loophole.

---

[38]   Certain types of transactions are referred to in tax parlance as "reorganizations," which is a term of art in the tax law. Corporate divisions and reorganizations are discussed in Chapters Eight and Nine.

[39]   Nonvoting preferred stock would be used because its subsequent disposition would not affect the control of the corporation, its terms could be set so as to prevent its participating in corporate income above its preference rights, and the terms could be designed to satisfy the requirements of a potential purchaser of the stock.

In the above example, A adopted a so-called "preferred stock bail-out." The government could attack the transaction as a sham or step transaction, but that contention was not successful in a 1953 case that upheld the taxpayer's use of a bail-out.[40] In *Chamberlin*, the stockholders negotiated the sale of unissued preferred stock to two insurance companies whose investment committees approved the purchase of the stock prior to the date on which the corporation's charter was amended to permit the corporation to issue the preferred stock as a dividend on its outstanding common stock. The terms of the preferred stock were tailored to comply with conditions set by the two insurance companies, and all but a few shares of the preferred stock were sold to the companies within two days after the stock dividend was declared. Pursuant to its terms, the preferred stock was redeemed from the insurance companies seriatim over a 7-1/2 year period. The Sixth Circuit allowed the stockholders to recognize capital gains on the sale of the preferred stock to the insurance companies.

In adopting the 1954 Code, Congress sought to close the "bail-out" loophole, not by taxing stock dividends, but rather by imposing a "taint" on stock in certain circumstances so that the disposition of such "tainted" stock can cause the recognition of ordinary income. Section 306 is the apposite provision of the Code, and that statute provides the "tainted" stock with the generic name "section 306 stock."[41]

¶ 6.08.1 Definition of "Section 306 Stock"

Section 306 stock is stock, including rights to acquire stock, that is described in any one of subparagraphs (1), (2), (3) or (4) below. However, except as provided in § 306(g), stock or stock rights acquired from a corporation will not constitute section 306 stock if no part of the distribution would have constituted a dividend if cash had been distributed in lieu of the stock or stock rights.[42]

(1) *Stock dividend.* Stock (other than common stock issued with respect to common stock) that was distributed to a shareholder is section 306 stock if by reason of § 305(a) any part of the distribution was not included in the shareholder's income.

---

[40]   Chamberlin v. Commissioner, 207 F.2d 462 (6th Cir. 1953).

[41]   The Code expressly designates such stock as "section 306 stock." § 306(c)(1). Preferred stock that meets certain requirements is classified as "nonqualified preferred stock" and is not treated as stock for certain purposes. § 351(g). Unless and until regulations provide otherwise, nonqualified preferred stock will be treated as stock for § 306 purposes and so is subject to that provision. § 351(g)(4).

[42]   Treas. Reg. § 1.306–3(a), (b).

The Commissioner has made clear the Service's view of what the meaning of "common stock" is for purposes of § 306. It has become clear that the crucial factor is the extent to which the stock participates in the corporation's growth.[43] For purposes of § 306, a class of stock that is restricted either as to the maximum amount of dividends payable thereon in a taxable year or as to the extent of its participation in liquidation will not qualify as common stock even if that class of stock is voting stock and even if it is not redeemable.[44]

The Commissioner has applied to § 306 the definition of "preferred stock" set forth in Treas. Reg. § 1.305–5(a).[45] In general, the Commissioner has defined preferred stock as stock that, in relation to other classes of stock, enjoys certain limited rights and privileges (typically relating to dividend and liquidation priorities) but that does not participate in corporate growth to any significant extent. If a class of stock is not preferred stock under the definition adopted in Treas. Reg. § 1.305–5(a), then presumably it will qualify as common stock. The Commissioner's definition of common and preferred stocks has not been tested in litigation; but in view of Treas. Reg. § 1.305–5(a), it appears likely that the Commissioner's position would be sustained if the issue were raised.

Section 306(e)(2) provides that common stock with respect to which the shareholder can convert to preferred stock or into property, regardless of whether the conversion privilege is contained in the stock, is treated as preferred stock.

(2) *Stock (other than common stock) received in a corporate reorganization or division.* Where a shareholder disposes of stock (other than common stock) that he previously received pursuant to a plan of reorganization[46] or pursuant to a tax-free or partially tax-free corporate division,[47] and where gain or loss from the transaction in which the stock was received

---

[43]   Rev. Rul. 82–191.

[44]   Rev. Rul. 79–163. See also Rev. Rul. 82–191.

[45]   Rev. Rul. 75–236.

[46]   "Reorganization" is a term of art defined in § 368(a). See Chapter Nine.

[47]   The stock must have been distributed under § 355 (or under so much of § 356 as applies to § 355). See Chapter Eight.

was not recognized in whole or in part, then the stock will constitute section 306 stock to the extent that the effect of the transaction was substantially the same as a stock dividend (or where the stock was received in exchange for section 306 stock).[48]

(3) *Stock whose basis in the hands of the shareholder disposing of the stock is determined by reference to the basis of section 306 stock.* If a taxpayer obtains stock whose basis is determined by reference to the basis of section 306 stock, the acquired stock will be section 306 stock in the taxpayer's hands.[49]

For example, where a taxpayer exchanges section 306 stock for other stock in a tax-free exchange (e.g., an exchange for the stock of a controlled corporation that is covered by § 351 (see Chapter Seven)), the newly acquired stock will also be section 306 stock in the taxpayer's hands. This provision does not require that the stock received in the exchange be preferred stock, and so it can apply to common stock.

However, this provision does not apply if the section 306 stock was issued with respect to common stock and was subsequently exchanged for common stock in the *same corporation*. In that case, the common stock that was received in exchange will not be treated as section 306 stock.[50]

Also, if a taxpayer receives stock that was section 306 stock in the hands of the transferor, and if the taxpayer's basis in that stock is determined by reference to the transferor's basis, the acquired stock will be section 306 stock in the hands of the taxpayer.[51] Thus, in the case of a transfer of section 306 stock to a controlled corporation in a § 351 exchange for stock of the controlled corporation, both the stock acquired by the controlled corporation and the controlled corporation's stock that the transferor acquired will be section 306 stock.

---

[48]   § 306(c)(1)(B). See Rev. Rul. 77–335.

[49]   § 306(c)(1)(C); Treas. Reg. § 1.306–3(e).

[50]   § 306(e)(1).

[51]   § 306(c)(1)(C); Treas. Reg. § 1.306–3(e).

> If both this paragraph (3) and paragraph (2) are applicable to the same stock, paragraph (2) has priority.[52]

(4) *Stock (other than common stock) of a controlled corporation acquired as part of a § 351 exchange.* When a person transfers property to a controlled corporation in exchange for the latter's stock and when the exchange qualifies for nonrecognition of gain or loss under § 351,[53] any non-common stock received by the transferor will constitute section 306 stock if receipt of money in lieu of that stock would have been treated as a dividend to any extent.[54]

When section 306 stock is included in a decedent's gross estate for estate tax purposes, the stock loses its "taint" and ceases to be section 306 stock.[55] Such stock does not constitute section 306 stock because it does not fall within any of the alternative conditions set forth in § 306(c). Since stock that is included in a decedent's gross estate acquires a basis under § 1014 equal to the fair market value of the stock at the estate tax valuation date, § 306(c)(1)(C) is inapplicable.

In no event will stock issued by a corporation constitute section 306 stock if the corporation has no current or accumulated *e and p* for the taxable year in which the distribution was made.[56] It should be emphasized that this exception to § 306 treatment rests, not merely on the *e and p* at the time of distribution of the stock, but rather on both the accumulated *e and p* and the total amount of the corporation's *e and p* for the year in which the distribution occurred.

Ex. (1) X Corporation, which had substantial *e and p*, had 100 shares of common voting stock outstanding—50 shares of which were owned by A and 50 shares of which were owned by B. X declared a dividend of one share of $10 par preferred stock for each outstanding share of common stock. Accordingly, X distributed 50 shares of preferred stock to A and 50 shares to B. The preferred stock dividend is not taxable to A or B because of § 305(a), but the preferred stock they received constitutes section 306 stock.

Ex. (2) Y Corporation, which had substantial *e and p*, had 100 shares of common stock outstanding—50 shares of Class A

---

[52]   Id.

[53]   See Chapter Seven.

[54]   § 306(c)(3).

[55]   Treas. Reg. § 1.306–3(e).

[56]   § 306(c)(2).

common stock that were owned by Jones and 50 shares of Class B common stock that were owned by Smith. Y distributed 50 shares of $10 par preferred stock to Jones as a dividend on his Class A stock, and Y distributed 20 shares of Class A common stock to Smith as a dividend on his Class B stock. The distributions of stock to Jones and Smith are § 301 distributions taxable to them because of the provisions of § 305(b)(3). Since no part of the stock dividends to Jones and Smith was excluded from their income by § 305(a), none of the stock received by them constitutes section 306 stock.

¶ 6.08.2 Disposition of Section 306 Stock

The tax consequence of a disposition of section 306 stock depends upon whether or not the disposition is a redemption and whether certain exceptions are applicable.

(1) *Not a redemption.* Where a shareholder disposes of section 306 stock in any manner other than where the stock is redeemed, then the amount realized by the shareholder will constitute ordinary income to the extent of the stock's ratable share of the corporation's *e and p* at the time that the stock was distributed to the shareholder. The balance of the amount realized will be treated as a payment for the purchase of the stock so that it will be treated as a return of capital to the extent of the shareholder's basis in the stock and as a gain (typically a capital gain) to the extent it exceeds the shareholder's basis in the stock.[57] While a shareholder can realize a loss on the sale of section 306 stock when the amount realized that exceeds the amount that is treated as ordinary income is less than the shareholder's basis in the stock, the shareholder cannot recognize any of that loss.[58] However, the shareholder's unused basis in the section 306 stock (i.e., the shareholder's basis in that stock in excess of that portion of the amount realized on the disposition that was not treated as ordinary income) will be reallocated back to the stock with respect to which the section 306 stock was issued.[59]

The ordinary income that a shareholder recognizes on the disposition of section 306 stock is

---

[57] § 306(a)(1).

[58] § 306(a)(1)(C).

[59] Treas. Reg. § 1.306–1(b)(2), Ex.(2).

treated as dividend income for purposes of applying the capital gain rate treatment accorded by § 1(h)(11).[60] However, for other tax purposes, unless Treasury specifies otherwise (and it has not yet done so), the ordinary income that the shareholder recognized on the disposition is not treated as a dividend. So, a disposition of section 306 stock by any means other than a redemption (or a constructive redemption) has no effect on the corporation's *e and p*. Also, if a shareholder who sells section 306 stock is itself a corporation, the ordinary income the corporate shareholder recognized will not be treated as a dividend; and so the shareholder will not qualify for the dividend-received deduction provided by § 243.

Ex. (3)   A owned 100 shares of common stock of the X Corporation. A received a tax-free stock dividend of ten shares of preferred stock having a fair market value of $1,000. X made no other distributions that year. The basis of the ten preferred shares (determined under § 307) was $600. The X Corporation had *e and p* in excess of $200,000. A subsequently sold five shares of preferred stock for $630 cash. The five shares of preferred stock's ratable portion of *e and p* at the time of distribution was $500 (i.e., their fair market value). Therefore, $500 of the $630 realized on the sale is ordinary income to A, but it may qualify for capital gain rate treatment under §§ 306(a)(1)(D) and 1(h)(11). The remaining $130 of amount realized is offset against A's $300 basis in the five shares of and is not income to him. Accordingly, A also realized a capital loss of $170, but the loss is not recognized.[61] The $170 of unused basis in the section 306 stock is added to A's basis in his common stock.[62] The *e and p* of the corporation are not reduced.

Ex. (4)   Several years later, A sold his remaining five shares of preferred stock for $1,200. For the same reasons that applied to the sale in Example (3), $500 of that amount was ordinary income; $300 of the amount realized was offset against A's basis in those five shares and was not income to him. The remaining $400 of the purchase price is treated as a capital gain. The $500 of ordinary income that A recognized is treated as dividend income for purposes of

---

60   § 306(a)(1)(D).

61   § 306(a)(1)(C).

62   Treas. Reg. § 1.306–1(b)(2), Ex.(2).

§ 1(h)(11), and likely will qualify for capital gain rates. The *e and p* of the corporation are not reduced.

(2) *Redemptions.* When a corporation redeems section 306 stock from a shareholder, the *total amount realized* by the shareholder constitutes a distribution to him under § 301.[63] Accordingly, the distribution will reduce the corporation's positive *e and p*. To the extent that the § 301 distribution constitutes a dividend, it likely will qualify for capital gain rates under § 1(h)(11).

The amount of ordinary income recognized under § 306 for a redemption of section 306 stock depends upon the corporation's *e and p* in the year of redemption. In contrast, the amount of ordinary income recognized on the sale of section 306 stock depends upon the historical *e and p* of the corporation at the time that the section 306 stock was distributed.

Ex. (5) Z Corporation had 100 shares of Class A common stock outstanding, and those shares were divided equally among D, E, F, and G, its four individual and unrelated shareholders. Each shareholder had held his Z stock for more than three years. Each shareholder had a basis of $24 in each of his shares of Class A stock; so, a shareholder's basis in 25 shares of Class A stock was $600.

As of January 1, Year One, Z had accumulated *e and p* of $1,000; and Z earned no positive or negative *e and p* during Year One. On March 8, Year One, Z distributed one share of Class B preferred stock, having a value of $20 per share, on each outstanding share of Class A stock. So, D, E, F, and G each received 25 shares of Class B preferred stock having a fair market value of $500. The Class B preferred stock constituted section 306 stock. Immediately after the distribution of the stock dividend, the fair market value of each share of Class A stock was $40. So, each shareholder had a basis of $200 in his 25 shares of Class B stock ($8 per share), and each shareholder had a basis of $400 in his 25 shares of Class A stock ($16 per share). Z made no other distributions that year.

On August 5, Year One, Z redeemed the Class B preferred stock that F and G held for which Z distributed $500 cash to each. Z made no other distributions that year. The $500 distributed to F and the $500 to G constituted § 301 distributions to each. Since Z had *e and p* of $1,000, F and

63   § 306(a)(2).

G each had $500 of dividend income. Z's accumulated *e and p* was reduced to zero because of making those distributions. Neither F nor G is allowed to recognize a loss on the redemption.[64] The $200 of basis that F had in his Class B stock is reallocated to F's basis in his 25 shares of Class A common stock; so, F then has a basis of $600 in his 25 shares of Class A stock. Similarly, G's basis in his 25 shares of Class A stock becomes $600.

¶ 6.08.3   Exemption from § 306 Treatment

Under § 306(b), the following transactions are exempted from the reach of § 306:

(1) the redemption or sale of all of the stock of the shareholder in the corporation in termination of his entire stock interests. For purposes of determining whether the shareholder's interest was terminated, the attribution rules of § 318 are applicable; but if the disposition was a redemption, the shareholder may use § 302(c)(2)(A) (the waiver of family attribution provision) and (b)(3) to avoid section 306 treatment.[65]

(2) a redemption of stock pursuant to a complete liquidation.

(3) a redemption of stock held by a noncorporate shareholder where the redemption is made pursuant to a partial liquidation and qualifies as a purchase under § 302(b)(4).

(4) a disposition of stock in which gain or loss is not recognized to the shareholder.

(5) where it is demonstrated to the satisfaction of the Commissioner that both the distribution of the stock and the subsequent disposition or redemption of the stock did not have avoidance of federal income tax as a principal purpose.[66] However, where the stock to which the section 306 was issued is disposed of either prior to or simultaneously with the disposition of the section 306 stock, it is not necessary to establish that the distribution of the section 306 stock did not have a tax avoidance purpose, and the disposition of the section

---

[64]   § 306(a)(1)(C).

[65]   Treas. Reg. § 1.306–2(a).

[66]   § 306(b)(4).

306 stock will ordinarily be treated as not having a tax avoidance purpose.[67]

---

[67] Treas. Reg. § 1.306–2(b)(3).

Chapter Seven

ORGANIZATION OF A CORPORATION

Analysis

Para.

7.01   Introduction

7.02   Basic Rules Apart from § 351

7.03   Basic Overview of § 351(a)

7.04   Basis Limitation Rules

7.05   § 351 Requirements—Business Purpose and Continuity of Interest

7.06   § 351 Requirements—"Persons in Control Immediately After the Exchange"

7.07   § 351 Requirements—the Transferor Must Transfer "Property"

7.08   § 351 Requirements—the "Exchange" Requirement

7.09   § 351 Requirements—Transfers "Solely in Exchange for Stock"

7.10   Contribution to Capital

7.11   Receipt of "Boot," Part I (in General)

7.12   The Receipt of Boot, Part II (Corporate Assumption of Transferor Liability and Netting of Obligations)

7.13   The Receipt of Boot, Part III (Corporate Obligations to Shareholder)

7.14   Overriding § 351

7.15   Non-Statutory Overrides

¶ 7.01 INTRODUCTION

As we discussed in Chapter One, an absolute rule treating corporations as taxable entities distinct from their shareholders would under many circumstances have undesirable "lock-in" effects, deterring people from transferring businesses to the corporate form at precisely the moment when it might be most beneficial for society to have them do so.[1] Section 351 of the Code exists to mitigate that lock-in effect by providing nonrecognition treatment for certain transfers of property to "controlled corporations." It reflects a belief that the tax laws should not impede changes in the form of business

---

[1]   See ¶ 1.03.

operations as long as the requisite continuity of investment is maintained.[2] In this chapter, we explore the manner in which § 351 affects the recognition of gain and loss by shareholders and corporations, as well as the related effects on inside and outside basis.

The Service will not provide a ruling on whether a transaction qualifies for non-recognition under § 351, but the Service will rule on some specific issues within § 351.[3]

In the litigation of issues involving the application of § 351, typically the taxpayer is seeking to have an exchange qualify for nonrecognition under that provision. However, there are circumstances where a taxpayer would benefit if the exchange did not qualify. In such cases, there sometimes is litigation in which it is the Service that is seeking to have § 351 apply, and the taxpayer contends that the exchange is a taxable transaction.

¶ 7.02   BASIC RULES APART FROM § 351

To appreciate the effects of § 351, it is useful to review the tax consequences of interactions between corporations and shareholders apart from § 351.[4] An individual who transferred appreciated or depreciated property to a corporation in exchange for stock or other property would ordinarily recognize a gain or loss to the extent the fair market value of the stock and other property received differed from his basis in the transferred property.[5] The corporation would not recognize any gain or loss on the sale or exchange of its own stock by virtue of § 1032, but it could recognize gain or loss in connection with any other property it transferred to the shareholder in the exchange.[6] If a corporation sells its own debt instrument, it normally does not recognize any gain or loss, since the transaction is treated as a loan.

Both the corporation and the shareholder would have a fair market value basis in the newly received property and the holding

---

[2]   See S. Rep. No. 275, 67th Cong., 1st Sess., 11 (1921), reprinted in 1939–1 C.B. (Pt. 2) 181, 188–89.

[3]   Rev. Proc. 2013–32 (Secs. 2.01 and 5.02).

[4]   For this purpose, we have separated out the discussion on pure contributions to capital (i.e., where the shareholder receives nothing in exchange for the contributed property). See ¶ 7.10.

[5]   § 1001(c). One important exception derives from § 267, which prohibits an individual from deducting a loss recognized on the sale or exchange of property to a corporation in which he owns, directly or indirectly (and after applying certain stock attribution rules), more than 50% in value of the outstanding stock.

[6]   Section 267 denies the corporation a loss deduction on account of a sale or exchange of property with an individual who owns, directly or indirectly (and after applying certain stock attribution rules), more than 50% in value of its outstanding stock.

period for each property would begin on the day after the date of the exchange.[7]

¶ 7.03   BASIC OVERVIEW OF § 351(a)

If a client walked into your office having formed a new corporation by exchanging property for newly issued stock of the corporation, he may have the following six questions on his mind:

(1) Will I recognize a gain or loss on the exchange of property for stock?

(2) Will the corporation recognize gain or loss on the exchange of stock for property?

(3) What is the basis in the newly acquired corporate stock?

(4) What is the corporation's basis in the exchanged property?

(5) What is the holding period in the stock?

(6) What is the corporation's holding period in the exchanged property?

This section will give a basic overview of the answers to those six questions.

If one or more "persons" transfer "property" to a corporation (other than an "investment company") "solely in exchange for stock" in that corporation and they are in "control" of the corporation immediately after the exchange, then those persons do not recognize any gain or loss on the exchange.[8] Under § 1032, the corporation also does not recognize any gain or loss on the sale or exchange of its own stock.[9] Thus, to answer the client's first two questions, when § 351(a) applies, neither the qualifying shareholders nor the corporation will recognize any gain or loss from the transaction.

As to the client's basis questions, when § 351 applies, generally the shareholder's outside basis in corporate stock and the corporation's inside basis in the transferred property are calculated to carry forward any realized-but-unrecognized gains or losses on the exchange. Under § 358, the shareholder's basis in the stock received is generally equal to the basis the transferor previously held in the

---

[7]   Rev. Rul. 66–7; Rev. Rul. 99–5.

[8]   § 351. A transfer to a corporation that constitutes an "investment company" will not qualify for § 351 treatment. § 351(e)(1). This provision is aimed at preventing the use of § 351 to obtain nonrecognition for an exchange of investment stocks and securities for a more diversified portfolio of stocks and securities or similar properties. See Treas. Reg. § 1.351–1(c)(1).

[9]   As noted in ¶ 7.02, this is true whether or not § 351 applies.

property transferred to the corporation, increased by any income the transferor recognized on the exchange, and decreased by the value of any boot received. When the shareholder receives stock of more than one class (such as common and preferred), the basis described above is allocated across stock classes according to the fair market value of the stock of each class received in the exchange.[10] Under § 362, the corporation's basis in the transferred property is equal to the basis that the transferor held in that property prior to the exchange, increased by any gain the transferor recognized on the exchange. As we will discuss in detail later in the chapter, these general basis rules are subject to modification in certain circumstances.

Finally, § 1223 provides the answers to the last two client questions regarding holding period. Under § 1223(1), when calculating the holding period of the corporate stock received in a § 351(a) exchange, a shareholder may include the holding period of the exchanged asset as long as the exchanged asset was either (1) a capital asset as defined in § 1221 or (2) § 1231 property. That is, if the shareholder exchanges an ordinary asset, such as inventory, the shareholder will not be able to tack that asset's holding period and the holding period for the corporate stock received in the exchange will begin on the day following the date of the § 351 exchange. For the transferee corporation, the answer to the holding period question is simpler. Under § 1223(2), when determining the corporation's holding period of the exchanged asset, the transferee corporation *always* includes the period in which the transferor shareholder held the asset (no matter what type of asset it is). That is, the corporation always tacks the shareholder's holding period.

Ex. (1)   A, an individual, forms X Corporation. A contributes Blackacre, unimproved land, in exchange for 100 shares of X voting common stock. Prior to the exchange, A's basis in Blackacre was $40,000. The fair market value of the 100 shares of X stock is $100,000.

Assume the exchange meets the requirements of § 351(a). Under that provision, A does not recognize the $60,000

---

[10]   Treas. Reg. § 1.358–2(b)(2). As we have noted elsewhere in this book, on January 21, 2009, the Treasury and the Service issued proposed regulations that relate to the determination of tax basis in various transactions that include distributions and exchanges involving corporate stock. It is not clear at this writing whether or when these proposed regulations will be finalized, but, if they are finalized, they will apply according to their terms only to transactions that take place after the final regulations are published in the Federal Register. The preamble to the proposed regulations states that the changes that are proposed to the § 358 regulations make "clarifying, but nonsubstantive, modifications." In that light, we have chosen in the discussion in this chapter with respect to tax basis to refer to the relevant provisions of the current regulations and not to include references to the corresponding provisions of the proposed regulations.

realized gain on the exchange. Under § 1032, X does not recognize any gain or loss on the exchange of its own stock. Thus, neither A nor X has any recognized gain or loss on the exchange.

A's basis in the 100 shares of X stock received in the transaction will be $40,000, the same basis that A had in Blackacre at the time of the exchange. X's basis in Blackacre will also be $40,000, the same basis that A had in Blackacre at the time of the exchange.

Unless Blackacre is an ordinary asset, A will be able to include his holding period in Blackacre when determining his holding period in the X stock. When determining its holding period in Blackacre, whether or not it was an ordinary asset to A, X will be able to tack the holding period that A had in Blackacre.

Ex. (2)   Same facts as Example (1) except that, in addition to the 100 shares of X voting common stock, A also receives 100 shares of X nonvoting Class B common stock. The fair market value of the 100 shares of X voting common stock is $80,000 and the fair market value of the 100 shares of X nonvoting Class B common stock is $20,000.

Again, under §§ 351 and 1032, neither A nor X recognizes any gain or loss on the exchange. A's $40,000 basis in the acquired X stock must be allocated between the two classes of stock by fair market value.[11] Thus, the basis in the X voting common stock is:

$$\frac{\$40,000}{\text{(A's old basis)}} \times \frac{\$80,000 \text{ (fmv of X voting common stock)}}{\$100,000 \text{ (total fmv of stock received by A)}}$$

A's basis in the X voting common stock is $32,000 ($40,000 × 80%) and A's basis in the X nonvoting Class B common stock is $8,000 ($40,000 × 20%).

All other results are the same as Example (1). Under § 362, X's basis in Blackacre is $40,000. Under § 1223, assuming Blackacre is not an ordinary asset to A, A will be able to tack the holding period of Blackacre to both classes of X stock received in the exchange. When calculating its own holding period, X will be able to tack A's holding period in Blackacre.

---

[11]   Treas. Reg. § 1.358–2(b)(2).

From a planning perspective, § 351 has two critical effects. First, any gain or loss that has already accrued and might otherwise have to be recognized is deferred (though not forgotten). If the property is appreciated, that effect is to the benefit of the taxpayer. Second, that accrued gain or loss is transferred to the corporation so that it will be subjected to the two-tier tax structure. If one assumes that corporate-level income taxes are ultimately borne by the shareholders, then that effect (in the case of appreciated property) will often be to the detriment of the taxpayer. In circumstances where the transferor will realize a net loss on the exchange, the parties sometimes will seek to avoid § 351 so that the transferor can recognize that loss. Moreover, as we shall see later in this chapter, there are limitations on the extent to which the accrued loss in a depreciated asset can be transferred to the corporation.

Ex. (3)   A owns Blackacre, undeveloped land worth $50,000 in which A has a basis of $10,000. A creates a new corporation X and transfers Blackacre to it in exchange for all 100 shares of X common stock. Under § 351, A recognizes no gain on the exchange. Under § 1032, X recognizes no gain or loss on the exchange. Under § 358(a)(1), A takes a basis of $10,000 in the X shares. Under § 362(a), X takes a basis of $10,000 in Blackacre. If A then sells the X stock for $50,000, A will recognize a gain of $40,000. If X sells Blackacre to Y for $50,000, X will be taxed on the $40,000 gain. The $40,000 gain reduced by X's tax liability will increase X's *e and p.* If X then distributes the after-tax proceeds to a shareholder (including A), the shareholder will be taxed on a dividend distribution as well if X has sufficient *e and p.* If § 351 did not exist, A would have recognized a $40,000 gain on the initial exchange with X, but neither X nor A would have incurred any tax liability on account of the subsequent sale to Y and distribution of the proceeds (assuming X has no other transactions).

¶ 7.04 BASIS LIMITATION RULES

As noted above, the general rule for § 351 transactions is that the corporation's basis in the transferred property is equal to the basis that the transferor held in that property prior to the exchange, increased by any gain the transferor recognized on the exchange. However, that general rule is subject to two important limitations. One limitation, set out in § 362(d), applies only when a corporation assumes liabilities of a transferor in excess of the basis of contributed property. We save discussion of that limitation until we discuss the tax consequences of a corporation assuming liabilities in a § 351 transaction.[12]

The other limitation was enacted in the American Jobs Creation Act of 2004. The purpose of the limitation is to prevent a taxpayer from duplicating a single economic loss and, subsequently, deducting that loss more than once. The following example illustrates how that duplication could occur before the 2004 amendment was adopted.

Ex. (1)   A, an individual, formed X Corporation. A exchanged Blackacre, undeveloped land, for 100 shares of X voting common stock. A's basis in Blackacre was $50,000 and its value was $30,000. The fair market value of the 100 shares of X stock that A received was $30,000.

Under §§ 351 and 1032, neither A nor X recognized any gain or loss on the exchange. Prior to 2004, A's basis in the X stock would have been $50,000 and X's basis in Blackacre would also have been $50,000. If X sold Blackacre to an unrelated party, X would have recognized a $20,000 loss. Also, if A sold the X stock to an unrelated party, A would have recognized a $20,000 loss. Thus, A would have taken a single economic loss (the $20,000 depreciation on Blackacre) and transformed it into two deductible losses (one $20,000 loss for A on the X stock and one $20,000 loss for X on Blackacre).

Congress felt this situation was abusive and enacted § 362(e)(2). Subsection 362(e)(2) applies if the *aggregate* adjusted basis that the transferee corporation would have in the properties transferred by a transferor is greater than the *aggregate* fair market value of the transferred properties (note that the test is applied by using the *transferee corporation's* basis). When § 362(e)(2) applies, the corporation's basis in the transferred property is reduced by that difference. This basis reduction is allocated among the depreciated properties in proportion to their built-in loss immediately before the transfer.[13] As noted below, the transferor and the transferee can elect to reduce the basis of the stock the transferor receives in lieu of reducing the basis of the property that the transferee receives. Unless an election is made, this reduction of basis applies only to the basis of property received by the transferee and does not affect the basis of the transferor in the stock received in the exchange. Note that this rule of basis reduction is applied separately to property transferred by each transferor. Note also that the transferee's basis is reduced for all purposes—not just for measuring a loss. Consequently, if the

---

12   See ¶ 7.12.2.

13   § 362(e)(2)(B).

transferred property appreciates in the hands of the transferee corporation, the transferee may recognize a gain on the disposition of that property.

Ex. (2)   Same facts as Example (1) except that the transfer takes place after 2004 and thus § 362(e) is applicable. The aggregate basis of the property in the hands of the transferee corporation ($50,000) exceeds the aggregate fair market value of the property ($30,000). Unless the election that is described below is made, X must reduce the basis of the property by the difference. Therefore, X's basis in Blackacre would be $30,000. A's basis in the X stock remains $50,000.

Ex. (3)   B, an individual, forms Y Corporation. B exchanges two pieces of undeveloped real estate property, Blackacre and Whiteacre, for 100 shares of Y voting common stock. B's basis in Blackacre is $40,000 and the fair market value of Blackacre at the time of the exchange was $50,000. B's basis in Whiteacre is $70,000 and the fair market value of Whiteacre at the time of the exchange was $50,000.

Section 362(e)(2) is applicable to this exchange. Y's aggregate basis of the transferred properties ($110,000) exceeds the aggregate fair market value of those properties ($100,000). Unless the election described below is made, Y must reduce the basis of the transferred properties by the $10,000 difference. Section 362(e)(2)(B) requires that the reduction be allocated among the transferred property in proportion to their respective built-in loss. Since Whiteacre is the only property with built-in loss, all of the basis reduction will be allocated to that property. Thus, Y's basis in Blackacre is $40,000 and Y's basis in Whiteacre is $60,000. B's basis in the Y stock is $110,000.

The transferor and the transferee corporation can make an election under § 362(e)(2)(C) to have the basis reduction apply to the corporate stock received by the transferor rather than apply to the transferee corporation's basis in the exchanged assets.[14] If such election is made, the transferor's basis in the stock will be the fair market value of the stock.

Ex. (4)   Same facts as Example (3) except that B and Y elect under § 362(e)(2)(C) to have the basis limitation apply to B, the transferor, rather than to Y. Y's basis in the exchanged

---

[14]   In certain circumstances, the transferor can unilaterally make the election. Notice 2005–70. For example, the common parent of a consolidated group can make the election on behalf of all members of the consolidated group.

properties will be determined under the regular § 362 rule. Thus, Y will have a $40,000 basis in Blackacre and a $70,000 basis in Whiteacre. B's basis in the Y stock will be limited to its fair market value at the time of the exchange. B's basis in the Y stock will be $100,000.

¶ 7.05 § 351 REQUIREMENTS—BUSINESS PURPOSE AND CONTINUITY OF INTEREST

The landmark decision of the Supreme Court in *Gregory v. Helvering*,[15] established that a transaction cannot qualify as a "reorganization" for tax purposes unless there was a business purpose for the transaction. The business purpose requirement has been adopted in the regulations defining reorganizations and those determining the requirements for qualifying a corporate division for nonrecognition treatment.[16] The scope of the requirement sometimes has been expanded to prevent favorable tax treatment in circumstances not involving a reorganization or a corporate division. The Service has taken the position that an exchange with a controlled corporation cannot qualify for nonrecognition treatment under § 351 unless there was a business purpose for the transaction.[17] The Service's position on this point is discussed in somewhat more detail at ¶ 7.15.3.

As discussed in Chapter Nine, one of the requirements for a transaction to qualify as an acquisitive "reorganization" is that a "continuity of interest" rule be satisfied. In general, that rule is satisfied if a significant portion of the consideration received in the transaction is stock. It appears unlikely that the § 351 nonrecognition rules have a continuity of interest requirement. In two 1980 rulings, the Service indicated that § 351 has a continuity of interest requirement; but those two rulings were repudiated and revoked four years later.[18]

---

[15]   293 U.S. 465 (1935).

[16]   See Chapters Eight and Nine.

[17]   E.g., Rev. Rul. 55–36; Chief Counsel Advisory (CCA) 200020035. One district court has sustained the Service's position on this issue; although, in that case, the court found that there was a business purpose for the transaction. Caruth v. United States, 688 F.Supp. 1129, 1138–41 (N.D. Tex. 1987), aff'd on a different issue, 865 F.2d 644 (5th Cir. 1989). One federal court of appeals has also expressly endorsed the Service's position. Estate of Kluener v. Commissioner, 154 F.3d 630 (6th Cir. 1998). Some commentators, however, have questioned whether there is an actual business purpose requirement for § 351 transfers. Martin D. Ginsburg & Jack S. Levin, Mergers, Acquisitions, and Buyouts at 9–11.

[18]   Rev. Rul. 80–284 and Rev. Rul. 80–285, both revoked by Rev. Rul. 84–71.

¶ 7.06 § 351 REQUIREMENTS—"PERSONS IN CONTROL IMMEDIATELY AFTER THE EXCHANGE"

Section 351 applies only where an identifiable group of persons (namely, those who transferred properties to the corporation) is in control of the corporation immediately after the exchange. A "person" can be an individual, estate, trust, company, partnership, association, or another corporation.[19] The group of persons can include organizations that are tax-exempt (and therefore may have only a limited interest in whether § 351 applies).

To "control" the corporation, the group of transferors must own stock possessing at least 80% of the total combined voting power of all classes of outstanding voting stock and at least 80% of the total number of shares of all classes of outstanding nonvoting stock.[20] As to the second requirement, the Service has ruled that the control group must hold 80% of the shares of *each class* of nonvoting stock.[21]

If a member of a consolidated group[22] transfers property to a corporation in exchange for stock, in applying the 80% control requirement, the stock owned by all the other members of the consolidated group are treated as held by the transferor.[23]

The reason behind a requirement of 80% control is a sense that nonrecognition treatment should be restricted to situations in which the taxpayer is not significantly altering the substance of his investment. The smaller the taxpayer's stake in the corporation, the more the exchange alters the source of his expected future profits.

Ex. (1)   A, who runs a printing company as a sole proprietorship, owns an offset printing press with a basis of $100 and a fair market value of $5,000. A transfers the press to Monolith Printing, Inc., in exchange for Monolith common stock worth $5,000. A did not previously own any Monolith stock, and the stock he receives represents only 0.001% of the outstanding Monolith common stock. A's expectation of future income from his investment will have little to do with the profitability of the particular press he transferred. It is therefore not surprising that § 351 does not apply to the transfer.

---

[19]   § 7701(a)(1).

[20]   §§ 351(a), 368(c).

[21]   Rev. Rul. 59–259.

[22]   A consolidated group is a group of affiliated corporations that file a consolidated return pursuant to § 1501.

[23]   Treas. Reg. § 1.1502–34.

If the objective is to identify situations in which there is no significant change in the source of a taxpayer's expectation of future profits, then it should not matter whether control is acquired during the exchange. The appropriate question is rather whether control is held immediately after the exchange. Accordingly, if a preexisting shareholder transfers property in a § 351 exchange, all of his stock is counted in applying the 80% control test. It is not necessary to acquire 80% of the stock in the § 351 exchange itself.[24]

In actual practice, § 351 would be of little value if it applied only to situations where a single individual controlled 80% of the corporation. It is usually the case that corporations are formed when several persons pool their resources to pursue a common enterprise. Accordingly, § 351 applies when "one or more persons" make qualifying transfers and constitute a control group. Moreover, the transfers need not take place simultaneously as long as they are made pursuant to a common plan.[25]

¶ 7.06.1 Accommodation Transfers

The Code's acceptance of a "control group" means that taxpayers can alter the source of their expectation of future profits and gain the benefits of nonrecognition treatment, provided that they act in concert to pool their resources with other investors.

The practical decision to apply § 351 to situations where several people act in concert has given rise to a number of problems associated with determining who should be included as a member of the control group. Existing shareholders in the corporation who do not transfer any property pursuant to the exchange are obviously not included (otherwise every transaction would satisfy the control test since all the shares of a control group member would be counted). Similarly, shareholders who make "accommodation transfers" of a nominal amount of property do not have their holdings counted in applying the 80% test.[26] An accommodation transfer is one made for the purpose of qualifying an exchange made by other persons for the nonrecognition provided by § 351.

Ex. (1)   A owns 3000 shares of common stock of the X Corporation, and B owns 1000 shares. X owns assets worth $400,000, and

---

[24]   Treas. Reg. § 1.351–1(a)(2), Ex. (3).

[25]   Treas. Reg. § 1.351–1(a)(1).

[26]   Treas. Reg. § 1.351–1(a)(1)(ii). See Estate of Kamborian v. Commissioner, 469 F.2d 219 (1st Cir. 1972), aff'g Kamborian v. Commissioner, 56 T.C. 847 (1971). The regulation refers to a transferor's transfer of property having a "relatively small value in comparison to the" stock already owned by the transferor or to be received for services. In addition, even if the value of the transferred property is small, the transferor's stock holdings will be counted if the purpose of making the transfer was not to qualify an exchange of other persons for § 351 treatment.

each share of X stock is worth $100. A owns Blackacre and has a basis of $30,000 in it; Blackacre's fair market value is $50,000. A and B adopt a plan whereby A contributes Blackacre to X in exchange for 500 shares of stock, while B contributes $500 cash to X in exchange for 5 shares of stock. After the exchange, A owns 3500 shares, and B owns 1005 shares. If A and B are both counted in the control group, the exchange will qualify under § 351. If it is determined that B's transfer was an accommodation transfer (that is, the transfer by B was made to allow B to be counted as part of the § 351 control group), the exchange will not qualify, since A owns less than 80% of the outstanding stock.

For advance ruling purposes, the Service has created a "safe harbor" to the effect that a transfer of property by an existing shareholder will not be deemed an accommodation transfer if the fair market value of the property transferred is worth at least 10 percent of the fair market value of the stock already owned (or, as we shall see, to be received in exchange for services[27]) by that shareholder.[28]

¶ 7.06.2 "Immediately After"

A problem related to the "accommodation transfers" issue concerns how long members of the control group must continue to hold stock once the § 351 exchange is completed. The statute speaks only of control "immediately after the exchange." But in practice the issue is more complicated.

Ex. (1)   A owns property having a basis of $1,000 and a fair market value of $10,000. Pursuant to a prearranged plan, A transfers the property to Newco in exchange for 50 shares of Newco stock while C transfers $10,000 cash to Newco in exchange for the other 50 shares. A immediately gives her 50 shares to her son B, but she was under no obligation to do so. Courts have tended to hold that such voluntary transfers do not defeat the application of § 351.[29] Note that in such situations no gain would be recognized if the order of transactions were reversed (i.e., if A transferred the

---

[27]   See ¶ 7.07.

[28]   Rev. Proc. 77–37 (Sec. 3.07). While this procedure refers to 10 percent of "stock and securities" already owned (or to be received in exchange for services), it preceded the 1989 amendment to § 351(a) that turned securities into boot—i.e., that deleted securities from the type of property that can be received without causing gain recognition. In light of that 1989 amendment, the safe harbor should be read to refer only to 10 percent of stock, and securities should be ignored for that purpose.

[29]   See, e.g., D'Angelo Assoc., Inc. v. Commissioner, 70 T.C. 121 (1978); Stanton v. United States, 512 F.2d 13 (3d Cir. 1975). But see Fahs v. Florida Mach. & Foundry Co., 168 F.2d 957 (5th Cir. 1948).

property to B, who then exchanged it for Newco stock pursuant to a plan with C.)

Ex. (2)   A owns property having a basis of $1,000 and a fair market value of $10,000. The property was a capital asset in A's hands, and A had held the property for five years before making the exchange. Pursuant to a prearranged plan, A transfers the property to Newco in exchange for 50 shares of Newco stock while C transfers $10,000 cash to Newco in exchange for the other 50 shares. A immediately sells her 50 shares to an unrelated party for $10,000. A was not under a binding obligation to sell the shares at the time of the exchange with Newco.

Although the decisions are not entirely uniform in this area, most courts have not viewed facts such as those in Example (2) as calling for the application of the so-called "step transaction" doctrine in the context of § 351 so as to cause A not to be part of the control group. On the other hand, if A were under a binding obligation to transfer the shares to the unrelated party at the time of the exchange with Newco, the judicial decisions weigh strongly against the application of § 351.[30] Thus, the general view of the judicial decisions is that the control group is broken when the subsequent disposition of stock either is pursuant to a legally binding commitment or is so economically interdependent with the transfer as to make the transfer to the corporation economically fruitless without the disposition.[31] The argument is that viewing the transactions as a whole (rather than each step independently) in such circumstances demonstrates that the persons transferring property (A and C) are not in control of the corporation after the exchange (C and the unrelated party are in control of the corporation).[32]

---

[30]   See, e.g., American Bantam Car Co. v. Commissioner, 11 T.C. 397 (1948), aff'd per curiam, 177 F.2d 513 (3d Cir. 1949). The Service has taken a more aggressive view in its revenue rulings, holding that a transfer of stock pursuant to any preconceived plan is sufficient to violate the "immediately after" requirement. Rev. Rul. 54–96, modified on other grounds by Rev. Rul. 56–100. However, the great weight of judicial authority is not consistent with that aggressive view; indeed, the Service itself has been known to rely on such judicial authority when it is seeking to rebut a taxpayer argument that § 351 does not apply to a transaction because of pre-planned disposition of stock following an asset transfer to a corporation.

[31]   Nevertheless, the Commissioner has ruled that the "immediately after the exchange" test is not violated if a partnership incorporates by transferring its assets to a corporation in exchange for stock and then immediately distributes that stock to its partners. Rev. Rul. 84–111, revoking and superseding Rev. Rul. 70–239. Similarly, the test is not violated when a business goes public by issuing the bulk of its stock to an underwriter who promptly resells the stock to the public. Treas. Reg. § 1.351–1(a)(3).

[32]   There is a possible argument that, in light of changes in the application of the doctrine of the "continuity of proprietary interest" in the reorganization area, one could question whether a transferor's prompt disposition of the transferee corporation's

In Rev. Rul. 80–24, the Service ruled that if a purported § 351 transaction is an integral part of a larger transaction that was attempted to be a tax-free reorganization under § 368 but failed to qualify as such, the initial exchange did not qualify for § 351 treatment. In Rev. Rul. 84–71, the Service revoked Rev. Rul. 80–24 and repudiated its holding. The Service ruled that the initial transaction is not disqualified for § 351 by being an integral part of a failed attempt to qualify a larger transaction as a reorganization under § 368.

¶ 7.07 § 351 REQUIREMENTS—THE TRANSFEROR MUST TRANSFER "PROPERTY"

The nonrecognition rule of § 351 applies only to "property" that is transferred to the corporation in exchange for stock. "Property" has been construed to include most items of value that would give rise to enforceable property rights. For example, "property" includes cash, accounts receivables, partnership interests, stock, and securities. Still, there are several significant exceptions.

Perhaps most significantly, services rendered to or for the benefit of the corporation are not "property."[33] Thus, a transferor who receives stock in exchange for "sweat equity" must recognize compensation income to the extent of the value of any stock or other property received for those services. Similarly, a transferor who transfers *only* services (or services and only a nominal amount of property[34]) is not counted as a member of the control group.[35] This rule is usually explained as reflecting a concern that taxpayers might otherwise use § 351 transactions to transform ordinary income into capital gains. It is sometimes difficult to distinguish a transfer of property from a transfer of services, especially where a property owner has worked to increase its value before or in the course of transferring it to a corporation.[36]

The Service takes the position that interests in intellectual property and intangibles do not constitute "property" for purposes of

stock should have any effect on the qualification of the exchange for nonrecognition under § 351. For a detailed discussion of that argument, see Corporate Income Taxation Hornbook at 281–284.

[33]   § 351(d)(1); Treas. Reg. § 1.351–1(a)(1)(i).

[34]   The accommodation transfer rules are discussed in ¶ 7.06.1.

[35]   Treas. Reg. § 1.351–1(a)(1)(ii).

[36]   See, e.g., James v. Commissioner, 53 T.C. 63 (1969)(holding that a taxpayer who transferred an option to purchase a tract of land, together with a loan commitment, to his controlled corporation was transferring "services"). Compare United States v. Stafford, 727 F.2d 1043 (11th Cir. 1984)(a financing institution's unenforceable letter of intent is "property" that may be exchanged for a partnership interest without recognition of gain, under § 721); Rev. Rul. 64–56 (demonstrating how to use the transferred property is not a "service" requiring separate taxation).

§ 351 unless the transferor transfers "all substantial rights" in a way that "would constitute a sale or exchange of property rather than a license."[37] At least one court has rejected the narrow "sale or exchange" test, upholding the application of § 351 to the transfer of a royalty-free nonexclusive license to make, use, and sell herbicides under certain patents.[38]

¶ 7.08 § 351 REQUIREMENTS—THE "EXCHANGE" REQUIREMENT

When a transferor gives a corporation only a part of a larger bundle of economic rights, the Service sometimes contends that the transferor has not given "property" to the corporation. In order for that contention to be determinative, one must also conclude that the transfer does not constitute an "exchange" of the *larger* bundle of rights. The Service has tended to conflate the two inquiries, suggesting that, *if* there is no exchange of the larger bundle of rights, *then* what is transferred is not "property." One court rejected that approach, concluding that once one had determined that the license at issue was "property," it was but a short step to find an "exchange," since the taxpayer "handed over something of value and received stock in return."[39]

A complementary question is whether an "exchange" exists for purposes of § 351 if the transferors receive no stock at all in return for their contributions and the shareholders' contributions are made in proportion to their stock interests.

Ex. A owns 70 shares of common stock in X corporation; B owns the remaining 30 shares. A transfers land worth $70,000 and having a basis of $10,000 to X at the same time that B transfers $30,000 cash. If X were to issue another 70 shares to A and 30 shares to B, § 351 would apply. Does § 351 apply if X does not issue any new stock at all? In *Lessinger v. Commissioner*,[40] the Second Circuit, altering its previous position, held that § 351 does not require the parties to undertake a "meaningless gesture."[41]

Even in the absence of § 351, a voluntary contribution of appreciated property to the capital of a corporation would ordinarily not trigger any gain for either the transferor or the corporation.[42]

---

[37] Rev. Rul. 71–564, amplifying Rev. Rul. 64–56. See also Rev. Rul. 69–156.

[38] E. I. Du Pont de Nemours & Co. v. United States, 471 F.2d 1211 (Ct. Cl. 1973).

[39] Id.

[40] 872 F.2d 519 (2d Cir. 1989).

[41] See also Utley v. Commissioner, 906 F.2d 1033 (5th Cir. 1990); Jackson v. Commissioner, 708 F.2d 1402, 1405 (9th Cir. 1983).

[42] See ¶ 7.10 for a discussion of contributions of capital. There are circumstances where the characterization of a transaction as a constructive § 351 exchange, instead

The term "exchange" has not been construed to require stock to be issued in proportion to the value of the property received from the members of the control group.[43] If stock is issued disproportionately, however, any excess may be treated as compensation for services or as compensation or a gift between shareholders.[44]

There are circumstances where recharacterizing a transaction with a corporation (such as a contribution to the capital of a corporation) as a § 351 exchange can be disadvantageous to the transferor. Consider the following example.

Ex. Sheila, the sole shareholder of Bilt Rite corporation, "sold" appreciated property to Bilt Rite for a bargain price that was less than Sheila's basis in the property. The price paid by Bilt Rite was paid in cash. If treated as a bargain sale and a contribution to Bilt Rite's capital of the value of the property in excess of the amount paid by Bilt Rite, Sheila would not recognize any income. If, instead, the transaction were recharacterized as a constructive § 351 exchange in which the cash paid by Bilt Rite constituted boot, Sheila would recognize income under § 351(b).[45]

¶ 7.09 § 351 REQUIREMENTS—TRANSFERS "SOLELY IN EXCHANGE FOR STOCK"

Section 351(a) applies only to transfers of property "solely in exchange for stock." Any property other than the transferee's stock that is received by the transferor is known as "boot." We shall discuss the consequences of receiving boot in the next section. In this section, we shall first consider how stock and boot are to be distinguished.

Before October 3, 1989, "securities" of the transferee corporation were not treated as "boot," but were instead treated in the same manner as stock and therefore did not trigger the recognition of gain. While the term "securities" was not defined by statute, it was understood to include debt instruments that reflected a permanent or long-term interest in the corporation but still did not rise to the level of "equity."[46] Thus, notwithstanding the different tax treatment given "debt" and "equity" in other provisions of the Code, certain forms of long-term debt were treated in the same way as equity under § 351. However, the Omnibus Budget Reconciliation Act of 1989[47]

---

of as a contribution to capital, can be disadvantageous. See the second Example in the text above.

[43]   See Treas. Reg. § 1.351–1(b)(1); Weisbart v. Commissioner, 79 T.C. 521 (1982).

[44]   § 351(h).

[45]   See ¶ 7.11, infra.

[46]   See Rev. Proc. 94–3 Sec. 4.01(30).

[47]   Pub. L. No. 101–239, 103 Stat. 2106.

deleted the term "securities" from § 351(a), so that all property other than "stock" is now treated as "boot."[48]

The statute does not define what is meant by "stock," but it is clear that it encompasses both common and preferred stock (other than "nonqualified preferred stock," which is discussed in ¶ 7.11.1) whether voting or nonvoting. To qualify, the stock must be stock of the transferee corporation itself and not of an affiliate. Stock rights and warrants do not qualify.[49] However, a nonassignable contingent right to acquire additional shares in the transferee corporation can constitute stock.[50]

Corporate debt may be treated as stock when a debt instrument bears too many of the characteristics of equity investment. Section 385 authorizes Treasury to promulgate regulations designating when a debt instrument will be treated as stock and lists five factors which may be included in those regulations. A debt instrument that is treated as stock is sometimes referred to as hybrid stock. The most important factor in determining whether a debt is hybrid stock is whether the corporation is thinly capitalized—that is its debt obligation is many times greater than its capital (a so-called high debt-capital ratio).Some other factors are whether the debt is convertible to stock and whether the debt is subordinated to other debts of the corporation.

¶ 7.10   CONTRIBUTION TO CAPITAL

If a shareholder transfers appreciated property to a corporation and receives nothing in exchange, that will ordinarily be treated as a "contribution to capital." While the appreciation will not give rise to any income for the transferor since he receives nothing in exchange, neither will the transfer of the property give rise to a deductible loss since the contribution will increase the value of his stock.[51] Instead, the transferor's basis in that stock will be increased by his basis in the transferred property.[52] Under § 118, the corporation will be exempt from taxation on the contribution to capital, and will take a basis in the property equal to the transferor's old basis in that property.[53]

---

[48]   Omnibus Budget Reconciliation Act of 1989 § 7203, 103 Stat. at 2333.

[49]   Treas. Reg. § 1.351–1(a)(1).

[50]   See Hamrick v. Commissioner, 43 T.C. 21 (1964). Stock that is placed in escrow under conditions that might require it to be returned to the transferee corporation may also qualify as "stock." See Rev. Proc. 84–42 Sec. 2.02.

[51]   § 263(a)(1).

[52]   § 1016(a)(1).

[53]   § 362(a). Since the contributed property is appreciated, the loss limitation rules described in ¶ 7.04 are not applicable.

If the net adjusted basis of the property contributed by a person to a corporation is greater than the net fair market value of the contributed properties, the limitation on basis described in ¶ 7.04 applies to reduce the corporation's basis in the property.[54] As explained in ¶ 7,04, unless an election is made, the corporation's basis in property that otherwise would have a built-in loss is reduced.

As noted in ¶ 7.08, what purports to be contributions to capital may be recharacterized as a § 351 exchange if the contributions are made in the same proportion as the stock of the transferee corporation is held by its shareholders. In such a case, any cash or property in kind received by a transferor might be treated as boot.

¶ 7.11 THE RECEIPT OF "BOOT," PART I (IN GENERAL)

While § 351(a) provides nonrecognition treatment for transactions in which property is transferred "solely" in exchange for stock,[55] § 351(b) extends partial nonrecognition treatment to transactions that would satisfy § 351(a) were it not for the fact that the transferor shareholder also received property other than stock ("boot"). Specifically, § 351(b) provides that under such circumstances no loss to the recipient is recognized, and gain is recognized only to the extent of the value of the boot received.

The presence of boot in a § 351 exchange influences the calculation of outside and inside basis. The shareholder takes a basis in the non-cash boot property equal to its fair market value.[56] The shareholder's basis in stock received from the corporation is equal to his basis in the transferred property, increased by the amount of gain recognized, and decreased by the amount of money received and the fair market value of any non-cash boot received.[57] The corporation's basis in the transferred property is equal to the basis that the transferor held in that property prior to the exchange, increased by any gain the transferor recognized on the exchange.[58]

In theory, the boot indicates the extent to which the taxpayer has taken advantage of the exchange to "cash out" appreciation in the transferred property. If one part of the transferred property's value corresponds to the transferor's basis in that property and the remainder of the transferred property's value reflects unrealized

---

[54]   § 362(a), (e).

[55]   Other than nonqualified preferred stock discussed in ¶ 7.11.1.

[56]   § 358(a)(2).

[57]   § 358(a)(1).

[58]   § 362(a). Recall, however, the basis limitations rules discussed in ¶ 7.04. Also, note that basis limitation rules may apply when the gain recognized by the transferor is attributable to the corporation's assumption of a liability. See ¶ 7.12.2.

appreciation, the effect of § 351(b) is to treat *all* of the boot as a cashing out of unrealized appreciation and none of it as a recovery of initial investment. Note the parallel with the treatment of dividends on corporate stock discussed in Chapter Two.[59]

Ex. (1) A is the sole shareholder of X Corporation. A owns unimproved Blackacre in which he has a basis of $30,000. The fair market value of Blackacre is $55,000. A transfers Blackacre to X in exchange for preferred stock of X having a value of $35,000, a 10-year bond of X having a value of $5,000, $3,000 in cash, and common stock of the Z corporation having a value of $12,000. The preferred stock is not nonqualified preferred stock.

A realizes a gain of $25,000 on the exchange. Since the $5,000 bond, the $3,000 cash, and the $12,000 in stock in the Z corporation are boot, A recognizes a gain of $20,000.

A takes a basis of $5,000 in the bond and a basis of $12,000 in the Z stock. A's basis in the preferred stock of X is $30,000 (the $30,000 basis in the property that A transferred, increased by the $20,000 gain that A recognized, and reduced by the $20,000 in boot that A received).

X takes a basis in Blackacre equal to $50,000 (A's $30,000 basis in Blackacre, increased by the $20,000 gain that A recognized).

Ex. (2) The same facts as in Example (1), except that A had a basis of $45,000 in Blackacre. A realizes a gain of $10,000 on an exchange in which he receives $20,000 in boot. He recognizes a gain of $10,000.

Once again, A takes a basis of $5,000 in the bond and a basis of $12,000 in the Z stock. A's basis in the preferred stock of X is $35,000 (the $45,000 basis in the property that A transferred, increased by the $10,000 gain that A recognized, and reduced by the $20,000 in boot that A received).

X takes a basis of $55,000 in Blackacre (A's $45,000 basis, increased by the $10,000 gain that A recognized).

Ex. (3) The same facts as in Example (1), except that A had a basis of $65,000 in Blackacre. A realizes a loss of $10,000 on an

---

[59] But note also the stark contrast with the treatment of nonrecourse loans secured by appreciated property (where taxpayers may cash out even *more* than their initial investment without recognizing gain, ending up with nonrecourse liabilities in excess of basis).

exchange in which he receives $20,000 in boot. He recognizes no gain or loss.

A's basis in the boot is as before. The parties did not make an election under § 362(e)(2)(C) to limit A's basis in the X stock he received. A's basis in the X preferred stock is $45,000 (his former $65,000 basis in Blackacre, reduced by $20,000 in boot received). Under the basis limitation rule of § 362(e)(2),[60] X takes a basis of $55,000 in Blackacre. However, if the parties did make an election under § 362(e)(2)(C), X would have a basis of $65,000 in Blackacre; and the election would limit A's basis in the preferred stock to its fair market value of $35,000.

When a shareholder transfers several assets to a corporation in exchange for the corporation's stock plus boot, several questions are presented. Are gains and losses netted against one another? How is the boot allocated? How is the gain characterized? Consider the following example:

Ex. (4)   B is the sole shareholder of Z Corporation. B owns unimproved Whiteacre in which he has a basis of $14,000. The fair market value of Whiteacre is $8,000. B also owns 100 shares of common stock of the publicly held Y corporation in which he has a basis of $6,000. The fair market value of that stock is $16,000. B transfers Whiteacre and the Y stock to Z in exchange for 150 shares of Z common stock (worth $15,000) and $9,000 in cash.

In tabular form, Example (4) looks like this:

Asset	B's Basis	FMV	Realized Gain (or Loss)
Whiteacre	$ 14,000	$ 8,000	($ 6,000)
Y Stock	6,000	16,000	10,000

The first question is whether B can net out the gain and loss on Whiteacre and the Y Stock to recognize a net gain of $4,000. The Commissioner has ruled that gains and losses may not be netted under § 351, so that (by virtue of § 351(b)(2)) the loss on Whiteacre must go entirely unrecognized.[61]

The second question is how much gain B must recognize on account of the $10,000 gain realized on the Y stock. In other

---

[60]   See ¶ 7.04.
[61]   Rev. Rul. 68–55.

words, how much of the $9,000 in boot should be allocated to the Y stock and how much (if any) should be allocated to Whiteacre? In Rev. Rul. 68–55, the Commissioner ruled that stock in the transferee corporation and boot should each be allocated among the transferred assets according to the fair market values of the transferred assets at the time of the exchange. In 2009, Treasury promulgated Prop. Reg. § 1.351–2(b) which adopts the same approach as set forth in Rev. Rul. 68–55. The Y stock's fair market value of $16,000 constitutes two thirds of the total fair market value of the assets transferred by B. Consequently, two thirds of the Z stock (worth $10,000) and two thirds of the boot (worth $6,000) are allocated to the transfer of the Y stock. Out of the $10,000 gain realized on the transfer of the Y stock, B thus recognizes a gain of $6,000 (the amount of boot allocated to the Y stock).

A third question concerns how the gain should be *characterized*—to what extent is it ordinary income, to what extent capital gain? In general, the gain's character is determined by the character of the asset transferred. Thus, gain recognized on account of the transfer of a capital asset is characterized either as long-term or short-term capital gain, depending on the transferor's holding period. But this general rule is overridden in a variety of situations. Gain recognized on account of the transfer of depreciable property is ordinary income to the extent required by § 1245 or § 1250 (depreciation recapture provisions). Similarly, gain recognized on certain transfers of property that will be depreciable *in the hands of the corporation* may be recharacterized as ordinary income by § 1239 (dealing, *inter alia*, with certain transfers of property by an individual who, directly or indirectly, is deemed to own more than 50% in value of the corporation's outstanding stock).[62]

¶ 7.11.1 Nonqualified Preferred Stock

The Taxpayer Relief Act of 1997 characterized a certain type of preferred stock as "nonqualified preferred stock."[63] Preferred stock that does not constitute nonqualified preferred stock (NQPS) is sometimes referred to as "qualified preferred stock" (QPS). Nonqualified preferred stock is preferred stock, defined in the provision as stock that is limited and preferred as to dividends and

---

[62]   See ¶ 7.14.2.
[63]   § 351(g)(2).

does not participate in corporate growth to any significant extent,[64] in which one of the following four conditions exists:

(i)   the holder of the stock has the right to require the issuing corporation (hereafter referred to as the "issuer") or a related person[65] to redeem or purchase the preferred stock (in other words, the holder has a "put");

(ii)   the issuer or a related person is required to redeem or purchase the preferred stock;

(iii)   the issuer or a related person has the right to redeem or purchase the preferred stock, and as of the date on which the preferred stock was issued, it is more likely than not that such right will be exercised; or

(iv)   the dividend rate on the preferred stock varies in whole or in part (directly or indirectly) with interest rates, commodity prices, or similar indices.

Conditions (i), (ii), and (iii) above apply only if the right or obligation referred to therein may be exercised within 20 years after the issue date of the preferred stock, and if, as of the issue date, such right or obligation is not subject to a contingency that makes remote the likelihood of such redemption or purchase. Moreover, in the following circumstances, a right or obligation that otherwise met the conditions of (i), (ii), or (iii) above will not satisfy those conditions and so will not classify stock as nonqualified preferred stock:

(1)   if the right or obligation refers to preferred stock that was transferred in connection with the performance of services for the issuer or a related person (and if the stock constitutes reasonable compensation for those services) and it may be exercised only upon the holder's separation from the service of the issuer or a related person; or,

(2)   if the right or obligation may be exercised only upon the death, disability, or mental incompetency of the holder.[66]

---

[64] § 351(g)(3)(A). There must be a real and meaningful likelihood of the shareholder actually participating in the earnings and growth of the corporation. This definition of preferred stock is similar to the one employed in other parts of the Code. For example, see the definition of preferred stock in the regulations dealing with stock dividends. Treas. Reg. § 1.305–5(a).

[65] For purposes of NQPS, a person shall be treated as related to another person if they bear a relationship to such other person described in §§ 267(b) or 707(b).

[66] This exception will not apply if the stock that was either relinquished or acquired in the exchange is either (1) stock of a corporation whose stock is readily

If a transferor, in an exchange that otherwise would have qualified for nonrecognition treatment under § 351(a), receives nonqualified preferred stock of the transferee corporation in the exchange, the consequences depend upon whether the transferor also received other stock of the transferee corporation. If the transferor received both nonqualified preferred stock and other stock of the transferee corporation (i.e., stock that is not nonqualified preferred stock), the nonqualified preferred stock is treated as boot, and so the provisions of § 351(b) will apply to the exchange. On the other hand, if the transferor receives no stock of the transferee corporation other than nonqualified preferred stock, then no part of § 351 applies to the exchange; instead, the exchange is treated as an ordinary taxable exchange.

It is important to note that, although nonqualified preferred stock is treated as boot, the Conference Report for the Taxpayer Relief Act of 1997 stated that, unless and until regulations are promulgated that provide otherwise, the nonqualified preferred stock will nevertheless be treated as outstanding stock for purposes of determining the control requirements of §§ 351 and 368(c).[67] Thus, unless and until such regulations are issued, the transferors of property must hold at least 80% of the transferee corporation's nonqualified preferred stock to satisfy the control requirement of § 351(a).

Ex. (1) Individual A transferred undeveloped Land, in which A had a basis of $70,000 and which had a fair market value of $120,000, to the newly created X Corporation. A had held the Land as an investment for more than 5 years before the exchange with X took place. At the same time as A's exchange, each of three other individuals transferred property with a fair market value of $100,000 to X. Except for the nonqualified preferred stock rules, the exchanges would all qualify for nonrecognition under § 351(a). Each of the four transferors received 100 shares of voting common stock of X. The voting common stock of X had a fair market value of $1,000 per share. In addition to the common shares, A received 20 shares of preferred stock of X that had a fair market value of $1,000 per share (i.e., $20,000 for the 20 shares). The terms of the preferred stock require X to redeem those 20 shares for their par value 10 years after

tradable on an established securities market or (2) stock of any other corporation if such exchange is part of a transaction in which such corporation will become a corporation that has stock readily tradable on an established securities market. § 351(g)(2)(C).

[67] H.R. Rep. No. 105–220. 105th Cong., 1st Sess., (1997), at p. 545.

their issue date. The preferred stock constitutes nonqualified preferred stock within the meaning of § 351(g).

Since the nonqualified preferred stock that A received is treated as boot, § 351(b) controls the tax consequences that A incurred on the exchange. A realized a gain of $50,000 on the exchange. Under § 351(b)(1), A will recognize his realized gain ($50,000) but only up to the extent of the amount of boot he received ($20,000). So, A recognized a gain of $20,000 on the exchange. Presumably, the gain will be either a long-term capital gain (most likely) or a § 1231 gain.

A will have a basis in the 20 shares of nonqualified preferred stock that he received that is equal to that stock's fair market value since the preferred stock is treated as boot.[68] So, A will have a basis of $20,000 in the 20 shares of preferred stock that he received, which gives him a basis of $1,000 per share in those shares. A's basis in the 100 shares of common stock that he acquired equals his basis in the Land ($70,000) increased by the gain recognized ($20,000), and reduced by the amount of boot he received ($20,000).[69] So, A has a basis of $70,000 in his 100 shares of common stock, or $700 per share. X's basis in the Land is equal to A's basis ($70,000) plus any gain recognized by A on the exchange ($20,000).[70] So, X has a basis of $90,000 in the Land.

A's holding period for the 100 shares of common stock that he acquired includes the 5-year period that he held the Land, assuming, as seems likely, that the Land was a capital asset or a § 1231 asset in A's hands.[71] A's holding period for the 20 shares of preferred stock that he acquired in the exchange begins on the day following the date on which the exchange took place. X's holding period for the Land it acquired from A includes the 5-year period that A held the Land.[72]

Ex. (2) The same facts as those stated in Example (1) except that A had a basis of $180,000 in the Land, and A received no common stock in the exchange. Instead, A received 120 shares of X's preferred stock, having a value of $1,000 per

---

[68]   § 358(a)(2).
[69]   § 358(a)(1).
[70]   § 362(a).
[71]   § 1223(1).
[72]   § 1223(2).

share. The preferred stock constituted nonqualified preferred stock. A realized a loss of $60,000 on the exchange. Since A did not receive any stock of X that was not nonqualified preferred stock, the provision of § 351(g)(1)(B), which would treat the preferred stock as boot to which § 351(b) applies, is inapplicable. Instead, only the provision of § 351(g)(1)(A), which prevents the nonrecognition of § 351(a) from applying, is operative. Consequently, § 351 does not apply to A at all, and so A is not prevented from recognizing the $60,000 loss he incurred on the exchange. The exchange is treated as a taxable exchange to which no nonrecognition rules apply. Since A does not own more than 50% of the value of X's outstanding stock, the deduction denial provision of § 267(a)(1) and (b)(2) is inapplicable, and A can deduct the $60,000 loss he recognized on the exchange.

¶ 7.11.2   Controlled Corporation's Recognition of Gain or Loss

Section 351(f) provides that the provisions of § 311 will control the determination of whether a controlled corporation recognizes a gain or loss on the transfer of non-cash boot as part of a § 351 exchange. Under § 311(a), a controlled corporation will not recognize a loss on transferring depreciated property that constitutes boot; but a controlled corporation will recognize gain under § 311(b) on the transfer of appreciated boot unless the boot is an obligation of the controlled corporation (i.e., a debt instrument of the controlled corporation) or is nonqualified preferred stock. Section 1032 precludes a corporation's recognition of gain or loss on the disposition of its own stock. Unless and until regulations provide otherwise, nonqualified preferred stock will be treated as stock for purposes of § 1032. In the authors' view, it is unlikely that Treasury will promulgate regulations excluding nonqualified preferred stock from § 1032.

¶ 7.12   THE RECEIPT OF BOOT, PART II (CORPORATE ASSUMPTION OF TRANSFEROR LIABILITY AND NETTING OF OBLIGATIONS)

In an ordinary exchange between A and B, if B accepts property from A subject to a liability (such as a mortgage), the principal amount of the liability is treated as consideration paid to A.[73] In *United States v. Hendler*,[74] the Supreme Court held that, in the

---

[73]   E.g., Crane v. Commissioner, 331 U.S. 1 (1947).

[74]   303 U.S. 564, reh. denied, 304 U.S. 588 (1938).

context of an otherwise nonrecognition exchange, such consideration should be treated as boot. Congress responded to *Hendler*, however, by enacting § 112(k) of the Internal Revenue Code of 1939,[75] the predecessor to what is now § 357.

Section 357(a) provides that, with two exceptions, a transferor is not deemed to have received boot in a § 351 exchange solely by virtue of a corporation's assumption of a liability.[76] Instead, the transferor's basis in stock received is reduced by the amount of the transferred liability.[77] That general rule is subject to two exceptions—where the liabilities were transferred for a tax-avoidance or non-business purpose and where the liabilities exceed the transferor's aggregate basis in transferred assets.[78] We consider those exceptions below.

The provision applies only to liabilities that are "assumed" by the transferee,[79] but § 357(d)(1) defines "assumes" in a very special and somewhat artificial way. Typically, when a debt is said to have been "assumed," it means that the transferee has accepted personal responsibility to pay the debt, including any deficiency that arises if the debt is secured by property that proves to be inadequate to satisfy the full amount of the debt. But in § 357(d)(1), the term "assume" is defined more broadly in some respects and more narrowly in others.

Section 357(d)(1)(B) provides that, when property is transferred to a transferee subject to a nonrecourse debt, the transferee is treated as having "assumed" that liability. However, if the nonrecourse debt to which the transferred property is subject also encumbers other property that is not transferred to the transferee, the nonrecourse debt may have to be divided between the properties, and only the portion allocated to the transferred property will be subjected to § 357 treatment.[80]

A recourse liability will be treated as having been assumed if, on the basis of all the facts and circumstances, it is determined that "the transferee has agreed to, and is expected to, satisfy such liability" (or a portion thereof), regardless of whether the transferor is relieved of

---

[75]   Revenue Act of 1939, ch. 247, § 213, 53 (Part 2) Stat 862, 870 (current version at § 357).

[76]   With one modification, for purposes of this provision, a corporation's acceptance of property subject to a nonrecourse liability is treated as an assumption of liability by the corporation. § 357(d).

[77]   § 358(d). The presence of liabilities has no effect on the corporation's basis in assets received unless the liabilities cause the transferor to recognize income. § 362(a).

[78]   §§ 357(b), (c).

[79]   § 357(a).

[80]   § 357(d)(2). The debt is allocated to the other property only to the extent of the amount that the owner of that property has agreed with the transferee (and is expected) to pay. In no event can the amount of debt allocated to the other property exceed that property's fair market value.

that liability.[81] Thus, as to a recourse debt, the transferor need only have the transferee expressly agree that it will not pay the debt, and the debt will then be excluded from § 357 treatment.[82]

¶ 7.12.1 Tax Avoidance Purpose

Under § 357(b), where any liability transferred to a controlled corporation as part of a § 351 exchange was assumed (as defined above) for the principal purpose of avoiding federal income taxes, or for some other purpose that was not a bona fide business purpose, then *all the liabilities* assumed by the corporation from that transferor (including those transferred for a bona fide business purpose) are treated as boot.[83]

Ex. A has a basis of $600,000 in an office building worth $1,000,000. A also owns 100% of the stock of Y corporation. If A were to contribute the building to Y in exchange for $500,000 worth of new stock and $500,000 in cash, A would recognize a gain of $400,000. Instead, A proceeds in three steps. First, she takes out a loan of $500,000 from Friendly Bank, secured by the office building. Second, she transfers the building to Y corporation, subject to the loan, in exchange for $500,000 worth of new Y stock. Third, Y pays off the loan when it finally comes due.

Section 357(b) provides the Commissioner with a statutory mechanism for challenging A's attempt to cash out the appreciation in the office building.[84] If § 357(b) is applied, the $500,000 liability would constitute boot to A. A would recognize a gain of $400,000; A would take a basis of $500,000 in the Y stock ($600,000 prior basis, plus $400,000 gain, minus $500,000 boot);[85] Y would take a basis of $1,000,000 in the building (A's $600,000 prior basis, plus A's $400,000 gain).[86]

---

[81] § 357(d)(1)(A).

[82] If the transferee corporation does not agree to pay a recourse debt so that § 357 does not apply to that debt, does that mean that the debt might be treated as boot under the Supreme Court's *Hendler* decision that § 357(a) replaced? In the view of the authors, it will not be treated as boot. The purpose of adopting a restricted definition of an assumption of a recourse debt in § 357(d) was to prevent a recourse debt that the transferor will satisfy from causing the transferor to recognize gain (and to prevent an increase in basis of the transferred assets). To reinstate the *Hendler* treatment of such liabilities would frustrate the congressional purpose for the amendments.

[83] § 357(b); Treas. Reg. § 1.357–1(c).

[84] The Commissioner might also resort to such nonstatutory tools as the step transaction doctrine.

[85] § 358(a).

[86] § 362(a).

The courts have had some difficulty applying § 357(b) in a consistent or predictable manner.[87] They have been more likely (but not certain) to find a tax avoidance purpose in situations where the liability was incurred shortly before the § 351 exchange[88] and where the proceeds of the loan were used for personal purposes rather than to acquire a business asset securing the liability.[89]

¶ 7.12.2 Liabilities in Excess of Basis

Under § 357(c), where the sum of liabilities assumed exceeds the aggregate basis of the property transferred, the excess constitutes gain to the transferor.[90] This provision is applied to each transferor separately.[91] The gain is allocated among the assets transferred by that transferor according to their respective fair market values, and is characterized accordingly as ordinary income or as long-term or short-term capital gain.[92] Note that, even though it is a form of an exception to § 357(a), *§ 357(c) does not require the excess to be treated as boot*; rather, it requires it to be *recognized as gain*.

Ex. (1)   B has a basis of $1,000 in a computer worth $9,000 that is subject to a mortgage with an outstanding principal amount of $8,000. B has a basis of $6,000 in a photocopy machine worth $1,000. B transfers both assets to X in a § 351 exchange, receiving X stock worth $2,000. For purposes of § 357, X's acceptance of the computer subject to the $8,000 encumbrance thereon is treated as an assumption of that liability. In tabular form:

Asset	B's Basis	FMV	Liability	Realized Gain (or Loss)
Computer	$ 1,000	$ 9,000	$ 8,000	$ 8,000
Photocopier	6,000	1,000	——	(5,000)

---

[87]   See generally Richard G. Greiner, et al., *Assumption of Liabilities and the Improper Purpose—A Re-examination of Section 357(b)*, 32 Tax Lawyer 111 (1978).

[88]   See, e.g., Campbell v. Wheeler, 342 F.2d 837 (5th Cir. 1965); Thompson v. Campbell, 353 F.2d 787 (5th Cir. 1965); Bryan v. Commissioner, 281 F.2d 238 (4th Cir. 1960).

[89]   See Drybrough v. Commissioner, 376 F.2d 350 (6th Cir. 1967); Thompson v. Campbell, 353 F.2d 787 (5th Cir. 1965).

[90]   If a liability is described by both § 357(b) and § 357(c), the rules of § 357(b) will apply and the rules of § 357(c) will not. § 357(c)(2)(A).

[91]   Rev. Rul. 66–142.

[92]   Treas. Reg. § 1.357–2(a)–(b). If § 1239 would require ordinary income treatment of a gain from the sale of a depreciable asset to a corporation, that section will require the same treatment of gain recognized under § 357(c) that is allocated to that asset. Alderman v. Commissioner, 55 T.C. 662 (1971); Rev. Rul. 60–302. See ¶ 7.14.2.

The aggregate liability of $8,000 exceeds B's aggregate bases by $1,000. If that amount were treated as boot, $900 would be allocated to the computer and $100 to the photocopier, so that B would recognize a gain of $900.[93] Under § 357(c), however, all $1,000 must be recognized as gain—according to the regulations, $900 characterized according to the character and holding period of the computer, $100 characterized according to the character and holding period of the photocopier.[94]

Because § 357(c) treats the excess of liability over basis as gain rather than as boot, the effects of a transaction subject to § 357(c) on the transferor's outside basis and on the corporation's inside basis deserve special discussion. As far as the *transferor's* outside basis is concerned:

- Section 358(a)(1)(B) provides that, to the extent the transferor recognizes a gain by virtue of § 357(c), the basis the transferor acquires in the stock received in the exchange is *increased*.

- Section 358(d) provides that the amount of the liability assumed is treated as money received by the transferor upon the exchange, so that the amount of basis remaining to be assigned to stock received in the exchange is *reduced*.[95]

The net effect of these two provisions is to ensure that, if § 357(c) applies, the transferor takes a basis in the transferee corporation's stock equal to *zero*.

Ex. (2) D has a basis of $1,000 in a computer worth $10,000 that is subject to a mortgage of $4,000. D transfers the computer, subject to the mortgage, to the X corporation, receiving stock worth $1,000, securities worth $2,000, and $3,000 cash. In tabular form:

Asset	D's Basis	FMV	Liability	Realized Gain (or Loss)
Computer	$ 1,000	$10,000	$ 4,000	$ 9,000

D recognizes $5,000 of gain on account of the boot received. In addition, § 357(c) requires that D recognize an additional $3,000 gain. Under § 358(a)(1), D takes a basis in the stock

---

[93] Rev. Rul. 68–55.

[94] Treas. Reg. § 1.357–2(b).

[95] § 358(a)(1)(A)(ii).

equal to $1,000 + $8,000 – $2,000 (value of non-cash boot) – $7,000 (total cash boot including the liability assumed) = $0. D's basis in the securities is $2,000.[96]

The situation is less clear with regard to the *transferee* corporation's inside basis in assets received. Consider the following example:

Ex. (3) E transfers three assets to Y in a § 351 exchange, where the assets have the following bases and fair market values and are subject to the following liabilities:

Asset	E's Basis	FMV	Liability	Realized Gain (or Loss)
Blackacre	$ 75,000	$ 75,000	$ 65,000	$ 0
Whiteacre	15,000	100,000	85,000	85,000
Truck	30,000	25,000	——	(5,000)
Total:	$120,000	$200,000	$150,000	$ 80,000

Since the amount of liabilities ($150,000) that Y assumes is greater than the total basis that E had in the transferred properties ($120,000), § 357(c) requires E to recognize $30,000 of gain on the transaction. Moreover, as noted earlier, the regulations provide that gain is *characterized* according to the relative fair market values of *all* the transferred assets—37.5% ($11,250) to Blackacre, 50% ($15,000) to Whiteacre, and 12.5% ($3,750) to the truck.[97] Note that the regulations allocate the gain in this fashion even though only Whiteacre is an appreciated asset.

Section 362(a) provides that Y should take a basis in the transferred assets equal to E's basis in those assets, "increased in the amount of gain recognized to the transferor on such transfer." If the basis increase under § 362(a) were allocated among the assets in the same way that gain is characterized—according to the fair market value of all transferred assets—the result would be anomalous: Y's basis in the Truck would be increased above what it had been in E's hands, even though it was not the subject of the liability that gave rise to the income under § 357(c) and even though in fact its value had declined. It would seem far more sensible to allocate the section 357(c) gain only among the transferred properties that were appreciated in E's hands or, alternatively, only among the transferred properties that were subject to liabilities in excess of their bases in E's hands. Prior to 1999, no definitive authority

---

[96] § 358(a)(2).
[97] Treas. Reg. § 1.357–2(b).

indicated how the basis increase should be allocated, but the amendments made by the 1999 Act have changed the landscape for this issue.

As a consequence of the 1999 Act's adoption of § 362(d)(1), the basis that Y (the transferee corporation) acquires in Blackacre and in the truck will be the same basis that E had therein—i.e., a $75,000 basis in Blackacre and a $30,000 basis in the truck. The basis in those assets cannot be increased because of E's § 357(c) gain since any increase in the basis of either of those assets would increase the basis above the asset's fair market value. Section 362(d)(1) prohibits a transferee corporation from increasing the basis of a transferred asset above its fair market value for a gain recognized by the transferor as a result of the transferee's assumption of a liability. Only the basis of Whiteacre can be increased.

E recognized a $30,000 gain under § 357(c). Should all of that $30,000 gain increase the basis of Whiteacre, thereby raising Y's basis in Whiteacre to $45,000? Alternatively, should the same formula that the regulations utilize for characterization purposes be applied also in determining Y's basis so that only 50% of the $30,000 gain will increase the basis in Whiteacre? If the latter construction were adopted, it would mean that there would be no basis increase to Y for $15,000 of the gain that E recognized. That result seems contrary to the spirit of the §§ 357 and 362 scheme. While there is no authoritative resolution of this issue, the authors believe that the best construction is to allocate the § 357(c) gain among the appreciated transferred assets in proportion to the amount of each asset's appreciation in the hands of the transferor. That approach is preferable even under the pre-1999 version of those statutory provisions (albeit it probably will not be adopted for those years); but it seems especially preferable for the post-1999 amendment period and much more likely to be adopted.[98]

In addition to the § 362(d)(1) limitation on the amount of increase in basis that can come from gain recognition attributable to the transferee's assumption of liabilities, § 362(d)(2) provides that, if transferred property is subject to a nonrecourse liability that is also secured by non-transferred property, and if the transferor recognizes gain because of the transferee corporation's assumption of that debt, and if no person is subject to tax on that gain (e.g., the transferor is a foreign person or a tax-exempt person), for purposes of determining

---

[98]   In light of the 1999 amendments, should the regulatory allocation of § 357(c) gain for characterization purposes be reexamined? Should the 1999 amendments be deemed to have invalidated the regulatory scheme for characterization? It seems unlikely that the amendments will invalidate the regulation, but it is possible that they will be held to do so. In any event, the regulations should be reconsidered and altered to conform to the basis adjustment rules of the amendments.

the transferee's basis in the transferred property, the transferor's gain is computed by prorating the nonrecourse debt among all of the properties subject to that liability according to their relative fair market values.

¶ 7.12.3 Liabilities That Would Give Rise to a Deduction

Section 357(c) once also posed special problems for cash-basis taxpayers who transferred the accounts receivable and accounts payable of an ongoing venture to controlled corporations. Typically, such a taxpayer will have a zero basis in the accounts receivable, while the accounts payable will constitute substantial liabilities. If the accounts payable were treated as liabilities to which § 357 applied, the transferor could incur a gain under § 357(c). At first, the courts held that § 357(c) applied to those liabilities, but a large majority of the Tax Court changed its view and held that an obligation that would be deductible by the transferor when paid is excluded from liabilities covered by § 357.[99] The Service acquiesced in that decision. Congress codified and amplified that approach in amendments adopted in 1978.[100]

In 1978, Congress added §§ 357(c)(3) and 358(d)(2) to the Code. In its current form, § 357(c)(3) protects taxpayers (whether or not they use cash-basis accounting) from having to recognize gain on account of the transfer of liabilities (whether or not accounts payable) that would give rise to a deduction when paid, *unless* the incurrence of the liability resulted in the creation of, or an increase in, the basis of any property.[101] Similarly, such liabilities do not reduce the shareholder's basis in the corporation's stock.[102]

---

[99]   Focht v. Commissioner, 68 T.C. 223 (1977) (reviewed by the court).

[100]   In Rev. Rul. 80–199, the Service stated that it would follow the *Focht* approach in cases arising before the statutory change was adopted.

[101]   § 357(c)(3)(B). According to the legislative history, this exception has in mind the situation of a cash basis taxpayer who, in January, buys $1000 worth of tools on credit, with payment due in July. Payment of the bill would give rise to an immediate deduction (and reduce the basis in the tools to zero), but between January and July the taxpayer is assumed to hold a $1000 basis in the tools. If in March the taxpayer transfers the tools, subject to the liability, to a controlled corporation, the $1000 obligation is treated as a "liability" for purposes of § 357(c). See S. Rep. No. 1263, 95th Cong., 2d Sess. 185 n.7.

[102]   There is one exception to this rule. If the basis of the shareholder in the transferee corporation's stock exceeds the fair market value of the stock, the basis may be reduced, but not below fair market value, for any liabilities assumed by the corporation that were ignored on account of § 357(c)(3). This exception does not apply if the trade or business that the liability was connected to was also transferred as part of the exchange or if substantially all the assets that are subject to the liability are transferred to the person assuming the liability. § 358(h).

While not expressly covered by the statute, the rationale for § 357(c)(3) would extend to exclude from §§ 357(c)(1) and 358(d)(1) liabilities the subsequent payment of which will constitute a capital expenditure (and so will increase the payor's basis in some item). In recognition of that principle, the Commissioner has ruled that a corporation's assumption of a liability whose subsequent payment will constitute a capital expenditure is not included in the liabilities of § 357(c)(1) that can cause gain recognition nor in the liabilities of § 358(d)(1) that cause a reduction of the shareholder's basis.[103] The Service has also ruled that, when the transferee corporation pays the liabilities, it may take a deduction in its own right or increase its basis for a capital expenditure.[104]

¶ 7.12.4 Avoiding § 357(c)

A series of cases has raised the question whether a transferor might under some circumstances avoid the application of § 357(c) either by not parting fully with responsibility for the liability or by undertaking an offsetting new liability to the corporation.

In *Lessinger v. Commissioner*,[105] the taxpayer transferred a business with a negative net worth to a controlled corporation, and authorized the corporation to show on its books an open account obligation from the transferor to the corporation in an amount equal to the excess of the business's liabilities over his preexisting basis in its assets. No interest was payable on the debt. Four years later, that open account was formalized in a promissory note. The Second Circuit concluded that the obligation was bona fide and would be enforced in favor of the corporation's creditors. It then concluded that, in applying § 357(c), (1) the obligation was an item of property transferred in the exchange, (2) the obligation's "adjusted basis" should be understood to mean its basis in the hands of the *transferee*, and (3) the transferee corporation's basis would not be determined pursuant to § 362(a) but rather would be equal to its face amount (which was assumed to also be equal to its fair market value).

Lessinger has been widely criticized by commentators.[106] One feature that the critics of *Lessinger* have found disturbing is that, if

---

[103] Rev. Rul. 95–74. While this circumstance typically will not arise if the transferor is on the accrual method, it can apply to an accrual method transferor if the liability had a contingent element at the time that it otherwise would have accrued.

[104] PLR 7830010; PLR 200013044; Rev. Rul. 80–198; Rev. Rul. 95–74.

[105] 872 F.2d 519 (2d Cir. 1989).

[106] See, e.g., Louis S. Nunes, Comment, *Taking Section 357(c) Out of the Scheme of Things: Has the Second Circuit Stranded This Section of the Internal Revenue Code?*, 65 Tul. L. Rev. 663 (1991); J. Clifton Fleming, Jr., *The Highly Avoidable Section 357(c): A Case Study in Traps for the Unwary and Some Positive Thoughts About Negative Basis*, 16 J. Corp. Law 1 (1990); Colleen M. Martin, *Lessinger and Section 357(c): Why a Personal Guarantee Should Result in* Owen *Taxes*, 10 Va. Tax Rev. 215 (1990);

read literally, it could result in a "negative basis" for the stocks received in the exchange:

Ex. (1)   A transfers to a controlled corporation (1) a demand note in the face amount of $9,000, and (2) an asset with a basis of $1,000, subject to a mortgage of $10,000, and receives in exchange stock worth a nominal amount. Under *Lessinger*, A recognizes no gain on the transaction. Under § 358(a)(1)(A)(ii), A should take a basis in the stock received equal to $1,000 (A's basis in the asset), decreased by the amount of "any money received by" A in the transaction. Under § 358(d), the $10,000 mortgage assumption should be treated as money received by A unless it is "a liability excluded under section 357(c)(3)." For most commentators,[107] a literal reading of *Lessinger* is that the mortgage is *not* excluded under § 357(c)(3) (it is instead treated as a liability that is matched against a higher *basis* amount than one might otherwise have expected). Thus, A should take a negative basis of ($9,000) in the stock.[108]

It is not entirely clear that a court following *Lessinger* would pursue the logic set forth in Example (1). After all, a court willing to adopt *Lessinger*'s rather casual interpretation of "adjusted basis" in § 357(c) might be equally casual in its interpretation of § 358(d) and conclude that A's basis in the stock received should be increased by the amount of the new obligation (since A certainly would not have any basis in that obligation). That would leave A with a basis of zero in the stock.

In *Peracchi v. Commissioner*,[109] in a divided decision, the Ninth Circuit reached the same result that the Second Circuit reached in

Michael M. Megaard & Susan L. Megaard, *Can Shareholder's Note Avoid Gain on Transfer of Excess Liabilities?* 71 J. Tax'n 244 (1989). However, there has been one notable exception to the criticism. See Kenneth Brewer, Peracchi v. Lessinger: *Two Circuits Divided by a Common Decision,* 79 Tax Notes 1063 (1998), p. 1063; Kenneth Brewer, *The Zero Basis Hoax,* 63 Tax Notes 457 (1994), p. 457.

[107]   In rejecting the reasoning of *Lessinger*, although reaching the same result, the Ninth Circuit observed in Peracchi v. Commissioner, 143 F.3d 487 (9th Cir. 1998) that § 357(c) was enacted in order to prevent there being a negative basis. While that purpose has been attributed to the adoption of § 357(c), other commentators have suggested a different motive. See Kliegman and Martin, *Whose Liability Is It Anyway? The Impact of Recent Amendments To Section 357,* 91 J. Tax'n 341, 342–343 (Dec. 1999).

[108]   In his defense of the Second Circuit's opinion in *Lessinger*, Brewer reads the court's opinion as holding that the transferor in *Lessinger* had "no basis" in his promissory note, which Brewer contends is quite different from saying that he had a zero basis. Brewer contends that the court held that the note was not "property" in the transferor's hands, and so basis does not come into play in his hands. Even if so, that would still leave the transferor with a negative basis in the corporation's stock. See Brewer note 106, supra.

[109]   143 F.3d 487 (9th Cir. 1998).

Lessinger, but the court repudiated the reasoning adopted in *Lessinger*.[110] In *Peracchi*, the taxpayer needed to contribute additional capital to his closely held corporation in order to bring the corporation into compliance with Nevada's premium-to-asset ratio requirement for insurance companies. Accordingly, the taxpayer contributed two parcels of real estate to the corporation. The transaction was treated as a § 351 exchange with the corporation. The realty was encumbered, and the aggregate liabilities thereon exceeded the taxpayer's basis in those two properties by more than half a million dollars. If the taxpayer had done nothing else, § 357(c) would have required the taxpayer to recognize a gain of over $500,000 on that transfer. To prevent that, taxpayer executed a promissory note in the amount of $1,060,000, payable over a term of ten years and bearing interest at 11%; and taxpayer transferred that promissory note to the corporation together with the two parcels of realty. The issue was whether the contribution of that note prevented § 357(c) from operating to cause taxpayer to recognize income on the transaction.

The Ninth Circuit rejected the Second Circuit's position that, while the taxpayer had zero (or no) basis in the note, the transferee corporation had a basis in the note equal to its face amount, and that, for purposes of applying § 357(c) in this circumstance, it is the basis of the note in the hands of the transferee that should control. Instead, the Ninth Circuit held that the note had a basis in the hands of the taxpayer equal to its face value, and so the liabilities that the corporation accepted did not exceed the basis that the taxpayer had in the transferred properties. Accordingly, the majority of the court held that the taxpayer did not recognize any gain under § 357(c).[111] Since the promissory note represents a debt of the taxpayer, it is somewhat awkward to say that the taxpayer has a "basis" in its own obligation. The more typical view is that one can have basis (i.e., investment) in property but not in one's liabilities.

In *Peracchi*, the court noted the possibility that the transferee corporation might never enforce the taxpayer's obligation under the note so long as the taxpayer was in control of the corporation. But the court pointed out that if the corporation became bankrupt, creditors could and would enforce the note. By transferring the note to the

---

[110]   Peracchi v. Commissioner, 143 F.3d 487, f.n. 17.

[111]   The Ninth Circuit's decision has generated its share of criticism. See, e.g., Lee Sheppard, *Negative Basis, Economic Exposure, and Runaway Metaphors*, 79 Tax Notes 676 (1998), p. 676; and Jasper Cummings, Jr., *Ninth Circuit Avoids* Lessinger *Misstep, But Makes Another*, 79 Tax Notes 781 (1998), p. 781. It has one defender in Kenneth Brewer, who also defends *Lessinger*, but even Brewer recognizes that the two courts had to strain to reach their result. Kenneth Brewer, Peracchi v. Lessinger: *Two Circuits Divided By a Common Decision*, note 106, supra.

corporation, the taxpayer made himself liable to creditors of the corporation if the corporation later became insolvent. The court held that this and other considerations were of sufficient significance to warrant treating the note as a bona fide debt.

The court may have been influenced in reaching that result by its observation that the taxpayer could have achieved the same result by borrowing a million dollars from a bank, contributing the proceeds to the corporation, and then having the corporation purchase the note from the bank. The ultimate circumstance would be identical to that reached when the taxpayer contributed the note directly to the corporation. However, there are some problems with identifying the transaction in question with the one proposed by the court. First, in the case of the loan from a bank, the bank (an independent third party) would have to have approved the loan to the taxpayer. More importantly, the entire transaction could be collapsed under the step transaction doctrine and treated as a direct contribution of the note from the taxpayer to the corporation. If the bank had been induced to make the loan to the taxpayer by assurances that the note would promptly be purchased by the corporation, the step transaction doctrine is especially likely to have come into play.

As previously noted, as a consequence of the 1999 Act, if the liabilities in question are recourse debts, the transferor to the corporation can avoid § 357(c) gain by having the transferee corporation expressly disclaim any intention to make payment on the debt.

¶ 7.12.5 Liabilities in Excess of Fair Market Value

In 2005, Treasury issued proposed regulations denying § 351 treatment in two circumstances where liabilities exceed the fair market value of certain assets. These exclusions will become effective when and if the proposed regulations are finalized.[112] First, § 351 would not be available if the fair market value of the transferred property did not exceed the sum of the liabilities assumed by the transferee corporation and the boot received by the transferor in the exchange.[113] For purposes of this calculation, any liability of the transferee corporation that is transferred as part of the exchange (and thus extinguished for tax purposes) would still be treated as a liability assumed by the transferee corporation.[114]

Second, § 351 treatment would not be available when the fair market value of all assets of the transferee corporation did not exceed

---

[112] Prop. Reg. § 1.351–1(a)(1)(iv).

[113] Prop. Reg. § 1.351–1(a)(1)(iii)(A).

[114] Id.

the entire amount of the transferee corporation's liabilities immediately after the exchange (i.e., the corporation is insolvent).[115]

¶ 7.13 THE RECEIPT OF BOOT, PART III (CORPORATE OBLIGATIONS TO SHAREHOLDER)

Until October 3, 1989, "securities" of the transferee corporation were not treated as "boot," but were instead treated in the same manner as stock and therefore did not trigger the recognition of gain. Since that date, all corporate debt obligations to shareholders have been treated as boot, regardless of whether they are evidenced by a "security."

Despite the boot characterization of such obligations, shareholders will often be able to defer recognition of gain under the installment sale rules of § 453. Under § 453, a taxpayer who does not elect out is directed to use the installment method to report gain from a disposition of property for which at least one "payment" is to be made after the close of the taxable year in which the disposition occurs. In general, the installment method provides that the amount of income recognized each year is equal to that year's total payments, multiplied by the ratio of the gross profit that will ultimately be realized to the total contract price.[116]

Installment reporting is not permitted for "recapture income" that would be characterized as ordinary income by virtue of §§ 1245 or 1250.[117]

The transferor's outside basis in the stock of the corporation is equal to the basis that he held in the transferred property, plus any gain recognized on the exchange, minus any liabilities assumed and any other boot received (which includes the installment obligation itself).[118] For this purpose, the gain is to be determined as if the installment method did not apply, so that the transferor's basis in the stock is increased immediately to reflect even gain that will not be recognized until subsequent installment payments are made.[119] The transferee corporation's inside basis in transferred assets is equal to the transferor's basis plus any gain recognized by the transferor on the exchange.[120] If the transferor recognizes additional income in later years under the installment method, the corporation's inside

---

[115]   Prop. Reg. § 1.351–1(a)(1)(iii)(B).

[116]   § 453(c).

[117]   § 453(i).

[118]   § 358.

[119]   Prop. Reg. § 1.453–1(f)(3).

[120]   § 362(a).

basis is increased at that time by the amount of that additional income. If the transferee corporation no longer owns the transferred assets at the time it makes the subsequent installment payments, the basis adjustment is not lost; the corporation may treat the amount of basis increase that it would have enjoyed if it still owned the assets as a deductible loss.[121]

¶ 7.14 OVERRIDING § 351

The Code subordinates the nonrecognition rule of § 351 to certain other provisions, some of which we have mentioned earlier in this chapter. In this section, we review those statutory limitations on the section's applicability.

¶ 7.14.1 Statutory Overrides—Depreciation Recapture (§ 1245)

The depreciation recapture provisions of § 1245 or § 1250 do not cause the recognition of gain that is entitled to nonrecognition treatment under § 351(a).[122] Rather, those sections require that under certain circumstances some or all of the § 1231 gain (in the case of trade or business property) or capital gain (in the case of investment property) that must be recognized under § 351(b) (by virtue of the transferor's receipt of boot) or § 357(c) (by virtue of the transfer of assets subject to liabilities in excess of their bases) must be recharacterized as ordinary income.

Nonetheless, §§ 1245 and 1250 do cause the recognition of gain whose recognition might otherwise be deferred under the installment method in a § 351 transaction. By virtue of an amendment made in the Deficit Reduction Act of 1984, "recapture income" is no longer eligible for installment reporting.[123]

---

[121]   Prop. Reg. § 1.453–1(f)(3)(ii), (iii) Ex. (1).

[122]   §§ 1245(b)(3), 1250(d)(3).

[123]   § 453(i). Section 46 currently provides for an investment credit in connection with certain qualified rehabilitation expenditures and certain investments in qualified energy property and qualified timber property. Prior to the effective date of the Tax Reform Act of 1986, the investment credit was available for a much broader range of business property (known as "section 38 property"). The old investment credit was subject to recapture where insufficient time passed before the taxpayer who claimed the credit "disposed" of the underlying property or before there was a "cessation" of the qualifying use, unless the disposition resulted in a "mere change in the form of conducting the trade or business." Treas. Reg. §§ 1.47–1; 1.47–3(f)(1). The Commissioner vacillated significantly over how often § 351 exchanges would qualify as "mere changes in form" and how often they would trigger investment credit recapture. Compare Rev. Rul. 76–514 with Rev. Rul. 83–65. See also Loewen v. Commissioner, 76 T.C. 90 (1981).

¶ 7.14.2 Statutory Overrides—Related Party Transactions (§ 1239)

Like the depreciation recapture provisions, § 1239 does not cause the recognition of gain that is entitled to nonrecognition treatment under § 351(a). Rather, it provides that gain that would be recognized as capital gain or § 1231 gain under either § 351(b) or 357(c) must be recharacterized as ordinary income where property that will be depreciable in the hands of the corporation has been received from a more-than-50% owner.[124]

The rationale for § 1239 is that related persons may have an incentive to overstate the value of property if the seller is taxed at capital gains rates while the (related) buyer expects to enjoy ordinary deductions.

¶ 7.14.3 Statutory Overrides—Reallocations by the Commissioner (§ 482)

Section 482 authorizes the Commissioner to reallocate income and deductions among commonly owned or controlled organizations, trades, or businesses where necessary to prevent evasion of taxes or clearly to reflect their incomes. The regulations state that the Commissioner may even use it in circumstances described by § 351.[125]

In such situations, the Commissioner does not generally use § 482 to cause recognition of gain on the transfer from shareholder to corporation, but rather to cause income subsequently realized by the corporation to be treated as if realized by the shareholder, or to require that deductions that would otherwise accrue to the

---

[124] See Alderman v. Commissioner, 55 T.C. 662 (1971); Rev. Rul. 60–302, 1960–2 C.B. 223. A person is a more-than-50% owner of a corporation if, after applying certain stock attribution rules, the person owns more than 50% in value of the corporation's outstanding stock. The stock attribution rules are a modified version of those found in § 267(c). See § 1239(c).

Section 1239 also applies to sales or exchanges between a corporation and its more-than-50% owners, and to sales or exchanges between corporations each of which is more-than-50% owned by the same person. In determining whether § 1239 applies to a § 351 exchange between an entity and a natural person, the more-than-50%-ownership test is applied *after* the transfer is completed if the transferor is a natural person; but if the transferor is an entity, it is deemed satisfied if it is met *either* immediately before *or* immediately after the transfer takes place. Treas. Reg. § 1.1239–1(c)(3). If the transfer is between two entities, the satisfaction of the test of whether the same person owns more than 50% of both entities is determined by applying the ownership requirement to the transferor before the transfer and to the transferee after the transfer. Treas. Reg. § 1.1239–1(c)(4). Note that the regulation cited above requires 80% ownership for control, but § 1239 was amended in 1986 to adopt the more-than-50% ownership requirement in place of the 80% ownership requirement that previously existed.

[125] Treas. Reg. § 1.482–1A(d)(5).

shareholder be taken at the corporate level. For example, in *National Securities Corp. v. Commissioner*,[126] the court upheld the Commissioner's reallocation of a loss on depreciated stock from a subsidiary to the parent, to the extent the decline in value had taken place in the hands of the parent, where there was no plausible business purpose for the transfer in the first place. In *Rooney v. United States*,[127] shareholders transferred a farm to their corporation just before harvest time, and the court upheld the Commissioner's reallocation of their deductions for planting expenses to the corporation.

Nonetheless, the courts seem reluctant to allow the Commissioner to range too far with § 482 in such contexts. This may reflect a sense that, because such efforts require the parties to pinpoint how much gain or loss had accrued in the shareholders' hands at the moment of incorporation, they create some tension with Congress's purpose in establishing the nonrecognition structure of § 351.[128]

¶ 7.14.4 Statutory Overrides—Anti-Bailout Rule I (§ 304)

Consider the following example:

Ex. For the past 3 years, A has owned all 100 shares of stock in corporation X, having a basis of $10,000 and a fair market value of $100,000. A also owns 80 of the 100 outstanding shares of stock in corporation Y, having a basis of $80 and a fair market value of $80,000. X and Y each have accumulated *e and p* of $80,000. Several years earlier, A borrowed $5,000 from bank B, secured by 50 shares of X stock. The debt is a nonrecourse debt.

A transfers the 50 shares of X stock that was encumbered by the bank loan to corporation Y, subject to the liability, in exchange for 20 new shares of Y stock (having a fair market value of $20,000) and $25,000 in cash. Thus, A has received $25,000 cash, relieved himself of the liability to B, and increased his stake in Y from 80% to 83.33% by transferring half his X stock to Y. A

---

[126]   137 F.2d 600 (3d Cir. 1943).

[127]   305 F.2d 681 (9th Cir. 1962).

[128]   See, e.g., Eli Lilly & Co. v. Commissioner, 856 F.2d 855 (7th Cir. 1988) (transfer of patents to Puerto Rico subsidiary); G. D. Searle & Co. v. Commissioner, 88 T.C. 252 (1987) (involving transfer of intangibles to Puerto Rico subsidiary). But see Foster v. Commissioner, 80 T.C. 34 (1983), aff'd on this issue, 756 F.2d 1430 (9th Cir. 1985); Stewart v. Commissioner, 714 F.2d 977 (9th Cir. 1983); Central Cuba Sugar Co. v. Commissioner, 198 F.2d 214 (2d Cir. 1952). See generally Patricia L. Martin, Note, *Section 482 and the Nonrecognition Provisions: Resolving the Conflict*, 77 Nw. U. L. Rev. 670, 685–87 (1982); Melvin S. Adess, *The Role of Section 482 in Nonrecognition Transactions—The Outer Edges of Its Application*, 57 Taxes 946 (1979).

had a basis of $5,000 in the 50 shares of X stock that he transferred to Y.

As noted in Chapter Three, until 1982 a transfer such as this satisfied the literal terms of both § 304 and § 351.[129] While A has realized a gain of $45,000 on the transfer of the X stock, neither § 304 nor § 351 would require the full amount of gain to be recognized. Seen from the § 351 perspective, A has transferred property (the X stock) to Y in exchange for Y stock and $30,000 worth of boot (the boot is the $25,000 cash plus the $5,000 liability to which the X stock was subject). Thus, $30,000 would be recognized, and it would be characterized as a capital gain by virtue of the character of the X stock in A's hands. Seen from the § 304 perspective, however, A has used a brother-sister stock purchase to withdraw $30,000 worth of Y's *e and p*, which should be taxed as ordinary income to reinforce the two-tier tax structure.

In 1982, Congress resolved this "choice of perspective" problem by amending § 304 to provide that, generally, only § 304 will apply to transactions that would otherwise be covered by both § 351 and § 304.[130] Thus, subject to a minor exception, § 351 applies to transfers of stock of a related corporation only in a pure stock-for-stock exchange.

¶ 7.14.5 Statutory Overrides—Anti-Bailout Rule II (§ 306)

Section 306 is intended to minimize the use of preferred stock to permit shareholders to enjoy capital gains treatment of their share of corporate income without reducing their voting interest in the corporation.[131] It operates by "tainting" certain preferred stock received by a shareholder. For present purposes, the question is, When can stock received in a § 351 transaction be § 306 stock? Section 306(c)(3) provides that preferred stock acquired in a § 351 exchange will be treated as Section 306 stock if, had money in lieu of stock been received, its receipt would have been a dividend to any extent (by virtue of § 304).

Another situation that can cause stock received in a § 351 exchange to be characterized as Section 306 stock is a transfer of Section 306 stock to a corporation in a § 351 exchange. In that event,

---

[129] For a comprehensive review of the confused state of the law before 1982, see Gunther v. Commissioner, 92 T.C. 39 (1989), aff'd, 909 F.2d 291 (7th Cir. 1990).

[130] § 304(b)(3)(A).

[131] See generally Chapter Six.

the stock received in exchange for the Section 306 stock will itself constitute Section 306 stock even if it is common stock.[132]

¶ 7.15 NON-STATUTORY OVERRIDES

The statutory overrides to § 351 discussed above are supplemented by traditional common law doctrines:

¶ 7.15.1 Non-Statutory Overrides—Assignment of Income

The anticipatory assignment of income principle is a judicially created doctrine providing that a person who earns the right to income cannot escape taxation by assigning the right to that income to a third party.[133] It is clear that § 351 does not preclude the application of the assignment of income doctrine,[134] but unfortunately the boundaries of the doctrine itself are somewhat less clear.

A former Chief Counsel of the Internal Revenue Service wrote an article while he was serving in that capacity indicating that the Service would not seek to apply the assignment of income doctrine to the transfer of accounts receivable in a § 351 exchange as long as:

- the assignment of the receivables to the controlled corporation had a bona fide business purpose;

- the accounts payable of the business were also transferred to the controlled corporation; and

- the corporate transferee agrees in a closing letter with the Commissioner that it will report the payments received on the transferred receivables in its gross income with the same characterization that the income would have had in the hands of the transferor.[135]

---

[132] § 306(c)(1)(C).

[133] Lucas v. Earl, 281 U.S. 111 (1930) and Helvering v. Horst, 311 U.S. 112 (1940) are two of the landmark cases in this area.

[134] See Davidson v. Commissioner, 43 B.T.A. 576 (1941), holding that an assignment of insurance commissions to a controlled corporation was an assignment of income and that the commissions were taxable to the transferor when paid to the corporation. See also Roubik v. Commissioner, 53 T.C. 365 (1969); Rev. Rul. 77–336.

[135] K. Martin Worthy, *IRS Chief Counsel Outlines What Lies Ahead for Professional Corporations*, 32 J. Tax'n 88, 90 (1970). See also Hempt Bros., Inc. v. United States, 490 F.2d 1172, 1176–78 (3d Cir. 1974); Raich v. Commissioner, 46 T.C. 604 (1966); Rev. Rul. 80–198.

¶ 7.15.2 Non-Statutory Overrides—the Tax Benefit Rule

The "tax benefit rule" is a judicially created doctrine of long standing. It provides that a taxpayer who claims a deduction in one year may be required to report income upon the occurrence of a certain type of event in a later year, at least to the extent the earlier deduction provided the taxpayer with a "tax benefit."[136] The issue in a § 351 transaction will come down to (1) is the § 351 transaction "fundamentally inconsistent" with the premise underlying the prior deduction and (2) does the nonrecognition rule of § 351 preclude the application of the tax benefit rule.[137]

¶ 7.15.3 Non-Statutory Overrides—Business Purpose Test and Court Holding Doctrine

We noted briefly at ¶ 7.05, that it is the position of the Service that a putative § 351 transaction must have a business purpose in order for § 351 to apply, and that one district court and one court of appeals have agreed with that position. The so-called "business purpose" doctrine is usually said to have originated in the Supreme Court's decision in *Gregory v. Helvering*,[138] a case involving a taxpayer who blended a spin-off under the Revenue Act of 1924 with a liquidation, for the sole purpose of avoiding the two-tier tax structure. The Court found that the absence of a business purpose put the transaction "outside the plain intent of the statute." As has been rightly observed, "over the years the decision has so permeated every crevice of the tax law that it must always be in the forefront of the tax lawyer's mind."[139] Section 351 is just such a "crevice."

The so-called *"Court Holding"* doctrine dates back to a 1945 Supreme Court opinion involving a corporate taxpayer that had negotiated a sale of all its assets to a third party and then distributed all those assets in liquidation to its shareholders, who promptly completed the sale.[140] The Supreme Court held that, in substance, the sale was made by the corporation, and should be taxed in that manner.[141] In the context of § 351, the Service has successfully relied

---

[136]   § 111. For a fuller discussion of the interplay of § 351 with the tax benefit rule, see Corporate Income Taxation Hornbook at 322–324.

[137]   See Nash v. United States, 398 U.S. 1 (1970). See also United States v. Bliss Dairy, Inc., 460 U.S. 370 (1983).

[138]   293 U.S. 465 (1935).

[139]   See, e.g., Bittker and Eustice at ¶¶ 1.05[2](c), 3.17(6).

[140]   Commissioner v. Court Holding Co., 324 U.S. 331 (1945).

[141]   The decision's significance in the context of liquidating distributions dwindled substantially over time as a result of the decision in United States v. Cumberland Pub. Serv. Co., 338 U.S. 451 (1950), the addition of the old version of § 337 to the Internal Revenue Code of 1954, and finally the repeal of the General Utilities doctrine in 1986.

on the *Court Holding* doctrine to challenge transactions where assets received in a § 351 transfer are promptly sold by the corporation in a sale that had been pre-arranged by the shareholder.[142] At times, the Service's *Court Holding* analysis incorporates the business purpose doctrine by reference, suggesting that "an important consideration in resolving the issue of who is the true seller of the property is whether [the shareholder] contributed the property to [the corporation] for any valid business purpose or just for tax avoidance reasons."[143]

While the Service has thus been quite resistant to pre-arranged sales of transferred property, it has looked much more favorably on so-called "double dropdown" cases, where the corporate transferee of property retransfers the property to its own controlled subsidiary.[144] Indeed, it has been willing to approve "triple dropdown" transactions.[145]

---

[142]   See, e.g., Murry v. Commissioner, 49 T.C.M. 403 (1984); Stewart v. Commissioner, 714 F.2d 977 (9th Cir. 1983); Hallowell v. Commissioner, 56 T.C. 600 (1971).

[143]   TAM 9016001.

[144]   Rev. Rul. 77–449. See also Rev. Rul. 83–156; Rev. Rul. 83–34.

[145]   See GCM 39138; PLR 8342030.

Chapter Eight

CORPORATE DIVISIONS

Analysis

Para.

8.01 Introduction

8.02 Types of Corporate Divisions

8.03 Nonrecognition Treatment and the Potential for Tax Avoidance

8.04 An Overview of §§ 355 and 356

8.05 "Stock or Securities"

8.06 Distribution of a Controlling Interest

8.07 The "Device" Test

8.08 The Five-Year Active Trade or Business Requirement

8.09 Nonstatutory Requirements—Business Purpose and Continuity of Interest

8.10 Boot

8.11 Tax Consequences for Shareholders When Boot Is Distributed

8.12 Basis Calculation

8.13 Taxation of the Distributing Corporation

8.14 Earnings and Profits

¶ 8.01 INTRODUCTION

This chapter concerns situations in which business activities that were once conducted through a single corporation (or a single corporate parent) are divided among two or more unaffiliated corporations. Such situations may involve separating two unrelated trades or businesses that were conducted under one corporate roof, separating two related divisions of a single enterprise, or separating the functions of what had previously been a single integrated operation.

These transactions are known as "corporate divisions." In some corporate divisions, the shareholders are divorced from each other so that one group of shareholders owns one or more of the previously conducted businesses and a different group of shareholders owns the other previously conducted businesses. In other corporate divisions, the same (or many of the same) shareholders continue to own all of the businesses, but the businesses are conducted in separate corporate entities.

While they need not do so, corporate divisions sometimes satisfy the definition of a reorganization in § 368, in which case they may be referred to as "divisive reorganizations," "divisive D reorganizations," or simply as "D reorganizations." The exchanges made pursuant to a corporate division may or may not qualify for full or partial nonrecognition treatment. The qualification for nonrecognition treatment depends upon whether the transaction satisfies certain statutory and common law requirements. It is not necessary for nonrecognition treatment that a corporate division qualify as a reorganization; some corporate divisions that provide nonrecognition treatment are divisive reorganizations and some are not.

Corporate divisions can occur for any of a variety of business reasons: for example, dissident shareholders may want to go their separate ways, shareholders may want to separate a risky business venture from a more stable one, it may be desirable for some shareholders to focus on a single business, an antitrust decree may require the break-up of a business, or federal or state laws might forbid certain enterprises to be carried on by a single corporation or chain of corporations. As we shall see, a corporate division will not provide nonrecognition treatment if the division fails to have a bona fide corporate business purpose.

As we saw with the organization of a corporation in Chapter Seven, the doctrine of realization can create "lock-in" effects; the prospect of a substantial tax liability might deter people from changing the form of their business operations. Just as Congress has mitigated that lock-in effect by providing nonrecognition treatment for certain transfers of property to controlled corporations, it has also granted favorable treatment to the participants in certain corporate divisions. The tax treatment provided by the Code is a product of an effort to strike an appropriate balance between the policy interest in minimizing lock-in and the policy interest in enforcing a two-tier tax on corporate income.

The principal provisions of the Code affecting corporate divisions are §§ 355 and 356, but there are other relevant provisions including ones directing the determination of basis and of earnings and profits. Depending on the facts of the transaction, a corporate division can be treated either as a taxable sale or exchange of stock, as a § 301 distribution, or as a wholly or partial nonrecognition transaction.

¶ 8.02 TYPES OF CORPORATE DIVISIONS

Tax lawyers divide corporate divisions into three categories: "spin-offs," "split-offs," and "split-ups." The differences in tax treatment associated with the different categories occur primarily when "boot" is received or the transaction fails to qualify for nonrecognition treatment under § 355 or § 356. If a corporation distributes both property that qualifies for nonrecognition and property that does not qualify, the nonqualified property is referred to as "boot." The characteristic features of the different categories of corporate divisions are as follows:

(a) *Spin-Offs.* The parent corporation distributes stock representing a controlling interest in a subsidiary corporation to one or more of the shareholders of the parent corporation, and the shareholders do not surrender any of their stock in the parent corporation in exchange. If neither § 355 nor § 356 applies, the taxation of a spin-off will be determined by § 301.

(b) *Split-Offs.* As in a spin-off, the parent corporation distributes stock representing a controlling interest in a subsidiary corporation to one or more of the shareholders of the parent corporation. In contrast to a spin-off, however, the shareholders surrender some (or all) of their stock in the parent corporation in exchange. If neither § 355 nor § 356 applies, the taxation of a split-off will be determined by § 302.

(c) *Split-Ups.* The parent corporation liquidates completely, distributing to its shareholders the stock of two or more subsidiary corporations. If neither § 355 nor § 356 applies, the taxation of a split-up will be determined by § 331.

¶ 8.03 NONRECOGNITION TREATMENT AND THE POTENTIAL FOR TAX AVOIDANCE

Suppose shareholder A in parent corporation P receives stock in subsidiary corporation S through a corporate division. If the requirements of § 355 are satisfied, A can receive nonrecognition treatment on the transaction, allocating whatever basis he previously had in the P stock across his remaining shares of P stock and the new S stock according to their relative fair market values.[1]

Nonrecognition treatment of corporate divisions creates the possibility for a shareholder to avoid ordinary income treatment of what might otherwise be characterized as a dividend out of corporate earnings and profits. Instead, the shareholder can receive capital gains treatment on a smaller amount and can defer recognizing that gain for some time. In addition, in many (but not all) circumstances,

---

[1]   § 358(b), (c).

the distributing corporation will not recognize gain or loss on making the distribution to the shareholder.[2]

As previously noted, qualified dividends to a noncorporate shareholder currently are taxed at capital gains rates. Even when capital gains rates are applicable, qualification for nonrecognition treatment is still significant because it defers the shareholder's tax consequences to a subsequent year, allows a tax-free recovery of basis, and can prevent the distributing corporation from ever recognizing a gain on its distribution of appreciated stock.

Until 1934, divisive reorganizations were widely used in the manner discussed above to avoid dividend treatment. In that year, Congress eliminated all nonrecognition treatment for spin-offs, while preserving nonrecognition for split-offs and split-ups. As you could predict, that elimination of nonrecognition for spin-offs was not effective since the same result could be obtained by having a proportional split-off or split-up. An example of the tax avoidance potential of divisive reorganizations is the much-cited case of *Gregory v. Helvering*.[3]

Gregory involved a spin-off under pre-1934 law. In *Gregory*, the taxpayer was the sole shareholder of X, which owned 1000 shares of Y. The taxpayer caused X to form Z Corporation and to transfer its 1000 shares of Y stock to Z in exchange for all of Z's stock which was distributed to the taxpayer as a spin-off. Four days later, the taxpayer liquidated Z and then sold the 1000 shares of Y.

Before 1934, for nonrecognition purposes, spin-offs were covered by the general reorganization provisions found in Section 112 of the Revenue Act of 1928. In *Gregory*, the Supreme Court held that, even though the spin-off transaction complied with the literal terms of that section, the "substance" of the transaction was indistinguishable from a dividend of the Y stock from X to its shareholder, and the transaction should be taxed accordingly. In particular, the entire transaction appeared to serve no purpose *other* than the avoidance of taxes, and the Court concluded that a "reorganization" within the meaning of the statute was a transaction that furthered some "business or corporate purpose." In essence, the Court defined the term "reorganization," as used in tax law, to include a requirement that the transaction have a bona fide business purpose.

Gregory's "business purpose" doctrine continues to serve as an important extra-statutory prerequisite to nonrecognition treatment

---

[2]   See ¶ 8.13.

[3]   293 U.S. 465 (1935).

for a corporate division regardless of whether it constitutes a reorganization.[4]

¶ 8.04 AN OVERVIEW OF §§ 355 AND 356

Section 355 allows nonrecognition treatment for certain transactions that are thought to involve merely a change in the corporate form through which one or more business enterprises are conducted.

It should be noted that § 355 applies to all three forms of corporate division—it does not matter whether a distributee surrenders stock in the distributing corporation.[5] It does not matter whether the subsidiary corporation whose stock was distributed was newly created or pre-existing. It also does not matter whether the distribution to the shareholders was made pro rata.[6]

For § 355 to apply, a corporation (hereafter referred to either as "the parent" or as "the distributing corporation") must distribute "solely"[7] stock or securities of at least one corporation "which it controls immediately before the distribution" (hereafter referred to either as "the subsidiary" or as "the controlled corporation").[8] The term "securities" refers to a debt instrument that reflects a long-term interest in the corporation, but that does not constitute an equity interest. While a security is a debt instrument, not all debt instruments qualify as a security.

Property that is distributed by the distributing corporation that does not qualify for nonrecognition to the distributee is sometimes referred to as "boot." As we shall see, if a distributing corporation distributes qualified stock and securities of a controlled corporation and also distributes boot, while § 355(a) will not apply to the distribution, § 356 can apply to provide the distributee with nonrecognition for some of the realized gain and can prevent recognition of any realized loss. A explained in ¶ 8.10, there are circumstances where certain stock or securities will be treated as boot.

The parent must distribute the subsidiary's stock or securities to shareholders of the parent in their capacity as shareholders or to

---

4   See Treas. Reg. §§ 1.355–2(b), 1.368–1(c), 2(g). See generally ¶ 8.09.

5   § 355(a)(2)(B).

6   § 355(a)(2)(A).

7   As we shall see, there can be some nonrecognition when the distributing corporation distributes other property in addition to stock and securities, but § 355(a) does not apply in that case. Instead, § 356 can apply to that distribution.

8   For this purpose, "control" is tested under the definition of § 368(c), which requires that the parent hold voting stock representing at least 80 percent of the voting power and at least 80 percent of each class of non-voting stock.

holders of the parent's securities in exchange for those securities. The parent must either distribute all of its stock and securities in the subsidiary or else distribute a controlling share of stock under circumstances where the Secretary is satisfied that retention of stock (or stock and securities) in the subsidiary was not in pursuance of a plan having tax avoidance as one of its principal purposes.[9]

The distribution itself must not be used principally as a device for the distribution of earnings and profits of the parent or the subsidiary.[10] Moreover, the transaction must satisfy *Gregory*'s extra-statutory business purpose requirement.[11] In addition, (according to the regulations) an extra-statutory "continuity of proprietary interest" requirement must be satisfied.[12]

Section 355 includes an important and distinctive restriction on the availability of nonrecognition treatment—the 5-year "active business" requirement found in § 355(b). "Immediately after the distribution," each subsidiary whose stock is distributed must be engaged in the active conduct of a trade or business that is deemed to have been conducted throughout the five-year period leading up to the distribution. Moreover, if immediately before the distribution, the parent had any assets other than the distributed stock or securities of the subsidiaries, then the parent also must be engaged in the active conduct of such a trade or business immediately after the distribution.[13]

If a spin-off would qualify for nonrecognition under § 355 were it not for the fact that boot was distributed in addition to the controlled corporation's qualified stock and securities, the amount of the boot (i.e., the amount of cash plus the fair market value of non-cash boot) is treated as a § 301 distribution, which will constitute a dividend to the shareholder to the extent of the amount of the distributing corporation's *e and p* that is allocated to that distribution.[14]

In the case of a split-off or a split-up, if the transaction would qualify the shareholder for nonrecognition under § 355 were it not for the fact that property other than stock or securities of the controlled corporation is distributed, the shareholder cannot recognize any loss realized on the exchange;[15] but the shareholder must recognize any

---

[9]   § 355(a)(1)(D).
[10]   § 355(a)(1)(B).
[11]   Treas. Reg. § 1.355–2(b).
[12]   Treas. Reg. § 1.355–2(c).
[13]   § 355(b)(1).
[14]   § 356(b).
[15]   § 356(c).

gain realized on the exchange to the extent of the cash received plus the fair market value of the non-cash boot received.[16] The gain recognized by the distributee on the exchange will be treated as dividend income to the extent that the exchange had the "effect of the distribution of a dividend."[17] Only gain that is recognized by the distributee can be treated as a dividend. If the gain recognized by the distributee exceeds the amount treated as a dividend, the excess amount is treated as gain from the sale or exchange of the stock, which typically will be a capital gain.[18] For purposes of determining the amount of recognized gain that will be treated as a dividend, only a ratable share of the distributing corporation's *accumulated e and p* is utilized. In other words, earnings and profits are determined only by reference to accumulated *e and p* rather than the more usual bifurcated system of applying current *e and p* first and then applying accumulated *e and p*.[19]

As was true of § 351, the rules of § 355 are in form mandatory. Taxpayers who wish to recognize a gain or loss in a transaction to which § 355 would otherwise apply can do so only by structuring the transaction so that it fails to satisfy one of the statutory or extra-statutory prerequisites.

When § 355 or § 356 applies to an exchange in a split-off or split-up, the distributee's basis in the nonrecognition property (i.e., generally the qualified stock and securities) is calculated to carry forward any realized-but-unrecognized gains or losses on the exchange.

¶ 8.05 "STOCK OR SECURITIES"

To qualify for complete nonrecognition treatment, the distributee must receive only stock and securities of a corporation controlled by the distributing corporation immediately prior to the distribution.[20] The amount of stock distributed must be sufficient to constitute control within the meaning of § 368(c).[21] The distributed

---

[16]   § 356(a)(1).

[17]   § 356(a)(2). The meaning of this reference is discussed at ¶ 8.11.4.

[18]   § 356(a)(2).

[19]   § 356(a)(2).

[20]   § 355(a)(1)(A).

[21]   § 355(a)(1)(D). The distributing corporation has "control" of a subsidiary corporation only where it owns stock possessing at least 80% of the total combined voting power of the voting stock of the subsidiary and owns at least 80% of the total number of shares of nonvoting stock of the subsidiary corporation. § 368(c). This is the same test of "control" applied for purposes of § 351. The IRS has ruled that the control group must hold 80% of the shares of each class of nonvoting stock. Rev. Rul. 59–259. It is unsettled whether disallowed nonqualified preferred stock is to be taken into account in determining whether stock constituting control of the subsidiary was

stock of the subsidiary may be either common or preferred, but preferred stock may be characterized as section 306 stock[22] or as disallowed nonqualified preferred stock.

As we shall see, certain stock, so-called "stock boot," will not qualify for nonrecognition; and the principal amount of securities received in excess of the principal amount of securities surrendered constitutes boot. Nonqualified preferred stock is not treated as a stock or security unless received in a distribution in exchange for, or with respect to, other nonqualified preferred stock[23] (such stock that does not qualify for nonrecognition is sometimes referred to hereafter as "disallowed nonqualified preferred stock").

Taxpayers and the Commissioner have expended substantial resources litigating the question whether the term "stock or securities" includes stock rights or stock warrants of the subsidiary. This matter was laid to rest by amendments made to the regulations in 1998.[24] With one exception, stock rights and warrants are treated as *securities* that have no principal amount.[25] Since they are deemed to have no principal amount, their receipt will not cause the distributee to recognize any income.[26] The one exception is that a warrant or right to acquire nonqualified preferred stock will not be treated as a security (and so will constitute boot) unless such warrants or rights are received in exchange for (or with respect to) other nonqualified preferred stock or the right to acquire such stock.[27]

¶ 8.06 DISTRIBUTION OF A CONTROLLING INTEREST

Section 355(a)(1)(D) requires that the distributing corporation distribute either (a) all of the subsidiary's stock and securities that it held immediately before the distribution, or (b) an amount of stock constituting "control" of the subsidiary within the meaning of § 368(c) if it can satisfy the Secretary that the retention of some subsidiary

---

distributed, but it seems likely that it will be unless regulations are promulgated excluding that stock.

[22]   Treas. Reg. § 1.355–4. See § 306(c)(1)(B); Rev. Rul. 59–197. Section 306 stock is discussed in Chapter Six.

[23]   § 355(a)(3)(D). Treas. Reg. § 1.356–6(a)(1).

[24]   Treas. Reg. §§ 1.355–1(c); 1.356–3(b), (c) Exs. (7)–(9); and 1.356–6.

[25]   Id.

[26]   The amount taxable when a shareholder receives "boot" (i.e., property other than property that qualifies for nonrecognition) is established by § 356. When the item distributed or exchanged is a security, the boot that is taxable cannot exceed the fair market value of the principal amount of that security. § 356(d)(2)(C). Since a warrant or right is treated as a security with no principal amount, the amount of the distributee's boot is zero. Id.

[27]   Treas. Reg. § 1.356–6(a)(2).

stock or securities was not in pursuance of a tax avoidance plan. The regulations under § 355 indicate that ordinarily it will be difficult to justify the retention of any stock or securities.[28]

¶ 8.07 THE "DEVICE" TEST

Section 355(a)(1)(B) requires that the distribution not be "used principally as a device for the distribution of the earnings and profits of the distributing corporation or the controlled corporation or both." The regulations elaborate on how the IRS will apply this "device" test.[29] Keep in mind that the test is whether the distribution was used *principally* as a device to avoid dividend treatment; the fact that such a device was one purpose of the distribution does not prevent § 355 from applying if that was not the principal purpose.

The regulations indicate that the "device" test is concerned primarily with situations in which a shareholder might use a nonrecognition corporate division to transform dividend income into capital gains. Currently, dividend income distributed by a domestic corporation to an individual shareholder usually is subject to capital gain rates—usually 20%. That raises the question of whether there is a justification for applying a device test in the current environment. Even given the same tax rates, there are tax advantages to qualifying for § 355 treatment, but it is an open issue as to whether those benefits are significant enough to justify the complexity imposed by the device test.

The question seems effectively resolved in the regulations. Even when long-term capital gains and dividend income are taxed at the same rates as those applied to ordinary income, a nonrecognition corporate division followed by a sale or liquidation could still be utilized to insulate a portion of the distribution from taxation as a recovery of the basis that is allocated to the distributed property. That potential for the utilization of basis, which is not available for section 301 distributions, is deemed sufficient under the regulations to cause the application of the device provision if the other conditions of that provision are present.[30] The regulations state that generally the determination of whether a transaction fails the "device" test depends on all the "facts and circumstances."[31]

---

[28] Treas. Reg. § 1.355–2(e)(2).

[29] Treas. Reg. § 1.355–2(d).

[30] Treas. Reg. § 1.355–2(d)(1) ("A device can include a transaction that effects a recovery of basis."). The question would be more interesting in the unusual context of a corporate division in which the distributees had little or no basis in their stock of the distributing corporation.

[31] Id.

The regulations provide explicit guidance about how those facts and circumstances should be appraised. They first identify three factors that support a finding that a distribution was a device, and then list three factors that support a contrary finding. Again, keep in mind that use as a device must be the principal purpose of the distribution for the provision to apply. Those six factors are not conclusive of a principal purpose, but rather provide evidence to be weighed in making the determination of whether the device provision applies. The weight to be assigned to a factor depends on all the facts and circumstances. The regulations also identify three classes of distributions that "ordinarily" are not motivated principally by a device purpose and so ordinarily are *not* subject to the device provision, notwithstanding the presence of factors that are listed as evidence of a device purpose.[32]

The following three factors are those listed in the regulations as evidencing a device purpose:

(1) *Pro rata distribution.*[33] The regulations state that a pro rata or "substantially pro rata" distribution presents "the greatest potential for the avoidance of the dividend provisions of the Code." As is true for all of the items that evidence a device purpose, this item can be rebutted by showing that there was a strong business purpose for the corporate division. The regulations contain an example of a situation in which the pro rata factor was outweighed by a strong business purpose.[34]

(2) *Subsequent sale or exchange of stock.*[35] If after the distribution, stock in either the distributing or the controlled corporation is sold or exchanged, that is evidence of a device.[36] The greater the percentage sold or exchanged, and the closer the sale or exchange comes on the heels of the distribution, the stronger this factor is. If the sale or exchange was prearranged, the

---

[32] Treas. Reg. § 1.355–2(d)(5).

[33] Treas. Reg. § 1.355–2(d)(2)(ii).

[34] Treas. Reg. § 1.355–2(d)(4), Ex. (2).

[35] Treas. Reg. § 1.355–2(d)(2)(iii).

[36] Where the sale is not prearranged, the statute suggests that this factor should ordinarily not, by itself, be given determinative weight. "[T]he mere fact that subsequent to the distribution stock or securities in one or more of such corporations are sold or exchanged by all or some of the distributees (other than pursuant to an arrangement negotiated or agreed upon prior to such distribution) shall not be construed to mean that the transaction was used principally as such a device." § 355(a)(1)(B).

regulations indicate that this factor will not merely be "evidence" but "substantial evidence" of a device.[37]

(3) *Nonbusiness or "secondary business" assets.*[38] If either the distributing or the controlled corporation has substantial assets that are not used in a trade or business that satisfies the five-year active business requirement of § 355(b) (discussed in ¶ 8.08), that is evidence of a device. The ratio of such nonbusiness assets to the corporation's business assets figures in determining the strength of this factor.[39]

Moreover, if a business activity of either the distributing or controlled corporation is a "secondary business" (one whose primary function is to serve the business needs of the other corporation or a corporation controlled by it), and if the secondary business could be sold without adversely affecting the corporation being served, that is evidence of a device as well.[40] Treasury may have been motivated to adopt this provision for device evidence because Treasury had to concede in the regulations that a secondary business can satisfy the five-year active conduct of a trade or business requirement.[41] Rather than totally abandon its objection to the division of a secondary business, Treasury left open the possibility that such a division will run afoul of the device standard.[42]

The factors that point against a finding of a device purpose are as follows:

(1) *Corporate business purpose.*[43] The more important the purpose is to the success of the business, the stronger this factor is. It is also stronger to the extent prompted by a disinterested third party, by factors beyond the parties' control, or by conditions calling for immediate action.[44] As previously noted, a strong corporate

---

[37] Treas. Reg. § 1.355–2(d)(2)(iii)(B). A sale or exchange will be deemed to have been prearranged if enforceable rights to buy or sell existed before the distribution. Moreover, if a sale or exchange was discussed by the buyer and seller *and* was reasonably to be anticipated by them before the distribution, the sale or exchange will *ordinarily* be considered to have been prearranged. Treas. Reg. § 1.355–2(d)(2)(iii)(D).

[38] Treas. Reg. § 1.355–2(d)(2)(iv).

[39] Treas. Reg. § 1.355–2(d)(2)(iv)(B). See also Rev. Rul. 86–4. However, a difference in that ratio for the distributing and controlled corporations ordinarily is not evidence of a device if the distribution is not made pro rata and the difference in the ratio is attributable to equalizing the value of the stock distributed to the value of the stock and securities surrendered by the distributees. Id.

[40] Treas. Reg. § 1.355–2(d)(2)(iv)(C).

[41] Treas. Reg. § 1.355–3(c), Exs. (9) and (11).

[42] Id.; Treas. Reg. § 1.355–2(d)(2)(iv)(C).

[43] Treas. Reg. §§ 1.355–2(b)(4), 1.355–2(d)(3)(ii).

[44] See Rev. Rul. 83–114 (response to antitrust decree).

business purpose often will outweigh existing evidence of a device. To be relevant, the business purpose must be one that serves a business of the distributing or controlled corporation as contrasted to the business or other commercial purposes of a distributee.

(2) *Distributing corporation publicly traded and widely held.*[45] If no shareholder is directly or indirectly the beneficial owner of more than five percent of any class of stock, and if the stock is publicly traded, that is evidence of a nondevice.

(3) *Distribution to domestic corporate shareholders.*[46] If one or more of the distributees was a domestic corporation that would have been entitled to a dividend-received deduction under § 243(a) if the distribution had been treated as a section 301 distribution, then it is much less likely that a corporate division was undertaken for tax avoidance purposes. Accordingly, the presence of such a domestic corporate distributee constitutes evidence of a nondevice.[47]

Beyond these factors, the regulations specify three classes of distributions that *ordinarily* are not considered to have a principal purpose of a device notwithstanding the presence of any of the device factors mentioned above.[48] The regulations do hedge on committing to nondevice treatment by employing the word "ordinarily." Those three circumstances that ordinarily receive nondevice treatment are:

(1) *Absence of earnings and profits.*[49] If neither the distributing nor any of the controlled corporations had accumulated earnings and profits at the beginning of the taxable year or current earnings and profits at the date of distribution, and if immediately before the distribution, the distributing corporation did not have appreciated assets that, if distributed, would create current earnings and profits, then there was no dividend income to be avoided. In that case, the device provision likely will not apply.

---

[45] Treas. Reg. § 1.355–2(d)(3)(iii).

[46] Treas. Reg. § 1.355–2(d)(3)(iv).

[47] Id. In addition, if the distributee is the parent of a foreign subsidiary and if § 245(b) would apply to § 301 distributions to the distributee, that also is evidence of a nondevice purpose.

[48] Treas. Reg. § 1.355–2(d)(5)(i).

[49] Treas. Reg. § 1.355–2(d)(5)(ii).

(2) *Section 303(a) transactions.*[50] If, in the absence of § 355, the distribution would have been a redemption to which § 303(a) applied "with respect to each shareholder distributee," then the corporate division would not have avoided any dividend income. This provision cannot apply to a spin-off since there would not be a redemption of stock in that case.

(3) *Section 302(a) transactions.*[51] If, in the absence of § 355, the distribution would have been a redemption to which § 302(a) applied "with respect to each shareholder distributee," then once again the corporate division would not have avoided any dividend income.[52]

¶ 8.08 THE FIVE-YEAR ACTIVE TRADE OR BUSINESS REQUIREMENT

In addition to the device test, § 355 relies on another mechanism to minimize the risk that a taxpayer might use a corporate division to distribute earnings and profits. That mechanism is the requirement that each of the relevant corporations be engaged in the "active conduct of a trade or business." In general outline, §§ 355(a)(1)(C) and 355(b) require that:

- Immediately after the distribution, the distributing corporation and each controlled corporation whose stock was distributed continue to actively conduct a trade or business that had been actively conducted throughout the five-year period preceding the distribution. In determining whether a corporation is actively conducting a trade or business, all the members of an affiliated group of which that corporation would be the common parent are treated as a single corporation.[53]

- None of the relevant trades or businesses was acquired during that five-year period in a transaction in which gain or loss was recognized in whole or in part.

---

[50]   Treas. Reg. § 1.355–2(d)(5)(iii).

[51]   Treas. Reg. § 1.355–2(d)(5)(iv).

[52]   For purposes of this exemption, in determining whether § 302(a) would apply, the regulations do not apply § 302(c)(2)(A)(ii) and (iii)—i.e., the provisions prohibiting a distributee from acquiring an interest in the corporation within 10 years after the distribution, and the provision requiring the distributee to notify Treasury if that prohibition is violated.

[53]   § 355(b)(3)(B). The determination of an affiliated group is made by applying § 1504(a) without applying § 1504(b), which latter provision excludes certain categories of corporations from being included in an affiliated group.

- Control of a corporation that was conducting one of the relevant businesses was not acquired during that five-year period by either the distributing corporation or one of the controlled corporations in a transaction in which gain or loss was recognized in whole or in part.

The five-year active trade or business requirement proved to be complex in practice and gave rise to a substantial amount of litigation. A 1989 amendment to the regulations revised the Treasury Department's position concerning how it will apply the requirement,[54] and thereby eliminated many of the troublesome issues. Some of the more significant issues that arise in this context are discussed below.

¶ 8.08.1 Active Conduct of a Trade or Business

The regulations define the "active conduct of a trade or business" in two steps. First, they define a "trade or business" quite broadly.[55] They indicate that under § 355, the term should include "a specific group of activities . . . carried on by the corporation for the purpose of earning income or profit, [including] every operation that forms a part of, or a step in, the process of earning income or profit."[56] The group of activities "ordinarily must include the collection of income and the payment of expenses."[57]

That generous understanding of a "trade or business" has little practical effect, however, because the statute also requires that the trade or business have been actively conducted. In general, the active trade or business requirement connotes substantial managerial and operational activities directly carried on by the corporation— activities that are sufficient to distinguish the corporation's entrepreneurial endeavors from mere passive investments.[58] These managerial and operational functions must be conducted by the corporation without taking any credit for activities performed by outsiders such as independent contractors.[59] In particular, holding property for investment and leasing property to others who use it in a trade or business do not constitute the "active conduct" of a trade

---

[54]　Treas. Reg. § 1.355–3.

[55]　The term "trade or business" is used widely throughout the Code, but has not been given a single definition. See Commissioner v. Groetzinger, 480 U.S. 23 (1987). It is commonly thought that virtually anything a for-profit corporation does is pursuant to a "trade or business." Cf. International Trading Co. v. Commissioner, 484 F.2d 707 (7th Cir. 1973).

[56]　Treas. Reg. § 1.355–3(b)(2)(ii).

[57]　Id.

[58]　See, e.g., Rev. Rul. 88–19; Rev. Rul. 86–126; Rev. Rul. 86–125; Rev. Rul. 79–394; Rev. Rul. 73–237; Rev. Rul. 73–234.

[59]　Treas. Reg. § 1.355–3(b)(2)(iii).

or business for purposes of § 355, unless the taxpayer provides significant services with respect to the operation and management of the leased property.[60]

Thus, the IRS has ruled that a taxpayer's ownership and management of an investment portfolio of stocks and securities that were held on the taxpayer's own behalf does not constitute the *active conduct* of a trade or business, even though the taxpayer had hired 20 employees "to analyze and review the portfolio, research and investigate corporate situations, purchase and sell, pick up and deliver the securities, and maintain books of account."[61] Similarly, the regulations indicate that the holding of undeveloped real estate does not constitute the active conduct of a trade or business unless the owner engages in "significant development activities," and the holding of mineral rights does not constitute the active conduct of a trade or business unless the owner engages in "significant exploitation activities."[62] For example, where a landowner leased vacant land to a parking lot operator but provided no services to the lessee, the IRS held that the landowner was not engaged in the active conduct of a trade or business.[63]

The regulations provide two examples:[64]

Ex. (1)   X, a bank, owns an eleven-story office building. It occupies the ground floor itself and rents the other ten floors to various tenants. Bank employees manage and maintain the entire building. X transfers the building to new subsidiary Y and then distributes the Y stock. Henceforth, Y will manage the building, negotiate leases, seek new tenants, and repair and maintain the building. Both X and Y satisfy the active business requirements.

Ex. (2)   X, a bank, owns a two-story building. It occupies 75% of the building itself and rents the remaining half floor as storage space (presumably requiring little maintenance) to a neighboring retail merchant. X transfers the building to new subsidiary Y and then distributes the Y stock. Henceforth, Y will lease the same 75% to X under a lease which provides that X will repair and maintain its portion and pay property taxes and insurance. Expressly declining to rule on whether X satisfied the active business requirement before the distribution, the regulation states

---

[60]   Treas. Reg. § 1.355–3(b)(2)(iv).
[61]   Rev. Rul. 66–204.
[62]   Treas. Reg. § 1.355–3(c), Exs. (2), (3).
[63]   Rev. Rul. 68–284.
[64]   Treas. Reg. § 1.355–3(c), Exs. (12), (13).

that Y does not satisfy the active business requirement afterwards.

Over the years, the courts have struggled with close questions about what degree and kind of activity suffices to make a financial venture "active." For example, in *Rafferty v. Commissioner*,[65] the First Circuit phrased the test as whether the "corporation [engages] in entrepreneurial endeavors of such a nature and to such an extent as to qualitatively distinguish its operations from mere investments." The court found that the subsidiary corporation in that case failed to satisfy that requirement, emphasizing that, during the relevant time period, the subsidiary paid no salaries or rent and earned income only by collecting rent from its parent. In *King v. Commissioner*,[66] however, the Sixth Circuit found that subsidiaries were engaged in active businesses even though their only assets were real estate that they leased to their parent under a net lease. The court was satisfied by the facts that the subsidiaries purchased land, negotiated with contractors for the construction of improvements to the real estate, and obtained insurance on the properties. While *Rafferty* and *King* reached different results on their respective facts, both courts expressed dissatisfaction with the bright-line position that the Service took at that time that no activity by a subsidiary could constitute an active business if it was completely dependent on its parent for all income. As we will see, in the 1989 amendment to the regulations, Treasury abandoned the Service's prior position and effectively agreed that each of several integrated activities can be an actively conducted business even though all of the income of one of those activities is derived from another of those activities.

The Service initially concluded that the active trade or business requirement is not satisfied unless the activities in question produced a substantial net income. See Rev. Ruls. 57–464 and 57–492. In 2019, the Service suspended those two rulings and said that Treasury and the Service are conducting a study to determine whether a business can qualify as an active trade or business if it has entrepreneurial activities (in contrast to investment or other non-business activities) even if no income has been collected.[67]

Inevitably, the line that is being drawn here is uncertain, and it is worth pausing to wonder why it is being drawn at all. In one sense, the potential for bailing out accumulated earnings and profits would not seem to depend on whether a corporation charges a high rent and pays its own employees to provide basic services or charges a low rent and leaves the tenant with all such obligations under a "net lease."

---

[65]   452 F.2d 767, 772 (1st Cir. 1971).

[66]   458 F.2d 245 (6th Cir. 1972).

[67]   Rev. Rul. 2019–09.

Nevertheless, however difficult the line-drawing may be, there is a point to making that distinction. The congressional purpose for adopting the "active business" requirement is derived from a concern that the "device" test alone is too impressionistic to prevent abuses, and therefore Congress added an additional test that requires that each of the separated businesses have sufficient longevity and substance to provide some assurance that their separation had economic significance apart from distributing the corporation's earnings.

¶ 8.08.2 Active Conduct of a Trade or Business Through a Subsidiary

Prior to 2006, § 355(b)(2)(A) provided that a corporation is treated as engaged in the active conduct of a trade or business if it is effectively a holding company—that is, if substantially all of its assets consist of stock and securities of corporations controlled by it that are so engaged. In 2006, Congress deleted the holding company provision from § 355(b)(2)(A) and added § 355(b)(3) to the Code. For purposes of applying the five-year active trade or business rule, that provision treats a corporation and all of the affiliated corporations of which the first corporation is the common parent as a single corporation. The common parent and the affiliated corporations are referred to as the common parent corporation's "separate affiliated group," or "SAG" for short.

It is noteworthy that the test for whether the corporations are affiliated for this purpose does not turn on whether they are connected by stock ownership that satisfies the "control" test of section 368(c), which otherwise applies for purposes of § 355. Rather, the test is whether they are connected through stock ownership that satisfies a slightly expanded version of the test of § 1504(a), which applies to the filing of consolidated federal income tax returns and which is similar to but nonetheless different from the control test of § 368(c).

Ex. (3)   P is a holding company that holds no assets other than all of the stock of four subsidiaries: S1, S2, S3, and S4. The stock in each subsidiary has roughly the same value. S1 and S2 are actively engaged in the conduct of trades or businesses. S3 and S4 are not. In a corporate division, P spins off all of its stock in S1 to its shareholder A. Note that P is the common parent of the separate affiliated group (SAG) of P, S1, S2, S3, and S4.

For purposes of § 355, prior to the 2006 amendment, P would not have been engaged in the active conduct of a trade or business either before or after the spin-off. After the spin-off, P's stock in S2 (which is itself engaged in the active conduct of a trade or business) is not substantially all its assets, and so the pre-2006 version of § 355(b)(2)(A) would not have applied.

As a consequence of the 2006 amendment, P and all four of its subsidiaries are treated as a single corporation for purposes of applying the active business rule to P. So, before the division, P is deemed to have actively conducted the businesses operated by S1 and S2. After the division, P and its three remaining subsidiaries are treated as a single corporation, and so P is deemed to actively conduct the business operated by S2. Thus, the corporate division complies with the five-year active conduct of a trade or business requirement.

¶ 8.08.3 The Five-Year Requirement

The five-year period leading up to the corporate division is an especially sensitive period for purposes of applying § 355. The Code contains several provisions to guard against the possibility that what appears to be an "active business" was itself merely a temporary investment of earnings and profits in anticipation of a distribution.

The primary rule is that for a corporation to satisfy the active business requirement, the corporation's trade or business must have been actively conducted *throughout* the five-year period.[68] Moreover, the business may not have been acquired during the five-year period in anything other than a wholly nonrecognition transaction.[69] Finally, control of a corporation that was conducting the trade or business cannot have been acquired by the distributing or a controlled corporation during the five-year period in anything other than a wholly nonrecognition transaction.[70]

We note here that the statute requires only that the distributing parent and the controlled subsidiaries each be engaged in the active conduct of *a* trade or business. There is no requirement that the trade or business in question comprise any particular percentage of the corporation's assets.[71] Obviously, however, the lower the percentage

---

[68] § 355(b)(2)(B).

[69] § 355(b)(2)(C). The actual statutory language disqualifies only an acquisition through "a transaction in which gain or loss was recognized in whole or in part." However, the regulations state that a purchase within the five-year period of a trade of business will fail the five-year active conduct of a trade or business requirement even if the seller did not recognize gain because the purchase price equaled the seller's basis. Treas. Reg. § 1.355–3(b)(4)(i).

[70] § 355(b)(2)(D).

[71] Thus, the IRS has ruled that the requirement was satisfied in the case of a company whose active business represented "a substantial portion" of the value of its assets, but "less than half of such value;" and, in a 1996 ruling, the IRS stated that having only 5% of a corporation's gross assets used in a trade or business may be deemed sufficient in some circumstances. Rev. Rul. 73–44, clarified by Rev. Rul. 76–54. See also Tech. Adv. Mem. 8308007; G.C.M. 37534; G.C.M. 34238. The last G.C.M.

of corporate assets used in the business, the greater the risk that the transaction will be found to have been used principally as a "device" for the distribution of earnings and profits.[72]

¶ 8.08.4 Division of an Integrated Business and the Problem of "Expansions"

A corporation may wish to use a corporate division to separate several components of what had previously been a single, integrated business. For example, the corporation may wish to separate its East Coast manufacturing-and-sales business from its West Coast manufacturing-and-sales business—a "vertical" division of a single business. Or it may wish to separate its manufacturing operations from its retail sales operations—a "horizontal" division of functions that previously were "vertically integrated."

Many people find the terminology of "horizontal" and "vertical" to be somewhat confusing in this context, so before proceeding further, we offer a diagram to help clarify the way in which the terms are used. Consider a business that engages in both production and sales activities, each on both the East Coast and the West Coast:

West Coast Productions	East Coast Productions
West Coast Sales	East Coast Sales

This business is "vertically" integrated in that production and sales are all carried out in a single company. A "horizontal" division would draw a horizontal line through the company, separating production from sales. A "vertical" division would draw a vertical line through the company, separating the business geographically into two new businesses, each of which is still "vertically" integrated because each still carries on both production and sales activities.

Historically, the active business requirement of § 355(b) posed two types of obstacles for the division of integrated businesses. First, where a division (whether "horizontal" or "vertical") serves to separate two facets of a business that have long been parts of an integrated whole, taxpayers have faced the argument that the division has failed to yield two distinct trades or businesses, each with its own distinct five-year history. Second, where the division

---

notes authorities in which as little as 2% of corporate assets were used directly in an active trade or business. In Rev. Proc. 96–43 (adding to Section 4 of Rev. Proc. 96–3), the Commissioner stated that the Service may rule that a trade or business whose gross assets have a fair market value that is less than 5% of the value of the corporation's total gross assets qualifies for § 355(b) if it is established that the trade or business is not de minimis when compared with other assets of the corporation.

[72] See ¶ 8.07.

(again, whether "vertical" or "horizontal") serves to separate the business in a way that corresponds to a recent expansion of the main business, taxpayers have faced the (in a sense, opposite) argument that the expansion constituted a distinct separate business that was not operated for a full five years.

The current regulations explicitly provide that § 355 can apply to the division of a single business that has been in active operation for at least five years into separate businesses.[73] For horizontal divisions, the current regulations include three examples of such transactions and conclude that they satisfy the "active business" requirement.[74]

Significantly, the examples indicate that the Treasury Department is even willing to accept a functional division where, before the division, one component generated no outside income directly for the integrated business and, after the division, that component derived all its revenue from the corporation with which it had previously been affiliated.[75] The regulations emphasize, however, that where the "principal function" of one of the separated businesses is to "serve the business of the other corporation (or a corporation controlled by it)," there is "evidence of device" that must be taken into account under the facts and circumstances test.[76]

To be sure, even under the liberalized regime of the current regulations, each surviving corporation after a functional division must establish that it is engaged in the *active conduct* of a trade or business in order to satisfy the requirements of § 355(b).[77] It cannot simply be a vehicle for passive investments.

There is still an issue when one of the separated businesses had a distinct identity *before* the § 355 distribution, but *not* a full five years before. This problem arises whenever a business might be said to have "expanded" during the five-year period, either by purchase or new construction.

Ex. (4) X has operated a furniture manufacturing plant in North Carolina for twenty years. In Year One, X builds a new furniture manufacturing plant in Virginia. In Year Three, X distributes the Virginia plant to one of its shareholders in a split-off. Is this a simple separation of a twenty-year-old manufacturing business that happens to have "expanded"

---

[73]   Treas. Reg. §§ 1.355–1(b); 1.355–3(c), Ex. (4).
[74]   Treas. Reg. § 1.355–3(c), Exs. (9), (10), (11).
[75]   Treas. Reg. § 1.355–3(c), Ex. (9).
[76]   Id.; Treas. Reg. § 1.355–2(d)(2)(iv)(C).
[77]   See generally ¶ 8.08.1.

recently? Or is it the spin-off of a two-year-old trade or business?

Ex. (5) The same facts as Example (4), except that instead of building the new plant in Virginia, X buys a preexisting furniture manufacturing plant in Virginia for cash.

The concern here is that X might have built or purchased the new plant as an elaborate ruse to distribute accumulated earnings and profits. But that is extremely unlikely to have occurred. There is usually substantial financial risk associated with investing one's profits in the construction or purchase of a new, relatively illiquid manufacturing plant. How much can one rely on the separate "device" test to catch the most aggressive tax avoidance schemes?

The current regulations are generous and realistic on this point. Under the regulations, the critical concern is the "character" of the operations at the several sites rather than their geographical separation or the manner in which the expansion took place. Now, the central question is whether the changes "are of such a character as to constitute the acquisition of a new or different business." The geographical location of the different operations, and the extent to which they are separately managed, are no longer factors in the analysis.[78] This is true whether the expansion was created or purchased by the taxpayer.

¶ 8.08.5 Corporate Divisions Followed by Corporate Acquisitions

Section 355(b)(1)(A) requires that, in addition to satisfying the active business requirement throughout the five-year period leading up to the distribution, each corporation be engaged in the active conduct of a trade or business "immediately after the distribution." This requirement has been implicated in transactions where, pursuant to a prearranged plan, one of the corporations involved in a corporate division is then acquired by an unrelated party or participates in a reorganization transaction.

Ex. (6) X has owned and operated both a hardware store and a grocery store for more than five years. Y is willing to join with the hardware business but wants no part of the grocery business. Accordingly, X transfers the grocery business to new subsidiary corporation S and then spins S off to its shareholders. X then merges into Y, with X's shareholders receiving Y stock in exchange for their X stock.

---

[78] Treas. Reg. § 1.355–3(b)(3)(ii), (c), Ex. (7).

The IRS challenged such transactions on the ground (among others) that "immediately after the distribution" X was no longer engaged in the active conduct of a trade or business since X had disappeared in the merger. In *Curtis v. United States*,[79] the Sixth Circuit affirmed a District Court decision accepting the IRS argument. In *Commissioner v. Morris Trust*,[80] however, the Fourth Circuit affirmed a Tax Court decision rejecting it. The court emphasized that the statute was literally satisfied in that "immediately" after the distribution (i.e., before the merger) X was continuing the business, and that the substantive values underlying the statute were satisfied because after the merger Y was continuing the business. The IRS subsequently announced that it was accepting the *Morris Trust* decision on that point.[81] However, in 1997, because of the belief that *Morris Trust* type transactions were being utilized to achieve tax results that were deemed to be abusive, Congress added subsection (e) to § 355 (the so-called anti-*Morris Trust* provision) to require the distributing corporation to recognize gain on the distribution of the controlled subsidiary's stock to its shareholders in many, though not necessarily all, *Morris Trust* transactions. However, the anti-*Morris Trust* provisions do not disturb the tax-free treatment that § 355 otherwise accords to the shareholders of the distributing corporation. Thus, they may be said to make the *Morris Trust* transaction only partially taxable. Section 355(e) is discussed at ¶ 8.13.3.

¶ 8.09 NONSTATUTORY REQUIREMENTS— BUSINESS PURPOSE AND CONTINUITY OF INTEREST

In addition to the statutory requirements set forth above, the regulations include two nonstatutory requirements—the "business purpose" and "continuity of interest" requirements. Both requirements are generalized tests that apply to corporate divisions under §§ 355 and 356, as well as to corporate reorganizations under § 368.[82] The continuity of interest requirement has two distinct elements—a continuity of proprietary interest and a continuity of business enterprise (COBE).

---

[79]   336 F.2d 714 (6th Cir. 1964).

[80]   367 F.2d 794 (4th Cir. 1966).

[81]   Rev. Rul. 68–603.

[82]   Reorganizations are discussed in Chapter Nine.

¶ 8.09.1 Business Purpose

The business purpose requirement is a generalization of the Supreme Court's holding in *Gregory v. Helvering*,[83] beyond the context of the old "reorganization" statute that gave rise to that case.[84] "The principal reason for this business purpose requirement is to provide nonrecognition treatment only to distributions that are incident to readjustments of corporate structures required by business exigencies and that effect only readjustments of continuing interests in property under modified corporate forms."[85] The business purpose requirement complements the statutory requirement that the transaction not be a "device" for the distribution of earnings and profits; while the presence of a business purpose is "evidence" of a nondevice,[86] the two requirements are not equivalent.[87]

Appendix A to Rev. Proc. 96–30[88] sets forth guidelines as to how the IRS will rule on corporate divisions. A major element of those guidelines is the so-called "fit and focus" standard.[89] The fit and focus standard refers to a corporate division for the purpose of either improving the structure and management of the businesses or permitting a division of ownership so that different persons can focus on separate businesses. As stated in the revenue procedure, "the separation will enhance the success of the businesses by enabling the corporations to resolve management, systematic, or other problems that arise (or are exacerbated) by the taxpayer's operation of different businesses within a single corporation or affiliated group."[90] While Appendix A of Rev. Proc. 96–30 was deleted by Rev. Proc. 2003–48, which announced that the IRS would no longer give advance rulings on whether the business purpose requirement was satisfied, the fit and focus standards are likely to continue to be used by the IRS in applying the business purpose rule on audits and in litigation.

The regulations provide a number of details about what the Treasury Department is willing to recognize as a legitimate business purpose. It is far from clear, however, that the courts will be as exacting. After some general observations about what should constitute an acceptable business purpose, we will comment

---

[83] 293 U.S. 465 (1935).

[84] See ¶ 8.03.

[85] Treas. Reg. § 1.355–2(b)(1).

[86] Treas. Reg. §§ 1.355–2(b)(4), –2(d)(3)(ii).

[87] For a peculiar case in which the trier of fact found neither a tax avoidance motive nor a legitimate business purpose, see Commissioner v. Wilson, 353 F.2d 184, 187–88 (9th Cir. 1965).

[88] Rev. Proc. 96–30 was modified by Rev. Proc. 2003–48.

[89] Id.

[90] Id.

specifically on two particular aspects of the regulations—their hostility to non-economic shareholder purposes, and their insistence that there be no convenient alternative mechanism to accomplish the business purpose.

The regulations state that the purpose must be "a real and substantial non-federal tax purpose germane to the business of the distributing corporation, the controlled corporation, or the affiliated group (as defined in § 1.355–3(b)(4)(iv)) to which the distributing corporation belongs."[91] Examples of such purposes may be found in the regulations themselves and in prior Revenue Rulings. Some of the approved purposes are:

- A desire to separate dissident shareholders.[92]

- A desire to separate a business that competes with the other business's customers.[93]

- A desire to facilitate a merger by reducing the value of the assets of the surviving corporation so that the shareholders of the other party to the merger will not be minority shareholders.[94]

- A desire to comply with an antitrust decree.[95]

- A desire to make it easier to hire a key employee who demands stock in the company and insists that it not be a subsidiary corporation.[96]

- A desire to eliminate the burdens of state regulatory requirements imposed on the parent on account of the subsidiary's business activities.[97]

- A desire to eliminate an unsuccessful subsidiary from the parent's balance sheet to facilitate a new public offering of the parent's stock.[98]

Over the years, substantial controversy has persisted about how to treat transactions that are motivated by desires of the

---

[91]   Treas. Reg. § 1.355–2(b)(2).

[92]   Badanes v. Commissioner, 39 T.C. 410 (1962); Rev. Rul. 69–460. See also Rev. Rul. 56–655; Treas. Reg. § 1.355–2(b)(5), Ex. (2) (no hostility between the shareholders, but they "anticipate that the operations of each business will be enhanced by the separation because each shareholder will be able to devote his undivided attention to the business in which he is more interested and more proficient"); PLR 9726013.

[93]   See Rev. Rul. 59–197.

[94]   See Rev. Rul. 72–530. See also Rev. Rul. 76–527.

[95]   Treas. Reg. § 1.355–2(b)(5), Ex. (1).

[96]   See Rev. Rul. 88–34.

[97]   Rev. Rul. 88–33.

[98]   Rev. Rul. 85–122.

shareholders that are not tax avoidance but cannot properly be deemed purposes of the corporation either. The regulations take a very strong stand on this question. A shareholder purpose is not acceptable unless it is "so nearly coextensive with a corporate business purpose as to preclude any distinction between them."[99]

The case law on this point is somewhat less stringent. In *Estate of Parshelsky v. Commissioner*,[100] the Second Circuit held that a shareholders' personal non-tax-avoidance reasons should be considered together with corporate reasons in applying the business purpose requirement. It found the appropriate inquiry to concern whether the taxpayer "had corporate *or* shareholder purposes such as would motivate a reasonable businessman to effect a spin-off." In *Rafferty v. Commissioner*,[101] the First Circuit rejected the *Parshelsky* view but seemed not to demand quite so much as the regulations, holding that "a distribution which has considerable potential for use as a device for distributing earnings and profits should not qualify for tax-free treatment on the basis of personal motives unless those motives are germane to the continuance of the corporate business."[102]

How central must the business purpose be to the distribution? At one point the regulations require only that the distribution be "motivated, in whole or substantial part, by one or more corporate business purposes."[103] But the regulations later indicate that a business purpose cannot count at all in this calculus if it "can be achieved through a non-taxable transaction that does not involve the distribution of stock of a controlled corporation and which is neither impractical nor unduly expensive."[104] They give an example of a regulated corporation that engages in a spin-off of a profitable business in order to be able to charge customers of the regulated business more for their product; since the corporation could have achieved the same goals by creating a holding company through a § 351 exchange, the regulations would deny nonrecognition treatment pursuant to § 355.[105]

---

[99]   Treas. Reg. § 1.355–2(b)(2)–2(b)(5), Ex. (2). For an example of such a situation, see Rev. Rul. 75–337 concerning an intra-family split-off designed to ensure that the only daughters with ownership interest in a car dealership would be those daughters active in the business, in order to ensure that the manufacturer would be willing to renew the franchise after the father's death.

[100]   303 F.2d 14 (2d Cir. 1962), rev'g. 34 T.C. 946 (1960).

[101]   452 F.2d 767 (1st Cir. 1971). Other aspects of the case are discussed in ¶ 8.08.1.

[102]   Id. at 770. In Rev. Rul. 2003–52, the Service found a sufficient corporate business purpose even though it determined that the spin-off in question also furthered the personal estate-planning objectives of the principal shareholders of the distributing corporation.

[103]   Treas. Reg. § 1.355–2(b)(1).

[104]   Treas. Reg. § 1.355–2(b)(3).

[105]   Treas. Reg. § 1.355–2(b)(5), Ex. (4).

Perhaps somewhat surprisingly, this crabbed understanding of what constitutes a legitimate "business purpose" has some support in the case law.[106] In our opinion, however, it is far too strict. One may well have reason to suspect the legitimacy of a putative business purpose that could have been achieved more simply and more directly than through a § 355 distribution. But that is a far cry from insisting that nonrecognition treatment should be denied whenever a creative second-guesser can identify an alternative non-taxable transaction that is just as complex as the § 355 approach (but not "impractical or unduly expensive"). Recall that the business purpose requirement is hardly the last bulwark against tax avoidance in the § 355 area; it is merely an additional arrow in the Commissioner's quiver. It should not be used to punish taxpayers who are not seeking to use § 355 as a device by leaving them *worse* off than they would have been had they chosen the alternative non-taxable transaction. On the other hand, it will be the rare case in which a tax advisor will structure a corporate division around a business purpose that is not supported by the Treasury regulations. Those regulations have existed for a great many years, and the courts have shown an increasing willingness to defer to the Treasury's judgment with respect to such regulations.

¶ 8.09.2 Continuity of Interest

As noted above, there are two elements to the continuity of interest requirement—continuity of business enterprise (COBE) and continuity of proprietary interest.

As applied to § 355, the continuity of business enterprise (COBE) requires no more than that the "business or businesses existing prior to the separation" be continued.[107] There is no indication of how long the business or businesses must be continued. If there were multiple businesses conducted prior to the corporate division, it is probable that COBE does not require the continuation of all of those businesses, but requires only that the distributing and controlled corporations each continue at least one substantial historic business.[108]

The second element embodied in the regulations is the "continuity of proprietary interest" requirement, although this is sometimes referred to simply as the "continuity of interest" requirement. The "continuity of proprietary interest" doctrine has a

---

[106]   See King v. Commissioner, 458 F.2d 245 (6th Cir. 1972) (McCree, J., dissenting); Estate of Parshelsky v. Commissioner, 303 F.2d 14 (2d Cir. 1962); Gada v. United States, 460 F.Supp. 859 (D. Conn. 1978). But see Hanson v. United States, 338 F.Supp. 602 (D. Mont. 1971).

[107]   Treas. Reg. § 1.355–1(b).

[108]   Ginsburg & Levin, ¶ 1008.

long and important history in the context of acquisitive reorganizations.[109] There, it has come to be understood as a requirement that a substantial portion of the consideration received by parties to a reorganization consist of an ongoing equity interest in the surviving enterprise. For advance ruling purposes, the Service has indicated that it will deem the requirement satisfied when at least 50% of the value of the consideration received by the shareholders of the acquired corporation (as a group) takes the form of stock in the surviving enterprise.[110] It is clear, however, that if 40% of the consideration is stock, that will be sufficient to satisfy the requirement.[111]

That standard does not translate very easily to the world of corporate divisions—especially to spin-offs where the shareholders are not giving anything up. One might simply take the position that what is required is that at least half the value of the distribution consist of nonrecognition property.[112] The current regulations, however, take a more stringent line. They require that "one or more persons who, directly or indirectly, were the owners of the enterprise prior to the distribution or exchange own, in the aggregate, an amount of stock establishing a continuity of interest in *each* of the modified corporate forms in which the enterprise is conducted after the separation."[113]

Ex. For more than five years, X has owned and operated a hardware store directly and has owned all the stock of corporation S, which has operated a grocery store directly. The businesses are of equal value. A and B each own half of X's 100 outstanding shares.

---

[109]   See Treas. Reg. § 1.368–1(b); Pinellas Ice & Cold Storage Co. v. Commissioner, 287 U.S. 462 (1933); Helvering v. Minnesota Tea Co., 296 U.S. 378 (1935); LeTulle v. Scofield, 308 U.S. 415 (1940). See generally ¶ 9.03.1.

[110]   Rev. Proc. 77–37, Sec. 3.02. The 50% of consideration in stock benchmark is adopted in Treas. Reg. § 1.368–1(e)(8), Ex. (1). However, as discussed in Chapter Nine with respect to corporate reorganizations, it is clear that the continuity of proprietary interest requirement will be satisfied if as little as 40% of the value of the aggregate consideration that the shareholders received is stock. Temp. Reg. § 1.368–1T(e)(2)(v), Ex. (1) provides an example of an acquisitive reorganization in which 40% of the consideration was in stock of the surviving corporation, and that was held to be sufficient to provide continuity of proprietary interest.

[111]   Id.

[112]   See Rev. Rul. 79–273 (S is a wholly owned subsidiary of P. Pursuant to an integrated plan, (a) X forms subsidiary Z and contributes cash equal to 85% of the value of outstanding P stock, (b) Z merges into P in a statutory merger, with X getting new P stock, (c) P uses the cash it acquired from Z to redeem pro rata from its preexisting shareholders 85% of their P stock, and (d) P distributes all the shares of S pro rata to its preexisting shareholders in exchange for the remaining 15% of their P stock. Section 355 held inapplicable because no continuity of interest.).

[113]   Treas. Reg. § 1.355–2(c)(1) (emphasis added).

New purchaser C is interested in X's hardware business, but not in S's grocery business. Pursuant to a prearranged plan, C first buys 40 shares of X stock from A for cash; X then splits off S by distributing all the S stock to B in exchange for all 50 shares of X stock that B held.

According to the current regulations, this transaction does *not* satisfy the continuity-of-interest requirement.[114] They state that, while A and B still have 60% of their original equity interests in the former X–S enterprise (all of the grocery business and $\frac{1}{5}$ of the hardware business), "the 20 percent interest of A in X is less than the minimum equity interest in the distributing corporation, X, that would be required in order to meet the continuity of interest requirement."[115]

As a consequence of the combination of changes that have taken place in the application of the continuity of interest doctrine to acquisitive reorganizations and of amendments that have been made to § 368(a)(2)(H)(ii) and to § 355 itself,[116] there may be a legitimate basis to challenge the validity of the current regulations. At the very least, one could argue that the current § 355 regulations relating to continuity of interest should be greatly modified to harmonize them with the treatment of continuity of interest with respect to corporate reorganizations. At this writing, however, Treasury has not yet revoked or modified its regulations in this area. Let us first examine the current regulations and then consider the arguments that could be asserted in support of their invalidity.

The regulations that deal with the continuity of proprietary interest requirement in the context of a § 355 transaction focus exclusively on changes in stock ownership that take place prior to the distribution or exchange of the controlled corporation's stock.[117] The regulations require that one or more persons who were the owners of the enterprise prior to the distribution or exchange own in the

---

[114]   Treas. Reg. § 1.355–2(c)(2), Ex. (4).

[115]   Id.

[116]   For example, it would appear that, in enacting section 355(d) in 1990, Congress implicitly indicated that, while such a transaction may be an occasion to tax the distributing corporation on the built-in gain in the controlled corporation stock, it is not appropriate to tax the shareholders in such circumstances. The same point could be made with respect to the 1997 enactment of section 355(e). One or both of these provisions would apply to many of the transactions where continuity was found lacking, but it would then be only the distributing corporation that would be taxed, not the shareholders receiving the distribution.

[117]   Treas. Reg. 1.355–2(c).

aggregate sufficient stock in *each* of the involved corporations to qualify for continuity of proprietary interest.[118]

The continuity of interest regulations under § 355 do not expressly require that the shareholders continue to hold their interest in the involved corporations for any specified period of time after the distribution or exchange took place.[119] In any case, a sale of stock after the division and as part of the same plan is an issue that is already more than adequately policed under the regulations that relate to the device restriction. That fact probably explains why the focus of the § 355 continuity regulations is on stock dispositions that occur *before* the corporate division. We have found no authority where the Service has successfully asserted a continuity of interest argument with respect to post-division sales of stock. In fact, § 368(a)(2)(H)(ii) now explicitly preempts such an argument in the case of corporate divisions that constitute D reorganizations,[120] and it seems virtually impossible to conceive a persuasive basis for a different continuity rule for divisions that constitute D reorganizations and those that do not, especially since we know that taxpayers can easily structure non-reorganization divisions to qualify for D reorganization treatment.

So long as the disposition is made to persons unrelated to the combining corporations, the current position of the Service is that neither prior nor subsequent dispositions of stock will violate the continuity requirements in the context of an acquisitive reorganization. Should there then be a different application of the continuity requirement if the transaction is a corporate division rather than an acquisitive reorganization? The authors believe that there is no persuasive reason why the requirement should be applied differently in the context of a corporate division.

¶ 8.10 BOOT

The distributed property must be stock and securities of the subsidiary to qualify the recipient shareholder for nonrecognition treatment under § 355. Thus, any property other than stock and securities of the subsidiary will constitute boot to the recipient shareholders. However, even some stock and securities will not

---

[118]   The examples in the regulations treat a 50% interest as qualifying for continuity of interest, but do not indicate to what extent a lesser figure would also be sufficient. As noted above, however, a 40% interest is acknowledged to be sufficient for purposes of corporate reorganizations, and there is no apparent reason why that same level of continuity should not be sufficient for corporate division purposes as well.

[119]   But see ¶ 8.07 as to whether the device exception to § 355 might apply.

[120]   The statute states quite explicitly that, in a D reorganization to which either § 355, or so much of § 356 as relates to § 355, applies, "the fact that the shareholders of the distributing corporation dispose of part or all of the distributed stock . . . shall not be taken into account."

qualify for nonrecognition treatment. Four provisions of the statute reclassify certain stock and securities as boot. In particular, "excess securities" can be treated as boot by virtue of § 355(a)(3)(A); "recently acquired stock" can be treated as boot by virtue of § 355(a)(3)(B); "nonqualified preferred stock" can be treated as boot by virtue of § 355(a)(3)(D); and stock and securities issued to satisfy accrued interest on securities can be treated as boot by virtue of § 355(a)(3)(C).

¶ 8.10.1 Excess Securities Boot

The excess securities boot provision significantly limits the extent to which a parent can distribute securities of a subsidiary and obtain nonrecognition treatment for the distributee under § 355. Specifically, nonrecognition is available to the distributee only to the extent that the parent receives its own securities in exchange.

Where securities of the parent that are held by the subsidiary are surrendered to the parent in exchange for securities of the subsidiary that are held by the parent, the amount of boot depends both on the *principal amounts* of both sets of securities and on the *fair market value* of the subsidiary's securities on the date of the exchange. The amount of boot is equal to the fair market value of the portion of the distributed securities whose principal is not matched by the surrender of securities of the parent in exchange.[121] Note that this is neither simply the difference in fair market value, nor simply the difference between the principal amounts.

Ex. A and B are the sole and equal shareholders of X, which is the sole shareholder of subsidiary S. A and B each hold a bond from X in the principal amount of $4,000, paying annual interest at the rate of 5% per year, with the principal payable in ten years. Each X bond has a fair market value of $3,700.

X holds two bonds from S, each in the principal amount of $10,000, paying annual interest at the rate of 10% per year, with the principal payable in ten years. Each S bond has a fair market value of $13,000.

X distributes its S shares equally to A and B, and also distributes an S bond to each of them. In exchange, A and B surrender their X bonds to X.

The amount of boot A and B receive in that Example is calculated as follows. A and B each receive an S bond in the principal amount of $10,000, in exchange for an X bond in the principal amount of $4,000. They each receive boot in an amount equal to the fair

---

[121] Treas. Reg. § 1.356–3.

market value of a hypothetical S bond in the principal amount of $6,000 but otherwise having the same terms. That would equal the fair market value of the actual $10,000 S bond ($13,000), multiplied by a fraction that reflects the ratio of the excess principal amount to the total principal amount (6,000/10,000 = 60%). Thus, the boot is equal to $13,000 (the fair market value of the distributed security) times 60%, or $7,800.

It may be helpful to diagram that Example this way:

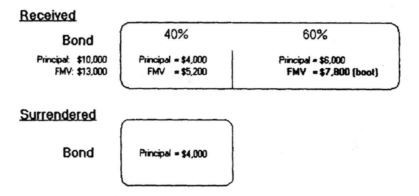

¶ 8.10.2 Stock Boot

Where the parent corporation acquired stock in the subsidiary "by reason of" something other than a nonrecognition transaction that took place during the five-year period leading up to the distribution,[122] the recently acquired stock is treated as stock for some purposes, but as "other property" for other purposes.[123] Such recently acquired stock is sometimes referred to as "stock boot" or as "hot stock." The stock boot is counted along with other stock in applying the requirement that all (or virtually all) of the parent's stock of the subsidiary be distributed.[124] It is not treated as stock for purposes of applying the general nonrecognition rule of § 355; instead it is treated as boot under § 356.[125] However, as noted below,

---

[122]　See ¶ 8.08.3.

[123]　§ 355(a)(3)(B).

[124]　§ 355(a)(1)(D), (a)(3)(B).

[125]　Moreover, if distributed to shareholders, it is not treated as stock for purposes of § 355(c), and so the parent corporation may recognize gain on making that distribution. See ¶ 8.13.1. However, if the distribution to shareholders is made pursuant to a D reorganization, then the question of the parent corporation's recognition of gain is determined by § 361(c) rather than by § 355(c). Nevertheless, the stock boot will not constitute "qualified property" within § 361(c)(2)(B)(ii) since it was not acquired by the distributing corporation as part of the exchange. Consequently, regardless of whether the corporate division is a reorganization, the distributing corporation will recognize gain on any appreciated stock boot that it distributes.

regulations that were promulgated in 2011 have so narrowed the scope of the stock boot rule as to render it of only minor significance.

The purpose of the stock boot restriction, like the restrictions imposed under the "active business" test of § 355(b), is to minimize the risk that a distributing corporation might use its retained earnings to purchase additional shares of the subsidiary in anticipation of the distribution.

As noted in ¶ 8.08.2, in applying the five-year active trade or business requirement, § 355(b)(3) treats a "separate affiliated group" (SAG) as a single corporation. With respect to any corporation, a "separate affiliated group" refers to the affiliated group that would be determined under § 1504(a) if such corporation were the common parent and § 1504(b) did not apply.[126] Affiliation with a corporation under § 1504(a)(2) requires ownership of stock possessing at least 80% of the voting power of the corporation's outstanding stock and at least 80% of the value of the corporation's outstanding stock. The standard for control for § 1504(a)(2) affiliation purposes is similar to the standard for control adopted in § 368(c). The difference is that § 368(c) does not require ownership of stock possessing 80% of the value of the corporation's stock, but rather requires ownership of 80% of the voting power and of the total number of outstanding shares of nonvoting stock. Thus, it is possible for a corporation to have "control" of a subsidiary corporation for purposes of § 368(c) and not to have "control" of that corporation for purposes of § 1504(a).

While § 355(b)(3) applies to the active trade or business requirement, § 355(b)(3)(D) authorizes Treasury to promulgate regulations applying the principles of the SAG rules to the stock boot rules. Treasury acted on that authorization by promulgating Treas. Reg. § 1.355–2(g)(2) in 2011. That regulation negates the stock boot rule if either: (1) the acquired stock was owned by the distributing corporation's SAG immediately before and after the stock was acquired, or (2) the stock was purchased from a member of the same affiliated group of corporations,[127] provided that such member corporation had not purchased that stock within the five-year pre-distribution period.[128] These exceptions narrow the scope of the stock boot rule.

---

[126]   § 355(b)(3)(B).

[127]   "Affiliated group" is defined for this purpose in Treas. Reg. § 1.355–3(b)(4)(iv) very similarly, but not identically, to the definition of members of the distributing corporation's SAG.

[128]   Treas. Reg. § 1.355–2(g)(1), (2)(ii).

¶ 8.10.3 Nonqualified Preferred Stock Boot

The concept of "nonqualified preferred stock" (NQPS) was introduced into the Code as part of the Taxpayer Relief Act of 1997. The term is defined in § 351(g), which is discussed at ¶ 7.11.1. Preferred stock that is not NQPS is sometimes conveniently referred to as "qualified preferred stock" (QPS), but that is not a term used in the Code or the Treasury Regulations.

Nonqualified preferred stock that is distributed in connection with a corporate division to which either § 355 or § 356 applies will not be treated as stock or a security unless either (1) it is received in exchange for (or in a distribution with respect to) other nonqualified preferred stock; or (2) it is received in exchange for (or in a distribution with respect to) qualified preferred stock that satisfies the conditions of Treas. Reg. § 1.356–7(b)(1)(i), and the stock received is substantially identical to the original preferred stock.[129] In other words, nonqualified preferred stock that is distributed in connection with a § 355 or § 356 corporate division will be treated as boot except to the extent that such stock either is received in exchange for (or in a distribution with respect to) other NQPS or is received in exchange for (or in a distribution with respect to) certain QPS having similar terms.[130]

¶ 8.11 TAX CONSEQUENCES FOR SHAREHOLDERS WHEN BOOT IS DISTRIBUTED

The general rule of § 355 regarding the tax treatment of shareholders is quite straightforward—nonrecognition of gain or loss. However, as we have noted, § 355 by its terms provides nonrecognition treatment only for certain transactions in which a parent corporation distributes "solely" stock or securities of a controlled corporation. Section 356 complements § 355 by extending partial nonrecognition treatment of gain to transactions that would satisfy § 355 were it not for the fact that the transferor received other property or money ("boot"). Section 356(c) prevents the recognition of any loss even though boot was received.

¶ 8.11.1 § 356—General Rules

Section 356(a) deals with gain from otherwise-qualifying split-offs or split-ups, and provides that, in such "exchanges," the shareholder recognizes any gain realized on the exchange to the extent of the value of the boot received. Section 356(b) deals with

---

[129]   §§ 355(a)(3)(D), and 356(e). Treas. Reg. § 1.356–6.

[130]   For greater elaboration on this point, please see pp. 386–387 of the Corporate Income Taxation Hornbook.

otherwise-qualifying spin-offs ("distributions") and says something quite different—the fair market value of any boot is to be treated as a § 301 distribution. Section 356(c) deals with losses, and provides that no loss is recognized even if boot is present.

¶ 8.11.2 § 356—Amount and Characterization of Gain

For purposes of allocating basis to the distributed properties, the regulations provide that a designation in the terms of an exchange as to what distributions were made in exchange for which properties will be respected if the designation is economically reasonable.[131] This matching will not affect the amount of boot received as excess securities boot since the Code requires that that amount of boot is determined by matching securities according to their principal amounts regardless of how the parties designated the exchange.[132] The regulations provide that, in the absence of an economically reasonable designation in the terms of the exchange, for purposes of determining basis, a pro rata portion of the shares of stock and securities and boot received will be treated as received in exchange for each share of stock and security surrendered based on the fair market value of the stock and securities surrendered.[133] In the view of the authors, better tax policy might match the securities received with the securities surrendered to the extent that their fair market values are equal, but the regulations provide otherwise.

¶ 8.11.3 § 356—Special Problems in Split-Offs with Boot

In a spin-off, the shareholder does not give anything up in exchange for the distribution. The shareholder does not give back any assets with basis that might limit the amount of gain below the full fair market value of the boot. Any boot distributed is, in effect, indistinguishable from a § 301 distribution, and it is taxed that way.[134] It gives rise to ordinary dividend income to the extent of the distributing corporation's *e and p*.[135]

In a split-off or split-up, the shareholder gives up shares of the parent corporation, and may therefore have realized gain that is less than the full fair market value of the boot, or may even realize a loss. Section 356(a)(1) provides that such a shareholder is taxed on the

---

[131]   Treas. Reg. § 1.358–2(a)(2)(ii).

[132]   §§ 355(a)(3)(A), 356(d)(2)(C).

[133]   Treas. Reg. § 1.358–2(a)(2)(ii).

[134]   § 356(b).

[135]   Treas. Reg. § 1.356–2. The *e and p* is determined in the usual manner by first applying the corporation's current *e and p* and then applying the corporation's accumulated *e and p*.

amount of any gain realized to the extent of the fair market value of boot received. The shareholder is able to use some of his basis in the parent stock to reduce the amount of gain, and the gain may be characterized as capital even if the distributing corporation had *e and p* available. If a loss is realized, none is recognized.

Yet a pro rata spin-off is indistinguishable in economic effect from a pro rata split-off where each shareholder returns a proportionate share of his or her stock in the parent corporation. For that reason, § 356(a)(2) provides that, if the exchange had "the effect of the distribution of a dividend," the *gain recognized* by the shareholder will be treated as a dividend to the extent of the shareholder's ratable portion of the corporation's earnings and profits accumulated after February 28, 1913, and the balance of the recognized gain, if any, will usually be a capital gain. The current capital gains rates for most dividend income reduces the significance of allowing capital gain treatment for the excess amount.

Somewhat strangely, § 356(a)(2) does not produce exactly the same tax treatment for pro rata split-offs that § 356(b) produces for pro rata spin-offs. It goes part way in that direction, but not all the way. Two important differences stand out. First, even a split-off that "has the effect of the distribution of a dividend" is taxable only to the extent that the shareholder realizes a gain on the stock that is surrendered. Second, § 356(a)(2) does not employ the traditional bifurcated dividend test of § 316 that is applied to § 301 distributions and to spin-offs under § 356(b); instead of looking both to current *e and p* and to accumulated *e and p*, § 356(a)(2) looks exclusively to accumulated *e and p*.

When boot is distributed as part of a § 356 exchange, and if the shareholder thereby recognized a gain, it must then be determined whether the exchange "has the effect of a distribution of a dividend."[136] If so, some or all of that shareholder's gain may constitute dividend income depending upon the amount of *e and p* that is allocated to that gain.[137] The standards for determining whether an exchange has the effect of a distribution of a dividend are discussed below.

¶ 8.11.4 § 356—Testing for Dividend Equivalency

As noted above, in the case of a split-off or split-up that is covered by § 356(a), the characterization of any ensuing gain depends

---

[136] § 356(a)(2).

[137] Only the amount of the shareholder's recognized gain that does not exceed the distributee's "ratable share" of the distributing corporation's accumulated *e and p* is a dividend. Id. The Code and regulations do not describe how a distributee's "ratable share" is to be determined.

on whether the exchange "has the effect of the distribution of a dividend." That phrase is not defined in statutes or regulations, and was the subject of substantial uncertainty for many years.

Originally, the IRS attempted to follow an "automatic dividend" rule, treating any recognized gain as a dividend distribution to the extent of the corporation's *e and p*.[138] After substantial criticism by courts and commentators,[139] the IRS abandoned the automatic dividend rule in favor of using the principles for determining dividend equivalency that were developed under IRC § 302 (the stock redemption rules).[140]

Even after that overriding issue was resolved, a number of smaller ones remained. The courts waffled for several years until Congress made it clear that the attribution rules of § 318 apply to determine dividend equivalency in this context.[141] A more complex question concerned how, in testing for dividend equivalency, one should respond to the fact that the shareholder received both nonrecognition property (usually stock in the subsidiary) as well as boot.

Ex. X corporation has substantial accumulated *e and p*. X owns all the stock of Y, which has a fair market value of $114,000. X also owns a Y bond with a face amount of $6,000, and a fair market value of $6,000. Y has conducted a jewelry business for more than five years. X has conducted a realty business for more than five years.

X has two unrelated shareholders, A and B. B owns 50 shares of X common stock, and A owns 450 shares. A has owned her stock for more than five years. She has a basis of $70,000 in those shares, and they are now worth $120,000.

In a split-off, A transfers all her X stock to X in exchange for all of the Y stock and the Y bond. After the split-off, X retains the realty business and B owns all the outstanding X shares. The parties did not designate which item was exchanged for which. Since A did not exchange any X securities, A received $6,000 of boot.

In that Example, in the aggregate, A realized a gain of $50,000 ($120,000 worth of property received minus a combined basis of

---

[138]   See Rev. Rul. 56–220.

[139]   See King Enterprises v. United States, 418 F.2d 511 (Ct. Cl. 1969); Hawkinson v. Commissioner, 235 F.2d 747 (2d Cir. 1956).

[140]   Rev. Rul. 74–515. See also Rev. Rul. 93–62; Rev. Rul. 84–114. The § 302 rules for determining dividend equivalency are discussed in Chapter Three.

[141]   Tax Equity and Fiscal Responsibility Act of 1982, Sec. 227(b), amending § 356(a)(2), Pub. L. No. 97–248, 96 Stat. 324, 492.

$70,000 for the property surrendered). She must recognize $6,000 of that gain because she has received $6,000 of excess securities boot. How that gain is characterized depends on whether it has the effect of a dividend distribution under § 356(a)(2), which in turn depends upon the percentage of change in A's ownership of X stock. But how should one analyze the effect of the distribution of boot on A's stock ownership? Even though the exchanges took place simultaneously, should the boot exchange for some of A's stock be treated as a separate transaction from the nonrecognition exchange of the rest of the transaction? If so, which exchange should be deemed to have taken place first?

Should one pretend that the $6,000 of boot was first distributed in redemption of $6,000 of X stock, and that X then followed that redemption by making a qualifying § 355 distribution of Y stock for A's remaining shares of X stock? If that order were followed, then one could compare the percentage of X stock that A held before the redemption for boot with the percentage of X stock that A held after that redemption took place and apply § 302 principles to see if the exchange had the effect of a dividend. Alternatively, should one pretend that X first made a qualifying § 355 distribution of Y stock for A's shares of X stock and X then followed that exchange by distributing the $6,000 of boot in redemption of A's remaining shares of X stock? If the latter order were adopted, the redemption of A's final shares of X stock would have terminated A's stock interest in X, and so the transaction clearly would not have had the effect of a dividend. Obviously, the method that is applied to order the exchanges (boot first followed by a nonrecognition exchange or vice versa) can have a significant effect on the tax treatment of the transaction.

Since it abandoned the "automatic dividend" rule, the IRS has consistently adhered to the first approach (pure boot transaction first, followed by a nonrecognition transaction).[142] Indeed, it applied that boot-first approach not only in the context of corporate divisions, but also in the context of acquisitive reorganizations (where the boot comes from a separate acquiring corporation). After many years of litigation, the Supreme Court rejected the use of the boot-first approach in the context of acquisitive reorganizations in *Commissioner v. Clark*.[143] Notwithstanding *Clark*, the IRS has ruled that it will continue to use the boot-first approach where corporate divisions are concerned.[144] The IRS maintains that the principle on

---

[142]   Rev. Rul. 74–516, superseded by Rev. Rul. 93–62.

[143]   489 U.S. 726 (1989), aff'g 828 F.2d 221 (4th Cir. 1987), aff'g 86 T.C. 138 (1986). We discuss the *Clark* case in Chapter Nine.

[144]   Rev. Rul. 93–62, superseding Rev. Rul. 74–516. See, e.g., PLR 200708012.

which the Supreme Court based its *Clark* decision requires a boot first treatment when applied to a corporate division.

The authors are of mixed minds about which of those two approaches is correct as a matter of good tax policy. For the present, the courts have yet to speak to the question of whether the IRS is correct in not applying the boot second approach to corporate divisions.

¶ 8.12 BASIS CALCULATION

Section 358 controls the calculation of shareholder basis after a § 355 distribution. The calculation of basis is simplest if, before the distribution, the distributee held only one class and block[145] of stock and no security, or if the distributee held only one class and block of security and no stock.

The basis rules for corporate divisions apply both to exchanges of stock that occur in split-offs and split-ups and to spin-offs in which there is only a distribution of stock of a controlled corporation and nothing is transferred in exchange for that stock. In the case of a spin-off, the basis rules are applied as if an exchange took place in which the retained stock and securities of the distributing corporation were transferred to the distributing corporation and received back as part of the exchange.[146]

The calculation of the shareholder's basis in the nonrecognition property that the distributee received and in the stock or security of the distributing corporation that the distributee retained proceeds in two steps—first an "aggregate basis amount" is calculated, and then that aggregate amount is allocated among the nonrecognition and the retained properties according to their fair market values. The distributee's basis in any non-cash boot he received will equal that property's fair market value.[147]

To calculate the aggregate basis amount, one begins with the shareholder's adjusted basis in the stock or securities of the distributing corporation that the distributee shareholder held before the corporate division took place. One includes the basis of *all* such stock or securities, whether or not they are retained by the distributee or transferred to the distributing corporation in the course of the corporate division.[148] Thus, the computation is made in the same manner whether the division takes the form of a spin-off, a

---

[145] The authors refer to a "block" of stock as a means of distinguishing blocks of stock of the same class that were purchased on different dates or have a different basis.

[146] § 358(c).

[147] § 358(a)(2).

[148] § 358(b)(2), (c).

split-off, or a split-up.[149] To that amount, one adds any amount treated as a dividend or recognized as a gain by the shareholder as a result of the division.[150] The resulting figure is then reduced by the amount of cash the distributee received and by the fair market value of any non-cash boot the distributee received.[151] The final figure is what we refer to as the "aggregate basis amount."

Boot received by a shareholder (other than cash) takes a basis equal to its fair market value.[152] Note that under § 358, "stock boot" and the portion of a security that is treated as "excess-security boot" under §§ 355 and 356 are treated as non-cash boot for basis calculation purposes.[153]

The aggregate basis amount is allocated among both the stock and securities that the shareholder retained in the distributing corporation and the non-boot stock and securities of the controlled corporation that the shareholder received in the distribution.[154] This allocation is made among the properties according to their fair market values.[155]

¶ 8.13 TAXATION OF THE DISTRIBUTING CORPORATION

Since the repeal of General Utilities in 1986, the general rule is that a corporation that distributes an appreciated asset without liquidating must recognize the unrealized appreciation,[156] but a corporation that distributes a depreciated asset without liquidating may not recognize the unrealized depreciation.[157] If the distribution is covered by § 355 or § 356, however, that general rule is modified in significant ways. The precise manner in which it is modified depends on whether the division is pursuant to a "reorganization" within the meaning of § 368.

---

[149]   Id. In the case of a spin-off, the transaction is treated as an exchange in which the stock and securities of the distributing corporation that are retained are treated as having been surrendered to the distributing corporation and received back as part of the exchange. § 358(c).

[150]   § 358(a)(1)(B).

[151]   § 358(a)(1)(A).

[152]   § 358(a)(2). By convention, the Code does not describe money in terms of "fair market value" or "basis," so cash boot is excluded from the statutory allocation of basis cited in the text. For analytic purposes, it is often easier to treat money as a good whose basis and fair market value are equal to its face value.

[153]   See Treas. Reg. § 1.358–2(a)(1).

[154]   § 358(b), (c).

[155]   Treas. Reg. § 1.358–2(a)(2)(iv).

[156]   The same requirement of recognition of gain applies to liquidating distributions of appreciated property unless the liquidating corporation is a controlled subsidiary or the liquidation is part of a reorganization. §§ 336(a), (c), 337.

[157]   § 311(a), (b).

In the next chapter, we will discuss the definition of a "reorganization" in some detail. For present purposes, you may think of a corporate division that constitutes a reorganization as one in which the parent corporation operated a business directly for many years and then, pursuant to a single plan, formed a *new* subsidiary, transferred the business to the subsidiary, and distributed the subsidiary stock to its shareholders.[158] You may think of a corporate division that does not constitute a reorganization as one in which an *old* subsidiary had been running the business for many years on its own, and the parent simply decided to distribute the subsidiary stock.

¶ 8.13.1 Not Pursuant to a Reorganization

If the distribution is not pursuant to a reorganization, the tax treatment of the distributing parent corporation is determined primarily by §§ 355(c), (d), and (e).[159] If a corporation makes a distribution of a *de*preciated asset that is covered by §§ 355 or 356 and is not pursuant to a reorganization, the corporation cannot recognize the loss.[160] If the corporation distributes *a*ppreciated property, the extent to which the corporation must recognize gain depends on the nature of the appreciated property.

To the extent the parent distributes appreciated property other than stock or securities of its subsidiary, § 355(c) applies the general rule ordinarily employed after the repeal of *General Utilities*: the parent must recognize gain as if it had sold such property to the distributee at its fair market value.[161] Section 355(c) preserves the old *General Utilities* rule, however, with regard to appreciated stock or securities of the controlled subsidiaries, as long as the stock or securities constitute "qualified property."

As an initial proposition, all stock and securities of the controlled subsidiaries are defined to be "qualified property" and are therefore spared taxation at the level of the distributing parent. There are four exceptions in which stock or securities of a controlled subsidiary will not constitute "qualified property" and so the distribution of appreciated stocks or securities within one of those exceptions will cause the distributing parent to recognize a gain. One of those

---

[158] See § 368(a)(1)(D).

[159] To the extent a split-off or spin-off covered by §§ 355 or 356 might otherwise be controlled by § 311, and to the extent a split-up covered by §§ 355 or 356 might otherwise be controlled by § 336(a), those sections are overridden. § 355(c)(3).

[160] § 355(c). Section 361(c) prevents a deduction for unrealized depreciation when a distribution is made pursuant to a reorganization; so the treatment of unrealized depreciation is the same regardless of whether the transaction constitutes a reorganization.

[161] § 355(c)(2)(A), (B). If the distributed property is subject to a liability, its fair market value is treated as being not less than the amount of such liability. § 355(c)(2)(C).

exceptions is for the distribution of nonqualified preferred stock (NQPS).[162] However, even the distribution of a controlled subsidiary's appreciated nonqualified preferred stock (NQPS) will not cause the distributing parent to recognize income to the extent that it is distributed in exchange for other nonqualified preferred stock of the parent.[163]

The fact that all or a portion of a distributed security of a controlled subsidiary is treated as "excess-security boot"[164] by virtue of § 355(a)(3)(A) (and may therefore defeat nonrecognition at the shareholder level) is not enough to keep it from being "qualified property" at the level of the distributing parent.[165] The distribution of such a security will not cause the distributing parent to recognize a gain.

A different approach is taken towards appreciated "stock boot"— i.e., stock of the subsidiary that was acquired by the parent corporation in a taxable transaction within the five-year period preceding the distribution. Stock boot is not treated as stock of the controlled corporation for all purposes under § 355, except for the requirement that all (or virtually all) of the subsidiary's stock be distributed.[166] Accordingly, it is not stock for purposes of § 355(c), and so is not "qualified property" for purposes of that provision; and its unrealized appreciation will be taxed in the same manner as other appreciated property. In many cases, however, there will be little or no appreciation in the stock boot so the gain recognized will be minimal. Moreover, as noted in ¶ 8.10.2, Treas. Reg. § 1.355–2(g)(2), which was promulgated in 2011, excluded many purchases from the stock boot rule and thereby limited its significance. This regulation expressly applies for purposes of treating what would otherwise have been stock boot as qualified property for purposes of § 355(c).

In 1990 and in 1997, Congress carved out two additional exceptions to the "qualified property" category. The two exceptions, which are set forth in § 355(d) and (e), are discussed in ¶ 8.13.3. Those two exceptions apply regardless of whether the distribution to the shareholders is made pursuant to a reorganization.

---

[162] "Nonqualified preferred stock" is defined in § 351(g)(2) and is discussed at ¶ 8.10.3.

[163] § 355(a)(3)(D). See ¶ 8.10.3.

[164] "Excess security boot" refers to the difference between the principal amount of securities received by a distributee and the principal amount of securities surrendered (if any) by that distributee.

[165] Section 355(a)(3)(A) does not reclassify the security as something other than a security of the controlled subsidiary; it simply provides that "Paragraph (1) [the provision giving nonrecognition at the shareholder level] shall not apply" to such a security.

[166] § 355(a)(3)(B).

¶ 8.13.2 Pursuant to a Reorganization

If the distribution is pursuant to a reorganization, the tax treatment of the distributing parent corporation is determined by § 361(c)[167] and by § 355(d) and (e)[168] If a corporation makes a distribution of a *de*preciated asset that is covered by §§ 355 or 356 and is pursuant to a reorganization, the corporation cannot recognize the loss.[169] If the corporation distributes *ap*preciated property, the extent to which the corporation must recognize gain depends on the nature of the appreciated property.

To the extent the parent distributes appreciated property other than "qualified property," § 361(c) (like § 355(c)) applies the general rule ordinarily employed after the repeal of *General Utilities*: the parent must recognize gain as if it had sold such property to the distributee at its fair market value.[170] Section 361(c)(2) diverges significantly from § 355(c), however, when it comes to defining the phrase "qualified property." In brief, the distributing corporation is able to escape taxation on a broader range of distributed properties when the corporate division occurs in the context of a reorganization than when the division occurs outside that context.

For example, as long as they were received by the distributing corporation from the new controlled corporation as part of the reorganization, "qualified property" also includes (in addition to stock and securities of the controlled corporation) *obligations* of the controlled corporation even when they do not qualify as "securities." In addition, qualified property includes the *right to acquire* stock in the controlled corporation.[171] While it is not free of doubt, it appears likely that nonqualified preferred stock (NQPS) will constitute qualified property for purposes of § 361(c), and so the distributing parent will not recognize gain from distributing NQPS pursuant to a reorganization.[172]

---

[167]   To the extent a split-off or spin-off covered by §§ 355 or 356 might otherwise be controlled by § 311, and to the extent a split-up covered by §§ 355 or 356 might otherwise be controlled by § 336(a), those sections are overridden. § 361(c)(4).

[168]   Subsections 355(d) and (e) are discussed below, in ¶ 8.13.3.

[169]   § 361(c)(1).

[170]   § 361(c)(2)(A), (B).

[171]   § 361(c)(2)(B)(ii). However, the tax consequence of a non-reorganization corporate division will be the same. Since a right to acquire stock is treated as a security, its distribution in a non-reorganization corporate division will not cause the distributing corporation to recognize a gain. § 355(c).

[172]   See the discussion of that issue at Corporate Income Taxation Hornbook at 388–389.

¶ 8.13.3 Gain Recognition Required by § 355(d) and (e)

In 1990, Congress added § 355(d) to the Code to provide another exception to the nonrecognition treatment that otherwise would be accorded to the distributing parent on the distribution of otherwise qualified property. In 1997, Congress added § 355(e) (the so-called anti-*Morris Trust* provision) to provide an even more extensive exception to the nonrecognition treatment that the distributing corporation usually enjoys. The exceptions provided by § 355(d) and (e) apply to distributions made pursuant to a corporate division whether the distribution is made pursuant to a reorganization (so that § 361(c) is invoked) or is not part of a reorganization so that § 355(c) is invoked.[173] The exclusive effect of § 355(d) and (e), when either of those subsections becomes operative, is to require the distributing corporation to recognize gain on the distribution of what otherwise would be qualified property; neither of those subsections has any effect on the question of whether the distributees recognize any income on the distribution or on the question of what basis the distributees have in the distributed property. Thus, the distributees' nonrecognition of gain or loss is not affected by those provisions; and the distributees' basis in the distributed property, which basis is determined by § 358, is not increased by any gain that the distributing corporation recognized under § 355(d) or (e).

Subsections 355(d) and (e) overlap. If both provisions would otherwise apply to a distribution, § 355(d) takes priority and that provision alone will apply.[174]

Both subsections § 355(d) and (e) are complex. We provide only a general overview here. We will examine § 355(d) first and then consider § 355(e).

¶ 8.13.3.1   § 355(d)

Section 355(d) applies when, immediately after a distribution that is subject to § 355(a) or § 356(a), (1) any person holds stock constituting a 50% or greater interest (by vote or value)[175] in *either*

---

[173] § 355(d)(1), (e)(1).

[174] § 355(e)(2)(D).

[175] The 50% or greater interest requirement is applied immediately after the distribution. § 355(d)(2). It is satisfied when, at that time, the relevant person holds "disqualified stock" possessing at least 50% of the total combined voting power of all classes of stock entitled to vote, *or* at least 50% of the value of all classes of stock. Disqualified stock is defined later in this section. The 50% or greater interest is satisfied if it applies *either* to the stock of the distributing corporation *or* to the stock of any subsidiary a controlling interest in which was distributed in the transaction. Id.

the distributing corporation[176] *or* in a controlled corporation,[177] and (2) such person's holding of such stock is attributable to actual or constructive purchases of that stock (or stock of the distributing corporation with respect to which stock of the controlled corporation was distributed to such person) during the five-year period ending on the date on which the distribution took place. The stock that comprises the 50% or greater interest is referred to as "disqualified stock,"[178] and it is described below.

Disqualified stock includes any stock of the distributing or a controlled corporation that, within the five-year period ending on the date of distribution, was acquired by purchase[179] or is treated as acquired by purchase under the stock attribution rules.[180] A "purchase" is defined as an acquisition in which all of the following three circumstances exist: (1) the acquirer's basis in the acquired property is not determined in whole or in part by reference to the adjusted basis of such property in the hands of the person from whom it was acquired, (2) the acquirer's basis in the acquired property is not determined by § 1014(a), and (3) with one exception, the property was not acquired in an exchange to which §§ 351, 354, 355, or 356 applied.[181] The one exception is that an acquisition in a § 351 exchange will constitute a purchase to the extent that the property was acquired in exchange for cash or cash items, any marketable stock or security, or any debt of the transferor.[182]

In addition, if a person who purchases an interest in an entity is deemed, through the attribution rules of § 355(d)(8)(A), to hold stock or securities that are held by that entity, the person will be deemed to have purchased that attributed stock or securities.[183] Such a constructive purchase is referred to as a "deemed purchase."

A distribution to which § 355(d) applies (i.e., a § 355 or § 356 distribution in which the relevant person holds disqualified stock that satisfies the 50% or greater interest requirement) is referred to as a "disqualified distribution."[184] In the case of a "disqualified

---

[176]   § 355(d)(2)(A). The distributing corporation is sometimes referred to herein as the "parent" since it is distributing the stock of a subsidiary, which is sometimes referred to as the "controlled corporation."

[177]   § 355(d)(2)(B). You will recall that a "controlled corporation" is a subsidiary a controlling interest of whose stock was distributed by the distributing corporation in the transaction.

[178]   § 355(d)(3).

[179]   § 355(d)(3)(A), (B)(i).

[180]   § 355(d)(8)(B).

[181]   § 355(d)(5).

[182]   § 355(d)(5)(B).

[183]   § 355(d)(8)(B).

[184]   § 355(d)(2).

distribution," *no* stock *or* securities of any of the controlled corporations will be treated as "qualified property," and any unrealized appreciation in such stock or securities will be taxed to the distributing corporation in the same manner as with other appreciated property.[185] Again, it should be emphasized that § 355(d) concerns only the extent to which the distributing corporation must recognize income; it has no bearing on the extent to which the distributee shareholders must recognize income.

A significant purpose of § 355(d) is to prevent a corporation from using the corporate division or reorganization provisions to avoid recognizing gain on the sale of a business. Consider the following example.

Ex. (1)   X Corporation operates a hardware business and a retail shoe business. The value of the hardware business constitutes 60% of the value of X. B owns all 40 shares of X's outstanding stock and has owned those shares for more than 10 years. X wishes to sell the hardware business to A (unrelated to B) for a substantial gain, but X does not wish to recognize taxable income on the sale. Accordingly, X and A pursue the following plan:

On January 1, Year One, X issues 60 new shares of stock to A for cash. X does not recognize income on that exchange because of § 1032. On January 1, Year Four, X transfers the assets of the hardware business to the newly formed Y Corporation in exchange for Y stock. No cash, marketable securities, or liabilities are included in that transfer. As noted in Chapter Seven, X does not recognize gain on that exchange, and X takes a basis in the Y stock equal to the basis X had in the transferred assets.[186]

Immediately after forming Y, X distributes the Y stock to A in exchange for A's 60 shares of X stock.

---

[185]   § 355(d).
[186]   §§ 351, 358, 361.

In diagrammatic form:

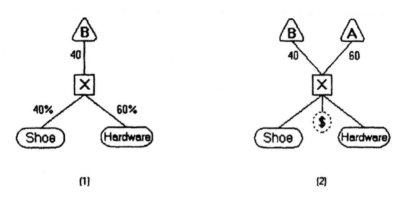

(1)   (2)

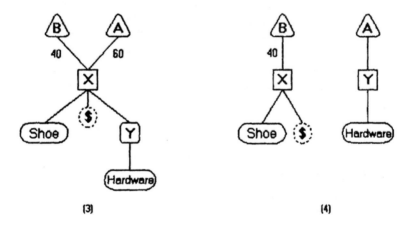

(3)   (4)

If the distribution to A in Example (1) could qualify under § 355, X would not recognize income on the distribution of the Y stock.[187] In the absence of § 355(d) or (e) (and assuming the other requirements of § 355 were satisfied), X would therefore be able to sell the hardware business for a profit (the excess of the money X received when it issued 60 new shares of stock to A over X's basis in the assets of the hardware business) without recognizing any gain.

---

[187] § 361(c). The distribution was part of a divisive reorganization. Note, however, the discussion at ¶8.09.2 of the continuity of interest requirement imposed by Treas. Reg. § 1.355–2(c). That requirement could provide a basis for asserting that the transaction does not qualify under § 355, but there are reasons to doubt that the regulation imposing such a strict continuity requirement on corporate divisions is still valid.

Of course, even if the nonrecognition rule were to apply, Y's basis in its assets would not be stepped up to reflect the amount paid by A for the hardware business. Accordingly, if Y were later to be liquidated, Y would recognize a gain. Presumably, therefore, A would pay X somewhat less for the X stock than it would be prepared to pay for the assets that X contributed to Y. Nevertheless, Congress did not wish to permit the continued deferral of taxation of any portion of the unrealized appreciation in the hardware business. Accordingly, § 355(d) requires X to recognize income on distributing the Y stock.[188]

A's acquisition of 60 shares of X stock for cash was a purchase of those shares under § 355(d)(5)(A), and the purchase took place within the 5-year period preceding X's distribution of its Y stock. A's shares of X therefore were "disqualified stock" under § 355(d)(3)(A). Since the distribution of Y stock to A is attributable to the disqualified X shares that A held, the Y shares also are disqualified stock. Immediately after the distribution, A held 100% of Y's stock all of which was disqualified stock. Consequently, the distribution was a disqualified distribution, and X will recognize gain in the amount by which the Y stock is appreciated in X's hands. A will not recognize any gain or loss because § 355(d) has no effect on the distributee. Under § 358, A's basis in the Y stock will equal the basis that A had in the 60 shares of X stock that A exchanged for the Y stock. A will not obtain any increase in basis for the gain recognized by X on the distribution.

The breadth of the § 355(d) provision incorporates transactions that do not constitute the type of abuse that Congress sought to address when it adopted that provision. In response to concerns that the provision is overly broad, Treasury, through its regulations, has excluded certain non-abusive transactions from that provision. In addition to providing specific exceptions, the regulations authorize the Commissioner to designate other transactions that will not be treated as disqualified distributions because they do not violate the purposes of § 355(d).[189]

Treas. Reg. § 1.355–6(b)(3)(i) provides that, regardless of the terms of the statute itself, "a distribution is not a disqualified distribution if the distribution does not violate the purposes of section 355(d) as provided in" that paragraph of the regulation. Since such distributions are not disqualified, they do not trigger gain recognition under § 355(d). The regulation states that a "distribution does not

---

[188]   See § 355(d)(2)(B). Note once again that § 355(d) does not affect the nonrecognition of income that A is allowed by § 355; it affects only the recognition of income by X.

[189]   Treas. Reg. § 1.355–6(b)(3)(v).

violate the purposes of § 355(d) if the effect of the distribution and any related transaction is neither—"

(A) to increase a "disqualified person's" (defined below) direct or indirect ownership in either the distributing corporation or in any controlled corporation; or

(B) to provide a disqualified person (defined below) with a "purchased basis" in the stock of any controlled corporation.

A "disqualified person" is any person who immediately after a distribution holds (after applying aggregation and stock attribution rules) disqualified stock in *either* the distributing *or* a controlled corporation that constitutes a 50% or greater interest in such corporation.[190] "Disqualified stock" is defined in ¶ 8.13.3.1. A "purchased basis" is basis in a controlled corporation's stock that constitutes disqualified stock unless the stock is disqualified stock only because of the application of the "deemed purchase" rules of § 355(d)(8)(B).[191]

¶ 8.13.3.2   § 355(e)

In the *Morris Trust*[192] case, discussed at ¶ 8.08.5, a bank had entered into an agreement pursuant to which it would be acquired by another corporation through a statutory merger. However, the prospective acquiring corporation did not want one of the departments of the target corporation.[193] To facilitate the merger, the target transferred the unwanted department to a newly created corporate subsidiary and then spun off the newly formed subsidiary to its shareholders. After the spin-off was completed, the target was merged into the acquiring corporation. The Fourth Circuit held that the spin-off qualified for nonrecognition under § 355, and the Commissioner conceded the correctness of that position.[194] Subsequent to that decision, transactions of this type, i.e., a combination of a corporate division and a corporate acquisition involving the distributing corporation, were referred to as "*Morris Trust*" transactions. While there was subsequent litigation over some variations of the *Morris Trust* theme, nonrecognition ultimately was sustained for most *Morris Trust* transactions, and they were generally regarded as benign.

---

[190] Treas. Reg. § 1.355–6(b)(3)(ii).

[191] For further elaboration, see the examples at pp. 422–423 of the Corporate Income Taxation Hornbook.

[192] Commissioner v. Morris Trust, 367 F.2d 794 (4th Cir. 1966).

[193] The unwanted department was an insurance department, and the acquiring corporation was prohibited by law from operating an insurance department.

[194] Rev. Rul. 68–603.

Over the years, a technique was developed that utilized the *Morris Trust* transaction to sell a corporation's business to a third party mostly for cash without causing the selling corporation to recognize income. This was accomplished in the following manner or in some variation of this approach.

Ex. (2)   For more than 5 years, X Corporation had owned and operated several businesses, one of which was a retail clothing store. Y Corporation wished to purchase the retail clothing business that X conducted, and was willing to pay cash. The assets of the retail clothing business were appreciated, and so X would have recognized income if it sold those assets for cash. Instead, X borrows from a bank an amount equal to 80% of the value of the assets of the retail clothing business (including its good will) and secures that loan with the assets of the retail clothing business. X then forms the S Corporation as a wholly owned subsidiary, and X transfers all of its assets, other than those of the retail clothing business, to S in exchange for all of the latter's voting common stock. Among the assets that X transferred to S was the cash that X had obtained from the bank loan. X then distributes all of its S stock pro rata to its shareholders in a spin-off. After the transfer to S and the spin-off, X owns only the assets of the retail clothing business and holds those assets subject to the encumbrance for the bank loan. X recognized no gain on making the transfer to S because of § 361, and neither X nor its shareholders recognized income on the spin-off because of §§ 355(a) and 361(c). Y then acquires X through a merger, and the shareholders of X exchange their X stock for Y stock. There is no gain recognized on those exchanges. After the merger, Y is liable for the bank loan; the S corporation owns all of the businesses that X conducted except for the retail clothing business; and S has the proceeds of the bank loan. In effect, X received cash for 80% of the value of the retail clothing business, continues to conduct its other businesses under the name of S, and recognized no gain on the transaction.

This abusive utilization of the *Morris Trust* transactions, as illustrated in Example (2) above, attracted attention and spurred Congress to seek a legislative remedy to close that loophole. However, instead of choosing a surgical remedy that identifies and attacks only the abusive situations, Congress chose a cruder instrument that reaches many nonabusive *Morris Trust* transactions. The remedy that Congress chose is set forth in § 355(e), which is sometimes referred to as the anti-*Morris Trust* provision.

Congress determined that a corporate division should not be permitted to be tax-free to the distributing corporation if it is accompanied by a significant change in the ownership interests in either the distributing or any of the controlled corporations, regardless of whether the change of ownership takes place in the context of a nonrecognition transaction or in the context of an outright purchase. There is no good reason to require recognition of income when the change of ownership occurs because of nonrecognition exchanges unless the transaction is structured to disguise what amounts to an outright purchase (such as the one described in Example (2) when the device of a loan was used to cloak a cash sale with the guise of a nonrecognition exchange). Section 355(e) reaches far more than the limited circumstances in which the *Morris Trust* technique can be abused.

Section 355(e) requires a distributing corporation that makes a distribution that qualifies under § 355, or under so much of § 356 as relates to § 355, to recognize gain on the distribution of appreciated stocks and securities of the controlled corporation if the distribution is part of a "plan" (or series of related transactions) pursuant to which "1 or more persons" acquire stock representing a 50% or greater interest in either the distributing corporation or in any of the controlled corporations. As is the case with § 355(d), § 355(e) does not affect the nonrecognition of the distributees—only that of the distributing corporation; and it does not permit the recognition of loss on the distribution of depreciated stocks or securities.

Although there is some overlap between § 355(d) and § 355(e), there are also some significant differences between the two provisions. Section 355(d) requires that one person make the proscribed acquisition (albeit aggregation and attribution rules apply). Section 355(e) applies if one or more persons make the acquisition; and § 355(e) utilizes the same aggregation rules for related persons that are employed in § 355(d), and contains a slightly broader version of the § 318(a)(2) attribution rule.[195] Section 355(d) applies only if the proscribed acquisition was a "purchase," whereas § 355(e) applies to any type of acquisition. The two subsections have different time periods: § 355(d) uses the five-year period preceding the distribution; whereas § 355(e) primarily uses the period spanning two years prior to and two years subsequent to the distribution.[196] The requisites for applying § 355(d) are objective; but the requisites under § 355(e) for determining whether a plan existed introduce a

---

[195] § 355(e)(4)(C).

[196] In the case of both subsections, the time periods can be extended if the stock or security holder's risk of loss on such property is substantially diminished by some device such as an option, short sale, or special class of stock. § 355(d)(6), (e)(5)(C).

subjective element. Finally, § 355(e) can apply when the assets of a corporation are acquired by another corporation in an acquisitive reorganization (as contrasted to an acquisition of a stock interest);[197] but § 355(d) contains no such provision.

The current regulations primarily address the meaning and operation of the statutory reference to a "plan (or series of related transactions)." In addition to setting out standards for applying the provision and a number of examples illustrating how it will be applied, the regulations also include nine safe harbors in which a distribution will not be treated as part of a plan, and so § 355(e) will not apply.[198]

The regulations prescribe a series of so-called "plan factors," non-plan factors, and "operating rules"—not unlike the approach that the regulations take in describing "device factors" and "non-device factors" for purposes of applying the device restriction.[199] The regulations provide that the plan and non-plan factors present in a transaction are to be evaluated in light of the underlying facts and circumstances, some but not all of which are referenced in the description of the factors themselves.[200]

¶ 8.14 EARNINGS AND PROFITS

When a corporate division qualifies for nonrecognition treatment under §§ 355 or 356, the Secretary has been granted broad discretion to promulgate regulations determining the reallocation of the distributing corporation's *e and p* among the distributing and controlled corporations.[201]

---

[197]　§ 355(e)(3)(B).

[198]　Treas. Reg. § 1.355–7(d).

[199]　See the discussion at ¶ 8.07.

[200]　For a detailed discussion of the factors and operating rules, see Corporate Income Taxation Hornbook 427–431.

[201]　§ 312(h)(1). If the corporate division was made pursuant to a D reorganization, the *e and p* allocation is prescribed by Treas. Reg. § 1.312–10(a). If the corporate separation was not made pursuant to a D reorganization, the *e and p* allocation is prescribed by Treas. Reg. § 1.312–10(b). See Corporate Income Taxation Hornbook at 431–432.

Chapter Nine

REORGANIZATIONS

Analysis

Para.

9.01   Introduction

9.02   General Tax Consequences of Mergers and Acquisitions That Qualify as Reorganizations

9.03   Reorganizations—Extra-Statutory Requirements

9.04   Overview of the Statutory Requirements of Reorganizations

9.05   A Closer Look at Statutory Reorganizations Including Determination of Basis

9.06   Tax Treatment of Shareholders Who Receive Boot in Qualifying Reorganization

9.07   Tax Treatment of Target Corporation (Distribution of Appreciated Assets)

9.08   The Rise of § 351 Exchanges as an Alternative to a Reorganization

¶ 9.01 INTRODUCTION

The study of reorganizations lies at the heart of the study of corporate taxation. Yet it is plagued by a linguistic problem: the term "reorganization" has at least three different meanings in general business parlance.

First, the term has a technical meaning in the law of bankruptcy. There, it refers to a specific mechanism for modifying the legal rights of persons who have claims on the assets of another legal person that is financially distressed. That is not what we mean when we refer to reorganizations in this chapter, although a bankruptcy reorganization can be—and often is—structured to satisfy the requirements of a tax reorganization.

Second, the term has a general, somewhat colloquial meaning in casual conversation among business lawyers. There, it refers to any significant change in the ownership structure of an enterprise, whether or not the change qualifies for special tax treatment. It encompasses a wide range of mergers, acquisitions, divisions, and other restructurings of investors' and creditors' interests in business enterprises. While we sometimes use the term that way in casual conversation with each other, that is not the way we are using it in this chapter.

Third, the term has a technical meaning for tax purposes. In that context, a reorganization is an adjustment of corporate ownership that qualifies for favorable tax treatment because it satisfies the statutory and extra-statutory requirements necessary to fall within one of the definitional subparagraphs of § 368(a)(1) of the Code. That is the meaning we intend when we speak of reorganizations in this chapter.

The potential for confusion is compounded by the fact that there often is substantial overlap between and among the three types of "reorganizations" noted above. For example, a tax reorganization will often be the means used to effect a restructuring of corporate business interests. Thus, while a business reorganization will not necessarily qualify for treatment as a tax reorganization, it is often desirable that it so qualify in order both to avoid a federal tax burden on the participants in the transaction and to preserve various tax attributes and characteristics of the corporate enterprise. Similarly, and for many of the same reasons, it will often be the case that a bankruptcy reorganization will be structured so that it qualifies as a tax reorganization. In any event, the point is that, while very few technical requirements need be satisfied for a bankruptcy or other business transaction to be considered a "reorganization" for bankruptcy or other purposes, there are a number of technical requirements that need to be fulfilled in order for such a reorganization to also qualify as a tax reorganization. In substantial part, this chapter is devoted to exploring those technical requirements.

¶ 9.02 GENERAL TAX CONSEQUENCES OF MERGERS AND ACQUISITIONS THAT QUALIFY AS REORGANIZATIONS

The Internal Revenue Code provides favorable[1] tax treatment to reorganization transactions that are described in § 368(a). As will be seen in detail later in this chapter, the precise consequences of different forms of reorganizations vary in important ways across the different categories. Yet it is a useful generalization to observe that, among other things, the reorganization provisions enable an acquiring corporation to acquire a target corporation's business in a way that triggers immediate recognition of *neither* outside gain (the inherent unrealized gain that the target shareholders have in their

---

[1]   When we say that the tax treatment of reorganizations is "favorable," we do not mean to deny that on occasion a taxpayer may find the treatment less favorable than the treatment provided to taxable transactions.

stock) *nor* inside gain (the inherent unrealized gain that the target corporation has in its assets). To be sure, the reorganization provisions do not *forgive* taxation of either level of gain. Rather, the recognition of both gains continues to be deferred into the future.

Why does the Code provide such favorable tax treatment to reorganizations? At a very high level of generality, the reason is familiar. It is similar to the reason that certain transfers of assets to controlled corporations receive favorable treatment under § 351 and certain corporate divisions (which may or may not qualify as reorganizations) receive favorable treatment under § 355. Congress is concerned that the doctrine of realization can create "lock-in" effects; the prospect of a substantial tax liability might deter people from engaging in economically desirable and productive business transactions. In the field of reorganizations, as in those other domains, Congress has attempted to strike an appropriate balance between the policy interest in minimizing lock-in and the policy interest in enforcing a two-tier tax on realized income.

As we saw in other contexts, things become more complicated as soon as one moves to a slightly less general plane and attempts to offer a unitary characterization of the *kinds* of transactions where Congress has found lock-in especially disturbing. Notwithstanding the difficulties associated with identifying a single objective, Congress has followed a characteristic pattern in attempting to implement that objective—i.e., in attempting to strike a balance between minimizing lock-in effects and enforcing a two-tier tax on realized income. Congress has established a set of bright-line rules that define specially favored categories of transactions. When a transaction falls into one of those categories, the relevant taxpayers are given partial or complete nonrecognition treatment: gain is generally recognized only to the extent boot is received in the transaction and losses are not recognized.[2] The realized-but-unrecognized gains or losses are deferred for later recognition through rules that assign the taxpayers below-market or above-market[3] bases in the nonrecognition property they receive in the transaction.

---

[2] §§ 356, 361. Even then, boot does not always cause the recognition of gain. See § 361(b). "Boot" refers to property received in a nonrecognition type of transaction that does not qualify for nonrecognition treatment.

[3] There are restrictions that can prevent or minimize a corporate transferee's obtaining a basis that is greater than the assets' fair market value. See § 362(d)(1), (e)(1).

¶ 9.03 REORGANIZATIONS—EXTRA-STATUTORY REQUIREMENTS

Before exploring the specific statutory requirements, it should be noted that the courts and the Treasury Department have had an active hand in developing and imposing extra-statutory requirements on reorganizations.[4]

¶ 9.03.1 Continuity of Proprietary Interest

In *Pinellas Ice & Cold Storage Co. v. Commissioner*,[5] the Supreme Court considered a case arising under the Revenue Act of 1926. A company exchanged its assets for $400,000 cash and $1,000,000 worth of promissory notes that were payable over the course of three and one half months. It realized more than $500,000 in gain on the exchange. The taxpayer argued that the notes were "securities," the transaction qualified as a reorganization, and the company should have to recognize gain only to the extent of the cash (the boot). The Supreme Court disagreed. While the Court could have simply held that the notes were not "securities" within the meaning of the statute, it instead wrote more broadly: it emphasized that the statute was intended to extend only to "things which partake of the nature of a merger or consolidation"; thus, "the seller must acquire an interest in the affairs of the purchasing company more definite than that incident to ownership of its short-term purchase-money notes."[6]

In a series of cases over the next few years, the Supreme Court elaborated this "continuity of proprietary interest" requirement. Those cases suggested that:

- The interest must be "definite and material", representing "a substantial part" of the consideration paid.[7]

- It does not matter if the consideration received reflects only a small share of the ownership of the acquiring corporation.[8]

- The receipt of any type of stock that constitutes an equity interest, including nonvoting preferred stock,

---

4   See generally Treas. Reg. § 1.368–1(b), and Rev. Rul. 2000–5.

5   287 U.S. 462 (1933).

6   287 U.S. at 470.

7   Helvering v. Minnesota Tea Co., 296 U.S. 378, 385 (1935).

8   Id. at 386. See also Kass v. Commissioner, 60 T.C. 218, 277 (1973), aff'd without opinion, 491 F.2d 749 (3d Cir. 1974). Bittker and Eustice offer a vivid metaphor: "a whale can swallow a minnow and satisfy the continuity of interest requirement." Bittker & Eustice, ¶ 12.21[2][b].

will constitute a continuation of a proprietary interest.[9]

- On the other hand, debt instruments (even long-term debt instruments) are simply inadequate to sustain continuity of proprietary interest; only stock will do.[10]

- It is not clear exactly what portion of the consideration must constitute stock, but 40% is now generally recognized as sufficient.[11]

Over the years, the lower courts and the IRS have developed the continuity-of-proprietary-interest requirement even further. Perhaps most significantly, continuity of proprietary interest is a characteristic of the *entire transaction*, not of any particular shareholder's activity in the course of a transaction. Thus, it is *not* necessary to satisfy the requirement with regard to each shareholder of the acquired corporation. If a corporation has four equal shareholders, and in a merger two receive cash and two receive stock, the continuity-of-proprietary-interest requirement is satisfied.[12] Conversely, if the requirement is not satisfied with respect to an entire transaction, an individual shareholder is not helped by the fact that he received nothing but stock.

One other aspect of the continuity-of-proprietary-interest doctrine warrants comment: the question of how long the continuity must continue *after* the reorganization. What happens if the acquiring corporation drops the acquired assets into a subsidiary immediately after the reorganization? And how long must the shareholders of the acquired corporation continue to hold the stock they receive in the reorganization? A related question is whether it violates the continuity requirement if stock of the target corporation is purchased shortly before and in anticipation of a subsequent reorganization. These questions have been resolved by regulations that were promulgated in 1998.

For many years, it was thought that if stock of a corporation involved in a reorganization was disposed of pursuant to a plan that preceded the reorganization, an application of the step transaction or *Court Holding* doctrine would treat the prior shareholders as not retaining a proprietary interest in the surviving corporations to that

---

[9] John A. Nelson Co. v. Helvering, 296 U.S. 374, 377 (1935). However, a subsequent amendment of the Code has provided that, if the stock is nonqualified preferred stock, it may be treated as boot and cause income recognition. See ¶ 9.06.

[10] Le Tulle v. Scofield, 308 U.S. 415, 420–21 (1940).

[11] Treas. Reg. § 1.368–1(e)(2)(v), Ex. (1).

[12] Rev. Rul. 66–224.

extent.[13] This was true regardless of whether the sale of the stock occurred shortly before or after the reorganization took place. In other words, the test for continuity did not rest exclusively on an examination of the nature of the consideration received by the shareholders of the target corporation. If some of the target's shareholders sold their stock for nonequity consideration prior to and in anticipation of the reorganization, those shares, and shares received in exchange therefor pursuant to the reorganization, would not be counted as continuity even though the purchasers held those purchased shares at the time that the reorganization took place. Similarly, if, shortly after the reorganization took place, prior shareholders of the target sold stock of a surviving corporation (whether those were shares of the acquiring corporation, of a parent of the acquiring corporation, or of the target corporation), those shares would not be counted as representing a continuity of interest if the sale was preplanned before the reorganization occurred.

The belief that the step transaction or *Court Holding* doctrine would cause the sold stock in the circumstances described above to be excluded from the measure of continuity was shattered when the Tax Court decided *J.E. Seagram Corp. v. Commissioner*,[14] in which the court held that a disposition of stock to a third party shortly before an acquisitive reorganization was completed did not violate the continuity-of-proprietary interest requirement. In so holding, the court upheld the position that the Service took in that case. Subsequent to the *Seagram* decision, in 1998, the Service amended the regulations dealing with the application of the continuity-of-proprietary-interest requirement to reorganizations.[15] As a consequence of those regulatory changes, the virtually *exclusive* focus of the continuity requirement is now on the nature of the consideration that was received for the target's stock.

Treas. Reg. § 1.368–1(e) makes the test for determining whether there was continuity of interest in a reorganization rest on the nature of the consideration received by the shareholders of the target corporation for their proprietary interest in the target. As noted above, a significant portion (at least 40%) of the consideration must consist of equity interests.[16]

---

[13] See Rev. Rul. 66–23, declared obsolete, Rev. Rul. 2003–99; G.C.M. 39150 (Mar. 1, 1984).

[14] 104 T.C. 75 (1995).

[15] Treas. Reg. § 1.368–1(e).

[16] In Treas. Reg. § 1.368–1(e)(2)(v), Ex. (1), Treasury concluded that the continuity of interest rule was satisfied when 40 percent of the consideration was stock (equity) and 60 percent was cash.

Under the amended regulations, a shareholder's disposition to a third party of stock of either the acquiring or the target corporation, regardless of whether the disposition occurred immediately prior or subsequent to the acquisition of the target and regardless of whether a subsequent disposition was pursuant to a binding preexisting agreement, does not affect continuity of proprietary interest unless the disposition of the target stock was made to a person related to the acquiring or target corporation or the disposition of the acquiring corporation's stock was made to the acquiring corporation or a person related to the acquiring corporation.[17] Any reference in this paragraph to an "acquiring corporation" also refers to a parent of an acquiring corporation when the parent's stock is used as consideration for the acquisition of the target's stock or assets.[18]

In sum, so long as the disposition is made to persons unrelated to the corporations, and neither the acquiring nor the target corporation was the source of the consideration that was paid, the current position of the Service, as reflected in Treasury regulations, is that prior or subsequent dispositions of stock will not violate the continuity requirements in the context of an acquisitive reorganization. As to redemptions or purchases by the target or related corporations, such redemptions or purchases will not always affect continuity. The difference may well depend on whether the form of reorganization is a "stock" reorganization, such as a B reorganization, where it will usually be feasible to trace the source of the funds, or an "asset" reorganization, such as an A or a C reorganization, where a tracing typically will not be possible.

As the preceding discussion reveals, in many contexts the judicial requirements of the general continuity-of-interest doctrine have been greatly relaxed over the years through the action of Congress, the courts, or the Treasury Department. In addition to the points discussed above, the regulations provide that the continuity of proprietary interest requirement does not even apply to certain categories of reorganization—e.g., "E" reorganizations (involving changes in a corporation's capital structure), and "F" reorganizations (typically involving a change in the state under whose law the corporation is organized).[19] Moreover, in several types of reorganization, the general continuity doctrine will not be significant

---

[17] The type of relationship to corporations to which this provision applies is defined in the regulations. For this purpose, only corporate entities are related persons. Treas. Reg. § 1.368–1(e)(4).

[18] As noted later in this chapter, the stock used as consideration for an acquisitive reorganization can be the stock of either the acquiring corporation or a parent of the acquiring corporation. For that reason, the regulations refer to the stock of the "issuing" corporation in order to refer to whichever stock was used.

[19] Treas. Reg. § 1.368–1(b).

because the statutory requirements of that form of reorganization are even more exacting.

¶ 9.03.2 Continuity of Business Enterprise

For many years, the Internal Revenue Service has contended that a "reorganization" necessarily implies that the acquiring corporation will continue some form of a business enterprise that had previously been conducted by the target corporation. The Treasury Department supported the IRS position through the promulgation of a regulation, which the IRS accompanied with the issuance of several Revenue Rulings.[20] Treas. Reg. § 1.368–1(d) sets forth a clear continuity-of-business-enterprise (COBE) requirement, providing that the "issuing" corporation (generally the acquiring corporation or its parent in the case of a triangular reorganization) must *either* (i) continue what was historically a significant line of business of the target, *or* (ii) use a significant portion of the target's historic business assets in a business. The COBE requirement applies to the business conducted by the target corporation; there is no requirement that the acquiring corporation be engaged in a business before the acquisition took place.[21] Note that the COBE requirement does not apply to a so-called E or F reorganization.[22] At least one commentator has criticized the COBE requirement and urged its repeal or liberalization.[23]

Consider the following interpretive issues:

(1) How long must a target corporation have conducted a business for it to be considered "historic"? The regulations say only that it is "the business it has conducted most recently" but "not one the corporation enters into as part of a plan of reorganization."[24]

(2) How long must the acquiring corporation continue the target's business or continue to use the target's historic business assets to provide adequate "continuity"? The regulations are silent. However, in an example added by a 1998 amendment of the regulation, the fact that the business assets of the target (fabric) were being consumed by the acquirer (who manufactured the fabric into sportswear that presumably the acquirer sold) did not prevent the acquirer from being treated

---

[20] See, e.g., Rev. Rul. 81–247.

[21] Rev. Rul. 81–25.

[22] Treas. Reg. § 1.368–1(b).

[23] David F. Shores, *Continuity of Business Enterprise: A Concept whose Time Has Passed*, 63 The Tax Lawyer 471 (2010).

[24] Treas. Reg. § 1.368–1(d)(2)(iii).

as having used the target's historic business assets.[25] The example does not indicate the time table for the manufacture and sale of the sportswear.

(3) If the target corporation conducted *several* businesses, how many must be continued? The regulations state that it is necessary only to continue one "significant" line of business.[26] Where the target conducted three businesses of approximately equal value, the acquiring corporation's continuation of only one of those three businesses was sufficient to satisfy the COBE requirement.[27]

(4) How does one determine if a line of the target's business is "significant"? The regulations say that all facts and circumstances must be considered, and provide an example in which one of three equal lines of business is found to be significant.[28] Moreover, one of the examples in the regulations treats the use of $1/3$ of the target's historic assets as the use of a significant portion that satisfies the COBE requirement, and, by analogy, a business that constitutes $1/3$ of the value of the target's several businesses should also be significant.[29]

(5) Is it sufficient to satisfy the alternative requirement of the continuation of the target's historic business that the acquiring corporation conducts the same type of business and continues to do so after the reorganization takes place? For example, if both P and T Corporations were in the business of manufacturing sweaters, and if P acquired T's assets in a reorganization, promptly sold those assets and used the proceeds in its business, but did not do business with any of T's customers, would the fact that P conducts the same line of business that T had conducted satisfy the COBE requirement? The regulations state that while P's conduct of the same line of business "tends to establish the requisite

---

[25]   Treas. Reg. § 1.368–1(d)(5), Ex. (11).

[26]   See Treas. Reg. § 1.368–1(d)(2)(ii).

[27]   Treas. Reg. § 1.368–1(d)(5), Ex. (1).

[28]   See Treas. Reg. § 1.368–1(d)(2)(iv), –1(d)(5), Ex. (1).

[29]   Treas. Reg. § 1.368–1(d)(5), Ex. (12).

continuity," that fact alone is not sufficient to satisfy the COBE requirement.[30]

(6) How does one determine if a group of assets constitutes "a significant portion" of the acquired corporation's historic business assets? The regulations say that the determination is "based on the relative importance of the assets to operation of the business," but that "all other facts and circumstances" including the "net fair market value of those assets" are also considered.[31] The regulations include an example in which the acquiring corporation discontinued the target's business but held the target's old equipment as a "backup source of supply" of intermediate goods for use in its own business. The regulations deem that use sufficient to satisfy the requirement.[32]

(7) Can the COBE requirement be satisfied if the target's historic assets (or a significant portion of them) are not used directly by the acquiring corporation, but rather are used by one or more corporations that are related to the acquiring corporation? Can the continuation of the target's historic business test be satisfied by having the target's business conducted by one or more corporations that are related to the acquiring corporation? These questions are addressed in the 1998 and 2007 amendments that Treasury made to the regulations. The resolution of those questions is described below.

The regulations provide that COBE requires that the "issuing corporation" either continue a significant historic business of the target or use a significant portion of the target's assets in a business.[33] The "issuing corporation" means the acquiring corporation unless the transaction is a triangular reorganization, in which case it means the corporation that is in control of the acquiring corporation.[34] For convenience, the issuing corporation will sometimes be labeled hereafter as "P" and the target corporation will sometimes be labeled as "T."

The issuing corporation is treated as holding all of the businesses and all of the assets of every member of a "qualified

---

[30] Treas. Reg. § 1.368–1(d)(2)(i).
[31] See Treas. Reg. § 1.368–1(d)(3)(iii).
[32] See Treas. Reg. § 1.368–1(d)(5), Ex. (2).
[33] Treas. Reg. § 1.368–1(d)(1).
[34] Treas. Reg. § 1.368–1(b).

group."[35] A "qualified group" is one or more chains of corporations connected through stock ownership with the issuing corporation, but only if: (1) the issuing corporation owns directly stock in at least one corporation, which stock possesses at least 80% of the voting power of all classes of voting stock of that corporation and constitutes at least 80% of each class of nonvoting shares of such corporation, and (2) stock meeting those 80% requirements in each of the corporations in the qualified group (other than the issuing corporation) is held directly by one or more of the other corporate members of the group.[36] As a consequence of that provision, T's historic business assets that are used by two or more members of the qualified group in their businesses are aggregated to determine whether the issuing corporation is deemed to use a significant portion of T's historic business assets in a business.[37]

¶ 9.03.3 Other Extra-Statutory Doctrines

Several other judicially created doctrines serve to check the extent of aggressive tax planning possible through the use of the reorganization provisions. Thus, the business purpose doctrine of *Gregory v. Helvering* applies to reorganizations.[38] And so does the step transaction doctrine.[39]

¶ 9.04 OVERVIEW OF THE STATUTORY REQUIREMENTS OF REORGANIZATIONS

Reorganizations (or "reorgs") are known by the capital letters of the seven subparagraphs of § 368(a)(1) in which they are described. A statutory merger described in § 368(a)(1)(A) is known as an "A reorganization" or an "A reorg." A stock-for-stock acquisition described in § 368(a)(1)(B) is known as a "B reorganization." And so on, up through a bankruptcy reorganization described in § 368(a)(1)(G), which is known as a "G reorganization."

The seven kinds of reorganization fall generally into three broad groupings: "divisive reorganizations" (some D reorgs), "acquisitive reorganizations" (A, B, C, some D, and G reorgs), and "nondivisive, nonacquisitive reorganizations" (E and F reorgs). In this section we present an overview of the requirements for each reorganization, together with diagrams of prototypical cases.

---

35   Treas. Reg. § 1.368–1(d)(4)(i).
36   Treas. Reg. § 1.368–1(d)(4)(ii).
37   Treas. Reg. § 1.368–1(d)(5), Ex. (6).
38   See ¶¶ 8.03, 8.09.1.
39   Treas. Reg. § 1.368–1(a). See ¶ 7.06.2.

¶ 9.04.1 A Reorganizations

The A reorganization is a statutory merger or consolidation. In the classic example, the target ("T") is merged into the acquiring corporation ("A"), the target is dissolved by operation of law (its stock disappearing), and the original shareholders of T receive stock in the acquiring corporation. For tax purposes, the stock of the acquiring corporation that a shareholder receives is deemed to be received in exchange for the shareholder's stock of the target that ceased to exist. As the term "statutory" implies, such a merger transaction must occur pursuant to the statutory law of the jurisdictions whose laws govern the acquiring and target corporations. Such an A reorganization may be diagrammed as follows:

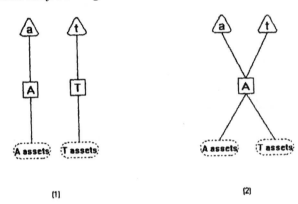

(1)　　　　　　　　　　　　　　　　　　(2)

A Reorganization

Section 368(a)(1)(A) speaks simply of "a statutory merger or consolidation." That makes the straightforward merger a refreshingly simple form of reorganization where all that is involved is a merger of two previously unrelated parties "effected pursuant to the statute or statutes necessary to effect the merger or consolidation."[40]

From a comparative standpoint, the A reorganization has two great virtues when compared with B or C reorganizations. First, it provides great flexibility with regard to the consideration paid by the acquiring corporation. As will be seen below, a B reorganization requires the acquiring corporation to give only voting stock, and a C reorganization requires the acquiring corporation to give voting stock

---

[40]　Treas. Reg. § 1.368–2(b)(1)(ii). For many years, a statutory merger could not qualify as an A reorganization if it occurred pursuant to the laws of a non-U.S. jurisdiction. However, the regulation has now been amended to permit an A reorganization to occur pursuant to non-U.S. law.

as consideration for at least 80% of the value of the target corporation's assets. In contrast, an A reorganization is constrained only by the continuity-of-proprietary-interest requirements discussed above.[41] Nonvoting stock works as well as voting stock, except that nonqualified preferred stock may constitute boot and cause income recognition.[42] Moreover, as much as 60% of the consideration can be boot (although, as will be seen below, gain will be recognized by a transferee to the extent of the boot received).

Second, the A reorganization also provides extra flexibility when the acquiring corporation does not want all of the target's assets. As will be seen below, a transaction will not qualify as a C reorganization if less than "substantially all" the target's assets are acquired. In contrast, an A reorganization is constrained only by the much less demanding continuity-of-business-enterprise requirements discussed above.[43]

In Rev. Rul. 2000–5, the Service ruled that compliance with a corporate law merger statute is not sufficient to qualify a transaction as an A reorganization. We have already noted that the extra-statutory requirements of business purpose, continuity of proprietary interest, and continuity of business enterprise must be satisfied. In that Revenue Ruling, the Service stated that there are other requirements, namely that the "transaction effectuated under a corporate law merger statute must have the result that one corporation acquires the assets of the target corporation by operation of the corporate law merger statute and the target corporation ceases to exist." Subsequently, the Treasury incorporated the result of Rev. Rul. 2000–5 into its regulations.[44]

One variant of the A reorganization involves a merger of T into a limited liability company ("LLC") in which the acquiring corporation ("A") is the sole member. Unless it elects to be treated as a corporation for U.S. tax purposes, such an LLC is treated as a "disregarded entity" under Treas. Reg. § 301.7701–2(a), which means that it is disregarded as an entity separate from its owner, A, for federal income tax purposes. Thus, if no election has been made to treat such an LLC as a corporation for federal income tax purposes, a statutory merger of T into such an LLC will be treated for federal income tax purposes as though T had effected a statutory merger directly into A.[45] This merger variant may be diagramed as follows:

---

[41]   See ¶ 9.03.1.

[42]   See ¶ 9.06.

[43]   See ¶ 9.03.2.

[44]   See Treas. Reg. § 1.368–2(b)(1)(ii).

[45]   Treas. Reg. § 1.368–2(b)(1).

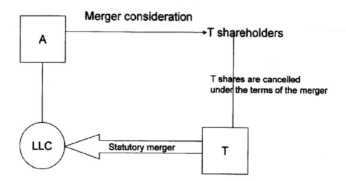

Two other, more complicated variants of the A reorganization—forward and reverse triangular mergers—are diagrammed later in this chapter, after we have introduced the B and C reorganizations. Some additional variants are discussed in a 2013 article by Linda Swartz and Richard Nugent.[46]

¶ 9.04.2 B Reorganizations

The B reorganization is sometimes called a *stock-for-stock* reorganization. Here the shareholders of the target corporation give up their stock in T, *solely* for *voting* stock in the acquiring corporation, so that afterwards the acquiring corporation has at least 80% *control* of the target under § 368(c). Note that, whereas T disappears in an A reorganization, T continues as a subsidiary of the acquiring corporation ("A") in a B reorganization.

---

[46]   Linda Swartz and Richard Nugent, *Big A, Little C: Baby Steps Towards Modernizing Reorganizations*, 140 Tax Notes 233 (2013).

Such a B reorganization may be diagrammed as follows:

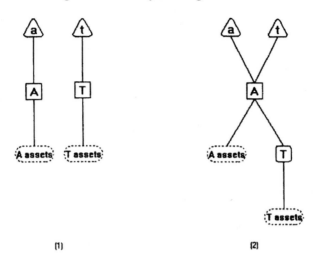

(1)   (2)

B Reorganization

One of the great virtues of a simple B reorganization is that *nothing happens directly to the target corporation*. It merely undergoes an ownership change. Its stock is transferred from one set of shareholders to a new, corporate shareholder. It retains all its old contractual rights and licenses. And while the target remains responsible for all its former liabilities, the acquiring entity does not need to worry about the prospect of undisclosed liabilities attaching to its own preexisting assets that are being deployed in other ventures.

Similarly, because nothing happens directly to the target corporation, a stock-for-stock acquisition ordinarily *does not trigger appraisal rights in dissenting shareholders*.[47] Dissenters to mergers and dissenters to massive sales of corporate assets often have the right to have their shares appraised and redeemed. They do not, however, have the right to keep their fellow shareholders from selling off their stock to a new purchaser.

---

[47]   In certain instances, a B reorganization may be effected by having a newly created subsidiary of the acquiring corporation merge into the target, where the terms of the merger require that the target's stock must be exchanged for voting stock of the acquiring corporation. Such a transaction is often referred to as a "forced B reorganization" and was sanctioned by the IRS in Rev. Rul. 67–448. See the discussion in the text accompanying note 99, infra. In such a forced B reorganization, it is possible that the target shareholders who dissent from approving the merger may be entitled to appraisal rights under the law of the jurisdiction governing the merger.

To qualify as a reorganization pursuant to § 368(a)(1)(B), however, the stock acquisition must leap two significant hurdles:

- The acquisition must be *solely for voting stock* of the acquiring corporation.

- Immediately after the acquisition, the acquiring corporation must have *control* of the target (within the meaning of § 368(c)).[48]

Note that there is no requirement that the acquiring corporation acquire control of the target by virtue of the transaction; it is only required that the acquiring corporation has control of the target immediately after the acquisition. For example, if A corporation has had 85% of T's outstanding stock for several years, an exchange of A's voting stock for some of the other outstanding T's shares will qualify as a B reorganization.

The "solely for voting stock" requirement is in many ways the most peculiar feature of a B reorganization. On its face, it would seem to imply that, if the acquiring corporation adds even a *single* share of nonvoting stock, or even a *single dollar's worth* of debt, cash, or other boot, then *all* of the former shareholders of the target corporation must recognize all of the gain they realize on the exchange. This is why many practitioners describe a B reorganization as the most unforgiving of the reorganization forms recognized by the tax law.

Such a result seems quite peculiar to most observers (at least, most observers who are familiar with the general patterns and practices of the tax laws). After all, in other contexts, the inclusion of a small amount of boot in what would otherwise be a tax-free exchange typically forces gain recognition only to the extent of the boot received.[49] And boot *may* be included in A reorganizations and C reorganizations. Nonetheless, with only a few exceptions described below, the statutory language has been accepted at face value by the Treasury and by the courts: a B reorganization is usually a bootless reorganization.

Ex. (1) A is a corporation that has one asset, an apartment building worth $500,000, in which it has a basis of $100,000. All 1000 shares of A's stock, worth a total of $500,000, are owned by P. P has a basis of $300,000 in those shares.

---

[48] That is, the acquiring corporation must own stock possessing at least 80% of the voting power of the target corporation plus at least 80% of the total number of shares of all nonvoting classes of stock of the target corporation. § 368(c). Where a corporation has several classes of nonvoting stock outstanding, the Service has ruled that the controlling corporation must own at least 80% of the shares of each separate class. Rev. Rul. 59–259.

[49] E.g., §§ 351(b), 356, 361(b), 1031(b).

T is a corporation that has one asset, a hotel worth $200,000, in which it has a basis of $80,000. T has 100 shares of stock outstanding. U owns 80 shares, V owns 15 shares, and W owns 5 shares.

On January 1, Year One, and pursuant to a single plan, (i) A issues 320 new shares of voting stock to U, in exchange for U's 80 shares of T, (ii) A issues 60 new shares of voting stock to V, in exchange for V's 15 shares of T, and (iii) A buys W's 5 shares of T, for $10,000 cash.

Ex. (2) The same facts as in Example (1), except that W did not own any shares of T. Instead, U owned 80 shares and V owned 20 shares. On January 1, Year One, A acquires all 80 of U's shares and 15 of V's shares in exchange for voting stock; A buys V's remaining 5 shares for cash.

In Example (1), A has acquired 95% of the T stock in exchange for voting stock. If A had done nothing else, that would clearly have qualified as a B reorganization, allowing U and V to enjoy nonrecognition treatment. But A did more. A acquired the remaining 5% by paying cash to W. Should that extra transaction between A and W force U and V to recognize gain? In Example (2), some of the "boot" went to a shareholder who also received voting stock. Should that preclude nonrecognition treatment for him or only trigger gain to the extent of the boot? Should it affect the other shareholder? The Treasury has clearly taken the position that neither of these Examples should qualify for nonrecognition treatment with regard to any of the shareholders;[50] and, subject to a few aberrational cases, the courts have sustained Treasury's position.

The no-boot requirement is applied quite strictly. The acquiring corporation may not use boot from a subsidiary to acquire target stock.[51] Nor may it assume any of the target shareholders' liabilities.[52] However, a few exceptions to the "solely for voting stock" rule do exist. The Service has ruled that an acquiring corporation may pay the bona fide reorganizational expenses of the target shareholders without violating the solely for voting stock requirement, as long as they are "solely and directly related" to the reorganization.[53] The distinction is, to be sure, a precarious one.[54]

---

[50] Rev. Rul. 75–123.

[51] Rev. Rul. 85–139.

[52] Rev. Rul. 79–4.

[53] Rev. Rul. 73–54. Similarly, if the acquiring corporation pays the bona fide reorganizational expenses of the target corporation in a C reorganization, the payments will not be treated as boot. Id.

[54] According to the Revenue Ruling, legitimate, qualifying, "bona fide" expenses include certain legal and accounting fees of the acquired corporation; appraisal fees;

Among other things, it implies that the acquiring corporation must pay the expenses directly, and must *not* give cash to the target shareholders with the expectation that they will use the cash to pay the fees.

A slightly more generous exception concerns the payment of cash for fractional shares.[55] The Service will treat such cash as consistent with the solely voting stock requirement, as long as the cash reflects nothing but a way to round off fractional shares and is not bargained for as separate consideration.[56]

What happens if an acquiring corporation has purchased a few shares of stock in a corporation and then later decides it wants to acquire the corporation in a B reorganization? Does the early acquisition of stock for cash mean that the "solely" requirement can never be satisfied?

The brief answer is no. As long as the previously acquired stock is "old and cold"—as long as it was acquired independently and not as an integral part of the later plan of acquisition—the "solely" requirement can be satisfied.[57] Indeed, the ownership of even a substantial amount of old and cold stock in the target does not preclude a B reorganization. See Treas. Reg. § 1.368–1(e)(1), (6), (8) Ex. (10). Note, however, that the regulations take the position that a series of acquisitions that occur "over a relatively short period of time such as 12 months" may be aggregated and treated as a single, integrated transaction.[58] If an acquiring corporation finds itself in possession of some "young and hot" stock, it may need to sell that stock unconditionally to an unrelated third party before undertaking a B reorganization.[59]

Ex. (3) T Corporation has 100 shares of stock outstanding, all owned by E. On January 1, Year One, A corporation

---

administrative costs directly related to the reorganization, such as those incurred for printing, clerical work, telephone, and telegraph; security underwriting fees; registration fees and expenses; transfer taxes; and transfer agents' fees and expenses.

In contrast, such bona fide transactional expenses do *not* include fees incurred by individual target shareholders for legal, accounting, investment, or estate planning advice, or for counsel pertaining to participation in, or action with respect to, the reorganization. Id.

[55] Mills v. Commissioner, 331 F.2d 321 (5th Cir. 1964), rev'g 39 T.C. 393 (1962); Rev. Rul. 66–365.

[56] Rev. Rul. 66–365.

[57] The regulations give as an example a transaction in which some shares were acquired for cash in 1939 and the reorganization took place in 1955. Treas. Reg. § 1.368–2(c).

[58] Id.

[59] See Rev. Rul. 72–354 holding that such an unconditional sale removed the taint that would have prevented the subsequent stock for stock exchange from qualifying as a B reorganization if the "young and hot" stock had not been sold.

acquires 60 shares of T from E, in exchange for $60,000 in cash. On January 1, Year Four, A acquires the remaining 40 shares of T from E, in exchange for new voting stock in A.

Example (3) presents a classic "creeping acquisition." The question is whether the acquisition of 40 shares of T in Year Four qualifies as a B reorganization. As noted above, as long as the acquisitions in Year One and Year Four are truly independent, the Year One acquisition should not lead to a violation of the "solely" requirement. But what of the requirement that the acquiring corporation be in "control" of the target immediately after the exchange?

"Control" means ownership of at least 80% of the total combined voting power of all classes of stock entitled to vote and at least 80% of each class of nonvoting stock of the corporation.[60] The 1954 Code added a parenthetical to the provision governing B reorganizations, to allow the control requirement to be satisfied "whether or not such acquiring corporation had control immediately before the acquisition." Thus, as long as any stock acquired with other than voting stock is "old and cold," a creeping acquisition can qualify.

Ex. (4) T Corporation has 100 shares of stock outstanding, all owned by E. On January 1, Year One, A corporation acquires 60 shares of T from E, in exchange for new voting stock of A. On August 1, Year One, A acquires the remaining 40 shares of T from E, in exchange for new voting stock of A.

Here, the taxpayer would *like* to aggregate the two stock acquisitions into a single acquisition for purposes of § 368(a)(1)(B). It is clear that the *August 1* transaction will qualify as a B reorganization. But the *January 1* transaction will not qualify if it stands alone, since when it was completed A did not have control of T. To qualify the January 1 acquisition of stock for nonrecognition treatment, it is necessary to conclude that the two transactions were part of a single acquisition. The regulations suggest that "an acquisition is permitted tax free in a single transaction or in a series of transactions taking place over a relatively short period of time such as 12 months."[61] Presumably, the several acquisitions will not be treated as a single, integrated transaction unless they were made pursuant to a single plan. Of course, the length of time over which the series of transactions extends is highly relevant to deciding

---

[60]   § 368(c).
[61]   Treas. Reg. § 1.368–2(c).

whether the series reflected a single plan, but other evidence should be relevant as well.

Ultimately, one of the most pressing planning problems presented by a B reorganization is the question of how to deal with dissenting shareholders who do not want to give up their target stock for voting stock in the acquiring corporation. If the dissenters own 20% or less of the target, the acquiring corporation can simply leave them alone and endure their continued presence as minority shareholders. But if that prospect is intolerable, the acquiring corporation has several options.

Sometimes it may be possible for the target itself to redeem the dissenters' shares prior to the reorganization. Such redemptions should not disqualify the reorganization as long as they are not being funded by the acquiring corporation, and as long as the continuity of proprietary interest doctrine is satisfied.[62] (Note that there is no requirement that "substantially all" the target's assets be retained in a B reorganization.)

Another solution is to have the acquiring corporation create a new corporation for the sole purpose of merging that new corporation into the target in what is often called a "forced B reorganization" and can sometimes also qualify as a reverse subsidiary merger, which we discuss later in this chapter. See the discussion at note 47, supra, and at the text to note 99, infra. The dissenting shareholders may demand cash for their shares in such a merger, but, as noted above, such cash payments will not preclude a B reorganization as long as the cash is provided solely by the target and is not funded indirectly by the acquiring corporation.

Another possibility may be to have a third party (such as a *noncorporate* shareholder of the acquiring corporation) purchase the dissenters' stock in the target.[63] In such a case, it is important that the third party not be acting as the agent of the acquiring corporation in making the purchase—the purchase price should not be furnished by the acquiring corporation either before or after the fact.

---

[62]   See Treas. Reg. § 1.368–1(e)(1)(ii), (7), Ex. (9). In light of the regulatory changes made to the application of the continuity of proprietary interest doctrine, the target's redemption prior to the reorganization and without using funds derived from the acquiring (or a related) corporation should not violate that requirement. See ¶ 9.03.1.

[63]   See Rev. Rul. 68–562. Of course, if the purchaser is a *corporation* that qualifies as related to the acquiring corporation under Treas. Reg. § 1.368–1(e)(3), a very large purchase could cause a problem with the general continuity-of-proprietary-interest requirement. See Treas. Reg. § 1.368–1(e)(3) and ¶ 9.03.1.

A final issue to consider with B reorganizations arises if, after completing a stock acquisition, the acquiring corporation liquidates the target:

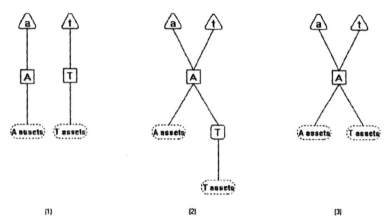

B Reorganization Followed by Target Liquidation

As we shall see, the result is economically indistinguishable from a stock-for-assets C reorganization. Applying the step-transaction doctrine, the IRS has ruled that, to qualify for nonrecognition treatment, the transaction must satisfy the rules that apply to C reorganizations.[64] However, if the liquidation of the target is effected pursuant to a statutory merger, the Service has indicated that the transaction needs to satisfy only the less rigorous requirements of an A reorganization.[65]

¶ 9.04.3 C Reorganizations

The C reorganization is sometimes called a *stock-for-assets* reorganization. Here the target corporation gives up *substantially all* of its assets, in exchange for *voting* stock of the acquiring corporation, and then the target corporation liquidates and distributes the stock of the acquiring corporation to its shareholders. Unlike the case of a B reorganization, where the acquiring corporation may not give boot, under some circumstances an acquiring corporation can give boot representing up to 20% of the total consideration and still qualify as a C reorganization.[66] Moreover, when the target liquidates, it may even be able to avoid having to recognize gain to the extent that it distributes the boot it received.[67]

---

[64]   Rev. Rul. 67–274. See also Rev. Rul. 2008–25.
[65]   Rev. Rul. 2001–46.
[66]   § 368(a)(2)(B).
[67]   § 361(b)(1)(A).

Such a C reorganization may be diagrammed as follows:

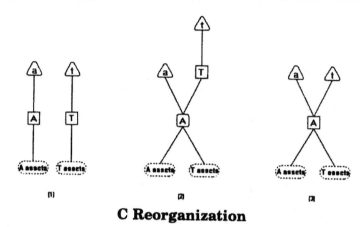

(1)   (2)   (3)

C Reorganization

Economically, a C reorganization has the same effect as a merger. For that reason, it is sometimes referred to as a "practical merger." To qualify as a reorganization pursuant to § 368(a)(1)(C), the asset acquisition must satisfy three significant tests:

- Consideration given: *either*

    (i)   the consideration given in the acquisition (and assumed liabilities are *disregarded* for this purpose) must be *solely voting stock* of the acquiring corporation,

    or

    (ii) the property acquired in exchange solely for such voting stock must constitute *at least 80%* of the total fair market value of all the target's property (and assumed or accepted liabilities[68] *are considered* as if the acquiring corporation had paid cash in the amount of such liabilities).

- The acquiring corporation must acquire *substantially all* of the target's properties in the acquisition.

- The target corporation must *liquidate* pursuant to the plan of reorganization.[69]

When, in 1934, Congress first added the "solely for voting stock" test in the stock-for-assets context, the test was the same as that in

---

[68]   For this purpose, it makes no difference whether a liability is assumed by the acquiring corporation or is an encumbrance on property that the acquiring corporation takes subject to that liability.

[69]   § 368(a)(2)(G).

the stock-for-stock context. Over the years, however, that requirement has undergone two significant amendments in the stock-for-assets context that have not been applied to B reorganizations.

The first change came in 1939 because, the year before, the Supreme Court had ruled that the assumption of target corporation liabilities by the acquiring corporation would violate the "solely" requirement.[70] In response, Congress amended the statute to provide that the assumption of target liabilities by the *acquiring* corporation does not violate the "solely" requirement.[71] The reason is the fairly straightforward one that Congress wanted to provide nonrecognition treatment when a corporation used its voting stock to acquire all of the operations of another corporation, encompassing all of the target's outstanding assets and liabilities. If that exception had not been enacted, there would be relatively few circumstances in which a C reorganization would be feasible.

The second change came in 1954, when Congress added the so-called "boot relaxation" provision of § 368(a)(2)(B). Under that provision, an acquisition may qualify as a C reorganization as long as the corporation uses voting stock to acquire property having a fair market value equal to at least 80% of the fair market value of all of the property of the other corporation before the acquisition. Significantly, under § 368(a)(2)(B), the assumption or acceptance of liabilities by the acquiring corporation is treated as compensation that is not made in the acquiring corporation's voting stock and so has the same effect as would the payment of cash for purposes of determining whether the 80% of fair market value rule was satisfied. Thus, the net effect of the 80% rule is to provide that up to 20% of the consideration in a C reorganization can be boot, *but* that any assumption of liabilities and any assets *retained* by the target corporation count against that 20% ceiling.

Ex. (5) T Corporation has assets valued at $200,000, subject to liabilities totaling $20,000. None of T's shareholders is a corporation that controls T.

On January 1, Year One, A Corporation transfers $165,000 worth of its own voting stock, together with $10,000 cash, to T in exchange for all T's assets other than a $5,000 machine. A assumes all $20,000 worth of liabilities on the exchange. T then liquidates, distributing the A stock, the machine, and the cash to its shareholders.

---

[70]   United States v. Hendler, 303 U.S. 564 (1938).

[71]   See § 368(a)(1)(C).

In Example (5), the 80% test is satisfied and the transaction qualifies as a C reorganization.

Ex. (6) The same facts as in Example (5), except that the assumed liabilities total $45,000, and A transfers $154,000 worth of voting stock together with only $1,000 cash.

In Example (6), the 80% test is not satisfied and the transaction does not qualify as a C reorganization. Note that the result in Example (6) would be the same if A had not assumed the liabilities, but had taken T's assets subject to those liabilities.

Ex. (7) The same facts as in Example (6), except that instead of transferring $154,000 worth of stock and $1,000 cash, A transfers $155,000 worth of stock and transfers no boot to T.

In Example (7) the transaction qualifies directly under § 368(a)(1)(C). The fact that it would not satisfy the 80% test of § 368(a)(2)(B) is irrelevant. No boot was paid, and so the boot relaxation rule is not applicable.

The requirement that the acquiring corporation obtain "substantially all" the target's properties in exchange solely for voting stock has been a source of substantial uncertainty in the context of C reorganizations. The purpose of the requirement is to make sure that *divisive* reorganizations are tested as D reorganizations and do not qualify "through the back door" as C reorganizations.[72] Unfortunately, knowing that purpose does not lend much additional precision to the statutory vagueness.

For advance ruling purposes, the IRS historically required a representation that the acquiring corporation obtain at least 90% of the fair market value of the target's "net" assets (the fair market value reduced by liabilities) and at least 70% of the fair market value of the target's "gross" assets.[73] For these purposes, many categories of expenditures by the corporation immediately before the acquisition are "clawed back" and taken into account.[74]

While the ruling guidelines have emerged as an important benchmark in the planning of reorganization transactions, the cases and Revenue Rulings confirm that failure to satisfy the guidelines is not always fatal. The Revenue Rulings often look more closely at "the

---

[72] See S. Rep. No. 1622, 83d Cong., 2d Sess., 274 (1954).

[73] Rev. Proc. 77–37, Sec. 3.01, as amplified by Rev. Proc. 86–42, Sec. 7.05(3).

[74] See Helvering v. Elkhorn Coal Co., 95 F.2d 732 (4th Cir. 1937). Rev. Proc. 86–42 refers specifically to "amounts paid by target to dissenters, amounts used by target to pay its reorganization expenses, amounts paid by target to shareholders who receive cash or other property, and all redemptions and distributions (except for regular, normal dividends)." Cf. Treas. Reg. § 1.368–2(j)(6), Ex. (3).

nature of the properties retained by the transferor, the purpose of the retention, and the amount thereof."[75] And the cases seem to look more favorably on the retention of assets to pay creditors than they do on the retention of assets to distribute to shareholders.[76]

The "solely" and "substantially all" tests can interact awkwardly where the acquiring corporation already owns stock in the target corporation. Until recently, even where the acquiring corporation's interest was "old and cold," it could prevent qualification as a C reorganization.

Ex. (8)   T is a corporation in the stereo business. It owns a store and a substantial quantity of inventory.

        21% of T's stock is owned by E, an individual. The remaining 79% is owned by A, a corporation. A has owned its T shares for the past fifteen years.

        On January 1, Year Sixteen, A issues new voting stock to T, in exchange for all T's assets.

        On January 15, Year Sixteen, T liquidates, distributing 79% of the A shares to A, and the remaining 21% to E.

Example (8) sets forth a stylized version of the facts of *Bausch & Lomb Optical Co. v. Commissioner*.[77] In that case, the Second Circuit, following an earlier Revenue Ruling,[78] held that in substance A had acquired only 21% of T's assets in exchange for voting stock; it had acquired the remaining 79% in exchange for its T shares. Accordingly, the court held that the transaction did not qualify as a C reorganization because it did not satisfy even the relaxed form of the "solely" test. This construction of the voting stock requirement was generally referred to as the *Bausch & Lomb* doctrine.

The *Bausch & Lomb* doctrine no longer exists. It has been repudiated by Treasury and is now obsolete. Regulations now permit an acquiring corporation to own previously acquired stock of the target.[79] Moreover, in applying the boot relaxation rule, the fact that the acquiring corporation owned previously acquired stock is not taken into account; the regulation focuses on whether the amount of consideration that constitutes boot and liability assumption exceeds

---

[75]   Rev. Rul. 57–518. See also Rev. Rul. 88–48; Rev. Rul. 78–47.

[76]   See Pillar Rock Packing Co. v. Commissioner, 90 F.2d 949 (9th Cir. 1937); Thurber v. Commissioner, 84 F.2d 815 (1st Cir. 1936); Western Indus. Co. v. Helvering, 82 F.2d 461 (D.C. Cir. 1936); Smith v. Commissioner, 34 B.T.A. 702 (1936).

[77]   267 F.2d 75 (2d Cir. 1959).

[78]   Rev. Rul. 54–396 (declared obsolete in T.D. 8885).

[79]   Treas. Reg. § 1.368–2(d)(4).

20% of the value of the target's assets.[80] Accordingly, the transaction described above in Example (8) will qualify as a C reorganization.

The requirement that the target corporation liquidate was added to the Code in 1984.[81] No specific time period is established for the liquidation; the statute says only that the target must distribute all its properties "in pursuance of the plan of reorganization." The provision was added in response to the perception that some taxpayers were effectively cashing out substantial businesses in the guise of C reorganizations.

¶ 9.04.4 Triangular Reorganizations

Section 368(a)(2)(C) provides that an A, B, or C reorganization is not disqualified if the acquiring corporation drops some or all of the acquired target stock or assets down into a controlled subsidiary.[82] The drop-down transaction is not treated as part of the reorganization (the subsidiary is not treated as a party to the reorganization), but is instead treated as a separate § 351 exchange.[83]

Ten years after it authorized post-acquisition drop-downs, Congress amended § 368(a)(1)(B) and § 368(b) to permit a B reorganization where the consideration consists solely of voting stock of a corporation that is in control of the acquiring corporation. In economic substance, the transaction is equivalent to a B reorganization at the *parent* level, followed by a "drop-down" of the target stock from the parent to its subsidiary.

This special variant of a B reorganization is known as a triangular B reorganization. It is called triangular because three corporations are involved: instead of using its own stock to acquire the target, the acquiring corporation uses its parent's stock.[84] This variant is also sometimes known as a subsidiary B reorganization.

---

[80]   Treas. Reg. § 1.368–2(d)(4)(ii), Ex. (1).

[81]   Deficit Reduction Act of 1984, Pub. L. No. 98–369, § 63, 98 Stat. 494, 583 (adding § 368(a)(2)(G)).

[82]   For this purpose, "control" is defined in § 368(c) to mean ownership of at least 80% of total combined voting power and at least 80% of each class of nonvoting shares. Rev. Rul. 59–259. The regulations expand the scope of the drop-down provision by permitting multiple drop downs to lower tier subsidiaries. Treas. Reg. § 1.368–2(k). An acquiring corporation does not lose its status as a "party to a reorganization" by dropping down the acquired stock or assets to lower tier subsidiaries. Treas. Reg. § 1.368–2(f).

[83]   See Chapter Seven. Accordingly, the acquiring corporation may have to recognize gain if it drops down property subject to liabilities in excess of the property's basis. § 357(c).

[84]   The first parenthetical in § 368(a)(1)(B) authorizes the acquiring corporation to receive the target's stock "in exchange solely for all or a part of the voting stock of a corporation which is in control of the acquiring corporation."

The term is useful because (a) in such a reorganization, the parent corporation usually makes the decision to undertake the acquisition, and (b) the transaction has the same non-tax consequences as an ordinary B reorganization, followed by a decision to "drop down" the target stock into a subsidiary of the acquiring corporation.

Thus, one could diagram a triangular B reorganization in either of the following two ways:

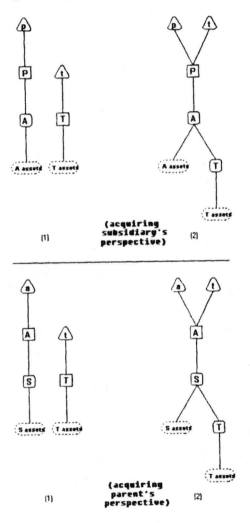

Triangular (Subsidiary) B Reorganization

If the acquiring corporation uses parent voting stock instead of its own in a triangular B reorganization, then it must use *only* parent stock; a B reorganization may use *either* the acquiring corporation's voting stock or its parent's voting stock, but *not* some of each.[85]

Just as the B reorganization has a triangular variant, there is a triangular C reorganization (also known as a subsidiary C reorganization) as well. Once again, the acquiring corporation uses stock of its parent instead of its own stock. And once again such a triangular C reorganization may be diagrammed as follows:

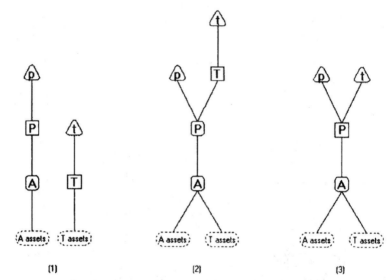

(1)   (2)   (3)

(shown only from acquiring subsidiary's perspective)

Triangular (Subsidiary) C Reorganization

As was true of triangular B reorganizations, if the acquiring corporation uses parent voting stock instead of its own in a triangular C reorganization, then it must use *only* parent stock. A C reorganization may use *either* the acquiring corporation's voting stock or its parent's voting stock, but *not* some of each.[86] However, if the consideration provided by the use of *either* the acquiring corporation's voting stock or its parent's voting stock is sufficient to satisfy the 80% test of § 368(a)(2)(B), it is arguable that the acquisition could then qualify as a C reorganization in which the voting stock of the other corporation is treated as boot. However, it is not clear whether the Service or the courts would ultimately determine that the boot relaxation rule should be applied in such a

---

85   Treas. Reg. § 1.368–2(c).

86   Treas. Reg. § 1.368–2(d)(1).

case, although the authors see no reason why it should not be applicable.

¶ 9.04.5 Triangular Mergers

There are two types of triangular mergers: forward (§ 368(a)(2)(D)) and reverse (§ 368(a)(2)(E)) triangular mergers.

¶ 9.04.5.1 *Forward Triangular (Subsidiary) Merger ((a)(2)(D))*

The forward triangular merger (also known as a forward subsidiary merger or an (a)(2)(D) reorganization), is a kind of hybrid between an A reorganization and a C reorganization.[87] The target corporation is merged into the acquiring corporation, but the target's shareholders receive stock in the *parent* of the acquiring corporation. While the reorganization takes the form of a merger, the parties end up in the same position as in a triangular C reorganization.

Such a forward triangular merger may be diagrammed as follows:

---

[87]   § 368(a)(2)(D).

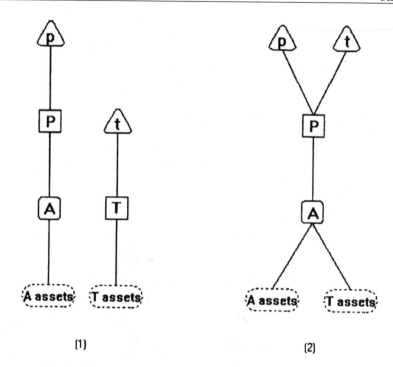

(1) (2)

(shown only from acquiring subsidiary's perspective)

Forward Triangular (Subsidiary) Merger ((a)(2)(D))

The reason that the forward triangular merger is sometimes said to be a hybrid between an A reorganization and a C reorganization is that it carries with it some of the requirements of each of those two reorganization forms. The acquiring subsidiary corporation in a forward triangular merger need not be a long-established going concern. It may be a newly formed subsidiary, created just for the purpose of the transaction.[88] To qualify under § 368(a)(2)(D), however, the transaction must satisfy five requirements:

- The parent must "control" the acquiring corporation within the meaning of § 368(c).[89]

- The acquiring corporation must acquire "substantially all" of the properties of the acquired corporation.

---

[88]   Treas. Reg. § 1.368–2(b)(2).

[89]   That implies ownership of stock with at least 80% of the total combined voting power of all classes of stock entitled to vote and at least 80% of the shares of each other class of stock.

- The acquiring corporation may not use *any* of its own stock; only its parent's stock may be used.[90]

- The transaction must otherwise be such that it would have qualified as an A reorganization if the target had merged into the *parent* instead of into the acquiring corporation.[91]

- If the acquiring corporation is a transitory corporation that was formed for the purpose of carrying out the merger, it must not liquidate too soon after the transaction. If it does, the merger into the acquiring corporation may be disregarded, and then the acquisition will be treated as a direct acquisition of the target's assets by the parent, and so will have to qualify as a C reorganization to receive nonrecognition treatment.[92]

Note that in a forward triangular merger, there is no statutory limitation on the amount of boot that can be paid. The only limitation on boot is that the continuity of propriety interest requirement must be satisfied. Consequently, boot constituting as much as 60% of the consideration can be paid. Note also that there is no requirement that voting stock be the consideration, and so non-voting stock can be used.

¶ 9.04.5.2   *Reverse   Triangular   (Subsidiary)   Merger ((a)(2)(E))*

The reverse triangular merger (also known as a reverse subsidiary merger or an (a)(2)(E) reorganization or occasionally a reverse B reorganization), is a kind of hybrid between an A reorganization and a B reorganization.[93] The "acquiring corporation" is merged into the target corporation, but at the same time the shareholders of the target exchange a *controlling* stake in the target for *voting* stock of the parent of the acquiring corporation. As a result, the original target shareholders end up holding stock in the *parent* of the acquiring corporation, and the parent ends up owning the target. This is sometimes called a "reverse B reorganization" because, if only

---

[90]   § 368(a)(2)(D)(i). To the extent boot is included in the reorganization, however, it may come from either the parent or the subsidiary. Similarly, either the parent or the subsidiary may assume liabilities of the target in the transaction. Treas. Reg. § 1.368–2(b)(2).

[91]   Note in particular that, if either the parent or the subsidiary had previously purchased a sizeable amount of target stock that it still owned, the ability of the transaction to satisfy the continuity-of-proprietary-interest doctrine may depend on whether the stock is "old and cold." See ¶ 9.03.1.

[92]   See Rev. Rul. 72–405.

[93]   § 368(a)(2)(E).

voting stock of the parent corporation is used and no amount of boot is used, the parties end up in the same position as in a B reorganization in which the T shareholders exchange their T stock for P voting stock.

Such a reverse triangular merger may be diagrammed as follows:

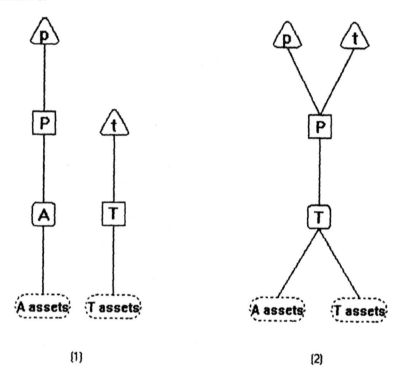

(1)   (2)

[shown only from acquiring subsidiary's perspective]

Reverse Triangular (Subsidiary) Merger ((a)(2)(E))

In a reverse triangular merger, the nominal target (the "A" corporation) disappears in the transaction and is therefore usually referred to as the "merged" corporation. The nominal acquiring corporation (T) is actually the target and effectively is acquired by A's parent.

As was true of forward triangular mergers, the merged corporation need not be a long-established going concern. It may be a thoroughly transitory subsidiary, created just for the purpose of the transaction.[94] To qualify under § 368(a)(2)(E), however, the transaction must satisfy three requirements:

- The parent must "control" the merged corporation within the meaning of § 368(c).[95]

- The surviving target corporation must, after the merger, hold "substantially all" of its pre-merger properties *and* "substantially all" the properties of the merged corporation that merged into it.[96]

- The former shareholders of the target corporation must exchange stock of the target corporation constituting control of that corporation in exchange for voting stock of the parent.

The last requirement differentiates reverse triangular mergers from *both* forward triangular mergers and B reorganizations. Unlike the forward triangular merger, a § 368(a)(2)(E) reverse triangular merger requires the use of *voting* stock of the parent corporation. And whereas the forward triangular merger required only the use of sufficient stock consideration to satisfy the continuity-of-proprietary-interest requirement, a § 368(a)(2)(E) reverse triangular merger requires the use of sufficient voting stock consideration to acquire "control" of the target—80% of the voting power of all the target's voting stock and 80% of the shares of each class of nonvoting stock.[97] Unlike a B reorganization, consideration can include some boot; but there is a "substantially all" the property requirement while there is none for a B reorganization.

The 80% requirement has two important implications. First, it effectively limits the use of boot to 20% of the consideration provided by the acquiring corporation and its parent in a reverse triangular merger.[98] (Of course, that is more flexibility than would be available in a B reorganization, where no boot at all is permitted.) Second, the

---

[94] Treas. Reg. § 1.368–2(j)(5). Indeed, because a failed reverse triangular merger is more likely to qualify as some *other* kind of reorganization (e.g., a B reorganization) if it makes use of a transitory subsidiary, some authorities recommend that a transitory subsidiary be used as a matter of course.

[95] That implies ownership of stock with at least 80% of the total combined voting power of all classes of stock entitled to vote and at least 80% of the shares of each other class of stock.

[96] The "substantially all" test also applies to forward triangular mergers and to C reorganizations, and for the most part it should be construed in the same manner (although here it is applied to *both* corporations). Note, however, that this is not a requirement for qualification as a B reorganization.

[97] § 368(c).

[98] In performing the 80% "control" calculation, one ignores any stock of the target corporation that is redeemed by the target out of its own funds. Treas. Reg. § 1.368–2(j)(3)(i), (6), Ex. (2). The funds used in such a redemption are *not* ignored, however, in applying the "substantially all" test. Treas. Reg. § 1.368–2(j)(3)(iii).

requirement that control be acquired *in the transaction* means that an (a)(2)(E) reorganization is unavailable if the acquiring corporation owns more than 20% of the target's voting stock (or more than 20 percent of any class of target nonvoting stock) before the reorganization. That is less flexibility than would be available in a B reorganization. Finally, the "substantially all" the properties requirement must be satisfied whereas B reorganizations are not subject to that requirement.

If the merged corporation (A) was created by P corporation for the purpose of merging it into T, it has a short life and is referred to as a "transitory corporation." When a transitory subsidiary corporation is merged into T, the merger can be ignored for tax purposes and the transaction can be recast as an exchange of P's stock for the stock of T. If that exchange qualifies as a B reorganization (i.e., if only voting stock of P is used in the exchange), the transaction can be treated as a B reorganization.[99] Such transactions are referred to as a "forced B reorganization."

One reason that it was necessary to adopt § 368(a)(2)(D) and (E) to permit forward and reverse triangular mergers was to negate the problem of remote continuity of interest. In both of those triangular mergers, the shareholders of the actual target do not hold stock of the surviving corporation, and so the continuity of proprietary interest requirement would not be satisfied. Those shareholders do hold stock of the parent of the surviving corporation, but two 1930s Supreme Court decisions held that such remote continuity did not satisfy the requirement.[100] That position, referred to as the *Groman-Bashford* doctrine, would prevent triangular reorganizations and drop-downs of target stock if Congress had not authorized those transactions. In view of Treasury's liberal application of the authorization of drop-downs in § 368(a)(2)(C) and its liberalization of the continuity-of-proprietary interest rule, there appears to be little or no continuing efficacy to the *Groman-Bashford* doctrine.

¶ 9.04.6 D Reorganizations

D reorganizations straddle the world of corporate divisions and corporate acquisitions. Some (but not all) corporate divisions qualify as D reorganizations.[101] Similarly, some (but not all) corporate acquisitions qualify as D reorganizations.

---

[99] Treas. Reg. § 1.368–2(j)(6), Exs. (4), (5).

[100] Groman v. Commissioner, 302 U.S. 82 (1937); Helvering v. Bashford, 302 U.S. 454 (1938).

[101] In general, a corporate division pursuant to § 355 also qualifies as a D reorganization if it involves two steps: the drop-down of a trade or business to a controlled subsidiary, followed by the qualifying spin-off or split-off of the subsidiary.

¶ 9.04.6.1   *Divisive D Reorganizations*

The classic divisive reorganization is a D reorganization: a transfer of assets from a corporation to a controlled subsidiary, followed immediately by a spin-off, split-off, or split-up with respect to that subsidiary.[102] It is sometimes helpful to think of a divisive D reorganization as a § 351 transfer, followed by a § 355 division. If § 368(a)(1)(D) applies, however, the transaction is treated differently from what would follow from the application of §§ 351 and 355, in that certain tax attributes (such as *e and p*) are allocated differently,[103] and the distributing corporation's receipt of securities of the controlled corporation will not constitute boot.[104] There also are some differences in the nonrecognition rules that apply to the distributing corporations.[105]

A sample divisive D reorganization involving a spin-off may be diagrammed as follows:

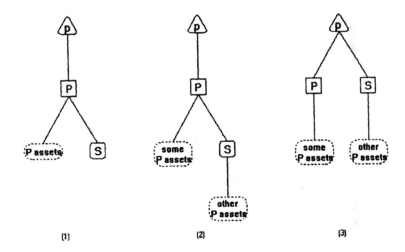

(1)   (2)   (3)

Divisive D Reorganization

Divisive D reorganizations are discussed in Chapter Eight.

¶ 9.04.6.2   *Acquisitive D Reorganizations*

The acquisitive D reorganization (sometimes known as a "reverse acquisition") is a variation on the divisive D reorganization.

---

[102]   See Chapter Eight.
[103]   See, e.g., Treas. Reg. § 1.312–10(a).
[104]   Compare § 351(a) with § 361(a).
[105]   Compare § 355(c) with § 361(c).

It begins with a transfer of substantially all the assets of the target corporation to a corporation that is "controlled" by the transferor or its shareholders or a combination thereof immediately after the transfer (using a relaxed 50% "control" standard and some fairly sweeping attribution rules that apply only to this type of reorganization). However, instead of being followed by a § 355 division, the asset transfer is followed by a liquidation of the target.[106]

Because this form of acquisitive reorganization can take place only if the target corporation (or its shareholders or a combination of the target and its shareholders) controls the acquiring corporation immediately after the initial transfer of assets, it occurs in contexts that can be described either as "reverse acquisitions" or as "affiliate acquisitions."

Such acquisitive D reorganizations may be diagrammed as follows:

---

[106]   §§ 368(a)(1)(D), 354(b). The liquidation involves an exchange of stock in a party to the reorganization that qualifies under §§ 354 and 356. See § 368(a)(1)(D).

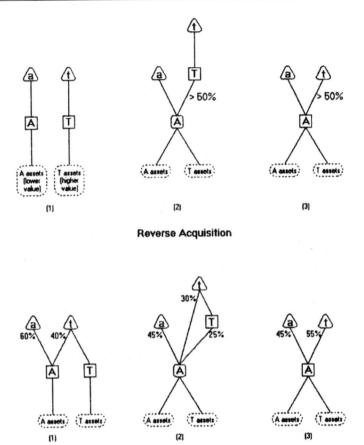

Reverse Acquisition

Affiliate Acquisition

Acquisitive D Reorganizations

An acquisitive D reorganization may be thought of as a specialized cousin of a C reorganization.[107] Seen from this perspective, what makes a D reorganization distinctive is that, immediately after the acquisition of the nominal "target's" assets, the nominal "target," together with its shareholders, is in *control* of the nominal "acquiring" corporation. For this purpose, "control" is defined in § 304(c) and generally requires only the ownership of stock possessing either: (1) at least 50% of the total combined voting power of all classes of voting stock, or (2) at least 50% of the value of all of

---

[107]   To be sure, the transaction need not satisfy the requirements of § 368(a)(1)(C) in order to qualify under § 368(a)(1)(D). If it satisfies both, however, it is treated *only* as a D reorganization and *not* as a C reorganization. § 368(a)(2)(A).

the corporation's outstanding stock.[108] To the extent one thinks of a C reorganization as a "practical merger," it is appropriate to think of a D reorganization as a "practical reverse merger."

Because of the direction in which "control" runs, it is sometimes easier to view a D reorganization from the perspective of the putative target. Seen from that perspective, an acquisitive D reorganization involves two steps: the transfer of a trade or business to a controlled subsidiary, followed by the liquidation of the parent.

More precisely, an acquisition of assets must satisfy three significant tests to qualify as an acquisitive reorganization pursuant to § 368(a)(1)(D):

- Immediately after the initial drop-down of assets, the nominal "target" corporation, in combination with its shareholders, must *control* the nominal "acquiring" corporation within the meaning of § 304(c) (so that the nominal acquiring corporation can be thought of as a subsidiary of the nominal target), and

- In pursuance of the plan of reorganization, the nominal target must distribute its assets in a transaction that qualifies under § 354 or § 356, which in turn means it must satisfy the two § 354(b) requirements that:

  (1) the nominal acquiring corporation must acquire *substantially all* of the nominal target's assets in the acquisition, and

  (2) after the exchange, the nominal target must *distribute all of its assets* (which will consist virtually entirely of the stock and securities of the nominal acquiring corporation).

¶ 9.04.7 E Reorganizations

The E reorganization is described in the Code simply as "a recapitalization." No further definition is provided. As a general matter, a recapitalization is a transaction in which a corporation's shareholders or creditors exchange their interests in the corporation for other forms of equity or debt in the same corporation. More specific guidance concerning which transactions qualify as a recapitalization *for tax purposes* is hard to come by. Over the years, the IRS and the Supreme Court have offered a few sporadic attempts. For example, in a 1925 ruling, the Service stated that a recapitalization "signifies an arrangement whereby the stock and

---

[108] § 368(a)(2)(H). A modified version of § 318 stock attribution rules applies. § 304(c)(3). In addition, the stock or securities of the nominal "acquiring" corporation must be distributed in a transaction that qualifies under §§ 354 or 356. § 368(a)(1)(D).

bonds of the corporation are readjusted as to amount, income, or priority, or an agreement of all stockholders and creditors to change and increase or decrease the capitalization or debts of the corporation, or both."[109] And in 1942, the Supreme Court stated that a recapitalization was a "reshuffling of a capital structure, within the framework of an existing corporation."[110]

However, in 1947, the Court cautioned against attempts to provide a unified theory of recapitalizations.[111] The Court declared that this is an area of the tax law where no abstract definition should be sought, and it would be especially inappropriate to attempt to borrow a definition from corporate law or accounting. "[T]he form of a transaction as reflected by correct corporate accounting opens questions as to the proper application of a taxing statute; it does not close them."[112]

While the lawyer attempting to predict whether a transaction qualifies as a recapitalization is therefore discouraged from seeking a single overarching principle, it is nonetheless possible to draw some useful generalizations. We offer two: (1) although the continuity-of-proprietary-interest and continuity-of-business-enterprise doctrines are inapplicable in the recapitalization context, the business purpose requirement remains significant,[113] and (2) the courts and the IRS tend to categorize recapitalizations according to the *types of securities* that are exchanged.

¶ 9.04.7.1   *Exchange of Stock for Stock*

Section 1036(a) provides for nonrecognition treatment whenever a shareholder exchanges common stock for common stock in the same corporation, or preferred stock for preferred stock in the same corporation, *regardless* of whether the exchange is also pursuant to a reorganization.[114] Section 1036(a) does not apply to nonqualified preferred stock as defined in § 351(g)(2), and thus it will not apply to the receipt of nonqualified preferred stock or the receipt of stock in exchange for nonqualified preferred stock.[115] However, if nonqualified preferred stock is received in exchange for other

---

[109]   S.M. 3710 (1925).

[110]   Helvering v. Southwest Consol. Corp., 315 U.S. 194, 202 (1942).

[111]   Bazley v. Commissioner, 331 U.S. 737 (1947).

[112]   Id. at 741.

[113]   See Hickok v. Commissioner, 32 T.C. 80 (1959); Treas. Reg. § 1.368–1(b). For the most part, the courts and the Service have been fairly lenient in accepting motivations for recapitalizations as legitimate "business purposes" for tax purposes.

[114]   See Treas. Reg. § 1.1036–1; Rev. Rul. 54–482 (common for common); Rev. Rul. 56–586 (preferred for preferred).

[115]   § 1036(b).

nonqualified preferred stock pursuant to a reorganization, the exchange can qualify for nonrecognition under § 354.[116]

If the shareholder exchanges common for preferred, or preferred for common, § 1036(a) does not apply. Nonrecognition treatment is available in such cases only if the transaction qualifies as a reorganization, so that § 354 will apply. The regulations suggest, however, that such straightforward stock-for-stock exchanges, pursuant to a plan and for a legitimate business purpose, are relatively unproblematic,[117] unless nonqualified preferred stock is involved. Nonetheless, a few problem areas are worth noting.

When, pursuant to a recapitalization, a shareholder receives preferred stock that is not nonqualified preferred on account of prior holdings of common stock, there is a risk that the preferred stock will be section 306 stock if (i) the shareholder is able, *to any extent*, to escape recognition of gain or loss, and (ii) the effect of the exchange is "substantially the same as the receipt of a stock dividend."[118] Under the regulations, such a situation exists if "cash received in lieu of such stock" would have been treated as a dividend under § 356(a)(2) or would have been treated as a § 301 distribution by virtue of § 356(b) or § 302(d).[119] The Service has tended to find that standard satisfied wherever the exchange of common for preferred has not substantially changed the proportionate interest of the common shareholder in the corporation.[120] Where, however, a shareholder exchanges preferred stock that is not section 306 stock for substantially similar preferred stock, the new preferred stock is also not section 306 stock.[121] Moreover, where a shareholder exchanges section 306 stock for new common stock, the exchange can effectively remove the section 306 taint.[122]

Even more unnerving than the potential receipt of section 306 stock in a recapitalization is the possibility that some of the stock received might be taxable as a § 301 distribution by virtue of §§ 305(b) and (c). Exercising the authority granted pursuant to that section, the Treasury Department has promulgated Treas. Reg. § 1.305–7(c). That regulation provides that a recapitalization will be deemed to result in a distribution of stock, taxable as a § 301 distribution if it falls within § 305(b), and if (1) it is pursuant to a plan to periodically increase a shareholder's proportionate interest in

---

[116]   § 354(a)(2)(C)(i).

[117]   Treas. Reg. § 1.368–2(e)(2), (3), (4).

[118]   § 306(c)(1)(B).

[119]   Treas. Reg. § 1.306–3(d).

[120]   See Rev. Rul. 70–199; Rev. Rul. 59–197; Rev. Rul. 59–84; Rev. Rul. 56–116.

[121]   Treas. Reg. § 1.306–3(d), Ex. (2); Rev. Rul. 79–287.

[122]   See §§ 306(c)(1)(B), 306(c)(1)(C), 306(e)(1).

the assets or *e and p* of the corporation, or (2) a shareholder owning preferred stock with dividends in arrears exchanges his stock for other stock and thereby increases his proportionate interest in the assets or *e and p* of the corporation.

¶ 9.04.7.2   Exchange of Bonds for Stock

A bondholder's exchange of bonds for stock in a recapitalization does not cause recognition of gain or loss.[123] The Code provides that the value of stock received in satisfaction of accrued but unpaid interest will constitute ordinary income to the bondholder to the extent that it had not previously been reported as income by the bondholder.[124] Conversely, to the extent the bondholder had previously reported income on account of accrued but unpaid interest that exceeded the value of the stock received, the bondholder may recognize a loss. At the corporate level, the issuance of stock in cancellation of old bonds can trigger cancellation of indebtedness income pursuant to § 61(a)(12) of the Code.[125]

¶ 9.04.7.3   Exchange of Bonds for Bonds

A bondholder's exchange of bonds for bonds can also qualify as a recapitalization. If, however, the principal amount of the bonds received exceeds the principal amount of the bonds surrendered, the fair market value of the excess constitutes excess-securities boot.[126] The bondholder is accordingly taxable to the extent of the lesser of that boot and the amount of gain realized on the exchange.[127] Moreover, to the extent the excess securities boot reflects a payment of accrued but unpaid interest or discount, it may be taxable as ordinary income.[128] As to the issuing corporation, if the issue price of the new bonds is less than the indebtedness satisfied in exchange for the new bonds, the difference can constitute cancellation of indebtedness income.[129]

¶ 9.04.7.4   Exchange of Stock for Bonds

When a stockholder exchanges stock (and no bonds) for bonds in the same corporation, then even if the transaction qualifies as a recapitalization, the extent of nonrecognition treatment that is available will be limited by the excess-securities boot rules of

---

[123]   Treas. Reg. § 1.368–2(e)(1); Rev. Rul. 59–98.

[124]   § 354(a)(2)(B).

[125]   For stock for debt exchanges made after the year 1994, see § 108(e)(8).

[126]   See ¶ 8.10.1.

[127]   §§ 354(a)(2), 356(a).

[128]   See § 354(a)(2)(B). See also § 1276(c), (d) (no recognition of market discount income on the exchange unless there is excess-securities boot).

[129]   § 108(e)(10).

§§ 354(a)(2) and 356(d).[130] The shareholder will recognize gain to the extent of the excess of the fair market value of the bonds over his basis in the stock surrendered.[131] Moreover, to the extent that the exchange has the effect of a dividend, some of that *gain* will be recharacterized as dividend income.[132]

In 1947, before the addition of the excess-securities-boot provisions to the Code, the Supreme Court decided *Bazley v. Commissioner*.[133] In that case, members of a family exchanged their stock in a family corporation for new stock and bonds of the same corporation in a transaction that did not alter their relative percentage interests in the corporation. The Court held that the transaction was not a reorganization, but rather a disguised effort to withdraw earnings and profits from the corporation; accordingly, it treated the bonds received as disguised dividends.

It is likely that *Bazley* survives the adoption of §§ 354(a)(2) and 356(d). Unfortunately, the precise contours of the *Bazley* holding remain somewhat nebulous. For example, it is not clear whether a non-pro-rata recapitalization might be treated differently, either within or outside the family context.[134]

¶ 9.04.8 F Reorganizations

The F reorganization consists of "a mere change in identity, form, or place of organization of one corporation." Typically, it involves the transfer of all of one corporation's assets to a newly created corporate shell. As with an E reorganization, whether a given change in identity qualifies as an F reorganization depends on facts and circumstances. The F reorganization has enjoyed a curious life. For the most part, that life can be characterized as one of quiescence, boom, and then bust.

Until the mid-1950s, the F reorganization was a sleeper provision, rarely heard from. Section 381(b)(3) of the 1954 Code provided that the acquiring corporation in an A, C, or D reorganization may not carry back the net operating losses of the target to offset its own pre-acquisition income (but, by implication, no such restriction applies to an F reorganization). In 1957, the IRS ruled that a transaction that qualifies *both* as an F reorganization and as an A, C, or D reorganization should be treated as an F reorganization. The combination of that ruling and the statutory treatment of loss carrybacks suddenly meant that there was a benefit

---

[130]   See ¶ 8.10.1
[131]   § 356(a)(1).
[132]   § 356(a)(2).
[133]   331 U.S. 737 (1947).
[134]   See, e.g., Seide v. Commissioner, 18 T.C. 502 (1952).

to stretching the definition of an F reorganization to overlap with the other reorganization provisions as much as possible.

In 1982, Congress amended § 368(a)(1)(F) to limit it to a change in identity, form, or place of incorporation "of one corporation." Taken literally, the language would exclude even the prototypical reincorporation in a different state, which typically is accomplished by creating a corporate shell in the other state and then merging the existing corporation into the newly created corporate shell. The legislative history indicates, however, that, "[t]his limitation does not preclude the use of more than one entity to consummate the transaction provided only one operating company is involved."[135] In its rulings, the Service has made clear that the merger of two corporations can qualify as an F reorganization provided that the merger involves only one "operating corporation."[136]

The 1982 amendment brought an end to the boom in F reorganizations. Nonetheless, the F reorganization remains important in the more-or-less cosmetic circumstances for which it was originally designed.

¶ 9.04.9 G Reorganizations

The G reorganization consists of a transfer by a corporation of some or all of its assets to another corporation in a bankruptcy, receivership, foreclosure, or similar proceeding. The provision, added by the Bankruptcy Tax Act of 1980, was intended to facilitate the rehabilitation of financially troubled businesses by deferring taxation whenever substantially all the assets of the troubled corporation are transferred to the acquiring corporation.[137]

¶ 9.05 A CLOSER LOOK AT STATUTORY REORGANIZATIONS INCLUDING DETERMINATION OF BASIS

As a general proposition, when an acquiring corporation uses nothing but its own voting stock to acquire a target, both the target and its shareholders are spared gain and loss recognition. Any unrealized *outside* gains that were lurking at the shareholder level are preserved in the hands of the target shareholders in the form of low basis in the acquiring corporation's stock. Any unrealized *inside* gains that were lurking at the corporate level are preserved in the hands of whichever corporation ends up owning the assets in

---

[135] H.R. Rep. No. 760, 97th Cong., 2d Sess. 541 (1982).

[136] Rev. Rul. 96–29.

[137] For a more detailed discussion of the G reorganization and its requirements, see Corporate Income Taxation Hornbook at pp. 528–530.

question, once again in the form of low basis.[138] That happy set of outcomes is achieved through the interaction of several different provisions of the Code:

- Section 368 is the *definitions* section. It prescribes what qualifies as a "reorganization" for corporate tax purposes, who counts as a "party" to the reorganization, and what constitutes "control."

- Section 354 is the *shareholder/distributee nonrecognition* section. It says that, if you are following a plan of reorganization, no gain or loss is recognized when a shareholder exchanges stock or securities in one party to the reorganization for stock or securities in the same corporation or in another party to the reorganization.

- Section 358 is the *shareholder/distributee basis* section. Among other things, it is designed to ensure that realized-but-unrecognized outside gain or loss is preserved as a built-in-gain or loss through the difference between the shareholder's basis and the fair market value of nonrecognition property.

- Section 361 is the *target corporate nonrecognition* section. It says that, if a corporation is following a plan of reorganization, the corporation will recognize no gain or loss when it exchanges *property* for stock or securities in another party to the reorganization, but it *may* recognize gain if it distributes certain appreciated property to its shareholders.

- Section 1032 is the *acquiring corporation nonrecognition* section. Unlike the other provisions, section 1032 applies whether or not the underlying transaction meets the definition of "reorganization" in § 368(a)(1). It protects a corporation from having to recognize any gain when it exchanges its own stock for property.

- Section 362(b) is the *corporate basis* section. Among other things, it is designed to ensure that realized-but-unrecognized inside gain or loss is preserved as a built-in-gain or loss through the difference between the

---

[138] Any unrealized losses may also be preserved, but there are restrictions on the preservation of built-in losses in some circumstances. § 362(d), (e).

transferee corporation's basis and the fair market value of nonrecognition property.[139]

- Section 381 (subjected to limitations by §§ 382, 383, and 384) is the *tax attributes* section. It determines what happens to the income tax attributes of the parties to the reorganization, such as earnings and profits, net operating losses, etc.[140]

However, not all qualifying reorganizations are transactions in which an acquiring corporation uses nothing but its own stock to acquire all of the stock or assets of a target. Sometimes the acquiring corporation includes cash or other boot in the consideration paid. And sometimes the acquiring corporation in an asset acquisition acquires less than all the assets of the target. Either form of departure from the "model reorganization" can cause some gain to be recognized on the target side of the ledger. The inclusion of boot can trigger gain for the target shareholders. And if the target corporation retains some appreciated assets and distributes them to its shareholders, it may have to recognize some gain as well.[141] If the acquiring corporation uses non-cash boot, it will recognize any built-in gain or loss in that non-cash boot.

In the following Sections, we provide some basic examples of how these Code provisions govern the different forms of reorganization.[142]

¶ 9.05.1 Tax Treatment of Simple A Reorganizations

Ex. (1) A is a corporation that has one asset, an apartment building worth $500,000, in which it has a basis of $100,000. All 1000 shares of A's stock, worth a total of $500,000, are owned by P. P has a basis of $300,000 in those shares. T is a corporation that has one asset, a hotel worth $200,000, in which it has a basis of $80,000. All 100 shares of T's stock, worth $200,000, are owned by F. F has a basis of $150,000 in those shares. On January 1, Year One, T merges into A in compliance with the state law. Title to T's hotel is transferred to A. All 100 shares of F's T stock are cancelled, and in exchange F receives from A 400 new shares of A stock worth $200,000. In effect, the transaction can be seen as a constructive transfer of the 400 A shares to T in exchange

---

[139] Id.

[140] We discuss the carryover of tax attributes in Chapter Ten.

[141] The taxation of reorganizations involving some form of boot is discussed at ¶¶ 9.06, 9.07.

[142] We focus on the A, B, C, D, and triangular reorganizations as those are the main reorganizations covered in the corporate tax course.

for T's assets, followed by a constructive distribution of those 400 shares to F in cancellation of his T stock.

The tax consequences of the merger, a valid A reorganization, are as follows:

- Although F realizes a gain of $50,000 on the exchange of T shares for A shares, F does not recognize any gain. § 354(a)(1).

- F takes an outside basis of $150,000 in the 400 shares of A stock. § 358(a)(1).

- T does not recognize gain on the constructive transfer of its hotel to A. § 361(a).

- A recognizes no gain or loss on the merger. § 1032.

- A takes over T's $80,000 inside basis in the hotel. § 362(b).

¶ 9.05.2 Tax Treatment of Simple B Reorganizations

Ex. (2) A is a corporation that has one asset, an apartment building worth $500,000, in which it has a basis of $100,000. All 1000 shares of A's stock, worth a total of $500,000, are owned by P. P has a basis of $300,000 in those shares. T is a corporation that has one asset, a hotel worth $200,000, in which it has a basis of $80,000. All 100 shares of T's stock, worth $200,000, are owned by F. F has a basis of $150,000 in those shares. On January 1, Year One, A issues 400 new shares of voting stock to F, in exchange for F's 100 shares of T.

In Example (2), a valid B reorganization, the tax consequences of the stock-for-stock acquisition are as follows:

- Although F realizes a gain of $50,000 on the exchange of T shares for A shares, F does not recognize the gain. § 354(a)(1).

- Instead, F takes an outside basis of $150,000 in the 400 shares of A stock. § 358(a)(1).

- A recognizes no gain or loss on the issuance of 400 shares of its stock to acquire the 100 shares of T stock. § 1032.

- A takes an outside basis of $150,000 in the 100 shares of T stock. § 362(b).

- T does not recognize any gain or loss and T's $80,000 inside basis in the hotel is unaffected.

¶ 9.05.3 Tax Treatment of Triangular B Reorganizations

Ex. (3) A is a corporation that has one asset, an apartment building worth $500,000, in which it has a basis of $100,000. All 1000 shares of A's stock, worth a total of $500,000, are owned by P. P has a basis of $300,000 in those shares. P is a corporation with total assets worth $1,000,000. All 100 shares of P stock are currently owned by E. T is a corporation that has one asset, a hotel worth $200,000, in which it has a basis of $80,000, and T has no liabilities. All 100 shares of T's stock, worth $200,000, are owned by F. F has a basis of $150,000 in those shares. On January 1, Year One, P issues 20 new shares of voting stock to F, and F transfers to A his 100 shares of T.

In Example (3), a valid triangular B reorganization, the tax consequences of the triangular stock-for-stock acquisition are as follows:

- Although F realizes a gain of $50,000 on the exchange of T shares for P shares, F does not recognize the gain. § 354(a)(1).

- Instead, F takes an outside basis of $150,000 in the 20 shares of P stock. § 358(a)(1).

- A recognizes no gain or loss on the acquisition of the 100 shares of T stock. Treas. Reg. § 1.1032–2(b).

- A takes an outside basis of $150,000 in the 100 shares of T stock. § 362(b).

- T does not recognize any gain or loss, and T's $80,000 inside basis in the hotel is unaffected.

- P's basis in its A shares is increased by $150,000.[143] Treas. Reg. § 1.358–6(c)(3), (4), Ex. (3).

When Congress amended § 368(a)(1)(B) to authorize triangular B reorganizations, it undoubtedly assumed that the transaction would be a nonrecognition transaction for the *acquiring* corporation as well as for the target shareholders. Unfortunately, it neglected to amend the statute to make that outcome certain. In the context of a two-party B reorganization, the acquiring corporation recognizes no

---

[143] The mechanism for determining P's basis in its A stock is referred to as the "over-the-top" approach and is explained below.

gain by virtue of § 1032. By its terms, however, that provision provides nonrecognition treatment only when a corporation acquires property in exchange for stock (including treasury stock) *of such corporation.*

The problem was solved by regulations (finalized in 1995) that treat a triangular B reorganization virtually the same as if P had acquired T's stock directly from T's shareholders in a 2-party type reorganization and P had then dropped down the T shares to its subsidiary, A (the acquiring corporation). In the latter case, P would not recognize any gain or loss on acquiring the T shares, P's basis in the T shares would be the same as the basis that T's shareholders had therein ($150,000 in Example (3)), neither P nor A would recognize any gain on P's contribution of the T shares to A, P would increase its basis in its shares of stock of A by the amount of its basis in the contributed T shares ($150,000), and A would have a basis in the T shares equal to the basis that P had therein ($150,000). The treatment of a triangular reorganization as if it were a two-party reorganization followed by a drop-down is sometimes referred to as an "over-the-top" approach. The 1995 regulations adopted that over-the-top approach.

Under the regulations, in Example (3), the A corporation will not recognize any gain on the receipt of the T shares to the extent that the consideration for those shares was voting stock of P that either was transferred directly from P to the T shareholders (as it was in that Example) or was obtained by A from P for the purpose of transferring those shares to the T shareholders.[144]

If for some reason an attempted triangular B reorganization failed to qualify as a reorganization, for many years there was a concern that A might then recognize gain on the transfer of P stock regardless of whether the stock was transferred directly by P to the T shareholders or was transferred by A. That concern has been largely dispelled, however, at least in the most typical circumstances, by regulations that the Treasury has issued under § 1032 of the Code.[145] Those regulations provide that, under circumstances described above and in which a nonrecognition provision does not apply, the transaction shall be treated as though A purchased the P stock from P at its fair market value immediately before A disposed of it. A is treated as though it received the cash used to purchase the P stock from P as a capital contribution. As a result, A will neither realize nor recognize any gain on the disposition of the P stock, and, while P will realize gain on the sale of its stock to A, that gain will, of course, not be recognized pursuant to § 1032. However, that

---

[144]   Treas. Reg. § 1.1032–2(b).
[145]   Treas. Reg. § 1.1032–3.

regulation applies only to P stock that either was directly transferred from P to T's shareholders or was transferred by P to A, which immediately used the stock to acquire the T shares. Thus, if, pursuant to the acquisition of T stock, A transferred to F stock of P that A had acquired previously in an unrelated transaction, A can recognize gain or loss on the exchange of that P stock.

Similarly, under the over-the-top model that the regulations have adopted for determining stock basis in triangular transactions that do satisfy the requirements for reorganization treatment, P's basis in its A stock is increased by the basis that P would have had in the T shares if it had acquired them directly.[146] The basis that P would have acquired in the T shares in a 2-party B reorganization would be determined by § 362(b) to be the same as the basis that the T shareholders had therein. Thus, in Example (3), P would have had a basis of $150,000 in the T shares. On P's constructive transfer of the T shares to A as a contribution to capital, P would increase its basis in its A shares, pursuant to § 358, by the basis it had in the contributed property ($150,000).[147] As a result, in Example (3), P will increase its basis in its A shares by $150,000.

¶ 9.05.4 Tax Treatment of Simple C Reorganizations

Ex. (4)   A is a corporation that has one asset, an apartment building worth $500,000, in which it has a basis of $100,000. All 1000 shares of A's stock, worth a total of $500,000, are owned by P. P has a basis of $300,000 in those shares. T is a corporation that has one asset, a hotel worth $200,000, in which it has a basis of $80,000. All 100 shares of T's stock, worth $200,000, are owned by F. F has a basis of $150,000 in those shares. On January 1, Year One, A issues 400 new shares of voting stock to T, in exchange for T's hotel. On January 15, Year One, T liquidates and distributes the A voting stock to F in cancellation of F's shares in T.

In Example (3), a valid C reorganization, the tax consequences of the stock-for-assets acquisition are as follows:

- A recognizes no gain or loss on the acquisition of the hotel from T. § 1032.

- A takes an inside basis of $80,000 in the hotel. § 362(b).

- Although T realizes a gain of $120,000 on the exchange of the hotel for A stock, T does not recognize the gain.

---

[146]   Treas. Reg. § 1.358–6(c)(3), (4), Ex. (3).

[147]   Id.

Instead T transfers its $80,000 basis in the hotel to the A stock that it received. §§ 361(a), 358(a)(1).

- Notwithstanding the repeal of *General Utilities*, T does not recognize any gain on liquidation, since all it is distributing is A stock. §§ 336(c), 361(c).

- Although F realizes a gain of $50,000 on the liquidation of T, F does not recognize the gain. § 354(a)(1).

- Instead, F takes an outside basis of $150,000 in the 400 shares of A stock. § 358(a)(1). Note that this makes the basis that T obtained in the A stock that T acquired totally irrelevant.

¶ 9.05.5 Tax Treatment of Triangular C Reorganizations

Ex. (5) A is a corporation that has one asset, an apartment building worth $500,000, in which it has a basis of $100,000. All 1000 shares of A's stock, worth a total of $500,000, are owned by P. P has a basis of $300,000 in those shares. P is a corporation with total assets worth $1,000,000. All 100 shares of P stock are currently owned by E. P and A do not file a consolidated return. T is a corporation that has one asset, a hotel worth $200,000, in which it has a basis of $80,000. All 100 shares of T's stock, worth $200,000, are owned by F. F has a basis of $150,000 in those shares. On January 1, Year One, P issues 20 new shares of voting stock to T, and T transfers its hotel to A. On January 15, Year One, T liquidates and distributes the P voting stock to F in cancellation of F's shares in T.

In Example (5), the tax consequences of the valid triangular C reorganization are as follows:

- A recognizes no gain or loss on the acquisition of the hotel from T. Treas. Reg. § 1.1032–2. Under the over-the-top approach, the exchange is treated as if P transferred its voting stock for T's assets, and so § 1032 prevents any gain recognition on the transfer of the P stock to the extent that the transferred P stock either was transferred directly by P to T or was acquired from P by A for the purpose of transferring it to T.

- A takes an inside basis of $80,000 in the hotel. § 362(b).

- Although T realizes a gain of $120,000 on the exchange of the hotel for P stock, T does not recognize the gain.

§ 361(a). Instead, T transfers its $80,000 basis in the hotel to the P stock it received. § 358(a)(1).

- Notwithstanding the repeal of *General Utilities*, T does not recognize any gain or loss on liquidation, since all it is distributing is P stock. §§ 336(c), 361(c)(2) and (4).

- Although F realizes a gain of $50,000 on the liquidation of T, F does not recognize the gain. § 354(a)(1).

- Instead, F takes an outside basis of $150,000 in the 400 shares of P stock that F received. § 358(a)(1).

- P's basis in its A shares is increased by $80,000. Treas. Reg. § 1.358–6(c)(1). Again, the over-the-top approach mandates this result.

The over-the-top approach is used only (1) for purposes of determining the effect of a triangular reorganization on the basis that the parent has in its stock in the surviving or acquiring corporation, and (2) in some circumstances, to prevent the acquiring corporation from recognizing a gain on the use of its parent's stock to acquire the target's assets. The transaction is not treated for *all* purposes as if the parent had acquired the target's assets and dropped them down. For example, what happens in a triangular C reorganization if the target has liabilities that are assumed or accepted by the acquiring corporation?

Let us first consider the situation when the target's liabilities are less than its basis in its assets. In determining the effect that a triangular reorganization would have on the basis that the parent has in the stock of the acquiring corporation, the over-the-top approach treats the transaction as if the parent acquired the assets subject to those liabilities and then transferred the assets subject to those liabilities to the acquiring corporation. The parent's basis in the constructively acquired assets would equal the basis that the target had therein.[148] On the parent's constructive contribution of the assets to the acquiring corporation, the regulations apply § 358 to determine the effect on the parent's basis in the acquiring corporation's stock. Under §§ 358(a)(1) and (d) and 357(d)(1)(B), the parent's basis in the acquiring corporation's stock is increased by the difference between the parent's basis in the target's assets and the amount of liabilities that are assumed or accepted by the acquiring corporation.

However, what if the amount of the target's liabilities that are assumed or accepted exceeds the parent's basis in the target's assets? If the constructive transfer from the parent to the acquiring corporation were treated as an actual transfer, the parent would

---

[148]   § 362(b).

recognize income under § 357(c) in the amount by which such liabilities exceeded the parent's basis in the transferred assets.[149] But the constructive transfer is *not* treated as an actual transfer, and so the parent corporation does not recognize any income under § 357(c).[150] The more difficult question is whether the excess amount of such liabilities will *reduce* the parent's basis in the acquiring corporation's stock or whether the excess liability will be ignored so that the parent's basis in that stock will not change. The answer to that question depends upon whether the parent and the acquiring corporation are part of a consolidated group (i.e., a group that files a consolidated return) following the reorganization. If the parent and the acquiring corporation are not part of a consolidated group, the excess liability is ignored, and the parent's basis in the acquiring corporation's stock is not changed.[151] However, if they are part of a consolidated group, the parent's basis in the acquiring corporation's stock is reduced by the excess of the liabilities over the parent's constructive basis in the target's assets, and it is possible for this reduction to result in the parent's having what amounts to a negative basis in its stock of the acquiring corporation.[152]

Ex. (6) The same facts as in Example (5) except that the hotel that T owned had a value of $230,000 and was subject to a mortgage liability of $30,000. A obtained the hotel from T subject to that liability and in exchange for voting stock of P that P transferred to T. What is the effect of the triangular C reorganization on P's basis in its A stock? Under the over-the-top approach, P is treated as having acquired T's asset, subject to the mortgage liability, and then transferred that asset subject to the liability to A. P's

---

[149] Section 357(c), of course, would apply only if such an actual drop-down were treated as a section 351 transaction. Even though the acquiring corporation (in a forward triangular merger) or the target corporation (in a reverse triangular merger) ordinarily does not issue any new shares of stock to P in such an actual drop-down, the courts have uniformly held that any such issuance of stock is a "meaningless gesture" in the context of a parent that owns 100% of the common stock of the transferee corporation and thus will be deemed to have occurred for federal income tax purposes. See, e.g., Lessinger v. Commissioner, 872 F.2d 519 (2d Cir. 1989); Utley v. Commissioner, 906 F.2d 1033 (5th Cir. 1990); and Jackson v. Commissioner, 708 F.2d 1402 (9th Cir. 1983).

Although it is not clear that the same principle would apply to create a section 351 and 357(c) transaction when the parent controls the acquiring corporation but owns less than 100% of its common stock, the doctrine of Crane v. Commissioner, 331 U.S. 1 (1947), and Commissioner v. Tufts, 461 U.S. 300 (1983), would independently require the parent to recognize gain where the parent effected an actual drop-down of assets and liabilities, section 351 did not apply to that drop-down, and the liabilities assumed (or taken subject to) exceeded the adjusted basis of the assets transferred.

[150] Treas. Reg. § 1.358–6(c)(1)(ii).

[151] Id.

[152] Treas. Reg. § 1.1502–30(b).

basis in the asset (the hotel) would be the same as T's, namely $80,000. The constructive transfer of the hotel to A would increase P's basis in its A stock by $80,000, and would decrease its basis in A's stock by the $30,000 liability to which the hotel was subject. Thus, P would increase its basis in its A stock by a net of $50,000.

Ex. (7)   The same facts as those in Example (6) except that the amount of the mortgage liability on the hotel was $90,000, and the value of the hotel was $290,000. Consequently, the liability exceeded T's basis in the hotel. A obtained the hotel from T in the manner described in Example (6), and A and P are not members of a consolidated group (i.e., they do not file a consolidated return). Note that T will not recognize any gain on transferring the hotel subject to the liability because § 357(c) does not apply on its terms to an exchange made pursuant to a C reorganization. Under the regulations, P will not recognize any gain because of the constructive transfer of the hotel to A, and P's basis in its A stock will not be changed as a result of this transaction.[153]

¶ 9.05.6   Tax Treatment of Triangular A Reorganizations: Forward and Reverse Triangular Mergers

Ex. (8)   P owned all of the stock of S Corporation, which P had newly created for purposes of the merger acquisition of T. P transferred 500 shares of its voting stock to S, and that was the only asset that S had. P therefore had a zero basis in its S stock. § 358(a). P had 10,000 shares of voting stock outstanding. T owned assets having a value of $400,000 and a basis of $200,000. T had no liabilities. A, an individual, owned all of T's outstanding stock. A had a basis of $60,000 in his T stock, which had a value of $400,000. T was merged into S. Pursuant to that merger, S transferred P stock to A in exchange for A's T stock.

This merger qualifies as a valid forward triangular merger under § 368(a)(2)(D). The tax results are as follows:

-   P recognizes no gain on the formation of S Corporation. § 351 or § 361(a) or § 354(a)(1).[154]

---

[153]   Treas. Reg. § 1.358–6(c)(1)(ii).

[154]   Clearly § 351 applies, and it is possible that either or both § 361(a) and/or § 354(a)(1) also applies. Each of those three sections provides for nonrecognition and the application of any one of them is sufficient. If P had received stock and securities of S in that exchange, it would be important to have § 361 apply since that section does not treat securities as boot whereas § 351 and § 354 treat securities as boot.

- S recognizes no gain on its formation. § 1032.

- S recognizes no gain on the exchange of its P stock for T's assets. Treas. Reg. § 1.1032–2(b), –2(d) Ex. 1.

- S acquires the T assets with a carryover basis of $200,000. § 362(b).

- Although A realizes a gain of $340,000 on the exchange of T shares for P shares, A does not recognize the gain. § 354(a)(1).

- A takes an outside basis of $60,000 in the 500 shares of P stock. § 358(a)(1).

- Under the over-the-top model that is employed by the regulations,[155] P's basis in its S stock will equal $200,000. P's basis in its S stock is determined by adding to the basis that P had in its S stock (zero) the amount that would have increased its basis in the S stock if P had acquired T's assets in a nonrecognition transaction and had then dropped those assets and liabilities down to S. If P acquired T assets, P would have obtained a basis of $200,000 in those assets (the same basis that T had therein). § 362(b). If P had then dropped those assets down to its subsidiary, S, P would have increased its basis in its subsidiary's stock by $200,000. § 358(a)(1). Thus, P's basis in its S stock is zero plus $200,000, which equals $200,000.

Ex. (9)   P owned all of the stock of S, and P had a basis of $100,000 in its S stock. The net value of S's assets was $150,000, and so the value of S stock that P held is also $150,000. S had operated a business for several years. P had 10,000 shares of voting stock outstanding. T owned assets having a value of $500,000 and a basis of $300,000. T had liabilities in the amount of $120,000. A owned all of T's outstanding stock. A had a basis of $80,000 in his T stock, which had a value of $380,000.

S was merged into T pursuant to a reverse triangular merger. Under the terms of that merger, A received 500 shares of voting stock of P, having a value of $380,000, in exchange for his T stock. In addition, the merger terms provided that P's S stock would be converted into T stock that would represent 100% of the T stock outstanding after the merger of S into T. That post-merger T stock would then be worth $530,000, which is the sum of T's original

---

[155]   See ¶ 9.05.3 and ¶ 9.05.5 for a discussion of the over-the-top approach.

enterprise value of $380,000 plus S's original enterprise value of $150,000, which had been absorbed into T as a result of the merger. Because the merger thus entitled P to receive such T stock in exchange for its S stock, the merger terms treated P and S economically as if before the merger P had increased the value of S by transferring to S the 500 shares of P voting stock that A received in exchange for his T stock when S merged into T. Thus, pursuant to the merger, A exchanged his pre-merger T stock worth $380,000 for P voting stock worth $380,000, and P exchanged its S stock, which the merger terms valued to include both the $150,000 value of S's business assets and the $380,000 value of P's voting stock that had been issued to A in the merger, for post-merger T stock that was worth $530,000.

In practice, P sometimes, but not always, actually transfers its voting stock to S prior to the merger. Often, it instead shortens the transaction by transferring its voting stock directly to A as part of the merger. Even when that shortened version of the transaction is adopted, by entitling P to acquire the entire post-merger value of T in exchange for the S stock, the transaction treats P economically as if it had constructively transferred the P voting stock to S, T had acquired the P voting stock upon the merger of S into T, and T had then transferred the P voting stock to A in redemption of A's stock.

This merger qualifies as a reverse triangular merger under § 368(a)(2)(E). The tax results are as follows:

- Although A realizes a gain of $300,000 on the exchange of T shares for P shares, A does not recognize the gain. § 354(a)(1).

- Although P realizes a gain of $430,000 on the receipt of post-merger T shares in exchange for its S shares, P does not recognize that gain. § 354(a)(1).

- A takes an outside basis of $80,000 in the 500 shares of P stock. § 358(a)(1).

- T does not recognize any gain or loss and T's $300,000 inside basis in the assets is unaffected.

- Under the over-the-top model that is employed by the regulations,[156] P's basis in its T stock will

---

[156] Id.

equal $280,000. P's basis in its T stock is determined by adding to the basis that P had in its S stock ($100,000) the amount that would have increased its basis in the T stock if P had acquired T's assets and liabilities in a nonrecognition transaction and had then dropped those assets and liabilities down to T as a subsidiary. If P acquired T's assets and liabilities, P would have obtained a basis of $300,000 in those assets (the same basis that T had therein). § 362(b). If P had then dropped those assets and the $120,000 of liabilities down to its subsidiary, P would have increased its basis in its subsidiary's stock by $180,000 (the difference between P's basis in those assets and the amount of the liabilities accepted by the subsidiary). § 358(a)(1). Thus, P's basis its T stock is $100,000 plus $180,000, which equals $280,000.

However, if a reverse triangular merger also qualifies as a B reorganization, which can occur if the merged corporation is a transitory corporation and no boot is used in the transaction[157], the parent corporation (P) can choose one of two alternative methods for determining its basis in the acquiring corporation's (T's) stock: either it can determine its basis in T's stock as if it were acquired by the parent in a two-party B reorganization (i.e., P would take the same basis in the T stock that T's shareholders had therein),[158] or P can elect to determine its basis in its T stock in the manner described above for a reverse triangular merger that does not also qualify as a B reorganization.[159] In Example (9), the transaction cannot be treated as a B reorganization because S was not a transitory corporation; and so P's basis in the T stock must be determined under the rules for a reverse triangular merger.

Ex. (10) The same facts as those stated in Example (9) except that P formed the S Corporation for the purpose of using it to carry out the reverse triangular merger. P transferred 500 shares of its voting stock to S, and that was the only asset that S had. P therefore had a zero basis in its S stock. S was then merged into T. P received T stock for its S stock, and A transferred his shares of T stock to T in exchange for the 500 shares of P stock that T held. Since S was a transitory corporation, its merger into T can be ignored, and the

---

[157] See Rev. Rul. 67–448.

[158] § 362(b).

[159] Treas. Reg. § 1.358–6(c)(4), Ex. (2)(c).

transaction can be recast as a two-party B reorganization in which A exchanged his T stock for voting stock of P. The regulations grant P an election as to how it can determine its basis in its T shares of stock. P can elect to determine its basis as if the transaction were a reverse triangular merger, in which case P will have a basis of $180,000 in its T stock. Alternatively, P can elect to determine its basis as if the transaction were a two-party B reorganization, in which case, P's basis in its T shares would be $80,000 (the same basis that A had therein). Obviously, P will choose the $180,000 basis since that is higher. However, if A's basis in his T stock had been $220,000 (instead of $80,000), P would have elected to determine its basis as if the transaction were a B reorganization so that P would then have taken a basis of $220,000 in its T shares.

¶ 9.05.7 Acquisitive D Reorganizations

Ex. (11) A is a corporation that has one asset, an apartment building worth $500,000, in which it has a basis of $100,000. P owns 700 shares of A's stock, worth a total of $350,000. P has a basis of $420,000 in those shares. The remaining 300 shares of A's stock (worth $150,000) are owned by F, who has a basis of $180,000 in those shares. T is a corporation that has one asset, a hotel worth $2,000,000, in which it has a basis of $80,000. All 100 shares of T's stock, worth $2,000,000, are owned by G, who is not related to F or P. G has a basis of $150,000 in those shares. On January 1, Year One, A issues 4,000 new shares of its voting stock to T, in exchange for T's hotel. On January 15, Year One, T liquidates and distributes the A voting stock to G in cancellation of G's shares in T.

Example (11) may be diagrammed as follows:

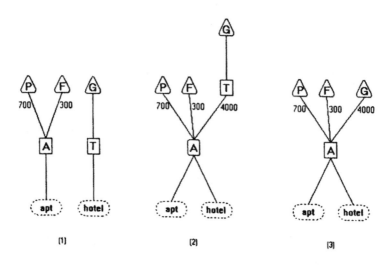

(1)   (2)   (3)

In Example (11), A acquires substantially all T's assets in the exchange, T controls A after the exchange (within the meaning of "control" in § 368(a)(2)(H)(i)), and T liquidates. The tax consequences are as follows:

- A recognizes no gain or loss on the acquisition of the hotel from T. § 1032.

- A takes an inside basis of $80,000 in the hotel. § 362(b).

- Although T realizes a gain of $1,920,000 on the exchange of the hotel for A stock, T does not recognize the gain. Instead T transfers its $80,000 basis in the hotel to the A stock. §§ 361(a), 358(a)(1).

- Notwithstanding the repeal of *General Utilities*, T does not recognize any gain on liquidation, since all it is distributing is A stock. §§ 336(c), 361(c)(2).

- Although G realizes a gain of $1,850,000 on the liquidation of T, G does not recognize the gain. § 354(a)(1).

- Instead, G takes an outside basis of $150,000 in the 4000 shares of A stock. § 358(a)(1).

¶ 9.06 TAX TREATMENT OF SHAREHOLDERS WHO RECEIVE BOOT IN QUALIFYING REORGANIZATION

Section 354(a) provides nonrecognition treatment for a target shareholder who gives up stock or securities in the target in exchange "solely for stock or securities" in a party to the reorganization. But § 354(a)(2) eliminates that protection (1) if the receipt of the stock or securities is attributable to accrued interest on securities held by the target shareholder, (2) if the shareholder receives securities having a higher principal amount than the securities she surrenders,[160] or (3) if the shareholder receives nonqualified preferred stock (other than in exchange for other nonqualified preferred stock).[161]

The net effect of § 354(a) is to define, for nonrecognition purposes, three categories of "boot" in the reorganization context. Those three categories, of course, are in addition to the general category of boot, comprising all property other than the stock or securities of a party to the reorganization.

Whenever a target shareholder receives boot in a qualifying reorganization in which he realizes a gain, he may be eligible for *partial* nonrecognition treatment pursuant to § 356(a). Section 356(a) is the same provision that governs partial nonrecognition treatment in the context of split-offs and split-ups in which boot is received.[162] It provides, generally, that the target shareholder should recognize the *lesser* of the amount of gain realized or the value of boot received. We will not repeat here the general discussion of § 356(a) that is found in Chapter Eight.[163] Rather, we shall flag only three distinctive points to be noted about the application of § 356(a) in the reorganization context.

The first point has to do with the applicability of § 356(a)(2). That section provides that, if the distribution of boot in a qualifying reorganization "has the effect of the distribution of a dividend," the *gain realized* (not the full amount of the distribution) is treated as a dividend to the extent of the shareholder's *ratable share* (not all) of the *accumulated e and p* (not the current *e and p*) "of the corporation" (more about *which* corporation below).[164] As we saw in Chapter Eight, several possibilities suggested themselves for how to

---

[160] See ¶ 8.10.1.

[161] See ¶ 8.10.3.

[162] Spin-offs are governed by § 356(b), which does not apply to reorganizations other than a D reorganization involving a spin-off.

[163] See ¶ 8.11.

[164] The relevant language of § 356(a)(2) dates all the way back to 1924. Rev. Act of 1924, Pub. L. No. 68–176, § 203(d)(2), 43 Stat. 253, 257.

determine whether a given distribution "has the effect of the distribution of a dividend."[165]

Originally, the IRS attempted to follow an "automatic dividend" rule under such circumstances, treating any recognized gain as a dividend distribution to the extent of the corporation's *e and p*.[166] After substantial criticism, the IRS abandoned the automatic dividend rule in favor of the principles for determining dividend equivalency that were developed under § 302.[167]

Yet, even knowing that § 302 principles would be applied, taxpayers and the IRS still found two alternative theories for *how* those principles should be applied. Consider the following example:

Ex. (1) T corporation has two unrelated shareholders, J and K. J owns 50 shares of T common stock, and K owns 450 shares. K has a basis of $300,000 in those shares, and they are now worth $450,000. T has been operating a cooking school for many years, and its cooking school operation is worth $250,000. T also holds $250,000 in cash. Corporation A is a conglomerate with $10,000,000 in assets and accumulated *e and p* of $1,200,000. A has 1,000 shares of common stock outstanding. On January 1, Year One, T merges into A. Pursuant to the merger, J receives 5 shares of A stock worth $50,000, and K receives 25 shares of A stock worth $250,000, along with $200,000 in cash.

In Example (1), K realizes a gain of $150,000, but receives $200,000 worth of boot. According to § 356(a)(1), K must recognize $150,000 worth of gain. According to § 356(a)(2), that $150,000 gain (*not* the full $200,000) will be characterized as ordinary dividend income if the transaction had the effect of a dividend distribution.

A first approach to Example (1) is "boot first." One would ask what the tax consequences would be if T had first redeemed 200 shares of its stock from K, in exchange for $200,000, and then T had merged into A. Such a redemption would have reduced K's ownership interest in T from 450/500 (90%) to 250/300 (83%). It would almost certainly be treated as having the effect of a dividend.[168]

A second approach to Example (1) is "boot second." One would ask what the tax consequences would be if T had first merged into A (with K receiving 45 shares of A stock), and A had then redeemed 20

[165] See ¶ 8.11.4.
[166] See Rev. Rul. 56–220.
[167] Rev. Rul. 74–515. See also Rev. Rul. 93–62; Rev. Rul. 84–114. In 1982, Section 356(a)(2) was amended to make it clear that the attribution rules of § 318 should be applied in this context.
[168] See Chapter Three.

of its shares from K, in exchange for $200,000. Such a redemption would have reduced K's ownership interest in A from 45/1050 (4.5%) to 25/1030 (2.5%). It would almost certainly *not* be treated as having the effect of a dividend, and would instead be treated as a sale or exchange.[169]

The boot-first approach is generally more likely to give rise to dividend treatment. Historically, such a result was usually more attractive to corporate shareholders but less attractive to individual shareholders.[170] At least for the present, however, a noncorporate shareholder may be indifferent as to the characterization of the gain so long as the tax rate applicable to dividend income is the same as the tax rate applicable to long-term capital gain.

The boot-first approach was initially the position taken by the IRS.[171] After a division in the courts, the Supreme Court resolved the dispute in *Commissioner v. Clark*.[172] *Clark* rebuffed the IRS, holding that only a boot-second approach would be consistent with the language and history of the statute.

A second point to be made about the application of § 356(a)(2) in the reorganization context is that, even if one concludes that a distribution has the effect of a dividend distribution under *Clark*, one still must make a judgment about *whose* earnings and profits should be considered available.[173] Before *Clark*, there was a split of authority over whose *e and p* should be considered in applying § 356(a)(2).[174] The Tax Court adhered steadfastly to the position that only the target's *e and p* should be considered. It is conceivable that the question will be revisited after *Clark*, but the occasions for the issue to arise are likely to be few and far between. After *Clark*, most acquisitions will receive sale or exchange treatment in the manner of Example (1) above.

The third point concerns the effect that dividend treatment to a corporate shareholder will have on the shareholder's basis. Of course, to the extent the target shareholder must recognize gain or dividend income as a result of the application of § 356(a), he receives an increased basis in the nonrecognition property he received in the

---

[169]   See § 302(b)(2) ("substantially disproportionate redemption").

[170]   See § 243, but see § 1059(e)(1)(B) (discussed at the end of this section).

[171]   See Rev. Rul. 75–83, revoked by Rev. Rul. 93–61.

[172]   489 U.S. 726 (1989), aff'g 828 F.2d 221 (4th Cir. 1987), aff'g 86 T.C. 138 (1986).

[173]   For a detailed discussion of this issue, see Corporate Income Taxation Hornbook 548–552.

[174]   Compare Davant v. Commissioner, 366 F.2d 874 (5th Cir. 1966) (target's *e and p* augmented by the acquiring corporation's *e and p*, up to the amount of the purchase price) with American Mfg. Co. v. Commissioner, 55 T.C. 204 (1970) (target only), Atlas Tool Co. v. Commissioner, 70 T.C. 86, 107 (1978), aff'd, 614 F.2d 860, 864 (3d Cir. 1980) (target only).

reorganization.[175] However, if the shareholder is a corporation, the amount that such corporate shareholder receives that is characterized as a dividend will be treated as a redemption of stock for purposes of applying § 1059.[176] If such constructive redemption is not part of a pro rata redemption to all shareholders (as it very likely will not be), the dividend will be an "extraordinary dividend" to the corporate shareholder and will cause a reduction of the shareholder's basis in its stock.[177]

¶ 9.07 TAX TREATMENT OF TARGET CORPORATION (DISTRIBUTION OF APPRECIATED ASSETS)

Section 361(a) provides nonrecognition treatment for a target corporation that receives "solely stock or securities in another corporation a party to the reorganization." Moreover, § 361(b)(1)(A) provides nonrecognition treatment for a corporation that receives *other* property in the reorganization, as long as it distributes it in pursuance of the plan of reorganization.[178] The distribution may be to creditors as well as to shareholders.[179] Since target corporations are now required to liquidate in the case of C, G, and acquisitive D reorganizations, the combined effect of those two provisions is to provide the target corporation with complete protection from gain recognition on account of its transfer of property to the acquiring corporation,[180] except to the extent that gain is recognized by virtue of § 357(b) (concerning the assumption or acceptance of certain target liabilities).[181]

On the other hand, the fact that target corporations must liquidate in such reorganizations is also important because the liquidation itself provides a second potential occasion for gain recognition by the target corporation. Section 361(c)(1) provides, as a general matter, that such liquidations will be tax-free for the target corporation.[182] However, with the general repeal of *General Utilities* in 1986 came greater concern for the possibility that appreciated

---

[175] § 358(a)(1)(B).

[176] § 1059(e)(1)(B).

[177] § 1059(a)(1), (e)(1). If the amount of such reduction exceeds the corporate shareholder's basis, the shareholder will recognize gain in the amount of the excess. § 1059(a)(2).

[178] § 361(b)(3).

[179] Id.

[180] See § 368(a)(2)(G) (C reorganizations); § 354(b)(1) (D and G reorganizations).

[181] Section 357(c), requiring gain recognition on certain transfers when liabilities exceed basis, does not apply to acquisitive reorganizations even when § 351 also applies to the transaction. Rev. Rul. 2007–8.

[182] Once again, transfers to creditors are included. § 361(c)(3).

assets might migrate from the corporate level to the shareholder level without triggering corporate-level taxation. Section 361(c)(2) is designed to guard against that danger.

Section 361(c)(2) requires the target corporation to recognize gain (but not loss) if in the course of its liquidation it distributes appreciated property other than "qualified property." Qualified property is defined to include stock, stock rights, and "obligations" of the target corporation itself, or of any other party to the reorganization if the target corporation acquired them "in the exchange" (by which the statute presumably means in the course of the plan of reorganization).

The net result is that the target corporation can be liable for tax on account of any nonqualified appreciated assets that it distributes in the course of the reorganization. However, as demonstrated in the example below, the basis rules of § 362(b) and § 358 operate to ensure that the *only* appreciated nonqualified assets that the target corporation can distribute are assets other than boot acquired from the acquiring corporation, i.e., assets that it held before the reorganization.

Ex. K owns all the outstanding stock of T corporation. T owns:

- assets used in a limousine business, with a basis of $400,000 and a fair market value of $500,000;

- a rare painting, with a basis of $10,000 and a fair market value of $20,000, but subject to a liability of $25,000;

- cash totaling $5,000.

A is a large, diversified corporation. In a qualifying C reorganization, A acquires the assets that T used in the limousine business in exchange for:

- voting common stock in A, with a fair market value of $475,000;

- a rare sculpture, with a basis of $10,000 and a fair market value of $25,000.

Pursuant to the plan of liquidation, T promptly liquidates and distributes the A stock, the painting (subject to the liability), the sculpture, and the cash to K.

In this Example, A must recognize $15,000 worth of gain in connection with the reorganization, on account of the exchange of the sculpture for T's limousine business.[183]

---

[183]   § 1001(c).

Under § 361(b), T does *not* recognize any gain in connection with the exchange of the limousine business for A stock and the sculpture. T does not recognize gain because of its receipt of the sculpture because T distributed the sculpture to its shareholder pursuant to the reorganization.[184] T takes a basis in the sculpture equal to its fair market value, or $25,000.[185] T takes a basis in the A stock equal to $375,000 (its $400,000 old basis in the limousine business assets minus the $25,000 fair market value of the sculpture).[186] T's basis in the A stock has no bearing on any tax consequences since T will not recognize any gain on distributing that stock to K, and K's basis in the A stock that K received from T is not determined by reference to T's basis.

Because T has taken a fair market value basis in the sculpture, its only appreciated asset at the time of liquidation is the painting. T must recognize a gain on the distribution of the painting as if it had sold the painting to K for its fair market value. Moreover, the painting's fair market value is deemed to be no less than the liability to which it is subject, $25,000.[187] Accordingly, T must recognize a $15,000 gain.

The painting and the cash will constitute boot to K, but, since the liability to which the painting is subject ($25,000) is greater than its value ($20,000), the painting should not cause K to recognize any gain. It seems unlikely, however, that the excess liability over the painting's value would prevent the $5,000 cash from being treated as boot to K.

¶ 9.08 THE RISE OF § 351 EXCHANGES AS AN ALTERNATIVE TO A REORGANIZATION

It is no doubt clear to the reader from the preceding review and analysis of the tax law relating to corporate reorganizations that this area of the law is replete with a variety of complexities and technical rules, each of which has the potential to be an obstacle to attainment of the desired tax-free result. Creative plans have been formulated to overcome some of those obstacles. One such plan utilizes the so-called "double dummy subsidiaries" approach. This plan utilizes the rule that the merger of a transitory subsidiary is ignored so that a

---

[184] § 361(b)(1)(A).

[185] It is unclear whether § 358(a)(2) or § 362(b) should apply to determine T's basis in the sculpture, but, regardless of which applies, T's basis will be $25,000. But note that it would make a difference which provision applies if the boot that A transferred to T had been a depreciated asset (e.g., if A had had a basis of $40,000 in the sculpture).

[186] § 358. See also § 362(b).

[187] § 361(c)(2)(C).

nominal reverse triangular merger can be recharacterized as a straight § 351 exchange.[188]

Ex. P and T are publicly traded corporations engaged in the same line of business. The businesses of P and T are about the same general size, although the parties have agreed that the business of P is somewhat more valuable. Both P and T have outstanding several classes of non-voting preferred stock that bears a very low preferred dividend rate in terms of the currently prevailing market conditions. If T were to merge into P, or P were to merge into T, the shareholders of the preferred stock of the merged corporation, and perhaps also of the surviving corporation, could elect to receive cash either pursuant to the dissenters' rights conferred by state corporate merger law or under the terms of the preferred stock itself. Because it would be very expensive to replace the capital represented by these classes of preferred stock, P and T want to effect an acquisition that will leave outstanding the shares of preferred stock of the acquired corporation.

Neither an A reorganization nor a C reorganization is acceptable because in both structures the outstanding preferred stock of the acquired corporation will need to be converted into new preferred stock of the acquiring corporation (triggering shareholder rights to cash out their stock) or be acquired for cash. Likewise, neither a B reorganization nor a reverse triangular A reorganization is acceptable because, if the preferred stock of the target corporation is left outstanding, the transaction will fail the control test of § 368(c) and the transaction will thereby fail to qualify as a reorganization.

Therefore, the parties undertake the following structure. An incorporator creates a new corporation, which is called "PT Holding," or "PTH." PTH in turn creates two transitory subsidiaries, one of which is called "P Sub" and the other is called "T Sub." (P Sub and T Sub are the "dummies" that give this transaction structure its common name.) P Sub then effects a statutory merger into P and T Sub effects a statutory merger into T. Under the terms of each merger, the common stock of the surviving corporation is converted into common stock of PTH (the only class of stock that PTH will have), the preferred stock of P and T will be unaffected, and the stock of P Sub and T Sub will be converted into common stock of the corporations into which each of them was merged. The mergers of the transitory subsidiaries are ignored for tax purposes, and the transaction is

---

[188]   See, e.g., Rev. Rul. 67–448 and GCM 37135 (1977).

treated as if the common shareholders of P and T transferred their common stock to PTH in exchange for the latter's stock.

At the end of the transaction, the common shareholders of P and T will be regarded as having exchanged their P stock and T stock for newly issued stock of PTH and, as a control group of transferors of property, will hold 100% of all the PTH outstanding stock and thus hold "control" of PTH within the meaning of § 368(c). In addition, PTH will hold 100% of all the outstanding common stock of P and T, but none of the preferred stock, which will remain in the hands of the same shareholders who held it before the transaction.

In the transaction described in the Example, the historic common shareholders of P and T are treated for tax purposes as a group of persons who pursuant to a common plan transferred property—i.e., their shares in P and T—to PTH in exchange for all of the outstanding stock of PTH. As such, the historic common shareholders of P and T collectively represent a control group that acquired control of PTH, within the meaning of § 368(c), in exchange for property. This is a § 351 transaction in which the P and T shareholders will recognize no gain or loss. Under this analysis, all that is important is that the P and T common shareholders acquire control of PTH; it is unimportant whether or not PTH acquires stock of P and T that represents control of P and T for purposes of § 368(c).[189]

There are, of course, a number of additional, collateral questions that arise in double dummy transactions. For a more detailed discussion of the structure and how it was developed, the reader may wish to review our Corporate Income Taxation Hornbook.[190]

We conclude this analysis by cautioning the reader not to view the double dummy structure as a ready panacea to circumvent most of the restrictions that surround reorganization transactions. Indeed, one should be mindful that this structure can have significant practical limitations. Potential acquiring companies, particularly if they are publicly held, will tend to resist using this acquisition structure in all but the largest and most strategically important transactions. This is because the double dummy structure will often require them to undertake a substantial change in their corporate structure and to hold a special shareholder meeting and vote with respect to the acquisition, which, for public companies, can involve major complexity and considerable expense that they have come not to expect for smaller or moderate acquisitions. As a result, acquirers

---

[189] Private Letter Rulings 199911028 and 199911029.

[190] See Corporate Income Taxation Hornbook at pp. 552–560.

will often find that the non-tax complexities and costs involved in implementing the double dummy structure outweigh the tax benefits, except with respect to larger and more significant combinations where such complexities and costs are often dwarfed by the economic value of the transaction.[191] Indeed, it has been with respect to such large acquisitive transactions that the double dummy structure has most frequently been applied.

---

[191] However, if the public company acquirer (P) is a Delaware corporation, P may be able to employ the double dummy technique without the need for a meeting and vote of the P shareholders. Subject to certain conditions, Delaware corporate law will often permit P to effect both a drop-down of its stock into a new holding company and a conversion of the outstanding P shares to holding company shares without a shareholder meeting or vote and solely on the strength of a resolution of P's board of directors. For an extensive discussion of this application of Delaware corporate law to simplify the corporate law mechanics of a double dummy transaction, see Ginsburg & Levin at ¶ 904.7.

Chapter Ten

ACQUISITION OR RETENTION OF TAX ATTRIBUTES

Analysis

Para.

10.01   Introduction

A.   *ACQUISITION OF TAX ATTRIBUTES*

10.02   Introduction
10.03   Liquidation of Subsidiary Corporations
10.04   Acquisitive Reorganizations
10.05   Triangular Reorganizations
10.06   Taxable Years and Carrybacks
10.07   Net Operating Losses
10.08   Earnings and Profits

B.   *STATUTORY LIMITATIONS*

10.09   Introduction
10.10   The § 382 Limitation—Overview
10.11   Objective of § 382 Limitation
10.12   Events That Cause the Application of the Limitation
10.13   The Amount of the § 382 Limitation
10.14   Continuity of Business Requirement
10.15   Insolvent Corporations
10.16   Recognized Built-In Gains and Losses
10.17   The § 383 Limitation on Carryovers of Net Capital Losses and of Certain Tax Credits
10.18   Limitation on Offsetting Preacquisition Losses and Credits of One Corporation Against Another's Built-In Gains
10.19   Acquisitions Made to Evade or Avoid Income Tax—§ 269

C.   *NON-STATUTORY LIMITATION ON SURVIVAL OF TAX ATTRIBUTES*

10.20   The De Facto Dissolution Doctrine

¶ 10.01   INTRODUCTION

One of the principal non-tax attributes of a corporation is that it has continuity of life. That is, changes in the stock ownership of the corporation do not affect its existence. The death, disability, or bankruptcy of a shareholder does not interrupt the corporation's existence, nor does a disposition of all or any part of its outstanding stock. Similarly, a corporation can discontinue the business that it previously operated and commence an entirely different business without disrupting the continuity of its life.

Because a corporation is a taxable entity, it will possess numerous tax attributes, some of which can be quite beneficial. Regardless of whether a tax attribute that a corporation possesses is beneficial, unfavorable, or neutral, it is important to know whether that tax attribute survives any of the following events: (1) a significant change in the ownership of the corporation's stock, (2) a significant change in the corporation's structure, (3) an absorption of the corporation's assets into a different corporation, (4) an amalgamation with one or more other corporations, or (5) a termination of the business previously conducted by the corporation. For many years, the tax law has struggled with the question of whether and to what extent a corporation's "identity" survives for purposes of its tax attributes when the corporate entity is involved in any of these events. Those issues have resulted in numerous court decisions and statutory enactments by Congress in an attempt to formulate a satisfactory policy that mitigates the arbitrary nature of the annual accounting concept while minimizing the opportunities for what is perceived as taxpayer abuse. The purpose of this chapter is to briefly describe the current state of the tax law in attempting to strike an appropriate balance in that regard.

The tax law must deal with two aspects of the issue of survival of tax attributes. The first is that there must be general rules that address the survival of specific attributes so that there is some order and predictability. For example, if X, which conducts business A on the cash receipts and disbursement method of accounting, is merged into Y, which conducts business B on the accrual method, the parties need to know whether Y should continue to report the income of business A on the cash method or whether Y is obliged to extend its accrual method to the newly acquired business.[1] These general rules

---

[1]   In general, an acquiring corporation must continue to use the same method of accounting for a business of the target corporation as the target used. § 381(a)(4). However, the acquiring corporation is permitted to change the method used by the target in the year in which in which the § 381 transaction took place. Rev. Proc. 2012–39. See also Treas. Regs. §§ 1.381(c)(4)–1(a)(5), 1.381(c)(5)–1(a)(5).

of survival will apply regardless of whether the retention of the attribute in question is beneficial.

Most of the general rules concerning the survival of tax attributes are set forth in § 381, which was first adopted in 1954. Section 381(c) lists 23 tax attributes to which that provision applies and describes the extent to which each survives.[2] Among the most important attributes included in that list are the net operating loss carryover, the earnings and profits account, the capital loss carryover, certain tax credits, and accounting methods (including inventory and depreciation methods and the installment method).

It eventually became clear, however, that, in addition to the general rules governing the survival of tax attributes, special rules were needed to prevent trafficking in favorable tax attributes. The extent to which favorable attributes should be allowed to survive turns on policy considerations.

Because of the perceived need to designate the circumstances in which a corporation's tax attributes will survive changes in corporate structure or ownership and to place limits on such attribute survival, a number of statutory provisions have been adopted. One Code provision (§ 381) establishes most of the general rules of survival, while other relevant statutory provisions create limitations on the extent to which certain tax attributes will survive specified changes of ownership. Several of the statutory limitations on attribute survival after a change of ownership do not apply to all tax attributes, but rather only to a few specifically designated attributes—primarily, net operating loss carryovers, capital loss carryovers, certain unused tax credits, and certain built-in losses (a built-in loss includes an asset whose basis at the time of change of ownership is greater than its value and also can include a deduction that is otherwise allowable after the change but that is attributable to a time prior to that change).

These statutory provisions are designed to deal with two separate circumstances: first, a significant shift in the ownership of a corporation's stock and, second, a corporate combination either through a transaction that meets the Code's definition of a reorganization or through the liquidation of a subsidiary. In addition, the statutory limitations on the survival of tax attributes are supplemented to a limited degree by common law tax doctrines.

---

[2]   While § 381(c) has 26 numbered provisions, 3 of those have been repealed.

A. ACQUISITION OF TAX ATTRIBUTES
¶ 10.02 INTRODUCTION

A number of questions arise concerning the survival of the tax attributes of two or more corporations that are a party to a reorganization or liquidation transaction. In addition to the survival question itself, it must be determined whether, and as of what date, a reorganization closes the taxable year of an acquired corporation and what significance the closing of a taxable year has for the availability of surviving tax attributes. There is also a question as to whether post-acquisition losses of the surviving corporation can be carried back and deducted from the pre-acquisition taxable income of either the acquired or the surviving corporation. Under current law, only certain losses can be carried back at all, and so the issue arises only when a loss could otherwise be deducted in a prior year.[3]

In adopting § 381 as part of the 1954 Code, Congress dealt with many, but not all, of these questions. Section 381 addresses the extent to which a surviving corporation succeeds to the tax attributes of a corporation whose assets were acquired in an A, C, F, or certain D and G reorganizations, as well as in a liquidation under § 332. Note that § 381 addresses only the survival of the acquired corporation's attributes, and then applies only to those attributes that are described in § 381(c).[4] There was no need to provide for the survival of the acquiring corporation's attributes since those attributes are held by the same taxpayer that had them before the reorganization.[5]

This chapter uses several different terms to refer to an acquired or an acquiring corporation. An acquired corporation is sometimes referred to by that name, sometimes as the "target," and sometimes as the "transferor" corporation. An acquiring corporation is sometimes referred to by that name, sometimes as the "surviving" corporation, and sometimes as the "transferee" corporation.

---

[3]   With a few exceptions, a corporation can carryback its capital losses to three prior years. § 1212(a). A corporation can not carry back its net operating losses unless it occurs in one of several designated businesses (farming business and insurance business other than life insurance). § 172.

[4]   Although § 381(c) deals with a substantial number of tax attributes, the legislative history of that provision makes it clear that it was not intended to be exclusive. Items not expressly covered by § 381 may be controlled by pre-1954 law, although the legislative direction of § 381 may well affect the treatment of such items. The non-exclusivity of § 381 is acknowledged at Treas. Reg. § 1.381(a)–1(b)(3). Note, however, that, when one corporation purchases the assets of another corporation in a taxable transaction, the tax attributes of the target corporation are not acquired by the purchasing corporation.

[5]   However, the availability of certain pre-acquisition tax attributes of a surviving corporation may be restricted by one of the statutory provisions described in Part B and the de facto dissolution doctrine discussed in Part C.

¶ 10.03   LIQUIDATION OF SUBSIDIARY CORPORATIONS

Section 381(a) provides for the carryover of tax attributes in two types of transactions—the liquidation of subsidiary corporations under § 332 and acquisitive corporate reorganizations (other than B reorganizations) as defined in § 368.

Generally, when a corporation is liquidated, its tax attributes end with the termination of the corporation's existence. One exception to this general result is provided in § 381(a)(1). If a controlled subsidiary is liquidated under § 332, those tax attributes of the subsidiary that are listed in § 381(c) are carried over to the parent under § 381.

¶ 10.04   ACQUISITIVE REORGANIZATIONS

Section 381(a)(2) provides for the carryover of tax attributes that are listed in § 381(c) in the following five types of reorganizations: A, C, D, F, and G. Section 381 will not apply to a D or G reorganization unless the asset acquisition and the distribution requirements of § 354(b)(1) are satisfied. In each of these reorganizations, the assets of the transferor corporation are integrated into the acquiring corporation and, in turn, its attributes carry over to the acquiring corporation. In contrast, corporate divisions under § 355 are not covered by § 381, and tax attributes generally are not reallocated because of those transactions.[6] Section 381(a)(2) also does not mention either the B or E reorganization. In a B reorganization (a stock-for-stock acquisition) the acquired corporation remains intact as the subsidiary of the acquiring corporation. In an E reorganization the capital structure of a single corporation is changed. Unlike the acquisitive reorganizations, in neither the B nor the E reorganization are the assets of a corporation transferred to another entity; consequently, nothing happens at the corporate level to interrupt the continued application of the tax attributes of a corporate entity. Nevertheless, the limitations and restrictions that are imposed by the statutory provisions discussed in Part B may apply to restrict the use of some of the continuing entity's tax attributes.

¶ 10.05   TRIANGULAR REORGANIZATIONS

An acquisitive reorganization can involve more than two corporations. For example, as discussed in Chapter Nine, there are triangular variants to A, B, and C reorganizations, and, even as to a two-party acquisition, the initial acquiring corporation can transfer

---

[6]   But see § 312(h) and Treas. Reg. § 1.312–10 for the determination of earnings and profits of corporations involved in a corporate division.

the target's assets or stock to a controlled subsidiary or subsidiaries. At the conclusion of a triangular C reorganization or a forward triangular A reorganization, the target's shareholders have exchanged their target stock for stock in the parent of an acquiring corporation, and that acquiring corporation has acquired the target's assets. (The parties could accomplish the same result by having the parent participate directly in the reorganization and then having it transfer the acquired assets to a controlled subsidiary.) At the conclusion of a reverse triangular A reorganization, the transferee corporation has become a controlled subsidiary of the parent corporation in which the transferee's former shareholders now hold stock, and the transferee continues to own its old assets together with the assets of the transferor corporation, which is a former subsidiary of that parent. Assuming that surviving corporations should retain their own former tax attributes, which corporation should acquire the tax attributes of the corporation that disappears in a triangular acquisition?

When tax attributes of a target are carried over pursuant to § 381, they are transferred to the "acquiring corporation," which term has a special meaning for purposes of § 381. The regulations provide that for this purpose there can be only one acquiring corporation in an acquisition no matter how many corporations are involved.[7] In a multiple corporation acquisition, the acquiring corporation will be the corporation that *directly* acquired the target's assets that were transferred as part of the reorganization even if that corporation ultimately retains none of those assets.[8]

Ex. (1)   In a C reorganization, X Corporation acquired all but a minor portion of the assets of the T Corporation in exchange for voting common stock of X. T was promptly liquidated, and its assets, including the X stock, were distributed to its shareholders. Since X acquired substantially all of T's assets, the acquisition qualified as a C reorganization. X is the acquiring corporation.

Ex. (2)   The same facts as in Example (1) except that, after acquiring most of T's assets, X transferred all of those acquired assets to Y, its wholly-owned subsidiary. X is the acquiring corporation for purposes of § 381.

Ex. (3)   The same facts as in Example (1) except that, after the acquisition of T's assets, X transferred 75% of the acquired assets to Y, and transferred the remaining 25% of the acquired assets to Z. Both Y and Z are wholly-owned

---

[7]   Treas. Reg. § 1.381(a)–1(b)(2).

[8]   Id.

subsidiaries of X. For purposes of § 381, X is the acquiring corporation.

¶ 10.06   TAXABLE YEARS AND CARRYBACKS

Section 381(b) provides general operating rules for terminating the taxable year of the transferor corporation and for limiting carrybacks of net operating losses and net capital losses. These rules apply to all of the transactions described in § 381(a) other than the F reorganization.[9]

The taxable year of a subsidiary corporation whose assets are distributed in a § 332 liquidation ends on the date that the distribution of the subsidiary's assets (or of substantially all of its assets) is completed. The taxable year of a transferor corporation (i.e., a target) whose assets are transferred pursuant to a reorganization (other than an F reorganization) ends on the date that the transfer of the target's assets (or of substantially all of its assets) is completed.[10]

Section 381(b)(3) provides that, if a parent corporation in a § 332 liquidation or the acquiring corporation in a reorganization (other than an F reorganization) has a net operating loss or a net capital loss in a taxable year ending after the date on which the distribution or transfer of the assets of the subsidiary or the transferor corporation is completed, that net operating loss or net capital loss cannot be carried back to an earlier year of the liquidated subsidiary or of the transferor corporation. Section 381(b)(3) does not prevent the carryback of a net operating loss or a net capital loss of the acquiring or parent corporation to its own prior taxable year. Consequently, the post-acquisition net operating losses and net capital losses of the surviving corporation cannot be deducted from pre-acquisition income of a liquidated subsidiary or of a target corporation; but such post-acquisition net losses can be carried back and deducted only from the pre-acquisition taxable income of the surviving corporation. However, under current law, there are only two designated types of businesses (farming and insurance other than life insurance) that are permitted to carryback a net operating loss. § 172. Thus, the consequences of the carryback of post-acquisition net operating losses and capital losses may be different depending on which corporation serves as the acquired corporation and which serves as the acquiring corporation. As a consequence of changes made by the 2017 Tax Cuts and Jobs Act, with only two

---

[9]   In the case of an F reorganization, the acquiring corporation is treated, for purposes of § 381, just as the transferor corporation would have been treated if the reorganization had not taken place. Treas. Reg. § 1.381(b)–1(a)(2).

[10]   § 381(b)(1).

exceptions, a net operating loss no longer can be carried back to prior years; but a net capital loss generally can be carried back to the preceding three years.[11]

¶ 10.07 NET OPERATING LOSSES

A net operating loss is one of the tax attributes with which § 381 deals. In this section, we will examine the extent to which the net operating losses of a subsidiary or target corporation are available to the acquiring corporation. We will not discuss in this section the special limitations that are imposed by §§ 382, 384, and 269 on the availability of acquired net operating losses, and we will defer discussion of those limitations to Part B of this chapter. The reader should bear in mind that the examples set forth in this section do not take into account the effect that those special limitations would have on the amount of such net operating losses that can be deducted by the acquiring corporation.

When § 381 applies to an acquisition, the acquiring corporation[12] obtains all of the net operating losses of the transferor corporation even if the acquiring corporation obtains less than 100% of the transferor's assets.[13] This treatment applies regardless of whether the § 381 transaction is a reorganization or a liquidation of a subsidiary.

Ex. S Corporation has $100,000 of net operating loss carryovers. P Corporation owns 80% of each class of stock of S. P causes the liquidation of S, and P receives 80% of S's assets as liquidating distributions. The remaining 20% of S's assets are distributed to S's minority shareholders. P acquires all $100,000 of S's net operating loss carryovers. The determination of the taxable years in which P can take deductions for those loss carryovers is discussed below.

Subject to exceptions for two specified businesses,[14] a net operating loss for a taxable year can not be carried back to the any of the taxpayer's preceding taxable years and deducted from the taxable income in those years.[15] A net operating loss can be carried forward to subsequent years and deducted from taxable income in each of those years. Except for an insurance company, there is no limitation

---

[11]   §§ 172(b), 1212(a)(1). See n. 3, supra.

[12]   As noted in ¶ 10.05, the acquiring corporation is the corporation that directly acquired the target's assets even if that corporation does not retain those assets.

[13]   Treas. Reg. § 1.381(c)(1)–1(c)(2).

[14]   The two exceptions are for losses incurred in a farming business and an insurance business (other than life insurance). The losses of those businesses can be carried back to the two years prior to the year of loss. § 172(b)(1)(B) and (C).

[15]   § 172(b)(1)(A).

on the number of subsequent years to which a net operating loss can be deducted.[16] The net operating losses are required to be deducted from the taxable income of the earliest years to which they can be applied.[17] However, a corporation that is permitted to carry back a net operating loss can waive that right and use only a carryforward.

¶ 10.08   EARNINGS AND PROFITS

When § 381 applies, the acquiring corporation[18] obtains the accumulated positive earnings and profits (*e and p*) or the accumulated deficit *e and p* that the transferor corporation had at the close of the date of transfer.[19] As used herein, a reference to a "transferor" corporation includes a liquidating subsidiary as well as the target of an acquisitive reorganization; a reference to a "transfer" includes a liquidating distribution; and a reference to an "acquiring corporation" includes the parent of a liquidating subsidiary. If a transferor corporation accumulates *e and p* or incurs a deficit in *e and p* after the transfer date but before the reorganization or liquidation is completed, such *e and p* or deficit is deemed to have been accumulated or incurred as of the close of the date of transfer.[20]

Any positive or deficit *e and p* acquired pursuant to § 381 are treated as accumulated *e and p* or as an accumulated deficit; they have no effect on the acquiring corporation's current *e and p*.[21]

If the § 381 transaction is a § 332 liquidation of a subsidiary and if the parent corporation receives less than 100% of the subsidiary's assets because some are distributed to minority shareholders, then the subsidiary's accumulated *e and p* acquired by the parent are first reduced to reflect the distributions to minority shareholders regardless of whether the distributions to the minority shareholders took place before, at, or after the date on which the distribution to the parent took place.[22]

Presumably, the reduction of the subsidiary's *e and p* will follow the rule that applies for reducing *e and p* in the case of a stock redemption or partial liquidation.[23] Accordingly, the subsidiary's *e*

---

[16]   Id. An insurance company (other than a life insurance company) is limited to a 20-year carryforward. § 172(b)(3).

[17]   § 172(b)(2).

[18]   The acquiring corporation is the corporation that directly acquired the target's assets even if that corporation does not retain those assets.

[19]   Treas. Reg. § 1.381(c)(2)–1(a)(2).

[20]   Treas. Reg. § 1.381(c)(2)–1(a)(1).

[21]   Treas. Reg. § 1.381(c)(2)–1(a)(2).

[22]   Treas. Reg. § 1.381(c)(2)–1(c)(2).

[23]   See § 312(n)(7). See also ¶ 3.08.

and p should be reduced by a percentage equal to the ratable share of *e and p* attributable to the stock of the minority shareholders.

If a § 381 transaction is a reorganization and if the transferor corporation distributes boot to its shareholders, in addition to distributing property that is not taxable to them because of § 354, then the accumulated *e and p* of the transferor, as of the close of the date of transfer, are reduced to reflect the amount of *e and p* that are properly applicable to the distribution of the boot, regardless of whether the boot is distributed before or after the transfer to the acquiring corporation.[24]

If the acquiring corporation and the transferor each had positive accumulated *e and p* as of the close of the date of transfer, the two are combined in the acquiring corporation to constitute a single *e and p* account. Similarly, if the acquiring corporation and the transferor each had a negative accumulated *e and p* as of the close of the date of transfer, the two are combined to form a single negative accumulated *e and p* in the acquiring corporation.[25]

The reason that tax consequences are more complicated when one corporation has a negative (i.e., deficit) accumulated *e and p,* and the other has positive accumulated *e and p* is that § 381 prohibits the blending of negative and positive *e and p* accounts.[26] An accumulated deficit *e and p* of either the transferor or the acquiring corporation can be used only to offset *e and p* that accumulate after the transfer date.[27] The acquiring corporation will keep two separate accumulated *e and p* accounts: a positive account and a negative account. The negative account will offset *e and p* arising after the transfer, but will have no other consequence.

Ex. As of January 1, Year One, A had accumulated *e and p* of $35,000. A made no distributions to its shareholders in Year One. A had no current *e and p* in Year One. On July 1, Year One, A acquired all of the assets of T in exchange for voting common stock of A. T promptly liquidated and distributed its assets (the A stock) to its shareholders. The acquisition of T's assets qualified as a C reorganization. As of January 1, Year One, T had a negative *e and p* of $18,000. Between January 1 and July 1 of Year One, T had current *e and p* of $2,000. Except for the liquidating distribution of its A stock, T made no distributions to its shareholders in that year.

---

[24]   Treas. Reg. § 1.381(c)(2)–1(c)(1).
[25]   Treas. Reg. § 1.381(c)(2)–1(a)(4).
[26]   § 381(c)(2)(B).
[27]   Id.

An acquiring corporation does not increase its current *e and p* by the amount of the target's current *e and p*. Instead, the target's current *e and p* is added to the accumulated *e and p* of the target, and the target's total accumulated *e and p* is acquired by the acquiring corporation.

Accordingly, T's accumulated negative *e and p* of $18,000 is reduced by its $2,000 of current *e and p*, and the resulting $16,000 of negative accumulated *e and p* is acquired by A.

A cannot combine its positive *e and p* with the negative *e and p* A acquired form T. Instead, the negative *e and p* it acquired is accounted for separately and can offset future earnings of A. Accordingly, immediately after the acquisition of T, A has two accumulated *e and p* accounts—a positive accumulated account of $35,000, and a negative *e and p* account of $16,000.

In Year Two, A had current *e and p* of $12,000. A distributed $5,000 to its shareholders in that year. The $5,000 distribution is treated as a dividend paid out of current *e and p*. If A did not have a separate negative *e and p* account, the remaining $7,000 of its current *e and p* would have been added to A's accumulated *e and p*. Instead, the $7,000 current *e and p* will reduce A's negative *e and p* account so that it will be $9,000 ($16,000 minus $7,000 = $9,000). As of January 1, Year Three, A will have two accumulated *e and p* accounts. A will have a positive accumulated *e and p* account of $35,000 and a negative accumulated *e and p* account of $9,000.

B. STATUTORY LIMITATIONS

¶ 10.09   INTRODUCTION

In Part A of this chapter, we discussed the general rules for the retention or acquisition of various tax attributes of a corporate entity. Once it has been determined that under those general rules a tax attribute has survived a change of ownership of a corporate entity or a change of the corporate structure, it becomes necessary to consider whether the availability of that tax attribute is subject to limitations imposed by one or more of several statutory provisions. These statutory limitations are designed to restrict the ability of taxpayers to market certain favorable tax attributes by selling them to persons who could put them to better use. While it is possible to argue on economic grounds that a taxpayer should be permitted to sell a favorable tax attribute, Congress and the Service have consistently indicated their hostility to that practice and have acted to limit the extent to which that can be accomplished or to prevent it entirely.

The principal statutory provisions that address the problem of trafficking in tax attributes can be divided into two groups. One group is comprised of §§ 382–384, and the second "group" is comprised of only a single statute—§ 269. We will sometimes refer to the §§ 382–384 group as the "§ 382 set." The scope of these two groups can overlap, and so it is possible for both groups to apply to a transaction in certain cases.

The standards for applying each of the two groups of statutes are very different. The § 382 set applies when specified objective conditions occur. In the case of § 269, however, not only must certain objective conditions occur, but there must also be a determination as to the subjective purpose of the transaction. While the rules governing the § 382 set are intricate, they turn on the presence of objective facts that can be determined on a fairly mechanical basis. On the other hand, even when the objective conditions of § 269 occur, the provision will not apply unless it is determined that the principal purpose of the transaction was the evasion or avoidance of some amount of the federal income tax by securing the benefit of a tax deduction, credit, or other allowance that the taxpayer could not have enjoyed if the transaction had not taken place.

Not all tax attributes are subject to these statutory limitations. The § 382 set deals exclusively with limitations on deductions for net operating and capital loss carryovers, limitations on the carryover of certain tax credits, and limitations on the availability of deductions for certain built-in losses. Section 269, while applying to the same tax attributes as does the § 382 set, also can apply to other tax attributes.

¶ 10.10   THE § 382 LIMITATION—OVERVIEW

As opposed to eliminating a corporation's net operation loss carryovers, § 382 limits the amount of such carryover loss that can be deducted in a taxable year after the change of ownership takes place.[28] Of course, if a § 382 limitation prevents a taxpayer from deducting the entire amount of a carryover loss before the period in which it can be deducted expires, the effect of the limitation is to reduce the amount of the carryover loss that can be deducted. In many circumstances, the application of § 382 will not prevent the deduction of the entire amount of a net operating loss, but rather will affect the timing of the deduction by spreading it over a number of years. Note that the limitations on the deduction of carryover losses

---

[28]   There is one exception that relates to the treatment of insolvent corporations. § 382(*l*)(5). Another exception arises when there has been both a significant change of ownership and a discontinuance of the business enterprise of the corporation that had a net operating loss. See ¶ 10.14.

can apply to carryover losses of the surviving corporation as well as to those of the acquired corporation.

The provisions of § 382 and the regulations thereunder are complex and intricate. We will not attempt to provide an exhaustive examination of this statute, but we will explain its basic operation in some detail.

There are two circumstances in which it might be reasonable to limit the availability of a corporation's loss carryovers and of its built-in losses. One circumstance is where there is a substantial change in the ownership of the corporation. The second circumstance is when the corporation abandons the conduct of the business that produced the loss or takes on a new business that produces income. The current version of § 382 applies a limitation only when there has been a substantial change of ownership of the corporation's stock. If there has not been a substantial change of stock ownership, a corporation's change from one type of business to another will have no effect on the availability of either its loss carryovers or its built-in losses. However, when, in addition to there being a substantial change of ownership, there also was a failure to continue the business enterprise of the corporation that had a net operating loss for at least two years after the transfer, no net operating loss deduction will be allowed.[29]

¶ 10.11　OBJECTIVE OF § 382 LIMITATION

Section 382 limits the extent to which net operating loss carryovers and built-in losses of a loss corporation can be utilized after there has been a substantial change in the ownership of the loss corporation's stock. The thrust of the approach is to permit a deduction for such losses to approximately the same extent as would have been allowed if there had been no change of ownership and if instead the assets of the loss corporation had been contributed to a partnership that produced the annual income that was subsequently earned by the surviving corporation. The operation of the provision only approximates an equivalent consequence, but a rough equivalence is the aim of the statute, which reflects the evident belief of Congress that such a rough equivalence should be sufficient to deter trafficking in the tax attributes affected by §§ 382 and 383.

Ex. (1)　As of January 1, Year Three, X Corporation had net assets valued at $100,000, and X had a net operating loss carryforward of $32,000 from Year One. At that date, Y Corporation had net assets valued at $400,000, and Y had no loss carryovers. On that date, the two corporations

---

[29]　See ¶ 10.14.

formed a partnership, the XY partnership, and each corporation transferred all of its assets to the partnership. X and Y obtained a 20% and 80% interest respectively in the partnership. X and Y continued in existence and the sole asset that each corporation possessed was its interest in the XY partnership. The partnership earned taxable income of $50,000 in Year Three of which $10,000 (20%) was allocated to X, and the remaining $40,000 (80%) was allocated to Y. Note that a partnership does not pay federal income taxes, and instead its tax attributes (including its income) are allocated among its partners. Y will pay federal income tax on the $40,000 of taxable income that was allocated to it. The $10,000 of taxable income that was allocated to X will be offset by a like amount of X's net operating loss carryover, and so X will pay no federal income tax. The remaining $22,000 of X's net operating loss carryover will be carried over to Year Four.

Ex. (2)   The same facts as those stated in Example (1) except that, instead of forming a partnership, X was merged into Y on January 1, Year Three, and the shareholders of X (the loss corporation) received shares of stock of Y constituting 20% of the latter's outstanding stock. The merger qualified as an "A" reorganization, and so, under § 381, Y acquired X's $32,000 of net operating loss carryover. In Year Three, Y earned taxable income (before taking into account any net operating loss carryover) of $50,000. The congressional goal for § 382 is to limit the amount of the acquired $32,000 net operating loss carryover that Y can deduct in Year Three to approximately the same amount that X would have deducted in that year if the partnership route that is described in Example (1) had been adopted instead of the merger. Thus, in principle, only about $10,000 of the carryover should be allowed in Year Three. We will examine later in this section exactly how the limitation of § 382 is determined, but this example illustrates the direction of the statute.

¶ 10.12   EVENTS THAT CAUSE THE APPLICATION OF THE LIMITATION

The § 382 limitation applies when there has been an "ownership change" of a "loss corporation." A "loss corporation" is a corporation that is entitled to use a net operating loss carryover, or has either a net operating loss in the taxable year in which an ownership change took place or a "net unrealized built-in loss."[30] The meaning of the term "net unrealized built-in loss" is explained later in this section. Before explaining what constitutes an "ownership change," it will be helpful to set forth the definition of several terms. The meaning of the term "loss corporation" is set forth three sentences above. Other important terms are:

Old loss corporation. The term "old loss corporation" refers to a corporation that has undergone an ownership change and was a loss corporation immediately before the ownership change took place.[31] The event that causes an ownership change may or may not result in the termination of the existence of an old loss corporation. If the old loss corporation continues to exist after an ownership change occurred, it then becomes a "new loss corporation." It is therefore possible for the same corporation to be both an old loss corporation and a new loss corporation.

New loss corporation. The term "new loss corporation" refers to a corporation that, immediately after an ownership change, is a loss corporation.[32] A new loss corporation may be the same corporate entity that previously had been an old loss corporation or it may be a different corporate entity. A successor corporation to a new loss corporation also constitutes a new loss corporation.

Successor corporation. A successor corporation is a corporation that acquired the tax attributes of a loss corporation pursuant to § 381 as a consequence of acquiring the assets of the loss corporation.[33]

Predecessor corporation. A predecessor corporation is a transferor corporation that transfers or distributes its assets to an acquiring corporation in a transaction to which § 381(a) applies.[34]

Stock. Unless expressly provided otherwise, the stock of a corporation does not include preferred stock that is described in § 1504(a)(4); in other words, it does not include nonvoting, nonconvertible stock that is limited and preferred as to dividends, does not participate in corporate growth to any significant extent, and has limited

---

[30]   § 382(k)(1).
[31]   § 382(k)(2); Temp. Reg. § 1.382–2T(f)(2).
[32]   § 382(k)(3); Temp. Reg. § 1.382–2T(f)(3).
[33]   Treas. Reg. § 1.382–2(a)(5).
[34]   Treas. Reg. § 1.382–2(a)(6).

redemption and liquidation rights.[35] To add further to the complexity, the regulations also provide that, in certain prescribed circumstances, nonstock interests in a corporation will be treated as stock for purposes of § 382; and conversely, in other specified circumstances, certain stock of a corporation will not be treated as stock.[36] A common element in each variation is whether the nonstock interest is structured so as to offer a potential for significant participation in corporate growth or, alternatively, whether the terms of the stock are such that it has a relatively low probability of participating in future corporate growth.

Owner shift. An "owner shift" is any change in the ownership of the stock of a loss corporation that affects the percentage of the value of the loss corporation's stock owned by a person who is a "5-percent shareholder."[37] The term "5-percent shareholder" is defined below. An owner shift can occur as a consequence of one of a number of different types of transactions. For example, any of the following may cause an owner shift: a shareholder's sale of a loss corporation's stock, the redemption of a loss corporation's stock, a recapitalization of the loss corporation, a § 351 exchange with a loss corporation, a loss corporation's issuance of new shares of stock, and a reorganization in which the loss corporation is a party.[38]

In general, any changes in a shareholder's proportionate share of the value of the loss corporation's outstanding stock that is attributable to fluctuations in the relative fair market values of different classes of the corporation's stock are not taken into account.[39]

Equity structure shift. An equity structure shift is a transaction that qualifies as a reorganization under § 368, except that the term does not apply to an "F" reorganization or to a divisive "D" or "G" reorganization. The term can also include taxable reorganization-type transactions, public offerings, and similar transactions to the extent that the regulations so provide.[40]

---

[35]   § 382(k)(6)(A).

[36]   Temp. Reg. § 1.382–2T(f)(18).

[37]   § 382(g)(2), (k)(5), (6)(C). Transactions between persons neither of whom is a 5-percent shareholder are disregarded. Temp. Reg. § 1.382–2T(e)(1)(ii).

[38]   Temp. Reg. § 1.382–2T(e)(1).

[39]   § 382(*l*)(3)(C).

[40]   § 382(g)(3).

Testing date. The "testing date" is the date on which a loss corporation is required to determine whether an "ownership change" has occurred.[41] The meaning of the term "ownership change" is explained later in this section. The loss corporation is obligated to make that determination immediately after an owner shift takes place.[42] While the determination must also be made immediately after an equity structure shift, the loss corporation must do so only if the equity structure shift also causes an owner shift.[43] Consequently, the crucial question is whether an owner shift took place.

Testing period. The testing period is the period of time during which increases in the percentage interests that shareholders have in the ownership of the loss corporation's stock are measured to determine whether an ownership change has occurred. The testing period is generally the three-year period that ends on the testing date.[44]

5-percent shareholder. A 5-percent shareholder is any person who at any time during the testing period held stock of the loss corporation having a fair market value of 5 percent or more of the value of all of the loss corporation's outstanding stock.[45] For this purpose, preferred stock that is described in § 1504(a)(4) is not taken into account in determining either the value of stock held by the shareholder or the aggregate value of the loss corporation's outstanding stock.[46]

A modified version of the stock attribution rules of § 318 is applied in determining the stock that is deemed to be owned by a shareholder.[47] In lieu of family attribution (as provided in § 318(a)(1)), an individual and his spouse, children, grandchildren, and parents are treated as a single shareholder.

The attribution of stock owned by an entity to its partners, beneficiaries, or shareholders that is provided by § 318(a)(2) is applicable except that the 50% limitation on the attribution of stock from a corporation to its shareholders

---

[41]   Temp. Reg. § 1.382–2T(a)(2) and Treas. Reg. § 1.382–2(a)(4).

[42]   Treas. Reg. § 1.382–2(a)(4).

[43]   Temp. Reg. § 1.382–2T(a)(2)(i)(B).

[44]   There are circumstances where the testing period can be shortened. See § 382(i).

[45]   § 382(k)(6)(C), (7).

[46]   Treas. Reg. § 1.382–2(a)(3).

[47]   § 382(*l*)(3)(A).

does not apply.[48] Except as provided otherwise in regulations, any stock that is attributed from an entity to an individual is treated as no longer being held by the entity.[49] In determining a person's percentage interest in the stock of a corporation for the purpose of determining the amount of stock owned by that corporation that is to be attributed to the person, preferred stock of the corporation that is described in § 1504(a)(4) is ignored.[50]

Unless provided otherwise by regulation, there is no attribution to a corporation, partnership, estate, or trust of stock held by a shareholder, partner, or beneficiary.[51]

Public group. A loss corporation may have a number of shareholders none of whom is a 5-percent shareholder. For purposes of § 382, those shareholders are combined, and the combined group will be treated as a single 5-percent shareholder.[52] For convenience, such a combined group of shareholders is referred to as a "public group."[53] In some circumstances a public group must be divided into two or more public groups each of which may be treated as a separate 5-percent shareholder.[54]

Ownership change. The limitations imposed by § 382 apply to a new loss corporation only after there has been an "ownership change."[55] An ownership change occurs when the percentage of stock of a loss corporation that is owned immediately after an owner shift by one or more 5-percent shareholders is more than 50 percentage points higher than the smallest percentage of stock of the loss corporation (or any predecessor corporation) owned by those shareholders at any time during the testing period.[56] The test for determining whether an ownership change has occurred is made by comparing the percentage of stock ownership (determined according to stock value) of each 5-percent shareholder immediately after an owner shift with the lowest percentage of stock ownership that that shareholder

---

[48]   § 382(l)(3)(A)(ii). Temp. Reg. § 1.382–2T(h)(2)(i). There are some *de minimis* limitations to prevent attribution to a shareholder who has less than a 5% interest in a corporation. Temp. Reg. § 1.382–2T(g)(2), (h)(2)(iii).

[49]   § 382(l)(3)(A)(ii)(II); Temp. Reg. § 1.382–2T(h)(2)(i)(A).

[50]   Temp. Reg. § 1.382–2T(h)(2)(ii)(A).

[51]   § 382(l)(3)(A)(iii); Temp. Reg. § 1.382–2T(h)(3).

[52]   § 382(g)(4)(A).

[53]   Temp. Reg. § 1.382–2T(f)(13).

[54]   § 382(g)(4)(B); Temp. Reg. § 1.382–2T(j).

[55]   Temp. Reg. § 1.382–2T(a)(1).

[56]   § 382(g)(1).

had at any time during the testing period. If the shareholder's percentage at the later date is higher, the amount of that increase is aggregated with the increase of other 5-percent shareholders. There is an ownership change if the aggregate increase of all such shareholders is greater than 50 percentage points.

In general, any changes in a shareholder's proportionate share of the value of the loss corporation's outstanding stock that is attributable to fluctuations in the relative fair market values of different classes of the corporation's stock are not taken into account.[57]

In certain circumstances when a shareholder acquired stock of a loss corporation from another person, the shareholder is deemed to have held the stock during the period that it was held by the other person.[58] This tacking of ownership applies in the following circumstances:

(1) the stock was acquired from a decedent, and the recipient's basis in the stock is determined by § 1014;

(2) the stock was acquired as a gift or a transfer in trust, and the recipient's basis is determined by § 1015;

(3) the stock was acquired from a spouse or former spouse, and basis is determined by § 1041(b)(2);

(4) the stock was received in satisfaction of a right to receive a pecuniary bequest; or

(5) the stock was acquired pursuant to a divorce or separation instrument.

The following examples illustrate how the determination of ownership change is made. In the following examples, "L" is a loss corporation; if there is more than one loss corporation, they are referred to as "L₁," "L₂," "L₃," etc.; "P" is a corporation that is not a loss corporation; A, B, C, D, and F are unrelated individuals. All corporations report their income on a calendar year basis.

Ex. (1)   Since Year One, A and B each owned 40 percent of L's common stock, and F owned the remaining 20 percent. L had no other stock outstanding, and each share of its outstanding stock had the same value. On March 23, Year Five, C purchased from A and B all of the L stock that they owned. C, A, and B are 5-percent shareholders of L since each owned, at a time during the testing period that

---

[57]   § 382(*l*)(3)(C).

[58]   § 382(*l*)(3)(B).

includes the testing date, 5% or more of the value of L's outstanding stock. Since the purchase by C resulted in a change in the percentage stock ownership of a 5-percent shareholder (indeed, it caused a change in the percentage stock ownership of three 5-percent shareholders), there was an owner shift on March 23, Year Five, and that date is a testing date. The testing period begins on March 24, Year Two, and ends at the close of the day, March 23, Year Five. The lowest percentage of L's stock that C owned at any time during the testing period was zero, and the percentage of stock (by value) owned by C immediately after the owner shift was 80 percent. Consequently, there was an increase of the percentage of stock ownership of a 5-percent shareholder of greater than 50 percentage points, and so there was an ownership change on March 23, Year Five. L became a new loss corporation, and the § 382 limitations became applicable to it.

Ex. (2)   L has outstanding 200 shares of common stock. As of January 1, Year Four, A, B, and C respectively owned 100, 50, and 50 shares of L's outstanding stock, and they had owned those shares since January 1, Year One. Each share of L's stock has the same value, and L has no other shares of stock outstanding. On January 12, Year Four, A sold 60 shares of L's stock to B. That sale increased B's percentage stock ownership by 30 percentage points (from 25% to 55%) and decreased A's percentage stock ownership by 30 percentage points (from 50% to 20%). The sale caused an owner shift since there was a change in the percentage stock ownership of a 5-percent shareholder. Therefore, a determination must be made as to whether there was an ownership change. January 12, Year Four becomes a testing date, and the testing period begins on January 13, Year One and ends at the close of the testing date. However, since B was the only 5-percent shareholder whose percentage of stock ownership increased and since her percentage of stock ownership did not increase by more than 50 percentage points, there was not an ownership change on January 12, Year Four.

Ex. (3)   L has 100 shares of common stock outstanding and has no other shares outstanding. Each share of L's common stock has the same value. A, B, and C respectively owned 48, 40 and 12 shares of L's stock, and they had owned those shares since Year One. On April 5, Year Six, D purchased from A the 48 shares of L's stock that A owned. While that purchase caused an owner shift, it did not cause an ownership change, and so it did not trigger the application of § 382 limitations. On October 25, Year Eight, G purchased from C three of the shares of L's stock that C owned. G is the daughter of D. Neither G nor D is related to any other individual mentioned in this example. The purchase by G causes an owner shift, and the testing period begins on October 26, Year Five. Although G alone holds only 3% of L's stock (and so would not be a 5-percent shareholder), the relationship of G and D is such that, under § 382(*l*)(3)(A)(i), they are treated as a single individual, and so their stock holdings are combined to make a single 5-percent shareholder. Since G and D are treated as one individual shareholder, their combined holdings of 51 shares of L stock provides that "single" shareholder with 51% of L's outstanding stock. Prior to D's acquisition of 48 shares of L stock in Year Six, which took place within the testing period, the single shareholder of G and D combined had a zero percentage of L's outstanding stock. Since the percentage of stock ownership of that "single" shareholder (a 5-percent shareholder) increased by more than 50 percentage points, there was an ownership change on October 25, Year Eight.

Ex. (4) A has owned all 1000 shares of the outstanding common stock of L for more than three years. L has no other shares of stock outstanding. Each share of L's stock has the same value; in any event, § 382 will be applied by treating each share of stocks having similar terms as being of equal value even if, in fact, they were unequal because of a blockage discount or a control premium. On June 15, Year Six, A sold 300 shares of L's stock to B. The sale constitutes an owner shift, but there is not an ownership change since B's percentage stock interest increased by only 30 percentage points. On February 10, Year Nine, L redeems 500 of its shares from A, leaving A with 200 shares remaining. The redemption of A's 500 shares increases the percentage of B's stock ownership to 60 percent. This constitutes an owner shift, and the testing period begins on February 11, Year Six. Since B had a zero percentage stock ownership at the beginning of the testing period, there is an increase of more than 50 percentage points in B's percentage of stock ownership over the lowest percentage that B had at any time during the testing period, and so the redemption results in an ownership change.

Changes Within a Public Group. You will recall that those shareholders who hold less than five percent of a loss corporation's stock are grouped together, and the resulting group (sometimes called a "public group") is treated as a single 5-percent shareholder. Transfers of stock between members of a public group (i.e., between persons none of whom is a 5-percent shareholder) are not treated as owner shifts and so do not cause an examination of whether an ownership change has taken place.[59] Similarly, transfers of stock between members of different public groups of the same loss corporation (in certain circumstances explained later in this section, a public group can be divided into two or more separate public groups) do not cause an examination of whether an ownership change has occurred.[60]

Ex. (5)   The 1000 shares of outstanding common stock of L are owned by 100 individuals none of whom owns as much as 5 percent of the value of L's stock. The 100 individuals are grouped together and treated as a single 5-percent shareholder. Sales of L's stock between members of that group or to persons outside of that group do not constitute an owner shift unless some individual acquires a 5 percent or greater share of the value of L's stock. This rule prevents the normal buying and selling of stock of a publicly held loss corporation from triggering a requirement that the stock holdings of shareholders over a three-year period be examined to see if there has been an ownership change.

The regulations prescribe a series of segregation rules under which a public group must be divided into separate groups each of which is treated as a separate 5-percent shareholder. This can occur when there is a reorganization involving publicly held corporations.[61] Another circumstance in which this occurs is when a substantial block of newly issued stock of a publicly held loss corporation is acquired by a public group. In such cases, the members of the public group that held the loss corporation's stock immediately before the issuance of the new shares are combined and treated as one 5-percent shareholder, and the persons who acquired the newly issued stock are treated as a separate 5-percent shareholder.[62] Subject to the loss corporation's actual knowledge of contrary facts, it is presumed that no person in one public group is also a member of another public group, and that all members of both public groups are unrelated.[63]

---

[59]   Temp. Reg. § 1.382–2T(e)(1)(ii).

[60]   Id.

[61]   Temp. Reg. § 1.382–2T(j)(2)(iii)(B). See Example (7), infra.

[62]   Temp. Reg. § 1.382–2T(j)(2)(iii)(B).

[63]   Temp. Reg. § 1.382–2T(j)(1)(iii) and (k)(2).

Reorganizations. Section 382 limitations can apply to reorganizations if there is an ownership change.[64]

Ex. (6)   A owned all of the stock of L, and B owned all of the stock of P. L merged into P in an A reorganization. As a consequence, A received stock of P constituting 40% of the value of P's outstanding stock. All of P's outstanding stock is common stock having equal value per share. Under § 381, P acquired L's net operating loss carryover. The merger constitutes an equity structure shift and also constitutes an owner shift since the percentage stock ownership of a 5-percent shareholder is changed. P is a successor corporation of L. The percentage stock ownership of B in L increased from zero to 60 percent (B's stock ownership of P is also treated as stock ownership of L since P is the successor to L). Since B's percentage stock ownership increased by more than 50 percentage points, there was an ownership change as to L, and § 382 limitations will apply to the net operating loss carryover that P acquired from L. P is a new loss corporation.

Ex. (7)   L had 20,000 shares of common stock outstanding, which were held by 200 shareholders none of whom was a 5-percent shareholder. L had no other stock outstanding. All of L's shareholders together constituted a public group (Public Group L) that is treated as a single 5-percent shareholder. P had 45,000 shares of common stock outstanding, which were held by 300 shareholders, none of whom was a 5-percent shareholder. P had no other stock outstanding. All of P's shareholders together constituted a public group (Public Group P) that is treated as a single 5-percent shareholder. In Year Six, P made a tender offer to L's shareholders to exchange 1 share of P's common stock for every set of 4 shares of L's stock that was transferred to P. At that time, the net value of P's assets was $9,000,000; and the net value of L's assets was $1,000,000. All of the shareholders of L accepted the offer, and so the shareholders of L received 5,000 shares of P stock in exchange for their 20,000 shares of L stock. The exchange qualified as a "B" reorganization. At the time of the exchange, L had a substantial net operating loss carryforward.

After the exchange, L became a wholly owned subsidiary of P; and P had 50,000 shares of stock outstanding of which

---

[64]   § 382(g)(3)(A); Temp. Reg. § 1.382–2T(e)(2)(i).

the former shareholders of L (Public Group L) held 5,000 shares (10%). The shares of L that P holds are attributed to P's shareholders by § 382(*l*)(3)(A)(ii). The "B" reorganization constitutes an equity structure shift, but the question is whether there was also an owner shift and whether an ownership change took place. If Public Group L simply became part of Public Group P, there would not be an owner shift since, after applying attribution rules, all of L's stock would continue to be owned by a public group, and so the percentage of stock ownership of a 5-percent shareholder would not have changed. But the fact is that, after the exchange, the former shareholders of L have only a 10% interest in the enterprise.

If L were permitted to continue to deduct its net operating loss carryforward free of a § 382 limitation, the former shareholders of L would have successfully "sold" the corporation's loss carryover to the shareholders of P. Obviously, that would contravene the purpose and spirit of § 382. To prevent that from occurring, Public Group L and Public Group P are treated as two separate groups each of which constitutes a 5-percent shareholder. By stock attribution, Public Group P is deemed to own 90% of the outstanding stock of L. Therefore, there was a change in the percentage of stock ownership of a 5-percent shareholder, and so a determination must be made as to whether an ownership change occurred. Since the lowest percentage that Public Group P had during the testing period is zero, there was an increase of more than 50 percentage points in the percentage of stock ownership of a 5-percent shareholder. There was an ownership change, and the § 382 limitation applies to the deduction of L's net operating loss carryover.

¶ 10.13   THE AMOUNT OF THE § 382 LIMITATION

Once it is established that there has been an ownership change, it is then necessary to determine the amount of the § 382 limitation. The § 382 limitation is the maximum amount of "pre-change loss" that can be deducted or credited by a new loss corporation in a taxable year. The § 382 limitation is applied not only to the tax attributes listed in § 382, but also in determining the limitation on the deduction of a capital loss carryover and the amount of pre-change credit that can be taken under § 383.[65] Section 383 is discussed in ¶ 10.17.

Before discussing the § 382 limitation, it will be useful to have a few definitions in mind.

Change date. The change date is the date on which an owner shift that is the last component of an ownership change took place.[66]

Post-change year. The term "post-change year" refers to any taxable year that ends after the change date.[67]

Pre-change loss. The term "pre-change loss" includes any of the following: (1) a net operating loss carryforward of the old loss corporation to the taxable year ending on the change date or in which the change date occurred; (2) a net operating loss of the old loss corporation for the taxable year in which the ownership change occurred to the extent that that loss is allocable to the pre-change period (defined below); (3) a recognized built-in loss that is recognized in a recognition period taxable year;[68] (4) pre-change capital losses; and (5) pre-change credits.[69]

While the same term also is employed in the § 383 regulations, for purposes of that provision the term refers only to the first four items listed above and does not refer to pre-change credits, which are separately defined in the regulations relating to that Code section.[70]

Change year. A change year is a taxable year of a loss corporation that includes a change date.[71]

Pre-change period. The pre-change period of a loss corporation is the portion of the change year that ends on the close of the change date.[72]

Post-change period. The post-change period of a loss corporation is the portion of the change year beginning with the day after the change date.[73]

---

[65]   Treas. Reg. § 1.383–1(b).
[66]   Temp. Reg. § 1.382–2T(f)(19).
[67]   § 382(d)(2).
[68]   See § 382(h).
[69]   Treas. Reg. § 1.382–2(a)(2).
[70]   Treas. Reg. § 1.383–1(c)(3) and (4).
[71]   Treas. Reg. § 1.382–6(g)(1).
[72]   Treas. Reg. § 1.382–6(g)(2).
[73]   Treas. Reg. § 1.382–6(g)(3).

The § 382 limitation is equal to the product of multiplying the value of the old loss corporation times the "long-term tax-exempt rate."[74] The value of the old loss corporation is the value of all of the outstanding stock of that corporation immediately before the ownership change occurred; for this purpose, the value of *all* of the old loss corporation's stock, including preferred stock that is described in § 1504(a)(4), is taken into account.[75]

The IRS publishes monthly revenue rulings that set forth the § 382 long-term tax-exempt rate for the next calendar month. That rate is the average market yield for long-term U.S. Treasury obligations adjusted to reflect the difference in yield between taxable and tax-exempt securities. The long-term tax-exempt rate applicable to any month for purposes of determining the § 382 limitation is the highest such rate in effect for any month during the three-month period ending with the month in which the change date occurred.

For the purpose of determining the § 382 limitation for a loss corporation, the value of an old loss corporation immediately before the ownership change will be reduced if a redemption of the corporation's stock (or other corporate contraction) occurs in connection with the ownership change regardless of whether the redemption or other corporate contraction occurs before or after the ownership change took place.[76] The value of the old loss corporation will reflect the redemption or other corporate contraction; for example, in the case of a redemption, the value of the corporation is determined by valuing only the shares of stock that were not redeemed.

In an effort to minimize the impact of the § 382 limitation, parties to a change might arrange to contribute a substantial amount of capital to the loss corporation shortly before the ownership change takes place. Such a contribution might be made to increase the value of the loss corporation's stock and so increase the amount of the § 382 limitation. A contribution, however, will not be taken into account in valuing the corporation's stock if a principal purpose of the contribution was to increase the § 382 limitation.[77] The statute provides that, except as regulations may provide otherwise, a contribution made to a loss corporation during the two-year period ending on the change date will be conclusively presumed to be part

---

[74]   § 382(b)(1).
[75]   § 382(e)(1).
[76]   § 382(e)(2).
[77]   § 382(*l*)(1).

of a plan to avoid the § 382 limitation and so will not be taken into account.[78]

Despite the statutory irrebuttable presumption mentioned above for contributions made within two years before the change date, it was the intent of Congress that Treasury issue regulations that except from the irrebuttable presumption certain contributions that occur in circumstances that strongly negate the likelihood of an avoidance purpose.[79] The following examples of such contributions that should not be excluded from the corporation's value were listed: contributions made on the formation of a corporation (not accompanied by the incorporation of assets with built-in losses), contributions made before the first year in which there was a pre-change loss, and contributions that were needed to continue the basic operations of the corporation's business.[80] While the Treasury for more than 22 years did not issue regulations, the Service published Notice 2008–78, in which it stated its intention, and that of Treasury, to issue regulations that effectively negate the statutory irrebuttable presumption. The Notice also sets forth safe harbors in which contributions under defined circumstances will not be treated as part of a plan. Taxpayers may rely on Notice 2008–78 until additional guidance is promulgated.

The statute also calls for an adjustment to the value of the old loss corporation if one-third or more of the assets of the new loss corporation, determined immediately after the ownership change, are "nonbusiness assets." In that case, the value of the old loss corporation is reduced by the excess (if any) of the value of its nonbusiness assets (immediately prior to the ownership change) over the nonbusiness assets' share of indebtedness for which the old loss corporation was liable at that time.[81] The nonbusiness assets' share of liabilities is determined by allocating the old loss corporation's liabilities among its assets according to their relative values.[82] A "nonbusiness asset" is an asset that is held for investment, and the term includes cash and marketable stocks and securities.

The § 382 limitation is a ceiling on the amount of pre-change losses that can be used to offset taxable income of a new loss corporation in a post-change year and on the amount of pre-change credits that can be used. If there were no pre-change credits, and if the § 382 limitation for a post-change year exceeds the amount of pre-change losses that were utilized in that year to offset taxable income,

---

[78]   § 382(*l*)(1)(B).

[79]   Conference Report for the Tax Reform Act of 1986 at II–189.

[80]   Id.

[81]   § 382(*l*)(4).

[82]   § 382(*l*)(4)(D).

the excess is carried over to the next post-change year and increases the amount of § 382 limitation for that year.[83]

The § 382 limitation operates only after applying other statutory limitations on deductibility.[84] Thus, the limitation applies only to pre-change losses that would be allowable if not barred by § 382 or § 383.

¶ 10.14   CONTINUITY OF BUSINESS REQUIREMENT

If the new loss corporation fails to continue the business enterprise of an old loss corporation for at least two years after the change date, then none of the pre-change losses of the old loss corporation can be utilized in any post-change year, except that the pre-change losses can be applied to offset gain recognized because of a § 338 election and certain recognized built-in gain.[85] The conditions that must be met to satisfy the continuity of business enterprise requirement are the same as those established by Treas. Reg. § 1.368–1(d) as the conditions for satisfying the reorganization requirement of continuity of business enterprise.[86] In general, this requires that the new loss corporation either continue the old loss corporation's historic business or use a significant portion of the old loss corporation's historic assets in a business.

¶ 10.15   INSOLVENT CORPORATIONS

Since the § 382 limitation is determined by multiplying a rate times the value of a loss corporation's stock, the amount allowable for an insolvent corporation that underwent an ownership change could be zero since the value of its stock is often zero or nearly so. Congress did not wish to prevent a reorganized insolvent corporation from utilizing its pre-change losses unless it was necessary to do so to prevent an abusive use of the insolvent's tax attributes. In most cases, much of the economic impact of an insolvent corporation's losses and other tax attributes will have been borne by its creditors in addition to its shareholders. Congress therefore thought it appropriate to provide some room for a corporation emerging from insolvency proceedings to derive some benefit from its prior tax attributes in order to allow for at least partial recovery by the creditors of that corporation. Consequently, § 382 includes special

---

[83]   § 382(b)(2).

[84]   Treas. Reg. § 1.383–1(d)(3).

[85]   § 382(c).

[86]   See ¶ 9.03.2.

provisions that can apply to ownership changes that take place in the context of a G reorganization or other Title 11 proceeding.[87]

¶ 10.16 RECOGNIZED BUILT-IN GAINS AND LOSSES

In general, a built-in gain or loss refers to an item of gain, income, loss, or deduction that is recognized by a loss corporation within five years after an ownership change occurred, but only to the extent that the item is attributable to economic changes that took place prior to the change date. Section 382(h) provides special treatment for such items. In certain circumstances, a carryover pre-change loss can offset a recognized built-in gain without using any of the § 382 limitation on the amount of pre-change losses that can be deducted in a post-change year. In certain other circumstances, explained below, a recognized built-in loss will be included in the loss corporation's pre-change losses and therefore subjected to the § 382 limitation on deductibility. Before examining how built-in gains and losses are treated, it will be useful to understand the meaning of the following terms.

Recognition period. The recognition period with respect to any ownership change is the five-year period beginning on the change date.[88] Except for income reported on the installment method, only income, gains, losses, and deductions recognized during the recognition period can qualify as a recognized built-in gain or loss.

Recognition period taxable year. A recognition period taxable year is any taxable year any portion of which is in the recognition period.[89]

Recognized built-in gain. Income or gain that is recognized by a new loss corporation during the recognition period will constitute a "recognized built-in gain" in either of the following two circumstances and to the extent indicated:

(1) If the gain is derived from the disposition of an asset that the old loss corporation had held at the change date, the gain recognized on that disposition will constitute a recognized built-in gain to the extent that the value of the asset at the change date exceeded the old loss corporation's basis in the asset at that time.[90]

---

[87]   See § 382(*l*)(5), (6). Those provisions are an extensive topic in themselves and a detailed analysis of them is outside the intended scope of this chapter.

[88]   § 382(h)(7)(A).

[89]   § 382(h)(7)(B).

[90]   § 382(h)(2)(A).

(2)   Any item of income that is recognized during the recognition period and that is attributable to a time before the change date is treated as a recognized built-in gain.[91] Clearly, only income items that are attributable to an old loss corporation should be included in the recognized built-in gains, but the statutory language is not as explicit on this issue as it might be. An example of a built-in income item is the collection of an account receivable that had been earned by a corporation on the cash method.

Since the presence of a recognized built-in gain can have favorable tax consequences, a gain that is recognized during the recognition period is presumed not to be a built-in gain. To qualify a gain as a recognized built-in gain, the new loss corporation has the burden of establishing the extent to which the gain is attributable to appreciation of the asset that existed at the change date. For example, on recognizing a gain from the sale of an asset during the recognition period, to obtain recognized built-in gain treatment, the new loss corporation has the burden of establishing that the asset had been held by the old loss corporation at the change date, and the extent to which the value of the asset at the change date exceeded the old loss corporation's basis in it.[92]

Recognized built-in loss. A loss or deduction that is recognized by or allowable to a new loss corporation during the recognition period will constitute a "recognized built-in loss" in either of the following two circumstances and to the extent indicated:

(1)   If the loss is derived from the disposition of an asset that the old loss corporation had held at the change date, the loss recognized on that disposition will constitute a recognized built-in loss to the extent that the old loss corporation's basis in the asset at the change date exceeded the value of the asset at that time.[93]

---

[91]   § 382(h)(6)(A).

[92]   § 382(h)(2)(A). Since the burden of proof is placed on the corporation by a statutory provision in the Code, the general burden-shifting rule of § 7491 is inapplicable. § 7491(a)(3).

[93]   § 382(h)(2)(B).

(2)   Any deduction that is allowable during the recognition period and that is attributable to a time before the change date is treated as a recognized built-in loss.[94]

Since the tax consequence of having a recognized built-in loss is unfavorable, it is presumed that any loss that is recognized or cost recovery deduction that is allowable in the recognition period is a recognized built-in loss. For the new loss corporation to avoid that treatment for any part of a loss or cost recovery deduction that is recognized or allowable during the recognition period, the new loss corporation must demonstrate that all or part of the loss or deduction is not attributable to the period prior to the change date. The burden of proof is on the taxpayer.[95]

Net unrealized built-in gain or loss. With respect to an old loss corporation, the net unrealized built-in gain is the excess of the fair market value of the corporation's assets immediately before an ownership change over the aggregate adjusted basis that the corporation had in its assets at that time. With respect to an old loss corporation, the net unrealized built-in loss is the excess of the aggregate basis that the corporation had in its assets immediately before an ownership change over the fair market value of those assets at that time.[96] If an item of income or deduction of the new loss corporation would be treated as a recognized built-in gain or loss if taken into account or allowable during the recognition period, the old corporation's net unrealized built-in gain or loss will be adjusted to take that item into account.[97]

If a corporation's net unrealized gain or loss does not exceed a threshold figure, it is treated as zero, with the result that § 382 will not apply to built-in gains or losses that are recognized during the recognition period. The threshold figure is the lesser of (1) 15% of the fair market value of the old loss corporation's assets immediately before the ownership change, or (2) $10,000,000.[98] For purposes of determining whether an old loss corporation's net unrealized gain or loss exceeds the first of the threshold

---

[94]   § 382(h)(6)(B).

[95]   § 382(h)(2)(B). Since the burden of proof is placed on the corporation by a statutory provision in the Code, the general burden-shifting rule of § 7491 is inapplicable. § 7491(a)(3).

[96]   § 382(h)(3)(A).

[97]   § 382(h)(6)(C).

[98]   § 382(h)(3)(B).

alternatives (i.e., exceeds 15% of the fair market value of the corporation's assets), the calculation disregards cash, cash items, and any marketable security that has a value that does not substantially differ from its basis.[99]

Treatment of recognized built-in loss. If the old loss corporation had a net unrealized built-in loss, a recognized built-in loss of the new loss corporation for any recognition period taxable year is treated as a pre-change loss and is subjected to the § 382 limitation on deductibility. However, the aggregate amount of recognized built-in losses that are treated as pre-change losses cannot exceed the net unrealized built-in loss of the old loss corporation. Thus, the amount of a recognized built-in loss that is treated as a pre-change loss in any year of the recognition period cannot exceed the difference between the old loss corporation's net unrealized built-in loss and the recognized built-in losses of the new corporation for prior taxable years.[100]

If the deduction for a portion of a recognized built-in loss for a taxable year is denied because of the § 382 limitation, the disallowed portion is carried over to the next year in the same manner as a net operating loss or a capital loss (as the case may be), and it is subjected to the § 382 limitation on pre-change losses in the next year.[101]

Treatment of recognized built-in gains. If the old loss corporation had a net unrealized built-in gain, the § 382 limitation for any recognition period taxable year is increased by the recognized built-in gains for such year. The effect of this provision is to permit pre-change losses to offset recognized built-in gains without using any of the § 382 limitation on the deductibility of such losses. However, the aggregate amount of recognized built-in gains that can qualify for this treatment cannot exceed the net unrealized built-in gain of the old loss corporation. Thus, the increase to a new loss corporation's § 382 limitation for a recognition period taxable year that is caused by a recognized built-in gain cannot exceed the difference between the old loss corporation's net unrealized built-in gain and the recognized built-in gains for prior years.[102]

---

[99] § 382(h)(3)(B)(ii).
[100] § 382(h)(1)(B).
[101] § 382(h)(4).
[102] § 382(h)(1)(A).

¶ 10.17   THE § 383 LIMITATION ON CARRYOVERS OF NET CAPITAL LOSSES AND OF CERTAIN TAX CREDITS

Section 383 imposes a limitation on the amount of an old loss corporation's net capital loss incurred prior to an ownership change that can be carried over and deducted in a post-change year. Section 383 also limits the amount of an old loss corporation's foreign tax credits, general business credits, and minimum tax credits that arose prior to an ownership change and can be carried over and utilized in a post-change year to reduce the tax liability of a new loss corporation. Section 383 utilizes the same concepts and terminology employed by § 382 and operates in essentially the same manner as does § 382.[103]

¶ 10.18   LIMITATION ON OFFSETTING PREACQUISITION LOSSES AND CREDITS OF ONE CORPORATION AGAINST ANOTHER'S BUILT-IN GAINS

While §§ 382 and 383 limit the use of pre-change losses and credits, Congress concluded that those provisions do not adequately deal with one area of trafficking in tax losses—namely, the acquisition of the stock or assets of a corporation in order to offset the built-in and carryover losses, deductions, and credits of one corporation against the built-in gains of another corporation. In 1987, Congress adopted § 384 and the purpose of that provision is to prevent for a five-year period (not just limit the amount of the annual tax benefit as in §§ 382 and 383) the use of the built-in and carryover losses, deductions, and credits of one corporate party to an acquisitive reorganization or stock acquisition from offsetting a recognized built-in gain (or the tax on a built-in gain) of another corporate party to that reorganization or stock acquisition.[104]

Much of the terminology that is employed in § 384 has the same meaning that those terms have when used in § 382. The reader can refer to the earlier discussion in this chapter of § 382 (especially the discussion of built-in gains and losses) for the meaning of those terms. We will indicate when terms used in § 384 are not derived from § 382.

---

[103]   For a detailed discussion of § 383, see Corporate Income Taxation Hornbook at pp. 628–630.

[104]   See H.R. Rep. No. 391, 100th Cong., 1st Sess. 1093–94 (1987).

Section 384 applies only when either:

(1)   one corporation acquires directly (or through one or more corporations) control of another corporation; or

(2)   a corporation acquires the assets of another corporation in an "A," "C," or "D" reorganization,

and either of the corporations is a "gain corporation."[105] A "gain corporation" is a corporation with a net unrealized built-in gain.[106] "Control" of a corporation means ownership of its stock that possesses at least 80% of both the voting power and the value of its outstanding stock (and nonvoting preferred stock that is described in § 1504(a)(4) is not taken into account in determining the percentage of value of stock held by a corporation).[107]

If the requisite acquisition of control of a corporation or of a corporation's assets takes place, then the income in a recognition period taxable year[108] that is attributable to recognized built-in gains cannot be offset by a preacquisition loss; but this restriction does not apply to a preacquisition loss of the gain corporation.[109] The effect of this provision is to prevent a deduction that is attributable to the preacquisition period of one corporation from being taken when the only income that it could offset is the recognized built-in gain of a different corporation that is a gain corporation. This limitation applies regardless of whether the gain corporation is the target or the acquiring corporation.

A preacquisition loss that is prevented from being used because of § 384 can be carried forward to the next year.[110]

Section 384 does not apply if the target and the acquiring corporation, in either a stock or an asset acquisition, were members of the same "controlled group" at all times during the five-year period ending on the "acquisition date."[111] The "acquisition date" is the date on which either the acquisition of control occurred or the assets of the target were transferred.[112] A "controlled group" refers to a group of corporations (defined in § 1563) that are either a chain of corporations with a common parent, two or more corporations a specified percentage of whose stock is owned by five or fewer persons,

---

[105]   § 384(a).

[106]   § 384(c)(4). The term "net unrealized built-in gain" is defined in § 382(h)(3)(A) and is explained in ¶ 10.16. § 384(c)(8).

[107]   § 384(c)(5).

[108]   That term is defined in § 382(h)(7)(B) and is discussed in ¶ 10.16.

[109]   § 384(a).

[110]   § 384(e)(1).

[111]   § 384(b)(1).

[112]   § 384(c)(2).

or a combination of two such groups. While one of the requirements of § 1563 for the inclusion of a corporation in a controlled group is that at least 80% of either the voting power or the value of the corporation's outstanding stock be held by one or more other corporations in the chain or by the five or fewer persons who hold stock in the brother-sister corporations, § 384 substitutes a "more than 50%" requirement for the "at least 80%" requirement and requires that the more than 50% test be met for both voting power and value.[113]

The following definitions are important to understanding how § 384 operates.

Preacquisition loss. This term refers to all of the following:

(1) a net operating loss carryforward to the taxable year that includes the acquisition date;

(2) a net operating loss for the taxable year that includes the acquisition date to the extent that it is attributable to the period in that year that ends on the acquisition date; unless the regulations permit another method (such as the interim closing method), the net operating loss for such a year is allocated ratably on a daily basis; and

(3) if the corporation had a net unrealized built-in loss, the term includes any recognized built-in loss.[114]

Recognized built-in gain. This term includes:

(1) any gain recognized during the recognition period on the disposition of an asset except to the extent that the corporation can establish either that (a) the asset was not held by the gain corporation on the acquisition date (in which event none of the gain is treated as a recognized built-in gain), or (b) the gain exceeds the difference between the fair market value of the asset on the acquisition date and the adjusted basis of the asset on that date (in which event only the excess gain is excluded from recognized built-in gain),

(2) an item of income that is attributable to periods before the acquisition date.

There is a ceiling on the amount of recognized built-in gain that a corporation can have in a recognition period taxable year. The amount cannot exceed the difference between the

---

[113] § 384(b)(2).
[114] § 384(c)(3).

gain corporation's net unrealized built-in gain and the amount of recognized built-in gain for prior years that would have been offset by preacquisition losses if § 384 had not prevented it.[115] In other words, the aggregate amount of preacquisition losses that are not permitted by § 384 to be deducted cannot exceed the net unrealized built-in gain of the gain corporation. To the extent that a corporation's gain exceeds the ceiling described above, it is not treated as a recognized built-in gain.

Note the contrast between the approaches that § 382 and § 384 take in determining whether gain from the disposition of an asset is recognized built-in gain. On the one hand, § 382 does not treat a gain from the disposition of an asset as a recognized built-in gain unless the corporation demonstrates that it is. A corporation's recognized built-in gains are beneficial to the taxpayer in § 382, and so, for purposes of that section, the burden is on the corporation to demonstrate the extent to which it has one. On the other hand, the presence of a recognized built-in gain causes unfavorable consequences to a taxpayer under § 384. Therefore, for purposes of that provision, the gain recognized on the disposition of an asset is presumed to be a recognized built-in gain, and the corporation has the burden of demonstrating that it is not.[116]

In the following example, G is a gain corporation, and L is not. Prior to the acquisition date, none of the corporations is a member of an affiliated group or of a controlled group. All losses are deductible unless barred by § 384.

Ex. L acquired 90% of the outstanding stock of G for cash in Year One. For Year Two, G and L file a consolidated return. In Year Two, G had $200,000 of taxable income of which $160,000 was a recognized built-in gain. Without taking into account its preacquisition losses, in Year Two, L had taxable income of $35,000. In that year, L also had $325,000 of preacquisition losses, and §§ 382 and 383 did not prevent the deduction of those losses. Section 384 does not prevent the deduction of those preacquisition losses to the extent of the income of L ($35,000) and the income of G that does not constitute a recognized built-in gain ($40,000). Thus, $75,000 of L's preacquisition loss is deductible, and the remaining $250,000 is carried over to the

---

[115]   § 384(c)(1)(C).
[116]   § 384(c)(1)(A).

next year where it will be subject to the same limitation. The $160,000 of recognized built-in gain will be taxed.

Section 384 limitations on preacquisition losses also apply to built-in capital losses and to the carryover of the same tax credits that are subject to § 383.[117] The carryover credits that are limited by § 384 are precluded from being used to reduce a tax liability that is attributable to recognized built-in gains.

¶ 10.19   ACQUISITIONS MADE TO EVADE OR AVOID INCOME TAX—§ 269

Section 269 provides for the disallowance, in the discretion of the Treasury, of certain tax benefits, in whole or in part, when an acquisition of control of a corporation or of its assets is one of the two types of acquisitions described in § 269(a), but only if the acquisition is made for the principal purpose of tax evasion or avoidance. The phrase refers to an evasion or avoidance of the income tax by securing the benefit of a deduction, credit, or other allowance that such person could not enjoy if the acquisition had not taken place.[118]

The initial determination of whether § 269 is applicable rests on a two-step analysis. The first step is to determine whether there has been an acquisition of a type described in § 269(a). The resolution of this classification step turns on objective standards. The two listed acquisitions are acquisition of control of a corporation or a tax-free acquisition of a corporation's assets. If a requisite acquisition did not take place, § 269 does not apply, and there is no reason to consider the issue any further. On the other hand, if a § 269(a) acquisition did take place, it becomes necessary to take the second step and determine whether the principal purpose of the acquisition was the evasion or avoidance of the federal income tax by securing a tax benefit that the parties would not otherwise enjoy. This latter determination is based, at least partly, on a subjective standard, but objective facts are utilized in making that subjective determination. The determination of the purposes for making an acquisition requires a "scrutiny of the entire circumstances in which the transaction or course of conduct occurred, in connection with the tax result claimed to arise therefrom."[119]

---

[117]   § 384(d).

[118]   Treas. Reg. § 1.269–1(b), 3(a).

[119]   Treas. Reg. § 1.269–3(a). In this regard, a substantial body of law has developed concerning the implications of the requirement that the tax benefit in question must be one that the taxpayer would not "otherwise enjoy" in the absence of the transaction that triggered the applicability of § 269. In appropriate factual circumstances, this requirement serves as a significant limitation on the Service's ability to successfully assert § 269. See Cromwell v. Commissioner, 43 T.C. 313 (1964), acq. 1965–2 C.B. 4, and Corporate Income Taxation Hornbook at pp. 641–643.

If both steps are satisfied, then and only then does the Commissioner have the authority to disallow the tax benefit in question.

Consequences of the application of § 269. If the requisite acquisition and tainted purpose are found to exist, the Service, in its discretion, may disallow all or any part of the deduction, credit, or other allowance that was the object of the acquisition.[120] Instead of denying a deduction, credit, or other allowance, the Service can distribute, apportion, or allocate among the corporations or properties involved all or part of gross income, deductions, credits, or other allowances and permit the use thereof only to the extent that the Service determines will not result in the federal income tax evasion or avoidance for which the acquisition was made.[121]

Overlap with §§ 382–384. Section 269 can apply to a transaction that also is subject to §§ 382, 383, or 384. They are not mutually exclusive. Thus, § 269 can be utilized by the Service to disallow a deduction or credit that otherwise would have been allowed by §§ 382–384. However, the fact that limitations are imposed by §§ 382–384 on the use of certain tax attributes is a factor to be taken into account in determining whether, in fact, the principal purpose of an acquisition was the evasion or avoidance of federal income tax.[122]

C. NON-STATUTORY LIMITATION ON SURVIVAL OF TAX ATTRIBUTES

¶ 10.20   THE DE FACTO DISSOLUTION DOCTRINE

To a substantial degree, judicial doctrines relating to the survival of tax attributes have been supplanted by the various Code provisions that have been enacted to address that issue. There is, however, one remaining non-statutory doctrine that relates almost exclusively to the retention of tax attributes and can serve to destroy such attributes despite strict adherence to both § 382 and § 269. That is the doctrine of de facto dissolution, and we will close this review of the tax principles that govern the survival of corporate tax attributes with a brief discussion of that judicial doctrine.

The de facto dissolution doctrine holds that a corporation can remain in existence for non-tax purposes with the same historical shareholders and yet still be treated for tax purposes as though it had dissolved and ceased to exist because of the absence of any

---

[120]   § 269(a), (c).

[121]   § 269(c); Treas. Reg. § 1.269–4.

[122]   Treas. Reg. § 1.269–7.

substantial assets and the lack of any significant business activity. The typical fact pattern involves a corporation that conducts business over a number of years and creates tax attributes that involve either a significant income history or a series of net operating loss, capital loss, or credit carryforwards potentially usable in future years. Then the corporation disposes of all or nearly all of its assets, ceases its business activity, and thereupon becomes "a corporation in name and semblance only, without corporate substance and serving no real corporate purpose," even though the corporation has not formally dissolved or liquidated for purposes of state law.[123]

In those circumstances, the Service has held in Rev. Rul. 61–191 that the corporation would be treated as having de facto dissolved for tax purposes and thus having ceased to exist as a corporation in the eyes of the tax law.[124] The ruling reviews a series of judicial decisions that support its position. As a consequence, if the shareholders were in a later year to reinvigorate the corporation by conveying assets to it and commencing business operations, any income earned by the corporation could not be offset by the carryforward of net operating losses or other tax attributes relating to its prior activity. All such attributes are deemed to have disappeared when the corporation de facto dissolved. By the same token, any losses or excess credits that the corporation might generate in its new activity could not be carried back against income and tax that had been generated in its prior activity during earlier taxable years. In essence, the reinvigoration of the corporation is treated for tax purposes as if a new corporation had been created without the historic tax attributes of the prior corporation.

Even though the corporation has remained in existence as a corporate shell, its tax attributes are deemed to disappear at that point in time when it has ceased to hold significant assets or to conduct significant business activity. As a result, the shareholders cannot just keep a loss corporation "on the shelf" to use as a vehicle to conduct future activity and expect to enjoy any accumulated tax attributes against future income and tax that may later be generated by a new business conducted by the corporation. If such a corporation has significant and potentially valuable tax attributes and the shareholders want to preserve the option to use those attributes in the future, it will be necessary to maintain a significant amount of assets and corporate activity relating to those assets in the corporation during the interim period.

---

[123]   Rev. Rul. 61–191.
[124]   Id.

Chapter Eleven

S CORPORATIONS

Analysis

Para.

11.01   Small Businesses—Introduction

11.02   Subchapter S—Introduction

11.03   Application of Subchapter C to S Corporations

11.04   Eligibility, in General

11.05   Qualified Subchapter S Subsidiary ("QSSS" or "QSub")

11.06   Trusts as Shareholders

11.07   One Class of Stock Requirement, in General

11.08   Debt as a Second Class of Stock

11.09   Call Options and Warrants as a Second Class of Stock

11.10   Buy-Sell Arrangements

11.11   Difference in Amounts or Timing of Actual Distributions

11.12   Election

11.13   Taxable Year

11.14   Taxation of the S Corporation

11.15   Earnings and Profits

11.16   Pass-Through of Tax Items, in General

11.17   Shareholder's Basis—Adjustments

11.18   Order of Adjustments to Shareholder's Basis

11.19   Limitations on Deductions, in General

11.20   At Risk and Passive Activity Loss Limitations

11.21   Distributions to Shareholders—No Earnings and Profits

11.22   Distributions to Shareholders—Accumulated Adjustments Account (AAA)

11.23   Distributions to Shareholders of Property

11.24   Distributions to Shareholders During Post-Termination Transition Period

11.25   Termination of S Election—Revocation

11.26   Termination of S Election—Cessation of Qualification

11.27   Termination of S Election—Passive Investment Income

11.28   New S Election After Termination

11.29   S Termination Year

11.30   Taxation of Passive Investment Income

11.31   Purpose and Operation of § 1374

11.32   LIFO Recapture Amount
11.33   Qualified Business Income Deduction

¶ 11.01   SMALL BUSINESSES— INTRODUCTION

A consequence of taxing a corporation separately from its shareholders and of imposing a double tax on corporate earnings distributed to the shareholders is that the choice of whether to conduct business in the corporate form, in the partnership form, or as a sole proprietorship will be influenced by the differences in the federal income tax obligations applied to those business forms. The influence of tax considerations in choosing a business form is most pronounced in small, closely held business ventures since the nontax reasons for incorporating are less significant to small operations than to the large, publicly held ventures. In 1958, responding to a concern for stimulating small business ventures, Congress adopted several provisions to mitigate (but not to eliminate) the differences in tax treatment accorded to corporations on the one hand and to partnerships and sole proprietorships on the other. The most important of these provisions was the addition to the Code of Subchapter S. The provisions of Subchapter S were substantially altered by the adoption of the Subchapter S Revision Act of 1982 and by the Small Business Job Protection Act of 1996 and were amended again, on a modest scale, by other legislation enacted from time to time. Subchapter S permits certain closely held corporations ("S corporations") to elect not to be taxed on most or all of their income and, instead, to have their income, deductions, and credits allocated to their shareholders.

S corporations are a popular form of conducting business, especially for small business operations. They combine the advantages of a corporate structure, including access to the nonrecognition tax provisions that apply to certain combinations of corporate entities, with the pass-through of tax attributes that partnerships provide. With the rise of the Limited Liability Company (LLC) form of conducting business, many predicted that the use of S corporations would shrink as most businesses would choose the LLC form. Contrary to those expectations, while the LLC has proved a popular vehicle, the use of S corporations has continued to thrive. In 2006, over 3.8 million returns were filed by S corporations.

¶ 11.02   SUBCHAPTER S—INTRODUCTION

The reference to Subchapter S is to Subchapter S of Chapter 1 of Subtitle A of Title 26 of the United States Code. The provisions of Subchapter S, which are set forth in §§ 1361–1379, apply to a corporation only if both the corporation and all of its shareholders make a valid election, and then only if the corporation qualifies for that treatment.[1]

A corporation for which a valid election for Subchapter S treatment is effective is commonly referred to as an "S corporation." Any corporation that is not an S corporation is referred to as a "C corporation."[2] While many of the provisions of Subchapter C also apply to S corporations, the latter are subject to Subchapter S provisions as well. The following is a very general description of the workings of Subchapter S. A more detailed explanation is set forth in subsequent sections of this chapter.

Subject to four exceptions,[3] one of which is virtually obsolete, a corporation for which a valid Subchapter S election has been made will pay no federal income tax. Instead of taxing an S corporation, the tax items of an S corporation (such as long-term and short-term capital gains and losses, section 1231 gains and losses, ordinary income and losses, tax-exempt income, charitable contributions, deductions, and credits) are passed through and allocated among the shareholders proportionately to their stock holdings; and the shareholders report those allocated items as if they were recognized directly by them. As we will see, an S corporation is permitted to have only one class of stock; and so the proportional allocation of the corporation's tax items is easy to calculate.

The purpose of Subchapter S is to prevent the double taxation of corporate income for certain qualified and electing corporations. In general, the shareholders will increase their basis in their corporate stock for income that passes through to them, and they will reduce their basis in the corporation's stock for losses or deductions that pass through to them. Since the corporation's income is taxed to its shareholders at the end of the corporation's taxable year, even when not distributed to the shareholders, an S corporation's actual distribution to a shareholder generally does not cause the shareholder to recognize income. Instead, the shareholder reduces his basis in his corporate stock. If the distribution exceeds the

---

[1]   The S corporation eligibility requirements are described in ¶ 11.04.
[2]   § 1361(a).
[3]   The four exceptions are discussed in ¶ 11.14.

shareholder's basis, the excess is treated as a gain from the sale of the stock.[4]

In effect, a shareholder's basis in his stock is increased when the corporation earns income, and then is reduced when the income is distributed to the shareholder. This treatment assures that the shareholder will be taxed only once on the corporation's income. As explained in ¶ 11.22, however, there can be different consequences to a distribution when the S corporation has *e and p*. If an S corporation has *e and p*, a distribution to a shareholder can be dividend income, but will not necessarily be so.

An S corporation is required to file a tax return showing its items of income, deductions and credits and allocating them among its shareholders. The return is due to be filed by the 15th day of the third month after the close of the corporation's taxable year.[5]

The 2017 Tax Cuts and Jobs Act added § 199A to the Code to allow a deduction for a percentage of certain business income. For Subchapter S corporations, the deduction is allowed to the shareholders of the S corporation for a percentage (typically 20%) of their share of the corporation's qualified business income. The provision granting the deduction is subject to a sunset provision and is scheduled to expire in 2025. The Congressional purpose for adopting this deduction is effectively to reduce the tax rate applicable to certain noncorporate business income to approximately what the rate would be if the income were earned by a C corporation.[6] The provision is sometimes referred to as a pass-through deduction even though it also applies to the income of a sole proprietorship. The provision for the deduction is discussed in ¶ 11.33.

¶ 11.03   APPLICATION OF SUBCHAPTER C TO S CORPORATIONS

Unless provided otherwise in the Code or inconsistent with the terms of Subchapter S, the provisions of Subchapter C are applied to an S corporation in the same manner as they apply to any other corporation.[7] However, there are numerous differences provided in the Code. For example, subject to a number of exceptions, the taxable income of an S corporation is computed in the same manner as is applied to individuals.[8] Thus, the dividend-received deduction provided by § 243(a) for dividends received by shareholders that are

[4]   § 1368(b).
[5]   § 6072(b).
[6]   A C corporation is a corporation other than an S corporation.
[7]   § 1371(a).
[8]   § 1363(b).

themselves corporations is not available to S corporations. Of the numerous statutory provisions that treat S corporations differently from C corporations, some treat an S corporation in the same manner as an individual; some treat it as a partnership; and some treat it as a so-called "pass-thru" entity.[9]

There are numerous examples in which the provisions of Subchapter C have been applied to S corporations. Thus, the reorganization provisions (including nonrecognition of gain or loss) apply to S corporations.[10] Also, in TAM 9245004, reversing his prior position, the Commissioner held that an S corporation qualifies to make a valid § 338 election for a target whose stock the S corporation had acquired in a qualified stock purchase. In that TAM, the Commissioner also ruled that the S corporation's subsequent liquidation of the target qualified as a § 332 liquidation.

Considerable care should be taken in determining how other Code provisions apply to S corporations. One illustration is the operation of the stock attribution rules of § 318. For purposes of attributing stock that is held by an S corporation to its shareholders or vice versa, § 318(a)(5)(E) treats the S corporation as a partnership and treats its shareholders as partners. Consequently, attribution to or from a shareholder of an S corporation is not subject to the 50 percent stock holding requirement that is applied to C corporations and their shareholders by § 318(a)(2)(C), (3)(C). However, for other purposes, § 318(a)(5)(E) treats an S corporation as a corporation. So, the outstanding stock of an S corporation is subject to the § 318 stock attribution rules, whereas an interest in a partnership is not.

¶ 11.04   ELIGIBILITY, IN GENERAL

To qualify for Subchapter S treatment, an electing corporation must satisfy the requirements that are set forth in § 1361. A corporation that qualifies to elect Subchapter S treatment is referred to as a "small business corporation." Note that while a "small business corporation" is one that meets the qualifications to make a Subchapter S election, it will not be an S corporation unless a valid election is made. The "small" in that term refers to the number of shareholders that an S corporation is permitted to have; there are no limitations on the size of an S corporation's net worth or on the amount of its income. Under § 1361(b), a corporation must satisfy the following requirements to be a "small business corporation":

(1)   It must be a domestic corporation.

---

[9]   See, e.g., §§ 1372(a), 1373(a), 267(e)(2), 67(c), Temp. Reg. § 1.67–2T(g)(1)(iii).

[10]   GCM 39768.

(2) It must not be one of four types of corporations that are declared to be ineligible for Subchapter S treatment by § 1361(b)(2). An example of an "ineligible corporation" is an insurance company that is subject to tax under Subchapter L.

(3) It must not have a nonresident alien as a shareholder.

(4) It must not have more than one class of stock.

(5) It must not have a shareholder who is not an individual, an estate, a type of trust described in § 1361(c)(2) or (d), or a tax exempt organization described in § 1361(c)(6). The types of trusts that are permitted to be shareholders of an S corporation are described in ¶ 11.06. The types of "estates" that are permitted to hold stock in an S corporation are a decedent's estate and the estate of a bankrupt individual. If the corporation's stock is held by the estate of a decedent, it is the estate that is treated as the shareholder, and not the beneficiaries of the estate.[11] Thus, the estate counts as one shareholder, and a beneficiary of the estate can be a person who is not qualified to hold an S corporation's stock. In contrast, a trust typically is not treated as the shareholder.

An S corporation is permitted to be a subsidiary of another S corporation if certain conditions are satisfied. Such a subsidiary is referred to as a "Qualified Subchapter S Subsidiary" (QSSS), which is often referred to in practice and in the regulations as a "QSub." In all other respects, a corporation—even an S corporation—is not a permitted shareholder of an S corporation. An S corporation may be a stockholder of another corporation without disqualifying its S election.[12] In addition, while an S corporation may be a member of a partnership, its S election will be terminated if a partnership acquires any stock of the S corporation.[13]

---

[11]   Treas. Reg. § 1.1361–1(e)(1).

[12]   Section 1504(b)(8), however, prohibits an S corporation from being included in a consolidated return.

[13]   At times, reference is made in this chapter to a person (such as a C corporation) that is not permitted to hold stock in an S corporation. Of course, the person is not prohibited from holding the stock; rather, this reference means that the person's holding of stock disqualifies the corporation for Subchapter S treatment.

(6)   It must have no more than 100 shareholders.

In counting the number of shareholders, all "members of a family" and their estates are treated as one shareholder.[14] The members of a family are defined to refer to a common ancestor, all lineal descendants of that ancestor, and the spouses and former spouses of the common ancestor and the lineal descendants. The generation spread between the common ancestor and the youngest generation of the ancestor's "family" who hold stock in the corporation cannot exceed six generations.[15]

¶ 11.05   QUALIFIED SUBCHAPTER S SUBSIDIARY ("QSSS" OR "QSUB")

With one exception, an S corporation cannot have any of its stock owned by a corporation since corporations are not one of the shareholders permitted by § 1361(b)(1)(B). The one exception to that prohibition is that an S corporation can be a wholly owned subsidiary of another S corporation if the parent S corporation elects to treat the subsidiary as a qualified subchapter S subsidiary (QSSS or QSub).[16] If that election is made, the subsidiary S corporation (i.e., the QSub) is not treated as a separate corporate entity. Instead, all of the assets, liabilities, and tax items of the QSub are treated as the assets, liabilities, and tax items of the parent S corporation.[17] In essence, since the corporate identity of the QSub is ignored, the parent S corporation and the QSub are treated as a single corporation for federal tax purposes.

¶ 11.06   TRUSTS AS SHAREHOLDERS

Prior to 1976, the only permissible shareholders of S corporations were individuals and estates. Trusts were not listed as a qualified shareholder. The Tax Reform Act of 1976 amended Subchapter S to permit certain types of trusts to hold stock in an S corporation and the provisions concerning trusts were modified and expanded by amendments in subsequent years. The current provisions concerning trusts, which are set forth in § 1361(c)(2) and (d), authorize seven types of trusts to hold stock in an S corporation. If stock is held by a trust that is not one of the seven authorized types,

---

[14]   § 1361(c)(1)(A)(ii).

[15]   § 1361(c)(1)(B)(ii). This provision, along with many open questions that arise on account of it, are described in more detail in the authors' article *All in the Family: Family Members as a Single Shareholder of an S Corporation*, 116 Tax Notes 791 (Aug. 27, 2007).

[16]   § 1361(b)(3).

[17]   § 1361(b)(3)(A).

the corporation cannot qualify for Subchapter S treatment. Also, with one exception,[18] if a trust that had qualified as one of the seven authorized types ceases to qualify, a corporation in which that trust holds stock will cease to qualify for Subchapter S treatment commencing with the date that the trust no longer fits within the authorized list.

Examples of qualified trusts are:

(1) A trust *all* of the assets of which are deemed by §§ 671–678 to be owned by one individual who is a citizen or resident of the United States (i.e., by an individual who qualifies as a shareholder of an S corporation). If the assets of a trust are deemed to be owned by the grantor, the trust is sometimes called a "grantor trust." If, under § 678, a trust's assets are deemed to be owned by a third party who is not the grantor (because of powers the third party has over the income or corpus of the trust), the trust is sometimes called a "Mallinckrodt trust."

(2) Upon the death of the deemed owner of the assets of a grantor or Mallinckrodt trust, which trust had qualified to hold stock of an S corporation under (1) above, the trust will continue to qualify to hold such stock for two years after the death of the deemed owner.[19]

(3) If stock of an S corporation that was held by a deceased shareholder is transferred pursuant to the decedent's will from the decedent's estate to a trust (i.e., to a testamentary trust or to a pour over trust), the trust will be permitted to hold that stock for a two-year period beginning on the day that the stock is transferred to the trust.[20]

(4) A voting trust is permitted to hold the stock of an S corporation.[21] Each beneficiary of the voting trust is treated as a shareholder.[22]

---

[18] The exception refers to Qualified Subchapter S trusts, discussed at paragraph (6) in the text. Failure to meet the income distribution requirement for such a trust will not disqualify the S corporation's status until the beginning of the next taxable year of the corporation. § 1361(d)(3)(B) and (4)(B).

[19] § 1361(c)(2)(A)(ii).

[20] § 1361(c)(2)(A)(iii).

[21] § 1361(c)(2)(A)(iv).

[22] § 1361(c)(2)(B)(iv).

(5)   An "electing small business trust" is permitted to hold stock of an S corporation.[23] An electing small business trust is defined in § 1361(e). In general, it is a trust none of whose beneficiaries is a person other than an individual, an estate, or certain charitable organizations. To qualify, no interest in the trust can have been obtained by "purchase" (i.e., acquired with a cost basis). The election is made by the trustee.

(6)   A special type of trust referred to as a "qualified Subchapter S trust" (QSST) is permitted to hold stock of an S corporation if there is a single income beneficiary of the trust, during that person's life no distribution can be made to anyone else, all of the trust's income is distributed (or required to be distributed) to that person, and that person makes a qualifying election.[24]

Even prior to the statutory liberalization of the restrictions prohibiting a trustee's ownership of stock of an S corporation, those restrictions did not apply to a person who holds stock as a mere nominee, agent, guardian or custodian of an individual; the person on whose behalf such stock is held is treated as the shareholder.[25] So, where stock is held by a custodian for a minor under either the Uniform Gift to Minors Act or the Uniform Transfers to Minors Act, the minor (and not the custodian) is deemed to be the shareholder.[26] The consent of a minor to a Subchapter S election must be made by the minor or by a legal representative of the minor, or, if none, by a natural or adopted parent of the minor.[27]

¶ 11.07   ONE CLASS OF STOCK REQUIREMENT, IN GENERAL

An S corporation is not permitted to have more than one class of stock.[28] In 1992, Treasury adopted final regulations that make the one class of stock requirement turn exclusively on whether the "outstanding shares of stock of the corporation confer identical rights to distribution and liquidation proceeds."[29] Differences in distribution and liquidation rights of stock do not affect the one class of stock requirement unless the differences are created by a

---

[23]   § 1361(c)(2)(A)(v).

[24]   § 1361(d).

[25]   Treas. Reg. § 1.1361–1(e)(1).

[26]   Id.

[27]   Treas. Reg. § 1.1362–6(b)(2)(ii).

[28]   § 1361(b)(1)(D).

[29]   Treas. Reg. § 1.1361–1(*l*)(1).

"governing provision," which is defined at Treas. Reg. § 1.1361–1(*l*)(2). See ¶ 11.11. As to differences in voting rights, that regulation states:

> Differences in voting rights among shares of stock of a corporation are disregarded in determining whether a corporation has more than one class of stock. Thus, if all shares of stock of an S corporation have identical rights to distribution and liquidation proceeds, the corporation may have voting and nonvoting common stock, a class of stock that may vote only on certain issues, irrevocable proxy agreements, or groups of shares that differ with respect to rights to elect members of the board of directors.

¶ 11.08   DEBT AS A SECOND CLASS OF STOCK

Corporate debt may be treated as stock for many tax purposes when a debt instrument bears too many of the characteristics of equity investment. The current regulations (Treas. Reg. § 1.1361–1(*l*)(4)) set forth a general rule that for Subchapter S purposes establishes a number of safe harbors that immunize certain debt instruments from second class of stock treatment regardless of the applicability of the general rule. This regulatory provision applies to an instrument, obligation, or arrangement (other than stock) that provides some rights against the corporation (whether or not designated as a debt instrument). For convenience, hereafter we will sometimes refer to all such instruments, obligations, and arrangements as "debt instruments."

A debt instrument will not be treated as a second class of stock unless *both* of the following two conditions exist: (1) the debt instrument is treated by the general principles of federal tax law as an equity interest in the corporation or causes the holder thereof to be treated by federal tax law as a shareholder; and (2) a principal purpose of issuing the debt instrument (or entering into the arrangement) is to circumvent either the requirement that all outstanding stock of an S corporation have identical rights to distribution and liquidation proceeds or the requirement that the number of shareholders cannot exceed a specified figure.[30] Because of this second requirement, a debt instrument will not constitute a second class of stock unless a subjective principal purpose of evading a statutory requirement is found to exist. It seems unlikely that there will be many cases in which that principal purpose exists, and so most debt instruments should not cause a loss of S corporation status.

---

[30]   Treas. Reg. § 1.1361–1(*l*)(4)(ii)(A).

In addition to establishing a narrow general rule for treating a debt instrument as a second class of stock, the regulations provide a number of safe harbors that preclude second class of stock treatment regardless of the debt instrument's characterization under that general rule.[31]

In the view of the authors, the treatment of debt that was adopted in the current regulations makes sense. The policies at stake in deciding whether an S corporation's obligation should be treated as debt or equity are significantly different from those at stake in deciding how a C corporation's obligation should be treated. In the typical C corporation context, the "integrity" of the double-tax system is at issue since dividends create income for a shareholder without generating a deduction for the corporation. In the typical S corporation context, however, dividends have nothing to do with double taxation. All that should be at issue is whether the corporation's capital structure has become so complex that it either is not feasible or for some reason is inappropriate to characterize the entity as a "small business corporation"—a question that has no logical connection with whether a similar C corporation is escaping the double tax.

¶ 11.09   CALL OPTIONS AND WARRANTS AS A SECOND CLASS OF STOCK

A call option, warrant, or similar instrument that is issued by a corporation is included within the instruments or arrangements that can be classified as a second class of stock. For convenience, all of these types of instruments and arrangements are referred to collectively as "call options." The regulations have several provisions, including safe harbors, that address call options.[32]

The general principle is that a call option will not be treated as a second class of stock unless, after taking into account all the facts and circumstances (1) the call option is substantially certain to be exercised (either by the holder or by a potential transferee), and (2) the call option has a strike price (i.e., the price payable for the stock on exercise of the option) that is substantially below the fair market value of the underlying stock at the date the option was issued.[33]

---

[31]   See Treas. Reg. § 1.1361–1(*l*)(4); § 1361(c)(5).

[32]   Treas. Reg. § 1.1361–1(*l*)(4)(iii).

[33]   While that regulation does not specify the extent to which a strike price must be below the stocks' fair market value to be substantial, the example treats a strike price that is 50% of the stocks' value as substantially below that value. Treas. Reg. § 1.1361–1(*l*)(4)(v), Ex. 1.

¶ 11.10   BUY-SELL ARRANGEMENTS

Buy-sell agreements among shareholders (so-called cross-purchase buy-sell arrangements), redemption agreements, and agreements restricting the transferability of stock will not cause second class of stock treatment unless the principal purpose of the arrangement is to circumvent the one class of stock requirement *and* the agreement establishes a purchase price that is substantially above or below the fair market value of the stock at the time at which the agreement was made.[34]

¶ 11.11   DIFFERENCE IN AMOUNTS OR TIMING OF ACTUAL DISTRIBUTIONS

As noted above, a corporation is treated as having only one class of stock if all outstanding shares of the corporation's stock confer identical rights to distribution and liquidation proceeds. With only a few exceptions, the identity of rights requirement applies to the timing of distributions as well as to the amounts distributed. Differences in voting rights are ignored. The determination of whether stock possesses identical rights rests exclusively on the terms of "governing provisions." The governing provisions consist of the "corporate charter, articles of incorporation, bylaws, applicable state law, and binding agreements relating to distribution and liquidation proceeds."[35] That is an exclusive list, and only rights created by a governing provision are taken into account for this purpose.

A commercial contractual agreement such as a lease, employment agreement, or loan agreement does not constitute "a binding agreement relating to distribution and liquidation proceeds" unless a principal purpose of that agreement was to circumvent the one class of stock requirement. So, unless the facts and circumstances demonstrate that the prohibited principal purpose exists, such commercial contractual agreements will not constitute a governing provision and therefore will not cause there to be more than one class of stock.

While differences in timing or amounts of distributions (including actual, constructive, and deemed distributions) that do not occur because of a governing provision do not cause a second class of stock treatment, the regulations warn that such differences can cause other income tax consequences.[36] The regulations offer little guidance as to the nature of those potential tax consequences, other

---

[34]   Treas. Reg. § 1.1361–1(*l*)(2)(iii).
[35]   Treas. Reg. § 1.1361–1(*l*)(2)(i).
[36]   Treas. Reg. § 1.1361–1(*l*)(2)(vi), Exs. (3), (4).

than to suggest that a difference in timing might cause recharacterization of part of the distributions under § 7872 (dealing with certain loans bearing inadequate interest) or some other provision.

¶ 11.12   ELECTION

The provisions of Subchapter S apply only to corporations that have made a valid election to be an S corporation. An election is made by the corporation's filing Form 2553 together with consents signed by each person who is a shareholder on the date that the election is made.[37] A shareholder's consent must be in the form of a written statement, containing the information required by Treas. Reg. § 1.1362–6(b)(1), and signed by the shareholder under penalties of perjury. A shareholder's consent can be made either in a separate written statement or on Form 2553. Once a valid election has been made, there is no requirement that persons who subsequently become shareholders consent even when they become shareholders before the election takes effect.[38]

Note that if an S corporation's election is terminated, then, subject to a waiver by the Service, the corporation (or successor corporation) is barred for a period of five years from the date of that termination from making a new election to be an S corporation.[39] However, in certain circumstances where the termination was inadvertent, the corporation may obtain relief from that disqualification by making a request of the Commissioner under § 1362(f).

A valid election can be made at any time in the taxable year preceding the year in which the election first becomes effective. Also, a valid election that is made before the 16th day of the third month after the first day of a taxable year can make that corporation an S corporation as of the beginning of that same taxable year provided that (1) the corporation met all of the requirements of a "small business corporation" (as defined in § 1361(b)) for each day of that taxable year up to the day of the election; and (2) every person who held stock in the corporation during that taxable year but prior to the day of the election makes a timely consent to the election.[40] If the corporation fails either of those two requirements or if the election is made after the 15th day of the third month, the election will not be effective for that taxable year but will be effective for the first day of the following taxable year. However, if the only reason that the

---

[37]   § 1362(a); Treas. Reg. § 1.1362–1(a), –6(a)(2).

[38]   Treas. Reg. § 1.1362–6(b)(3)(ii), Ex. (2).

[39]   § 1362(g).

[40]   § 1362(b).

election was not effective for the beginning of the taxable year when made is that the election was not made timely, a late election will be permitted if the Commissioner determines that there was reasonable cause for the failure to make a timely election.[41] In the latter event, the Commissioner can treat the election as having been timely made for that year.

¶ 11.13 TAXABLE YEAR

An S corporation's taxable year is restricted to a calendar year unless the corporation can establish a business purpose for using a different accounting period.[42] The Revenue Act of 1987 added § 444 to the Code to permit certain entities, including S corporations, to elect a fiscal year as their taxable year in certain circumstances when that fiscal year would otherwise not be permitted. To make this election, the entity must make the payments required by § 7519; these payments essentially constitute an interest-free loan from the entity to the government, which is intended to compensate the government for the deferral in payment of the tax under the fiscal year arrangement as compared with a calendar year.

¶ 11.14 TAXATION OF THE S CORPORATION

A valid Subchapter S election does not eliminate the electing corporation as an entity for tax purposes. It does, however, relieve the corporation from federal income tax liability for most tax items. Subject to four exceptions (one of which is nearly obsolete), an S corporation is not subject to federal income taxation and instead serves as a conduit whose tax attributes are passed through to its shareholders. One of those exceptions occurs when a C corporation that uses the LIFO (last in-first out) method to account for its inventory becomes an S corporation.[43] A second occurs when an S corporation recaptures an investment credit that was taken by the corporation when it was a C corporation; in that event, the corporation (rather than its shareholders) will be liable for the recapture of the tax credit.[44] Third, in certain circumstances, all or part of an S corporation's recognized gains that are attributable to

---

[41]　§ 1362(b)(3), (5).

[42]　§ 1378(b).

[43]　§ 1363(d). While the tax on the so-called "LIFO recapture amount" is imposed on the corporation in its status as a C corporation, the tax will be paid in four equal installments beginning with the return for the last year in which it was a C corporation. Payments therefore will be made by the corporation after it attains S corporation status. The corporation's basis in its inventory will be adjusted to reflect the taxation of the LIFO recapture amount. § 1363(d)(1). See ¶ 11.32.

[44]　§ 1371(d)(2). It is this exception that is nearly obsolete because the investment credit was repealed, subject to a number of transition rules, more than twenty years ago as part of the Tax Reform Act of 1986.

appreciation that took place at a time when the corporation was a C corporation (or took place in the hands of another corporation that was a C corporation) will be taxed to the S corporation under § 1374.[45] A fourth circumstance in which a federal income tax is imposed on an S corporation is where the corporation is subjected to a tax on passive investment income under § 1375.[46]

With two exceptions, all elections affecting the computation of tax items of an S corporation are made by the corporation. For example, the choice of a method of depreciation for the depreciable assets of the corporation and the decision whether to elect nonrecognition under § 1033 for gain recognized from the involuntary conversion of the corporation's assets are to be made by the corporation. The two tax elections that are made by the shareholders (as contrasted to the corporation) are listed in § 1363(c)(2) and apply to the foreign tax credit and the tax treatment of certain mining expenditures.

¶ 11.15   EARNINGS AND PROFITS

A corporation will not accumulate any *e and p* that arise from earnings that it has in a year in which it is an S corporation.[47] There are two situations that can cause an S corporation to have accumulated *e and p*. An S corporation can have accumulated *e and p* if (1) it accumulated the *e and p* in a year when it was a C corporation, or (2) it inherited the *e and p* of another corporation that the S corporation acquired pursuant to either a reorganization or a § 332 liquidation of a controlled subsidiary corporation.

When an S corporation does possess accumulated *e and p*, its *e and p* will be reduced for its distributions to a shareholder to the extent that the distributions are treated as dividend income to the shareholder under § 1368(c)(2).[48] The corporation's *e and p* also will be adjusted because of reorganizations, stock redemptions, corporate divisions, and liquidations in the same manner as they would if the corporation were a C corporation.[49]

¶ 11.16   PASS-THROUGH OF TAX ITEMS, IN GENERAL

The taxable income of an S corporation is computed in a similar manner to the computation of a partnership's taxable income, but there are some differences. While § 1363(b) states that an S

---

[45]   See ¶ 11.31.
[46]   See ¶ 11.30.
[47]   § 1371(c)(1).
[48]   See ¶ 11.22.
[49]   § 1371(c)(2).

corporation's taxable income is computed in the same manner as an individual's, that provision and § 1366(a) divide the S corporation's income into separate categories in a manner that is similar to the division of a partnership's income; and an S corporation is denied the same deductions that are denied to a partnership by § 703(a)(2) (a partnership provision). Those items of corporate income (including tax-exempt income), losses, deductions (including charitable contributions), and credits, the separate treatment of which could affect a shareholder's liability, are separately stated and allocated among the shareholders; for convenience, those items are referred to as "separately stated items." The balance of the corporation's taxable income or loss (which is determined by excluding all of the "separately stated items") is also allocated among the shareholders; this figure is referred to as the "nonseparately computed income or loss."[50]

The pass-thru of tax items for the taxable year of an S corporation is made to each shareholder for his taxable year in which the taxable year of the S corporation ends (or the final year of a shareholder who dies or a trust or estate that terminates during the corporation's taxable year). This conduit aspect of an S corporation is sometimes referred to as a pass-thru of tax items, and that term is also used for partnerships. All of the S corporation's tax items are allocated among its shareholders on a daily basis.[51] The reason for the "one class of stock" requirement is to simplify that allocation.

Subject to two exceptions, the character of any item of the S corporation's income, loss, deduction, or credit that pass through to the shareholders is determined at the corporate level rather than by reference to the shareholders.[52] The two exceptions apply when a shareholder contributed to the S corporation either non-capital gain property or capital loss property if (and only if) the S corporation was formed or availed of for the principal purpose of selling or exchanging the property that, if sold by the shareholder, would have produced a gain or loss of a different character.

Deductions, losses, and credits that pass through to a shareholder are subject to the limitations on their deduction or application imposed by both the at risk rules of § 465 and the passive activity loss and credit limitation rules of § 469. Those limitations, discussed at ¶ 11.20, are applied to each shareholder rather than to the S corporation itself. As noted in ¶ 11.19, a deduction or loss that passes through to a shareholder can be deducted only to the extent that the shareholder has a basis in stock and indebtedness of the

---

[50]   § 1366(a).

[51]   §§ 1366(a)(1), 1377(a)(1).

[52]   Treas. Reg. § 1.1366–1(b).

corporation. There is an order of priority for the application of the several limitations on the deduction of pass-thru losses. First, the basis limitation rules are applied. Next the at risk limitations of § 465 are applied to whatever amount was allowed by the basis rules. Lastly, whatever amount has passed muster through the basis and at risk limitations then is subjected to the passive activity loss limitation rules.[53]

The various tax items of an S corporation are passed through to its shareholders, who report them as having the same characteristics as they have in the hands of the S corporation. For example, capital gains and capital losses pass through as long-term or short-term depending upon the corporation's holding period. Similarly, tax-exempt income will pass through as such, and § 1231 gains and losses pass through as such.

The deduction provided shareholders for the pass-thru of qualified business income of the S corporation is discussed in ¶ 11.33.

¶ 11.17   SHAREHOLDER'S BASIS—ADJUSTMENTS

A shareholder's basis in stock of an S corporation usually is determined under the same rules that are generally applicable to the determination of basis of other items. The most significant special treatment for the basis of the stock of an S corporation is the adjustments that are made to that basis. Under § 1367, a shareholder's basis in his stock in an S corporation is adjusted to reflect the corporation's items that have been allocated to that shareholder—e.g., his stock basis is increased by his share of the corporation's income items (including tax-exempt income); and his stock basis is reduced (but not below zero) by his share of losses, deductions, and non-capital expenses that are not deductible, and by § 301 distributions received from the corporation and not included in the shareholder's income under § 1368.[54]

The adjustments to stock basis are made on a per-share, per-day basis.[55] The adjustments generally are made as of the end of the corporation's taxable year, and are effective as of that date. However, if a shareholder disposes of any of a corporation's stock during the corporation's taxable year, the shareholder's basis in that stock will be adjusted immediately prior to the disposition, and that

---

[53]   See ¶ 11.20.

[54]   See ¶¶ 11.21 to 11.24 for a discussion of the treatment of distributions made to a shareholder.

[55]   Treas. Reg. § 1.1367–1(b)(2), (c)(3).

adjustment can thus affect the shareholder's gain or loss from that disposition.[56]

A shareholder's basis in a share of stock cannot be reduced below zero; but, if the amount of reduction attributable to a share exceeds the share's basis, the excess is applied to reduce (but not below zero) the remaining bases of the shareholder's other shares of the corporation's stock in proportion to the remaining basis of each of those shares.[57] If the total amount of basis reductions that are caused by an allocation of items to a shareholder's stocks (exclusive of reductions of basis that are attributable to the shareholder's receipt of distributions from the corporation) exceeds the aggregate basis of the shareholder's stocks, the excess is applied to reduce the shareholder's basis (but not below zero) in any indebtedness of the corporation that is held by the shareholder at the close of the corporation's taxable year.[58] The apparent reason for reducing the basis of stock before reducing the basis of a debt is to minimize the situations when a shareholder will recognize income from collecting on the debt.

A net increase (i.e., the excess of the positive adjustments allocable to that shareholder over the negative adjustments) in a subsequent year with respect to the shareholder will first be applied to restore the shareholder's basis in such debt to the extent that it was reduced in prior years, and only after the reductions of a shareholder's basis in such debt are fully restored can the basis of the shareholder's stock be increased.[59]

One issue that reached the Supreme Court was the effect on a shareholder's basis of cancellation of an S corporation's debt on which income was not recognized under § 108(a)(1)(B) because the corporation was insolvent. The Supreme Court ruled that the shareholder's basis was increased by his share of the nonrecognized gain.[60] Congress then repudiated the Supreme Court's decision by amending § 108(d)(7)(A) to prohibit the pass through to shareholders of any cancellation of indebtedness that is excluded from the corporation's income by § 108(a).

---

[56] Treas. Reg. § 1.1367–1(d)(1).

[57] Treas. Reg. § 1.1367–1(c)(3).

[58] § 1367(b)(2)(A); Treas. Reg. § 1.1367–2(b)(1).

[59] Treas. Reg. § 1.1367–2(c).

[60] Gitlitz v. Commissioner, 531 U.S. 206 (2001).

¶ 11.18   ORDER OF ADJUSTMENTS TO SHAREHOLDER'S BASIS

When several separate events cause adjustments to be made to a shareholder's basis in an S corporation's stock or in debt of the corporation that is owed to the shareholder, the order in which the adjustments are to be made can be important.

The order of adjustments is set forth in Treas. Reg. § 1.1367–1(f). According to that regulation, the adjustments to stock basis are made in the following order:

(1)   first, basis of stock is increased by its share of the corporation's income (including tax-exempt income) and by its share of the excess of depletion deductions over the basis of depletable property;

(2)   next, basis of stock is reduced by § 301 distributions received by the shareholder that year from the corporation that are not included in the shareholder's income under § 1368;

(3)   next, basis of stock is reduced by its share of non-capital, nondeductible expenses, and for its share of the oil and gas depletion deduction that does not exceed its share of the adjusted basis of the depletable property;

(4)   finally, basis of stock is reduced by its share of losses and deductions.

¶ 11.19   LIMITATIONS ON DEDUCTIONS, IN GENERAL

A shareholder can deduct a loss or deduction passed through to him from an S corporation only to the extent of his basis in the S corporation's stock and in any indebtedness owing to him from the corporation. As described above, for this purpose, the shareholder's basis in the S corporation's stock is determined at the end of the S corporation's taxable year after taking into account adjustments under § 1367(a)—e.g., positive adjustments for the sum of the shareholder's portion of the corporation's income and negative adjustments for distributions made to the shareholders.

A loss or deduction that is disallowed to a shareholder because of inadequate basis is carried over with the same character and treated as a loss or deduction incurred by the corporation in the succeeding year with respect to that shareholder.[61] Thus, the shareholder can utilize the loss or deduction in a later year in which

---

[61]   § 1366(d)(2)(A).

he has a basis in his stock or debt. This treatment is similar to the treatment accorded to partners by § 704(d) except that partners are not permitted to utilize their basis in partnership debt instruments to qualify for deductions allocated to them.

A loss that is carried over to a subsequent year is sometimes referred to as a "§ 1366(d) loss." The character of the loss deduction that passes through to a shareholder is determined by allocating the deduction proportionately among the corporation's deductible items for that year.[62] Similarly, the character of the § 1366(d) loss that is carried over is determined by making a proportional allocation among the corporation's deductible items.

Treas. Reg. § 1.1366–2(a)(5) states that the carryover of a disallowed loss (i.e., a § 1366(d) loss) is personal to the shareholder to whom that loss was allocated, and cannot be transferred to another person. That regulation was promulgated prior to a 2004 amendment that created a single exception to the provision that the carryover is exclusive to the shareholder who was denied the deduction. Section 1366(d)(2)(B) provides that when a shareholder who has rights to a carryover § 1366(d) loss transfers stock in a transaction covered by § 1041(a) to a spouse (or to a former spouse incident to a divorce), beginning with the next year, the carryover § 1366(d) loss that was attributable to the transferor will be deemed to have been incurred by the corporation with respect to the transferee.

¶ 11.20 AT RISK AND PASSIVE ACTIVITY LOSS LIMITATIONS

In addition to the limitations imposed by § 1366(d) on the deductibility of a shareholder's share of an S corporation's losses and deductions, a shareholder is also subject to the "at risk" limitations of § 465 and the passive activity loss and credit limitations of § 469. The at risk limitations and the passive activity loss and credit limitations are not applied to the S corporation itself.[63] Since the tax items of an S corporation are passed through to its shareholders, who themselves are subject to the at risk and passive activity loss and credit limitations, there is no reason to subject an S corporation to those limitations.

There is an order of priority to the application of these limitations to a shareholder's share of an S corporation's deductions and losses. First, the basis limitation imposed by § 1366(d) is applied. Any amount that is deductible after applying § 1366(d) is then subjected to the at risk limitation of § 465. Finally, any amount of

---

[62] Treas. Reg. § 1.1366–2(a)(4).
[63] §§ 465(a)(1); 469(a)(2); Temp. Reg. § 1.469–1T(b), (g)(2).

deduction that is not precluded by §§ 1366(d) and 465 is subjected to the limitations imposed on passive activity losses by § 469.[64] Note that corporate losses allocated to a shareholder and deductible under § 1366(d) will reduce the shareholder's basis in his stock or corporate debt regardless of whether the shareholder is prevented from deducting the loss by the at risk or passive activity loss rules.

Generally, the at risk limitation is applied separately to each activity from which a taxpayer has income.[65] A loss that is disallowed by the at risk limitation can be carried forward and deducted in a subsequent year when the at risk rule is satisfied, provided that the deduction is not then denied by the passive activity loss limitation of § 469.[66]

Unlike the at risk rules, the limitation on the deduction of passive activity losses does not operate on each activity separately. Instead, the tax items from all passive activities are aggregated and the limitation is applied to the net loss (if any).[67] In general, an activity of an S corporation is passive as to a shareholder if it involves the conduct of a trade or business[68] in which the shareholder does not materially participate.[69] A loss that is disallowed by the passive activity loss limitation rule can be carried forward and deducted in a subsequent year in which that rule is satisfied.[70]

¶ 11.21   DISTRIBUTIONS TO SHAREHOLDERS— NO EARNINGS AND PROFITS

Distributions of cash or other property by an S corporation to a shareholder will not be treated as a dividend if the corporation has no *e and p*.[71] As previously noted, an S corporation can have *e and p* only if it accumulated *e and p* in a prior year in which it was a C

---

[64] See Temp. Reg. § 1.469–2T(d)(6). The manner in which such disallowed losses are allocated among the shareholder's share of the corporation's losses is also described in that regulation.

[65] § 465(c).

[66] § 465(a)(2).

[67] § 469(d)(1).

[68] Many activities that do not constitute a trade or business for purposes of § 162 (the business expense deduction provision) nevertheless will be treated as a trade or business for purposes of the passive activity loss limitation provision. See § 469(c)(5), (6).

[69] § 469(c)(1). A taxpayer materially participates in a trade or business if the taxpayer and his spouse are involved in the operation of that trade or business on a basis that is "regular, continuous and substantial." § 469(h)(1), (5). A temporary regulation establishes seven tests for determining whether there has been material participation in a trade or business, and those seven tests are exclusive. Temp. Reg. § 1.469–5T(a). Satisfaction of any one of the seven tests is sufficient to establish material participation.

[70] § 469(b).

[71] § 1368(a), (b).

corporation, or if it inherited the *e and p* of another corporation pursuant to a reorganization or liquidation. If the corporation has no *e and p*, the amount of the distribution will reduce the shareholder's basis in his stock (but not in his debt instruments) and any excess of the distribution over the stock's basis is treated as a gain from the sale of the stock.[72]

¶ 11.22   DISTRIBUTIONS TO SHAREHOLDERS—ACCUMULATED ADJUSTMENTS ACCOUNT (AAA)

If an S corporation has accumulated *e and p*, a § 301 distribution to a shareholder will be dividend income to the extent that *e and p* are allocated to that distribution unless all or part of the distribution is insulated from dividend treatment by the accumulated adjustments account. The operation of the accumulated adjustments account provision is described below.

If an S corporation has accumulated *e and p*, the portion of the distributions that it makes to its shareholders in a taxable year that is not in excess of the corporation's "accumulated adjustments account" is treated in the same manner as if that portion were distributed by a corporation that had no *e and p*—i.e., it reduces a distributee's basis in his stock, and any excess over his basis in his stock is treated as gain from the sale of that stock.[73] The accumulated adjustments account provision applies to distributions of cash, property in kind, or both. The portion of the corporation's distributions that is in excess of its accumulated adjustments account is treated as dividends to the extent of the corporation's *e and p*.

The corporation's "accumulated adjustments account," which term is defined in § 1368(e)(1), is a compilation of the aggregate amount of most of the adjustments made under § 1367 to the basis that shareholders have in their stocks and debt instruments of the corporation because of distributions to the shareholders and the allocation to the shareholders of tax items of the corporation. The accumulated adjustments account is sometimes referred to as the "AAA." In determining a corporation's AAA, only the adjustments to basis that took place within the most recent continuous period that the corporation was an S corporation are taken into account. The period during which adjustments to basis are taken into account is referred to as the "S period."

For taxable years beginning after August 17, 1998, the order in which the several adjustments to AAA are made is set forth in Treas.

---

[72]   § 1368(b).
[73]   § 1368(c)(1).

Reg. § 1.1368–2(a)(5). Note that the AAA is the S corporation's account; the shareholders do not have their own accounts, nor is the account apportioned among them.[74]

On the first day that a corporation is an S corporation, its AAA is zero. Its AAA is then increased or decreased by the adjustments required by § 1368(e)(1). Those adjustments are similar to those made to the shareholder's basis in stock or debt by § 1377.[75]

An S corporation's AAA is reduced for distributions made to its shareholders that are not made out of its *e and p*, even if that distribution resulted in gain to a shareholder, but a distribution cannot cause or increase the amount of a negative AAA. However, it is possible for a corporation to have a negative AAA.[76] If that occurs, the corporation will not have a useful accumulated adjustments account until its subsequent net positive adjustments exceed that negative figure.

A "net negative adjustment" is the excess of reductions in the AAA for a taxable year (other than reductions for corporate distributions) over increases in the AAA for such year. If there is a "net negative adjustment" to the corporation's AAA for a taxable year, the amount of AAA at the end of the year that is to be applied to distributions made during that year is determined without making any adjustment for the "net negative adjustment."[77] In other words, the "negative adjustment" for a taxable year is not taken into account when determining the AAA to be applied to corporate distributions made during that year.

Adjustments that are made to a corporation's AAA are independent of adjustments to be made to its *e and p*. The normal rules for adjusting *e and p* are applied to an S corporation's *e and p* for dividend distributions, redemptions, liquidations, reorganizations, and divisions. An S corporation's *e and p* are not adjusted for income or deductions arising while it is an S corporation and are not reduced for distributions to the extent that the AAA is allocated to them.

---

[74]   However, unless the corporation's taxable year is divided into several parts under one of two special provisions, if the amount distributed to shareholders during the corporation's taxable year exceeds the accumulated adjustments account, then the accumulated adjustments account is apportioned among the distributions in proportion to the amounts distributed that are not treated as dividends. § 1368(c) (flush line).

[75]   However, there are a few differences. For example, no adjustment is made to the AAA for tax-exempt income and expenses related to that income.

[76]   See § 1368(e)(1)(A).

[77]   § 1368(e)(1)(C).

In general, the purpose of the AAA is to permit an S corporation to make nondividend distributions to its shareholders in an amount equal to its net post-1982 income that was previously taxed to its shareholders. The availability of this provision to a distributee does not depend upon the distributee's having been a shareholder at the time that the corporation earned the income that constitutes the AAA. Thus, a distribution to a shareholder can be insulated from dividend treatment by the AAA provision even though that shareholder had not previously been taxed on any of the corporation's income because, for example, the shareholder had only recently acquired stock of the corporation.

If all of the shareholders who received a distribution from the corporation during a taxable year consent, the corporation can waive the accumulated adjustments account provision as to all the distributions made in that year.[78] This election eliminates the AAA provision for the taxable year for which the election is effective. If this election is made, the corporation's distributions will constitute dividends to the extent of the corporation's accumulated *e and p*. One reason for making this election is to reduce accumulated *e and p* to zero and thereby preclude a tax on passive investment income under § 1375[79] and to preclude a termination of the Subchapter S election under § 1362(d)(3).[80]

¶ 11.23   DISTRIBUTIONS TO SHAREHOLDERS OF PROPERTY

As is true for C corporations, if an S corporation makes a distribution of appreciated property (other than its own obligation or stock) with respect to its stock, the corporation will recognize gain as if the corporation had sold the property to the distributee at its fair market value.[81] A similar recognition rule applies to liquidating distributions of appreciated property.[82] The S corporation will be taxed on such recognized gains only to the extent that they constitute a "recognized built-in gain" that is taxed under § 1374 or passive investment income that is taxed under § 1375. Regardless of whether the S corporation is taxed on the gain from distributing appreciated property, that recognized gain will pass through to the shareholders and can be taxed to them.

---

[78]   § 1368(e)(3).
[79]   See ¶ 11.30.
[80]   See ¶ 11.27.
[81]   § 311(b).
[82]   § 336(a).

If an S corporation distributes depreciated property as a nonliquidating distribution, it will not recognize any loss.[83] If an S corporation distributes depreciated property as a liquidating distribution, its loss will be recognized in some circumstances, but not in others as is the case with liquidating distributions by C corporations.[84]

Unless the distribution of appreciated property constitutes a dividend or the shareholder's adjusted basis in his stock (after adjusting his basis for the shareholder's share of the corporation's gain) is less than the amount distributed to him, a shareholder will not recognize income on the receipt of the distribution. Of course, each shareholder will recognize income from the pass through of the S corporation's recognized gain; but the distribution itself usually will not cause a second tax to the shareholders.

¶ 11.24   DISTRIBUTIONS TO SHAREHOLDERS DURING POST-TERMINATION TRANSITION PERIOD

A distribution of *cash* from a corporation to a shareholder after the termination of the corporation's Subchapter S status, but during a "post-termination transition period" (PTTP)[85] will not be taxed as a dividend to the shareholder to the extent that the distribution does not exceed the corporation's accumulated adjustments account (AAA), but instead such cash distributions will be applied against and reduce the shareholder's basis in his stock.[86] This provision applies only to distributions to persons who were shareholders of the corporation at the time that its S corporation status was terminated.[87] Moreover, it appears that the amount excluded from dividend treatment by this provision cannot exceed the shareholder's basis in the corporation's stock since the provision requires that the distribution reduce the shareholder's basis in his stock. Note that only cash distributions qualify for this treatment, and the exclusion from dividend treatment applies even if the distributing corporation has current *e and p.*

---

[83]   § 311(a).

[84]   § 336(a), (d). See ¶ 4.02.

[85]   The PTTP is defined in § 1377(b). It is possible for there to be as many as three post-termination periods. See § 1377(b)(1). The main one is the period beginning on the day after its S status terminated and ending the later of one year afterwards or the due date (with extensions) for its last return as an S corporation. § 1377(b)(1)(A).

[86]   § 1371(e)(1).

[87]   Treas. Reg. § 1.1377–2(b).

¶ 11.25 TERMINATION OF S ELECTION—REVOCATION

A Subchapter S election can be terminated by the revocation of shareholders who hold "more than one-half of the shares of stock of the corporation on the day on which the revocation is made." If the revocation is made on or before the 15th day of the third month of a taxable year, it will be effective on the first day of that year; if the revocation is made later, it will be effective for the first day of the following taxable year. Notwithstanding the preceding rules, if the revocation specifies an effective date that is on or after the date on which the revocation is made, the effective date will be the date that is specified in the revocation.[88]

¶ 11.26 TERMINATION OF S ELECTION—CESSATION OF QUALIFICATION

A corporation's election will terminate at any time that it ceases to qualify as an S corporation. For example, the issuing of a second class of stock or the acquisition of any of its stock by a C corporation will terminate the election. The termination is effective on and after the date on which the corporation ceases to qualify.[89] Such a termination will occur whether the terminating event is deliberate or unintentional. However, in certain circumstances, the Commissioner will exempt an S corporation from having its status terminated by an inadvertent event.

If (1) the terminating event was inadvertent, (2) within a reasonable period of time after discovery of the terminating event, steps are taken to bring the corporation into conformity with the S corporation requirements, and (3) each person who was a shareholder during the period that the corporation otherwise had lost its status as an S corporation consents to adjustments to such shareholder's income as are required by the Commissioner to provide equivalent tax consequences to what the shareholder would have incurred if the corporation had never lost its S corporation status, then the corporation will be treated as if it had continued to qualify as an S corporation (i.e., as if a termination had not occurred).[90]

---

[88] § 1362(d)(1).

[89] § 1362(d)(2).

[90] § 1362(f). This provision also applies to inadvertent invalid elections of S corporation status.

¶ 11.27 TERMINATION OF S ELECTION— PASSIVE INVESTMENT INCOME

Unless an S corporation has accumulated *e and p*, there is no penalty for having passive investment income—i.e., such income does not cause the termination of the election nor does it cause the imposition of any federal income taxes. You will recall that there are only two circumstances in which an S corporation can have accumulated *e and p*: (1) it accumulated *e and p* during a time when it was a C corporation, or (2) it acquired the *e and p* of another corporation as a consequence of an acquisitive reorganization or a liquidation of that corporation.

A Subchapter S election will be terminated if:

(1) the corporation had accumulated earnings and profits at the close of each of three consecutive taxable years in each of which it was an S corporation; and

(2) in each of such taxable years, more than 25 percent of the corporation's gross receipts was passive investment income (as defined in § 1362(d)(3)(C)).

A termination that is caused by the corporation's having passive investment income takes place on the first day of the taxable year following the close of the third consecutive year referred to above.[91]

"Passive investment income" is defined in § 1362(d)(3)(C).[92] In general, passive investment income means gross receipts from royalties, rents,[93] dividends, interest, annuities, and gains from the sales or exchanges of stocks or securities.

¶ 11.28 NEW S ELECTION AFTER TERMINATION

If an S corporation's status is terminated, the corporation (or a successor corporation) is barred from making a new election for S corporation treatment for a taxable year that begins prior to the fifth taxable year after the year in which the termination occurred—i.e., the election is not available for a five-year period. The Commissioner can waive that bar and grant permission to a corporation to elect S corporation status prior to the expiration of the five-year period when

---

[91]   § 1362(d)(3). In the absence of such a restriction, a closely held C corporation could easily avoid the double-tax Subchapter C regime by selling its business assets and, instead of liquidating and thereby triggering a tax to its shareholders, becoming a corporate investment vehicle for its shareholders and electing S corporation status to avoid corporate tax on the investment income.

[92]   See also Treas. Reg. § 1.1362–2(c)(5).

[93]   Rents derived from the active conduct of the trade or business of renting property are not treated as passive investment income. Treas. Reg. § 1.1362–2(c)(5).

the Commissioner deems it appropriate.[94] The Commissioner is not likely to consent to an early election if the termination was deliberate.

¶ 11.29   S TERMINATION YEAR

A taxable year in which an election for Subchapter S treatment is terminated (other than one that terminates on the first day of the taxable year) is called an "S termination year."[95] An S termination year is divided into two short years.[96] The portion of the S termination year that ends on the day prior to the day on which the termination occurred is called an "S short year," and the remainder of the S termination year is called a "C short year."[97] Subject to certain exceptions, the tax items of a corporation for the S termination year are allocated pro rata between the S short year and the C short year according to the relative lengths of those two periods.[98]

The normal Subchapter S provisions apply to the S short year of an S termination year. In order to maintain the progressivity built into the corporate tax structure, the taxable income of the C short year is annualized.[99]

¶ 11.30   TAXATION OF PASSIVE INVESTMENT INCOME

As noted in ¶ 11.27, an S corporation that has accumulated earnings and profits and has a substantial portion of its gross receipts from passive investment income is given three consecutive years to get its house in order before the election will be terminated. But the corporation is subject to tax consequences in any taxable year in which it has substantial passive investment income if it also has accumulated *e and p* at the end of that taxable year. Section 1375

---

[94]   § 1362(g).

[95]   § 1362(e)(4).

[96]   The division of an S termination year into two parts does not affect the taxable year of the shareholder in which the corporation's tax items are to be reported. Also, for purposes of determining the exhaustion of a carryover loss or credit, the two short years are treated as a single taxable year. § 1362(e)(6)(A).

[97]   § 1362(e)(1).

[98]   § 1362(e)(2). Instead of a pro rata allocation, at the corporation's election, the allocation of tax items will be made under normal accounting rules according to the actual amounts incurred in each of those short years if consents to a normal accounting allocation are obtained from all persons who were shareholders at any time during the S short year and from all persons who were shareholders on the first day of the C short year. § 1362(e)(3). This method of allocation is sometimes referred to as the "interim closing method." If, during the S termination year, there is a sale or exchange of 50 percent or more of the corporation's stock, the tax items must be allocated under normal accounting rules rather than pro rata. § 1362(e)(6)(D).

[99]   § 1362(e)(5).

imposes a tax on an S corporation for any taxable year in which it has both:

(1) accumulated earnings and profits at the close of that taxable year; and

(2) gross receipts more than 25 percent of which are passive investment income.

The § 1375 tax is computed by multiplying the "excess net passive income" by the highest ordinary income tax rate that is applicable to corporations (currently, that rate is 21 percent).[100] The "net passive income" of a corporation is generally the difference between its passive investment income and the corporation's deductions that are directly connected with the production of such income.[101] "Passive investment income" is defined in § 1362(d)(3)(C) and generally includes gross receipts from royalties, rents, dividends, interest, annuities, and sales or exchanges of stock or securities. The "excess net passive income" is an amount that has the same ratio to net passive income as the excess of passive investment income over 25 percent of gross receipts has to the corporation's passive investment income.

The amount of excess net passive income for a taxable year cannot exceed a modified version of the corporation's taxable income for that year.

It may be helpful to express the manner in which "excess net passive income" (ENPI) is determined as a formula. In the following formula:

ENPI = excess net passive income

PII = passive investment income

NPI = net passive income

GR = gross receipts

$$\text{ENPI} = \frac{\text{PII}-25\% \text{ of GR}}{\text{PII}} \times \text{NPI}$$

Ex. X Corporation conducted a personal service business as a C corporation in Year One, but it became an S corporation beginning January 1, Year Two. X reports its income on a calendar year basis. In Year Two, X had gross receipts of $100,000 of which $37,500 constitute interest from bonds of

---

[100] § 11(b). By "ordinary" rate, we refer to the corporate income tax rates exclusive of surtaxes.

[101] § 1375(b)(2).

publicly held corporations and $62,500 constitute receipts from the conduct of a personal service business. Individual A is the sole shareholder of X. X made no distributions to its shareholder in Year Two. X had deductible expenses in Year Two of $25,000 of which $7,500 is attributable to the interest it earned. The remaining $17,500 of deductible expenses are attributable to the receipts from the personal service business. At the beginning of Year Two, X had accumulated *e and p* of $18,000.

Of X's gross receipts, only the interest it received constitutes passive investment income. X's net passive income for Year Two is $30,000 (i.e., $37,500 interest minus the $7,500 of deductible expenses that are directly attributable thereto). X's passive investment income ($37,500) exceeds 25 percent of its gross receipts for that year (25% × $100,000 = $25,000) by $12,500. X's excess net passive income is determined by multiplying the net passive income ($30,000) by a fraction the numerator of which is the passive investment income in excess of 25 percent of X's gross receipts ($12,500) and the denominator of which is X's passive investment income ($37,500). So, in tabular form,

$$\frac{12,500}{37,500} \times \$30,000 = \$10,000 \text{ (excess net passive income)}$$

Since the amount of X's taxable income for Year Two ($75,000) is greater than its excess net passive income, the tax is determined by applying the current corporate tax rate to the ENPI. The $10,000 of excess net passive income is currently taxed to X at a 21 percent rate. This provides a tax of $2,100.

The $37,500 of interest income of X that is passed through to A is reduced by the $2,100 tax that X incurred under § 1375(a), and so A will report $35,400 of interest income from the S corporation.

¶ 11.31   PURPOSE AND OPERATION OF § 1374

In the absence of a remedial provision, a C corporation that has appreciated assets could avoid the imposition of a corporate tax on that appreciation by making an election to become an S corporation. Once the election became effective, the corporation's recognized gain would be passed through to its shareholders and therefore would be taxed only once at individual rates. Without the S election, the gain would have been taxed twice—once at the corporate level and again at the individual shareholder's level when the proceeds are distributed to the shareholders. To prevent the use of the Subchapter S election as a device for escaping corporate taxation of appreciation that arose prior to the effective date of the election, Congress imposed a corporate tax on the "net recognized built-in gains" of an S corporation when it is recognized within a specified period. This tax is set forth in § 1374.[102]

In examining the built-in gains tax, it is best to begin with an analysis of the definitions of the key terminology used to determine the tax.

(a) *Recognition Period.* The "recognition period" of an S Corporation is ordinarily the five-year period beginning with the date on which the Subchapter S election of the corporation became effective.[103]

(b) *Built-In Gain and Loss.* For convenience, the excess of the fair market value of an asset of an S corporation on the day on which the Subchapter S election first became effective over the adjusted basis that the S corporation had in the asset at that date is referred to herein as the "built-in gain" of that asset. The excess of adjusted basis over fair market value of an asset on the date on which the Subchapter S election first became effective is referred to herein as the "built-in loss" of that asset.

(c) *Net Unrealized Built-In Gain.* Subject to specified adjustments, Treas. Reg. § 1.1374–3(a) states that an S corporation's "net unrealized built-in gain" is equal to the amount that would have been realized on the first day of the recognition period if the corporation had sold all of its assets at fair market value to an unrelated person who assumed all of its liabilities, decreased by the sum of (i) any liability that would be included in the determination above of the amount realized, but only to the extent that the liability would entitle the corporation to a deduction when paid, and

---

[102] This provision works in conjunction with the tax on excess passive income imposed by § 1375 in restricting the ability of C corporations to use the S corporation provisions to circumvent the double tax regime of Subchapter C.

[103] § 1374(d)(7). A separate five-year period can apply to any asset that the S corporation acquires from a C corporation in a nonrecognition transaction. For that particular asset, the five-year recognition period begins on the date that the S corporation acquired the asset. § 1374(d)(8)(B). If an S corporation reports gain from a sale on the installment method, the recognition period for the year in which the sale took place will apply to the installment payments. § 1374(d)(7)(B).

(ii) the aggregate adjusted bases of the corporation's assets on the first day of the recognition period.[104]

(d) *Recognized Built-In Gain.* The "recognized built-in gain" of an S corporation is the amount of built-in gain recognized on the disposition of an asset by the S corporation in a taxable year that is within the "recognition period." The presumption is that any gain recognized by an S corporation on the disposition of an asset during the recognition period is a recognized built-in gain unless the S corporation establishes either that that asset was not held by the corporation at the date that the Subchapter S election became effective or that the built-in gain for that asset is less than the gain recognized on its disposition.[105]

A corporation's recognized built-in gains for a taxable year within the recognition period also include any item of income that is properly taken into account for that taxable year and that is attributable to periods prior to the first taxable year in which the Subchapter S election became effective (i.e., prior to the beginning of the recognition period). Treas. Reg. § 1.1374–4(b) states that this provision applies only to an item of income that is taken into account during the recognition period and that would have been included in gross income before the recognition period if the taxpayer had been using the accrual method of accounting.

(e) *Recognized Built-In Loss.* Part of the determination of a "net recognized built-in gain" is a netting of recognized built-in gains and losses for a taxable year that began within the recognition period. A "recognized built-in loss" is any loss recognized by an S corporation during the recognition period on the disposition of an asset that was held by the S corporation at the date on which the recognition period began, but only to the extent of the excess of the adjusted basis that the

---

[104] A separate net unrealized built-in gain calculation is made each time an S corporation acquires assets from a C corporation in a nonrecognition transaction. § 1374(d)(8) and Treas. Reg. § 1.1374–8(e), Exs. (1) and (2).

[105] § 1374(d)(3). The S corporation must also show that the asset was not acquired from a C corporation in a nonrecognition transaction. § 1374(d)(8). In order to be able to distinguish such built-in gains from gains that accrued after the S election became effective, practitioners ordinarily advise C corporations that are making an S election to obtain a professional appraisal of the C corporation's assets as of the day before the effective date of the S election.

corporation had in such asset at the date on which the recognition period began over the fair market value of the asset at that date (i.e., only to the extent of the built-in loss of that asset). The S corporation has the burden of establishing that it held the asset at the operative date and the burden of establishing the spread between basis and value at that date.[106]

A corporation's recognized built-in loss for a taxable year within the recognition period also includes any amount that is allowable as a deduction for such year (determined without regard to any carryover) and that is attributable to periods prior to the recognition period. Treas. Reg. § 1.1374–4(b)(2) states that such items are included as a recognized built-in loss only if the item is properly deductible during the recognition period and would have been properly allowed against gross income before the recognition period by a taxpayer using the accrual method.

(f)   *Net Recognized Built-In Gain.* An S corporation's "net recognized built-in gain" with respect to a taxable year in the recognition period is the amount of difference between the corporation's recognized built-in gain for such taxable year and the corporation's recognized built-in loss for such taxable year.[107] This final figure is the amount that is subject to taxation under § 1374.

A corporation's net recognized built-in gain is subject to two limitations: (1) the taxable income limitation, and (2) the net unrealized built-in gain limitation.

A corporation's net recognized built-in gain for a year cannot exceed the difference between the corporation's net unrealized built-in gain and the aggregate net recognized built-in gain for all prior taxable years that began in the recognition period. This limitation is referred to as the "net unrealized built-in gain limitation."

If an S corporation's modified taxable income for a taxable year is less than the amount of difference between its recognized built-in gains and losses for

---

[106]   § 1374(d)(4). Thus, note that when gain is recognized during the recognition period, the burden is on the taxpayer to show that the gain was not part of a built-in gain; but if a deduction is recognized during the recognition period, the burden is on the taxpayer to show that the deduction was part of a built-in loss.

[107]   Such excess can be reduced by certain carryforward losses and credits from years when the corporation was a C corporation. See § 1374(b)(2), (3).

such year, then the net recognized built-in gain for that year is equal to the corporation's modified taxable income.[108] This is referred to as "the taxable income limitation." For this purpose, an S corporation's taxable income is generally determined in the normal manner that applies to C corporations.[109] If this limitation applies, the additional amount that would have been taxed under § 1374 if taxable income had not been the smaller figure will be carried over and added to the corporation's recognized built-in gains for the next taxable year.[110]

If left unchecked, shareholders of a C corporation could transfer depreciated assets to it shortly prior to the corporation's making a Subchapter S election in order to reduce the size of the corporation's net unrealized built-in gain. To counter this, the regulations have adopted an anti-stuffing rule. This rule provides that if an asset is acquired by a corporation prior to or during the recognition period for the principal purpose of avoiding the built-in gain tax, the asset and its tax attributes are ignored for most purposes concerning § 1374.[111]

If the S corporation owns a partnership interest on the first day of the recognition period, subject to certain exceptions, complex rules apply to treat the S corporation as a direct owner of a share of partnership assets.[112]

The corporation's net recognized built-in gain is taxed at the highest ordinary[113] rate applicable to a C corporation's taxable income, which currently is 21 percent.[114]

---

[108]   § 1374(d)(2)(A)(ii).

[109]   No deduction can be taken under § 172 for a carryforward or carryback net operating loss and no deduction can be taken under §§ 243 through 247 and 249. The special computation of taxable income of an S corporation that ordinarily is required by § 1363(b) does not apply for the purpose of determining the taxable income limitation.

[110]   § 1374(d)(2)(B). A recognized built-in gain carryover that is unused in one year will carryover to the next year for so long as the recognition period has not expired. Note that while the tax imposed by § 1375 on excess net passive income also contains a taxable income limitation, there is no carryover of the amount of excess net passive income that is not taxed because of that limitation.

[111]   Treas. Reg. § 1.1374–9.

[112]   Treas. Reg. § 1.1374–4(i).

[113]   "Ordinary" refers to the tax rate applied to a C corporation's taxable income exclusive of surtaxes.

[114]   § 1374(b)(1).

It is possible that gain recognized by an S corporation from the disposition of an asset could constitute both passive investment income and a recognized built-in gain. To prevent a double tax to the S corporation, the amount of passive investment income is determined by excluding any of the corporation's recognized built-in gains and losses that occur during the recognition period.[115]

¶ 11.32   LIFO RECAPTURE AMOUNT

When an S corporation sells inventory during the recognition period,[116] it becomes necessary to determine whether the inventory that was sold was an asset that was held by the corporation on the first day of the recognition period and, if so, the amount of built-in gain or loss that the asset had at that time. If the inventory item that was sold is deemed to have been acquired after the first day of the recognition period, the gain or loss from that sale does not constitute a recognized built-in gain or loss.

Treas. Reg. § 1.1374–7(b) states that the inventory method that an S corporation employs for tax purposes will be used to identify the items of inventory that are sold during a taxable year. So, if an S corporation uses the FIFO (first-in, first-out) inventory method, the oldest inventory in its stock will be deemed to be sold first, and that will cause the earliest recognition of built-in gains from the inventory held at the beginning of the recognition period. On the other hand, if the corporation uses the LIFO (last-in, first-out) method, the later acquired inventory will be deemed to have been sold first, and that will delay the recognition of built-in gains on inventory. Indeed, the LIFO method could delay the recognition of such gain to years beyond the recognition period so that they will never be subjected to the built-in gains tax.

If a C corporation was using the LIFO method prior to electing S status, that could be advantageous for built-in gains tax purposes; but the tax benefit obtained thereby is offset by the requirement that the C corporation recognize the so-called LIFO recapture amount as income in its return for its last taxable year as a C corporation. The tax on that income is payable in four equal annual installments beginning with the return for the last year in which the corporation was a C corporation. The corporation's basis in the inventory will be increased by the LIFO recapture amount.[117]

---

[115]   § 1375(b)(4).

[116]   The recognition period usually is the five-year period beginning with the first day on which the election to be an S corporation became effective. § 1374(d)(7). However, there are circumstances in which a separate recognition period may apply to certain assets of the corporation.

[117]   § 1363(d).

The "LIFO recapture amount" is defined in § 1363(d)(3) as the excess of the inventory amount that the corporation would have had at the close of its last taxable year as a C corporation if it had reported its inventory on the first-in, first-out (FIFO) method over the inventory amount that the corporation actually had at that date as a consequence of using the LIFO method.

¶ 11.33 QUALIFIED BUSINESS INCOME DEDUCTION

The 2017 Tax Cuts and Jobs Act added § 199A to the Code providing a deduction for a percentage (usually 20%) of certain business income derived from a partnership, an S corporation, or self-employment. The deduction is subject to a sunset provision and does not apply to years after 2025. § 199A(i). The purpose of this provision is to serve as a device effectively to reduce the tax rate imposed on certain noncorporate business income to approximately what the rate would be if the TP were a corporation.

The deduction is neither itemized nor nonitemized. It is not taken into account in determining AGI, but it can be taken when the TP uses the Standard Deduction. § 63(b)(3).

¶ 11.33.1 Amount of the Deduction

The amount of the deduction is equal to the "combined qualified business income" of the TP, but the amount cannot exceed the difference between the TP's taxable income for that year and the TP's net capital gain[118] for that year.[119] The terms "qualified business income" and "combined qualified business income" are defined below.

¶ 11.33.2 Qualified Business Income

Qualified business income means the net amount of qualified items of income, gain, deduction, and loss with respect to a qualified trade or business of a noncorporate taxpayer. § 199A(c)(1).The term does not include qualified REIT dividends or qualified publicly traded partnership income. Id. To be qualified, the items must be connected with a trade or business within the United States[120] and included or allowed in determining taxable income. § 199A(c)(3)(A). The items listed in § 199A(c)(3)(B) are excluded from qualified business income. Some of those excluded items are: capital gains and losses, dividend

[118] A net capital gain is the excess of the TP's net long-term capital gain over TP's net short-term capital loss. § 1222(11). For the purpose of this provision, the term does not include gain which is treated as investment income under § 164(d)(4)(B)(iii). § 1(h)(2).

[119] § 199A(a).

[120] Qualified business income from sources within the commonwealth of Puerto Rico may qualify for the deduction. § 199A(f)(1)(C).

income or its equivalent, interest income other than interest properly allocable to a trade or business, an amount from an annuity that is not received in connection with a trade or business. Wages and other compensation for services also are excluded from qualified business income.[121]

¶ 11.33.3   Combined Qualified Business Income

The combined qualified business income of a noncorporate TP is equal to the sum of 20% of the TP's qualified REIT dividends and qualified publicly traded partnership income[122] plus the lesser of either:

(1)   20% of the TP's qualified business income with respect to a qualified trade or business, or

(2)   The greater of either 50% of the W-2 wages that the TP paid or incurred with respect to the qualified trade or business, or 25% of such wages and 2.5% of the adjusted basis of all qualified property[123] immediately after its acquisition.

If the TP's taxable income[124] for the taxable year does not exceed a threshold amount, item (2) above (i.e., 50% of W-2 wages or 25% of such wages plus 2.5% of unadjusted basis of qualified property) does not apply[125]. The threshold amount is described in ¶ 11.33.5 and is indexed for inflation.

If the TP's taxable income[126] is less than the threshold amount or if taxable income exceeds the threshold amount by less than $50,000 ($100,000 for a joint return), item 2 will not apply, but the deduction will be reduced by a fraction of the "excess amount" (described below). The numerator of the fraction is the excess of taxable income[127] over $50,000 ($100,000 for a joint return), and the denominator is $50,000 (or $100,000 if a joint return). The "excess amount" is the difference between item (1) (determined without

---

[121]   § 199A(c)(4).

[122]   The terms "qualified REIT dividends" and "qualified publicly traded partnership income" are defined in § 199A(e)(3) and (4).

[123]   Qualified property is defined in § 199A(b)(6). In general, it refers to depreciable property used in a qualified trade or business.

[124]   For this purpose, taxable income is determined without taking the qualified business income deduction. § 199A(e)(1).

[125]   § 199A(b)(3)(A).

[126]   For this purpose, taxable income is determined without taking the qualified business income deduction. § 199A(e)(1).

[127]   Id.

regard to the reduction in this provision) and item (2) (determined without the reduction in this provision).[128]

Ex. Roger was a shareholder of the Win All corporation which is an S corporation. Roger is not married. In 2019, Roger 's share of Win All's qualified business income was $100,000. Roger has no REIT dividends or publicly traded partnership income. Roger's share of Win All's W-2 wages was $15,000, and Roger's share of Win All's unadjusted basis in its qualified property was $50,000. Roger's taxable income in 2019 was $135,000, which amount is less than the threshold amount ($157,000).[129] Since his taxable income is less than the threshold amount, Roger's business income deduction is $20,000 (20% of his qualified business income of $100,000). The limitation based on W-2 wages and unadjusted basis does not apply when taxable income is less than the threshold amount[130] so only the 20% of qualified business income provision applies.

¶ 11.33.4   Qualified Trade or Business

A qualified trade or business is any trade or business other than a "specified service trade or business" or the trade or business of providing services as an employee. A specified service trade or business includes a trade or business involving the performance of services in the fields of health, law, accounting, actuarial services, performing arts, consulting, athletics, financial services, brokerage services, and any trade or business in which the principal asset is the reputation or skill of one or more of its employees, employers, or owners.[131] A specified service trade also includes services that consist of investing and investment management, trading or dealing in securities, partnership interests or commodities. Section 199A(d) expressly provides that neither engineering nor architecture is a specified service trade or business. If the TP's taxable income is less than the threshold amount plus $50,000 ($100,000 for a joint return), any specified trade or business of the TP will qualify for the § 199A business income deduction; but in determining that deduction, if the TP's taxable income exceeds the threshold amount, the income, gain, deduction and loss and the W-2 wages and the unadjusted basis of qualified property are reduced by a fraction in which the numerator is the amount by which taxable income exceeds the threshold

---

[128]   § 199A(b)(3).

[129]   The threshold amount is described in ¶ 11.33.5.

[130]   § 199A(b)(3)(A).

[131]   § 199A(d)(2)(A).

amount, and the denominator is $50,000 ($100,000 for a joint return).[132]

¶ 11.33.5   Threshold Amount

The threshold amount for 2018 was $157,500 ($315,000 for a joint return). The amount is increased to reflect increases in the cost of living for years subsequent to 2018.[133]

¶ 11.33.6   Anti-Abuse Rules

Section 199A contains several anti-abuse for certain transactions between related parties and for property acquired in a like-kind exchange or in an involuntary conversion.[134]

---

[132]   § 199A(d)(3).
[133]   § 199A(e)(2).
[134]   § 199A(h).

Table of Cases

Alderman v. Commissioner, 182, 193

American Bantam Car Co. v. Commissioner, 167

American Mfg. Co. v. Commissioner, 311

Anderson v. Commissioner, 25, 76

Associated Wholesale Grocers, Inc. v. United States, 104

Atlas Tool Co. v. Commissioner, 311

Badanes v. Commissioner, 222

Bashford, Helvering v., 284

Bausch & Lomb Optical Co. v. Commissioner, 275

Bazley v. Commissioner, 289, 292

Bennett v. Commissioner, 79

Bliss Dairy, Inc., United States v., 197

Breech, Jr. v. United States, 100

Bryan v. Commissioner, 182

Byrd, Estate of v. Commissioner, 74

Campbell v. Wheeler, 182

Caruth v. United States, 163

Central Cuba Sugar Co. v. Commissioner, 194

Cerone v. Commissioner, 58, 63, 64

Chamberlin v. Commissioner, 146

Chared Corp. v. United States, 39

Charles McCandless Tile Service v. United States, 40

Cherry-Burrell Corp. v. United States, 101

Clark, Commissioner v., 235, 311

Court Holding Co., Commissioner v., 197

Crane v. Commissioner, 179, 302

Cromwell v. Commissioner, 355

Crowley v. Commissioner, 39

Cumberland Pub. Serv. Co., United States v., 197

Curtis v. United States, 220

D'Angelo Assoc., Inc. v. Commissioner, 166

Davant v. Commissioner, 311

Davidson v. Commissioner, 196

Davis, United States v., 53

Day & Zimmermann, Inc., Commissioner v., 103

Drybrough v. Commissioner, 182

Dunn v. Commissioner, 65

E. I. Du Pont de Nemours & Co. v. United States, 169

Edenfield v. Commissioner, 79

Edwin's Inc. v. United States, 40

Eisner v. Macomber, 132

Eli Lilly & Co. v. Commissioner, 194

Elkhorn Coal Co., Helvering v., 274

Enoch v. Commissioner, 79

Exacto Spring Corporation v. Commissioner, 40

Fahs v. Florida Mach. & Foundry Co., 166

Focht v. Commissioner, 186

Foster v. Commissioner, 194

G. D. Searle & Co. v. Commissioner, 194

Gada v. United States, 224

Gallagher v. Commissioner, 100

General Utilities & Operating Co. v. Helvering, 37

George L. Riggs, Inc. v. Commissioner, 104

Gitlitz v. Commissioner, 376

Gregory v. Helvering, 163, 197, 202, 221

Groetzinger, Commissioner v., 212

Groman v. Commissioner, 284

Gunther v. Commissioner, 195

H.K. Porter Co. v. Commissioner, 103

Haft Trust v. Commissioner, 58

Hallowell v. Commissioner, 198

Hamrick v. Commissioner, 171

Hanson v. United States, 224

Hawkinson v. Commissioner, 234

Hempt Bros., Inc. v. United States, 196

Hendler, United States v., 179, 273

Henry T. Patterson Trust v. United States, 55, 59

Hersloff v. United States, 91

Hickok v. Commissioner, 289

Hillsboro Nat'l Bank v. Commissioner, 106

Hodge v. Commissioner, 104
Holsey v. Commissioner, 79
Honigman v. Commissioner, 39
Horst, Helvering v., 196
International Trading Co. v.
    Commissioner, 212
J.E. Seagram Corp. v.
    Commissioner, 256
Jackson v. Commissioner, 169,
    302
James v. Commissioner, 168
Jaques v. Commissioner, 39
John A. Nelson Co. v. Helvering,
    255
Kamborian v. Commissioner, 165
Kamborian, Estate of v.
    Commissioner, 165
Kass v. Commissioner, 254
Kimbell-Diamond Milling Co. v.
    Commissioner, 115
King Enterprises v. United
    States, 234
King v. Commissioner, 214, 224
Kluener, Estate of v.
    Commissioner, 163
Lennard, Estate of v.
    Commissioner, 63
Lessinger v. Commissioner, 169,
    187, 302
LeTulle v. Scofield, 225, 255
Littriello v. United States, 7
Loewen v. Commissioner, 192
Lucas v. Earl, 196
Lynch v. Commissioner, 64
Makransky, Commissioner v., 39
Mazzocchi Bus Co. v.
    Commissioner, 20
Menard, Inc. v. Commissioner,
    40
Messer v. Commissioner, 91
Metzger Trust v. Commissioner,
    58, 59
Mills v. Commissioner, 268
Minnesota Tea Co., Helvering v.,
    225, 254
Morris Trust, Commissioner v.,
    220, 246
Morrissey v. Commissioner, 7
Murry v. Commissioner, 198
Nash v. United States, 197
National Securities Corp. v.
    Commissioner, 194
Parshelsky, Estate of v.
    Commissioner, 223, 224
Penn v. Robertson, 6
Peracchi v. Commissioner, 188,
    189

Performance Systems, Inc. v.
    United States, 105
Pillar Rock Packing Co. v.
    Commissioner, 275
Pinellas Ice & Cold Storage Co.
    v. Commissioner, 225, 254
Rafferty v. Commissioner, 214,
    223
Raich v. Commissioner, 196
Rooney v. United States, 194
Roubik v. Commissioner, 196
Seda v. Commissioner, 64
Seide v. Commissioner, 292
Smith v. Commissioner, 79, 275
Southwest Consol. Corp.,
    Helvering v., 289
Stafford, United States v., 168
Stanton v. United States, 166
Stewart v. Commissioner, 194,
    198
Taschler, Estate of v. United
    States, 39
Telephone Answering Serv. Co.
    v. Commissioner, 100
Thompson v. Campbell, 182
Thurber v. Commissioner, 275
Transport Mfg. & Equip. Co. v.
    Commissioner, 39
Tufts, Commissioner v., 302
Utley v. Commissioner, 169, 302
Weisbart v. Commissioner, 170
Western Indus. Co. v. Helvering,
    275
Williams v. Commissioner, 39
Wilson, Commissioner v., 221
Wright v. United States, 55

Table of Internal Revenue Code Sections

§ 1(h)(2) 394
§ 1(h)(11) 3, 144, 151, 152
§ 1(h)(11)(B)(iii)........................18
§ 1(h)(11)(D)(ii) 34
§ 11(b)........................3, 387
§ 61(a)(12) 291
§ 63(b)(3) 394
§ 108(a)........................22, 376
§ 108(a)(1)(B)........................376
§ 108(b)........................22
§ 108(d)(7)(A) 376
§ 108(e)(4)........................109
§ 108(e)(8)........................291
§ 108(e)(10)........................291
§ 111 197
§ 112(k)........................180
§ 118 171
§ 162 ....3, 40, 379
§ 162(a)........................39
§ 163(j)........................ 4
§ 163(j)(2)........................ 4
§ 163(j)(3)........................ 4
§ 163(j)(7)........................ 4
§ 163(j)(8)........................ 4
§ 164(d)(4)(B)(iii)........................394
§ 165(c)(2)........................98
§ 165(g)........................109
§ 165(g)(3)........................109
§ 167(j)........................ 4
§ 168 ....28, 119
§ 168(b)(1) 29
§ 168(c)........................29
§ 168(g)........................29, 30
§ 168(g)(2)........................29, 33
§ 168(g)(3)........................29
§ 172 ....322, 325, 392
§ 172(b)........................326
§ 172(b)(1)(A)........................326
§ 172(b)(1)(B)........................326
§ 172(b)(1)(C)........................326
§ 172(b)(2)........................327
§ 172(b)(3) 327
§ 199A........................394
§ 199A(a) 394
§ 199A(b)(3)........................396
§ 199A(b)(3)(A)................395, 396
§ 199A(b)(6)........................395
§ 199A(c)(1) 394
§ 199A(c)(3)(A) 394
§ 199A(c)(3)(B) 394

§ 199A(c)(4) 395
§ 199A(d) 396
§ 199A(d)(2)(A) 396
§ 199A(d)(3) 397
§ 199A(e)(1) 395
§ 199A(e)(2) 397
§ 199A(e)(3) 395
§ 199A(e)(4) 395
§ 199A(f)(1)(C) 394
§ 199A(h) 397
§ 199A(i) 394
§ 243 ......35, 36, 78, 83, 144, 151, 311
§§ 243–247........................ 392
§ 243(a) 30, 210, 362
§ 243(a)(1)........................ 17
§ 243(a)(2)........................ 18
§ 243(a)(3)........................ 18
§ 243(c) 17, 31
§ 243(c)(2) 17
§ 244 .... 35, 78
§ 245 .... 35, 78
§ 245(b) 210
§ 246 17
§ 246A........................ 17
§ 249 392
§ 263(a)(1) 171
§ 267 .... 20, 93, 156
§ 267(a)(1)..........93, 95, 102, 179
§ 267(b)........................ 176
§ 267(b)(2)........................ 93, 179
§ 267(b)(3)........................ 94
§ 267(c) 93, 193, 363
§ 267(e)(2)........................ 363
§ 267(f)........................ 93, 94
§ 269 ....326, 330, 355, 356
§ 269(a) 355, 356
§ 269(c) 356
§ 269A(b)(2) 4
§ 291(a)(1)........................ 107
§ 301 .....10, 11, 12, 16, 21, 22, 23,
28, 30, 31, 33, 36, 37, 38, 39,
41, 42, 43, 48, 50, 51, 52, 55,
57, 58, 68, 69, 72, 73, 75, 76,
77, 78, 81, 82, 83, 84, 85, 99,
100, 128, 132, 134, 135, 136,
137, 138, 139, 140, 141, 142,
144, 150, 152, 201, 204, 210
§§ 301–385........................ 2
§ 301(b) 37

§ 301(b)(1) 11, 141
§ 301(b)(2) 11
§ 301(c)(1)................................11
§ 301(c)(2)...........................33, 83
§ 301(c)(3)...........................34, 83
§ 301(d)..............................36, 141
§ 301(e)...........................31, 32, 33
§ 301(e)(2).................................31
§ 302 .....47, 48, 67, 68, 72, 81, 82,
84, 100, 137, 201, 234, 235, 310
§ 302(a)..................68, 75, 86, 211
§ 302(b)..............65, 67, 82, 83, 85
§ 302(b)(1) 42, 43, 52, 53, 54,
55, 56, 57, 58, 68, 69
§ 302(b)(2) 52, 59, 60, 61, 62,
68, 69, 137, 311
§ 302(b)(2)(D) 61
§ 302(b)(3) 52, 62, 66, 67, 68,
69, 76, 153
§ 302(b)(4) 67, 68, 70, 153
§ 302(b)(5) 53
§ 302(c)(1).......................43, 59, 62
§ 302(c)(2)..........49, 62, 63, 64, 65
§ 302(c)(2)(A)..........62, 63, 65, 66,
153
§ 302(c)(2)(A)(i) 64
§ 302(c)(2)(A)(ii) 211
§ 302(c)(2)(A)(iii) 211
§ 302(c)(2)(B).......................65, 66
§ 302(c)(2)(C).......................66, 67
§ 302(d).................43, 49, 50, 290
§ 302(e)...................68, 69, 70, 78
§ 302(e)(1)................................69
§ 302(e)(1)(A)............................69
§ 302(e)(1)(B)............................69
§ 302(e)(2).........................69, 70
§ 302(e)(2)–(4) 69
§ 302(e)(3)................................69
§ 302(e)(4).........................69, 70
§ 302(e)(5).........................67, 68
§ 303 ......42, 73, 74, 75, 81, 82, 83
§ 303(a)..............................74, 211
§ 303(b)(1) 74
§ 303(b)(2)(A)............................73
§ 303(b)(2)(B)......................73, 74
§ 303(b)(3) 74
§ 303(c) 75
§ 303(d)....................................73
§ 304 ....79, 80, 81, 87, 195
§ 304(a).................................79, 81
§ 304(a)(1)..........80, 82, 84, 85
§ 304(a)(2) 80, 85, 86
§ 304(b)(1) 81, 82, 84, 85
§ 304(b)(2) 83, 85, 86
§ 304(b)(3) 87
§ 304(b)(3)(A)...........................195
§ 304(c) 81, 82, 85

§ 304(c)(3)............................. 288
§ 304(c)(3)(B)(ii) 81
§ 305 ....133, 134, 138, 142, 143
§ 305(a)...........133, 141, 142, 145,
146, 149, 150
§ 305(b).....28, 133, 139, 140, 141,
290
§ 305(b)(1)........134, 135, 140, 142
§ 305(b)(2).......135, 136, 137, 139,
140
§ 305(b)(3)...................... 137, 150
§ 305(b)(4)...................... 138, 141
§ 305(b)(5)............................. 139
§ 305(c) 139, 140, 290
§ 305(d)................................. 134
§ 305(d)(2)............................. 136
§ 305(e)(5)(B)......................... 138
§ 306 ....61, 132, 138, 144, 145,
146, 147, 149, 152, 153, 195
§ 306(a)(1).............................. 150
§ 306(a)(1)(C).......... 150, 151, 153
§ 306(a)(1)(D) 144, 151
§ 306(a)(2).............................. 152
§ 306(b)................................. 153
§ 306(b)(4)............................. 153
§ 306(c) 61, 149
§ 306(c)(1)............................. 146
§ 306(c)(1)(B) 148, 290
§ 306(c)(1)(C) 148, 149, 196,
290
§ 306(c)(2)............................. 149
§ 306(c)(3)...................... 149, 195
§ 306(d)................................. 142
§ 306(e)(1)...................... 148, 290
§ 306(e)(2)............................. 147
§ 306(g) 146
§ 307 .... 143, 151
§ 307(a) 142
§ 307(b) 143
§ 311 .... 179, 238
§ 311(a)...........21, 38, 72, 90, 179,
237, 383
§ 311(b)..............72, 179, 237, 382
§ 311(b)(1)............................... 38
§ 311(b)(2)............................... 38
§ 312 .... 28, 31
§ 312(a) 22, 25
§ 312(a)(1)............................... 23
§ 312(a)(2)............................... 28
§ 312(a)(3)......................... 23, 26
§ 312(b)................................... 23
§ 312(b)(2)............................... 27
§ 312(c) 24, 26, 27
§ 312(d)................................... 28
§ 312(f)(1) 19, 29
§ 312(h)................................. 323
§ 312(h)(1) 249

§ 312(k)...............................31, 33
§ 312(k)(3).....................29, 30, 33
§ 312(l)(1)..................................22
§ 312(n)...........................31, 32, 33
§ 312(n)(5)....................28, 32, 33
§ 312(n)(7)........31, 33, 75, 76, 77, 108, 327
§ 312(o).....................................28
§ 316.................................25, 233
§ 316(a).............................13, 25
§ 317(a)....................................11
§ 317(b)....................................42
§ 318.....31, 43, 44, 45, 46, 54, 58, 59, 62, 80, 81, 82, 84, 115, 153, 234, 310, 335, 363
§ 318(a)...................43, 58, 65, 66
§ 318(a)(1).......45, 47, 62, 66, 335
§ 318(a)(2) 335
§ 318(a)(2)(C)..............81, 82, 363
§ 318(a)(3) 66
§ 318(a)(3)(B)(i).......................46
§ 318(a)(3)(C).........45, 46, 81, 82, 363
§ 318(a)(4) 78, 115
§ 318(a)(5)(A).......................44, 45
§ 318(a)(5)(B)...........................47
§ 318(a)(5)(C)...........................47
§ 318(a)(5)(E)..........................363
§ 331 201
§ 331(a)..............................89, 98
§ 332.......71, 90, 92, 98, 100, 101, 102, 103, 104, 105, 106, 107, 108, 109, 114, 128, 322, 323, 325, 327
§ 332(b)............................102, 106
§ 332(b)(1) 101
§ 332(b)(2) 101, 107
§ 332(b)(3) 101, 102
§ 332(d)(3) 102
§ 334(a)..............................98, 107
§ 334(b)......98, 104, 105, 107, 109
§ 334(b)(1) 100, 106, 107
§ 334(b)(1)(A)..........................104
§ 334(b)(1)(B)...................104, 107
§ 334(b)(2) 115
§ 336(a)...........89, 90, 91, 92, 105, 238, 382, 383
§ 336(b)....................................38
§ 336(c) 90, 92, 300, 301, 308
§ 336(d)................90, 92, 93, 383
§ 336(d)(1) 93, 94
§ 336(d)(1)(A) 94
§ 336(d)(2) 93
§ 336(d)(2)(A) 96, 97
§ 336(d)(2)(B)(i)(II)...................96
§ 336(d)(2)(B)(ii)......................96
§ 336(d)(3) 105, 106

§ 336(e) 125, 126, 127, 128
§ 337 ....71, 90, 106, 108, 116, 197
§ 337(a).............92, 105, 106, 107
§ 337(b)(1)......................108, 109
§ 337(b)(2)...............................106
§ 337(c) 106, 108
§ 338.......114, 115, 116, 120, 122, 124, 125, 127, 128, 346
§ 338(a)(1)...............................116
§ 338(a)(2).............. 116, 119, 122
§ 338(b) 120
§ 338(b)(1)...............................122
§ 338(b)(3)...............................125
§ 338(b)(4)...............................123
§ 338(b)(5)........................112, 125
§ 338(b)(6)(A)......... 117, 118, 123
§ 338(b)(6)(B).........................123
§ 338(d)(3)...............................115
§ 338(e) 116
§ 338(f)....................................116
§ 338(g) 116
§ 338(g)(1)...............................116
§ 338(g)(3)...............................116
§ 338(h)(2) 116
§ 338(h)(3) 115, 123
§ 338(h)(8) 115, 123
§ 338(h)(9) 119
§ 338(h)(10) 116, 118, 120, 121, 122, 123, 124, 125, 127, 128
§ 338(h)(11) 117
§ 346 .... 67, 69
§ 351 ...47, 82, 87, 95, 96, 99, 148, 149, 156, 157, 159, 160, 161, 165, 168, 169, 170, 172, 174, 177, 182, 190, 194, 195, 242, 243, 253, 303, 312, 316, 334
§ 351(a)...........157, 158, 164, 166, 170, 171, 172, 177, 179, 192, 193, 285
§ 351(b).....87, 170, 172, 173, 177, 178, 179, 192, 193, 266
§ 351(b)(1)............................... 178
§ 351(b)(2)............................... 174
§ 351(d)(1)............................... 168
§ 351(e)(1)............................... 157
§ 351(f).................................... 179
§ 351(g) 146, 178, 231
§ 351(g)(1)(A).......................... 179
§ 351(g)(1)(B).......................... 179
§ 351(g)(2)............. 175, 239, 289
§ 351(g)(2)(C).......................... 177
§ 351(g)(3)(A)................. 138, 176
§ 351(g)(4)............................... 146
§ 351(h)................................... 170
§ 354 ....242, 294, 303, 328
§ 354(a)........................... 105, 309

§ 354(a)(1) 296, 297, 300, 301, 303, 304, 305, 308

§ 354(a)(2) 28, 291, 292, 309

§ 354(a)(2)(B)...........................291

§ 354(a)(2)(C)(i) 290

§ 354(b).....................................286

§ 354(b)(1) 312, 323

§ 355 ....69, 71, 147, 200, 203, 207, 211, 212, 216, 218, 220, 223, 226, 227, 231, 237, 238, 239, 242, 253, 323

§ 355(a)....................203, 241, 247

§ 355(a)(1) 92

§ 355(a)(1)(A)..........................205

§ 355(a)(1)(B)..................204, 207

§ 355(a)(1)(C)..........................211

§ 355(a)(1)(D) 204, 205, 206, 229

§ 355(a)(2)(A)..........................203

§ 355(a)(2)(B)..........................203

§ 355(a)(3) 28

§ 355(a)(3)(A)..........228, 232, 239

§ 355(a)(3)(B)..........228, 229, 239

§ 355(a)(3)(C)..........................228

§ 355(a)(3)(D) 228, 231, 239

§ 355(b).....69, 204, 209, 211, 217, 230

§ 355(b)(1) 204

§ 355(b)(1)(A)..........................219

§ 355(b)(2)(A)...................215, 216

§ 355(b)(2)(B)..........................216

§ 355(b)(2)(C)..........................216

§ 355(b)(2)(D) 216

§ 355(b)(3) 215, 230

§ 355(b)(3)(B)...................211, 230

§ 355(b)(3)(D) 230

§ 355(c) 92, 229, 238, 239, 240, 241, 285

§ 355(c)(2)(A) 238

§ 355(c)(2)(B) 238

§ 355(c)(2)(C) 238

§ 355(c)(3)...............................238

§ 355(d)...226, 238, 239, 240, 241, 242, 243, 244

§ 355(d)(1) 241

§ 355(d)(2) 241, 242

§ 355(d)(2)(A) 242

§ 355(d)(2)(B) 242, 245

§ 355(d)(3) 242

§ 355(d)(3)(A) 242, 245

§ 355(d)(3)(B)(i) 242

§ 355(d)(5) 242

§ 355(d)(5)(A) 245

§ 355(d)(5)(B) 242

§ 355(d)(8)(A) 242

§ 355(d)(8)(B) 242

§ 355(e) 220, 226, 238, 239, 241, 244, 247

§ 355(e)(1)............................... 241

§ 355(e)(2)(D)......................... 241

§ 355(e)(3)(B) 249

§ 355(e)(4)(C) 248

§ 356 ....100, 147, 200, 203, 206, 220, 227, 231, 237, 238, 242, 253, 266

§ 356(a)...........231, 233, 241, 291, 309, 311

§ 356(a)(1)........205, 232, 292, 310

§ 356(a)(2).......205, 233, 234, 235, 290, 292, 309, 310, 311

§ 356(b)...........204, 231, 232, 233, 290, 309

§ 356(c) 204, 231

§ 356(d)............................ 28, 292

§ 356(d)(2)(C).................. 206, 232

§ 356(e) 231

§ 357 .... 180, 182, 185

§ 357(a) 180, 181, 182

§ 357(b) 180, 181, 182, 312

§ 357(c) 180, 182, 183, 184, 185, 186, 187, 189, 192, 193, 276, 302, 312

§ 357(c)(1) 187

§ 357(c)(2)(A) 182

§ 357(c)(3) 186, 187, 188

§ 357(c)(3)(B) 186

§ 357(d)...........11, 12, 180, 181

§ 357(d)(1)............................. 180

§ 357(d)(1)(A).................... 11, 181

§ 357(d)(1)(B)........... 11, 180, 301

§ 357(d)(2)....................... 11, 180

§ 358 ....82, 157, 158, 191, 236, 241, 243, 294, 299, 313, 314

§ 358(a)........................... 181, 303

§ 358(a)(1).......160, 172, 178, 183, 296, 297, 300, 301, 304, 305, 306, 308

§ 358(a)(1)(A)........................ 237

§ 358(a)(1)(A)(ii) 183, 188

§ 358(a)(1)(B).......... 183, 237, 312

§ 358(a)(2).......172, 178, 184, 236, 237, 314

§ 358(b)............................ 201, 237

§ 358(b)(2)............................. 236

§ 358(c) 201, 236, 237

§ 358(d) 180, 183, 188

§ 358(d)(1)............................. 187

§ 358(d)(2)............................. 186

§ 358(h).................................. 186

§ 361 ....243, 253, 294, 303

§ 361(a)...........285, 296, 300, 301, 303, 308

§ 361(b).................. 253, 266, 314

§ 361(b)(1)(A)..........271, 312, 314
§ 361(b)(3) 312
§ 361(c) 92, 229, 238, 240, 241,
 244, 247, 285, 300
§ 361(c)(1).......................240, 312
§ 361(c)(2)........240, 301, 308, 313
§ 361(c)(2)(A)..........................240
§ 361(c)(2)(B)..........................240
§ 361(c)(2)(B)(ii) 229, 240
§ 361(c)(2)(C)..........................314
§ 361(c)(3).............................312
§ 361(c)(4).............................240
§ 362 ....84, 158, 159, 185
§ 362(a).....84, 160, 171, 172, 178,
 181, 184, 187, 191
§ 362(b)...........294, 296, 297, 299,
 300, 301, 304, 306, 308, 313,
 314
§ 362(d)............................160, 294
§ 362(d)(1) 185, 253
§ 362(d)(2) 185
§ 362(e) 92, 93, 98, 162, 172,
 294
§ 362(e)(1)...............................253
§ 362(e)(2)...............161, 162, 174
§ 362(e)(2)(B)...................161, 162
§ 362(e)(2)(C)...................162, 174
§ 367(e)(2)...............................106
§ 368 ....100, 168, 200, 220, 237,
 294, 323, 334
§ 368(a)............................147, 252
§ 368(a)(1) 252, 261, 294
§ 368(a)(1)(A)..........105, 261, 262
§ 368(a)(1)(B).........261, 266, 269,
 276, 297
§ 368(a)(1)(C)..........272, 273, 274,
 287
§ 368(a)(1)(D) 238, 285, 286,
 287, 288
§ 368(a)(1)(E)..............................50
§ 368(a)(1)(F)............................293
§ 368(a)(1)(G)............................261
§ 368(a)(2)(A)............................287
§ 368(a)(2)(B).........271, 273, 274,
 278
§ 368(a)(2)(C)...................276, 284
§ 368(a)(2)(D) 279, 280, 284,
 303
§ 368(a)(2)(D)(i).......................281
§ 368(a)(2)(E)..........279, 281, 283,
 284, 305
§ 368(a)(2)(G) 272, 276, 312
§ 368(a)(2)(H) 288
§ 368(a)(2)(H)(i)......................308
§ 368(a)(2)(H)(ii)..............226, 227
§ 368(b)....................................276

§ 368(c) 164, 177, 203, 205,
 206, 215, 230, 264, 266, 269,
 276, 283, 315, 316
§ 381 ....72, 100, 129, 295, 320,
 323, 325, 326, 327, 328, 332,
 333, 341
§ 381(a)...........104, 323, 325, 333
§ 381(a)(1)................................ 323
§ 381(a)(2)................................ 323
§ 381(a)(4)................................ 320
§ 381(b)................................... 325
§ 381(b)(1)............................... 325
§ 381(b)(3)...................... 292, 325
§ 381(c) 321, 322, 323
§ 381(c)(2)............................... 104
§ 381(c)(2)(B) 104, 328
§ 382 ....295, 326, 331, 332, 334,
 336, 338, 341, 342, 346, 351,
 356
§§ 382–384...................... 330, 356
§ 382(b)(1)............................... 344
§ 382(b)(2)............................... 346
§ 382(c) 346
§ 382(d)(2)............................... 343
§ 382(e)(1)............................... 344
§ 382(e)(2)............................... 344
§ 382(g)(1)............................... 336
§ 382(g)(2)............................... 334
§ 382(g)(3)............................... 334
§ 382(g)(3)(A)........................... 341
§ 382(g)(4)(A)........................... 336
§ 382(g)(4)(B)........................... 336
§ 382(h)........................... 343, 347
§ 382(h)(1)(A) 350
§ 382(h)(1)(B) 350
§ 382(h)(2)(A) 347, 348
§ 382(h)(2)(B) 348, 349
§ 382(h)(3)(A) 349
§ 382(h)(3)(B) 349
§ 382(h)(3)(B)(ii)..................... 350
§ 382(h)(4) 350
§ 382(h)(6)(A) 348
§ 382(h)(6)(B) 349
§ 382(h)(6)(C) 349
§ 382(h)(7)(A) 347
§ 382(h)(7)(B) 347, 352
§ 382(i)..................................... 335
§ 382(k)(1) 333
§ 382(k)(2) 333
§ 382(k)(3) 333
§ 382(k)(5) 334
§ 382(k)(6)(A)........................... 334
§ 382(k)(6)(C)................... 334, 335
§ 382(k)(7) 335
§ 382(*l*)(1) 344
§ 382(*l*)(1)(B) 345
§ 382(*l*)(3)(A) 335

§ 382(*l*)(3)(A)(i).......................339
§ 382(*l*)(3)(A)(ii)..............336, 342
§ 382(*l*)(3)(A)(ii)(II) 336
§ 382(*l*)(3)(A)(iii)....................336
§ 382(*l*)(3)(B) 337
§ 382(*l*)(3)(C) 334, 337
§ 382(*l*)(4) 345
§ 382(*l*)(4)(D) 345
§ 382(*l*)(5) 330, 347
§ 382(*l*)(6) 347
§ 383 ....295, 331, 343, 346, 351, 356
§ 384 ....295, 326, 351, 352, 356
§ 384(a)....................................352
§ 384(b)(1) 352
§ 384(b)(2) 353
§ 384(c)(1)(A)...........................354
§ 384(c)(1)(C)...........................354
§ 384(c)(2)................................352
§ 384(c)(3)................................353
§ 384(c)(4)................................352
§ 384(c)(5)................................352
§ 384(c)(8)................................352
§ 384(d)....................................355
§ 384(e)(1)................................352
§ 385 171
§ 441 4
§ 441(i)(2) 4
§ 444 372
§ 448 3
§ 448(a)(3) 4
§ 448(b)(1) 3
§ 448(b)(2) 3
§ 448(b)(3) 4
§ 448(c)(1)................................... 4
§ 448(d)(2) 3
§ 453 191
§ 453(c) 191
§ 453(i)..............................191, 192
§ 453B......................................107
§ 453B(d) 107
§ 465 ....374, 378
§ 465(a)(1) 378
§ 465(a)(2) 379
§ 465(c) 379
§ 469 ....374, 378
§ 469(a)(2) 378
§ 469(b)....................................379
§ 469(c)(1)................................379
§ 469(c)(5)................................379
§ 469(c)(6)................................379
§ 469(d)(1) 379
§ 469(h)(1) 379
§ 469(h)(5) 379
§ 482 ....193, 194
§§ 671–678 366
§ 678 366

§ 703(a)(2)............................. 374
§ 704(d) 378
§ 707(b) 176
§ 721 168
§ 1001(c) 156, 313
§ 1014 .... 75, 149, 337
§ 1015 337
§ 1016(a)(1)........................... 171
§ 1017 22
§ 1031 .... 19, 112
§ 1031(b)............................... 266
§ 1032 ....38, 156, 157, 159, 160, 161, 179, 294, 296, 298, 299, 300, 304, 308
§ 1033 373
§ 1036(a) 289, 290
§ 1036(b) 289
§ 1041(a) 378
§ 1041(b)(2) 337
§ 1059 ....34, 36, 68, 78, 312
§ 1059(a) 34, 35, 78
§ 1059(a)(1)..................... 35, 312
§ 1059(a)(2)..................... 35, 312
§ 1059(b) 35
§ 1059(c) 35
§ 1059(c)(2) 35
§ 1059(c)(3)(A) 36
§ 1059(c)(4) 35
§ 1059(d)(1)............................. 34
§ 1059(d)(4)............................. 35
§ 1059(e)(1) 36, 312
§ 1059(e)(1)(A)(i) 78
§ 1059(e)(1)(A)(ii) 78
§ 1059(e)(1)(A)(iii)(I) 78
§ 1059(e)(1)(A)(iii)(II)........ 79, 83
§ 1059(e)(1)(B)............... 311, 312
§ 1060(a) 112
§ 1060(c) 112
§ 1211 98
§ 1211(b) 18
§ 1212 98
§ 1212(a) 322
§ 1212(a)(1)........................... 326
§ 1221 158
§ 1222(11)............................. 394
§ 1223 .... 158, 159
§ 1223(1) 82, 158, 178
§ 1223(2) 158, 178
§ 1223(4) 142
§ 1223(5) 143
§ 1223(9) 75
§ 1231 ....91, 92, 158, 178, 192, 193, 375
§ 1239 .... 175, 182, 193
§ 1239(c) 193
§ 1245 ....91, 175, 191, 192
§ 1245(b)(3)................... 107, 192

§ 1250 ....175, 191, 192
§ 1250(d)(3) 107, 192
§ 1273 28
§ 1275(a)(4) 28
§ 1276(c) 291
§ 1276(d) 291
§ 1361 363
§§ 1361–1379............................361
§ 1361(a)...................................361
§ 1361(a)(1) 2
§ 1361(a)(2) 2
§ 1361(b)........................363, 371
§ 1361(b)(1)(B)........................365
§ 1361(b)(1)(D) 367
§ 1361(b)(2) 364
§ 1361(b)(3) 365
§ 1361(b)(3)(A)........................365
§ 1361(c)(1)(A)(ii) 365
§ 1361(c)(1)(B)(ii) 365
§ 1361(c)(2)........................364, 365
§ 1361(c)(2)(A)(ii)....................366
§ 1361(c)(2)(A)(iii) 366
§ 1361(c)(2)(A)(iv)....................366
§ 1361(c)(2)(A)(v)....................367
§ 1361(c)(2)(B)(iv)....................366
§ 1361(c)(5)..............................369
§ 1361(c)(6)..............................364
§ 1361(d)................364, 365, 367
§ 1361(d)(3)(B) 366
§ 1361(d)(4)(B) 366
§ 1361(e) 367
§ 1362(a)...................................371
§ 1362(b)...................................371
§ 1362(b)(3) 372
§ 1362(b)(5) 372
§ 1362(d)(1) 384
§ 1362(d)(2) 384
§ 1362(d)(3) 382, 385
§ 1362(d)(3)(C) 385, 387
§ 1362(e)(1)..............................386
§ 1362(e)(2)..............................386
§ 1362(e)(3)..............................386
§ 1362(e)(4)..............................386
§ 1362(e)(5)..............................386
§ 1362(e)(6)(A)........................386
§ 1362(e)(6)(D)........................386
§ 1362(f)...........................371, 384
§ 1362(g)..........................371, 386
§ 1363(b).................362, 373, 392
§ 1363(c)(2)..............................373
§ 1363(d)..........................372, 393
§ 1363(d)(1) 372
§ 1363(d)(3) 394
§ 1366(a)...................................374
§ 1366(a)(1) 374
§ 1366(d)...................................378
§ 1366(d)(2)(A) 377

§ 1366(d)(2)(B)......................... 378
§ 1367 .... 375, 380
§ 1367(a).................................. 377
§ 1368 .... 375, 377
§ 1368(a).................................. 379
§ 1368(b)................ 362, 379, 380
§ 1368(c)(1) 380
§ 1368(c)(2) 373
§ 1368(e)(1) 380, 381
§ 1368(e)(1)(A) 381
§ 1368(e)(1)(C) 381
§ 1368(e)(3)............................. 382
§ 1371(a)........................... 2, 362
§ 1371(a)(2)............................... 68
§ 1371(c)(1) 373
§ 1371(c)(2) 373
§ 1371(d)(2)............................. 372
§ 1371(e)(1) 383
§ 1372(a).................................. 363
§ 1373(a).................................. 363
§ 1374 .....373, 382, 389, 391, 392
§ 1374(b)(1)............................. 392
§ 1374(b)(2)............................. 391
§ 1374(b)(3)............................. 391
§ 1374(d)(2)(A)(ii) 392
§ 1374(d)(2)(B)........................ 392
§ 1374(d)(3)............................. 390
§ 1374(d)(4)............................. 391
§ 1374(d)(7).................... 389, 393
§ 1374(d)(7)(B)........................ 389
§ 1374(d)(8)............................. 390
§ 1374(d)(8)(B)........................ 389
§ 1375 .....373, 382, 386, 389, 392
§ 1375(a).................................. 388
§ 1375(b)(2)............................. 387
§ 1375(b)(4)............................. 393
§ 1377 381
§ 1377(a)(1)............................. 374
§ 1377(b).................................. 383
§ 1377(b)(1)............................. 383
§ 1377(b)(1)(A)........................ 383
§ 1378 4
§ 1378(b).................................. 372
§ 1501 164
§ 1504 115
§ 1504(a)................. 211, 215, 230
§ 1504(a)(2)............. 101, 121, 230
§ 1504(a)(4)...... 17, 101, 333, 335,
    336, 344, 352
§ 1504(a)(4)(C)........................ 101
§ 1504(b).................................. 230
§ 1504(b)(8)............................. 364
§ 1563 352
§ 1563(a)............................. 93, 94
§ 1563(a)(2)............................... 94
§ 1563(a)(3)............................... 94
§ 2053 .... 73, 74

§ 2054 73
§ 2106 74
§ 2611 73
§ 6072(b) 362
§ 6166(b)(6) 73
§ 7491(a)(3) 348, 349
§ 7519 372
§ 7701(a)(1) 164
§ 7701(a)(3) 6
§ 7701(a)(4) 2
§ 7701(a)(5) 2
§ 7872 ....39, 371

Table of Treasury Regulations

Prop. Reg. § 1.301–2(a).............33
Prop. Reg. § 1.302–5(a)(1) 50
Prop. Reg. § 1.302–5(a)(2) 50
Prop. Reg. § 1.302–5(a)(3) 52
Prop. Reg. § 1.302–5(b)(2) 34, 50
Prop. Reg. § 1.302–5(b)(4) 52
Prop. Reg. § 1.302–
5(b)(4)(i)(B) 53
Prop. Reg. § 1.302–5(e),
Ex. (1) 51
Prop. Reg. § 1.302–5(e),
Ex. (3) 57
Prop. Reg. § 1.304–2(a)(3) 82
Prop. Reg. § 1.304–2(c),
Ex. (1) 48, 83
Prop. Reg. § 1.304–2(c),
Ex. (3) 83
Prop. Reg. § 1.332–2(b)...........103
Prop. Reg. § 1.336–
2(b)(1)(i)(B)(2).....................128
Prop. Reg. § 1.336–
2(b)(1)(iii)............................128
Prop. Reg. § 1.336–
2(b)(2)(i)(B)(2).....................128
Prop. Reg. § 1.336–3 128
Prop. Reg. § 1.336–4 128
Prop. Reg. § 1.351–
1(a)(1)(iii)(A).........................190
Prop. Reg. § 1.351–
1(a)(1)(iii)(B).........................191
Prop. Reg. § 1.351–
1(a)(1)(iv)..............................190
Prop. Reg. § 1.351–2(b)...........175
Prop. Reg. § 1.453–1(f)(3) 191
Prop. Reg. § 1.453–
1(f)(3)(ii)...............................192
Prop. Reg. § 1.453–1(f)(3)(iii),
Ex. (1) 192
Temp. Reg. § 1.67–
2T(g)(1)(iii) 363
Temp. Reg. § 1.368–
1T(e)(2)(v), Ex. (1) 225
Temp. Reg. § 1.382–
2T(a)(1)................................336
Temp. Reg. § 1.382–
2T(a)(2)................................335
Temp. Reg. § 1.382–
2T(a)(2)(i)(B)........................335
Temp. Reg. § 1.382–
2T(e)(1) 334

Temp. Reg. § 1.382–
2T(e)(1)(ii)................... 334, 340
Temp. Reg. § 1.382–
2T(e)(2)(i) 341
Temp. Reg. § 1.382–
2T(f)(2) 333
Temp. Reg. § 1.382–
2T(f)(3) 333
Temp. Reg. § 1.382–
2T(f)(13) 336
Temp. Reg. § 1.382–
2T(f)(18) 334
Temp. Reg. § 1.382–
2T(f)(19) 343
Temp. Reg. § 1.382–
2T(g)(2) 336
Temp. Reg. § 1.382–
2T(h)(2)(i)............................. 336
Temp. Reg. § 1.382–
2T(h)(2)(i)(A)........................ 336
Temp. Reg. § 1.382–
2T(h)(2)(ii)(A) 336
Temp. Reg. § 1.382–
2T(h)(2)(iii) 336
Temp. Reg. § 1.382–
2T(h)(3) 336
Temp. Reg. § 1.382–2T(j) 336
Temp. Reg. § 1.382–
2T(j)(1)(iii) 340
Temp. Reg. § 1.382–
2T(j)(2)(iii)(B) 340
Temp. Reg. § 1.382–
2T(k)(2) 340
Temp. Reg. § 1.469–1T(b) 378
Temp. Reg. § 1.469–
1T(g)(2) 378
Temp. Reg. § 1.469–
2T(d)(6) 379
Temp. Reg. § 1.469–5T(a) 379
Treas. Reg. § 1.47–1............. 192
Treas. Reg. § 1.47–3(f)(1)....... 192
Treas. Reg. § 1.162–8.............. 39
Treas. Reg. § 1.269–1(b) 355
Treas. Reg. § 1.269–3(a) 355
Treas. Reg. § 1.269–4............. 356
Treas. Reg. § 1.269–7............. 356
Treas. Reg. § 1.301–1(g) 11
Treas. Reg. § 1.301–1(j) 39
Treas. Reg. § 1.302–2(a) 56
Treas. Reg. § 1.302–2(b) 54, 58
Treas. Reg. § 1.302–2(c)..... 49, 84
Treas. Reg. § 1.302–3(a) 60, 61

Treas. Reg. § 1.302–4(a) 63
Treas. Reg. § 1.302–4(c)............62
Treas. Reg. § 1.302–4(d) 65
Treas. Reg. § 1.304–2(a) 83, 84
Treas. Reg. § 1.304–2(c),
   Ex. (1) 61
Treas. Reg. § 1.305–1(b)(1)... 134,
   141
Treas. Reg. § 1.305–1(d) 134
Treas. Reg. § 1.305–2(a) 134
Treas. Reg. § 1.305–2(b),
   Ex. (1) 141
Treas. Reg. § 1.305–3(b)(2).....135
Treas. Reg. § 1.305–3(b)(4).....136
Treas. Reg. § 1.305–3(c).........137
Treas. Reg. § 1.305–3(d) 137
Treas. Reg. § 1.305–3(e),
   Ex. (1) 135
Treas. Reg. § 1.305–3(e),
   Ex. (2) 137
Treas. Reg. § 1.305–3(e),
   Ex. (3) 137
Treas. Reg. § 1.305–3(e),
   Ex. (4) 137
Treas. Reg. § 1.305–3(e),
   Ex. (10) 140
Treas. Reg. § 1.305–3(e),
   Ex. (11) 140
Treas. Reg. § 1.305–5(a) 138,
   147, 176
Treas. Reg. § 1.305–5(d),
   Ex. (9) 138
Treas. Reg. § 1.305–7(c).........290
Treas. Reg. § 1.306–1(b)(2),
   Ex. (2) 150, 151
Treas. Reg. § 1.306–2(a) 153
Treas. Reg. § 1.306–2(b)(3).....154
Treas. Reg. § 1.306–3(a) 146
Treas. Reg. § 1.306–3(b) 142,
   146
Treas. Reg. § 1.306–3(d) 290
Treas. Reg. § 1.306–3(d),
   Ex. (2) 290
Treas. Reg. § 1.306–3(e) 148,
   149
Treas. Reg. § 1.307–1(a) 142
Treas. Reg. § 1.307–1(b),
   Ex..142
Treas. Reg. § 1.307–2.............144
Treas. Reg. § 1.312–1(d) 28,
   141
Treas. Reg. § 1.312–3...............26
Treas. Reg. § 1.312–6(a) 20
Treas. Reg. § 1.312–10............323
Treas. Reg. § 1.312–10(a) 249,
   285
Treas. Reg. § 1.312–10(b) 249

Treas. Reg. § 1.316–2(b) 14, 16
Treas. Reg. § 1.316–2(c), Ex. ... 15
Treas. Reg. § 1.318–1(b)(3) 44
Treas. Reg. § 1.318–3(a),
   Ex. (1)(a) 46
Treas. Reg. § 1.331–1(c).......... 99
Treas. Reg. § 1.331–1(e).......... 98
Treas. Reg. § 1.332–2(b) 102,
   109
Treas. Reg. § 1.332–2(c).......... 91
Treas. Reg. § 1.332–2(d) 105
Treas. Reg. § 1.332–2(e),
   Ex.. 105
Treas. Reg. § 1.332–4(a) 102
Treas. Reg. § 1.332–5............. 105
Treas. Reg. § 1.332–7............. 108
Treas. Reg. §§ 1.336–1—5 125
Treas. Reg. § 1.336–1(b)(3).... 126
Treas. Reg. § 1.336–1(b)(6).... 126
Treas. Reg. § 1.336–
   1(b)(6)(i) 128
Treas. Reg. § 1.336–
   1(b)(6)(ii) 125
Treas. Reg. § 1.336–
   1(b)(6)(ii)(A) 125
Treas. Reg. § 1.336–1(b)(7).... 126
Treas. Reg. § 1.336–1(b)(8).... 126
Treas. Reg. § 1.336–
   1(b)(17)................................. 127
Treas. Reg. § 1.336–2(a) 126
Treas. Reg. § 1.336–
   2(b)(1)(i)(A) 126, 127
Treas. Reg. § 1.336–
   2(b)(1)(i)(B) 127
Treas. Reg. § 1.336–
   2(b)(2)(i)(A) 127
Treas. Reg. § 1.336–2(d)(1).... 127
Treas. Reg. § 1.336–2(d)(2).... 127
Treas. Reg. § 1.336–2(d)(3).... 127
Treas. Reg. § 1.336–2(g)(1).... 127
Treas. Reg. § 1.336–2(g)(2).... 125
Treas. Reg. § 1.336–2(h) 126
Treas. Reg. § 1.336–3(a) 127
Treas. Reg. § 1.336–3(b) 127
Treas. Reg. § 1.336–3(c)......... 127
Treas. Reg. § 1.336–4(a) 128
Treas. Reg. § 1.338(h)(10)–
   1(b)(2)................................... 121
Treas. Reg. § 1.338(h)(10)–
   1(b)(3)................................... 121
Treas. Reg. § 1.338(h)(10)–
   1(c)(1) 121
Treas. Reg. § 1.338(h)(10)–
   1(c)(3) 121
Treas. Reg. § 1.338(h)(10)–
   1(c)(4) 120

Treas. Reg. § 1.338(h)(10)–
  1(d)(1) 123
Treas. Reg. § 1.338(h)(10)–
  1(d)(4) 122
Treas. Reg. § 1.338(h)(10)–
  1(d)(5)(i)................122
Treas. Reg. § 1.338(h)(10)–
  1(d)(7)(i)...............122
Treas. Reg. § 1.338(h)(10)–
  1(e), Ex. (4) 121
Treas. Reg. § 1.338(h)(10)–
  1(e), Ex. (5) 121
Treas. Reg. § 1.338–1(a) 120
Treas. Reg. § 1.338–1(a)(1).....116
Treas. Reg. § 1.338–1(a)(3).....117
Treas. Reg. § 1.338–1(b) 119,
  120
Treas. Reg. § 1.338–1(b)(1).....119
Treas. Reg. § 1.338–1(b)(3).....120
Treas. Reg. § 1.338–
  1(b)(3)(i).............................120
Treas. Reg. § 1.338–
  2(c)(17)................................119
Treas. Reg. § 1.338–3(b)(1).....115
Treas. Reg. § 1.338–4..............117
Treas. Reg. § 1.338–
  4(b)(1)(i) 117
Treas. Reg. § 1.338–
  4(b)(2)(ii)............................117
Treas. Reg. § 1.338–4(c)(1) 118
Treas. Reg. § 1.338–4(d) 117,
  121
Treas. Reg. § 1.338–4(e) 118
Treas. Reg. § 1.338–4(g),
  Exs. (1)–(4) 118
Treas. Reg. § 1.338–5......120, 128
Treas. Reg. § 1.338–5(b)(1).....122
Treas. Reg. § 1.338–
  5(b)(2)(ii)............................122
Treas. Reg. § 1.338–5(c)..........123
Treas. Reg. § 1.338–5(d) 125
Treas. Reg. § 1.338–6.....118, 120,
  127, 128
Treas. Reg. § 1.338–6(b) 112,
  125
Treas. Reg. § 1.338–7.....118, 120,
  127
Treas. Reg. § 1.338–7(a) 117
Treas. Reg. § 1.338–8..............116
Treas. Reg. § 1.338–10(a) 119
Treas. Reg. § 1.338–
  10(a)(2)................................118
Treas. Reg. § 1.338–
  10(a)(2)(iii)..................119, 120
Treas. Reg. § 1.346–1(b)(2).......70
Treas. Reg. § 1.351–1(a)(1)... 165,
  171

Treas. Reg. § 1.351–
  1(a)(1)(i) 168
Treas. Reg. § 1.351–
  1(a)(1)(ii)................... 165, 168
Treas. Reg. § 1.351–1(a)(2),
  Ex. (3).............................. 165
Treas. Reg. § 1.351–1(a)(3).... 167
Treas. Reg. § 1.351–1(b)(1)... 170
Treas. Reg. § 1.351–1(c)(1) ... 157
Treas. Reg. § 1.355–1(b) 218,
  224
Treas. Reg. § 1.355–1(c)......... 206
Treas. Reg. § 1.355–2(b) 203,
  204
Treas. Reg. § 1.355–2(b)(1) ... 221,
  223
Treas. Reg. § 1.355–2(b)(2) 222
Treas. Reg. § 1.355–2(b)(2)–
  (5), Ex. (2) 223
Treas. Reg. § 1.355–2(b)(3) 223
Treas. Reg. § 1.355–2(b)(4) ... 209,
  221
Treas. Reg. § 1.355–2(b)(5),
  Ex. (1).............................. 222
Treas. Reg. § 1.355–2(b)(5),
  Ex. (2).............................. 222
Treas. Reg. § 1.355–2(b)(5),
  Ex. (4).............................. 223
Treas. Reg. § 1.355–2(c)........ 204,
  226, 244
Treas. Reg. § 1.355–2(c)(1) 225
Treas. Reg. § 1.355–2(c)(2),
  Ex. (4).............................. 226
Treas. Reg. § 1.355–2(d) 207
Treas. Reg. § 1.355–2(d)(1).... 207
Treas. Reg. § 1.355–
  2(d)(2)(ii) 208
Treas. Reg. § 1.355–
  2(d)(2)(iii) 208
Treas. Reg. § 1.355–
  2(d)(2)(iii)(B) 209
Treas. Reg. § 1.355–
  2(d)(2)(iii)(D) 209
Treas. Reg. § 1.355–
  2(d)(2)(iv) 209
Treas. Reg. § 1.355–
  2(d)(2)(iv)(B) 209
Treas. Reg. § 1.355–
  2(d)(2)(iv)(C) 209, 218
Treas. Reg. § 1.355–
  2(d)(3)(ii) 209, 221
Treas. Reg. § 1.355–
  2(d)(3)(iii) 210
Treas. Reg. § 1.355–
  2(d)(3)(iv) 210
Treas. Reg. § 1.355–2(d)(4),
  Ex. (2)................................ 208
Treas. Reg. § 1.355–2(d)(5).... 208

Treas. Reg. § 1.355–
2(d)(5)(i) 210
Treas. Reg. § 1.355–
2(d)(5)(ii) 210
Treas. Reg. § 1.355–
2(d)(5)(iii) 211
Treas. Reg. § 1.355–
2(d)(5)(iv) 211
Treas. Reg. § 1.355–2(e)(2) 207
Treas. Reg. § 1.355–2(g)(1) 230
Treas. Reg. § 1.355–2(g)(2) ... 230,
239
Treas. Reg. § 1.355–
2(g)(2)(ii) 230
Treas. Reg. § 1.355–3 212
Treas. Reg. § 1.355–
3(b)(2)(ii) 212
Treas. Reg. § 1.355–
3(b)(2)(iii) 212
Treas. Reg. § 1.355–
3(b)(2)(iv) 213
Treas. Reg. § 1.355–
3(b)(3)(ii) 219
Treas. Reg. § 1.355–
3(b)(4)(i) 216
Treas. Reg. § 1.355–
3(b)(4)(iv) 222, 230
Treas. Reg. § 1.355–3(c),
Ex. (2) 213
Treas. Reg. § 1.355–3(c),
Ex. (3) 213
Treas. Reg. § 1.355–3(c),
Ex. (4) 218
Treas. Reg. § 1.355–3(c),
Ex. (7) 219
Treas. Reg. § 1.355–3(c),
Ex. (9) 209, 218
Treas. Reg. § 1.355–3(c),
Ex. (10) 218
Treas. Reg. § 1.355–3(c),
Ex. (11) 209, 218
Treas. Reg. § 1.355–3(c),
Ex. (12) 213
Treas. Reg. § 1.355–3(c),
Ex. (13) 213
Treas. Reg. § 1.355–4 206
Treas. Reg. § 1.355–
6(b)(3)(i) 245
Treas. Reg. § 1.355–
6(b)(3)(ii) 246
Treas. Reg. § 1.355–
6(b)(3)(v) 245
Treas. Reg. § 1.355–7(d) 249
Treas. Reg. § 1.356–2 232
Treas. Reg. § 1.356–3 228
Treas. Reg. § 1.356–3(b) 206

Treas. Reg. § 1.356–3(c),
Exs. (7)–(9) 206
Treas. Reg. § 1.356–6 ..... 206, 231
Treas. Reg. § 1.356–6(a)(1) 206
Treas. Reg. § 1.356–6(a)(2) 206
Treas. Reg. § 1.356–
7(b)(1)(i) 231
Treas. Reg. § 1.357–1(c) 181
Treas. Reg. § 1.357–2(a)–
(b) 182
Treas. Reg. § 1.357–2(b) 183,
184
Treas. Reg. § 1.358–2(a)(1) 237
Treas. Reg. § 1.358–
2(a)(2)(ii) 232
Treas. Reg. § 1.358–
2(a)(2)(iv) 237
Treas. Reg. § 1.358–2(b)(2) ... 158,
159
Treas. Reg. § 1.358–6(c)(1) 301
Treas. Reg. § 1.358–
6(c)(1)(ii) 302, 303
Treas. Reg. § 1.358–6(c)(3) ... 297,
299
Treas. Reg. § 1.358–6(c)(4),
Ex. (2)(c) 306
Treas. Reg. § 1.358–6(c)(4),
Ex. (3) 297, 299
Treas. Reg. § 1.368–1(a) 261
Treas. Reg. § 1.368–1(b) 225,
254, 257, 258, 260, 289
Treas. Reg. § 1.368–1(c) 203
Treas. Reg. § 1.368–1(d) 258,
346
Treas. Reg. § 1.368–1(d)(1) 260
Treas. Reg. § 1.368–
1(d)(2)(i) 260
Treas. Reg. § 1.368–
1(d)(2)(ii) 259
Treas. Reg. § 1.368–
1(d)(2)(iii) 258
Treas. Reg. § 1.368–
1(d)(2)(iv) 259
Treas. Reg. § 1.368–
1(d)(3)(iii) 260
Treas. Reg. § 1.368–
1(d)(4)(i) 261
Treas. Reg. § 1.368–
1(d)(4)(ii) 261
Treas. Reg. § 1.368–1(d)(5),
Ex. (1) 259
Treas. Reg. § 1.368–1(d)(5),
Ex. (2) 260
Treas. Reg. § 1.368–1(d)(5),
Ex. (6) 261
Treas. Reg. § 1.368–1(d)(5),
Ex. (11) 259

Treas. Reg. § 1.368–1(d)(5),
Ex. (12) 259
Treas. Reg. § 1.368–1(e) 256
Treas. Reg. § 1.368–1(e)(1) 268
Treas. Reg. § 1.368–
1(e)(1)(ii) 270
Treas. Reg. § 1.368–1(e)(2)(v),
Ex. (1) 255, 256
Treas. Reg. § 1.368–1(e)(3) 270
Treas. Reg. § 1.368–1(e)(4) 257
Treas. Reg. § 1.368–1(e)(6) 268
Treas. Reg. § 1.368–1(e)(7),
Ex. (9) 270
Treas. Reg. § 1.368–1(e)(8),
Ex. (1) 225
Treas. Reg. § 1.368–1(e)(8),
Ex. (10) 268
Treas. Reg. § 1.368–2(b)(1) 263
Treas. Reg. § 1.368–
2(b)(1)(ii) 262, 263
Treas. Reg. § 1.368–2(b)(2) ... 280,
281
Treas. Reg. § 1.368–2(c) 268,
269, 278
Treas. Reg. § 1.368–2(d)(1) 278
Treas. Reg. § 1.368–2(d)(4) 275
Treas. Reg. § 1.368–2(d)(4)(ii),
Ex. (1) 276
Treas. Reg. § 1.368–2(e)(1) 291
Treas. Reg. § 1.368–2(e)(2) 290
Treas. Reg. § 1.368–2(e)(3) 290
Treas. Reg. § 1.368–2(e)(4) 290
Treas. Reg. § 1.368–2(f) 276
Treas. Reg. § 1.368–2(g) 203
Treas. Reg. § 1.368–
2(j)(3)(i) 283
Treas. Reg. § 1.368–
2(j)(3)(iii) 283
Treas. Reg. § 1.368–2(j)(5) 283
Treas. Reg. § 1.368–2(j)(6),
Ex. (2) 283
Treas. Reg. § 1.368–2(j)(6),
Ex. (3) 274
Treas. Reg. § 1.368–2(j)(6),
Ex. (4) 284
Treas. Reg. § 1.368–2(j)(6),
Ex. (5) 284
Treas. Reg. § 1.368–2(k) 276
Treas. Reg. § 1.381(a)–
1(b)(2) 324
Treas. Reg. § 1.381(a)–
1(b)(3) 322
Treas. Reg. § 1.381(b)–
1(a)(2) 325
Treas. Reg. § 1.381(c)(1)–
1(c)(2) 326
Treas. Reg. § 1.381(c)(2)–
1(a)(1) 327

Treas. Reg. § 1.381(c)(2)–
1(a)(2) 327
Treas. Reg. § 1.381(c)(2)–
1(a)(4) 328
Treas. Reg. § 1.381(c)(2)–
1(c)(1) 328
Treas. Reg. § 1.381(c)(2)–
1(c)(2) 108, 327
Treas. Reg. § 1.381(c)(4)–
1(a)(5) 320
Treas. Reg. § 1.381(c)(5)–
1(a)(5) 320
Treas. Reg. § 1.382–2(a)(2) 343
Treas. Reg. § 1.382–2(a)(3) 335
Treas. Reg. § 1.382–2(a)(4) 335
Treas. Reg. § 1.382–2(a)(5) 333
Treas. Reg. § 1.382–2(a)(6) 333
Treas. Reg. § 1.382–6(g)(1) 343
Treas. Reg. § 1.382–6(g)(2) 343
Treas. Reg. § 1.382–6(g)(3) 343
Treas. Reg. § 1.383–1(b) 343
Treas. Reg. § 1.383–1(c)(3) 343
Treas. Reg. § 1.383–1(c)(4) 343
Treas. Reg. § 1.383–1(d)(3) 346
Treas. Reg. § 1.482–
1A(d)(5) 193
Treas. Reg. § 1.1032–2 300
Treas. Reg. § 1.1032–2(b) 297,
298, 304
Treas. Reg. § 1.1032–2(d),
Ex. 1 304
Treas. Reg. § 1.1032–3 298
Treas. Reg. § 1.1036–1 289
Treas. Reg. § 1.1060–
1(b)(2) 112
Treas. Reg. § 1.1239–
1(c)(3) 193
Treas. Reg. § 1.1239–
1(c)(4) 193
Treas. Reg. § 1.1361–
1(e)(1) 364, 367
Treas. Reg. § 1.1361–
1(l)(1) 367
Treas. Reg. § 1.1361–
1(l)(2) 368
Treas. Reg. § 1.1361–
1(l)(2)(i) 370
Treas. Reg. § 1.1361–
1(l)(2)(iii) 370
Treas. Reg. § 1.1361–
1(l)(2)(vi), Ex. (3) 370
Treas. Reg. § 1.1361–
1(l)(2)(vi), Ex. (4) 370
Treas. Reg. § 1.1361–
1(l)(4) 368, 369
Treas. Reg. § 1.1361–
1(l)(4)(ii)(A) 368

Treas. Reg. § 1.1361–
1(*l*)(4)(iii)..............................369
Treas. Reg. § 1.1361–
1(*l*)(4)(v), Ex. 1.....................369
Treas. Reg. § 1.1362–1(a) 371
Treas. Reg. § 1.1362–
2(c)(5)..................................385
Treas. Reg. § 1.1362–
6(a)(2)..................................371
Treas. Reg. § 1.1362–
6(b)(1)..................................371
Treas. Reg. § 1.1362–
6(b)(2)(ii) 367
Treas. Reg. § 1.1362–
6(b)(3)(ii), Ex. (2) 371
Treas. Reg. § 1.1366–1(b) 374
Treas. Reg. § 1.1366–
2(a)(4)..................................378
Treas. Reg. § 1.1366–
2(a)(5)..................................378
Treas. Reg. § 1.1367–
1(b)(2)..................................375
Treas. Reg. § 1.1367–
1(c)(3) 375, 376
Treas. Reg. § 1.1367–
1(d)(1) 376
Treas. Reg. § 1.1367–1(f) 377
Treas. Reg. § 1.1367–
2(b)(1)..................................376
Treas. Reg. § 1.1367–2(c)........376
Treas. Reg. § 1.1368–
2(a)(5)..................................380
Treas. Reg. § 1.1374–3(a) 389
Treas. Reg. § 1.1374–4(b) 390
Treas. Reg. § 1.1374–
4(b)(2)..................................391
Treas. Reg. § 1.1374–4(i) 392
Treas. Reg. § 1.1374–7(b) 393
Treas. Reg. § 1.1374–8(e),
Ex. (1) 390
Treas. Reg. § 1.1374–8(e),
Ex. (2) 390
Treas. Reg. § 1.1374–9...........392
Treas. Reg. § 1.1377–2(b) 383
Treas. Reg. § 1.1502–30(b) 302
Treas. Reg. § 1.1502–34.........101,
164
Treas. Reg. §§ 301.7701–2—3 ... 7
Treas. Reg. § 301.7701–2(a) 7,
263
Treas. Reg. § 301.7701–2(b) 6
Treas. Reg. § 301.7701–
2(b)(1)................................... 7
Treas. Reg. § 301.7701–2(b)(3)–
(8)... 7
Treas. Reg. § 301.7701–3(a) 7

Treas. Reg. § 301.7701–
3(b)(1).................................... 8

Table of Revenue Rulings

Rev. Proc. 75–17 19
Rev. Proc. 77–37 .....166, 225, 274
Rev. Proc. 77–41 137
Rev. Proc. 84–42 171
Rev. Proc. 86–42 274
Rev. Proc. 90–52 100
Rev. Proc. 94–3 170
Rev. Proc. 96–30 221
Rev. Proc. 96–30, Apx. A 221
Rev. Proc. 96–43 217
Rev. Proc. 2003–48 221
Rev. Proc. 2012–39 320
Rev. Proc. 2013–32 156
Rev. Proc. 2015–3 19
Rev. Proc. 2018–3 ....6, 66, 70
Rev. Rul. 54–96......................167
Rev. Rul. 54–396....................275
Rev. Rul. 54–482....................289
Rev. Rul. 55–36......................163
Rev. Rul. 56–100....................167
Rev. Rul. 56–116....................290
Rev. Rul. 56–220.............234, 310
Rev. Rul. 56–556......................66
Rev. Rul. 56–584......................66
Rev. Rul. 56–586....................289
Rev. Rul. 56–655....................222
Rev. Rul. 57–387......................66
Rev. Rul. 57–464....................214
Rev. Rul. 57–492....................214
Rev. Rul. 57–518....................275
Rev. Rul. 58–614......................79
Rev. Rul. 59–84......................290
Rev. Rul. 59–98......................291
Rev. Rul. 59–197.....206, 222, 290
Rev. Rul. 59–259...........164, 205,
    266, 276
Rev. Rul. 59–296....................109
Rev. Rul. 60–302.............182, 193
Rev. Rul. 61–156....................100
Rev. Rul. 61–191....................357
Rev. Rul. 64–56...............168, 169
Rev. Rul. 66–7................141, 157
Rev. Rul. 66–23......................256
Rev. Rul. 66–142....................182
Rev. Rul. 66–204....................213
Rev. Rul. 66–224....................255
Rev. Rul. 66–365....................268
Rev. Rul. 67–274....................271
Rev. Rul. 67–448.....265, 306, 315
Rev. Rul. 68–55.......174, 175, 183
Rev. Rul. 68–284....................213
Rev. Rul. 68–562....................270

Rev. Rul. 68–602............ 102, 109
Rev. Rul. 68–603............ 220, 246
Rev. Rul. 69–156................... 169
Rev. Rul. 69–440..................... 17
Rev. Rul. 69–460................... 222
Rev. Rul. 69–608..................... 79
Rev. Rul. 70–199................... 290
Rev. Rul. 70–239................... 167
Rev. Rul. 70–489................... 109
Rev. Rul. 71–326................... 101
Rev. Rul. 71–350................... 142
Rev. Rul. 71–562..................... 65
Rev. Rul. 71–564................... 169
Rev. Rul. 72–71..................... 142
Rev. Rul. 72–354................... 268
Rev. Rul. 72–405................... 281
Rev. Rul. 72–530................... 222
Rev. Rul. 73–44..................... 216
Rev. Rul. 73–54..................... 267
Rev. Rul. 73–234................... 212
Rev. Rul. 73–237................... 212
Rev. Rul. 74–33....................... 76
Rev. Rul. 74–44....................... 40
Rev. Rul. 74–338......... 25, 76, 77
Rev. Rul. 74–396................... 106
Rev. Rul. 74–501....................... 6
Rev. Rul. 74–515........... 234, 310
Rev. Rul. 74–516................... 235
Rev. Rul. 75–83..................... 311
Rev. Rul. 75–123................... 267
Rev. Rul. 75–223............. 71, 72
Rev. Rul. 75–236................... 147
Rev. Rul. 75–337................... 223
Rev. Rul. 75–502............... 54, 55
Rev. Rul. 76–54..................... 216
Rev. Rul. 76–317................... 101
Rev. Rul. 76–364..................... 55
Rev. Rul. 76–385..................... 56
Rev. Rul. 76–429................... 100
Rev. Rul. 76–496..................... 62
Rev. Rul. 76–514................... 192
Rev. Rul. 76–527................... 222
Rev. Rul. 77–218..................... 54
Rev. Rul. 77–245..................... 70
Rev. Rul. 77–293..................... 66
Rev. Rul. 77–335................... 148
Rev. Rul. 77–336................... 196
Rev. Rul. 77–426..................... 54
Rev. Rul. 77–449................... 198
Rev. Rul. 77–467..................... 65
Rev. Rul. 78–47................... 275
Rev. Rul. 78–401............... 54, 55

Rev. Rul. 79–4..........................267
Rev. Rul. 79–8..........................40
Rev. Rul. 79–67........................66
Rev. Rul. 79–163.............138, 147
Rev. Rul. 79–184.......................71
Rev. Rul. 79–273....................225
Rev. Rul. 79–287....................290
Rev. Rul. 79–394....................212
Rev. Rul. 80–24......................168
Rev. Rul. 80–58.......................... 6
Rev. Rul. 80–189.......................87
Rev. Rul. 80–198.............187, 196
Rev. Rul. 80–199....................186
Rev. Rul. 80–284....................163
Rev. Rul. 80–285....................163
Rev. Rul. 81–25......................258
Rev. Rul. 81–41.......................60
Rev. Rul. 81–247....................258
Rev. Rul. 82–191.............138, 147
Rev. Rul. 83–34......................198
Rev. Rul. 83–65......................192
Rev. Rul. 83–68......................135
Rev. Rul. 83–114....................209
Rev. Rul. 83–156....................198
Rev. Rul. 84–71.............163, 168
Rev. Rul. 84–111....................167
Rev. Rul. 84–114.......55, 234, 310
Rev. Rul. 85–19.......................66
Rev. Rul. 85–122....................222
Rev. Rul. 85–139....................267
Rev. Rul. 86–4........................209
Rev. Rul. 86–125....................212
Rev. Rul. 86–126....................212
Rev. Rul. 88–19......................212
Rev. Rul. 88–33......................222
Rev. Rul. 88–34......................222
Rev. Rul. 88–48......................275
Rev. Rul. 90–13.......................70
Rev. Rul. 90–68......................135
Rev. Rul. 93–61......................311
Rev. Rul. 93–62.......234, 235, 310
Rev. Rul. 95–74......................187
Rev. Rul. 96–29......................293
Rev. Rul. 99–5.................141, 157
Rev. Rul. 2000–5.............254, 263
Rev. Rul. 2001–46..................271
Rev. Rul. 2003–52..................223
Rev. Rul. 2003–99..................256
Rev. Rul. 2008–25..................271
Rev. Rul. 2019–09..................214

Table of Miscellaneous Decisions

IRS GCM 34238......................216
IRS GCM 37135......................315
IRS GCM 37534......................216
IRS GCM 39138......................198
IRS GCM 39150......................256
IRS GCM 39570........................76
IRS GCM 39768......................363
Private Letter Rul.
   7830010 187
Private Letter Rul.
   8342012 76
Private Letter Rul.
   8342030 198
Private Letter Rul.
   8944076 64
Private Letter Rul.
   9018028 62
Private Letter Rul.
   9144017 65
Private Letter Rul.
   9723044 102
Private Letter Rul.
   9726013 222
Private Letter Rul.
   199911028 316
Private Letter Rul.
   199911029 316
Private Letter Rul.
   200013044 187
Private Letter Rul.
   200533002 6
Private Letter Rul.
   200708012 235
Private Letter Rul.
   200752035 6

Index

References are to Pages

ACCUMULATED ADJUSTMENTS ACCOUNT (AAA)
See, S Corporations

ADJUSTED GROSS ESTATE, 73

ADJUSTED GROSSED-UP BASIS (AGUB), 120, 122–125

AFFILIATED GROUP
See, Separate Affiliated Group

AGGREGATE DEEMED SALES PRICE (ADSP), 117–119, 121–122

ALTERNATE DEPRECIATION SYSTEM
See, Earnings and Profits (E & P)

APPRECIATED PROPERTY DEFINITION OF, 23, 90

ASSET CLASSES, 113

ASSOCIATION
See, Corporation, Classification as

AT RISK LIMITATIONS
See, S Corporations

ATTRIBUTION OF STOCK OWNERSHIP, 43–48
"Bad blood," 58–59
Constructive Redemptions, 79–87
Entity, from and to, 44–45
Estates, future interests in, 45–46
Family, 44–48, 62–67
Five-percent shareholder, 335–336
Options, 45
Reattribution, 47–48
S corporation stock, 365
Sideways, 47
Waiver of family attribution, 62–67

BAIL-OUT
See, Section 306 Stock; Stock Dividends

BASIS, 35–36
See, Controlled Corporations, Transfers to; Corporate Division; Reorganizations; S Corporations; Section 301 Distributions; Section 306 Stock; Stock Dividends

BAUSCH & LOMB DOCTRINE
See, Reorganizations

BOOT
See, Controlled Corporations, Transfers to; Corporate Division; Reorganizations

BUILT-IN LOSS
See, Controlled Corporations, Transfers to; Limitations on Use of Tax Attributes

BUSINESS PURPOSE, 163, 202–204, 209–210, 220–224
See, Controlled Corporations, Transfers to; Corporate Divisions; Reorganizations

C CORPORATIONS
Definition of, 2

C SHORT YEAR
See, S Corporations

CAPITAL GAINS AND LOSSES, 4

CHECK THE BOX
See, Corporation, Classification as

COMMON STOCK
Defined, 137–138, 147

COMPLETE LIQUIDATION
See, Liquidations

CONSISTENCY RULES
See, Stock, Purchase of (§ 338)

CONSOLIDATED GROUP, 118, 121–122, 302
Section 336(e) election, 125–129
Section 338 election, 121–122

CONSTRUCTIVE DIVIDEND
See, Dividends; Stock Dividends

**CONSTRUCTIVE
    REDEMPTIONS (§ 304)**
Generally, 80–87
Acquiring corporation, 80
Attribution of stock, 82
Basis, effect on, 82–87
Brother-sister corporations, 81–84
Control, 80–81, 84
Earnings and profits,81–87
Extraordinary dividend, 78–79
Issuing corporation, 80
Overlap with § 351, 87, 195
Parent-subsidiary corporations, 85–
    87

**CONTINUITY OF BUSINESS
    ENTERPRISE**
See, Limitations on Use of Tax
    Attributes; Reorganizations

CONTINUITY OF INTEREST
See, Controlled Corporations,
    Transfers to; Corporate
    Division; Reorganizations

CONTRIBUTIONS TO CAPITAL
See, Controlled Corporations,
    Transfers to

CONTROLLED CORPORATIONS
Liquidation of, 100–109
Minority shareholders, 105

**CONTROLLED
    CORPORATIONS,
    TRANSFERS TO**
Accommodation transfers, 165–166
Accounts receivable, 168
Assignment or anticipation of income,
    196–197
Basis and limitation on, 157–162,
    171–174
Basis of transferee corporation, 157–
    162, 171–174, 181–182
Basis of transferor, 157–162, 171–
    174, 181–182
Boot, basis of, 172–174
Boot, corporation's gain or loss, 179
Boot defined, 170–171
Boot, transferor's receipt of, 172–179,
    181–182
Built-in loss, 161–162
Business purpose requirement, 163,
    197
Constructive exchange, 82, 169–170
Constructive redemptions, overlap
    with, 87, 195
Continuity of interest, 167–168
Contributions to capital, 171
Control, 164–168
Corporation's gain or loss, 156–157,
    179

Court Holding doctrine, 197–198
Debt treated as stock, 170
Depreciable property,
    characterization of gain from,
    192
Dropdown by transferee, 198
Exchange, requirement of, 169–170
Gain or loss of transferor, 157–160,
    171, 181–182, 191–192
Holding period, 158
Immediately after, 166–167
Installment reporting, 191–192
Liability assumed
    Basis, limitation on
        transferee's, 160–162,
        183–186
    Boot, treatment as or exclusion
        from, 181–182
    Deductible liability, 186–187
    Exceeds basis of property
        transferred, 182–191
    Fair market value, in excess of,
        190
    Meaning of "assumed", 180
    Tax avoidance purpose, 181–
        182
Nonqualified preferred stock, 175–
    179
Overlap with § 304, 87, 195
Promissory note of transferor, 187–
    190
Property, restricted to transfers of,
    168–169
Qualified preferred stock, 175–176
Reallocation of corporate income and
    loss, 193–194
Recapture of depreciation, 192
Reorganization, alternative to, 314–
    317
Sale or exchange requirement, 169–
    170
Section 304, conflict with, 87, 195
Section 306 stock, 148, 195–196
Securities, 170, 191–192
Services, contribution of, 168–169
Stock, 170–171
Stock rights and warrants, 171
Tax benefit rule, 197

**CORPORATE BUSINESS, SALE
    OR PURCHASE OF**
See, Stock, Purchase of (§ 338)

CORPORATE DISTRIBUTIONS
See, Liquidations; Partial
    Liquidation; Section 301
    Distributions; Stock
    Redemptions

CORPORATE DIVISION
See also, Reorganizations
Active business requirement, 204, 211–220
Anti-*Morris Trust* provision, 241, 246–249
Attribution of stock ownership, 242, 248
Automatic dividend rule, 234
Basis of shareholder, 205, 236–237
Boot, 204–206, 227–236
Business purpose requirement, 202–204, 209–210, 220–224
Continuity of business enterprise (COBE), 224
Continuity of proprietary interest, 204, 220, 224–227
Corporate division, 200–201
D reorganization, 200
Device to distribute *e and p*, 201, 207–211
Disqualified distribution, 242–246
Disqualified person, 246
Disqualified stock, 241–246
Distribution requirement, 202–204, 206
Dividend equivalency, 233–236
Divisive D reorganization, 200
Divisive reorganization, 200
Earnings and profits, effect on, 249
Excess securities boot, 228–229, 234–235, 239
Expansion problem, 217–219
Fit and focus standard, 221
Five-year requirement, 216–219
Forms of, 200–201
Functional division, 218
Gain or loss
    Corporation's recognition of, 237–249
    Recognition by distributing corporation, 237–249
    Recognition by shareholder, 231–233
Horizontal division, 217–218
Nonqualified preferred stock, 206, 228, 231, 239
Nonrecognition, 201–205
Pro-rata, 208
Purchase, 241–248
Qualified preferred stock, 231
Qualified property, 238–241
Reorganization, as, 200, 240
Reorganization following a division, 219–220
Reorganization, not required to be, 200
Retention of subsidiary stock, 206–207
Secondary business, 209
Section 306 stock, 206
Securities, 203–205, 206–207, 228–229
Separate Affiliated Group (SAG), 215–216, 230
Single business, division of, 217–219
Spin-offs, 200–201
Split-offs, 200–201
Split-ups, 200–201
Stock boot, 206, 229–231, 237
Stock rights and warrants, 206
Stock, treated as boot, 206, 229–231, 237
Stock warrants as securities, 206
Subsequent sale of stock, 208–209, 219–220
Subsidiary, conduct of business by, 215–216
Trade or business, 212–219
Vertical division, 217–218

CORPORATION, CLASSIFICATION AS, 6–8

CORPORATION, PURCHASE OF
See, Stock, purchase of

CORPORATION'S SALE OF ITS OWN DEBT INSTRUMENT, 38, 156

CORPORATION'S, SALE OF ITS OWN STOCK, 38, 156, 294

COURT HOLDING DOCTRINE, 256

DEATH TAXES, REDEMPTION TO PAY, 73–75

DECEDENT'S GROSS ESTATE, STOCK INCLUDED IN, 73–75

DE FACTO DISSOLUTION, 356–357

DISGUISED DIVIDEND
See, Dividends

DISQUALIFIED PROPERTY, 95

DISTRIBUTION OF CORPORATE STOCK (§ 336(e)), 125–129

DISTRIBUTIONS OF PROPERTY
See also, Liquidations; *General Utilities* Doctrine; Partial Liquidations; Section 301 Distributions; Stock Dividends; Stock Redemptions
Amount distributed, 11–12
Basis, 36

Distributor's recognition of gain or
    loss, 37–38, 124–138
General Utilities doctrine, 37–38, 91

DIVIDENDS
    See also, Dividend-Received
        Deduction; Earnings and
        Profits (E&P);
        Reorganizations; Section
        306 Stock; Stock
        Dividends; Stock
        Redemptions
Bargain sale as, 38–39
Capital gains rates, 12, 17–18, 48–49
Constructive, 38–39
Defined, 12–17
Disguised, 38–39
Earnings and profits, 13–17, 18–33
Earnings and profits as
    measurement of dividend, 13
Extraordinary to a corporate
    shareholder, 34–36, 68, 78–79,
    82
Loans to shareholder, 39
Ordinary income, 11, 12, 18
Qualified dividend income, 18
Section 301 distribution,
    distinguished from, 10

**DIVIDENDS-RECEIVED
    DEDUCTION**
    Generally, 17–18
S corporations, 362–363

DIVISIVE REORGANIZATION
See, Corporate Division;
    Reorganizations

DOUBLE TAX
See, Two-Tier Tax Structure

**EARNINGS AND PROFITS
    (E & P)**
    Generally, 13, 18–33
Accounting method, 20
Accumulated, 13
Acquisition of, 327–329
Allocation of, 13–17
Alternative depreciation, 28–31, 33
Bifurcated system, 13
Capital expenditure, 20
Constructive redemptions, 83–87
Current, 13
Debt obligation, distribution of, 28
Deferred gain or loss, 19
Deficit, creation of, 22
Depreciation deductions, 28–31, 33
Discharge of indebtedness, 22
Distributions in excess of, 23, 33
Distributions of property, 22–27
Function of, 13, 19
Installment sale, 28, 32–33

Liability effect on, 23, 26
Loss carryover or back, 20
Nonrecognized gain or loss, 19
S corporations, 373, 379–383
Section 301 distributions effect on,
    22–28
Stock, distribution of, 28
Stock dividends effect on, 28, 141
Stock redemptions effect on, 75–78,
    151–153
Tax-exempt interest, 19
Tax liability, 19–20
Twenty-percent corporate
    shareholder, distributions to,
    31–33

EX-DIVIDEND DATE, 34–35

**EXTRAORDINARY DIVIDEND
    TO CORPORATE
    SHARERHOHOLDER,** 34–
    36, 78–79, 312

FAMILY ATTRIBUTION, 44–48,
    62–66

**GENERAL UTILITIES
    DOCTRINE,** 37–38, 91, 114,
    120

**GROSS ESTATE, STOCK
    INCLUDED IN,** 73–75

INSTALLMENT SALES
See, Earnings and Profits (E & P);
    Liquidations

***KIMBELL-DIAMOND* RULE,** 114–
    115

LIMITATIONS ON LOSSES
See, Limitations on Use of Tax
    Attributes

**LIMITATIONS ON USE OF TAX
    ATTRIBUTES**
    See also, Tax Avoidance
        Acquisition (§ 269)
Attribution of stock, 335–336
Built-in gains and losses, 351–355
Capital loss carryovers, 343, 351
Change date, 343
Change year, 343
Continuity of business requirement,
    346
Credit carryover, 351
De Facto disillusion, 356–357
Earnings and profits, 327–329
Equity structure shift, 334–335
Five-percent shareholder, 335
Insolvent corporations, 346
Long-term tax-exempt rate, 344
Loss corporation, 331–333
Net operating loss, 326–327

Net unrealized built-in gain or loss, 349–350
New loss corporation, 333
Old loss corporation, 333
Owner shift, 335, 338–342
Ownership change, 332, 336–342, 344
Post-change period, 343
Post-change year, 343, 345
Pre-change loss, 343, 345
Pre-change period, 343
Public group, 336, 339–342
Recognition period, 347
Recognized built-in gains and losses, 347–350, 353–355
Reorganizations, 323–325
Section 382 limitation, 330–350
Tacking of stock ownership, 337
Testing date, 335, 338–339
Testing period, 335, 338–339

LIQUIDATING DISTRIBUTION, 10

LIQUIDATIONS
Generally, 89–91
See, Partial Liquidations
Basis, 97, 104, 107–109
Corporate division, pursuant to, 92
Defined, 90–91
Disqualified property, 95–96
80-percent distributee defined, 106
Gain or loss, distributing
corporation's recognition of, 90–98, 103, 105–109
Indebtedness to parent corporation, 108–109
Insolvent subsidiary, 102, 108–109
Installment sales, 107
Losses, limitations on, 92–98
Minority shareholders, 105
Parent corporation's nonrecognition of gain or loss, 100–106, 114
Reincorporation, 98–99
Reorganization, pursuant to, 90
Shareholders' gain or loss, 98, 101–103
Subsidiary corporation, 90, 100–109
Subsidiary's nonrecognition of gain or loss, 105–108
Tax attributes, inheritance of, 104

MORRIS TRUST, 220, 241, 246–249

NONLIQUIDATING DISTRIBUTION, 10

NONQUALIFIED PREFERRED STOCK
See, Controlled Corporations, Transfers to; Corporate

Divisions; Reorganizations; Stock Dividends

ORGANIZING A CORPORATION
See, Controlled Corporations, Transfers to

PARTIAL LIQUIDATIONS
Generally, 67–72
See also, Stock Redemptions, Defined, 69
Extraordinary dividend, as, 68, 78–79
S corporations, 68
Safe harbor, 69–70

PASSIVE ACTIVITY LOSS LIMITATION
See, S Corporations

PREFERRED STOCK BAIL-OUT
See, Section 306 Stock; Stock Dividends

PREFERRED STOCK
Defined, 137–138, 147
Dividend of, 147

PUBLICLY HELD PARTNERSHIPS, 7

QUALIFIED BUSINESS INCOME DEDUCTION, 394–397

QUALIFIED PREFERRED STOCK, 175

QUALIFIED STOCK PURCHASE, 115

RECAPITALIZATION, 288–292

REDEMPTION OF STOCK
See, Stock Redemptions

REATTRIBUTION OF STOCK, 47–48

REINCORPORATION, 98–99

REORGANIZATIONS
"A" reorganization, 262–264, 279–284, 295–296, 303–307
"B" reorganizations, 264–271, 276–278, 296–297
Bausch & Lomb doctrine, 275
Boot defined, 170–171
Boot relaxation rule, 273
Business purpose, 261
"C" reorganization, 271–276, 278–279, 299–303
Consolidation, 262
Continuity of business enterprise (COBE), 258–260
Continuity of proprietary interest, 254–258

Control, 264–266, 269, 280, 283
Corporate division prior to, 219–220
Court Holding doctrine, 256
Creeping acquisition, 269
"D" reorganization, acquisitive, 287–288, 307–308
Defined, 251–252
Dividend, effect of, 309–311
Divisive, 285–287
Double dummy structure, 314–317
"E" reorganization, 288–292
Expenses of, 267–268
"F" reorganization, 292–293
Forced "B" reorganization, 270, 284
Forward subsidiary merger, 279–281, 284, 303–304
Forward triangular merger, 279–281, 284, 303–304
Fractional shares, 268
"G" reorganizations, 293
Gain or loss of distributing corporation on liquidation, 312–314
Liabilities, 272–274, 301–303
Liquidation pursuant to, 271–272
Merger or consolidation, 262–264, 279–284, 295–296, 303–307
Nonqualified preferred stock, 289–290, 309
Over-the-top model, 298–299, 301–303
Pre-reorganization redemption, 257
Recapitalization, 288–292
Reincorporation, 98–99
Reverse acquisition, 281–284, 303–307
Reverse subsidiary merger, 281–284, 303–307
Reverse triangular merger, 281–284, 303–307
S corporations, 336
Section 351 exchange as alternative to, 314–317
Step transaction, 256
Stock for stock, 264–271, 289–291, 297–299
Subsidiary "B" reorganization, 276–277, 297–299
Subsidiary "C" reorganization, 278–279, 299–303
Substantially all, 271–272, 274–275, 280, 283–284, 288
Transitory, 283–284, 314–315
Triangular, 276–284, 297–307
Triangular "B" reorganization, 276–277, 297–299
Triangular "C" reorganization, 278–279, 300–303

RESCISSION DOCTRINE, 4

REVERSE MERGER
See, Reorganizations

S CORPORATIONS
Generally, 2, 360–361
Accumulated adjustments account (AAA), 380–382, 383
At risk limitation, 378–379
Basis, adjustments to shareholder's, 361, 375–377
Built-in gain or loss, 388–393
Buy-sell agreements, 370
C corporation, definition of, 360
C short year, 386
Call options, 369
Carryover loss, 378
Cessation of qualification, 384
Debt, 368–369
Disproportionate distributions, 370–371
Distributions, differences in timing, or amounts of, 370–371
Dividend-received deduction, 362–363
Earnings and profits, 373, 379–385
Electing small business trust, 367
Election
    Making of, 371–372
    Renewal after termination, 371–372, 385–386
    Termination, 384–385
    Validity of, 371–372
Eligibility, 363–365
Estate as shareholder, 364
Excess net passive income, 387–388
Governing provisions, 367–368, 370
LIFO recapture, 393–394
Limitations on deductions and credits, 377–379
Loss, deduction of, 377–379
Mallinckrodt trust, 366
Net recognized built-in gain, 391–392
Net unrealized built-in gain, 391–392
Nonresident alien, 364
Nonseparately stated items, 374
One class of stock, 364, 367–371
Partial liquidations, 68
Passive activity loss limitation, 378–379
Passive investment income
    Defined, 385, 387
    Tax on, 386–388
    Termination of S status, 385
Pass-through of tax items, 373–375
Post-termination transition period, 382–383
Property in kind, distribution of, 382–383
Qualified subchapter S subsidiary (QSSS) or (Qsub), 364–365

Qualified subchapter S trust (QSST),
    367
Recognition period, 389
Recognized built-in gain, 390–393
Recognized built-in loss, 390–391
Reorganization, 363
Restricted stock, 370
Revocation of election, 384
S short year, 386
S termination year, 386
Sale of stock with § 338 election, 363
Separately stated items, 374
Shareholders
    Basis in stock and debts,
        adjustments to, 361, 375–
        379
    Distributions to, 379–383
    Estate, 364
    Family, members of, 365
    Loss, deduction of, 375–379
    Maximum number, 365
    Non-resident alien, 364
    Permissible person, 364
    Spouses, 365
    Trust as, 364–367
Small business corporation, 363
Subchapter C, application of, 362–
    363
Summary of treatment, 360–361
Taxable year, 372, 386
Taxation of, 372–373
Termination of S status, 384–385
Trust as shareholder of, 364–367
Voting rights, 368, 370
Voting trust, 366
Warrants, 369

S SHORT YEAR
See, S Corporations

SAFE HARBOR
See, Partial Liquidations; Stock
    Redemptions

SAG
See, Separate Affiliated Group

SALE OF CORPORATE ASSETS,
    111–113
Allocation of purchase price, 112–113
Residual method, 112–113

SALE OF CORPORATE STOCK,
    113–129
Acquisition date, 116–125
Adjusted Grossed-Up Basis (AGUB),
    120, 122–125
Affiliated group, 121, 125
Aggregate deemed sales price
    (ADSP), 117–119, 121–122
Election of § 336(e), 125–129
Election of § 338, 115–116, 119–125

Liability for tax, 116, 119–122
Nonrecently purchased stock, 123–
    124
Purchase, 115
Qualified stock purchase, 115–116,
    122, 124–125
Recently purchased stock, 117, 123–
    124
Residual method, 112–113
S Corporation, 363
Section 336(e) election, 125–129
Section 338(h)(10), 121–122
Twelve-month acquisition period, 115

SECTION 301 DISTRIBUTIONS
    Generally, 11–40
    See also, Dividends; Earnings
        and Profits (E&P);
        Section 306 Stock; Stock
        Redemptions
Amount distributed, 11–12
Basis of distributed property, 36–37
Basis of stock, effect on, 33–34, 48–52
Distributor's recognition of gain or
    loss, 37–38
Dividend, distinguished from, 10
Excess distribution, 33–34, 48–53
Stock redemption, 42–43, 48–52

SECTION 306 STOCK
Bail-out, 144–146
Basis, effect of disposition on, 150–
    153
Decedent's gross estate, stock
    included in, 149
Defined, 146–149
Disposition by redemption, 152–153
Disposition other than by
    redemption, 150–152
Dividend, treatment as, 150–153
Earnings and profits, effect on, 150–
    153
Exemption from treatment, 153–154
Preferred stock bail-out, 144–146
Preferred stock defined, 138, 147
Redemption, 152–153
Reorganization or division, 147–148,
    290
Section 301 distribution, treated as,
    152–153
Section 351 exchange, acquired in,
    148–149
Stock dividend as, 146
Substituted basis, 148

SECTION 336(e) ELECTION, 125–
    129

SECTION 338(h)(10) ELECTION,
    121–122

SECURITIES, 170, 191–192, 203–205, 206–207, 228–229

SEPARATE AFFILIATED GROUP (SAG), 215, 230

SIDEWAYS ATTRIBUTION
See, Attribution of Stock Ownership

SMALL BUSINESS CORPORATION
See, S Corporations

STEP TRANSACTIONS, 167, 256

STOCK DIVIDENDS
Basis of stock and rights, 141–144
Combined with property distribution, 135–138
Constructive dividend, 140
Conversion ratio, change of, 138–141
Definition of, 131–132
Earnings and profits, 141
Election to receive property, 134–135
Equivalent of, 139–141
Exclusion from income, 132–133
Fractional share of stock, cash received for, 137
History of tax treatment, 132–133
Holding period, 142–143
Preferred stock bail-outs, 144–146
Preferred stock, convertible to common, 138–139
Preferred stock, defined, 138, 147
Preferred stock, dividend on, 138
Recapitalization, 140
Section 301 distributions, as, 141
Section 303 stock, distribution on, 74–75
Section 306 stock, 144–154
Security convertible to stock, 136–137
Stock rights or warrants, distribution of, 134, 144
Stock split, 131–132
Taxable, 134–139, 141–142

STOCK INCLUDED IN DECEDENT'S GROSS ESTATE
See, Stock Redemptions

STOCK, PURCHASE OR DISTRIBUTION OF (§§ 338 AND 336(e))
See, Sale of Corporate Stock

STOCK REDEMPTIONS
See also, Attribution of Stock Ownership; Constructive Redemption (§ 304); Distributions of Property; Liquidations; Partial

Liquidations; Section 301 Distributions
Adjusted gross estate, 73
Another shareholder's stock, 79
Attribution of stock ownership, 43–48
Bad blood, 44, 58–59
Basis of retained shares, 48–52
Constructive, 80–87
Constructive recapitalization, 50–51
Decedent's gross estate, stock included in, 73–75
Deferred loss, 42–53
Defined, 42
Distributor's recognition of gain or loss, 37–38
Dividend, treated as, 41–43, 48–49
Earnings and profits, effect on, 75–76
Equivalence to a dividend
  Generally, 41–42, 53–67
  Bad blood, 44, 58–59
  Friendly shareholders, 58
  Hostility, 44, 58–59
  Meaningful reduction of interest, 54
Extraordinary dividend, 78–79
Generation-skipping tax, stock subject to, 73
Inclusion date, 52–53
Lost basis, 49–53
Minority shareholder, 55–56
New section 303 stock, 75
Nonvoting stock, 56–57
Partial liquidations, 67–72
Purchase, treated as, 41–42
Safe harbors, 53–67
Section 301 distribution, treated as, 42–43, 48–49
Substantially disproportionate redemption, 59–61
Termination of interest, 62–67
  Family attribution, waiver by entity, 66–67
  Family attribution, waiver by individual, 62–66
  Related persons, 66

SUBCHAPTER S
See, S Corporations

TAX ATTRIBUTES, ACQUISITION AND SURVIVAL OF
  Generally, 319–322
  See also, Limitation on Use of Tax Attributes
Acquisitive reorganizations, 324
Carryback of loss, 325
Earnings and profits, 327–329
F reorganization, 325
Net operating loss, 326–327
Taxable year, 325

Triangular reorganization, 323–324

TAX AVOIDANCE ACQUISITION (§ 269), 355–356

TAX RATES, 2–4

TAXABLE YEAR, 4

TWELVE-MONTH ACQUISITION PERIOD, 115

TWO-TIER TAX STRUCTURE
Generally, 1–2
Compromise system, 5